How to Divide When There Isn't Enough

How to Divide When There Isn't Enough develops a rigorous yet accessible presentation of the state of the art for the adjudication of conflicting claims and the theory of taxation. It covers all aspects one may wish to know about claims problems: the most important rules, the most important axioms, and how these two sets are related. More generally, it also serves as an introduction to the modern theory of economic design, which in the last twenty years has revolutionized many areas of economics, generating a wide range of applicable allocation rules that have improved people's lives in many ways. In developing the theory, the book employs a variety of techniques that will appeal to both experts and nonexperts. Compiling decades of research into a single framework, William Thomson provides numerous applications that will open a large number of avenues for future research.

William Thomson is the Elmer Milliman Professor of Economics at the University of Rochester. He is the author of several books including *A Guide for the Young Economist*, which has appeared in four translations, and over one hundred articles. In 2001, he won the University Award for Excellence in Graduate Teaching at the University of Rochester. He is a Fellow of the Econometric Society, the Society for Economic Theory, and the Game Theory Society.

Econometric Society Monographs Series

The Econometric Society is an international society for the advancement of economic theory in relation to statistics and mathematics. The Econometric Society Monograph series is designed to promote the publication of original research contributions of high quality in mathematical economics and theoretical and applied econometrics.

Books in the Series

O. Compte & A. Postlewaite, *Ignorance and Uncertainty*, 2019
I. Molchanov & F. Molinari, *Random Sets in Econometrics*, 2018
B. Honoré, A. Pakes, M. Piazzesi, & L. Samuelson (eds.), *Advances in Economics and Econometrics: Eleventh World Congress, Vols. I & II*, 2017
S. Maurer, *On the Shoulders of Giants: Colleagues Remember Suzanne Scotchmer's Contributions to Economics*, 2017
C. P. Chambers & F. Echenique, *Revealed Preference Theory*, 2016
J.-F. Mertens, S. Sorins, & S. Samir, *Repeated Games*, 2015
C. Hsiao, *Analysis of Panel Data: 3rd ed.*, 2014
C. Cameron & P. Trivedi, *Regression Analysis of Count Data, 2nd ed.*, 2013
A. Harvey, *Dynamic Models for Volatility and Heavy Tails, with Applications to Financial and Economic Time Series*, 2013
D. Acemoglu, M. Areilano, & E. Dekel (eds.), *Advances in Economics and Econometrics: Theory and Applications, Tenth World Congress, Vols. I, II, & III*, 2013
M. Fleurbaey & F. Maniquet, *A Theory of Fairness and Social Justice*, 2011
R. Vohra, *Mechanism Design: A Linear Programming Approach*, 2011
K. Samphantharak & R. Townsend, *Households as Corporate Firms: An Analysis of Household Finance Using Integrated Household Surveys and Corporate Financial Accounting*, 2009
I. Gilboa, *Theory of Decision under Uncertainty*, 2009
F. Vega-Redondo, *Complex Networks*, 2007
R. Blundell, W. Newey, & T. Persson, (eds.), *Advances in Economics and Econometrics: Theory and Applications, Ninth World Congress, Vols. I, II, & III*, 2006
J. Roemer, *Democracy, Education, and Equality*, 2006
C. Blackorby, W. Bossert, & D. Donaldson, *Population Issues in Social Choice Theory, Welfare Economics and Ethics*, 2005
R. Koenker, *Quantile Regression*, 2005
C. Hsiao, *Analysis of Panel Data, 2nd ed.*, 2003
M. Dewatripont, L. P. Hausen, & S. J. Turnovsky (eds.), *Advances in Economics and Econometrics: Theory and Applications, Eighth World Congress, Vols. I, II, & III*, 2003
E. Ghysels, N. Swanson, & M. Watson (eds.), *Essays in Econometrics: Collected Papers of Clive W. J. Granger, Vols. I & II*, 2001
S. Strøm (ed.), *Econometrics and Economic Theory in the 20th Century: The Ragnar Frisch Centennial Symposium*, 1999
A. C. Cameron & P. K. Trivedi, *Regression Analysis of Count-Data*, 1998
D. Jacobs, E. Kalai, & M. Kamien (eds.), *Frontiers of Research in Economic Theory: The Nancy L. Schwartz Memorial Lectures*, 1998
D. M. Kreps & K. F. Wallis (eds.), *Advances in Economics and Econometrics: Theory and Applications, Seventh World Congress, Vols. I, II, & III*, 1997
R. Guesnerie, *A Contribution to the Pure Theory of Taxation*, 1995
C. Sims (ed.), *Advances in Econometrics, Sixth World Congress, Vols. I & II*, 1994

Continued on page following the index

How to Divide When There Isn't Enough

From Aristotle, the Talmud, and Maimonides to the Axiomatics of Resource Allocation

William Thomson
University of Rochester

CAMBRIDGE
UNIVERSITY PRESS

University Printing House, Cambridge CB2 8BS, United Kingdom

One Liberty Plaza, 20th Floor, New York, NY 10006, USA

477 Williamstown Road, Port Melbourne, VIC 3207, Australia

314–321, 3rd Floor, Plot 3, Splendor Forum, Jasola District Centre, New Delhi – 110025, India

79 Anson Road, #06–04/06, Singapore 079906

Cambridge University Press is part of the University of Cambridge.

It furthers the University's mission by disseminating knowledge in the pursuit of education, learning, and research at the highest international levels of excellence.

www.cambridge.org
Information on this title: www.cambridge.org/9781107194625
DOI: 10.1017/9781108161107

First published 2019

Printed in the United Kingdom by TJ International Ltd. Padstow Cornwall

A catalogue record for this publication is available from the British Library.

Library of Congress Cataloging-in-Publication Data
Names: Thomson, William, 1949– author.
Title: How to divide when there isn't enough : from Aristotle, the Talmud, and Maimonides to the axiomatics of resource allocation / William Thomson, University of Rochester.
Description: Cambridge, United Kingdom ; New York, NY : Cambridge University Press, 2019. | Series: Econometric Society monograph series
Identifiers: LCCN 2019006500 | ISBN 9781107194625
Subjects: LCSH: Scarcity – Econometric models. | Resource allocation – Econometric models.
Classification: LCC HB801 .T5285 2019 | DDC 330.01/5195–dc23
LC record available at https://lccn.loc.gov/2019006500

ISBN 978-1-107-19462-5 Hardback
ISBN 978-1-316-64644-1 Paperback

To Lisa and Rachèle

Contents

Figures

Tables

Acknowledgments

I thank the National Science Foundation for its support under grants SBR-9731431 and SES-0214691. I delivered a series of lectures at the University of Caen on the problem of adjudicating conflicting claims, and I thank Maurice Salles for giving me the opportunity to do so. I thank my coauthors on various related papers, Christopher Chambers, Youngsub Chun, Diego Dominguez, Toru Hokari, James Schummer, and Chun-Hsien Yeh, for sharpening my understanding of the subject. I also thank Youngsub Chun, Myeonghwan Cho, Sungick Cho, Lars Ehlers, Makoto Hagiwara, Eun Jeong Heo, Toru Hokari, Paula Jaramillo, Biung-Ghi Ju, Hyunkyu Jun, Bawoo Kim, Sun Young Kim, Yehhyun Lee, Lauren Merrill, Eiichi Miyagawa, Sunha Myong, John Stovall, Yuki Tamura, Michael Trubsky, Rodrigo Velez, and Hyeon Yang for their extremely useful comments. Most of all, I thank Çağatay Kayı, Toyotaka Sakai, Cori Vilella, and Chun-Hsien Yeh for their extensive and detailed readings of successive drafts of this manuscript. My greatest debt is to Patrick Harless and Juan Moreno-Ternero for their extremely careful reading of the final version. Finally, I thank the eagle-eyed referees of Cambridge University Press for their multiple suggestions to make my text more readable.

General Notation

Set of natural numbers	$\mathbb{N}$
Set of real numbers	$\mathbb{R}$
The closed interval in $\mathbb{R}$ with endpoints a and b	$[a, b]$
The open interval with endpoints a and b	$]a, b[$
Given $x, y \in \mathbb{R}$, for each $i \in N$, $x_i \leq y_i$	$x \leqq y$
$x \leqq y$ and $x \neq y$	$x \leq y$
For each $i \in N$, $x_i < y_i$	$x < y$
Vector x from which ith coordinate has been deleted	x_{-i}
Vector x in which ith coordinate has been replaced by x'_i	(x'_i, x_{-i})
Vector x with coordinates rewritten in increasing order	$\tilde{x}$
Interior of $A \subset \mathbb{R}^\ell$	$\text{int}\{A\}$
Interior of $A \subset \mathbb{R}^\ell$ relative to $\mathbb{R}^\ell_+$	$\text{rel.int}\{A\}$
Sets of claimants	$N, N', \bar{N}, \ldots$
Generic claims vectors	$c, c', \bar{c}, \ldots$
Generic endowments	$E, E', \bar{E}, \ldots$
Generic claims problems	$(c, E), (c', E'), (\bar{c}, \bar{E}), \ldots$
Domain of problems with claimant set N	$\mathcal{C}^N$
Awards space for claimant set N	$\mathbb{R}^N_+$
Set of awards vectors of $(c, E) \in \mathcal{C}^N$	$X(c, E) \equiv \{x \in \mathbb{R}^N : 0 \leqq x \leqq c, \sum x_i = E\}$
Claimant i's claim c_i truncated at E	$t(c_i, E)$
Vector of claims c each truncated at E	$(t(c_i, E))_{i \in N} = t(c, E)$
Cardinality of the set A	$\|A\|$
Family of finite subsets of $\mathbb{N}$	$\mathcal{N}$
Union $\bigcup_{N \in \mathcal{N}} \mathcal{C}^N$	$\mathcal{C}$
Class of strict orders on N	$\mathcal{O}^N$
Class of weak orders on N	$\tilde{\mathcal{O}}^N$

Class of bijections on N	Π^N
ith unit vector in $\mathbb{R}^N$	e_i
Unit simplex in $\mathbb{R}^N$	$\Delta^N \equiv \{x \in \mathbb{R}_+ : \sum x_i = 1\}$
Vector of equal coordinates in Δ^N	e_N
Given $N' \subset N$, projection of $x \in \mathbb{R}^N$ onto $\mathbb{R}^{N'}$	$x_{N'}$
Segment connecting x and $y \in \mathbb{R}^N$	$\text{seg}[x, y]$
Broken segment connecting $x^1, \ldots, x^k \in \mathbb{R}^N$	$\text{bro.seg}[x^1, \ldots, x^k]$
Given $x, y \in \mathbb{R}^N$ such that $x \leqq y$, set of vectors z such that $x \leqq z \leqq y$	$\text{box}[x, y]$

Notation for Division Rules

Generic rules	$S, S', \bar{S} \ldots$
Path of awards of S for c	$p^S(c)$

Individual Rules

Proportional rule	P
Concede-and-divide (for $\|N\| = 2$)	CD
Reverse concede-and-divide (for $\|N\| = 2$)	CD^r
Constrained equal awards rule	CEA
Constrained equal losses rule	CEL
Talmud rule	T
Reverse Talmud rule	T^r
Piniles' rule	Pin
Constrained egalitarian rule	CE
Random arrival rule	RA
Minimal overlap rule	MO
Random stakes rule	RS
Adjusted proportional rule	AP
Average of CEA and CEL	Av

Families of Rules

Sequential priority rule relative to order $\prec \in \mathcal{O}^N$	$SP^{\prec}$
Sequential Talmud rule relative to order $\preceq \in \tilde{\mathcal{O}}^N$ and weights $w \in \Delta^N$	$ST^{\preceq, w}$
Young rule of representation $f \in \Phi$	Y^f
Equal sacrifice rule relative to $u \in \mathcal{U}$	ES^u
ICI rule relative to $H \in \mathcal{H}^N$	ICI^H
CIC rule relative to $H \in \bar{\mathcal{H}}^N$	CIC^H

TAL rule of parameter $\theta \in \Delta^N$	T^θ
Reverse TAL rule of parameter $\theta \in \Delta^N$	U^θ

Operating on Rules

Rule S subjected to the	
attribution of minimal rights operator	S^m
claims truncation operator	S^t
duality operator	S^d
operator p and then to operator p'	$S^{p' \circ p}$

CHAPTER 1

Introduction

1.1 CLAIMS PROBLEMS

How to divide when there isn't enough? When a group of agents has claims on a resource that add up to more than what is available, how should the resource be divided? A "division rule," or "rule" for short, associates with each such "claims problem" a division among the claimants of the amount available. Our goal is to survey the literature devoted to identifying the most desirable rules.

A primary concern of this literature is with a firm going bankrupt, its liquidation value having to be apportioned among its creditors. The model we study here, however, can be given many other interesting interpretations; covered are all situations in which a group of agents has entitlements over a resource that cannot be jointly honored.

Our search for answers begins with the description of several rules that are commonly used in practice or have been discussed in the theoretical literature. Then – and this constitutes the bulk of our work – we formulate properties that one may want rules to satisfy; we compare the rules on the basis of the properties they enjoy; we investigate the existence of rules satisfying various combinations of the properties; and, when rules exist that satisfy a given list of properties, we describe the family they constitute. These properties are formally stated as *axioms*. Finally, we appeal to the conceptual apparatus of modern game theory to construct rules. Both the cooperative branch of the field and its strategic branch are rich in concepts and techniques that proved very helpful in our endeavor.

Only one good is to be allocated here and, for all agents, more is preferred to less. Thus, agents' preferences are the same and they do not appear explicitly in our model. This is an important way in which the class of problems we investigate should be distinguished from other classes most often considered in the theory of economic design. When allocating resources on which agents have equal rights, the issue is typically how best to take account of how their preferences differ. Here, by contrast, agents differ only to the extent that their rights and identities differ. The central question in the discipline of economics is commonly stated as pertaining to the allocation of scarce and valuable resources and, in its standard specification, the reason for scarcity is that preferences are non-satiated. Preferences do not reach satiation here but there are natural upper bounds on consumptions – no agent should be assigned more than their claim – and our focus is on situations where there is not enough to reach these bounds simultaneously. Also, we will not take into account the intensity of the satisfaction that claimants derive from their assignments, as captured by what are usually called "utility functions." In spite of these significant differences, many of the general ideas that underlie properties of rules studied in other contexts are just as pertinent to the understanding of how to adjudicate conflicting claims. They will be fundamental concepts in our evaluation of candidate rules, and they will direct our search for the most desirable ones.

The best-known rule is the "proportional" rule, for which awards are proportional to claims. In fact, proportionality is often taken as the definition of fairness for claims problems. It was already so for Aristotle. But is there any reason to believe the proportional rule superior to the others? Beside Aristotle, an important source of inspiration for the work we present here is ancient literature, such as the Talmud, and a number of medieval authors, in particular Maimonides, where numerical examples are described, and for these examples, recommendations are made that conflict with proportionality. Can these recommendations be rationalized by means of well-behaved rules? The answer is yes, and we will exhibit such rules. Are there grounds for preferring one or the other to the proportional rule and to the other rules that have been proposed more recently? Here, the answer is more complex. We will indeed produce interesting axiomatic underpinnings for a rule that accounts for all of the numbers in the Talmud, and uncover good reasons to promote certain rules encountered in medieval texts, or inspired by these texts, as well as newly defined rules. We will also find that the proportional rule does satisfy many appealing properties, and, in fact, it will frequently emerge out of our axiomatic analysis. So will two rules found in Maimonides. However, a central conclusion to be drawn from our investigation is that, depending upon the viewpoint taken and the intended application of the theory, one or the other of several rules is preferable. On the other hand, certain a priori reasonable rules have rarely come out of axiomatic considerations, and some not at all. This should not be seen as a fatal flaw of these rules, but it diminishes their appeal to a degree.

Real-life claims problems are of course more complicated affairs than our stylized model can adequately represent, but many enlightening lessons can still be learned from its study. Besides, it can be enriched in a number of ways so as to accommodate additional features of resource allocation conflicts that are relevant to their resolution in practice, as we will indicate in various places. A concluding chapter lists even more significant ways in which it can be further generalized.

An important question that we will not address is the extent to which the choice of a particular division rule affects agents' incentives to make commitments that, in the end, one party may be unable to honor. In the context of bankruptcy, these are the incentives to loan and to borrow. Think of a legislature considering reforming bankruptcy laws so as to bring about some goal deemed socially desirable: a higher rate of investment, for example. Enhancing the safety of investing for certain categories of individuals might be achieved by the choice of particular rules, and this legislature would have to take such incentives into account. In many of the other applications, the parameters of the problems to be solved also result from decisions that agents have made in the past. Whatever rule they know would be used at the division stage will in general have had an effect on these earlier choices. In order to handle these kinds of issues, we would need to work with a more general model than the one that is our focus. Risk-taking, effort, and other variables under the control of agents, such as lenders, borrowers, tax payers, government agencies, and others, would have to be explicitly described, stochastic returns to economic activities factored in, and so on. But the theory developed here, which mostly ignores incentives, is a necessary component of the comprehensive treatment – it would have to be formulated in a general-equilibrium and game-theoretic framework – that we envision.[1]

1.2 THE MODEL

Here is the formal model. An amount $E \in \mathbb{R}_+$ of an infinitely divisible resource, the **endowment**, has to be allocated among a **group N of agents** having **claims** on it, $\boldsymbol{c_i} \in \mathbb{R}_+$ being the claim of agent $i \in N$, our generic agent. Up to Chapter 10, we take N to be a finite and fixed subset of the set of natural numbers $\mathbb{N}$, usually $\{1, \ldots, n\}$. Using the notation $\mathbb{R}^N_+$ for the cross-product of $|N|$ copies of $\mathbb{R}_+$ indexed by the members of N,[2] the claims vector $\boldsymbol{c} \equiv (c_i)_{i \in N}$ is therefore an element of $\mathbb{R}^N_+$. To complete the model, we add that the endowment is not sufficient to fully honor all claims.

In summary, a claims problem, or simply a **problem**, is a pair $(\boldsymbol{c}, \boldsymbol{E}) \in \mathbb{R}^N_+ \times \mathbb{R}_+$ such that $\sum c_i \geq E$. Let $\mathcal{C}^N$ denote the domain of all problems.[3]

Figures 1.1 and 1.2 illustrate the definition for $N \equiv \{1, 2\}$ and $N \equiv \{1, 2, 3\}$ respectively.

In Chapters 10–12 and in Section 15.3 we extend the model so as to allow the population of claimants to vary and generalize the notation accordingly.

Although the model just described is extremely simple, it is rich enough to be given several interesting and diverse interpretations, and it is mathematically nontrivial, as we will see.

[1] Steps in these various directions are taken by Araujo and Páscoa (2002), Karagözoğlu (2014), and Kıbrıs and Kıbrıs (2013). They are briefly discussed in Section 15.7.

[2] Alternatively, the superscript N may refer to a set pertaining to the agents in N. Which interpretation is intended should be unambiguous from the context.

[3] We allow the equality $\sum c_i = E$ for convenience, although in this boundary case, all claims can in fact be honored.

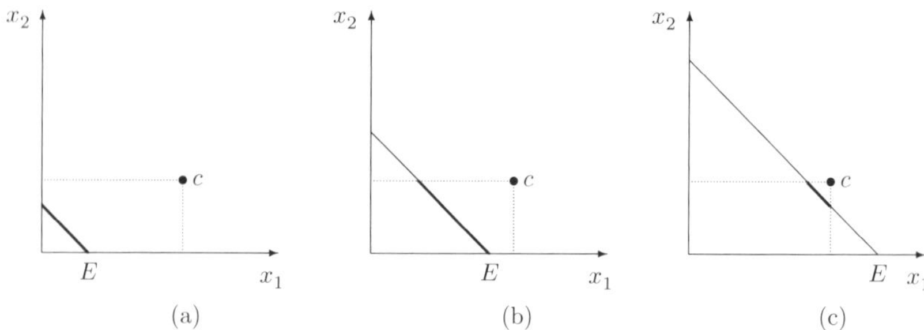

Figure 1.1: **Identifying the awards vectors of a two-claimant problem.** The claimant set is $N \equiv \{1, 2\}$. The claims vector is $c \in \mathbb{R}^N_+$. The endowment is $E \in \mathbb{R}_+$. Axes are indexed by claimants. Along each axis we measure an agent's claim and possible awards to that agent. The objective is to choose a vector satisfying the following conditions: it should be nonnegative and bounded above by c, and it should be on the line of equation $\sum x_i = E$. These are the "awards vectors" of (c, E). In this sequence of panels, c is fixed and E is given three values. In each case, the thick segment represents the set of vectors to choose from. (a) Here, there is no awards vector at which even one claimant is fully compensated. (b) Here, claimant 2 could be fully compensated, if alone; claimant 1 could not. (c) Here, each claimant could be fully compensated, if alone.

One application, already mentioned, is to bankruptcy: there, E is the liquidation value of a bankrupt firm, and each coordinate of c represents the claim held against it by one of its creditors.

A closely related application is to estate division: a man dies and his estate is insufficient to cover the debts he leaves behind. How should it be divided among his creditors? We will sometimes refer to such situations, often discussed in ancient literature, and use then the language of estate division.

The financial decisions faced by the organizer of a scientific meeting whose budget is too limited to fully cover the expenses of all participants, a situation familiar in academia, is another example.

Our next application is to rationing: a group of customers of a firm has placed orders for a good produced by the firm, but the total quantity it can supply turns out to be insufficient to satisfy everyone; orders can only be partially filled. Being able to demonstrate that it has done its best to be even-handed in dealing with the situation might help the firm remain on good terms with all of its customers. So how much should it assign to each of them?

The problem can also occur at the level of nations, when a scarce resource has to be distributed to states or provinces – food, clean water, medical supplies, or shares of the global carbon budget[4] come to mind here – and at the multinational level. For instance, an international agency distributing aid to impoverished countries rarely has enough to cover all of these needs.

[4] Giménez-Gómez, Teixedó-Figueras, Vilella (2016).

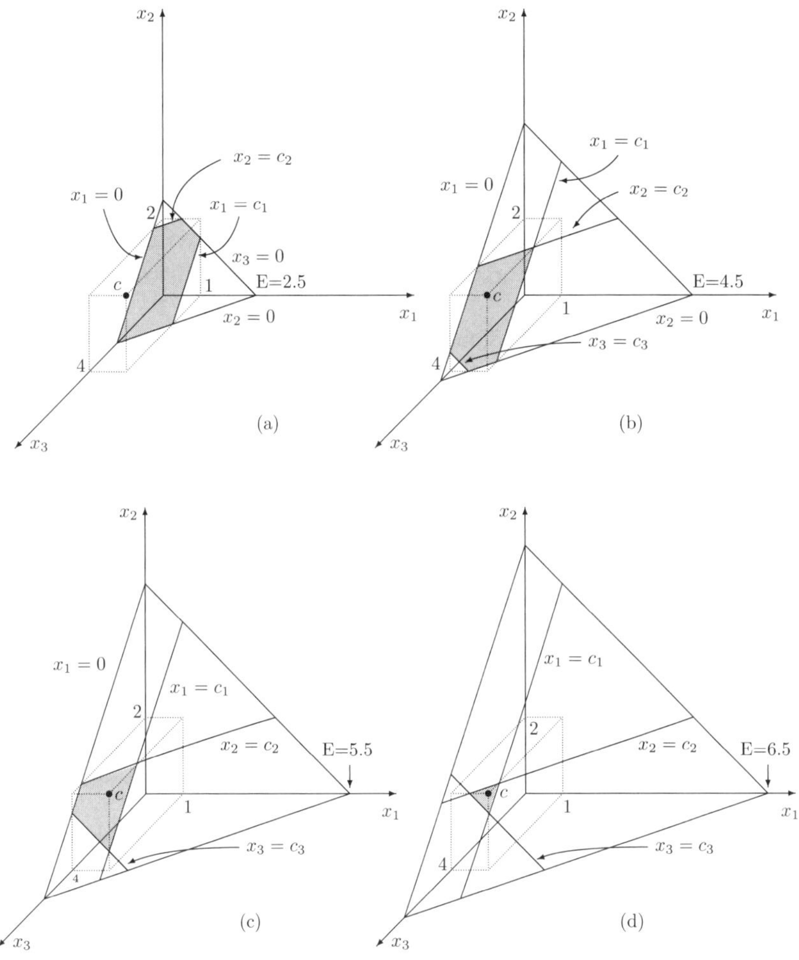

Figure 1.2: **Identifying the awards vectors of a three-claimant problem.** The claimant set is $N \equiv \{1, 2, 3\}$. The claims vector is $c \equiv (1, 2, 4) \in \mathbb{R}^N_+$ and the endowment E is given four values – 2.5 in panel (a), 4.5 in panel (b), 5.5 in panel (c), and 6.5 in panel (d). In each case, the shaded area represents the set of awards vectors of (c, E): they are nonnegative, bounded above by c, and belong to the plane of equation $\sum x_i = E$. Among the vectors $x \in \mathbb{R}^N$ satisfying these conditions, the subset of vectors such that $x_1 = c_1$, say, is indicated by a line in the plane of equation $\sum x_i = E$ labeled "$x_1 = c_1$." Only the constraints that are binding in identifying the set of awards vectors are labeled.

More generally, our model encompasses any situation in which some amount of a resource has to be allocated among a group of agents when that amount is insufficient to satisfy their commensurable claims, needs, or demands.

In most of the applications just listed, these parameters are objective amounts, typically supported by legal documents. Alternatively, they could be given a subjective interpretation, and their values could even be a matter of debate. In the case of needs, for instance, one can certainly imagine experts disagreeing on the aid required by different countries facing medical emergencies. Nevertheless, some reasonable brackets may well be agreed upon, the question being how to select a division that achieves the best compromise among these approximate measures of need. To simplify the analysis we work with precise values of all variables of the model instead of with intervals or distributions.[5]

In our personal and professional lives, misunderstandings sometimes occur as to how much of some resource each of us is entitled to. What should we do? In such situations claims are not supported by legal documents, but it doesn't necessarily mean that they should be ignored. The behavior of agents is often affected by informal agreements and subjective views of the situation they are facing, not just by objective factors. When claims are made in good faith, everyone involved may accept that they should be taken into consideration. In practice, expectations, beliefs, perceptions of fairness, and so on, play an important role in how agents respond to proposed settlements. Thus, the use of a rule whose good behavior can be demonstrated should contribute to dissipate conflicts, and help societies to function more smoothly.

Alternatively, one can simply think of each of the coordinates of the claims vector as a bound on the consumption of the agent to which it pertains, a bound that should not be exceeded for reasons that need not be explicitly specified.

Our model can also be interpreted as a formalization of a simple class of tax assessment problems: there, agents are taxpayers whose incomes are given by the coordinates of c, and who among themselves must cover the cost E of a project. The sum of their incomes is larger than the cost: they can afford the project. The question is how much each taxpayer should contribute.[6] This application differs from the previous one in that what is to be divided is a collective obligation (an agent's welfare decreases when their share of the dividend increases). This difference has no significant mathematical consequences for the theory, but this alternative interpretation of the variables should be kept in mind when evaluating axioms and rules.

Finally, we consider the closely related problem of cost allocation. Now, agents are the users of a public project. The parameter c_i represents the benefit agent i derives from the project, and E is the cost of undertaking it. The sum

[5] A model in which the parameters of the problem are intervals is studied by Branzei and Alparslan (2008). See Section 15.7 for a discussion and additional references.

[6] Note, however, that in practice the problem of taxation is not generally specified by first stating an amount to be collected, perhaps due to the uncertainty pertaining to the taxpayers' incomes. In most cases, taxation schedules are published first, and the amount collected falls wherever it may, depending upon realized incomes.

of the benefits is larger than the cost, indicating that the project is worth undertaking. How much should each user contribute? This problem has been the subject of a considerable literature, both normative and strategic. An issue that has preoccupied many investigators is that users may misrepresent the benefits they derive from the project, resulting in a distorted decision. The question then is how to elicit the information needed for the correct decision to be made (undertake it if the sum of the valuations exceeds the cost, and not otherwise; achieve a desirable distribution of welfare among the participants).

For convenience, in most of our treatment of the problem, we maintain the interpretation of the model as pertaining to the adjudication of conflicting claims, and we use language that fits that interpretation.

We are tasked with identifying a list of "awards," one for each claimant, whose sum is equal to the endowment. Instead of considering each problem separately, however, we will look for a general method of handling all problems – that is, for a function that associates with each problem a division of the endowment among the claimants. We will require that each claimant receive an amount that is nonnegative and at most as large as their claim. The division is to be thought of as a recommendation for the problem.

Formally, an **awards vector for $(c, E) \in \mathcal{C}^N$** is a vector $x \in \mathbb{R}^N$ such that $0 \leqq x \leqq c$ and satisfying the **balance** requirement $\sum x_i = E$.[7] Let $\boldsymbol{X(c, E)}$ be the set of awards vectors for (c, E). A division rule, or simply a **rule**, is a function that associates with each claims problem $(c, E) \in \mathcal{C}^N$ an awards vector for it; that is, a vector in $X(c, E)$. Our generic notation for a rule is the letter S.

We stress that a rule is a **single-valued** mapping, that is, a rule selects a unique awards vector for each problem. This is desirable because it means that the issue of how much to assign to each claimant has been completely resolved. Among the various recommendations that a multi-valued mapping may make for a given problem, on what grounds should one choose? *Single-valuedness* is particularly justified here because, for our model, a great variety of interesting mappings enjoy the property. This fact is worth emphasizing. Indeed, *single-valuedness* is a luxury that one can rarely afford: in most other types of allocation problems, it comes at a high price, excluding many natural mappings or preventing certain appealing properties from being satisfied by any mapping.

The set of awards vectors of each problem is a convex set. Thus, an arbitrary convex combination of rules is a rule.[8] This observation will shed much light on the structure of the space they constitute.

[7] Vector inequalities: $x \geqq y$ allows x and y to be equal; $x \geq y$ does not; $x > y$ means that each coordinate of x is larger than the corresponding coordinate of y.

[8] By the convex combination of two rules S^1 and S^2 with weights $(\lambda^1, \lambda^2) \in \Delta^1$ (where Δ^1 is the unit simplex of $\mathbb{R}^2_+$), we mean the rule that associates with each problem $(c, E) \in \mathcal{C}^N$ the awards vector $\lambda^1 S^1(c, E) + \lambda^2 S^2(c, E)$.

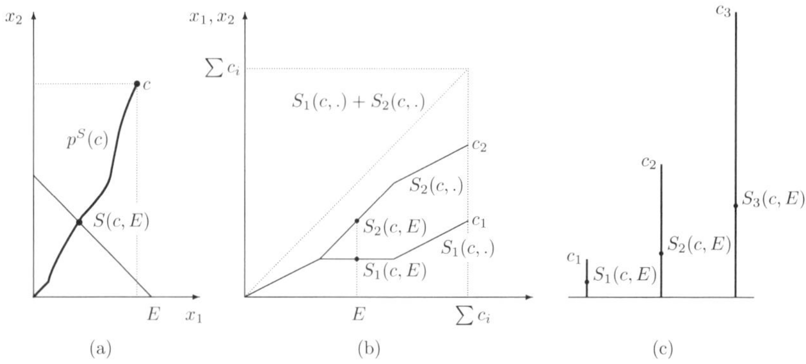

Figure 1.3: **Three ways of depicting a division rule.** In each case, the claims vector is fixed at $c \in \mathbb{R}^N_+$. (a) Here, $N \equiv \{1, 2\}$. We follow the awards vector $S(c, E)$ as E varies from 0 to $\sum c_i$, thereby obtaining the "path of awards" of S for c, $p^S(c)$. Diagrams of this sort are very useful for two claimants and for three claimants. (b) Here, $N \equiv \{1, 2\}$ also. We plot each claimant's award separately as a function of E, measured on the horizontal axis, as E varies from 0 to $\sum c_i$. The sum of the functions is the identity. These "schedules of awards" of S for c can be drawn for any number of claimants. (c) Here, $N \equiv \{1, 2, 3\}$. We represent claims and awards as vertical segments, and given $E \leq \sum c_i$, we indicate by dots the amounts that S awards to the various claimants. This amount is the vertical distance from the horizontal line to the dot. These diagrams can accommodate any number of claimants but only a few values of the endowment.

Figure 1.3 shows three ways of depicting a typical rule, called S. For the important class of Young's rules of Subsection 2.2.2, below, a fourth representation is possible. However, we will wait until then for a formal introduction of the concept and a description of these representations.[9] In each of the panels of Figure 1.3, the claims vector is kept fixed.

1. Graphs of the type represented in panel (a) give, in a Euclidean space of dimension equal to the number of claimants, the path followed by the awards vector chosen by S as the endowment increases from 0 to the sum of the claims. In "awards space," the award to each claimant is measured along the claimant's own axis. We call this path **the path of awards of the rule for the claims vector**. We use the notation $\boldsymbol{p^S(c)}$ for the path of S for c. In our illustrations, we almost always draw paths of awards as continuous, this property being very natural (we formally introduce continuity requirements on rules in Section 3.2). Moreover, as we will see, continuity with respect to the endowment is in fact satisfied by all interesting rules, and we have encountered no

[9] Hendrickx, Borm, van Elk, and Quant (2005) propose to represent a rule by specifying, for each $c \in \mathbb{R}^N_+$ and each $i \in N$, a function defined on $[0, \sum c_i]$ whose integral, for each E in that interval, gives claimant i's award.

situation where it has a cost in terms of other properties. However, paths could in principle be discontinuous.

Paths of awards are most suggestive of the behavior of rules. For example, we will discover that a rule can very usefully be evaluated by assessing, for each claims vector, how close to the 45° line – or to the ray emanating from the origin and passing through the claims vector – its path lies, whether it exhibits any concavity or convexity property, whether it is smooth or has kinks, and so on. Such qualitative features are revealed by simple visual inspection. Depicting rules by means of their paths of awards is also very useful for proofs. Paths are harder to draw and to visualize for three claimants, but we will still find them very useful. Of course, this representation cannot accommodate any larger number of claimants, but most of the difficulties in developing our theory already occur for two or three claimants.

2. Graphs of the type illustrated in panel (b) can handle an arbitrary number of claimants: for each claims vector, we simply plot the award chosen by the rule for each claimant as a function of the endowment. The domain of definition of this function is the interval from 0 to the sum of the claims. The sum of the functions is the identity function. We call these plots **schedules of awards of the rule for the claims vector**. The functions could be discontinuous too, but once again, in our illustrations, we almost always draw them continuous.

3. On a graph of the type illustrated in panel (c), where claims and awards are represented as vertical segments, only a few of the awards vectors chosen by a rule can be shown without clutter (for no more than three or four choices of the endowment), but such graphs are nevertheless very convenient for certain proofs. In particular, they too can accommodate an arbitrary number of claimants. (On rare occasions, we will prefer to represent claims as horizontal segments as opposed to vertical segments.)

1.3 TWO PUZZLES IN THE TALMUD

To someone not familiar with economic design, the need to go beyond whatever is generally done in practice, in our case proportionality, is not always obvious. However, we hope to convince readers of the great benefit of making a clean slate of any preconceived notions about which rules are better. Besides, proportionality is not as universal as one may think. Although it has been advocated since Aristotle, we describe in this section several problems discussed in the Talmud[10] for which the Talmud does not recommend proportional division. Only a few numerical examples are specified there, but several other examples appear in ancient literature, which we will describe in due time and for which outcomes other than the proportional outcomes were suggested. We expect that these intriguing examples will whet our readers' appetite as much as they have whetted the appetite of many of the researchers who have contributed to the subject.

[10] The Talmud is the collection of writings that constitute the basis for Jewish Law.

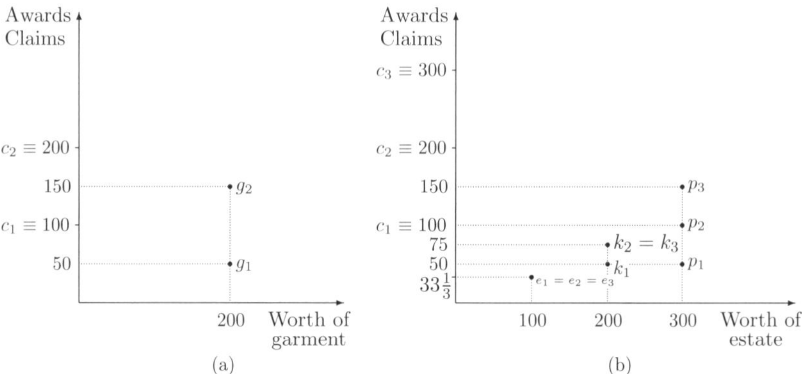

Figure 1.4: **Two puzzles in the Talmud**. The numbers in the Talmud that have to be explained pertain to the problems represented here. (a) In the "contested garment" problem there are two claimants, with claims 100 and 200, over a garment worth 200. The Talmud recommends the division $g \equiv (50, 150)$. (b) In the "marriage contract" problems, there are three claimants with claims 100, 200, and 300. If the estate is worth 100, the Talmud recommends $e \equiv (33\frac{1}{3}, 33\frac{1}{3}, 33\frac{1}{3})$; if worth 200, it recommends $k \equiv (50, 75, 75)$; and if worth 300, it recommends $p \equiv (50, 100, 150)$. Can one make sense of these choices?

The **contested garment problem** (Figure 1.4a) has to do with two men disagreeing over the ownership of a garment and making incompatible claims on it. How should the garment – rather its worth – be divided between them? Here is the description of the problem and the recommendation made for it:[11]

> Two hold a garment...If one of them says, "It is all mine," and the other says "Half of it is mine," ...the former receives three quarters and the latter receives one quarter.

To fix the ideas, let us assign a worth of 200 to the garment. Then, one man claims 100 and the other claims 200. Thus, the suggestion made in the Talmud is the division (50, 150).[12]

[11] See Baba Metzia, Babylonian Talmud I. All references to the relevant passages of the Talmud and of the secondary literature are taken from O'Neill (1982), Aumann and Maschler (1985), and Dagan (1996). For additional citations, see Callen (1987) and Aumann (2010).

[12] A variant of this numerical example also appears in a Tosefta to Baba Metzia, in which the smaller claim is one-third of the garment, the larger claim still being the entire garment. The recommendation there is that the smaller claimant gets one-sixth of the garment and the other the remainder. Another example in which two principles of liability conflict is in Baba Kamma 53a. First, the owner of a wild ox is responsible for half of the damages the ox may cause. Second, someone having dug an open pit on public property is liable for all of the damages it may cause. The example involves a wild ox causing an animal to fall in an open pit. The numerical values attached to the example are as in the contested garment problem and the recommendations made for it in the Talmud are the same as for the contested garment problem. References and a discussion are in Aumann (2010).

The **marriage contract** problem (Figure 1.4b)[13] concerns estate division. It involves the three wives of a man who signed contracts when marrying each of them specifying, as is the tradition, how much she should receive in case of dissolution of their marriage (divorce or his death). The man dies and his estate is found to be insufficient to simultaneously honor all three contracts. How should his estate be divided among his wives:[14]

> If a man who was married to three wives died and the kethubah of one was one maneh (100 zuz), of the other two hundred zuz, and of the third three hundred zuz, and the estate (was worth) only one maneh (one hundred zuz), (the sum) is divided equally. If the estate (was worth) two hundred zuz (the claimant) of the maneh (one hundred zuz) receives fifty zuz (and the claimants respectively) of the two hundred and three hundred zuz (receive each) three gold denarii (seventy-five zuz). If the estate (was worth) three hundred zuz (the claimant) of the maneh receives fifty zuz and (the claimant) of the two hundred zuz (receives) a maneh (one hundred zuz) while (the claimant) of the three hundred zuz (receives) six gold denarii (one hundred and fifty zuz). Similarly if three persons contributed to a joint fund and they had made a loss or profit they share in the same manner.

We will search for a formula that convincingly interpolates and extrapolates these recommendations. The formula should be justifiable historically in terms of what we know of the modes of reasoning and the mathematics of the times. The graphs of Figure 1.4 show that we have very little information to go by; many reasonable-looking schedules of awards can probably be made to pass through the few points that are specified. Yet, we will produce a recently discovered formula and argue that it is likely to capture what the Sages of the Talmud had in mind. Moreover, we will discover compelling arguments in its favor.

However, the elucidation of the numbers given in the Talmud and other historical documents, in particular texts due to Ibn Ezra and Maimonides (see below), is for us only a side benefit of the general theory that we will develop. The elaboration of such a theory is our principal objective.

1.4 THREE APPROACHES

Apart from what we will learn about how to solve claims problems and related problems, our study will illustrate the various approaches that can be taken when studying any domain of problems. We distinguish three main ones.

[13] The notation g in panel (a) is intended to remind us of the fact that a garment is to be divided, and in panel (b), e stands for equal division, p for proportional division, and k for a division that lies between equal division and proportional division. At this point, we prefer avoiding these expressions, however, since they are too suggestive of particular rules. For now, our intention is only to present the numbers to be explained, without prejudging the explanation.

[14] Kethubot 93a; the author of this Mishna is Rabbi Nathan.

1.4.1 Direct Approach

The **direct approach** starts from rules.[15] A rule may be used in practice, or it may be the formal representation of an investigator's ideas about how to deal with the class of situations under study. A rule may be given explicitly, by a formula or a geometric construction, or it may be defined implicitly, by a system of equations or an algorithm. A rule is evaluated by the appeal of its definition, and by testing it by means of examples. We confront it with situations in which common sense or experience with resource allocation in general suggests particular resolutions and we check whether the rule makes recommendations that agree with these expectations.

A challenge in carrying out this program is specifying a set of examples that are sufficiently representative of the entire range of situations that one may encounter. If there are often good arguments to exclude for each problem certain awards vectors as being unreasonable or unappealing, it is quite another matter to identify a set of examples that satisfy the twin requirements that (i) intuition points to a unique recommendation for each of them as being most desirable, at least to a reasonably narrow range of recommendations, and (ii) when contemplated together, they constitute a sufficiently powerful battery of tests to judge rules in their entirety, and to differentiate among them.

1.4.2 Axiomatic Approach

We will go into somewhat more detail in presenting the **axiomatic approach**, as it is the main focus of this book. This approach starts from properties of rules, formulated as "axioms." An axiom is the mathematical expression of the intuition we have about how a rule should handle a certain class of situations. A typical axiomatic study focuses on a few properties, studies their logical relations, and investigates the implications of the properties when imposed in various combinations.

Results are of two kinds. Sometimes, we find that certain properties are incompatible. The outcome then is an **impossibility theorem**. Or, we discover that a list of properties are compatible and we are able to describe the family of rules satisfying them. In some cases, only one rule is admissible. A theorem identifying a particular rule as being the only one to satisfy a given list of properties is an **axiomatic characterization** of the rule. Alternatively, a characterization theorem may identify a particular *family* of rules as being the only ones to satisfy a given list of properties. A central objective of the **axiomatic program** as a whole is to trace out the boundary separating those that are compatible from those that are not, and, when compatible, to obtain complete and explicit descriptions of which rules, or which families of rules, satisfy all of them.[16]

[15] We use this term for lack of a better alternative. It should become a little clearer after the other approaches have been defined.

[16] For a users' guide and a detailed discussion of the relative merits of the axiomatic method and other methods, see Thomson (2001, 2018c).

A rule characterized in a theorem typically satisfies a number of properties that do not appear in the statement of the theorem, but these additional properties occasionally come as a surprise. Uncovering in this manner unexpected relations among properties – unexpected because, separately, none of the properties that are imposed seems to have anything to do with the property that they jointly imply – is one of the benefits of axiomatic work.

For a characterization to be most useful, the axioms it involves should express conceptually distinct ideas so as to make it as clear as possible where the features of rules that are characterized come from. They should also be logically independent. That is, no axiom should be implied by the conjunction of the others. Then, if any one of them is dropped, the class of admissible rules expands. If, instead, one of the axioms is implied by the others, the theorem has not fully revealed the power of these other axioms; conversely, the freedom gained by relaxing them is obscured, which is undesirable.

We will follow each characterization by an examination of the independence of the axioms on which it is based. A characterization may involve only one axiom, and of course the issue of independence is moot then. However, in such a case there may be weaker versions of the axiom that are worth considering. The question arises then of how much leeway would be gained by weakening the axiom in these various ways, and in particular in determining the extent to which less demanding formulations would allow satisfying axioms with which the original axiom was incompatible. Similarly, for an impossibility, independence means that if one axiom were dropped, the remaining axioms would be compatible.

Exploring variants of axioms and understanding how substituting them for axioms appearing in theorems affects the conclusions reached is very important because there is almost always more than one way of giving mathematical form to some general idea we have about how rules should behave.

Some properties are very natural and everyone would probably endorse the idea underlying them and its formal expression. "Equal treatment of equals," the requirement that agents with the same characteristics be treated in the same way, is of this kind for many applications of our theory. Some properties are so compelling that it seems even desirable to incorporate them in the definition of what is understood by the term "rule." This is in fact why we have required that, for each problem, the vector chosen by a rule be balanced, nonnegative, and bounded above by the claims vector. Of course, a property being compelling does not guarantee that it will be easily met. In the theory of coalitional games, the requirement that a solution select for each game a payoff vector in the core of the game may well appear necessary to guarantee the stability of the outcomes we choose, but many games have empty cores. Similarly, in various theories of resource allocation, one may ask that a rule always provide each agent the incentive to be truthful about the information the agent holds privately (typically information about their preferences),[17] but this requirement

[17] A strategy is "dominant" for a player in a game if it is best no matter what strategies the other players choose. This property of a rule known as "strategy-proofness" is the requirement that,

is often incompatible with very minimal demands of efficiency and fairness in distribution. The case for imposing other properties is sometimes not as strong, and whether we should insist on them depends on the application we have in mind. The invariance (and covariance) properties that have played an important role in the theory to be presented, as well as in other branches of the theory of fair allocation, are illustrations. A property of this type describes two ways of looking at the same situation and states that they should result in the same outcome (or in "equivalent" outcomes).

It is useful to organize properties in categories. First, we can distinguish among **universal** versus **model-specific** axioms. Some properties indeed express ideas that are meaningful very generally, beyond the specific model under study. An example is the requirement, most commonly known as "efficiency," that there be no feasible outcome that everyone prefers to the one that is chosen. Here, it means that the endowment should be fully allocated. We referred to it as "balance." Another example is equal treatment of equals. In our context, apart from their name, the only characteristic an agent has is their claim, and it says that two claimants with equal claims should be awarded equal amounts. Other properties are inspired by the particular features of the situation that is the focus of the analysis. An example here is the requirement that no agent receive more than their claim. We will also encounter lower bounds on awards that are expressed as a function of the data defining a claims problem. These various requirements would not be meaningful in other settings.

Another useful distinction between axioms has to do with whether they apply to each problem in the domain of definition of a rule separately, "point by point," or whether they apply to pairs, triples, etc., of problems that are related in certain ways – they may also pertain to sequences of problems – and relate the choices made for these problems – and for their limits. We refer to the properties in the first category as **punctual** and to the properties in the second category as **relational**. Examples in the former are balance and equal treatment of equals. An example in the latter for our model is the requirement that, if the endowment increases, no claimant be assigned less.

Many relational axioms are **monotonicity axioms**: such an axiom states that a particular increase in one of the parameters entering the description of a problem should be accompanied by an increase in some variable(s) chosen by a rule, here the amounts awarded to one claimant, or to several claimants separately, or to a group of claimants in total; and many are **invariance axioms**: such an axiom describes circumstances under which a change in a problem should not affect the choice that is made, or some component of this choice.

A final distinction between properties is based on whether they involve a fixed population of agents or a variable population. All of the examples

for each economy and each agent, truth-telling be a dominant strategy in the manipulation game associated with the rule.

mentioned so far are **fixed-population axioms**. Requiring that if a population expands, all agents initially present be affected in the same direction, here that if new claimants arrive, none of the initial claimants be assigned more, is a **variable-population axiom**. Dealing with variable populations requires a more general model as well as proof techniques that are quite different from those needed in the fixed-population case, and often more delicate because the dimensionality of the space in which the analysis takes place is not fixed. For that reason we present our studies of these two kinds of properties in sets of separate chapters, although the analysis in the chapters in which population is allowed to vary still involves fixed-population properties.

Other principles can be invoked in organizing properties,[18] but at this point the broad distinctions just made should suffice.

1.4.3 Game-Theoretic Approach

Our third and final approach to studying a class of problems, the **game-theoretic approach**, consists in modeling the situation under consideration as a game (the term "game" is understood in its technical sense, as any situation in which a group of agents have conflicting interests); then applying a solution concept developed in the theory of games to solve the game: this means identifying "payoff vector(s)" representing either the recommendation(s) that an arbitrator could make to the agents involved, or prediction(s) of where they might end up if left to their own devices; finally, in the natural outcome space of the original situation, identifying the outcomes yielding the payoff vector(s) chosen for the game.

A number of ways of modeling conflicts as games have been proposed in the literature, and several of these modeling choices are available here. They give us the opportunity to take different types of solutions for games as starting points in defining rules to solve claims problems.

The organization of this book reflects the three approaches described in Subsections 1.4.1–1.4.3, and it should help illustrate the merits and limitations each has. It will be particularly instructive to uncover the extent to which they lead to the same awards vectors and rules.

Because our formal model can be given several concrete interpretations, for each of the approaches we follow we should have the application in mind when evaluating rules. A rule that is intuitively appealing in a bankruptcy situation may not be as compelling in the context of taxation or estate division. Similarly, when we follow the axiomatic approach, the relevance of a given axiom may depend on the application. As for the game-theoretic approach, the context will certainly affect the attractiveness of the model that we adopt; in particular, whether the behavioral assumptions underlying it are strategic or cooperative.

18 Thomson (2017c).

1.5 HISTORICAL NOTE

How to adjudicate conflicting claims has been a concern for all societies for many centuries. Aristotle addressed the issue, and in addition to the examples from the Talmud described above, we will give others from medieval sources, Maimonides in particular. How to deal with circular priorities (Section 15.7) has also been the object of some literature in legal journals in the first part of the twentieth century. However, the first formal analysis of claims problems is the work of O'Neill (1982). O'Neill understood how the three approaches briefly introduced in the previous subsection – the direct approach, the axiomatic approach, and the game-theoretic approach – could be called upon to help compare division rules and identify the most desirable ones, and his fascinating paper is rich in developments illustrating the power of each of them. It offers historical puzzles and analysis and mathematical reasoning, and can also serve as an introduction to game theory and economic design. It is the foundation stone of the literature reviewed in this book.

1.6 ROAD MAP

We continue with a short summary of the remaining chapters. In Chapter 2, we introduce the various rules that have been discussed in the literature or used in practice. We then identify several infinite yet simple families of rules that contain most of these rules as particular cases, allowing us to organize and expand our inventory in useful ways. These families link rules to one another. Many of the rules discussed in this chapter are quite appealing intuitively, but few of them have actually been used in practice. Why not, and should they be?

To answer these questions, we turn to axioms, and it is to axiomatic analysis that the bulk of this work is devoted (Chapters 3–13). We begin with a model in which the population of claimants is fixed and then turn to a more general model in which it may vary. The first properties we consider are basic punctual properties. The properties we study next are relational. They can be broadly divided into monotonicity and invariance properties. We then examine how rules affect the distribution of resources in a society, exploiting concepts developed in the literature devoted to the evaluation of income distributions.

In Chapter 14, we use concepts and tools of game theory to analyze claims problems.

In Chapter 15, we describe a number of extensions of the base model.

In Chapter 16, we collect basic information about the most important rules for easy reference, diagrams illustrating them for two claimants (Figures 16.1 and 16.2), and a table summarizing which of the main properties introduced in Chapters 3–12 they satisfy (Table 16.1). We also offer concluding comments.

In Chapter 17, we gather technical appendices.

In the chapters devoted to the axiomatic approach, properties of rules are our point of departure. As a result, possible characterizations of a given rule based on different combinations of properties do not appear consecutively. This organization comes from our position that properties of rules are the primary concepts, not rules themselves; a rule is of interest mainly to the extent that it possesses appealing properties. However, it is convenient to collect in one place all interesting rules, and we have chosen to do so right away, in Chapter 2. Another advantage of so structuring our presentation is practical. Having at our disposal a large number of rules is very useful when conducting axiomatic analysis: the rules help us appreciate the strength of an axiom when we first introduce it, test the validity of conjectures about compatibilities or incompatibilities of axioms, and provide powerful tools to establish the independence of axioms in characterizations.

1.7 HOW TO USE THIS BOOK

1. **To learn about a specific rule,** consult Section 2.1 where we may have defined and illustrated it, and informally compared it with other rules. Check Section 2.2 to see if it belongs to any of the various families of rules introduced there – another way to get insight into its structural connection to others, and to then easily identify a number of axioms it may or may not satisfy. Throughout Chapters 3–12, we may have used the rule to illustrate a newly stated axiom: we may have given it as an example of a rule satisfying the axiom or as an example of a rule violating it. Most results of this kind are straightforward, however, and readers should certainly not expect to find explicit answers concerning all rules that have appeared in the literature and all axioms; for such illustrative purposes we have only invoked the rules that have been most central in the theory. An alternative means of finding out whether a rule of interest satisfies a certain axiom is to exploit logical relations among axioms. A final way to learn about the rule is to search for characterizations it may have been given. Such results are distributed throughout the text, as we have organized our exposition around axioms and not around rules, as we just explained. However, the index lists all the places where each rule has been characterized.

2. **To learn about a specific axiom,** find the section where we introduced it. We have accompanied each definition by examples of rules that satisfy it, and examples of others that do not. We may also have presented a number of logical connections between the axiom and others, and the axiom may appear in subsequent characterizations. In addition to scanning the pages that follow its introduction to search for results of this kind, consulting the index is useful. Ideally, for each combination of axioms, we would like to have a complete description of the class of rules satisfying that combination. For lists involving only punctual requirements, this is (most frequently) easily done, the only issue being whether, for each problem, there are awards vectors satisfying all

of them. But when relational axioms are imposed too, matters are often much more delicate. The question is not so much how large the class of rules satisfying a certain list of axioms is, but rather how complex it is; how transparent its structure is.

To illustrate, many rules satisfy the punctual requirement, mentioned above, that two agents with equal claims receive equal amounts but the class they constitute can be completely described: for each problem to which the hypotheses of the axiom apply, choose an awards vector satisfying its conclusion. Similarly, the class of rules satisfying the requirement that the awards vector chosen for a replica problem be the replica of the awards vector chosen for the problem that is subject to the replication is easily described, even though it is a relational requirement. However, the class of rules satisfying this latter axiom, together with the second relational requirement that an agent whose claim increases receive at least as much as the agent did initially, is not well understood, and no characterization is available at this point.

3. **To learn about axiomatic reasoning,** an overview of the table of contents is a good place to start. The table shows how axioms can be organized in categories. Manipulating definitions to understand how axioms are related is a useful exercise. Inspecting a few characterization proofs reveals how such proofs are structured. In a characterization of a particular rule, the fact that the rule satisfies the axioms listed in the theorem is often straightforward, as the work is done axiom by axiom. The uniqueness part is more delicate because it has to do with the interplay of the axioms. It typically starts with simple situations for which the punctual requirements by themselves allow us to conclude which awards vectors should be chosen, and it proceeds to more complex situations by relating them by means of the relational requirements to ones already settled.[19]

4. **To learn about game theory,** Chapter 14 is of course the principal source. The main branches of the theory are presented there and a number of solution concepts that have been central to the theory are introduced.

For readers interested in a more elementary treatment of the theory concerning the adjudication of conflicting claims, several surveys are available.[20]

1.8 CONCLUDING COMMENT

Apart from what it will tell us about the resolution of claims problems, we hope that the present study will have a number of broader benefits. The main one is the introduction of many of the principles that have played an important role in the recent literature on the design of allocation rules. This is done in the context of a simple model where their meaning is transparent and their

[19] The components of an axiomatic study are discussed by Thomson (2001a, 2017c).

[20] Herrero and Villar (2001); Thomson (2003, 2015a). Didactic pieces are Malkevitch (undated, 2008, 2009).

manipulation relatively easy. The model is simple because it is defined in terms of a very small number of real-valued parameters. In particular, preferences do not enter its specification. Description of preferences and of their properties (the conceptual apparatus of microeconomic theory, indifference curves, the derivation of demand and supply correspondences, and the identification of conditions guaranteeing the existence of equilibria, and so on), are often what denies the lay reader access to the sort of analysis that professional economists engage in. Here, no such background is needed. We have attempted to write so as to be understood by anyone comfortable with mathematical reasoning. Moreover, few advanced mathematical definitions, results, and techniques are actually required. Much of the intuition for the concepts and the proofs can be gained by a geometric presentation. For that reason, we have included a large number of figures to illustrate rules, axioms, and proofs. Captions are often detailed and, on occasions, they include sketches of proofs. We therefore strongly urge readers to study them, as they should provide useful stepping stones to the complete arguments.

The chapters are roughly ordered in terms of increasing complexity. Chapter 2 consists of an enumeration of rules, and although some formulae appear there, the reader will gain insights into the subject by simply thinking of a rule in terms of its paths of awards, which are geometric objects in a Euclidean space of dimension equal to the number of claimants; often, looking at the two-claimant case will suffice. The collection of its paths of awards indexed by claims vectors constitutes a very useful "portrait" of a rule.

Proofs start appearing in Chapter 3, where axiomatic work begins. They first require the understanding of logical relations among properties, and then uncovering their implications when imposed in various combinations. Chapters 10–12 are similar in their methodology to Chapters 3–9 but the material there is more difficult because the model is generalized so as to allow the population of claimants to vary; thus, the analysis requires relating geometric objects that lie in spaces of different dimensions. Chapter 13 draws upon public finance, in particular, concepts designed for the evaluation of how skewed or even an income distribution can be. Chapter 14 relies on game theory. Some knowledge of the subject would be useful, but it is not necessary, as we will restate all of the definitions and background results that are needed.

In any case, we hope that readers who are not familiar with these various literatures will be sufficiently intrigued to want to consult supplementary material. We also hope that our exposition will help a new public appreciate the power of the theory of economic design, which in the last thirty years has revolutionized entire areas of economics, and of axiomatic reasoning, which has been a principal mode of reasoning in its development. Economic institutions are not God-given; they should be the object of informed choice, and, thanks to this literature, they can be. The axiomatics of resource allocation has radically changed how we think about a wide range of practical problems of design. Examples are assigning medical students to residency problems, arranging in a queue customers waiting for a service and specifying a fee schedule to cover its cost, assigning students to schools in school choice programs, allocating organs to patients waiting for transplants, rationing a good in short supply, assigning frequencies to telecommunication companies and determining charges for their use, locating a facility that a group of people will jointly use, building a network of communication and sharing its cost among its users, and so on. If this book can inspire readers to explore these new literatures, it will have achieved something important.

CHAPTER 2

Inventory of Division Rules

In this chapter, we first introduce the various rules that have been discussed in the literature, compiling a rich inventory of examples, some familiar, some less so, and some rather intriguing; we also define a number of new ones (Section 2.1). In the second part of this chapter, we introduce several ways of gathering rules in families (Section 2.2).

We begin with the "proportional" rule, the most common rule, already discussed by Aristotle. We introduce two other rules also found in ancient writing: the "constrained equal awards" and "constrained equal losses" rules. Next, we exhibit for two claimants a rule based on a simple scenario consisting of a concessions stage followed by an equal division stage, under the name of "concede-and-divide." The rule is very important because many ways of thinking about the adjudication of conflicting claims yield the same formula. We provide a nineteenth-century proposal, Piniles' rule, that delivers all of the numbers given in the Talmud for the marriage contract problems (Section 1.3), and a late twentieth-century definition that generates the numbers given in the Talmud for the contested garment problem as well as for the marriage contract problems (again, see Section 1.3). For two claimants, this rule is sometimes called the "contested garment rule" and for arbitrarily many claimants, it is referred to as the "Talmud rule." We define four more rules: the "constrained egalitarian" rule is inspired by the literature on rationing; the "random arrival" rule is defined by means of a simple first come, first served scenario that underlies a central concept in the theory of coalitional games; the "minimal overlap" rule is a twentieth-century rule that generalizes to the entire domain of problems an incompletely specified proposal made in the twelfth century; finally, the "random stakes" rule is based on a probabilistic scheme in which agents' claims are stochastically distributed over the endowment.

Next, in a first attempt at organizing and structuring this inventory, we look for patterns among them. This search results in the identification of several simple families of rules (Section 2.2). These families, which partially overlap, contain all of the rules that will be important in the axiomatic work of Chapters 3–13, but they are considerably broader.

We have deliberately left out certain rules that nevertheless will play a role in the axiomatic chapters. A few of those are exotic examples constructed so as to demonstrate the independence of axioms in characterizations; they have little intrinsic interest. Fortunately, we will almost always be able to settle the independence issue by appealing to natural examples, as is desirable. More important omissions are various families uncovered at various points in Chapters 3–12 as by-products of axiomatic work, but it would be difficult to justify them without bringing up the axioms that led to them. Properties of rules indeed provide a second way of structuring the space of rules.

Finally, not described in the present chapter are particular rules obtained by subjecting existing ones to certain "operators" (Chapter 9). These operators provide a third way of structuring the space of rules. Here too, what underlies their definitions are properties of rules, and it would be premature to discuss them at this point.

An implication of these omissions is that the richness of rules available will only be partially reflected in this chapter. This richness, and the various ways in which the space of rules can be structured, unique to the model of conflicting claims, contribute importantly to making it such a fascinating object of study.

It is of course pointless to introduce rules without *any* mention of the properties they have, and on a few occasions here, we will have to suggest elementary ones. We will wait until Chapter 3 to formally state these properties and others. Only then will we embark on a systematic cataloging of properties and investigating their implications, individually when first introduced, and then in conjunction with others. This work will constitute the bulk of our study.

2.1 AN INVENTORY OF RULES

We begin by introducing individual rules. Several of these rules belong to one or several of the families defined in Section 2.2. In the various branches of the theory of fair allocation where these notions make sense, equal division and proportional division are often perceived as two focal points in a spectrum of reasonable choices to which one can legitimately confine oneself. We will start with these two ideas, making an adjustment when writing down equal division so as to ensure that no one receives more than their claim.

2.1.1 Proportional Rule

In solving bankruptcy problems, common practice in most countries is to make awards proportional to claims. In fact, proportionality has a long documented history as the primary method of handling the simple allocation problems of the kind considered here. For Aristotle,[1] who is frequently quoted in this connection, proportionality amounts to equity:

[1] In his *Ethics*; the quote below is borrowed from Young (1994). The rule is also known as the "pari passu" rule.

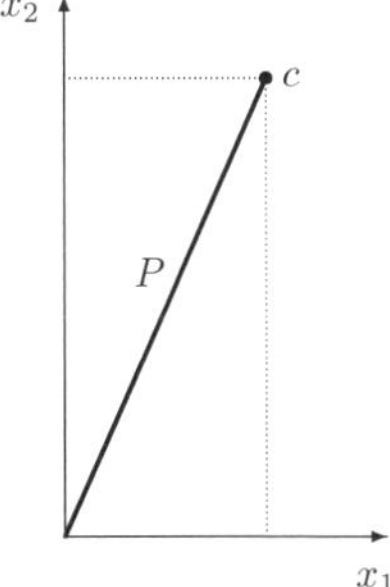

Figure 2.1: **Proportional rule.** Typical path of awards for $N \equiv \{1, 2\}$ and $c \in \mathbb{R}^N_+$ such that $c_1 < c_2$.

> A just act necessarily involves at least four terms: two persons for whom it is in fact just, and two shares in which its justice is exhibited. And there will be the same equality between the shares as between the persons, because the shares will be in the same ratio to one another as the persons... What is just in this sense is what is proportional and what is unjust is what violates the proportion.

Proportional rule, P: For each $(c, E) \in \mathcal{C}^N$,

$$P(c, E) \equiv \lambda c,$$

where $\lambda \in \mathbb{R}_+$ is chosen so as to achieve *balance*.[2]

The rule is illustrated in Figure 2.1.

Proportional division can be understood as a form of equal division. Indeed, using language appropriate for our current setting, the adjudication of conflicting claims, place all "units of claims" on the same footing, independently of who holds them, and perform equal division among units; then have each claimant collect the partial payments assigned to the units they holds Proportionality of awards to claims is the end result.[3]

2.1.2 Constrained Equal Awards Rule

Next, we turn to equal division in absolute terms as opposed to equal division in relative terms, equality per unit of claim. The extent to which one should take into account differences in claims is the question that our theory should address, and ignoring these differences should be seen as an extreme position that one may take. It may be acceptable for some configurations of the parameters and some interpretations of the model, and we certainly will value

[2] Then $\lambda = \frac{E}{\sum c_i}$. For this expression to be well defined, we exclude the degenerate case $\sum c_i = 0$, for which, by definition of a claims problem, $E = 0$, and the only choice is $(0, \ldots, 0)$.

[3] For this argument to be formally correct, claims should be integer multiples of some common number. This is of course not always the case in our model, but this situation can always be approximated. Such an approximation appears formally in the proof of Theorem 12.5.

it as a useful reference point. However, adjustments are needed to guarantee that no one ever gets more than their claim, as we require throughout. The next rule preserves the spirit of egalitarianism, but it does not suffer from this difficulty. In fact, one could say that it departs from egalitarianism in the minimal way that ensures that no agent receives more than their claim: it makes awards as equal as possible subject to this constraint. The rule has been advocated by many authors, in particular Maimonides, who is very explicit:[4]

> If [dividing the property into equal portions] would give the person owed the least more than he is owed, [this is what should be done]: We divide the sum [equally among the creditors], so that the person owed the least will receive the money he is owed. [He then withdraws.] The remaining creditors then divide the balance [of the debtor's resources] in the following manner.
>
> What is implied? [A person] owed three debts: one of a *maneh* (100 zuz), one for 200 and one for 300. If all [the resources to the debtor] total 300 [zuz], they are divided 100 for each. Similarly, if [his resources are less than 300], they should be divided equally [among the three].
>
> If [his resource] total more than 300 [zuz], the 300 should be divided equally and then the person owed 100 should withdraw. The remaining money should be divided equally in this same manner.
>
> What is implied? If [the debtor's resources] total 500 or less, the 300 should be divided equally, and then the person owed 100 should withdraw. The balance of 200 or less should then be divided equally [among the remaining creditors], and then the second one withdraws.
>
> If [the debtor's resources] total 600, the 300 should be divided equally, and then the person owed 100 should withdraw. They then divide 200 between the two equally, and then the second one withdraws. The 100 that remains should be given to the person owed 300; he thus receives only[5] 300.

A first illustration of the rule is Figure 2.2.

Constrained equal awards rule, *CEA*: For each $(c, E) \in \mathcal{C}^N$

$$CEA(c, E) \equiv (\min\{c_i, \lambda\})_{i \in N},$$

where $\lambda \in \mathbb{R}_+$ is chosen so as to achieve *balance*.

Although the extent to which the constrained equal awards rule departs from egalitarianism does not seem much of a step towards recognizing differences in claims, we will nevertheless offer interesting axiomatic justifications for it. Moreover, it is an ingredient in the construction of other important rules to be defined shortly, as well as a meaningful baseline.

It is intuitive from its definition that, for each problem, the constrained equal awards rule favors those claimants whose claims are relatively smaller. This is made precise in Chapter 13 in several ways.

[4] The passage is taken from his *Laws of Lending and Borrowing*, Chapter 20, Section 4.

[5] Footnote in the translation: "The commentaries question why the Ramban adds the word 'only.' For this creditor has also received all the money owed him."

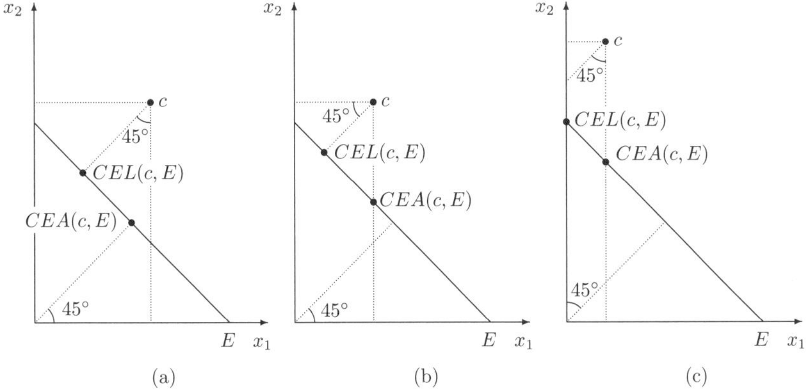

Figure 2.2: **Constrained equal awards and constrained equal losses rules.** Let $N \equiv \{1, 2\}$ and $(c, E) \in \mathcal{C}^N$. (a) Here, the constrained equal awards vector has equal coordinates (the constraint that each agent's award should be at most as large as their claim is not binding at the balanced vector of equal coordinates). Also, the losses claimants experience at the constrained equal losses vector are equal (the constraint that each agent's award should be nonnegative is not binding at the balanced vector at which losses are equal). (b) Here, $c_1 \leq \frac{E}{2}$, and the constrained equal awards rule fully compensates claimant 1. (c) Here, in addition, c_2 is sufficiently large in relation to c_1 that the constrained equal losses rule assigns the entire endowment to claimant 2.

A way to calculate the constrained equal awards vector of a problem is to start from equal division and to make adjustments if somebody's assignment exceeds their claim. A recursion is necessary (Figure 2.3).[6] If no agent receives more than their claim, equal division is what we choose. Suppose otherwise, namely that at equal division, at least one agent receives more than their claim. Then we calculate the difference for each such agent between an equal share of the endowment and their claim, and redistribute the sum of these differences equally among the agents who had received less than their claims. These transfers may bring the awards of some of these agents above their claims, so we repeat the operation with them. That is, we calculate the difference for each of them between what they now receive and their claim, and redistribute the sum of these differences equally among the agents who, after the first transfer, still receive less than their claims. We proceed in this way until no one receives more than their claim.

[6] One of our secondary objectives is to understand whether and how certain methods of resolving claims problems could have been used centuries ago. Providing simple descriptions of them is important. By a "simple" description, we mean one that involves elementary mathematics. In particular, we suspect that operating the algorithm described here is more compatible with the mathematics known at the time than solving an equation of the kind that appears in our formal definition of the constrained equal awards rule.

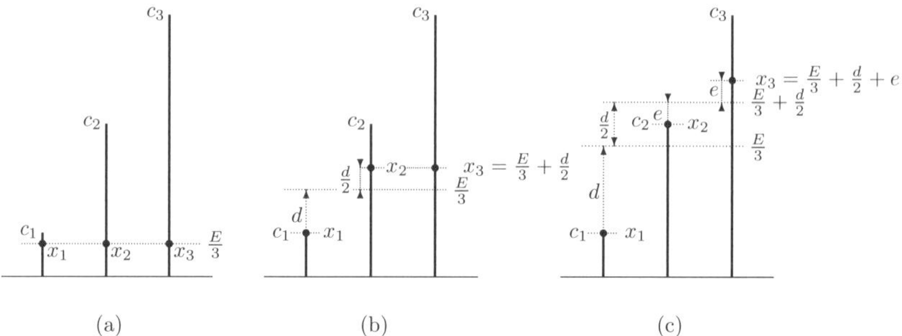

Figure 2.3: **A simple way to calculate the constrained equal awards vector for a fixed claims vector and three values of the endowment.** Let $N \equiv \{1, 2, 3\}$ and $c \in \mathbb{R}^N_+$. In each panel, $x \equiv CEA(c, E)$ for some $E \in [0, \sum c_i]$. (a) For E small enough, at equal division, each agent receives at most their claim, so x is equal division. (b) Here, E is such that, at equal division, claimant 1 receives d units more than c_1. We give claimant 1 c_1 instead and divide d equally between claimants 2 and 3. After this adjustment, agent 2 still receives at most their claim (and thus, so does agent 3), so we obtain x in two steps. (c) Here, E is even larger and such that, after the transfer from claimant 1, claimant 2 receives more than c_2. We obtain x by giving claimant 2 c_2 instead and transferring to agent 3 the difference, e, between claimant 2's tentative award of Step 2 and c_2.

For instance, let $N \equiv \{1, 2, 3\}$ and consider the problem $((13, 30, 60), 75) \in \mathcal{C}^N$. The starting point, equal division, is $(25, 25, 25)$. One claimant, namely claimant 1, receives more than their claim, which is 13, so we give them 13 instead and we divide equally between the other two the difference, $25 - 13$. This yields the revised awards vector $(13, 31, 31)$, at which claimant 2's award is raised above their claim of 30. So we give them 30 instead and we transfer to claimant 3 the difference, $31 - 30$, ending up with the awards vector $(13, 30, 32)$.

The path of awards of the constrained equal awards rule for a two-claimant claims vector and the schedules of awards for the marriage contract claims vector of the Talmud (Section 1.3) are represented in Figure 2.4a,b.

2.1.3 Constrained Equal Losses Rule

Here, we define a rule that is similar in spirit to the constrained equal awards rule – it too can be understood as an implementation of the goal of equality – but it involves a shift of perspectives from what claimants receive to the losses they incur. If we were to insist on equal losses, some claimants could receive negative amounts, so in order to satisfy the nonnegativity requirements, the rule makes losses as equal as possible subject to no one receiving a negative amount. This rule also appears in Maimonides, although his text is not quite as clear in that regard as the passage we quoted earlier in connection with

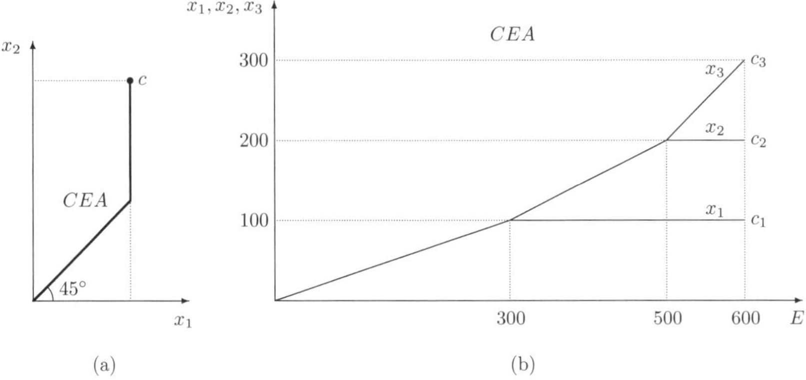

Figure 2.4: **Constrained equal awards rule.** (a) Typical path of awards for $N \equiv \{1, 2\}$ and $c \in \mathbb{R}_+^N$ such that $c_1 < c_2$. The path follows the 45° line until the smaller claimant is fully compensated. Any further increment in the endowment goes entirely to the other claimant until that claimant too is fully compensated. (b) Schedules of awards for the marriage contract claims vector of the Talmud.

the constrained equal awards rule. The rule is illustrated in Figures 2.2, 2.5, and 2.6.[7]

Constrained equal losses rule, CEL: For each $(c, E) \in \mathcal{C}^N$,

$$CEL(c, E) \equiv (\max\{c_i - \lambda, 0\})_{i \in N},$$

where $\lambda \in \mathbb{R}_+$ is chosen so as to achieve *balance*.

Whereas the previous rule appeared to favor for each problem those claimants whose claims are relatively smaller, this rule seems to favor those claimants whose claims are relatively larger. Several senses in which this is true are made precise in Chapter 13.

An algorithmic way of identifying the constrained equal losses awards vector of a problem is illustrated for a three-claimant example in Figure 2.5, which should be compared to Figure 2.3. For the general n-claimant case, we start with each agent receiving their claim, a generally infeasible choice. We calculate the shortfall $\sum c_i - E$ and distribute it equally. If each claimant ends up with a nonnegative amount, we have the desired awards vector (panel (a) of Figure 2.5). Suppose otherwise, namely that at the point of equal losses, some claimants receive negative amounts. Then we give them 0 instead, calculate the sum of these negative amounts, and distribute it equally among the claimants who had received a nonnegative amount. These transfers may bring below 0 the awards to some members of this latter group, so we repeat the operation with them. That is, we give them 0 instead, calculate the sum of the negative

7 In the context of taxation, the constrained equal awards rule is known as "head tax" and the constrained equal losses rule as "leveling tax."

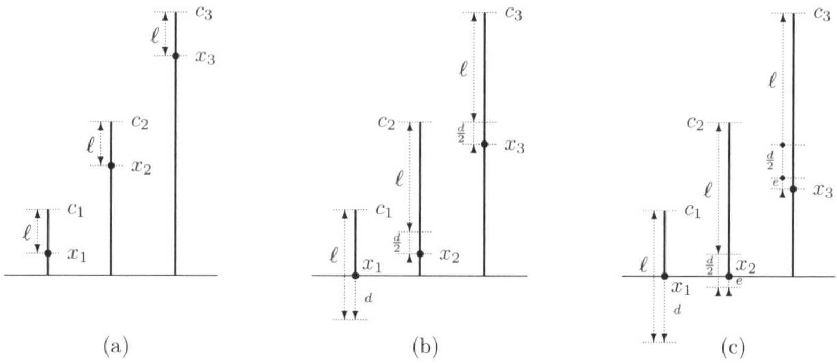

Figure 2.5: **Calculating the constrained equal losses vector for a fixed claims vector and three values of the endowment.** Let $N \equiv \{1, 2, 3\}$ and $c \in \mathbb{R}^N_+$. In each panel, $\ell \equiv \frac{\sum c_i - E}{3}$ designates the per-capita shortfall, and $x \equiv CEL(c, E)$ for some $E \in [0, \sum c_i]$. (a) For E large enough, at the vector of equal losses, each agent receives a nonnegative amount, so x is this awards vector. (b) Here, E is such that at the vector of equal losses, claimant 1 receives d units less than 0. We give claimant 1 0 instead and impose on each of claimants 2 and 3 an additional loss of $\frac{d}{2}$. After this adjustment, claimant 2 still receives a nonnegative amount (and thus, so does agent 3), so we obtain x in two steps. (c) Here, E is even smaller and such that after the negative transfer from claimant 1, claimant 2 receives less than 0. We give claimant 2 0 instead and impose on claimant 3 an additional loss equal to the difference, e, between claimant 2's tentative award of Step 2 and 0.

amounts they receive after the first revision, and redistribute it equally among the claimants who at the end of the previous step still receive nonnegative amounts. We continue in this way until everyone's award is nonnegative.

The path of awards of the constrained equal losses rule for a two-claimant example and its schedules of awards for the marriage contract claims vector of the Talmud are represented in Figure 2.6a,b.

2.1.4 Concede-and-Divide

Suppose that there are only two claimants and consider the following scenario to obtain a division (Figure 2.7).[8] Calling them i and j, what underlies it is the idea that agent i, by claiming c_i, can be understood as conceding to agent j the amount $E - c_i$ if this amount is nonnegative and 0 otherwise, namely $\max\{E - c_i, 0\}$. Similarly, by claiming c_j, agent j is implicitly conceding $\max\{E - c_j, 0\}$ to agent i. Let us then first assign to each claimant the amount conceded to them by the other; this can be done because the sum of these concessions is no larger than the endowment, as is easily verified. In a second step, let us divide the remainder, the part that is truly contested, equally. If both claims

[8] It is formalized by Aumann and Maschler (1985).

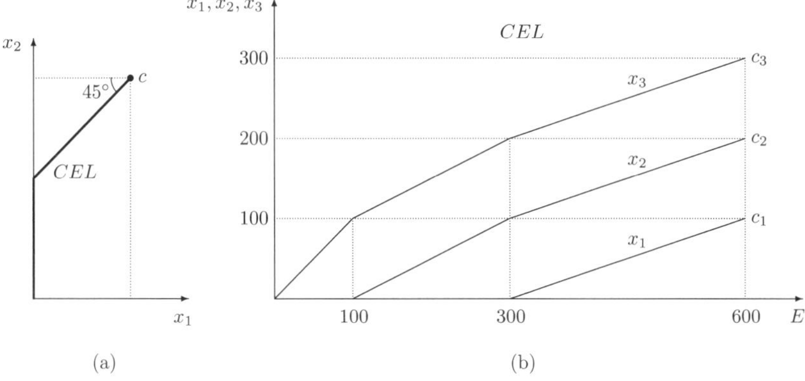

Figure 2.6: **Constrained equal losses rule.** (a) Typical path of awards for $N \equiv \{1, 2\}$ and $c \in \mathbb{R}^N_+$ such that $c_1 < c_2$. Starting from c, the path follows a line of slope 1 downwards until the smaller claimant receives 0. Any further shortfall is imposed entirely on the other claimant until that claimant too receives 0. (b) Schedules of awards for the marriage contract claims vector of the Talmud.

are at most as large as the endowment, after revision, they are equal. If one claim exceeds the endowment, that is still the case after being revised. The two claims will not be equal then, as shown in Figure 2.7b, but one could argue that any part of a claim that exceeds the residual endowment should be ignored (the idea is formally developed in Section 5.1). If truncated in this way, the two claims are equal once again. If both claims exceed the endowment, no concessions are made in the first stage but, of course, after truncation at the endowment, they are equal. In each of these cases, equal division at the second stage makes sense. It is easy to see that no agent ends up with more than their claim. We therefore obtain a well-defined rule, illustrated in Figure 2.8. Here is the formula:[9]

Concede-and-divide, CD: For $|N| = 2$. For each $(c, E) \in \mathcal{C}^N$,

$$CD(c, E) \equiv (\max\{E - c_j, 0\} + \frac{E - \max\{E - c_j, 0\} - \max\{E - c_i, 0\}}{2})_{i \in N}.$$

This rule, when applied to the contested garment problem, delivers the recommendation made in the Talmud.

Can the scenario underlying the rule be generalized to accommodate more than two claimants? Not entirely. The most straightforward way of doing so seems to proceed as follows: first, assign to each claimant the difference between the endowment and the sum of the claims of the others, or 0 if the difference is negative – again, we can think of this amount as what they conceded to that claimant – then divide the residual endowment equally among everyone.

9 If a group consists of two claimants and i denotes an arbitrary one of them, the notation j should be understood to refer to the other one; we will not explicitly state that $j \neq i$ then.

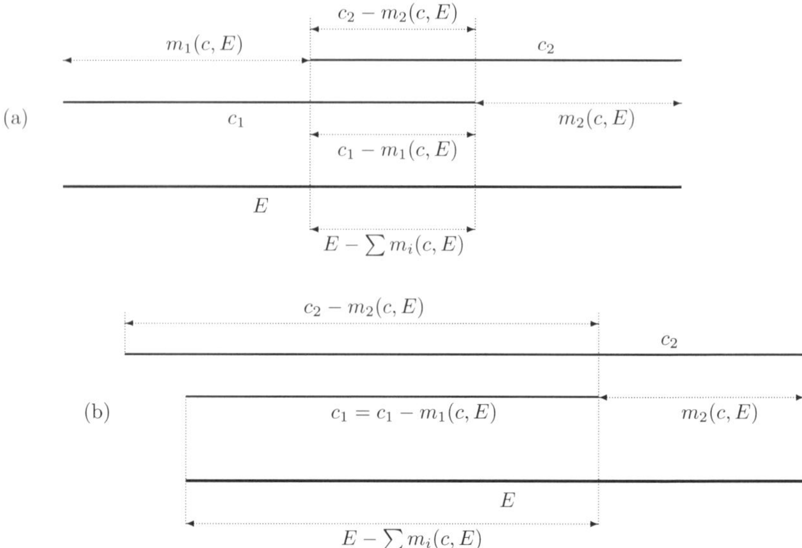

Figure 2.7: **Scenario underlying concede-and-divide, a two-claimant rule.** (a) Let $N \equiv \{1, 2\}$. Here, no claim is larger than the endowment. Each claimant $i \in N$ is first awarded the amount conceded by the other, claimant j, namely the difference $m_i(c, E) \equiv E - c_j$. Claimant 1's claim is revised down by this amount and the endowment down by the sum of these concessions. Revised claims are both equal to the residual endowment. This remainder is divided equally. (b) Here, agent 2's claim is larger than the endowment, so claimant 2's "concession" to claimant 1, $m_1(c, E)$, is 0. If agent 2's claim is revised down by agent 1's concession to them, $m_2(c, E)$, and *truncated at the residual endowment*, we end up in a situation similar to that illustrated in panel (a). If both claims were larger than the endowment, no concession would be made by either claimant, the endowment would remain the same, claims would not have to be revised down, but after truncation at the endowment, both would be equal to the endowment.

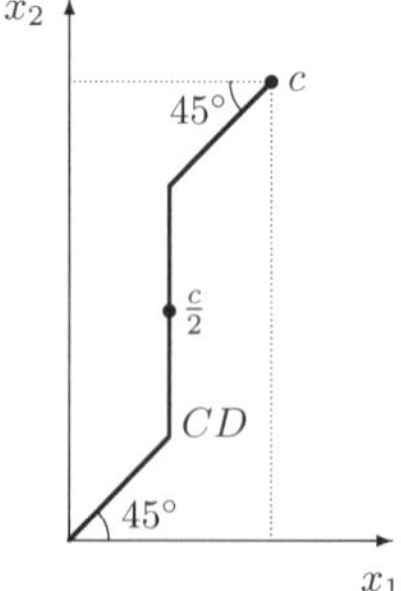

Figure 2.8: **Concede-and-divide.** Typical path of awards for $N \equiv \{1, 2\}$ and $c \in \mathbb{R}^N_+$ such that $c_1 < c_2$. The path is bro.seg$[(0, 0), (\frac{1}{2}c_1, \frac{1}{2}c_1), (\frac{1}{2}c_1, c_2 - \frac{1}{2}c_1), c]$. (When $c_1 = c_2$, it is simply seg$[(0, 0), c]$.)

The second step is not as appealing as it is for two claimants however, because, if $|N| > 2$, after claims are revised down by the conceded amounts, and even if truncated at the residual endowment, they are not necessarily equal. Thus, and even if all revised claims are smaller than the residual endowment, equal division does not stand out as the best choice for this second-step problem.

The following examples show these possibilities. First, given $(c, E) \in \mathcal{C}^N$ and $i \in N$, we use the notation $m_i(c, E) \equiv \max\{E - \sum_{N\setminus\{i\}} c_j, 0\}$ for claimant i's award at the first step. Now, let $N \equiv \{1, 2, 3\}$ and $(c, E) \in \mathcal{C}^N$ be equal to $((3, 5, 6), 10)$. Then $m(c, E) = (0, 1, 2)$ and $c - m(c, E) = (3, 4, 4)$. Here, all revised claims are smaller than the remainder, the difference $7 = 10 - (0 + 1 + 2)$, but they are not all equal. To see that at the second step of our scenario, equal division may bring some agents' awards above their claims, let $N \equiv \{1, 2, 3\}$ and $(c, E) \in \mathcal{C}^N$ be equal to $((1, 10, 12), 20)$. Then $m(c, E) = (0, 7, 9)$ and $c - m(c, E) = (1, 3, 3)$. The remainder is $4 = 20 - (0 + 7 + 9)$, and dividing it equally leads to a total award to claimant 1 (namely $0 + \frac{4}{3}$) that is larger than the agent's claim of 1.[10]

We will discover a surprisingly large number of ways of adjudicating conflicting claims that coincide for two claimants with concede-and-divide, and therefore recommend the awards vector selected by the Talmud for the contested garment problem but, for more than two claimants, these various approaches generally produce different recommendations.

2.1.5 Piniles' Rule

Piniles' (1861) rule can be understood as resulting from a "double" application of the constrained equal awards rule: first, this rule is applied to divide the lesser of two amounts, the endowment and the half-sum of the claims, using in the formula not the claims themselves but the half-claims.[11] If the endowment is larger than the half-sum of the claims, each agent is first assigned their half-claim, then the constrained equal awards rule is applied to divide the remainder, once again using the half-claims instead of the claims themselves. Working with half-claims is an important insight of Piniles' that is key to solving the mystery of the numbers in the Talmud, as we will see.

Piniles' rule, *Pin*: For each $(c, E) \in \mathcal{C}^N$ and each $i \in N$,

$$Pin_i(c, E) \equiv \begin{cases} \min\{\frac{c_i}{2}, \lambda\} & \text{if } E \leq \sum \frac{c_j}{2}, \\ \frac{c_i}{2} + \min\{\frac{c_i}{2}, \lambda\} & \text{otherwise,} \end{cases}$$

where in each case, $\lambda \in \mathbb{R}_+$ is chosen so as to achieve *balance*.

[10] An alternative would be, for each agent $i \in N$, to distribute in some fashion among the others what the agent concedes to them, namely the difference $\max\{E - c_i, 0\}$, and then to distribute the remainder. Here too, the issue is what principles should guide these distributions, keeping in mind that in the end, one should have an awards vector of the problem to be solved.

[11] A justification for proceeding in this manner is given in Chapter 7.

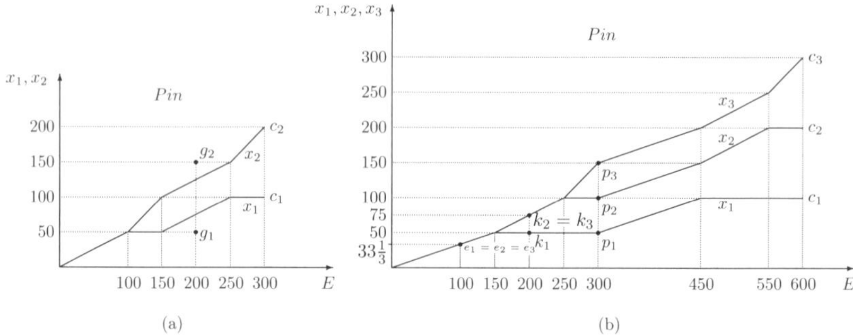

Figure 2.9: **Piniles' rule applied to the examples in the Talmud.** (a) Schedules of awards for the contested garment claims vector. The rule differs from the Talmud rule: for $E = 200$, the Talmud recommends the vector g indicated by the two dots on the vertical line of abscissa 200 (reproduced from Figure 1.4a). (b) Schedules of awards for the marriage contract claims vector. The rule makes the same recommendation as the Talmud does for each of the three values of the estate considered there: these recommendations are the vectors e, k, and p, indicated by the sets of dots on the vertical lines of abscissa 100, 200, and 300 respectively (also reproduced from Figure 1.4b). The two rules coincide for any endowment that is at most as large as the half-sum of the claims, and in general, they differ thereafter.

The rule is illustrated in Figure 2.9 for the examples in the Talmud. Piniles' rule accounts for the awards vectors proposed there for the three instances of the marriage contract problem but it does not account for the resolution the Talmud suggests for the contested garment problem.

Figure 2.10a shows a typical path of awards of Piniles' rule for two claimants. Concede-and-divide is reproduced in Figure 2.10b to facilitate the comparison between the two rules.

2.1.6 Talmud Rule

None of the rules described so far accounts for all of the numbers in the Talmud. For instance, the proportional rule produces the correct numbers in only one case (the vector p of Figure 1.4b). So does concede-and-divide (the vector g of Figure 1.4a; in fact, recall that this rule is defined only for two-claimant problems). As we observed when discussing Piniles' rule, if claims are first divided by two, the constrained equal awards rule accounts for all the numbers proposed for the marriage contract problems and, whether or not claims are first divided by two, the constrained equal losses rule accounts for the numbers pertaining to the contested garment problem (again, the vector g Figure 1.4a). Since under this operation the constrained equal awards and constrained equal losses rules together account for all of the numbers in the Talmud, it is natural to attempt to formally combine them in some way. It is this approach that will

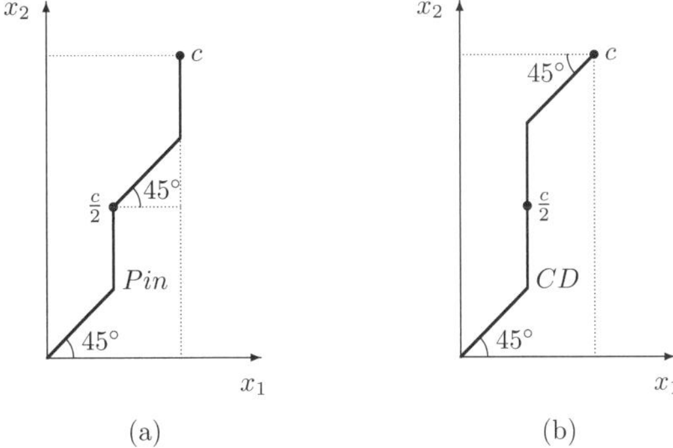

Figure 2.10: **Comparing Piniles' rule and concede-and-divide for two claimants.** (a) Typical path of awards of Piniles' rule for $N \equiv \{1, 2\}$ and $c \in \mathbb{R}^N_+$ such that $c_1 < c_2$. It is obtained by concatenating to itself the path of the constrained equal awards rule for $\frac{c}{2}$. (b) Concede-and-divide and the two-claimant version of the Talmud rule coincide. Their path for c is obtained by concatenating the path of the constrained equal awards rule for $\frac{c}{2}$ to that of the constrained equal losses rule for $\frac{c}{2}$.

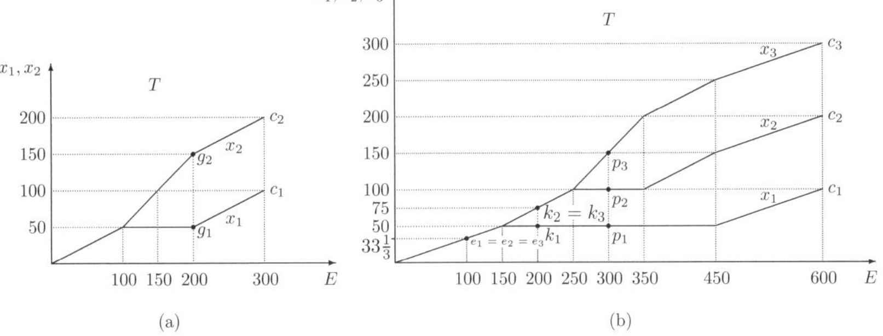

Figure 2.11: **The Aumann–Maschler proposal, which simultaneously rationalizes the recommendations made in the Talmud for the contested garment and marriage contract problems**. The awards vectors in the Talmud, reproduced from Figure 1.4, are the vectors g, e, k, and p, indicated by sets of dots on the vertical lines of abscissas 200 in panel (a) and 100, 200, and 300 in panel (b). (a) For the contested garment problem, claims are $(c_1, c_2) \equiv (100, 200)$. (b) For the marriage contract problems, claims are $(c_1, c_2, c_3) \equiv (100, 200, 300)$.

provide a solution to our puzzle; indeed, here is a "hybrid" of these two rules that generates all of these numbers.

Let $N \equiv \{1, \ldots, n\}$ and assuming $c_1 \leq \cdots \leq c_n$, we define the rule by means of an algorithm, progressively increasing the estate from 0 to $\sum c_i$ (see Figure 2.10b for the resulting path of awards for two claimants and Figure 2.11 for applications to the problems in the Talmud). We divide the first units equally until each claimant receives $\frac{c_1}{2}$. Then claimant 1 stops receiving anything for a while. We divide the next units equally among all others until each of them receives $\frac{c_2}{2}$. Then claimant 2 also stops receiving anything for a while. We divide the next units equally among the other $n-2$ claimants, and so on. We proceed in this way until the estate is worth $\sum \frac{c_i}{2}$. At that point, each agent has received their half-claim. If the estate increases beyond $\sum \frac{c_i}{2}$, we assign the next units entirely to claimant n until their loss is reduced to $\frac{c_{n-1}}{2}$. If there is more to allocate, we divide the next units equally among claimants n and $n-1$ until the loss each incurs is reduced to $\frac{c_{n-2}}{2}$, at which point claimant $n-2$ reenters the scene, and so on. We pursue this process until the estate is worth $\sum c_i$, at which point each claimant's loss is reduced to 0.

Alternatively, when the estate is worth more than $\sum \frac{c_i}{2}$, we can describe awards in a symmetric way to when it is worth less than $\sum \frac{c_i}{2}$, as follows. Starting from a worth equal to $\sum c_i$ – then each claimant receives their claim – consider shortfalls of increasing sizes. We divide initial shortfalls equally until the loss experienced by each claimant is $\frac{c_1}{2}$. Then claimant 1's loss is stopped and we divide additional shortfalls equally among the others, until their common loss is $\frac{c_2}{2}$. Then claimant 2's loss is also stopped, and we divide additional shortfalls equally among claimants $3, \ldots, n$, and so on. This goes on until each claimant's loss is their half-claim.

It is a simple matter to check that the algorithm, when applied to the problems in the Talmud, does deliver the numbers given there. Hence the name we choose for the rule it defines.[12] Here is its algebraic definition:[13]

Talmud rule, T: For each $(c, E) \in \mathcal{C}^N$ and each $i \in N$,

$$T_i(c, E) \equiv \begin{cases} \min\{\frac{c_i}{2}, \lambda\} & \text{if } E \leq \sum \frac{c_j}{2}, \\ c_i - \min\{\frac{c_i}{2}, \lambda\} & \text{otherwise,} \end{cases}$$

where in each case, $\lambda \in \mathbb{R}_+$ is chosen so as to achieve *balance*.

The restriction of the Talmud rule to the two-claimant case is often referred to as the "contested garment rule." Of particular interest, and easy to verify, is the fact that this rule coincides with concede-and-divide (Figure 2.10b).

2.1.7 Constrained Egalitarian Rule

The next rule is inspired by a solution to a certain class of simple allocation problems, exemplified by rationing in a two-good economy, so we will

[12] The algorithm is proposed by Aumann and Maschler (1985). Of course, the Talmud does not offer any example for $|N| > 3$; one has to speculate as to what it would have recommended then. However, we find the sort of considerations that led Aumann and Maschler to the interpolation and extrapolation they propose to be compelling, which is why we refer to the rule as the Talmud rule. A more complete justification is developed in Thomson (1994b).

[13] The expression for the second case can be written as $\max\{\frac{c_i}{2}, c_i - \lambda\}$.

refer to them as "rationing problems."[14] The following informal description will suffice. An amount M of a commodity has to be fully allocated among a group of agents each of whom has preferences that are monotone increasing up to a point, called the "peak amount," and monotone decreasing thereafter. A solution for this class of problems, called the **uniform rule**, is central in this context, having emerged from numerous axiomatic perspectives. It will be convenient to describe it parametrically as a function of M, keeping preferences fixed. For each $i \in N$, let $p(R_i)$ be agent i's peak amount. For simplicity, let $N \equiv \{1, \ldots, n\}$ and suppose that agents are indexed in such a way that $p(R_1) \leq \cdots \leq p(R_n)$. We divide the first units of the commodity equally until each agent receives agent 1's peak amount. Then agent 1 stops receiving anything for a while. We divide the next units equally among the other agents until each of them receives agent 2's peak amount. Then agent 2 also stops receiving anything for a while, and so on. This process goes on until each agent receives their own peak amount. The next units beyond the sum of the peak amounts go entirely to agent 1 until agent 1 receives agent 2's peak amount. We divide the next units equally between agents 1 and 2 until each receives agent 3's peak amount, and so on. This process goes on until each of agents 1 to $n - 1$ receives agent n's peak amount. We divide additional units equally among all agents.

The uniform rule has been shown to be the only rule to satisfy certain egalitarian objectives subject to efficiency.[15] In attempting to define a division rule that might enjoy similar properties, the most natural way to proceed seems to have claims play the role of peak amounts. However, given the several ways in which rationing problems and claims problems differ, some care should be exercised. First, in a claims problem, the sum of the claims is by definition at least as large as the endowment ($\sum c_i \geq E$). In a rationing problem as we defined it, no comparable restriction on the sum of the peak amounts in relation to the endowment is meaningful ($\sum p(R_i)$ may or may not be larger than M). Also, in a rationing problem, no upper bound is imposed on what agents should receive, whereas in a claims problem, it makes sense to require that no agent receive more than their claim, as we do throughout this book.

Second, it seems desirable in solving claims problems to require that awards be ordered as the claims are (a property formally defined in Section 3.7). The corresponding requirement for rationing problems, that payments be ordered as the peak amounts, is not compelling in general unless perhaps the rule depends only on the peak amounts, (which, as the reader may have noticed, is the case for the uniform rule).[16]

[14] The first axiomatic analysis of these problems is due to Sprumont (1991). The literature devoted to their study is surveyed in Thomson (2014). The rule is defined by Chun, Schummer, and Thomson (2001).

[15] For formal statements of these characterizations, see Schummer and Thomson (1997).

[16] This property is also satisfied by the proportional rationing rule, for which payments are proportional to the peak amounts.

A good starting point in using the uniform rule as the basis for the definition of a division rule is the Talmud rule, as it seems to correspond to the "first half" of the uniform rule (up to the point where each agent receives their peak amount). To obtain a rule for claims problems that reflects the totality of the uniform rule, we proceed as in the definition of the constrained equal awards rule but take from the Talmud rule its switch-point of $E = \sum \frac{c_i}{2}$. As noted earlier, numerous passages where the midpoint is viewed as an important reference can be found in the Talmud.[17]

Also, for payments to respect the order of the claims, we have to make sure that for each $i \in N$, if $c_i < c_{i+1}$, then when agent i starts receiving more, agent i should not receive so much as to overtake agent $i + 1$.

In spite of their similarities, the Talmud rule and the resulting rule differ significantly. In particular, for a rationing problem with single-peaked preferences, under the uniform rule, it is the agent with the smallest peak amount who receives the first additional units after the switchpoint of $\sum p(R_i)$. Thus, when adapted to claims problems, it is the smallest claimant who receives the first additional units after the switchpoint of $\sum \frac{c_i}{2}$. By contrast, under the Talmud rule, it is the largest claimant who does so.

We now propose an explicit description of the rule, once again assuming agents to be ordered by claims: $c_1 \leq \cdots \leq c_n$. As the endowment increases up to $\sum \frac{c_i}{2}$, we compute awards as for the Talmud rule. At that point, we assign the next units to claimant 1 until that claimant reaches their claim or half of the second smallest claim, whichever is smaller. If $c_1 \leq \frac{c_2}{2}$, claimant 1 stops at c_1. If $c_1 > \frac{c_2}{2}$, we divide the next units equally between claimants 1 and 2 until they reach c_1, at which point claimant 1 drops out, or they reach $\frac{c_3}{2}$. In the first case, we assign the next units to claimant 2 until that claimant reaches c_2 or $\frac{c_3}{2}$. In the second case, we divide the next units equally among claimants 1, 2, and 3 until they reach c_1, at which point claimant 1 drops out, or they reach $\frac{c_4}{2}$, and so on. Here is a compact formula:

Constrained egalitarian rule, CE: For each $(c, E) \in \mathcal{C}^N$ and each $i \in N$,

$$CE_i(c, E) \equiv \begin{cases} \min\{\frac{c_i}{2}, \lambda\} & \text{if } E \leq \sum \frac{c_j}{2}, \\ \max\{\frac{c_i}{2}, \min\{c_i, \lambda\}\} & \text{otherwise,} \end{cases}$$

where in each case, $\lambda \in \mathbb{R}_+$ is chosen so as to achieve *balance*.

For each claims vector, as the endowment increases from 0 to the half-sum of the claims, the value of λ for which *balance* holds in the formula, the "equilibrium" λ, increases from 0 to half of the largest claim. As the endowment increases from the half-sum of the claims to the sum of the claims, the equilibrium λ increases from half of the largest claim to the largest claim. The rule is illustrated in Figure 2.12 for two claimants, and in Figure 2.13 for the three-claimant examples in the Talmud.

[17] Such passages are noted by Aumann and Maschler (1985).

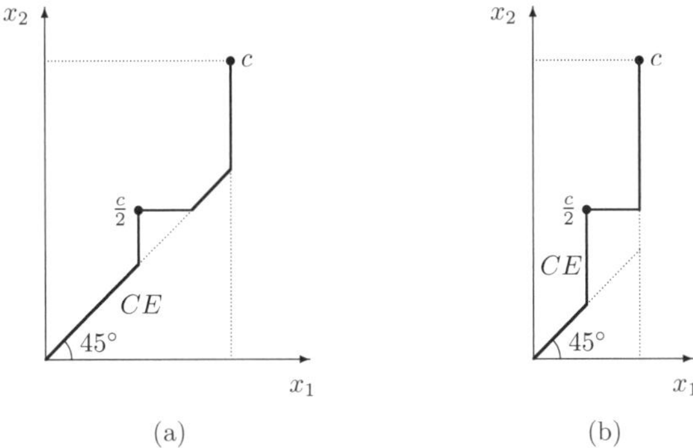

Figure 2.12: **Constrained egalitarian rule applied to two-claimant examples.** (a) Typical path of awards for $N \equiv \{1, 2\}$ and $c \in \mathbb{R}^N_+$ such $c_1 \leq c_2 \leq 2c_1$. The path contains two segments that lie in the 45° line. (b) If $c_2 > 2c_1$, the path contains only one such segment.

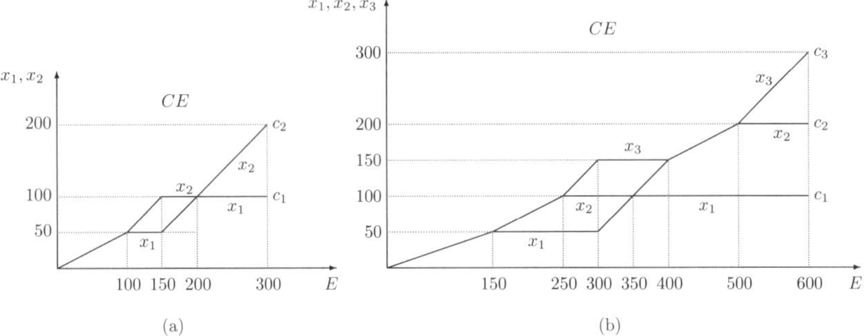

Figure 2.13: **Constrained egalitarian rule applied to the two claims vectors in the Talmud.** Schedules of awards for (a) the contested garment claims vector and (b) the marriage contract claims vector of the Talmud.

2.1.8 Random Arrival Rule

Imagine claimants arriving one at a time to get compensated, and suppose that each claim is fully honored until money runs out. For example, let $N \equiv \{1, 2, 3\}$ and $(c, E) \in \mathcal{C}^N$ be equal to $((50, 100, 150), 90)$. Using the notation $i \prec j$ to indicate that agent i precedes agent j, if $1 \prec 2 \prec 3$, we obtain the awards vector $(50, 40, 0)$. If instead, $3 \prec 2 \prec 1$, we obtain $(0, 0, 90)$. To remove the unfairness of the first come, first served scheme associated with any particular order of arrival, let us take the average of the awards vectors calculated in this way when all orders are equally probable.

For $N \equiv \{1, 2\}$, claimants can arrive in only two ways. If claimant 1 arrives first, that claimant receives $\min\{c_1, E\}$ and claimant 2 receives what is left. If claimant 2 arrives first, that claimant receives $\min\{c_2, E\}$ and claimant 1 receives what is left. Altogether then, claimant 1 gets $\frac{1}{2}[\min\{c_1, E\} + E -$

Table 2.1: ***Random arrival scenario applied to a marriage contract problem in the Talmud****. Here, $N \equiv \{1, 2, 3\}$, $c \in \mathbb{R}^N_+$ is equal to (100, 200, 300), and $E \equiv 200$. Claimants arrive randomly to be compensated. For each order in which they can arrive, each of them is fully compensated until money runs out. For instance, if they arrive in the order $1 \prec 2 \prec 3$, claimant 1 is fully compensated, claimant 2 only receives 100, and there is nothing left when claimant 3 arrives. All orders of arrival are equally likely. The choice is the average of the 3! resulting awards vectors, namely $(33\frac{1}{3}, 83\frac{1}{3}, 83\frac{1}{3})$.*

		Agent 1's claim: 100	Agent 2's claim: 200	Agent 3's claim: 300
	$1 \prec 2 \prec 3$	100	100	0
	$1 \prec 3 \prec 2$	100	0	100
The 3! orders	$2 \prec 1 \prec 3$	0	200	0
of the three agents	$2 \prec 3 \prec 1$	0	200	0
	$3 \prec 1 \prec 2$	0	0	200
	$3 \prec 2 \prec 1$	0	0	200
	Average	$33\frac{1}{3}$	$83\frac{1}{3}$	$83\frac{1}{3}$

$\min\{c_2, E\}]$ and claimant 2 gets $\frac{1}{2}[\min\{c_2, E\} + E - \min\{c_1, E\}]$. It is a simple exercise to check that these formulas coincide with the formulas for concede-and-divide.

For a formal definition of the rule in the general case, let $\mathcal{O}^N$ denote the class of strict orders on N, with generic element $\prec$.[18]

Random arrival rule, *RA*: For each $(c, E) \in \mathcal{C}^N$,

$$RA(c, E) \equiv \frac{1}{|N|!}\Big(\sum_{\prec \in \mathcal{O}^N} \min\{c_i, \max\{E - \sum_{j \in N, j \prec i} c_j, 0\}\}\Big)_{i \in N}.$$

Table 2.1 gives the complete calculation for one of the three-claimant examples in the Talmud. The rule is also fully illustrated in Figure 2.14 for the claims vectors found there.[19]

2.1.9 Minimal Overlap Rule

To introduce the next rule, we start from another historical precedent, known as Ibn Ezra's problem:[20]

> Jacob died and his son Reuben produced a deed duly witnessed that Jacob willed to him his entire estate on his death. The son Simeon also produced

[18] O'Neill (1982) proposes a "method of recursive completion" that is equivalent to the random arrival rule, as he shows. The random arrival rule is sometimes referred to as "run-to-the-bank."

[19] Chun (2005) defines a rule, inspired by the Talmud rule, that coincides with the random arrival rule for up to three claimants.

[20] This citation is from Rabinovitch (1973), pp. 162–3. It is also reproduced and discussed by O'Neill (1982).

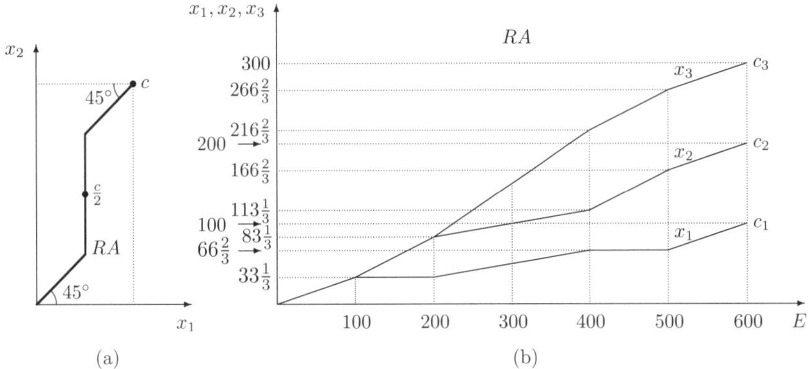

Figure 2.14: **Random arrival rule.** (a) Typical path of awards for $N \equiv \{1, 2\}$ and $c \in \mathbb{R}^N_+$ such that $c_1 < c_2$. (b) Schedules of awards for the marriage contract claims vector of the Talmud.

a deed that his father willed to him half of his estate. Levi produced a deed giving him one third, and Judah brought forth a deed giving him one quarter. All of them [the deeds] bear the same date. The gentile sages would divide the estate in accordance with the ratio of the face value of each, while the Jewish sages divide it in proportion to each one's claim.

Thus the mathematicians [*i.e.* the gentile sages] say that the amount is 1 and when you add to it $\frac{1}{2}$ plus $\frac{1}{3}$ plus $\frac{1}{4}$ the sum is $2\frac{1}{12}$ .... In short, Simeon takes half of Reuben's share, and Levi one third of Reuben's share and Judah one fourth of Reuben's share.

Ibn Ezra then illustrates by taking an example where the estate is worth 120 and he calculates each share, Reuben receiving $57\frac{3}{5}$ and so on. He then proceeds to explain the Talmudic rule.

In accordance with the views of the Jewish sages, the three older brothers say to Judah, "Your claim is only on 30 [one fourth], but all of us have an equal claim on them. Therefore, take $7\frac{1}{2}$, which is one quarter and depart." Each of the brothers take a similar amount. Then Reuben says to Levi, "Your claim is only on 40 [one third]. You have already received your share of the 30 which all four of us claimed: therefore take one third of the [remaining] 10, and go." Thus, Levi's share is $10\frac{5}{6}$ [that is, $30 \times \frac{1}{4} + 10 \times \frac{1}{3}$]. Reuben also says to Simeon, "Your claim is for only half of the estate which is 60, while the remaining half is mine. Now, you have already received your share of 40, so that the amount at issue between us is 20–take half of that and depart." Thus Simeon' share is $20\frac{5}{6}$ and Reuben' share is $80\frac{5}{6}$ [$= 30 \times \frac{1}{4} + 10 \times \frac{1}{3} + 20 \times \frac{1}{2} + 60 \times 1$].

A rule, only defined for some configurations of claims and estate, that produces these numbers for the above example, is suggested by Rabad (twelfth century):[21]

[21] This is noted by Aumann and Maschler (1985). Exact attribution of the various proposals is difficult. These authors cite precursors to Rabad dating to the third century. O'Neill (1982) credits

Rabad's proposal (specified only for problems in which the estate is at most as large as the largest claim). Let $c \in \mathbb{R}_+^N$ and let the estate E grow from 0 to $\sum c_i$. We divide equally any E that is at most as large as the smallest claim; as E increases from the smallest to the second smallest claim, the smallest claimant continues to receive $\frac{1}{|N|}$ of their claim; each of the others receives that amount plus an equal share of the difference between E and the smallest claim. In general, when E increases from the kth smallest claim to the $(k+1)$-th smallest claim, the k smallest claimants continue to receive the amounts they receive when E reaches the kth smallest claim, and each of the others receives the amount they receive then plus an equal share of the difference between E and the kth smallest claim.

Here is one way to extend Rabad's proposal to arbitrary problems.[22] Imagine that claims are not placed on an abstract share of the estate but on specific parts of it. Then, treating each claim that is larger than the estate as if it were equal to the estate, we choose which parts are claimed by the various agents so as to maximize the size of the part claimed exactly once (we do not mean "by one specific agent," but "by no more than one agent").

Since this maximization may have several solutions, we choose among them so as to maximize the size of the part claimed exactly twice (here, we do not mean "by a specific group of two agents," but "by no more than two agents"). This second maximization may also have several solutions, so we select among them by turning to the part claimed by exactly three agents, and so on. When we are done, we divide each part equally among all agents claiming it, and have each claimant collect their partial awards for the parts they claimed.

The idea underlying this definition is that the fewer agents claim a particular part of the estate, the better the situation is for this part. So, we maximize first the number of best cases, when a certain part is claimed exactly once. When this maximization has several solutions, we focus on the second-best cases, when a certain part is claimed exactly twice, and perform a similar maximization with them, and so on. Returning to our general language, here is a formal statement of the lexicographic maximization that underlies the rule.

Minimal overlap rule, *MO*: For each $c \in \mathbb{R}_+$, we proceed as follows. If a claim is larger than the estate, we replace it by the endowment. We then arrange claims on specific parts of the endowment so as to maximize the size of the part claimed exactly once, and for each $k = 2, \ldots, |N|$ successively, subject to the previous $k-1$ maximizations being achieved, we maximize the

Ibn Ezra, speaking of "Ibn Ezra's method." Rabad being explicit, we name the proposal after him. It bears some similarity to a rule defined for the so-called "airport problem" (Littlechild and Owen, 1973, discussed in Section 14.1).

[22] This proposal is due to O'Neill (1982) who simply refers to it as the "extended Ibn Ezra's method." He also notes several of the properties stated below. The expression "minimal overlap rule" is used by Thomson (2003).

size of the part claimed exactly k times. Once claims are so arranged, we divide each part equally among all agents claiming it. Each agent receives the sum of the partial compensations calculated for the parts they claimed.

The proposition below states that up to inessential relabeling of parts of the endowment there is only one way to arrange claims so as to satisfy the lexicographic maximization just described; thus, the rule is well defined. Moreover, when at least one claim is at least as large as the endowment, the optimal arrangement consists in nesting the claims and the resulting awards vector is what Rabad proposed. It is in this sense that the minimal overlap rule can be seen as a generalization of it. The proof of the proposition is in Section 17.1.

Proposition 2.1 *Up to relabeling of units, there is a unique arrangement of claims achieving minimal overlap. It is obtained as follows:*

Case 1: $\max\{c_j\} \geq E$. *Then each agent* $i \in N$ *such that* $c_i \leq E$ *claims* $[0, c_i]$ *and each other agent* i *claims* $[0, E]$.

Case 2: $\max\{c_j\} < E$. *Then there is* $t^* \in [0, E]$ *such that*

(a) *each agent* $i \in N$ *such that* $c_i \leq t^*$ *claims* $[0, c_i]$*;*
(b) *each agent* $i \in N$ *such that* $c_i \geq t^*$ *claims* $[0, t^*]$ *as well as a part of* $[t^*, E]$ *of size* $c_i - t^*$*, with no overlap among the subsets of* $[t^*, E]$ *claimed by any two of these agents.*

When Case 1 holds, claims truncated at the endowment are nested (Figure 2.15a). Figure 2.15b represents an example in which claims are configured so as to satisfy the requirements of Case 2.

The minimal overlap rule is illustrated in Figure 2.16 for the examples in the Talmud.

The minimal overlap rule can also be seen as the concatenation of Rabad's incompletely specified rule (recall that it is limited to problems in which the endowment is no larger than the largest claim), and the constrained equal losses rule. Specifically, if the endowment is at most as large as the largest claim, we apply Rabad's proposal. Otherwise, we first apply Rabad's proposal to the problem in which the endowment is equal to the largest claim; in a second step, we revise claims down by the awards of the first step and apply the constrained equal losses rule to divide the residual endowment.[23]

Variants. (i) When a claim exceeds the endowment, and in order to recognize the difference, one could proceed as follows. For each $i \in N$, let $k_i \in \mathbb{N}$ be such that $kE \leq c_i < (k+1)E$. Then we let agent i claim E k times exactly and

[23] Formally, and using RAB to denote Rabad's proposal, $MO(c, E) = RAB(c, E)$ if $E \leq \max\{c_i\}$ and $MO(c, E) = RAB(c, \max\{c_i\}) + CEL(c - RAB(c, \max\{c_i\}), E - \max\{c_i\})$ if $E > \max\{c_i\}$ otherwise. This formula is derived by Alcalde, Marco, and Silva (2008). See also Hendrickx, Borm, van Elk, and Quant (2007).

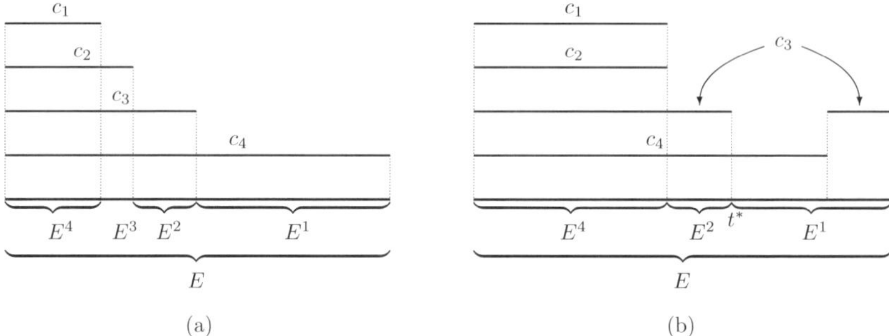

Figure 2.15: **Configurations of claims yielding minimal overlap**, as described in Proposition 2.1. Here, $N \equiv \{1, \ldots, 4\}$. For each agent, we indicate on a horizontal line the part of the estate that he claims. For each $k \in \{1, \ldots, 4\}$, E^k is the part claimed by exactly k claimants. We divide it equally between them. The minimal overlap awards vector is obtained by adding up the partial compensations each claimant receives for the parts they claim. (a) Configuration of claims for Ibn Ezra's problem – then $N \equiv \{1, 2, 3, 4\}$ and $(c, E) \in \mathcal{C}^N$ is equal to ((30, 40, 60, 120), 120). We achieve minimal overlap by nesting claims as in Case 1 of Proposition 2.1. (b) Four-claimant example in which $c_1 = c_2 < c_3 < c_4 < E$. Here, Case 2 of the proposition applies. As c_4 increases to E, less and less of E needs to be covered with some of agent 3's claim, and when c_4 reaches E, claims are nested.

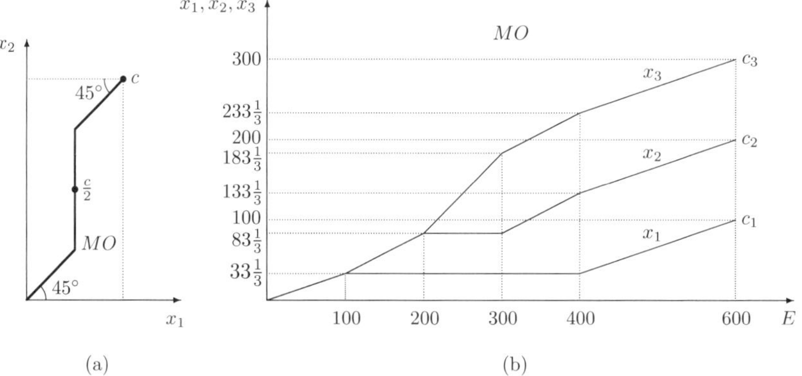

Figure 2.16: **Minimal overlap rule.** (a) Typical path of awards for $N \equiv \{1, 2\}$ and $c \in \mathbb{R}^N_+$ such that $c_1 < c_2$. For two claimants, the minimal overlap rule coincides with concede-and-divide. (b) Schedules of awards for the marriage contract claims vector of the Talmud. The general shape of each schedule of awards is the same as for the Talmud rule, but the points at which agents temporarily stop receiving additional compensations and at which they resume receiving more (the breakpoints in the schedules) are different for the two rules. A comparison to Figure 2.11 suggests that the minimal overlap rule is more generous to the relatively larger claimants than the Talmud rule is, and less generous to the relatively smaller claimants. This impression is given formal confirmation in Chapter 13.

we arrange the differences $(c_i - k_i E)_{i \in N}$ over E as explained in the definition above. Then, we perform equal division for each part of the endowment among all agents claiming it, taking into account the fact that each claimant may claim the same part more than once.

(ii) In defining an "optimal" arrangement of claims, instead of paying attention to the best cases first, namely the parts claimed by the smallest number of agents, we could focus on the worst cases first: we would identify the part claimed by the largest number of agents and arrange claims so as to minimize its size. Since several arrangements of claims would typically solve this minimization problem, we would then narrow down our attention to those minimizing the size of the part claimed by the second largest number of agents, and so on. It is easy to see that this objective is met by arranging claims in such a way that each part is claimed exactly k or $k+1$ times for some k. In fact, *each* such arrangement solves the exercise. After the equal division stage, these arrangements do not all produce the same awards vector, so we do not obtain a well-defined rule.

(iii) Another way to extend Rabad's proposal to problems in which the estate is larger than the largest claim is to apply it recursively, revising claims and estate down at each step, as follows. If the estate is at most as large as the largest claim, we proceed as Rabad suggested. If the estate is larger than the largest claim, we first give to each claimant what Rabad would give them if the estate were equal to the largest claim, we revise each agent's claim down by the amount just assigned to them and the estate down by the largest claim. If the revised estate is at most as large as the largest revised claim, we reapply Rabad's proposal and we are done in two steps. Otherwise, we assign to each claimant what Rabad would give them if the estate were equal to the largest revised claim, revise claims and estate down a second time, and keep going. It turns out that a full distribution of the endowment is reached in a finite number of steps (unless $\sum c_i = E$, in which there is no need for the recursion, of course). In fact, finite convergence occurs very generally, for any mapping defined on the domain of problems in which the estate is at most as large as the largest claim, not just for Rabad's proposal (Section 9.6).

2.1.10 Rule Based on Random Stakes

The rule defined next is based on a random process that is intended to give "equal chances to each unit of claim to be compensated":[24]

Random stakes rule, RS: For each $(c, E) \in \mathcal{C}^N$, we have each $i \in N$ randomly claim each part of E equally, for a total equal to $\min\{c_i, E\}$. Then we divide each part of E equally among all agents claiming it. If a part of E is not claimed by anyone, we reapply the process, after revising claims down by the partial compensations received in the first round. We iterate. The award to

[24] This definition is proposed by O'Neill (1982).

each claimant is the limit of the sum of the compensations that they receive at each step as the number of steps increases.

Proposition 2.2 *The random stakes rule is well defined.*

Proof: Let $(c, E) \in \mathcal{C}^N$. For simplicity, suppose that $N \equiv \{1, 2, 3\}$ and that E can be divided into units sufficiently small that each claim is a multiple of that unit. Since each claim that is larger than the endowment is treated as if it were equal to E, for each $i \in N$, let $c'_i \equiv \min\{c_i, E\}$. For each unit of E, the probability that agent 1, say, claims it, is the ratio $\frac{c'_1}{E}$, and the probability that no other agent claims it is $\frac{E-c'_2}{E}\frac{E-c'_3}{E}$. Using the notation $p_i \equiv \frac{c'_i}{E}$ for each $i \in N$, the probability that agent 1 is the only one claiming is equal to $p_1(1 - p_2)(1 - p_3)$. Similarly, the probability that a given unit is claimed by agent 1 and exactly one other agent is equal to $p_1 p_2(1 - p_3) + p_1(1 - p_2)p_3$, and they get half of it. Finally, the probability that a given unit is claimed by all three claimants is equal to $p_1 p_2 p_3$, and claimant 1 gets one third of it. Altogether, for each unit, claimant 1's award is

$$[p_1(1-p_2)(1-p_3)+\frac{1}{2}[p_1 p_2(1-p_3)+p_1(1-p_2)p_3]+\frac{1}{3}p_1 p_2 p_3]E.$$

Similar expressions give the awards to claimants 2 and 3. The sum of the three awards is not in general equal to E (it cannot be larger than E), and we therefore repeat the procedure to allocate the remainder. At each step, we revise each agent's claim down by the total amount awarded to them in the previous step. Note that the claim of at least one claimant is at least $\frac{E}{n}$, so that at the first round the endowment decreases by at least that much. By the same reasoning, what remains of the endowment after two rounds is at most $\frac{1}{n}\frac{E}{n}$. After k iterations, it is at most $\frac{E}{n^k}$, and as k increases, it vanishes to 0. The procedure is well defined. □

Variants. Other natural formulations of the basic idea underlying the definition given above are explored here.

(i) First, let us note that if we did not revise claims at each step, an agent could end up with more than their claim. Simple two-claimant examples suffice to illustrate the possibility.[25]

(ii) We may want to recognize the validity of the part of a claim that exceeds the endowment. One way to do this is to first let each agent claim the whole endowment as many times as this amount is contained in their claim, as for a variant that we defined for the minimal overlap rule. For each $i \in N$, let c'_i be the part of agent i's claim that remains. We then apply to the c'_is the procedure described earlier. At the division stage, we divide each part of the endowment as many times as it is claimed and, as before, each agent collects the partial compensations they receive for the parts they claim.

[25] See O'Neill (1982).

(iii) Alternatively, we may think of each agent having a number of tokens equal to the size of their claim, which they throw randomly onto the endowment. Then several of their own tokens may land on the same part of the estate. We divide each part of the endowment among the claimants proportionally to the number of tokens of each of them that have landed on it. An agent with a large claim is more likely to have multiple tokens land on the same part of the endowment. Thus, in the division, their advantage will be somewhat diminished, as compared to the original formulation.

Note that, here too, if we did not adjust the claims before the second operation of the random process, an agent could end up with more than their claim.

2.2 FAMILIES OF RULES

In this section, we pass from individual rules to families of rules. Given the rich inventory of rules that we presented in Section 2.1, it is natural to attempt to organize it in some way, to group the rules according to features they share. By examining their definitions and inspecting their graphs, one may be able to establish links among them, which may be helpful in understanding the structure of the space of rules. (In the following chapters, identifying properties that rules have in common will be another way to link them.)

We introduce several families. The members of the first family are parameterized by a strict order on the claimant set. The parameterizations of the other families are more complex. Members of the second family are indexed by a function of two variables. The members of the third family are indexed by a list of $2|N| - 1$ real-valued functions defined on $\mathbb{R}_+^{|N|}$, as are the members of the fourth family. The constrained equal awards and constrained equal losses rules are the only rules in common to the last three families.

2.2.1 Sequential Priority Family

With each strict order on the claimant set – we will use the expression "priority order" – is associated a rule in our first family. To solve a problem, we first fully compensate the highest-priority claimant, if possible; if not, we give them the entire endowment. We then fully compensate the second-highest-priority claimant, if possible; if not, we give them whatever is left; and so on.

For the formal definition, recall that $\mathcal{O}^N$ is the class of strict orders on N and that $\prec$ is our generic notation for these orders (Subsection 2.1.8), with $i \prec j$ meaning that claimant i has priority over claimant j.

Sequential priority rule relative to $\prec \in \mathcal{O}^N$, $SP^{\prec}$: For each $(c, E) \in \mathcal{C}^N$, $SP^{\prec}(c, E)$ is the awards vector obtained as follows: for some $k \in \{0, \ldots, n-1\}$, the first k agents according to $\prec$ are fully compensated, the agent ranked $k + 1$ receives what remains of the endowment, and the remaining agents (if any) receive nothing:

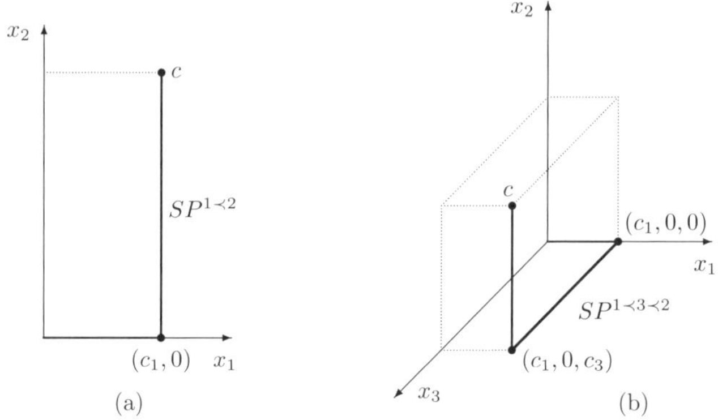

Figure 2.17: **Two sequential priority rules.** (a) The path of awards for $N \equiv \{1, 2\}$ and $c \in \mathbb{R}^N_+$ of $SP^{1\prec 2}$, the sequential priority rule relative to the strict order $1 \prec 2$, is bro.seg$[(0, 0), (c_1, 0), c]$. (b) The path of awards for $N \equiv \{1, 2, 3\}$ and $c \in \mathbb{R}^N_+$ of $SP^{1\prec 3\prec 2}$, the sequential priority rule relative to the strict order $1 \prec 3 \prec 2$, is bro.seg$[(0, 0, 0), (c_1, 0, 0), (c_1, 0, c_3), c]$.

$$SP^{\prec}(c, E) \equiv (\min\{c_i, \max\{E - \sum_{j \in N:\, j \prec i} c_j, 0\}\})_{i \in N}.$$

Figure 2.17 illustrates two examples. Paths of awards are monotone paths consisting of consecutive edges of a hyper-parallelogram having the origin and the claims vector as opposite vertices and whose edges are parallel to the axes.

Because of their systematic bias in favor of particular claimants, the ones listed first in the order to which they are associated, the sequential priority rules do not appear very attractive at first sight, but we will discover a number of reasons to be interested in this family of rules.

2.2.2 Young's Family

The members of the second family are indexed by a function whose inverse, for each claim that some agent may hold, can be interpreted as specifying a numerical evaluation of how well the agent is treated as a function of how much the agent is awarded. For each problem, the awards vector that is chosen is the vector at which all claimants are treated equally well.[26]

[26] These rules are introduced by Young (1987a). Kaminski (2000) develops a "hydraulic" metaphor to describe them. Generalizations are due to Stovall (2014a). The definition is adapted by Moreno-Ternero and Roemer (2006) to a model in which claims are replaced by utility functions. This model is analyzed further by Chun, Jang, and Ju (2014). Another adaptation, to the airport problem (footnote 21), is formulated by Thomson (2007b). Young's family is usually referred to as "the parametric family" but we prefer not using that expression because a number of other families have been defined to which it applies just as well. This is in particular the case for all of the other families introduced in this section.

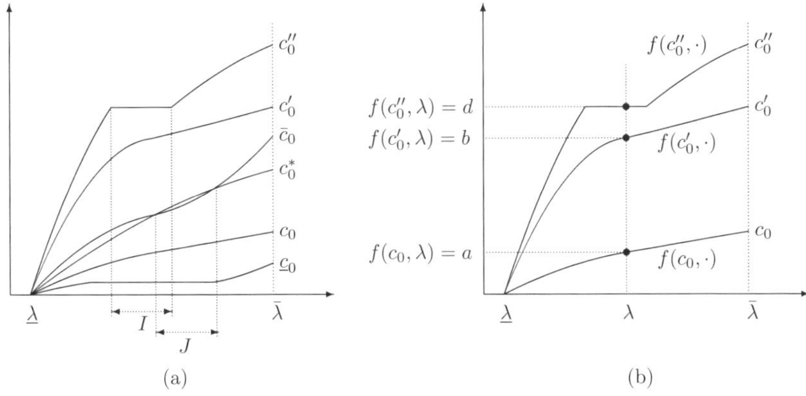

Figure 2.18: **Defining a Young rule**. (a) We specify a real-valued function f defined over the cross-product $\mathbb{R}_+ \times [\underline{\lambda}, \bar{\lambda}]$ where $[\underline{\lambda}, \bar{\lambda}] \subseteq \bar{\mathbb{R}}$ and such that for each $c_0 \in \mathbb{R}_+$, as a function of its second argument, $f(c_0, \cdot)$ is continuous and nowhere decreasing, its value at $\underline{\lambda}$ is 0, and its value at $\bar{\lambda}$ is c_0. This figure represents the graphs of such a function for six values of its first argument. (b) To solve a particular problem $(c, E) \in \mathcal{C}^N$, we pull out the functions $\{f(c_i, \cdot)\}_{i \in N}$ obtained from $f(c_0, \cdot)$ by giving c_0 the specific values of the claims listed in the problem, and identify a value λ of their second argument such that the sum of the values they take is equal to the endowment. The list of these values define the awards vector. In the example illustrated here and for the problem $((c_0, c_0', c_0''), a + b + d)$, this vector is (a, b, d).

For a formal definition, let $\mathbf{\Phi}$ be the family of functions $f: \mathbb{R}_+ \times [\underline{\lambda}, \bar{\lambda}] \mapsto \mathbb{R}_+$, where $-\infty \leq \underline{\lambda} < \bar{\lambda} \leq \infty$, that are continuous and nowhere decreasing with respect to their second argument, and such that for each $c_0 \in \mathbb{R}_+$, we have $f(c_0, \underline{\lambda}) = 0$ and $f(c_0, \bar{\lambda}) = c_0$. An example is shown in Figure 2.18. Given a problem $(c, E) \in \mathcal{C}^N$, we identify λ such that the values taken by the functions $\{f(c_i, \cdot)\}_{i \in N}$ when their second argument is λ add up to E, and choose $(f(c_i, \lambda))_{i \in N}$ as awards vector.

Young rule of representation $f \in \mathbf{\Phi}$, Y^f: Let $\mathbb{R}_+ \times [\underline{\lambda}, \bar{\lambda}]$ be the domain of definition of f. Then for each $(c, E) \in \mathcal{C}^N$,

$$Y^f(c, E) = (f(c_i, \lambda))_{i \in N},$$

where $\lambda \in [\underline{\lambda}, \bar{\lambda}]$ is chosen so as to achieve *balance*.

We refer to any λ achieving *balance* as an **equilibrium λ**.

The following are important observations.

First, if the functions $\{f(c_0, \cdot)\}_{c_0 \in \mathbb{R}}$ are not strictly increasing, there may be problems such that multiple values of the parameter λ exist for which *balance* is achieved. However, the awards vector itself is uniquely defined. That is why we have a well-defined rule. To illustrate, in the example of Figure 2.18a, if there are two agents and their claims are $\underline{c}_0$ and c_0'', there is an endowment such that a whole interval of λs achieve *balance* (the interval I), but the corresponding awards are independent of which one is chosen.

Second, given $c_0, c_0' \in \mathbb{R}_+$ such that $c_0 < c_0'$, the graph of $f(c_0, \cdot)$ may lie partly above that of $f(c_0', \cdot)$. This is illustrated in Figure 2.18a for the claims c_0^* and $\bar{c}_0$ (in the interval J). Consequently, for any problem in which some agent's claim is c_0^* and some other agent's claim is $\bar{c}_0$, and for some values of the endowment, the first agent would get more than the second agent, which is counter to intuition. (The intuition is formalized in Section 3.7 as an axiom.) At this stage, this is indeed a possibility. To prevent it, it is clearly necessary and sufficient that for each pair $\{c_0, c_0'\} \subset \mathbb{R}_+$ such that $c_0 < c_0'$, the graph of $f(c_0, \cdot)$ lies everywhere on or below the graph of $f(c_0', \cdot)$.

Third, if $f\colon \mathbb{R}_+ \times [\underline{\lambda}, \bar{\lambda}] \mapsto \mathbb{R}_+$ is a Young representation of some Young rule, and $g\colon [\underline{\lambda}, \bar{\lambda}] \mapsto \mathbb{R}$ is a one-to-one and increasing function, the function $\tilde{f}\colon \mathbb{R}_+ \times [g(\underline{\lambda}), g(\bar{\lambda})] \mapsto \mathbb{R}_+$ defined by setting for each $c_0 \in \mathbb{R}_+$ and each $\lambda \in [\underline{\lambda}, \bar{\lambda}]$, $\tilde{f}(c_0, \lambda) \equiv f(c_0, g(\lambda))$ is another representation of the rule.

If there is a nondegenerate interval in their domain of definition over which all functions $\{f(c_0, \cdot)\}_{c_0 \in \mathbb{R}_+}$ are constant, the representation is **degenerate**; it is **nondegenerate** otherwise. We will always work with nondegenerate representations.

We interpreted $f(c_0, \lambda)$ as the award needed for someone whose claim is c_0 to achieve a welfare evaluated at λ. This evaluation is independent of the identity of this claimant and of the identities of the other claimants and of their claims. As a result, Young's rules enjoy a large number of strong independence and separability properties, as we will see on multiple occasions in Chapters 3–12.

Many of the rules encountered above are Young rules. Lemma 2.1 identifies six of them by exhibiting representations of them. Figures 2.19–2.21 show these representations. For three of these rules, the representation is limited to situations in which there is an upper bound on claims. The bound is denoted c_{max}. Its existence restricts somewhat the scope of the definition but it has the advantage of permitting a significantly simpler (piecewise linear) representation.[27,28]

Lemma 2.1 *The proportional, constrained equal awards, constrained equal losses, Talmud, Piniles', and constrained egalitarian rules are Young rules.*

Proof: We omit the straightforward verification that the functions defined below are Young representations of the rules listed in the theorem.

[27] See Chun, Schummer, and Thomson (2001). See Young (1987a) for a Young representation of the Talmud rule without the upper bound.

[28] Several of these representations are in Chun, Schummer, and Thomson (2001).

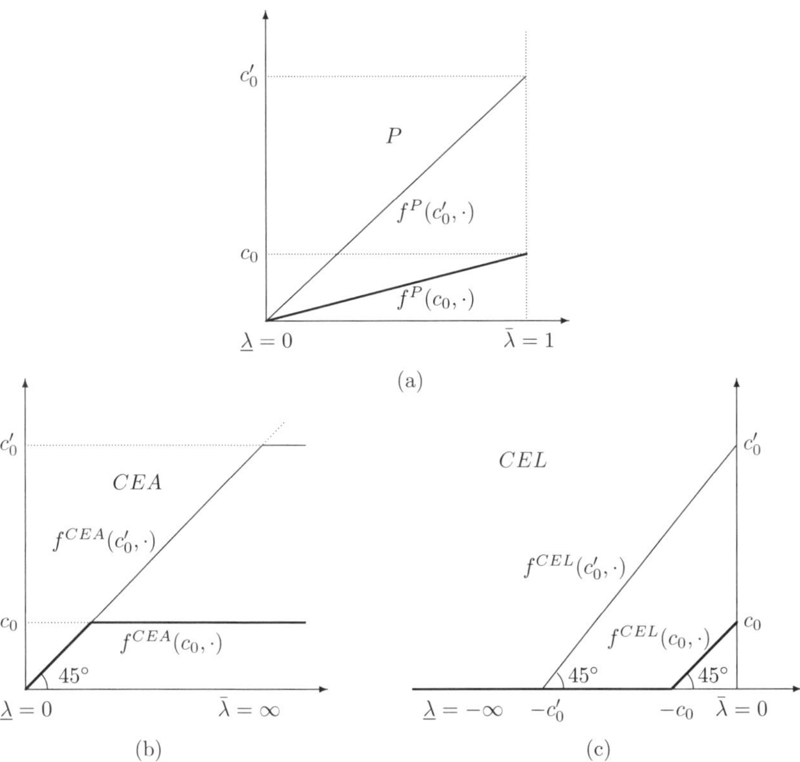

Figure 2.19: **Young representations of the proportional, constrained equal awards, and constrained equal losses rules**. (a) Proportional rule: $[\underline{\lambda}, \bar{\lambda}] \equiv [0, 1]$ and for each $c_0 \in \mathbb{R}_+$, the graph of $f^P(c_0, \cdot)$ is $\text{seg}[(0, 0), (1, c_0)]$. (b) Constrained equal awards rule: $[\underline{\lambda}, \bar{\lambda}[\equiv [0, \infty[$ and for each $c_0 \in \mathbb{R}_+$, the graph of $f^{CEA}(c_0, \cdot)$ follows the 45° line up to (c_0, c_0) and terminates with a horizontal half-line. (c) Constrained equal losses rule: $]\underline{\lambda}, \bar{\lambda}] \equiv]-\infty, 0]$ and for each $c_0 \in \mathbb{R}_+$, the graph of $f^{CEL}(c_0, \cdot)$ follows the horizontal axis until $(-c_0, 0)$ and terminates with a segment (it has slope 1) to $(0, c_0)$.

The proportional rule admits the following representation $f^P \colon \mathbb{R}_+ \times [0, 1] \mapsto \mathbb{R}_+$:

$$f^P(c_0, \lambda) \equiv \lambda c_0.$$

The constrained equal awards rule admits the following representation $f^{CEA} \colon \mathbb{R}_+ \times [0, \infty[\; \mapsto \mathbb{R}_+$:

$$f^{CEA}(c_0, \lambda) \equiv \begin{cases} \lambda & \text{if } \lambda \in [0, c_0]; \\ c_0 & \text{otherwise.} \end{cases}$$

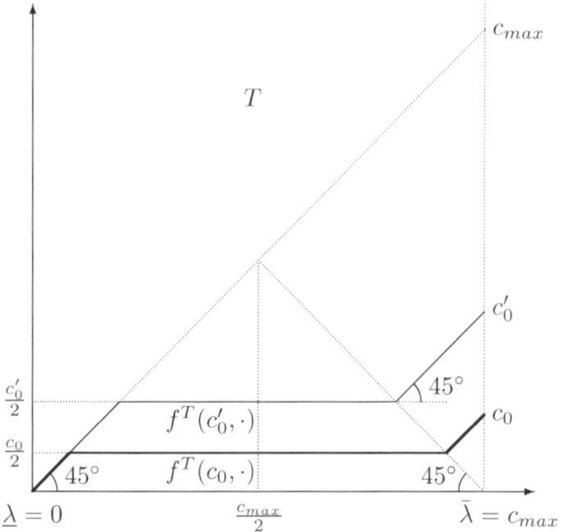

Figure 2.20: **Young representation of the Talmud rule when there is a maximal value that a claim can take, c_{max}.** Here, $[\underline{\lambda}, \bar{\lambda}] \equiv [0, c_{max}]$ and for each $c_0 \in \mathbb{R}_+$, the graph of $f^T(c_0, \cdot)$ follows the 45° line up to $(\frac{c_0}{2}, \frac{c_0}{2})$, continues horizontally until it meets the line of slope -1 emanating from $(c_{\max}, 0)$, and terminates with a segment (it has slope 1) to (c_{max}, c_0).

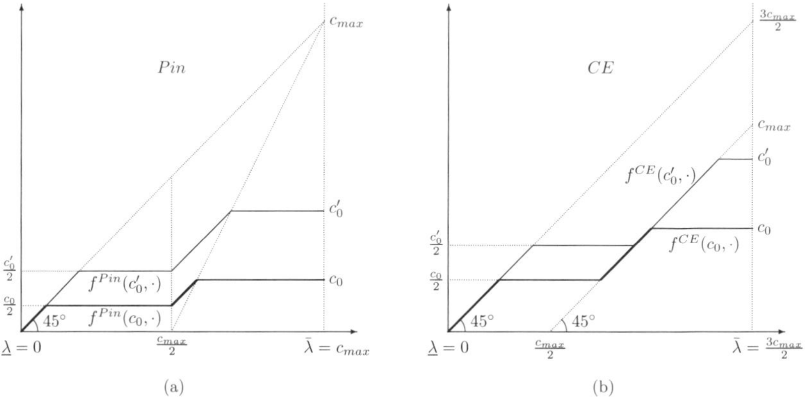

Figure 2.21: **Young representations of Piniles' and constrained egalitarian rules when there is a maximal value that a claim can take, c_{max}.** (a) Piniles' rule: $[\underline{\lambda}, \bar{\lambda}] \equiv [0, c_{max}]$ and for each $c_0 \in \mathbb{R}_+$, the graph of $f^{Pin}(c_0, \cdot)$ follows the 45° line up to $(\frac{c_0}{2}, \frac{c_0}{2})$, continues horizontally until $(\frac{c_{max}}{2}, \frac{c_0}{2})$, follows the line of slope 1 until the point of ordinate c_0 (the locus of this point as c_0 varies is a segment of slope 2 emanating from $(\frac{c_{max}}{2}, 0)$), and terminates with a horizontal segment to (c_{max}, c_0). (b) Constrained egalitarian rule: here, $[\underline{\lambda}, \bar{\lambda}] \equiv [0, 3\frac{c_{max}}{2}]$ and for each $c_0 \in \mathbb{R}_+$, the graph of $f^{CE}(c_0, \cdot)$ follows the 45° line up to $(\frac{c_0}{2}, \frac{c_0}{2})$, continues horizontally until it meets the line of slope 1 emanating from $(\frac{c_{max}}{2}, 0)$, follows that line until the point of ordinate c_0, then terminates with a horizontal segment to $(\frac{3c_{max}}{2}, c_0)$.

The constrained equal losses rule admits the following representation $f^{CEL}: \mathbb{R}_+ \times [-\infty, 0] \mapsto \mathbb{R}_+$:

$$f^{CEL}(c_0, \lambda) \equiv \begin{cases} 0 & \text{if } \lambda \in [-\infty, -c_0]; \\ \lambda + c_0 & \text{otherwise.} \end{cases}$$

As announced, for the next three rules, we limit attention to situations in which no claim is larger than some number called c_{max}.

The Talmud rule admits the following representation $f^T: [0, c_{max}] \times [0, c_{max}] \mapsto \mathbb{R}_+$:

$$f^T(c_0, \lambda) \equiv \begin{cases} \lambda & \text{if } \lambda \in [0, \frac{c_0}{2}]; \\ \frac{c_0}{2} & \text{if } \lambda \in [\frac{c_0}{2}, c_{max} - \frac{c_0}{2}]; \\ \lambda + c_0 - c_{max} & \text{if } \lambda \in [c_{max} - \frac{c_0}{2}, c_{max}]. \end{cases}$$

Piniles' rule admits the following representation $f^{Pin}: [0, c_{max}] \times [0, c_{max}] \mapsto \mathbb{R}_+$:

$$f^{Pin}(c_0, \lambda) \equiv \begin{cases} \lambda & \text{if } \lambda \in [0, \frac{c_0}{2}]; \\ \frac{c_0}{2} & \text{if } \lambda \in [\frac{c_0}{2}, \frac{c_{max}}{2}]; \\ \lambda - \frac{c_{max}}{2} + \frac{c_0}{2} & \text{if } \lambda \in [\frac{c_{max}}{2}, \frac{c_{max}}{2} + \frac{c_0}{2}]; \\ c_0 & \text{if } \lambda \in [\frac{c_{max}}{2} + \frac{c_0}{2}, c_{max}]. \end{cases}$$

The constrained egalitarian rule admits the following representation $f^{CE}: [0, c_{max}] \times [0, 3\frac{c_{max}}{2}] \mapsto \mathbb{R}_+$:

$$f^{CE}(c_0, \lambda) \equiv \begin{cases} \lambda & \text{if } \lambda \in [0, \frac{c_0}{2}]; \\ \frac{c_0}{2} & \text{if } \lambda \in [\frac{c_0}{2}, \frac{c_{max}}{2} + \frac{c_0}{2}]; \\ \lambda - \frac{c_{max}}{2} & \text{if } \lambda \in [\frac{c_{max}}{2} + \frac{c_0}{2}, \frac{c_{max}}{2} + c_0]; \\ c_0 & \text{if } \lambda \in [\frac{c_{max}}{2} + c_0, 3\frac{c_{max}}{2}]. \end{cases}$$ □

Figure 2.22 shows Young representations g^T and g^{Pin} of the Talmud and Piniles' rule when no bound is imposed on claims. In each case, the domain of definition of the representation is a compact interval $[\underline{\lambda}, \bar{\lambda}]$ with $\underline{\lambda} = 0$. It is divided into two subintervals, $[0, \lambda^*]$ and $[\lambda^*, \bar{\lambda}]$ (we chose $\lambda^* = \frac{\bar{\lambda}}{2}$ in the figure, but we did not have to do so).

For the Talmud rule, we specify a continuous and increasing real-valued function whose domain is $[0, \lambda^*[$, taking the value 0 at 0, and whose graph C is asymptotic to the vertical line of abscissa λ^*. Similarly, we specify a continuous and increasing real-valued function whose domain is $]\lambda^*, \bar{\lambda}]$, taking the value 0 at $\bar{\lambda}$, and whose graph D is asymptotic to the vertical line of abscissa λ^*. (We chose D to be the symmetric image of C with respect to $(\lambda^*, 0)$, which is possible because $\lambda^* = \frac{\bar{\lambda}}{2}$, but we could have chosen D independently of C.)

For Piniles' rule, we specify a continuous and increasing real-valued function whose domain is $[0, \lambda^*[$, which takes the value 0 at $\bar{\lambda}$, and whose graph C is asymptotic to the vertical line of abscissa λ^*. We also specify a continuous and increasing real-valued function whose domain is $[\lambda^*, \bar{\lambda}[$, which takes

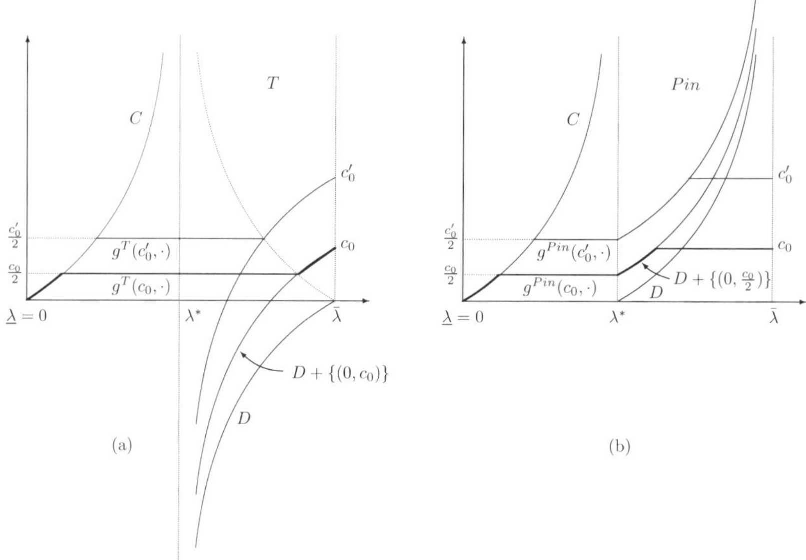

Figure 2.22: **Young representations of the Talmud and Piniles' rules when no upper bound is imposed on claims.** In each case, the domain of definition of the representation is some compact interval $[\underline{\lambda}, \bar{\lambda}]$ with $\underline{\lambda} = 0$. (a) Talmud rule: for each $c_0 \in \mathbb{R}_+$, the graph of $g^T(c_0, \cdot)$ follows the curve C until it reaches a point of ordinate $\frac{c_0}{2}$, continues horizontally until it reaches the vertical translate of the curve D by c_0 (the locus of this meeting point is the curve obtained by symmetry of D with respect to the horizontal axis); and it follows this vertical translate to $(\bar{\lambda}, c_0)$. (b) Piniles' rule: for each $c_0 \in \mathbb{R}_+$, the graph of $g^{Pin}(c_0, \cdot)$ follows C until it reaches a point of ordinate $\frac{c_0}{2}$, continues horizontally until it reaches the vertical line of abscissa λ^*; continues along the vertical translate of D by $\frac{c_0}{2}$ until it reaches a point of ordinate c_0; and it terminates with a horizontal segment to $(\bar{\lambda}, c_0)$.

the value 0 at λ^*, and whose graph D is asymptotic to the vertical line of abscissa $\bar{\lambda}$. (We chose $\lambda^* = \frac{\bar{\lambda}}{2}$ and D to be obtained from C by a horizontal translation, but we could have chosen D independently of C.)

The rules defined next constitute an important subfamily of Young's family. Let $\mathcal{U}$ be the class of functions $u: \mathbb{R}_{++} \mapsto \mathbb{R}$ that are continuous, strictly increasing, and such that $\lim_{x \to 0_+} u(x) = -\infty$.

Equal-sacrifice rule relative to $u \in \mathcal{U}$, ES^u: For each $(c, E) \in \mathcal{C}^N$, $ES^u(c, E)$ is the awards vector $x \in \mathbb{R}^N_+$ such that for each $i \in N$ with $c_i = 0$, $x_i = 0$, and there is $\lambda \geq 0$ such that for each $i \in N$ with $c_i > 0$, $u(c_i) - u(x_i) = \lambda$.[29]

[29] This definition is due to Young (1988), who frames it in the context of taxation.

In the context of taxation, the following members of Young's family have been discussed: for **Stuart's rule** (1889), $f^{St}(c_0, \lambda) \equiv \max\{c_0 - c_0^{1-\lambda}, 0\}$ and for **Cassel's rule** (1901), $f^C(c_0, \lambda) \equiv \frac{c_0^2}{c_0 + \frac{1}{\lambda}}$.

2.2.3 ICI and CIC Families

• **ICI family.** The hybrid character of the Talmud rule seems to bear little connection to the lexicographic minimization exercise that underlies the definition of the minimal overlap rule. Yet, Figure 2.11, which illustrates the Talmud rule, and Figure 2.16, which illustrates the minimal overlap rule, reveal a striking resemblance between them. What is similar is not only that each claimant's award is a piecewise linear function of the endowment – many other rules share this feature – but rather the specific pattern of increases in the awards as the endowment grows from 0 to the sum of the claims. First, each claimant's award increases initially, then it remains constant, then it increases again until the claimant is fully compensated, full compensation occurring only when the endowment reaches the sum of the claims (all claimants simultaneously reach full compensation at the very end). Second, claimants drop out of the distribution in the order of increasing claims (a first phase) and return for more in the reverse order (a second phase). Third, any two awards that are increasing at a given time do so at the same rate.

These observations underlie the family that we define next. It consists of all rules exhibiting these characteristics. For each such rule, each problem, and each claimant, the interval of constancy of the award depends on where their claim stands in the ordered list of claims, as claims are handled in increasing order during the first phase, and in decreasing order in the second phase. This is why we refer to the family as the "Increasing–Constant–Increasing" family, or ICI for short. (For the largest claimant(s), the interval of constancy is degenerate.)

Proceeding in this way is easily justified. If there is too little to divide, we may judge differences in claims irrelevant, and equal division makes sense. Awards are "consolation prizes" then. As the endowment increases, we may reach a point at which we feel that the smallest claimant is starting to receive too significant a part of their claim as compared to the others, so we exclude that claimant from the distribution of new increments. We may still judge differences in the claims of the others irrelevant, though, at least for a while, and we continue with equal division for them until, once again, we reach a point at which we feel that the smallest claimant in this group (that is, the second smallest claimant overall) is starting to receive too significant a part of their own claim as compared to them. Then we drop that claimant off and continue with equal division for the others, and so on. We do so until only one agent is left, and for a while that claimant gets the totality of each new increment. At some point, we start inviting claimants back in, but in the reverse order, repeating the process with a shift of focus from the compensations they receive to the losses they incur. We divide each increment among all claimants whose losses we still judge too small in relation to their claims to justify that they be treated differently. We proceed in a sequential manner until every one is fully compensated.

The richness in the family just introduced comes from the freedom in choosing the various points at which we drop agents off or invite them back in, and the fact that these drop-off and pick-up points are allowed to depend on the claims vector. These points cannot be completely arbitrary however, as we will see.

Here is the formal definition.[30] Let $H \equiv (F^k, G^k)_{k=1}^{n-1}$, where $n \equiv |N|$, be a list of pairs of real-valued functions defined on $\mathbb{R}_+^n$, such that for each $c \in \mathbb{R}_+^N$, the sequence $(F^k(c))_{k=1}^{n-1}$ is nowhere decreasing, the sequence $(G^k(c))_{k=1}^{n-1}$ is nowhere increasing, $G^1(c) \leq \sum c_i$, and the following relations, which we call the **ICI relations**, hold. We will show that these relations are necessary and sufficient to guarantee that, at the end of the process we described, each claimant is indeed fully compensated. In order to better show the symmetry between the two regimes we write one relation per claimant, but the relations are not independent: multiplying the first one by n, the second one by $n-1$, $\ldots$, and the last one by 1, and adding the results yields an identity. Assuming for simplicity of notation that $c_1 \leq \cdots \leq c_n$,

$$\begin{array}{ccccccc}
 & & \frac{F^1(c)}{n} & + & \frac{\sum c_i - G^1(c)}{n} & = & c_1 \\
c_1 & + & \frac{F^2(c)-F^1(c)}{n-1} & + & \frac{G^1(c)-G^2(c)}{n-1} & = & c_2 \\
\vdots & + & \vdots & + & \vdots & = & \vdots \\
c_{k-1} & + & \frac{F^k(c)-F^{k-1}(c)}{n-k+1} & + & \frac{G^{k-1}(c)-G^k(c)}{n-k+1} & = & c_k \\
\vdots & + & \vdots & + & \vdots & = & \vdots \\
c_{n-1} & + & \frac{-F^{n-1}(c)}{1} & + & \frac{G^{n-1}(c)}{1} & = & c_n
\end{array}$$

When two agents have equal claims, the ICI relations imply that they are dropped off together and that they are invited back in together. Thus, some of the breakpoints in the schedules of awards are equal then.

Let $\mathcal{H}^N$ be the family of lists of pairs of functions $H \equiv (F^k, G^k)_{k=1}^{n-1}$ satisfying the ICI relations. We refer to the rules we have just defined as **ICI rules** and to the family they constitute as the **ICI family**. Summarizing, we have:

ICI rule relative to $H \equiv (F^k, G^k)_{k=1}^{n-1} \in \mathcal{H}^N$, ICI^H: For each $c \in \mathbb{R}_+^N$, the awards vector is given by the following algorithm as the endowment increases from 0 to $\sum c_i$. Assuming for simplicity that $c_1 \leq \cdots \leq c_n$, as E increases from 0 to $F^1(c)$, equal division prevails among everyone. As E increases

[30] This definition is proposed and studied by Thomson (2000, 2008b). Huijink, Borm, Reijnierse, and Kleppe (2015) proceed differently but the family of rules they define, which they call the "claim-and-right" rules, happens to coincide with the ICI family, as they show. A particularly interesting member of their family is discussed in Chapter 14.

from $F^1(c)$ to $F^2(c)$, claimant 1's award remains constant, and equal division prevails among the other claimants. As E increases from $F^2(c)$ to $F^3(c)$, claimants 1 and 2's awards remain constant, and equal division prevails among the other claimants. This process continues until E reaches $F^{n-1}(c)$. The next increments go entirely to claimant n until E reaches $G^{n-1}(c)$, at which point equal division prevails among claimants n and $n-1$. This continues until E reaches $G^{n-2}(c)$, at which point equal division prevails among claimants n through $n-2$, and so on. This process continues until E reaches $G^1(c)$, at which point claimant 1 reenters the scene and equal division prevails among all claimants until E reaches $\sum c_i$ and everyone is fully compensated.

This algorithm has $2n-1$ steps, the middle step being when the largest claimant is the only one whose award increases. As noted earlier, when two agents have equal claims, they are dropped off together and invited back in together. Thus, some of the breakpoints are equal.

The ICI rules are well defined, as shown by the following calculations, illustrated in Figure 2.23. Claimant 1's award increases twice, at Step 1 by the amount $\frac{F^1(c)}{n}$, and at Step $2n-1$ by the amount $\frac{\sum c_i - G^1(c)}{n}$, for a total of c_1 (by the first ICI relation). Claimant 2's award increases along with claimant 1's award, on both occasions and at the same rate, therefore also for a total of c_1, and in addition it increases at Step 2 by the amount $\frac{F^2(c)-F^1(c)}{n-1}$ and at Step $2n-2$ by the amount $\frac{G^1(c)-G^2(c)}{n-1}$. Altogether, claimant 2 ends up with c_2 (by the second ICI relation). Similar statements can be made about the

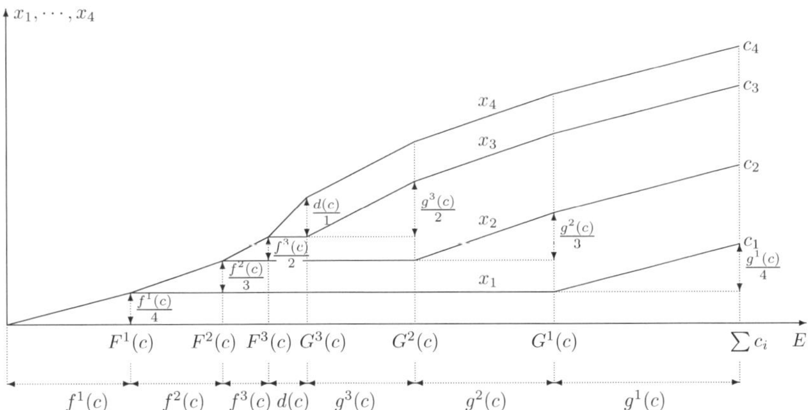

Figure 2.23: **Schedules of awards of a four-claimant ICI rule for a particular claims vector.** Here $N \equiv \{1,2,3,4\}$ and $c \in \mathbb{R}^N_+$. The ICI rule parameterized by $H \equiv (F^k, G^k)_{k=1}^3 \in \mathcal{H}^N$ is denoted ICI^H. Let $f^1(c) \equiv F^1(c)$, and for $k = 2, 3$, let $f^k(c) \equiv F^k(c) - F^{k-1}(c)$. Let $g^1(c) \equiv \sum c_i - G^1(c)$, and for $k = 2, 3$, let $g^k(c) \equiv G^{k-1}(c) - G^k(c)$. Finally, let $d(c) \equiv G^3(c) - F^3(c)$.

remaining claimants. So, for the first claimant, there are two terms; for each of the others except for the last claimant, there are two more terms than for the previous one; for the last claimant, there is only one more term than for the penultimate one.

The class of functions $\mathcal{H}^N$ is convex: a weighted average of functions in the class is also in the class.[31]

For any two ICI rules, each $c \in \mathbb{R}^N_+$, and each $k \in \{1, \ldots, n\}$, the difference $\delta^k(c) \equiv G^k(c) - F^k(c)$ is the same. Each $\delta^k(c)$ can be easily calculated from the ICI relations:

$$\begin{array}{rl} \delta^1(c) &= -(n-1)c_1 + c_2 + \ldots + \ldots + c_{n-1} + c_n \\ \delta^2(c) &= -(n-2)c_2 + c_3 + \ldots + c_{n-1} + c_n \\ \ldots &= + \ldots + \ldots + c_{n-1} + c_n \\ \delta^{n-2}(c) &= -2c_{n-2} + c_{n-1} + c_n \\ \delta^{n-1}(c) &= -c_{n-1} + c_n \end{array}$$

To describe a member of the family, it therefore suffices to select, for each $c \in \mathbb{R}^N_+$, a sequence $(F^k(c))_{k=1}^{n-1}$ of real numbers, and derive the sequence $(G^k(c))_{k=1}^{n-1}$ by adding to $F^k(c)$, for each $k = 1, \ldots, n-1$, the number $\delta^k(c)$. Any nowhere-decreasing sequence $(F^k(c))_{k=1}^{n-1}$ such that (i) $F^1(c) \geq 0$ and (ii) the resulting sequence $(G^k(c))_{k=1}^{n-1}$ is nowhere increasing and $G^1(c) \leq \sum c_i$, is acceptable. Alternatively, it suffices to select, for each $c \in \mathbb{R}^N_+$, a sequence $(G^k(c))_{k=1}^{n-1}$ of real numbers and derive the sequence $(F^k(c))_{k=1}^{n-1}$ by subtracting from $G^k(c)$, for each $k = 1, \ldots, n-1$, the number $\delta^k(c)$. Any nowhere-increasing sequence $(G^k(c))_{k=1}^{n-1}$ such that (i) $G^1(c) \leq \sum c_i$ and (ii) the resulting sequence $(F^k(c))_{k=1}^{n-1}$ is nowhere decreasing and $F^1(c) \geq 0$, is acceptable.

Several interesting ICI rules result from particular choices of $H \equiv (F, G) \in \mathcal{H}^N$. In each case, we only specify either F or G. Indeed, using the ICI relations, one can deduce G from F and conversely:

Lemma 2.2 *The constrained equal awards, constrained equal losses, Talmud, and minimal overlap rules are ICI rules.*

Proof:

(a) Constrained equal awards rule: for each $c \in \mathbb{R}^N_+$, let $G(c) \equiv (\sum c_i, \ldots, \sum c_i)$.
(b) Constrained equal losses rule: for each $c \in \mathbb{R}^N_+$, let $F(c) \equiv (0, \ldots, 0)$.
(c) Talmud rule: for each $c \in \mathbb{R}^N_+$ such that, to simplify notation, $c_1 \leq \cdots \leq c_n$, let $F(c) \equiv (n\frac{c_1}{2}, \frac{c_1}{2} + (n-1)\frac{c_2}{2}, \ldots, \frac{c_1}{2} + \frac{c_2}{2} + \cdots + \frac{c_{k-1}}{2} + (n-k+1)\frac{c_k}{2}, \ldots, \frac{c_1}{2} + \frac{c_2}{2} + \cdots + \frac{c_{n-2}}{2} + 2\frac{c_{n-1}}{2})$.

[31] However, the convex combination of two ICI rules is not (in fact, is never) an ICI rule. Convex operations on the space of rules are studied in Section 9.3.

(d) Minimal overlap rule: for each $c \in \mathbb{R}^N_+$ such that, to simplify notation, $c_1 \leq \cdots \leq c_n$, let $F(c) \equiv (c_1, c_2, \ldots, c_{n-1})$. □

We obtain a particularly simple subfamily of the ICI family as follows. Given $\theta \in [0, 1]$, let $F(c) \equiv (\theta n c_1, \theta[c_1 + (n-1)c_2], \ldots, \theta[c_1 + c_2 + \ldots + (n-k+1)c_k], \ldots, \theta[c_1 + c_2 + \cdots + 2c_{n-1}])$, and let the sequence $(G^k(c))_{k=1}^{n-1}$ be derived from the sequence $(F^k(c))_{k=1}^{n-1}$ by means of the ICI relations. Let us denote by $\boldsymbol{T^\theta}$ the rule so defined and refer to the subfamily $\{T^\theta\}_{\theta \in [0,1]}$ of the ICI family as the **TAL family**.[32] The constrained equal awards rule is obtained for $\theta = 1$, the constrained equal losses rule for $\theta = 0$, and the Talmud rule for $\theta = \frac{1}{2}$. The minimal overlap rule is an ICI rule but it is not a member of the TAL family. Finally, a TAL rule is always a Young rule.

For two claimants, the sequence H consists of a single pair (F^1, G^1) of functions, but because when $|N| = 2$, for each $c \in \mathbb{R}^N_+$, $F^1(c)$ and $G^1(c)$ have to satisfy the ICI relations (there are two of them then but they are not independent), we obtain a family indexed by a single parameter, which is a function of c. This family links the constrained equal awards and constrained equal losses rules, passing through concede-and-divide (which for two claimants coincides, as we saw, with the random arrival and minimal overlap rules). Paths of awards are easily determined and four ICI rules are illustrated in Figure 2.24. Supposing, to fix the ideas, that $N \equiv \{1, 2\}$ and that $c \in \mathbb{R}^N_+$ is such that $c_1 < c_2$, the path for c consists of the segment connecting the origin to the point $a(c) \equiv (\frac{F^1(c)}{2}, \frac{F^1(c)}{2})$, the vertical segment with endpoints $a(c)$ and $b(c) \equiv a(c) + (0, c_2 - c_1)$, and the segment (it has slope 1) connecting $b(c)$ to c.[33]

We noted earlier that the class of functions $\mathcal{H}^N$ is convex. Suppose $|N| = 2$ and let S and S' be two members of the ICI family associated with the functions H and $H' \in \mathcal{H}^N$. Then for each $c \in \mathbb{R}^N_+$, the path of awards of the rule associated with a convex combination of H and H' is obtained by "averaging" the paths of S and S' parallel to the 45° line: each line of slope 1 that crosses the path of one crosses the path of the other, and the average of the intersections (an intersection can be a point or a segment; when a segment, the average is an average of sets) gives part of the path of the rule associated with a convex combination of H and H'.

• **CIC family.** An alternative algorithm to the one underlying the definition of the ICI family suggests itself, by reversing the timing of the application

[32] It is proposed and studied by Moreno-Ternero and Roemer (2006a,b). For an up-to-date survey of the properties of its members, see Moreno-Ternero (2018).

[33] For each $\theta \in [0, 1]$, we obtain the rule T^θ by simply setting $a(c) = \theta(c_1, c_1)$ where according to our convention, $c_1 \leq c_2$. Thus, for two claimants and for each claims vector, the path of T^θ has the same shape as the path of a typical ICI rule, but we can recover each T^θ from only one of its paths for a claims vector of unequal coordinates, whereas for a general ICI rule, the kinks in paths of awards can depend in a very general way on the claims vector.

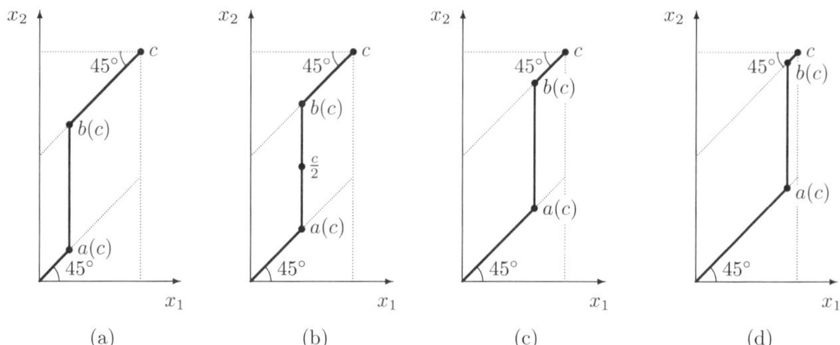

Figure 2.24: **Paths of awards of four two-claimant ICI rules.** Let $N \equiv \{1, 2\}$ and $c \in \mathbb{R}^N_+$ be such that $c_1 < c_2$. The four panels represent the paths of awards for c of ICI rules associated with progressively larger and larger values of the endowment at which equal division of each increment stops ($F^1(c)$) and then resumes ($G^1(c)$). These switches of regime are reflected in the kinks in the paths, the points $a(c) \equiv (\frac{F^1(c)}{2}, \frac{F^1(c)}{2})$ and $b(c) \equiv a(c) + (0, c_2 - c_1)$. Panel (b) shows the Talmud rule itself. At one extreme, when $a(c)$ and $b(c)$ belong to the vertical axis (then $a(c) = (0, 0)$), we obtain the constrained equal losses rule. At the other extreme, when $a(c)$ and $b(c)$ belong to the vertical line through c (then $b(c) = c$), we obtain the constrained equal awards rule. (These cases are not represented.)

of the constrained equal awards and constrained equal losses rules in the formulas. Fix the claims vector and let the endowment grow from 0 to the sum of the claims. There, we began with equal division and dropped claimants off in the order of increasing claims. Here, we introduce agents in the order of decreasing claims. We begin by giving everything to the largest claimant; throughout the process, we divide each increment in the endowment equally among all claimants who have been introduced, and drop each one off as soon as they are fully compensated. The family defined in this way can be indexed by a list of pairs of functions of the claims vector, $H \equiv (F^k, G^k)_{k=1}^{n-1}$, where $n \equiv |N|$: the first units are assigned to the largest claimant; when the endowment reaches $F^1(c)$, the second largest claimant comes in and equal division prevails between them; when the endowment reaches $F^2(c)$, the third largest claimant comes in and equal division prevails among the three largest claimants, and so on. When the smallest claimant has been introduced, equal division prevails among all claimants until that claimant is fully compensated; this occurs when the endowment reaches $G^{n-1}(c)$. The claimant drops out and equal division prevails among the others until the second smallest claimant is fully compensated; this occurs when the endowment reaches $G^{n-2}(c)$, and so on. The process concludes with the largest claimant being the only one left and that claimant gets the next increments until the claimant too is fully compensated. To guarantee that the rules are well defined, these functions should satisfy relations parallel to those that we imposed on the parameters indexing the ICI family, for the same reason. We call them the **CIC relations**. We describe them in an appendix (Section 17.2).

We show in that appendix that the constrained equal awards and constrained equal losses rules are members of the family. These two rules are the only ones to be both ICI and CIC rules. The CIC family also contains a rule defined like the Talmud rule except for a reversal of the timing of the application of the constrained equal awards and constrained equal losses rules: for each claims vector, we apply the latter in the lower half of the range of the endowment, and the former in the upper half. As for the Talmud rule, in each case, we use the half-claims instead of the claims themselves in the formulas. Thus, the name "reverse Talmud rule" under which the rule is known. Figure 2.25 illustrates it for the examples in the Talmud.[34]

Reverse Talmud rule, T^r: For each $(c, E) \in \mathcal{C}^N$ and each $i \in N$,

$$T_i^r(c, E) \equiv \begin{cases} \max\{\frac{c_i}{2} - \lambda, 0\} & \text{if } E \leq \sum \frac{c_j}{2}, \\ \frac{c_i}{2} + \min\{\frac{c_i}{2}, \lambda\} & \text{otherwise,} \end{cases}$$

where, in each case, $\lambda \in \mathbb{R}_+$ is chosen so as to achieve *balance*.

The reverse Talmud rule is a Young rule. Assuming once again that there is a maximal value c_{max} that a claim can take, it admits the following Young representation (Figure 2.26), $f^{T^r} : [0, c_{max}] \times [0, c_{max}] \mapsto \mathbb{R}_+$:

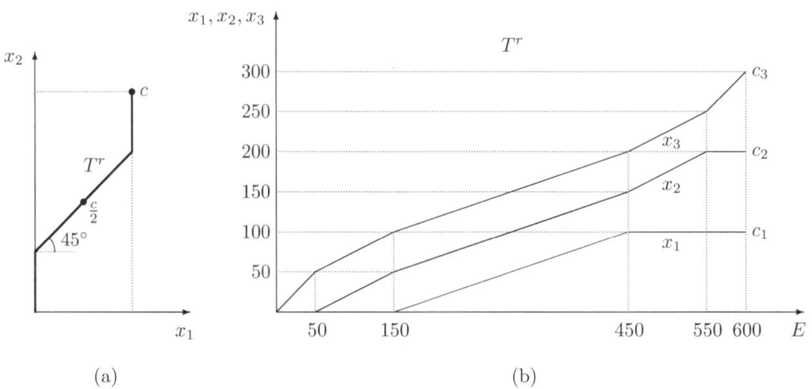

Figure 2.25: **Reverse Talmud rule.** (a) Typical path of awards for $N \equiv \{1, 2\}$ and $c \in \mathbb{R}_+^N$ such that $c_1 < c_2$. We obtain it by applying the constrained equal losses rule if the endowment is at most as large as the half-sum of the claims, and the constrained equal awards rule otherwise, in each case using the half-claims in the formula instead of the claims themselves. (b) Schedules of awards for the marriage contract claims vector of the Talmud.

[34] The rule is defined by Chun, Schummer, and Thomson (2001).

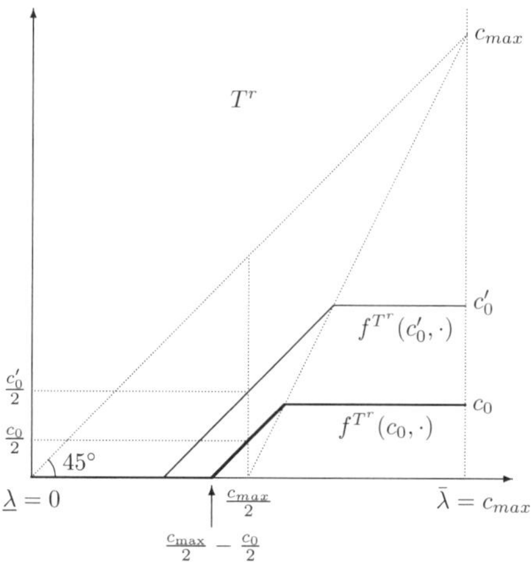

Figure 2.26: **Young representation of the reverse Talmud rule when there is a maximal value that a claim can take, c_{max}**. Here $[\underline{\lambda}, \bar{\lambda}] \equiv [0, c_{max}]$ and for each $c_0 \in \mathbb{R}_+$, the graph of $f^{T^r}(c_0, \cdot)$ follows the horizontal axis until the point of abscissa $\frac{c_{max}}{2} - \frac{c_0}{2}$, continues along a line of slope 1 until it meets the line of slope 2 passing through (c_{max}, c_{max}), and it terminates with a horizontal segment to (c_{max}, c_0).

$$f^{T^r}(c_0, \lambda) \equiv \begin{cases} 0 & \text{if } \lambda \in [0, \frac{c_{max}}{2} - \frac{c_0}{2}]; \\ \lambda - \frac{c_{max}}{2} + \frac{c_0}{2} & \text{if } \lambda \in [\frac{c_{max}}{2} - \frac{c_0}{2}, \frac{c_{max}}{2} + \frac{c_0}{2}]; \\ c_0 & \text{if } \lambda \in [\frac{c_{max}}{2} + \frac{c_0}{2}, c_{max}]. \end{cases}$$

For two claimants, we obtain a family indexed by a parameter that depends on the claims vector. Four members are illustrated in Figure 2.27 when applied to a particular claims vector.

We can also define a subfamily of CIC rules parallel to the TAL family (the family $\{T^\theta\}_{\theta \in [0,1]}$) by giving the switchpoints the following very simple form: let $\theta \in [0, 1]$ and for each $c \in \mathbb{R}^N$ with $c_1 \leq \cdots \leq c_n$, let $F(c) \equiv \theta(-c_{n-1} + c_n, -2c_{n-2} + c_{n-1} + c_n, \cdots, -kc_{n-k} + c_{n-k+1} + \cdots + c_n + \cdots, -(n-1)c_1 + c_2 + \cdots + c_n)$. Let $\boldsymbol{U^\theta}$ denote the rule associated with θ in this manner, and $\boldsymbol{\{U^\theta\}_{\theta \in [0,1]}}$ be the resulting **reverse TAL family**. Note that $U^0 = CEA$, $U^1 = CEL$, and $U^{\frac{1}{2}} = T^r$. This family is a subfamily of Young's family.[35]

2.3 SUMMARY

This chapter has displayed a surprisingly large number of rules to solve what appeared to be a very simple class of allocation problems, and offered several

[35] An exhaustive study of the properties of the family is due to van den Brink and Moreno-Ternero (2017).

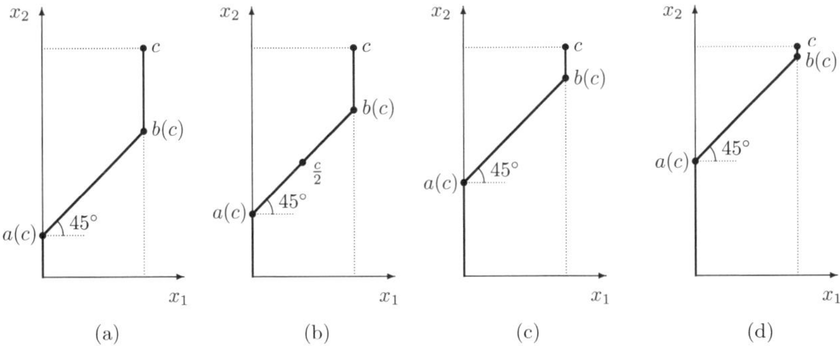

Figure 2.27: **Paths of awards of four two-claimant CIC rules.** Let $N \equiv \{1, 2\}$ and $c \in \mathbb{R}^N_+$ be such that $c_1 < c_2$. The four panels represent the paths of awards for c of CIC rules associated with progressively larger and larger values of the endowment at which equal division of each increment starts ($F^1(c)$) and then stops ($G^1(c)$). These switches of regime are reflected in the kinks in the paths, the points $a(c) \equiv (0, F^1(c))$ and $b(c) \equiv a(c) + (c_1, c_1)$. Panel (b) shows the reverse Talmud rule itself. At one extreme, when $a(c)$ and $b(c)$ belong to the 45° line (then $a(c) = (0, 0)$), we obtain the constrained equal awards rule. At the other extreme, when $a(c)$ and $b(c)$ belong to the line of slope 1 passing through c (then $b(c) = c$), we obtain the constrained equal losses rule. (These cases are not represented.)

ways of organizing this inventory of rules in families. The next chapters, in which we investigate properties of rules, will result in "grade sheets" for each of these rules that will be of great help in assessing their relative merits. At this point, a number of preliminary observations can be made.

First, what underlies many of the rules is the basic notion of equality, applied to gains or to losses, subject to natural constraints, in absolute or in relative terms. We obtain many of the rules that we have presented by exploiting the various ways in which these ideas can be combined.

Second, multiple ways of thinking about claims problems give us the same recommendation for two claimants. Attributing to each claimant the amount conceded to them by the other, and dividing the remainder equally – the scenario we called concede-and-divide – produces awards vectors that coincide with the awards vectors selected by several other rules, namely the Talmud rule, the random arrival rule, and the minimal overlap rule. In Chapter 5, we will discover yet other routes to that rule, and in Chapter 10, we will describe a natural way to extend it to general populations.

CHAPTER 3

Basic Properties of Division Rules

In the next ten chapters we focus on properties of division rules and examine their implications. In the current chapter, we start with basic ones: properties that seem desirable for most if not all of the interpretations of the model under study. They also happen to be satisfied by virtually all of the rules that have been discussed in the literature. In the subsequent chapters, we formulate requirements whose appeal will be more dependent on the application, in particular on the legal or informational constraints that have to be respected.

Almost all of the properties we study in this chapter apply to each problem separately, "point by point." We referred in Chapter 1 to such properties as "punctual." In Chapters 4–12, we turn to what we called there "relational" properties: such a property links the recommendations made by a rule for problems that are related in a certain way. Until Chapter 10, the population of claimants is fixed. This is in accordance with the model as we formulated it in Chapter 1. By contrast, we consider in Chapters 10–12 the possibility that population varies and generalize the model accordingly.

We present each known characterization as soon as all the axioms it involves have been stated.

3.1 BALANCE

First we require of a rule that, for each problem, it allocate the entire endowment. We introduced the idea as a property of an awards vector for a particular problem and in Chapter 2, we incorporated it in the definition of a rule. Here, we write it as a separate axiom. As in the statements of all axioms throughout this book, the notation S designates a generic rule:

Balance: For each $(c, E) \in \mathcal{C}^N$, $\sum S_i(c, E) = E$.

Obviously we cannot distribute more than there is, but conceivably we could distribute less. Depending upon which additional properties we impose on a rule and the consequent cost of budget balance, we could be satisfied with this weaker notion.[1] In other types of allocation problems, budget balance is not as innocuous a requirement as it appears at first sight, however. Also, in certain settings, not insisting on it has proved extremely useful. For example, suppose that the issue is to raise taxes to cover the cost of a public good as a function of its users' valuations of it – recall that this is one of the interpretations of our model (Section 1.2). In that context, the so-called Clarke–Groves rule succeeds in eliciting from users their true valuations only because it allows violations of budget balance.[2] In most of our other applications, this is not an issue and there would be little benefit from dropping the requirement, so we will impose it throughout.

3.2 CONTINUITY

Next we require that small changes in the data of the problem to be solved not lead to large changes in the chosen awards vector. Errors in specifying these data, or corrections of these errors, should not radically affect the recommendation. Such continuity requirements are often described as "technical," but they make much intuitive sense.[3] There is always some arbitrariness in the data of a problem, and they prevent rules from depending on details of problems of arguably little relevance.

Continuity: For each sequence $\{(c^\nu, E^\nu)\}$ of elements of $\mathcal{C}^N$ and each $(c, E) \in \mathcal{C}^N$, if $(c^\nu, E^\nu) \to (c, E)$, then $S(c^\nu, E^\nu) \to S(c, E)$.

Weaker versions of *continuity* are obtained by imagining small changes only in the claims vector, or only in one of its coordinates, or only in the endowment. We refer to them as **claims continuity**, **component-wise claims continuity**, and **endowment continuity** respectively.

All of the rules encountered in Section 2.1 are *continuous*, but some members of the various families of Section 2.2 are not. For a Young rule of representation $f \in \Phi$ defined on $\mathbb{R}_+ \times \Lambda$ where $\Lambda \subset \mathbb{R}$, and for each $\lambda \in \Lambda$, continuity of $f(c_0, \lambda)$ as a function of c_0 is what guarantees *claims continuity*. For an ICI rule associated with $H \equiv (F^k, G^k)_{k-1}^{n-1} \in \mathcal{H}^N$ to be *claims continuous*, the functions $(F^k)_{k=1}^{n-1}$, $(G^k)_{k=1}^{n-1}$, which give the breakpoints in the schedules of awards as a function of the claims vector, should be continuous. A similar requirement should be imposed on the functions giving the breakpoints in the schedules of awards of a CIC rule for it to be *claims continuous*.

[1] In the model of bankruptcy considered by Csóka and Herings (2017c), some of the endowment may be awarded to the firm, which amounts to dropping *balance*.

[2] For a discussion, see Green and Laffont (1979).

[3] Apart from *anonymity*, defined in Section 3.6, *continuity* is the only relational axiom discussed in this chapter.

3.3 HOMOGENEITY

We now require that if claims and endowment are multiplied by the same positive number, then so should all awards. There should be no "scale" effect.[4]

Homogeneity: For each $(c, E) \in \mathcal{C}^N$ and each $\lambda > 0$, $S(\lambda c, \lambda E) = \lambda S(c, E)$.

Most of the rules that we have seen satisfy this property, but Young's, ICI, and CIC rules do not necessarily do so. We omit the restrictions that should be imposed on the functions parameterizing them for *homogeneity* to be satisfied.

Note that *homogeneity* does not (only) say that "units of measurement [here, units of account] do not matter," and, of course, it is hard to see why they should, but rather that we can calculate awards without knowing the units in which these data are entered, which is a substantial assumption. Consider a rule that coincides with the proportional rule if the endowment is less than \$10, and with the constrained equal awards rule otherwise. This rule is not *homogeneous*. Suppose now that problems were specified in pounds instead of dollars. Then, we would most naturally adjust the definition of the rule as follows: up to an endowment equal in pounds to 10 times the rate of exchange of pounds for dollars, we would apply the proportional formula and otherwise we would apply the constrained equal awards formula. Invariance with respect to choices of units of account would be satisfied but not *homogeneity*.

Much confusion exists on this issue, both in the context of claims problems and also in other contexts where counterparts of the property have been invoked. Its source is that in specifying a claims problem, we do not usually bother indicating a unit of account. In order to be able to talk about whether a rule is invariant under changes of units of account, we should work with a model in which currencies are explicitly indicated and may vary from problem to problem, and where rates of exchange between currencies are specified, as we did in describing the example in the previous paragraph. Consider, for example, the domain consisting of all problems whose parameters are expressed in dollars together with all problems whose parameters are expressed in pounds. We say that "a problem expressed in dollars is equivalent to one expressed in pounds" if we pass from the former to the latter by subjecting its data to the pre-specified rate of exchange between these currencies. A rule defined on a domain of such problems is **invariant with respect to choices of units of accounts** if we always pass by a similar operation from the recommendation it makes for the first problem to the recommendation it makes for the second problem.[5]

Although most rules are *homogeneous*, there are good reasons to not insist on this property. Large values of the data of the problem at hand may justify that different division principles be applied than for small values. In the context

[4] For that reason, this property is often called "scale invariance."

[5] Marchant (2008) has independently made the same point.

of taxation, the need to go beyond *homogeneity* is particularly evident. In fact, most taxation rules used in practice are not *homogeneous*.

3.4 LOWER AND UPPER BOUNDS ON AWARDS AND LOSSES

Here, we specify bounds on awards, either lower bounds or upper bounds. We then investigate the recursive application of bounds.[6]

3.4.1 Defining Bounds

In assessing any type of allocation problem, we often find it natural to impose floors or ceilings on agents' utilities, welfares, or payoffs as the case may be. A variety of such bounds have been proposed for claims problems.

We begin with lower bounds on awards. Formally, a **lower bound function** is a function $b \colon \mathcal{C}^N \mapsto \mathbb{R}^N_+$ that specifies for each problem a vector that is weakly dominated by the claims vector and whose coordinates add up to no more than the endowment. Each coordinate of this vector is interpreted as a minimal amount that the corresponding claimant should get. Symmetrically, an **upper bound function** is a function $u \colon \mathcal{C}^N \mapsto \mathbb{R}^N$ that specifies for each problem a vector that is weakly dominated by the claims vector and whose coordinates add up to at least the endowment. Each coordinate of this vector is interpreted as a maximal amount that the corresponding claimant should get.

• Our first example is a lower bound: awards should be nonnegative. A violation would imply that for at least one problem, there is at least one claimant who, in addition to not getting any of the money due to them, would contribute to honoring the claims held by the others. The requirement is embodied in the definition of a rule since a rule has to take its values in $\mathbb{R}^N_+$. It is certainly very natural for most of the intended interpretations of the model, but not for all. For instance, when what has to be decided is how to share the cost of a public good, a situation our model covers, it says that every household should always contribute. Yet, it may well be thought desirable to sometimes transfer income to those households whose resources are too limited (negative income tax):

Nonnegativity: For each $(c, E) \in \mathcal{C}^N$, $S(c, E) \geqq 0$.

A stronger requirement is that, if the endowment is positive, each agent whose claim is positive receive a positive amount:

Positive awards: For each $(c, E) \in \mathcal{C}^N$ and each $i \in N$, if $c_i > 0$ and $E > 0$, then $S_i(c, E) > 0$.

[6] Luttens (2010) formulates axioms having to do with the manner in which rules respond to changes, not in the data of a problem directly, but in the resulting changes in certain endogenously defined lower bounds.

The next requirement is part of the definition of a rule as well. It provides an upper bound on awards: simply, each agent should receive at most their claim:

Claims boundedness: For each $(c, E) \in \mathcal{C}^N$, $S(c, E) \leqq c$.

Claims boundedness can be strengthened by requiring that if a loss has to be incurred, each agent whose claim is positive bear some of it:

Positive losses: For each $(c, E) \in \mathcal{C}^N$ and each $i \in N$, if $c_i > 0$ and $E < \sum c_j$, then $c_i - S_i(c, E) > 0$.

• Our next lower bound for a claimant's award in a problem is the difference between the endowment and the sum of the claims of the other agents if this difference is nonnegative, and 0 otherwise. Formally, for each $(c, E) \in \mathcal{C}^N$ and each $i \in N$, the **minimal right of claimant *i* in (c, E)** is the quantity $\boldsymbol{m_i(c, E)} \equiv \max\{E - \sum_{N\setminus\{i\}} c_j, 0\}$.[7] Let $\boldsymbol{m(c, E)} \equiv (m_i(c, E))_{i\in N}$. We require that each claimant receive at least their minimal right:

Minimal rights lower bounds on awards: For each $(c, E) \in \mathcal{C}^N$, $S(c, E) \geqq m(c, E)$.

Figure 3.1 illustrates for two claimants the possible locations of the vector of minimal rights for a fixed claims vector with unequal coordinates and three values of the endowment chosen so as to illustrate the three cases

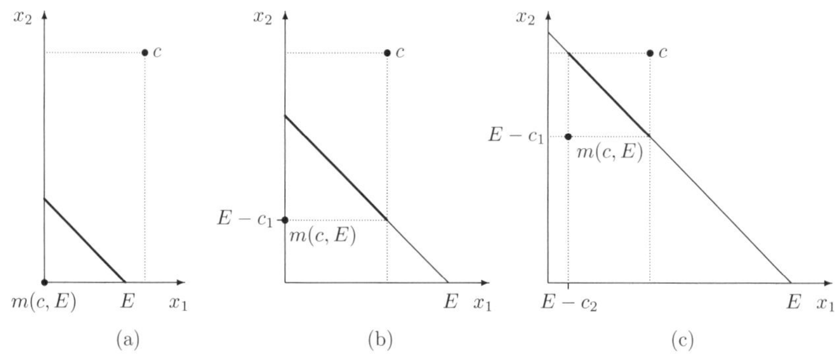

Figure 3.1: **The minimal rights lower bounds for two claimants.** The set of awards vectors (balanced vectors x such that $0 \leqq x \leqq c$) is indicated as a thick segment. For two claimants, it is also the set of balanced vectors at which minimal rights are respected. In each panel, $N \equiv \{1, 2\}$ and $c \in \mathbb{R}^N_+$ is such that $c_1 < c_2$. (a) Here, $E \leq c_1$, so both minimal rights are 0 (we have $m(c, E) = 0$). (b) Here, $c_1 < E \leq c_2$, and only claimant 2's minimal right is positive ($m(c, E) = (0, E - c_1)$). (c) Here, $c_2 < E$, and both minimal rights are positive ($m(c, E) = (E - c_2, E - c_1)$).

[7] In Subsection 2.1.4, we took a different perspective, and called this amount a concession made to claimant i by the others.

that may occur: (i) $E \leq \min\{c_i\}$: then both coordinates of $m(c, E)$ are 0; (ii) $\min\{c_i\} < E \leq \max\{c_i\}$: here, one coordinate is 0 and the other is positive; and (iii) $\max\{c_i\} < E$; now, both coordinates are positive. It is readily seen that for two claimants the set of balanced vectors satisfying the minimal rights and the set of awards vectors are the same. Figure 3.2 illustrates the *minimal rights lower bounds* for these three claimants. In this case, the latter includes the former. These relations are formally proved below.

The next bounds are based on the notion of a truncated claim already encountered as part of the scenario underlying concede-and-divide (Subsection 2.1.4): given $(c, E) \in \mathcal{C}^N$, the **truncated claim of agent $i \in N$ in (c, E)** is the minimum of the claim and the endowment: recall that $t_i(c, E) \equiv \min\{c_i, E\}$ designates agent i's claim truncated at E and that $t(c, E) \equiv (t_i(c, E))_{i \in N}$.

Truncated-claims upper bounds on awards: For each $(c, E) \in \mathcal{C}^N$, $S(c, E) \leq t(c, E)$.

∗ `Relating axioms` ♦ Together, *balance*, *nonnegativity*, and *claims boundedness*, all of which are incorporated in the definition of a rule, imply the *minimal rights lower bounds*. Indeed, let $(c, E) \in \mathcal{C}^N$ and $x \in \mathbb{R}^N$ be a vector

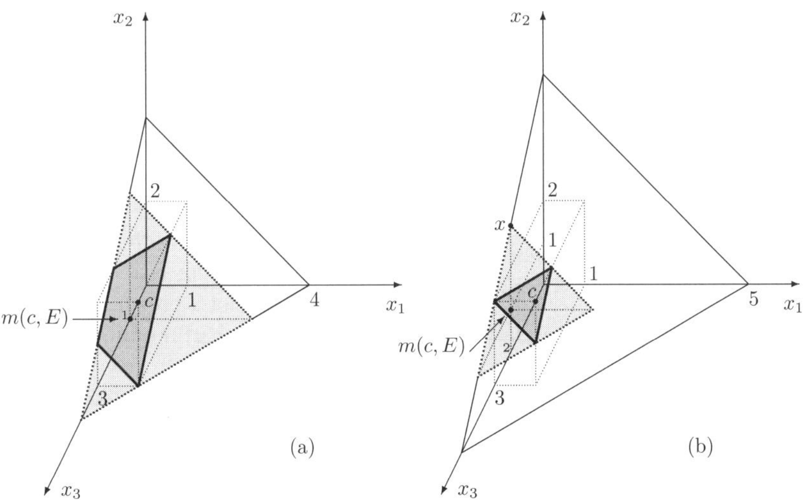

Figure 3.2: **The minimal rights lower bounds for three claimants.** Here, $N \equiv \{1, 2, 3\}$ and $c \in \mathcal{C}^N$ is equal to $(1, 2, 3)$. The endowment is given two values. The set of awards vectors (balanced vectors x satisfying $0 \leqq x \leqq c$) is indicated by dark shading. It is a subset of the set, indicated as the entire shaded region, of balanced vectors that weakly dominate the vector of minimal rights, $m(c, E)$. (a) When $E = 4$, only claimant 3's minimal right is positive ($m(c, E) = (0, 0, 1)$). (b) When $E = 5$, claimants 2 and 3's minimal rights are both positive ($m(c, E) = (0, 1, 2)$).

satisfying, for each $j \in N$, the *claims boundedness* inequality $x_j \leq c_j$. For each $i \in N$, let us sum over $j \in N\backslash\{i\}$ the statements $-x_j \geq -c_j$, and add E to both sides of the resulting inequality. Invoking the *balance* requirement $\sum x_i = E$, we obtain

$$x_i = E - \sum_{N\backslash\{i\}} x_j \geq E - \sum_{N\backslash\{i\}} c_j.$$

Combining this inequality with the *nonnegativity* requirement $x_i \geq 0$, we conclude that $x_i \geq \max\{E - \sum_{N\backslash\{i\}} c_j, 0\} \equiv m_i(c, E)$, as announced. From the existence of awards vectors (recall that the expression "awards vector" refers to a balanced vector that is bounded below by 0 and above by c), we deduce the existence of awards vectors at which the *minimal rights lower bounds* are respected.

♦ Conversely, for two claimants, *balance* and the *minimal rights lower bounds* together imply *nonnegativity* and *claims boundedness* (Figure 3.1). However, for three claimants or more, *nonnegativity*, *balance*, and the *minimal rights lower bounds* together do not imply *claims boundedness*. In the examples of Figure 3.2, $N \equiv \{1, 2, 3\}$ and $c \in \mathbb{R}^N_+$ is equal to $(1, 2, 3)$. If $E = 5$ (Figure 3.2b), the vector of minimal rights is $(0, 1, 2)$. The nonnegative balanced vector $x \equiv (0, 3, 2)$ dominates it, but $x_2 > c_2$.

♦ The *truncated-claims upper bounds* are satisfied by all awards vectors and for two claimants, any awards vector satisfies the bounds.

• Our next lower bound for an claimant's award is $\frac{1}{|N|}$ of their claim truncated at the endowment.[8]

$\frac{1}{|N|}$-truncated-claims lower bounds on awards: For each $(c, E) \in \mathcal{C}^N$, $S(c, E) \geqq \frac{1}{|N|}t(c, E)$.

Note that an agent's component of this lower bound function does not depend on the other agents' claims. One could think of using as a lower bound a pre-specified proportion of their claim instead (and not a pre-specified proportion of their truncated claim), but that is not a meaningful option. Indeed, the profile of bounds so obtained would be compatible with feasibility for all problems only if that proportion is 0, but then all rules would qualify.

[8] This bound is proposed by Moreno-Ternero and Villar (2004) under the name of "securement." It has also been referred to as the "reasonable lower bound" and the "average truncated lower bounds on awards." Bosmans and Lauwers (2011) propose to strengthen the bound on a claimant's award by dividing their truncated claim by the number of agents whose claims are positive. Moreno-Ternero and Villar (2004) and Moreno-Ternero (2006c) also propose the requirement for $|N| = 2$ that for each $(c, E) \in \mathcal{C}^N$ and each $i \in N$, if $c_i \leq E$, then $S_i(c, E) \geq \frac{c_i}{2}$, under the name of "lower securement." For general populations, the natural generalization is that under the same hypothesis, $S_i(c, E) \geq \frac{c_i}{|N|}$. Finally, they introduce for $|N| = 2$ the requirement that for each $(c, E) \in \mathcal{C}^N$ and each $i \in N$, if $c_i \geq E$, then $S_i(c, E) \geq \frac{E}{2}$, under the name of "upper securement." For general populations, and under the same hypothesis, this becomes $S_i(c, E) \geq \frac{E}{|N|}$.

Using proportions of *truncated* claims is a natural alternative, and in fact, $\frac{1}{|N|}$ is the highest proportion that ensures compatibility with feasibility for all problems:

Proposition 3.1 *The largest fraction such that, for each problem, each agent can be guaranteed to receive at least this fraction of his truncated claim is* $\frac{1}{|N|}$.

Proof: Let $(c, E) \in \mathcal{C}^N$ be such that for each $i \in N$, $c_i = E$. If α is such that for each $i \in N$, $x_i \geq \alpha t_i(c, E) = \alpha E$, then $E = \sum x_i \geq |N|\alpha E$. This inequality can be met only if $\alpha \leq \frac{1}{|N|}$. □

Let $N \equiv \{1, 2\}$, and $c \in \mathbb{R}^N_+$ be such that $c_1 \leq c_2$. Let $E \leq c_1$. Then, if S meets the $\frac{1}{|N|}$*-truncated-claims lower bounds on awards*, and since awarding each agent at least half of the endowment is possible only at equal division, its path of awards for c contains seg$[(0, 0), (\frac{c_1}{2}, \frac{c_1}{2})]$. In Subsection 2.2.3 we presented the view that if the endowment is small in relation to claims, equal division should prevail, and the bound under discussion can be seen as an implementation of the idea. The path continues in the subset of box$[(\frac{c_1}{2}, \frac{c_1}{2}), c]$ bounded below by the lower envelope of the 45° line and the horizontal line of ordinate $\frac{c_2}{2}$. Two cases can be distinguished depending upon whether or not $c_1 \leq \frac{c_2}{2}$ (Figure 3.3). If $c_1 \leq \frac{c_2}{2}$, the constraint that agent 2 should get at least their half-claim is binding for no endowment, in the sense that if an awards vector x satisfies the $\frac{1}{|N|}$*-truncated-claims lower bounds on awards* for claimant 1, then $x_2 \geq \frac{c_2}{2}$ whenever $c_2 \leq E$ (Figure 3.3a). If $c_1 > \frac{c_2}{2}$, it is binding for each endowment in the nonempty interval $]c_2, c_1 + \frac{c_2}{2}[$ (Figure 3.3b).

Of the main rules of Chapter 2, the only ones to violate the $\frac{1}{|N|}$*-truncated-claims lower bounds on awards* are the proportional and constrained equal losses rules. (This can be seen on Figure 3.3a for two claimants, as the paths of these rules do not lie in the required region for the bounds to be met.) The random arrival rule satisfies the bounds because each agent appears first in exactly the fraction $\frac{1}{|N|}$ of all orders, and for each such order, the agent receives their truncated claim. For the minimal overlap rule, consider the two cases described in Proposition 2.1. If Case 1 holds, the calculation is obvious. The maximal value of the endowment for which Case 1 holds is the largest claim: at that point, each claimant receives $\frac{1}{|N|}$ of their claim. Moreover, as we will see, for this rule, each award is a nowhere-decreasing function of the endowment. Thus, the bounds are still met if the endowment exceeds the largest claim.

The constrained equal awards, Talmud, and Piniles' rules all meet the $\frac{1}{|N|}$*-truncated-claims lower bounds on awards*. This is an easy consequence of the fact that a Young rule of representation $f \in \Phi$ defined on some interval $[\underline{\lambda}, \bar{\lambda}]$ meets the $\frac{1}{|N|}$*-truncated-claims lower bounds on awards* if and only if the schedules $\{f(c_0, \cdot)\}_{c_0 \in \mathbb{R}_+}$ have a well-defined upper envelope and this envelope – let us call it C – is such that, for each $c_0 \in \mathbb{R}_+$, the schedule for c_0 follows C from $(\underline{\lambda}, 0)$ up to a point of ordinate at least $\frac{c_0}{2}$. Let $(c, E) \in \mathcal{C}^N$

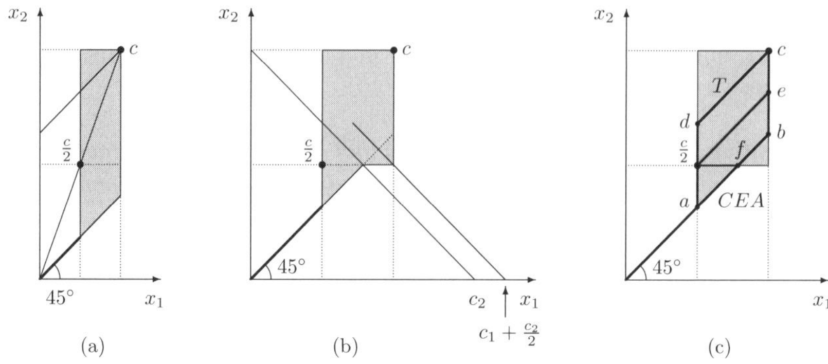

Figure 3.3: **The $\frac{1}{|N|}$-truncated-claims lower bounds on awards for two claimants.** This figure illustrates the bounds for $N \equiv \{1, 2\}$ and $c \in \mathbb{R}^N_+$ such that $c_1 < c_2$. For a rule to meet the bounds, its path of awards for c should lie in the region consisting of seg$[(0, 0), \frac{1}{2}(\min\{c_i\}, \min\{c_i\})]$ (here, $\min\{c_i\} = c_1$) and the shaded area. (a) Here, $c_1 < \frac{c_2}{2}$ and the constraint $x_2 \geq \frac{c_2}{2}$ is binding for no endowment. This panel shows that neither the proportional rule nor the constrained equal losses rule satisfies the bound. (b) Here, $c_1 > \frac{c_2}{2}$ and the constraint $x_2 \geq \frac{c_2}{2}$ is binding for each endowment in the interval $[c_2, c_1 + \frac{c_2}{2}]$. (c) The path of the constrained equal awards rule for c is bro.seg$[(0, 0), b, c]$, that of the Talmud rule is bro.seg$[(0, 0), a, d, c]$, that of Piniles' rule is bro.seg$[(0, 0), a, \frac{c}{2}, e, c]$, and that of the constrained egalitarian rule is bro.seg$[(0, 0), a, \frac{c}{2}, f, b, c]$. Thus, all of these rules meet the $\frac{1}{|N|}$*-truncated-claims lower bounds on awards* for $|N| = 2$. (In fact, they do so for arbitrary $|N|$.)

and λ be a solution of the equation giving the awards vector of (c, E). Then, there is $N' \subseteq N$ such that at λ, for each $i \in N'$, the schedule for c_i is still following C. The members of N' are receiving a common amount that is the maximal amount anyone is getting, this common amount being therefore at least as large as equal division. Each $i \in N \setminus N'$ (this set could be empty) is getting $f(c_i, \lambda) \geq \frac{c_i}{2} \geq \frac{c_i}{|N|}$.

The $\frac{1}{|N|}$*-truncated-claims lower bounds on awards* are defined by focusing on what claimants receive. By switching attention to the losses they incur, we obtain an upper bound: if in problem (c, E), agent i's claim is at most as large as the deficit, $\sum c_j - E$, agent i should receive at most $c_i - \frac{1}{|N|}c_i$; otherwise, agent i should receive at most $c_i - \frac{1}{|N|}(\sum c_j - E)$. This can be written as a lower bound on the loss agent i incurs. We impose this bound on each claimant[9]:

$\frac{1}{|N|}$-min-of-claim-and-deficit lower bounds on losses: For each $(c, E) \in \mathcal{C}^N$, $c - S(c, E) \geq \frac{1}{|N|}t(c, \sum c_j - E)$.

[9] This property is due to Moreno-Ternero and Villar (2004), who refer to it as "securement*."

A result similar to Proposition 3.1 holds. We omit its statement.

• Another lower bound on a claimant's award, which is obviously more demanding than the $\frac{1}{|N|}$-*truncated-claims lower bounds on awards*, is the minimum of the agent's claim and an equal share of the endowment.[10]

Min-of-claim-and-equal-division lower bounds on awards: For each $(c, E) \in \mathcal{C}^N$, $S(c, E) \geq t(c, \frac{E}{|N|})$.

These bounds are in fact quite restrictive. In particular, for two claimants, they are met only by the constrained equal awards rule. Indeed, let $N \equiv \{1, 2\}$ and $c \in \mathbb{R}^N_+$ be such that $c_1 \leq c_2$. If $E \leq 2c_1$, the bounds are met only at equal division. If $E \geq 2c_1$, the bound is met for claimant 1 only if claimant 1 is assigned c_1, and we then know what claimant 2 is assigned. In each case, we have obtained the awards vector recommended by the constrained equal awards rule. However, for more than two claimants, other rules qualify. Only the awards to those agents whose claims are no larger than equal division are specified; these claimants have to be fully compensated. The award to each other claimant is only required to satisfy a certain inequality, and there are infinitely many ways the resulting list of inequalities can be jointly satisfied.

For each agent, the *min-of-claim-and-equal-division lower bound* only depends on their claim and the endowment. In fact, we have:

Proposition 3.2 *The* ***min-of-claim-and-equal-division lower bounds on awards*** *are the greatest lower bounds to be independent of the agents' identities and to only depend, for each agent, on their claim and the endowment.*

Proof: Let $b\colon \mathbb{R}^2_+ \mapsto \mathbb{R}^N_+$ be a function satisfying the hypotheses (the first requirement being reflected in the fact that b has no agent subscript) and $(c, E) \in \mathcal{C}^N$. Let $i \in N$. By definition of a rule, $(*)$ $b(c_i, E) \leq c_i$. Also, compatibility with feasibility of the profile $(b(c_j, E))_{j\in N}$ requires $(**)$ $\sum b(c_j, E) \leq E$. Again, let $i \in N$. In the problem (c', E) in which for each $j \in N$, $c'_j = c_i$, $(**)$ yields $(***)$ $|N| b(c_i, E) \leq E$. Together, $(*)$ and $(***)$ imply $b(c_i, E) \leq \min\{c_i, \frac{E}{|N|}\}$, as asserted. □

Lower bounds on losses can be defined in a symmetric way to the way we defined lower bounds on awards:

Min-of-claim-and-equal-division-of-deficit lower bounds on losses: For each $(c, E) \in \mathcal{C}^N$, $c - S(c, E) \geq t(c, \frac{\sum c_i - E}{|N|})$.

For two claimants, these bounds are met only by the constrained equal losses rule, but that is not the case for more than two claimants. A result similar to Proposition 3.2 holds. We omit its statement.

10 This bound is proposed by Moulin (2002b), who simply refers to it as the "lower bound."

`* Relating axioms` ♦ We have already noted that if a rule satisfies the *min-of-claim-and-equal-division lower bounds on awards*, it satisfies the $\frac{1}{|N|}$-*truncated-claims lower bounds on awards*. ♦ Similarly, if a rule satisfies the *min-of-claim-and-equal-division-of-deficit lower bounds on losses*, it satisfies the $\frac{1}{|N|}$-*min-of-claim-and-deficit lower bounds on losses*.

Now consider the following family of bounds, parameterized by $\alpha \in [0, 1]$. Given $\alpha \in [0, 1]$, the **min-of-α-claim-and-equal-division lower bound on awards** says that $S(c, E) \geq t(\alpha c, \frac{E}{|N|})$. The **min-of-$\alpha$-claim-and-equal-division-of-deficit lower bound on losses** says that $c - S(c, E) \geq t(\alpha c, \frac{\sum c_j - E}{|N|})$. By setting $\alpha = \frac{1}{|N|}$ or $\alpha = 1$, we obtain the four bounds defined above.[11]

3.4.2 Recursive Assignment of Lower Bounds

Given a claims problem, a lower bound function specifies a minimal amount that claimants should receive. To guarantee that this be the case, let us assign these amounts. Let us then revise claims down by these assignments and the endowment down by their sum. Presumably, for the lower bound to be meaningful, the list of revised claims and the revised endowment together constitute a well-defined problem. If the lower bound function is to be taken seriously, it is quite natural to want to reapply it to the revised problem. Several possibilities emerge. One is that in this problem, the lower bounds are 0. Another is that the lower bounds of some claimants are not 0. This invites a further round of assignments, revisions, and reapplications of the lower bound function, and so on. The question then is whether recursively assigning the lower bounds exhausts the endowment, in finitely many steps or in the limit. If so, we are led to a rule.[12]

We illustrate these possibilities next. When we take the lower bounds to be the minimal rights, the process stops after only one step, before the endowment is exhausted, because the minimal rights in the revised problem are all 0 (Lemma 3.1). However, when we use the $\frac{1}{|N|}$-truncated-claims lower bounds on awards, assigning them recursively exhausts the endowment in the limit (Theorem 3.1). The rule that results is not one encountered in Chapter 2.

Can some general properties of lower bounds be identified that guarantee such a conclusion? The answer is yes. In fact, as we will see, not much is required of a lower bound function to guarantee that their recursive assignment does exhaust the endowment in the limit (Theorem 3.2).

• **Minimal rights.** First, let us verify that starting from any $(c, E) \in \mathcal{C}^N$, the pair $(c - m(c, E), E - \sum m_i(c, E))$ that results after minimal rights have been assigned and the endowment revised accordingly is a well-defined

[11] These definitions are proposed by Moreno-Ternero and Roemer (2006a) under the names "lower bound of degree α" and "upper bound of degree α."

[12] This proposal is made by Dominguez and Thomson (2006), to whom Theorem 3.1 is due.

problem. Indeed, we already know that $S(c, E) \geqq m(c, E)$ so that (i) $E - \sum m_i(c, E) \geq 0$. Since $c \geqq S(c, E)$, we have (ii) $c - m(c, E) \geqq 0$. One also easily calculates that (iii) the sum of the coordinates of $c - m(c, E)$ is at least as large as $E - \sum m_i(c, E)$. The desired conclusion follows from (i), (ii), and (iii).

An implication of the following lemma is that the minimal rights lower bounds cannot provide the basis for the definition of a rule in the manner suggested above.

Lemma 3.1 *For each $(c, E) \in \mathcal{C}^N$, in the (well-defined) problem obtained from (c, E) by revising claims down by the minimal rights and the endowment down by the sum of these quantities, minimal rights are 0.*

Proof: Let $(c, E) \in \mathcal{C}^N$, $i \in N$, and let us calculate the minimal right of claimant i in $(c - m(c, E), E - \sum m_j(c, E))$. It is given by

$$\max\{E - \sum_N m_j(c, E) - \sum_{N \setminus \{i\}} (c_j - m_j(c, E)), 0\}.$$

After canceling out terms, we obtain the expression

$$\max\{E - \sum_{N \setminus \{i\}} c_j - m_i(c, E), 0\},$$

which, using the definition of $m_i(c, E)$, is easily seen to be equal to 0. □

• **The $\frac{1}{|N|}$-truncated-claims lower bounds on awards.** Our next result will serve as point of departure for the definition of a new rule.

Theorem 3.1 *For each problem, recursively assigning the* ***$\frac{1}{|N|}$-truncated-claims lower bounds on awards*** *exhausts the endowment in the limit.*

defining a rule by recursive application of the $\frac{1}{|N|}$-truncated-claims lower bounds on awards

For each $(c, E) \in \mathcal{C}^N$ and each $i \in N$, let $\mu_i(c, E) \equiv \frac{1}{|N|} \min\{c_i, E\}$ and $\mu(c, E) \equiv (\mu_i(c, E))_{i \in N}$.

Proof: Let $(c, E) \in \mathcal{C}^N$. Let $(c^1, E^1) \equiv (c, E)$ and for each $k \geq 2$, let (c^k, E^k) be the problem obtained at the kth step of the process described in the theorem, namely

$$(c^k, E^k) \equiv \left(c^{k-1} - \mu(c^{k-1}, E^{k-1}), E^{k-1} - \sum_{i \in N} \mu_i(c^{k-1}, E^{k-1})\right).$$

Obviously no agent's claim ever increases from one step to the next, and the same is true for the endowment. Since the endowment is bounded below by 0, the sequence $\{E^k\}$ has a limit. Let it be denoted $\bar{E}$. We will show that $\bar{E} = 0$. Suppose, by way of contradiction, that $\bar{E} > 0$. Let $k \in \mathbb{N}$ be such that $E^k - \bar{E} \leq \frac{\bar{E}}{|N|^2}$. Since (c^k, E^k) is a well-defined problem, there is $i \in N$

such that $c_i^k \geq \frac{E^k}{|N|}$. At the $(k+1)$-th step, agent i receives $\frac{1}{|N|}\min\{c_i^k, E^k\}$, and since all agents receive nonnegative amounts, the endowment decreases by at least $\frac{1}{|N|}\min\{c_i^k, E^k\}$. Thus, $E^{k+1} < E^k - \frac{1}{|N|}\min\{c_i^k, E^k\} < \bar{E}$, which contradicts the definition of $\bar{E}$. □

It follows from the proof of Theorem 3.1 that for each problem, recursively assigning the $\frac{1}{|N|}$-truncated-claims lower bounds on awards defines a rule. For an explicit expression of the awards vector it selects, let $(c, E) \in \mathcal{C}^N$. Let $\mu^1(c, E) \equiv \mu(c, E)$, and for each $k \geq 2$,[13]

$$\mu^k(c, E) \equiv \mu\left(c - \sum_{\ell=1}^{k-1} \mu^\ell(c, E), E - \sum_{i \in N}\sum_{\ell=1}^{k-1} \mu_i^\ell(c, E)\right).$$

DT rule, DT: [14] For each $(c, E) \in \mathcal{C}^N$,

$$DT(c, E) \equiv \sum_{k=1}^{\infty} \mu^k(c, E).$$

Alternatively, for each $(c, E) \in \mathcal{C}^N$, let $\bar{c} \equiv \lim c^k$. Then let $DT(c, E) \equiv c - \bar{c}$.

If all claims are positive, there is $k \in \mathbb{N}$ at which there is nothing left to divide; conversely, finite convergence requires that all claims be positive.

Incidentally, the order of claims is never reversed by the attribution of the $\frac{1}{|N|}$-truncated-claims lower bounds on awards. Let $i, j \in N$ be such that $c_i < c_j$. If $E \leq c_i$, both claims decrease by $\frac{E}{|N|}$. If $c_i < E \leq c_j$, c_i is replaced by $\tilde{c}_i \equiv c_i - \frac{c_i}{|N|}$ and c_j by $\tilde{c}_j \equiv c_j - \frac{E}{|N|}$. Thus, $\tilde{c}_i \leq \tilde{c}_j$. Thus, in the proof of Theorem 3.1, agent i could be chosen to be the largest claimant (one of the largest claimants if there are several of them).

The construction of the DT rule is illustrated in the appendix (Section 17.3). Paths of awards are piecewise linear in (usually) infinitely many pieces.

• **A general convergence result.** Theorem 3.1 identifies a lower bound function whose recursive application exhausts the endowment in the limit and therefore leads to a well-defined rule, a rule that we had not encountered before. A natural question is whether other lower bound functions would also lead us to well-defined rules. A general positive answer is given by our next theorem, whose proof we omit. It uncovers a natural continuity property of

[13] Note that $\mu_i^k(c, E)$ depends on the other agents' claims, c_{-i}, since the endowment at step k depends on the entire claims vector.

[14] This rule is defined and studied by Dominguez and Thomson (2006) under the name of "recursive rule." We avoid this name here (and instead designate the rule by these authors' initials) because many other rules can be defined in a recursive way, as Theorem 3.2 shows. We will have yet other occasions to introduce recursive processes on the basis of which rules can be defined.

such functions that, together with a boundary property they should satisfy, guarantees this conclusion. These requirements are very mild:[15]

defining rules by recursive application of lower bounds

Theorem 3.2 *Consider a lower bound function that is continuous and, for each nonzero claims vector and positive endowment, specifies a positive lower bound for at least one claimant. Then, for each problem, its recursive application exhausts the endowment in the limit, thereby defining a rule.*

• **Deriving lower bounds from a family of rules.** So far, we have defined lower and upper bounds on awards for a problem by applying some function to it. Another way to generate bounds is as follows. Suppose that the decision has been made to use a rule in a certain family, but that no particular member of the family has been identified as being most desirable. The family may be given explicitly, or it may be defined through a list of properties its members have. Given a problem, for each claimant, let us calculate the smallest amount awarded to them by any of the rules in the family. The decision to only use these rules should certainly imply that the claimant is entitled to at least this amount: a lower bound has been derived.

The idea can be applied recursively here too. Let us award to each claimant their lower bound, revise their claim down accordingly, revise the endowment down by the sum of the amounts awarded in this way, and iterate. That is, let us calculate for each claimant the smallest amount awarded to them by any of the rules in the chosen family when applied to the problem obtained by revising claims and endowment as just proposed – it is well defined – and award them this amount. Let us once again revise the data of the problem accordingly and apply the rules in the family, and so on. If the residual endowment converges to zero, we have obtained an awards vector for the problem under consideration; if this is so for each problem, we have defined a rule.[16]

We will give an example of such a situation (Theorem 14.8), but we have to wait for a formal statement of this result until all the properties of rules it involves have been introduced.

3.5 CONDITIONAL FULL COMPENSATION, CONDITIONAL NULL COMPENSATION, AND RELATED PROPERTIES

If, in a given problem, an agent's claim is low enough, the agent is easily compensated, and it may make sense to take advantage of the opportunity and do so. The issue though is specifying a test that a claim should pass for its holder to be so treated. A plausible test is that if we substitute the claim for that of each larger claimant, we now have enough to compensate everyone.

[15] Theorem 3.2 is due to Dominguez (2013).

[16] This process, which is similar to that underlying a strategic game studied in Subsection 14.2.2, is formulated by Giménez-Gómez and Marco (2014).

Then one could argue that its holder was not "responsible" for the shortfall. The argument is particularly compelling for someone whose claim is at most as large as equal division, but since in fact there is no reason why someone whose claim is less than equal division should get equal division, we propose that the relevant test for a claimant to be fully compensated is the following: once those claimants holding claims that are no larger than the claimant's have been fully compensated, the claimant's claim is at most as large as an equal share among the other claimants of the residual endowment. Let us say that a claim passing this test is **sustainable**.[17] The formal requirement is the following:

Conditional full compensation: For each $(c, E) \in \mathcal{C}^N$ and each $i \in N$, if $\sum_{j \in N} \min\{c_j, c_i\} \leq E$, then $S_i(c, E) = c_i$.

Note that nothing is said about how much the agents whose claims are not sustainable should receive. Since a non-sustainable claim is clearly larger than a sustainable one, it seems natural to add to the requirement that the holder(s) of non-sustainable claims receive at least as much as the holder(s) of the largest sustainable one, or to impose the requirement in conjunction with the one, formulated below, that awards be ordered as claims are.

The constrained equal awards rule satisfies *conditional full compensation*, but among the rules of Chapter 2, it is the only one to do so. For instance, neither the proportional rule nor the constrained equal losses rule does. Indeed, for the proportional rule, no matter how close to the sum of the claims the endowment is, and no matter how small an agent's claim is (provided it is positive), the claimant is never fully compensated. (Full compensation only occurs when $\sum c_i = E$.) For the constrained equal losses rule, the smallest claimant receives nothing until the endowment reaches a certain value that may be larger than $|N|$ times this claimant's claim. The same logic shows that concede-and-divide also violates the property.

Nevertheless, it is easy to construct rules other than the constrained equal awards rule satisfying *conditional full compensation*, and in fact to characterize the family they constitute. This is because it is a punctual property. For two claimants, and letting $N \equiv \{1, 2\}$, *conditional full compensation* only places restrictions on the choice made by a rule for $(c, E) \in \mathcal{C}^N$ such that $E \geq 2\min\{c_1, c_2\}$. The smaller claimant should be fully compensated then, and whatever is left should go to the other. In Figure 3.4a, $c_1 < c_2$ and this first occurs at the point $x^1 \equiv (c_1, c_1)$. However if $E < 2\min\{c_1, c_2\}$, we have complete freedom in selecting the awards vector. This freedom is illustrated in Figure 3.4a.

For three claimants – now, let $N \equiv \{1, 2, 3\}$ and let us suppose that $c_1 \leq c_2 \leq c_3$ – the awards vector should have reached the plane of equation $x_1 = c_1$ when E reaches $3c_1$ (this occurs at the point x^1 in Figure 3.4b; this point is

[17] It may make the most sense in the context of taxation, as it protects taxpayers whose resources are too limited. The property is introduced by Herrero and Villar (2002) under the name of "sustainability."

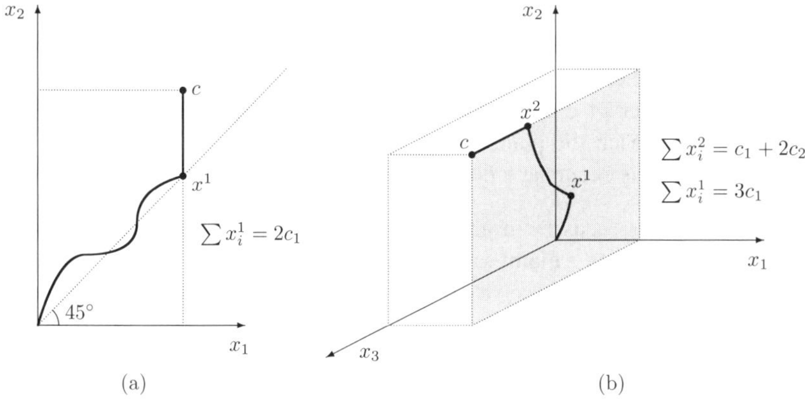

Figure 3.4: **Conditional full compensation.** (a) For two claimants, *conditional full compensation* says that if the endowment is at least as large as twice the smaller claim, the smaller claimant should be fully compensated. Here, $N \equiv \{1, 2\}$. For $c \in \mathbb{R}_+^N$ such that $c_1 < c_2$, $x^1 \equiv (c_1, c_1)$ should be chosen when $E = 2c_1$. From x^1 on, the path of awards should follow the line of equation $x_1 = c_1$. (b) Here, $N \equiv \{1, 2, 3\}$ and $c \in \mathbb{R}_+^N$ is such that $c_1 < c_2 < c_3$. If $E \geq 3c_1$, agent 1 should be fully compensated. Let x^1, a point whose first coordinate is c_1, designate the point reached when $E = 3c_1$. The path from x^1 on should belong to the plane of equation $x_1 = c_1$ (the shaded region for *nonnegativity* and *claims boundedness* to be satisfied). If $E \geq c_1 + 2c_2$, agent 2 should also be fully compensated. Thus $x^2 \equiv (c_1, c_2, c_2)$ is the point reached when $E = c_1 + 2c_2$. From x^2 on, the path should follow the line defined by the equations $x_1 = c_1$ and $x_2 = c_2$.

(c_1, c_1, c_1) if the rule respects the order of claims), and it should stay in that plane from then on; moreover, it should have reached the plane of equation $x_2 = c_2$ when E reaches $c_1 + 2c_2$ (this occurs at the point $x^2 \equiv (c_1, c_2, c_2)$), and it should stay in that plane until E reaches $\sum c_i$ and everyone is fully compensated. This means that to satisfy the two constraints that are binding for $E \geq c_1 + 2c_2$, the awards vector should follow the line defined by the equations $x_1 = c_1$ and $x_2 = c_2$. For the general case with $N \equiv \{1, \ldots, n\}$ and assuming $c_1 \leq \cdots \leq c_n\}$, for each $k \in N$, claimant k should be fully compensated if $E \geq c_1 + \cdots + c_{k-1} + (n - k + 1)c_k$.

The first step in the logic underlying *conditional full compensation* was the idea that any agent whose claim is at most as large as equal division should be fully compensated. Let us write this as a separate requirement, **equal-division–conditional full compensation**.[18] If a claim is at most as large as equal division it is clearly sustainable, so *conditional full compensation* is stronger than *equal-division–conditional full compensation*. For two claimants,

[18] This property is introduced by Herrero and Villar (2002) under the name of "exemption."

the two properties are of course equivalent. In Figure 3.4b, the path of a rule satisfying the property should reach the plane of equation $x_1 = c_1$ when the endowment reaches $3c_1$ (again, this occurs at the point (c_1, c_1, c_1) if the rule respects the order of claims) and it should stay in the plane from then on; also, it should reach the plane of equation $x_2 = c_2$ when E reaches $3c_2$ (if $\sum c_i > 3c_2$). This occurs at a point between x^2 and c on the figure.

Switching our focus from gains to losses, let us now require that if in a problem some agent i's claim satisfies the hypotheses of *conditional full compensation*, then agent i receive nothing in the related problem in which the endowment is equal to the sum of the claims minus its value in the initial problem. We refer to it as **conditional null compensation**. The hypothesis can equivalently be written as follows: when replacing each agent j's claim by 0 if it is smaller than c_i and by the difference $c_j - c_i$ otherwise, there still is not enough.[19]

Let us call **equal-division-of-deficit–conditional null compensation** the requirement that if agent i's claim is no larger than an equal division of the deficit, agent i's award be 0.

Weaker versions of these properties, which are useful in exploring trade-offs between general ideas of bounds with other properties, are **weak conditional full compensation**, which says that if an agent's claim is no larger than $\frac{2E-\sum c_i}{|N|}$, they should be fully compensated, and **weak conditional null compensation**, which says that if an agent's claim is no larger than $\frac{\sum c_i - 2E}{|N|}$, the agent's award should be 0.[20] For two claimants, letting $N \equiv \{1, 2\}$ say and, without loss of generality, considering $c \in \mathbb{R}^N_+$ such that $c_1 \leq c_2$, *weak conditional full compensation* says that the path of awards for c should contain seg$[(c_1, \frac{c_1+c_2}{2}), c]$; *weak conditional null compensation* that it should contain seg$[(0, 0), (0, \frac{c_2-c_1}{2})]$. For more than two claimants, *weak conditional full compensation* is weaker than *equal-division–conditional full compensation*; *weak conditional null compensation* is weaker than *equal-division-of-deficit–conditional null compensation*.

Parameterized versions of these properties can also be defined: Given $\alpha \in [0, 1]$, **α-conditional full compensation** says that for each $i \in N$, if $\alpha c_i \leq \frac{\alpha E-(1-\alpha)(\sum c_i - E)}{|N|}$, agent i should be fully compensated. Also, **α-conditional null compensation** says that for each $i \in N$, if $\alpha c_i \leq \frac{\alpha(\sum c_i - E)-(1-\alpha)E}{|N|}$, agent i's award should be 0. For $\alpha = 1$, these two properties become *equal-division–conditional full compensation* and *equal-division-of-deficit–conditional null compensation* respectively; for $\alpha = \frac{1}{2}$, we obtain

19 This property is introduced by Herrero and Villar (2002) under the name of "independence of residual claims."

20 These properties are introduced by Herrero and Villar (2002) under the names of "exemption" and "exclusion," respectively.

weak conditional full compensation and *weak conditional null compensation* respectively.[21]

Equal-division–conditional full compensation and *equal-division-of-deficit–conditional null compensation* are in general incompatible.[22] For two claimants, they are compatible only for problems in which the larger claim is at most as large as three times the smaller claim.

3.6 SYMMETRY PROPERTIES

The properties discussed in this section express a central idea in the theory of fair allocation, namely that agents with the same characteristics should be treated in the same way. When agents differ in dimensions that are not captured by a formal model, unequal treatment may be called for, however, and we explain next how rules can be generalized and the resulting rules parameterized so as to allow fine differentiations among claimants. It is then up to a user of the theory to specify the parameter so that the departure from equal treatment best reflects his or her perceived need to recognize differences in the claimants' merits that are not already reflected in their claims.

• First, we require that two agents with equal claims receive equal amounts:

Equal treatment of equals: For each $(c, E) \in \mathcal{C}^N$ and each pair $\{i, j\} \subseteq N$, if $c_i = c_j$, then $S_i(c, E) = S_j(c, E)$.

• A strengthening of this axiom is invariance under permutations of agents: their names should not matter. Denoting by Π^N the class of bijections from N into itself, the requirement is as follows:

Anonymity: For each $(c, E) \in \mathcal{C}^N$, each $\pi \in \Pi^N$, and each $i \in N$, $S_{\pi(i)}(c', E) = S_i(c, E)$, where $c' \equiv (c_{\pi(j)})_{j \in N}$.

• The next requirement is that there be no endowment at which two claimants are treated in a maximally asymmetric way: if both have positive claims, neither one should be fully compensated if the other receives nothing. It represents a tiny step towards *equal treatment of equals* but, together with other properties, we will sometimes see that this stronger property is in fact implied:[23]

Minimal sharing: For each $(c, E) \in \mathcal{C}^N$, and each pair $\{i, j\} \subseteq N$ such that $c_i, c_j > 0$, $S_i(c, E) = 0$ and $S_j(c, E) = c_j$ do not simultaneously hold.

• In most applications, *equal treatment of equals* and even *anonymity* are natural and basic fairness requirements. If the only information available is

[21] These properties are proposed by van den Brink, Funaki, and van der Laan (2013).

[22] Herrero and Villar (2001).

[23] This property is introduced by García-Jurado, González-Díaz, and Villar (2006) under the name of "acceptability."

that contained in the description of a problem, it is indeed difficult to justify treating agents with equal claims differently, or not exchanging their awards if their claims are exchanged. However, we may well have external reasons to differentiate among agents that are independent of the relative values of their claims. In actual bankruptcy proceedings for instance, claims are often given different priorities that reflect characteristics of their holders other than their claims. If two agents belong to different priority classes, nothing is assigned to the one who belongs to the lower class until the other is fully compensated. This is an extreme way of allowing a differential treatment of agents. Formally, this is accomplished by enriching the model with a partition of the claimant set into "priority classes." For example, and pursuing the application to bankruptcy, there may be three classes: tax authority, secured claimants, and unsecured claimants. We treat claimants in the same priority class differently only to the extent that their claims differ, but we may assign to claimants in different priority classes different awards even though their claims are equal.

We will represent such a partition of the claimant set by means of a complete and transitive binary relation on N, $\preccurlyeq$, with asymmetric part $\prec$ and symmetric part $\sim$. **Priority classes** are the equivalence classes of the relation. Given $\{i, j\} \subseteq N$, $i \prec j$ means that claimant i belongs to a higher priority class than claimant j – i.e. should come first in the distribution – and $i \sim j$ that claimants i and j belong to the same priority class.[24] Summarizing, a **claims problem with priority classes** is a list $(c, \preccurlyeq, E)$ where $(c, E) \in \mathcal{C}^N$ and $\preccurlyeq$ is a complete and transitive binary relation on N. Let $\boldsymbol{\mathcal{P}}^N$ be the domain of these problems.

For a rule defined on this domain, let us give a name to the requirement that if two claimants belong to distinct classes, nothing be assigned to the claimant belonging to the lower class unless the other claimant is fully compensated:

Respect of priority assignments: (for problems with priority classes) For each $(c, \preccurlyeq, E) \in \mathcal{P}^N$ and each pair $\{i, j\} \subseteq N$, if $i \prec j$ and $S_i(c, \preccurlyeq, E) < c_i$, then $S_j(c, \preccurlyeq, E) = 0$.

To adapt a standard rule to the domain of claims problems with priority classes so that it *respects priority assignments*, simply apply its definition to priority classes in succession. Formally, given the ordered partition $\{N^1, \ldots, N^K\}$ of the claimant set induced by $\preccurlyeq$, let $E^1 \equiv \min\{E, \sum_{i \in N^1} c_i\}$, $E^2 \equiv \min\{E - E^1, \sum_{i \in N^2} c_i\}$, $E^3 \equiv \min\{E - E^1 - E^2, \sum_{i \in N^3} c_i\}$, and so on. Letting the endowment grow from 0 to the sum of the claims, these are the amounts to be distributed to each of the successive classes in the ordered partition. To illustrate, we obtain a version of the proportional rule for such problems by making awards proportional to claims within each priority class

[24] The notation may be a little confusing here as "coming earlier in the order" means being given preferential treatment. In common language, we also use interchangeably phrases such as "first priority" and "high priority."

but, before attempting to satisfy the claims of the members of any class, fully satisfying the claims of the members of all classes with higher priorities.

We can also treat each priority class in its own particular way, that is, use different formulas for different classes. For example, we can apply the proportional formula for the class with the highest priority, the constrained equal awards formula for the class with the second highest priority, then switch to the random arrival formula for the class with the third highest priority, and so on. Such composite rules may appear strange at first sight but, by sorting claimants into classes of agents that we feel should be placed on the same level, it becomes possible to better tailor to each class the division method that we use for it. To show the usefulness of such generalizations in the context of bankruptcy, one class could consist of corporations, and another of individual investors. In the context of taxation, one class could consist of businesses and another of households. It is easy to conceive of reasons why such groups should not be all handled in the same way.

Note that priority classes are given beforehand and specified so as to reflect characteristics of claimants not explicitly incorporated in the model. In principle, the partition of claimants into priority classes could be performed endogenously, as a function of their claims: for instance, we could put in the same class the three agents with the largest claims, in a second class the two agents with the next largest claims, and in a third class the remaining agents; and here too, treat each class in its own way. But possible ties among claims will prevent rules from satisfying certain desirable properties, an obvious example being continuity with respect to claims (see Section 3.2).

On the other hand, the partitioning of the claimant set into priority classes may be implied by an axiom system. We will encounter situations of that kind, especially in our analysis of the variable-population version of our model, when agents involved in a problem are drawn from an infinite population of potential claimants (Sections 11.3–11.4). In that context, the partitioning of the claimant set could actually depend on who is actually present, but we will see that certain variable-population consistency requirements imply that it is induced in a natural way from a reference partition of the entire set of potential claimants.

Returning to the previous proposal pertaining to situations in which priority classes are exogenously given, a particular case is when each class contains only one claimant. Then to specify a rule, it suffices to indicate a strict order on the claimant set, $\prec$, and the resulting rule is the sequential priority rule relative to $\prec$ (Subsection 2.2.1).

In social choice and game theory, the adjective "dictatorial" is often applied to a rule that chooses, for each possible configuration of the data of the problem to be solved, an alternative that an agent specified beforehand and once and for all, the "dictator," prefers, some tie-breaking protocol being invoked when the dictator has more than one most preferred alternative. A "lexicographic dictatorial" rule is defined by specifying a strict order in which agents are accommodated; alternatively, they can be thought of as tie-breakers when earlier agents have expressed indifference: if the agent who is first in the order has a unique most preferred alternative, that is what is chosen; otherwise, the agent who is second is given the chance to break the tie: if, among the alternatives that are most preferred by the first agent, the second agent has a unique most preferred alternative, once again, that is what is chosen; otherwise, the agent who is third is brought in to break that second-round tie, and so on. The sequential priority rules considered here can be understood in this way but they are less distasteful than in most other situations because of the bound on how much each agent can receive, their claim. This is why we used the milder expression "sequential priority rule" to designate them. If an agent's claim is small in relation to the endowment, there may in fact be a lot left for the others even if the agent has high priority.

In our discussion so far, we have assumed that the priority relation is transitive. However, non-transitive priorities occur in real life and, in fact, they had been the object of some discussion in legal journals well before the emergence of the theory under review here. A very recent literature has returned to this issue, which we briefly introduce in Section 15.7.

• An alternative way to accommodate the need to not put all claimants on the same level is by enriching the definition of a claims problem by assigning weights to claimants: a **claims problem with weights** is a list (c, w, E), where $(c, E) \in \mathcal{C}^N$ and $w \in \text{int}\{\Delta^N\}$ is a point in the interior of the $(|N|-1)$-dimensional simplex indicating the *relative* importance (as opposed to the *absolute* priorities just described) that should be given to claimants. Let $\mathcal{W}^N$ be the domain of these problems.[25] We will maintain throughout the notational convention that a relatively larger weight assigned to a claimant is to be interpreted as a desired more favorable treatment for that claimant.

This definition suggests the requirement on a rule defined on this enlarged class of problems that in a claims problem with weights in which two agents have equal claims, the ratios awards/weights be equal for them unless the agent with the larger weight is fully compensated:

Respect of weight assignments: (for problems with weights) For each $(c, w, E) \in \mathcal{W}^N$ and each pair $\{i, j\} \subseteq N$ such that $w_i > w_j > 0$ and $c_i = c_j$, either $S_i(c, w, E) = c_i$ or $\frac{S_i(c,w,E)}{w_i} = \frac{S_j(c,w,E)}{w_j}$.

In adapting rules to this setting, difficulties sometimes occur. Most are easily handled, but others are more fundamental. We will discuss them in connection with an examination of the rules introduced in Chapter 2. We consider these rules in related groups, and show how to define weighted generalizations

[25] Casas-Méndez, Fragnelli, and García-Jurado (2011) study this class of problems when the weights are natural numbers. They provide characterizations of several of the rules defined below. The weights are parameters of some of their axioms.

for them. It is most natural, as we have done, to assume all weights to be positive. If not, we find ourselves in a situation similar to that discussed earlier in which the set of claimants is partitioned into priority classes, but within each priority class, a vector of positive weights is used to divide among the members of the class whatever is left when all classes with higher priorities have been fully compensated if possible.[26]

• The most general definition is that of a **claims problem with priority classes and weights**, namely a list $(c, \preccurlyeq, w, E)$, where $(c, \preccurlyeq, E)$ is a claims problem with priority classes, and $w \in \text{int}\{\Delta^N\}$ is a vector of weights. Within each priority class as specified by $\preccurlyeq$, we use the components of w pertaining to the members of the class to provide more favorable treatment to certain claimants at the expense of the others.

— **Proportional rule.** To obtain a weighted version of the proportional rule, a first thought of course is to make awards proportional to claims multiplied by weights $w \in \text{int}\{\Delta^N\}$ assigned to claimants. However, because of *claims boundedness*, awards cannot be proportional to the vector of weighted claims $(w_1c_1, \ldots, w_nc_n)$ no matter how much is available, so adjustments are necessary. Most natural here is a "minimum operation" of the kind performed in the definition of the constrained equal awards rule (Figure 3.5a):

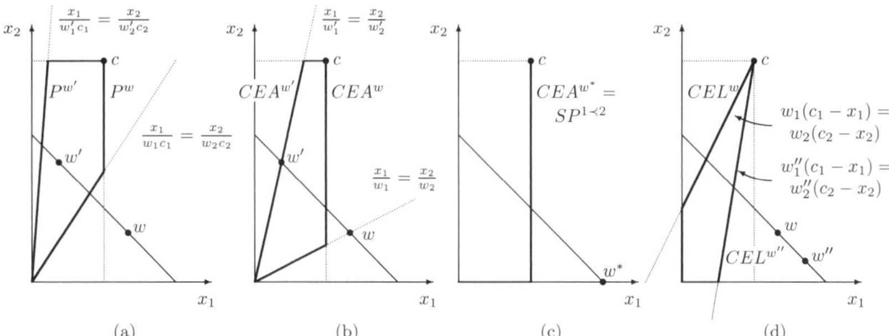

Figure 3.5: **Weighted versions of the proportional, constrained equal awards, and constrained equal losses rules.** Figures are drawn for $N \equiv \{1, 2\}$ and weights $w \equiv (\frac{2}{3}, \frac{1}{3}) \in \Delta^N$. (a) Weighted proportional rule with weights w. (b) Weighted constrained equal awards rule with weights w. For a sufficiently large transfer of weight from claimant 1 to claimant 2, the second part of the path of awards would be a horizontal segment instead of a vertical segment. (c) Extreme case of the weighted constrained equal awards rule, when $w^* = (1, 0)$, gives the sequential priority rule $SP^{1 \prec 2}$. (d) Weighted constrained equal losses rule with weights w. For a sufficiently large transfer of weight from agent 2 to agent 1, the path would begin with a horizontal segment instead of with a vertical segment.

26 Alternatively, a lexicographic system of weights can be used.

Weighted proportional rule with weights $w \in \text{int}\{\Delta^N\}$, P^w: For each $(c, E) \in \mathcal{C}^N$,

$$P^w(c, E) \equiv (\min\{\lambda w_i c_i, c_i\})_{i \in N},$$

where $\lambda \in \mathbb{R}_+$ is chosen so as to achieve *balance*.

— **Constrained equal awards, constrained equal losses, and constrained egalitarian rules.** Defining weighted generalizations of the constrained equal awards rule is straightforward. We simply distribute the endowment proportionally to a fixed vector of positive weights, once again, taking care not to award to an agent more than their claim. If the endowment is large enough, for some $k \in \{1, \ldots, n\}$, the agents with the k smallest claim/weight ratios are fully compensated and the others' awards are set proportional to their weights (Figure 3.5b).[27]

Weighted constrained equal awards rule with weights $w \in \text{int}\{\Delta^N\}$, CEA^w: For each $(c, E) \in \mathcal{C}^N$,

$$CEA^w(c, E) \equiv (\min\{c_i, w_i \lambda\})_{i \in N},$$

where $\lambda \in \mathbb{R}_+$ is chosen so as to achieve *balance*.

If $|N| = 2$, it is also convenient to define the weighted constrained equal awards rule with weights $(1, 0)$ as the rule whose path of awards for each claims vector is the limit of the paths of sequences of weighted constrained equal awards rules relative to weights converging to $(1, 0)$: it is simply the sequential priority rule $SP^{1 \prec 2}$. A similar definition can be given for the weights $(0, 1)$.

The following rule is a similarly defined extension of the constrained equal losses rule (Figure 3.5c).

Weighted constrained equal losses rule with weights $w \in \text{int}\{\Delta^N\}$, CEL^w: For each $(c, E) \in \mathcal{C}^N$,

$$CEL^w(c, E) \equiv (\max\{c_i - \frac{\lambda}{w_i}, 0\})_{i \in N},$$

where $\lambda \in \mathbb{R}_+$ is chosen so as to achieve *balance*.

Here too, it is convenient to extend the definition to the weights $(1, 0)$ and $(0, 1)$ by setting $CEL^{(1,0)} = SP^{1 \prec 2}$ and $CEL^{(0,1)} = SP^{2 \prec 1}$.

We omit the formula for the weighted version of the constrained egalitarian rule; it is obtained by simply adapting the formula offered above for the weighted constrained equal awards rules.

[27] N.-C. Lee (1994) studies these rules. They are essentially the "proportional solutions" of bargaining theory introduced by Kalai (1977), and called "weighted egalitarian" by Thomson (1996).

— **Concede-and-divide.** For concede-and-divide, what seems most natural in breaking the symmetry with which the two claimants are treated in the original definition is the following. We still start by attributing to each of them the amount conceded by the other, but we divide the remainder, what earlier we referred to as "the contested part," according to weights assigned to them (here, one of the weights could be 0):

Weighted concede-and-divide with weights $w \in \Delta^N$, CD^w: For $|N| = 2$. For each $(c, E) \in \mathcal{C}^N$,

$$CD^w(c, E) \equiv (\max\{E - c_j, 0\} + w_i[E - \sum_N \max\{E - c_k, 0\}])_{i \in N}.$$

The paths of awards for a typical claims vector and several choices of w are plotted in Figure 3.6.

— **Random arrival rule.** To obtain a version of the random arrival rule that does not necessarily assign equal awards to agents with equal claims, we choose $w \in \Delta^N$ and draw claimants with probabilities equal to the coordinates of w; once a first claimant has been drawn, we repeat the process by assigning probabilities to the remaining claimants that are proportional to their coordinates of w, and so on, until all claimants have been drawn. The calculations for two claimants are as follows. Let $N \equiv \{1, 2\}$ and $w \in \Delta^N$. (Here, w_1 or w_2 could be equal to 0.) We obtain the following awards vector for the **weighted random arrival rule with weights $w \in \Delta^N$:**

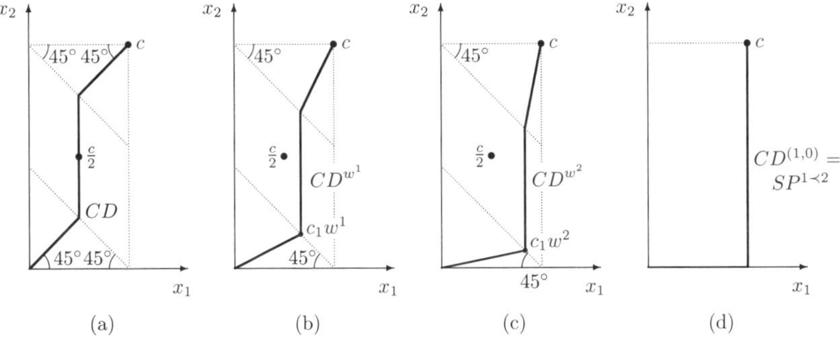

Figure 3.6: **Weighted versions of concede-and-divide**. Typical path of awards for $N \equiv \{1, 2\}$ and $c \in \mathbb{R}^N_+$ such that $c_1 < c_2$. Starting from concede-and-divide itself, we progressively increase the weight placed on agent 1's claim relative to the weight placed on agent 2's claim. The kinks in the paths of awards still occur when the endowment is either c_1 or c_2. (a) Concede-and-divide itself. (b) Weighted concede-and-divide rule with weights $w^1 \equiv (\frac{2}{3}, \frac{1}{3})$. (c) Here, the weight vector is $w^2 \equiv (\frac{5}{6}, \frac{1}{6})$. (d) At the limit, when $w \equiv (1, 0)$, we obtain the sequential priority rule relative to the order $1 \prec 2$.

$$\begin{array}{lll} (w_1E, w_2E) & \text{if} & E \leq c_1, \\ (w_1c_1, E - w_1c_1) & \text{if} & c_1 < E \leq c_2, \\ (w_2(E - c_2) + w_1c_1, w_1(E - c_1) + w_2c_2) & \text{if} & c_2 < E. \end{array}$$

Interestingly, the rule so defined coincides with weighted concede-and-divide with weights $w \in \Delta^N$, CD^w.

An alternative is to choose a vector of probability weights with which orders of arrival occur. By placing relatively larger weights on orders in which a particular claimant arrives early, we obtain rules that favor that claimant.

— **Minimal overlap and random stakes rules.** Our proposal for a weighted version of the minimal overlap rule is as follows: we arrange claims as in the original definition, but instead of dividing equally each unit among all agents claiming it, we divide it proportionally to the weights assigned to these claimants. We thereby obtain the **weighted minimal overlap rule with weights $\boldsymbol{w} \in \boldsymbol{\Delta}^N$**. We omit the formula.

Remarkably, when $|N| = 2$, for each $w \in \Delta^N$, this rule too coincides with the weighted concede-and-divide rule with weights $w \in \Delta^N$, CD^w.

For the random stakes rule, we can use weights in a similar way: for each unit available, we perform the division among all agents who have staked their claims on it proportionally to the weights assigned to these agents.

— **Talmud and Piniles' rules.** For a weighted version of the Talmud rule, several options are available because we have discovered that the rule can be seen from different perspectives, and each of them suggests a generalization.

The first option is to take as starting point the two-claimant weighted generalizations, defined in the previous paragraphs, of concede-and-divide, the random arrival, and minimal overlap rules, since after all, in the symmetric case, the Talmud rule coincides with each of them, and to look for extensions of these generalizations to the case of more than two claimants. We will submit in Section 10.4 that the most compelling way to extend concede-and-divide itself from two claimants to an arbitrary number of claimants is by imposing a "consistency" requirement, and it makes sense to also appeal to consistency in extending the weighted generalizations of concede-and-divide. We will uncover at that point certain constraints that have to be respected in pursuing this approach.

To describe the second option to define weighted versions of the Talmud rule, let us remember the initial definition we gave of the rule as a hybrid of the constrained equal awards and constrained equal losses rules. Here, after selecting a weight vector $w \in \Delta^N$, we would start from the weighted generalizations of the two rules with weights w, and create a hybrid rule from them in a similar manner. Geometrically, this means concatenating the path of awards of the weighted constrained equal awards rule with weights w for the half-claims vector to that of the weighted constrained equal losses rule with weights w, also for the half-claims vector. The paths of the resulting weighted hybrid rules are shown in Figure 3.7 for $N \equiv \{1, 2\}$ and several choices of the weight vector. Note that when claimant 1 has priority over claimant 2 (then the weight vector is the unit vector $(1, 0)$), the path for each claims vector $c \in \mathbb{R}_+^{\{1,2\}}$ consists of the concatenation with itself of the path for $\frac{c}{2}$ of the priority rule associated with the order $1 \prec 2$ (Figure 3.7d). It is not the path we obtain as limit of weighted concede-and-divide rules when the relative weight of claimant 1 goes to 1. That path is that of the priority rule associated with the order $1 \prec 2$.

For Piniles' rule the only meaningful way to proceed seems to be along the lines of this second option, namely to select a weight vector $w \in \Delta^N$ and for each $c \in \mathbb{R}_+^N$ to concatenate with itself the path of awards for $\frac{c}{2}$ of the weighted constrained equal awards rule with weights w. The limit rules, for $|N| = 2$ and when $w = (1, 0)$ for example, delivers the same path as the path we obtained when our starting point was the Talmud rule, namely the concatenation with itself of the path for $\frac{c}{2}$ of the priority rule associated with the order $1 \prec 2$.

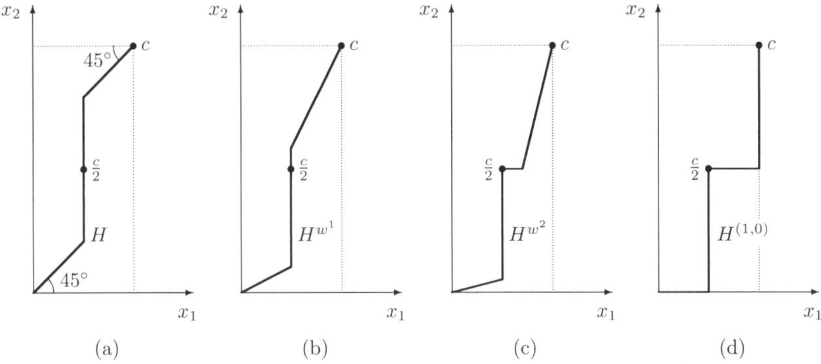

Figure 3.7: **Weighted versions of the Talmud rule seen as a hybrid of the constrained equal awards and constrained equal losses rules**. Typical path of awards for $N \equiv \{1, 2\}$ and $c \in \mathbb{R}_+^N$ such that $c_1 < c_2$. (a) The Talmud rule itself. Its path of awards for c is obtained by concatenating the paths of the constrained equal awards and constrained equal losses rules for $\frac{c}{2}$. In each of the three other panels, we concatenate instead the paths of weighted versions of these two rules for $\frac{c}{2}$, assigning progressively larger and larger weight to claimant 1 relative to claimant 2. The slope of the segment emanating from the claims vector is the inverse of that of the segment emanating from the origin. (b) Here, $w^1 \equiv (\frac{2}{3}, \frac{1}{3})$. (c) Here, $w^2 \equiv (\frac{4}{5}, \frac{1}{5})$. (d) At the limit, for the weights $(1, 0)$, we obtain a rule whose path for c is the concatenation with itself of the path for $\frac{c}{2}$ of the sequential priority rule in which claimant 1 is first.

We should also note that the weights can in principle depend upon which of the two "regimes" that are considered in the original definition: for endowments that are at most as large as the half-sum of the claims, we can use one set of weights, and for endowments at least as large as the half-sum of the claims, we can bring in another set of weights.

Similarly, the only straightforward way of defining weighted versions of the reverse Talmud rule yields rules whose limit has paths of awards for each claims vector that are the concatenation with itself of the path for the half-claims vector of a priority rule.

— **Young's family.** We obtain natural generalizations of Young's rules that do not satisfy *equal treatment of equals* by selecting, for each $i \in N$, a function $f_i \in \Phi$ satisfying the properties listed in the definition of a Young rule in Subsection 2.2.2 but whose second argument ranges over the same interval in $\mathbb{R}$ for all claimants. Then for each $(c, E) \in \mathcal{C}^N$, we find λ in that interval such that $\sum f_i(c_i, \lambda) = E$, and assign to each $i \in N$ the amount $f_i(c_i, \lambda)$. Let us call such a rule a **generalized Young rule** and to the list $(f_i)_{i \in \mathbb{N}}$ a **generalized Young representation** of it.

A special case is when, given $w \in \text{int}\{\Delta^N\}$, we subject, for each $i \in \mathbb{N}$, the function $f\colon \mathbb{R}_+ \times \Lambda \mapsto \mathbb{R}_+$, where without loss of generality, the left end-point of Λ is set equal to 0, to the following simple transformation: for each $(c_0, \lambda) \in \mathbb{R}_+ \times \Lambda$, let $f_i(c_0, \lambda) \equiv f(c_0, \frac{\lambda}{w_i})$. Then, given $(c, E) \in \mathcal{C}^N$, let $\lambda \in \mathbb{R}_+$ be such that $\sum f_i(c_i, \lambda) = E$ and choose $x \equiv (f_i(c_i, \lambda))_{i \in N}$. We then have a family of nonsymmetric generalizations of S that are indexed by points in the interior of the simplex.

— **ICI family.** To adapt an ICI rule S to accommodate an asymmetric treatment of claimants, we select a weight vector $w \in \text{int}\{\Delta^N\}$. Given $c \in \mathbb{R}^N_+$, we divide the interval $[0, \sum c_i]$ in the same intervals as in the definition of S. Until the middle interval, we divide each unit of the endowment proportionally to the weights assigned to the agents who are supposed to be sharing it. Thereafter we divide each unit proportionally to the inverse of the weights assigned to the agents who are supposed to be sharing it. We needed the ICI relations (Subsection 2.2.3) that we imposed on the parameters defining S to guarantee that when the endowment reaches the sum of the claims, everyone is fully compensated. We have to adapt them to accommodate weights, the result being ***w*-weighted ICI relations**.

Setting some weights equal to 0 amounts to assigning the corresponding claimants to lower priority classes. To formally accommodate such a possibility, we define an ordered partition of the set of claimants into priority classes, and for each class, specify a vector of positive weights for the members of the class; then for each claims vector, we distribute the endowment by moving from class to class, starting with the class with the highest priority. We can proceed in this way more generally, and for instance, make the weights depend on the interval in which the endowment falls.

We close this section with a generalization of the idea underlying *equal treatment of equals* to groups of claimants: two groups whose aggregate claims are equal should receive equal aggregate amounts:[28]

Equal treatment of equal groups: For each $(c, E) \in \mathcal{C}^N$ and each pair $\{N', N''\}$ of subsets of N, if $\sum_{N'} c_i = \sum_{N''} c_i$, then $\sum_{N'} S_i(c, E) = \sum_{N''} S_i(c, E)$.

This is a very significant strengthening of *equal treatment of equals*. Of our main rules, only the proportional rule satisfies it.

3.7 ORDER PRESERVATION PROPERTIES

In addition to *anonymity*, another strengthening of *equal treatment of equals* is the requirement on a rule that the choice it makes for each problem "reflect" or "respect" the order of the claims: if agent i's claim is at most as large as agent j's claim, agent i should receive at most as much as agent j does. We also require that the losses the two claimants incur be ordered in the same way: agent i's loss should be at most as large as agent j's loss.[29]

Order preservation: For each $(c, E) \in \mathcal{C}^N$ and each pair $\{i, j\} \subseteq N$, if $c_i \leq c_j$, then $S_i(c, E) \leq S_j(c, E)$. Also, $c_i - S_i(c, E) \leq c_j - S_j(c, E)$.

We refer to the first part of this property as **order preservation in awards** and to the second part as **order preservation in losses**.

Figure 3.8a,b shows, for two claimants, the two ways in which this two-part property can be violated. Figure 3.8c illustrates, also for two claimants and for a particular claims vector, what it takes for a rule to satisfy the property. Figure 3.9 concerns a three-claimant example: $N \equiv \{1, 2, 3\}$ and $(c, E) \in \mathcal{C}^N$ is equal to $((1, 2, 4), 5)$. Figure 3.9a represents the set of awards vectors of this problem. The set of balanced vectors satisfying the order preservation inequalities is the triangle with vertices a, b, and d in Figure 3.9b.

All of the rules of Chapter 2 *preserve order* except, obviously, the sequential priorities rules and some of Young's rules. For a Young rule – let $f \in \Phi$ be a representation of it – to satisfy *order preservation in awards*, as we noted in Subsection 2.2.2 when we informally introduced the property, for each pair $\{c_0, c_0'\} \subset \mathbb{R}_+$ such that $c_0 < c_0'$, the graph of $f(c_0, \cdot)$ should lie everywhere on or below the graph of $f(c_0', \cdot)$. Now, for each $c_0 \in \mathbb{R}_+$, let $g(c_0, \lambda) \equiv c_0 - f(c_0, \lambda)$. Then for *order preservation in losses* to hold, for each pair $\{c_0, c_0'\} \subset \mathbb{R}_+$ such that $c_0 < c_0'$, the graph of $g(c_0, \cdot)$ should lie everywhere on or below the graph of $g(c_0', \cdot)$.

[28] We obtain a weaker version of this property by applying it only to groups having equal numbers of claimants.

[29] This property appears in Aumann and Maschler (1985).

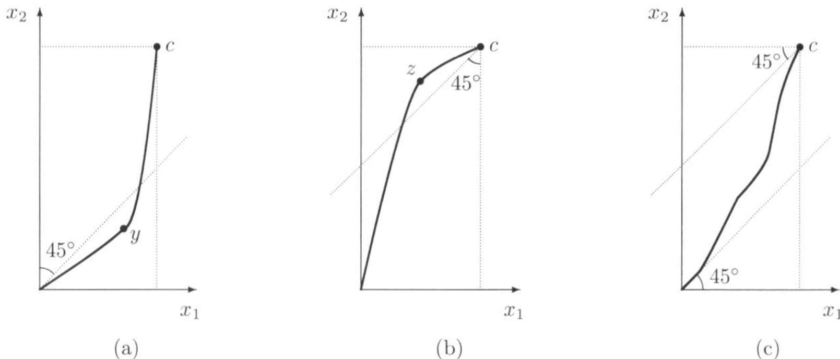

Figure 3.8: **Two rules violating order preservation and one rule satisfying the property for a particular claims vector.** Let $N \equiv \{1, 2\}$ and $c \in \mathbb{R}^N_+$ be such that $c_1 < c_2$. (a) For the path of awards represented here, at y, claimant 2's award is smaller than claimant 1's. Thus *order preservation in awards* is violated. (b) Here, at z, claimant 2's loss is smaller than claimant 1's, in violation of *order preservation in losses*. (c) For a rule to *preserve order*, its path for each c should lie between the line of slope 1 passing through the origin and the line of slope 1 passing through c, as shown here.

Starting from a sequential priority rule, we obtain a less radical way of favoring some claimants over the others by performing the sequential maximization of the definition subject to the *order preservation* requirements. Let us refer to the resulting rule as an **order-preservation–constrained sequential priority rule**. Suppose that $N \equiv \{1, 2\}$, and that $1 \prec 2$. Then for a claims vector below the 45° line, the path of awards is that of the constrained equal losses rule and for a claims vector above the 45° line, it is that of the constrained equal awards rule.

Few of the rules of Chapter 2 satisfy **strict order preservation**, which says that in addition to *order preservation*, (and unless $E = 0$ of course,) if agent i's claim is smaller than agent j's, then (i) agent i should receive less than agent j does (equality is not permitted any more), (ii) a parallel statement being made about their losses (here, unless $E = \sum c_k$). Let us refer to these two requirements as **strict order preservation in awards** and **strict order preservation in losses**. For a Young rule – let $f \in \Phi$ be a representation of it – these strict inequalities are met if for each pair $\{c_0, c_0'\} \subset \mathbb{R}_+$ such that $c_0 < c_0'$, (i) the graph of $f(c_0, \cdot)$ lies everywhere below the graph of $f(c_0', \cdot)$ (except of course at the left endpoint of their domain of definition where they have to meet); and (ii) recalling that $g(c_0, \cdot) \equiv c_0 - f(c_0, \cdot)$, the graph of $g(c_0, \cdot)$ lies everywhere below the graph of $g(c_0', \cdot)$ (here, except at the right endpoint of their domain of definition).

The following is a generalization, from individuals to groups, of *order preservation*: given two groups, if the aggregate claim of the first group is at most as large as the aggregate claim of the second group, then the aggregate award to the first group should be at most as large as the aggregate award to the second group, similar inequalities holding for the aggregate losses incurred by the two groups:[30]

Group order preservation: For each $(c, E) \in \mathcal{C}^N$ and each pair $\{N', N''\}$ of subsets of N, if $\sum_{N'} c_i \leq \sum_{N''} c_i$, then $\sum_{N'} S_i(c, E) \leq \sum_{N''} S_i(c, E)$. Also, $\sum_{N'}(c_i - S_i(c, E)) \leq \sum_{N''}(c_i - S_i(c, E))$.

We refer to the first part of this property as **group order preservation in awards** and to the second part as **group order preservation in losses**. Obviously, this property implies *equal treatment of equal groups*.

The definition allows one-claimant "groups," so this property also implies *order preservation*. As with *order preservation*, we obtain a more demanding version of the property, **strict group order preservation**, by adding that whenever the inequality appearing in the hypothesis is strict, so should the inequalities appearing in the conclusions (unless $E = 0$ for the first one, and unless $E = \sum c_i$ for the second one).

The sequence of four panels of Figure 3.9 shows how to identify the set of awards vectors satisfying the *group order preservation* inequalities for $N \equiv \{1, 2, 3\}$ and $(c, E) \in \mathcal{C}^N$ equal to $((1, 2, 4), 5)$.

When $c_1 \leq c_2 \leq c_3$, neither the comparison of c_1 to $c_2 + c_3$ nor that of c_2 to $c_1 + c_3$ adds any inequality to those coming from comparing individual claims (for instance, if $x \in \mathbb{R}^N_+$ satisfies $x_1 \leq x_2$, then of course $x_1 \leq x_2 + x_3$). Thus, in addition to the *order preservation* inequalities, we have only two more, whose direction is determined by comparing $c_1 + c_2$ and c_3:

Case 1: $c_1 + c_2 \geq c_3$. Then $x_1 + x_2 \geq x_3$ and $c_1 - x_1 + c_2 - x_2 \geq c_3 - x_3$.

Case 2: $c_1 + c_2 \leq c_3$ (as in the example of Figure 3.9). Then $x_1 + x_2 \leq x_3$ and $c_1 - x_1 + c_2 - x_2 \leq c_3 - x_3$.

The set of awards vectors satisfying the *group order preservation* inequalities for the example is the shaded area of panel (d). Note that a balanced vector may meet these inequalities but assign to an agent more than their claim: the vector y in that panel illustrates this possibility.

The figure shows that, for our example, there are awards vectors satisfying all of the *group order preservation* inequalities, and of course the question is whether this is true in general. The answer is yes. Indeed, the proportional awards vector always does, as is easily verified. In fact, it satisfies the strict version of the property. Of the rules of Chapter 2 it is the only one to satisfy *group order preservation* – we have already pointed out that this is already the case for *equal treatment of equal groups*, a weaker property – but infinitely many other rules do too. This is because the requirement is punctual. For each problem, the set of awards vectors from which to choose is a nonempty polygonal

[30] This property is formulated by Thomson (1998). Here too, we obtain a weaker version by requiring that the groups have equal numbers of claimants.

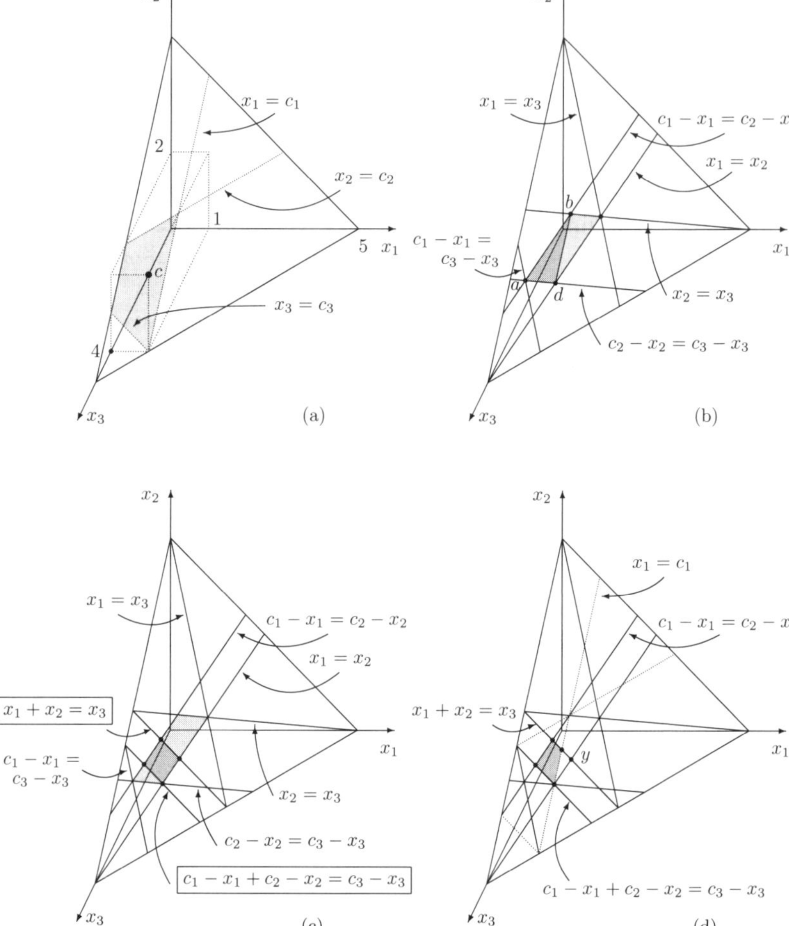

Figure 3.9: **Group order preservation for three claimants.** Let $N \equiv \{1, 2, 3\}$ and $(c, E) \in \mathcal{C}^N$ be equal to $((1, 2, 4), 5)$. In the simplex of balanced vectors, the arrow labeled "$x_1 = c_1$" points to those vectors satisfying this equality. The other arrows are interpreted in a similar way. The shaded area of panel (a) is the set of awards vectors of (c, E). That of panel (b) is the set of balanced vectors satisfying the order preservation inequalities. This set is also the entire shaded area of panel (c). The darker area in that panel is the set of balanced vectors satisfying the two inequalities coming from comparing groups that are not already implied by *order preservation* (the set of balanced vectors satisfying an inequality at equality is labeled in a rectangle). The shaded area of panel (d) is the set of awards vectors satisfying all of the *group order preservation* inequalities (here, only the ones that are binding are labeled).

region – it is not empty because it contains the proportional awards vector, as we just mentioned – and we have complete freedom in making the selection. Whether this can be done so as to obtain rules satisfying other properties of interest is another issue of course, especially for relational properties.

Rules in the spirit of the order-preservation–constrained sequential priority rules can be defined in which the constraint is that the group order preservation inequalities be met. Following our naming conventions, let us refer to them as **group-order-preservation–constrained sequential priority rules**.

* Relating axioms ♦ *Anonymity* is not logically related to either *order preservation* or *group order preservation*.

CHAPTER 4

Monotonicity Properties

On any domain of allocation problems, a "monotonicity" requirement pertains to changes in a parameter entering the description of the problems to be solved, when the parameter belongs to a space that is equipped with an economically meaningful order structure and the outcome space, or some component of it, does too. The requirement expresses the intuitive idea that the order structure of the space to which the parameter belongs should be reflected in the order structure of the space to which the solution outcome, or the corresponding component of it, belongs.

Monotonicity requirements have played an important role in the development of the axiomatic program. Requirements of this type pertaining to changes in certain variables, such as a social endowment of unproduced resources, or of factors of production, or of a production technology, can be interpreted as solidarity requirements or as concrete expressions of the abstract idea of common ownership. They have often been shown to be remarkably, and of course disappointingly, restrictive. In some contexts, they are even incompatible with efficiency and very elementary punctual notions of fairness in distribution. Monotonicity requirements with respect to individual parameters, private endowments say, can be motivated by both fairness and incentive considerations. These are typically not as demanding.

Here, in the context of claims problems, monotonicity, in its various forms, whether in response to an increase in the endowment or in response to an increase in some agent's claim, is not restrictive at all.

We will also formulate a variety of bounds on the impact that such increases may have, as well as order preservation requirements. These too turn out to be quite mild. The same cannot be said about their "strict" version obtained by adding that, when meaningful, there be an actual change in the chosen award vector, or in the relevant component(s) of it, in response to a change in the parameter ("meaningful" because, for example, if someone's claim is 0 and the endowment increases, obviously this claimant cannot be asked to receive more; or if the endowment is 0, an increase in someone's claim cannot be made to benefit them).

4.1 ENDOWMENT MONOTONICITY AND RELATED PROPERTIES

In this section, we formulate various monotonicity requirements pertaining to changes in the endowment.

• First is the requirement that if the endowment increases, each claimant receive at least as much as initially.[1] The property is illustrated in Figure 4.1a, and a violation in Figure 4.1b. Geometrically, paths of awards should be monotone curves:

Endowment monotonicity: For each $(c, E) \in \mathcal{C}^N$ and each $E' > E$, if $\sum c_i \geq E'$, then $S(c, E') \geqq S(c, E)$.

This property is not demanding: all of the rules of Chapter 2 satisfy it. However, a few interesting rules do not (Section 9.5).

We obtain a strict version of the property by requiring that, under the same hypotheses, the inequality appearing in the conclusion be strict for each agent whose claim is positive:

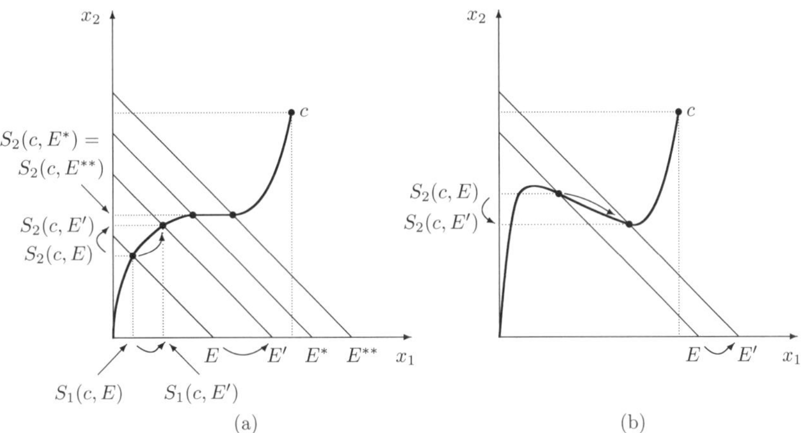

Figure 4.1: **Endowment monotonicity.** Let $N \equiv \{1, 2\}$ and $c \in \mathbb{R}^N_+$. If a rule S is *endowment monotonic*, its path of awards for c is a monotone curve from the origin to c. (a) Here, the property is met strictly when the endowment varies in the intervals $[0, E^*]$ and $[E^{**}, \sum c_i]$ – consider for instance the passage from E to E' – and weakly when the endowment varies in $[E^*, E^{**}]$ (indeed claimant 2's award remains constant as the endowment increases from E^* to E^{**}). (b) The property is violated by the rule represented in this panel: as the endowment increases from E to E', claimant 2's award decreases.

[1] Properties expressing the same idea are standard in all branches of game theory and economics. For a survey, see Thomson (1999b).

Strict endowment monotonicity: For each $(c, E) \in \mathcal{C}^N$ and each $E' > E$, if $\sum c_i \geq E'$, then for each $i \in N$ such that $c_i > 0$, $S_i(c, E') > S_i(c, E)$.

This strengthening is significant; the proportional rule is one of the few examples of Chapter 2 satisfying it. For a Young rule – let $f \in \Phi$ be a nondegenerate representation of it – the property holds if and only if the functions $\{f(c_0, \cdot)\}_{c_0 \in \mathbb{R}_+}$ are all increasing.[2] None of the sequential priority, ICI, or CIC rules is *strictly endowment monotonic*.

Conditional versions of *strict endowment monotonicity*, requiring that the inequality appearing in its conclusion be strict only for each claimant i whose initial award is neither 0 nor c_i (this eliminates corner situations) can be stated. Let us call **null-compensation–conditional strict endowment monotonicity** the variant according to which, in our previous notation, if $E' > E$, a rule is excused from the strict inequality $S_i(c, E') > S_i(c, E)$ for any claimant $i \in N$ who is assigned nothing initially, and **full-compensation–conditional strict endowment monotonicity** the variant according to which, if $E' > E$, it is excused from the strict inequality for any claimant $i \in N$ who is fully compensated initially. The constrained equal losses rule is an example of a rule that is not *strictly endowment monotonic* but passes the first one of these less demanding tests; the constrained equal awards rule is an example of a rule that is not *strictly endowment monotonic* but passes the second one of these tests.

• If it is natural to require that no claimant be hurt by an increase in the endowment, it is just as natural to require that no claimant's award increase by more than the amount by which the endowment increases:

Bounded gain from endowment increase: For each $(c, E) \in \mathcal{C}^N$ and each $E' > E$, if $\sum c_i \geq E'$, then for each $i \in N$, $S_i(c, E') - S_i(c, E) \leq E' - E$.

∗ Relating axioms ♦ *Endowment monotonicity* implies *endowment continuity*. The proof of this implication is standard and we omit it. ♦ Obviously, *endowment monotonicity* implies *bounded gain from endowment increase*. The reverse is not true except for two claimants.

• The next property provides one formal expression – we will see several others – of the general idea that the comparative impact on claimants of a change in a parameter of a problem should be related to how their claims are ordered. Specifically here, if the endowment increases, given any two claimants, the smaller one should receive a share of the increment that is at most as large as the share received by the larger one:[3]

[2] Recall that nondegeneracy implies that there is always exactly one solution to the equation in λ giving the awards vector. We can indeed ignore any subinterval of the interval of definition of the functions $\{f(c_0, \cdot)\}_{c_0 \in \mathbb{R}_+}$ over which all of them are constant. See Subsection 2.2.2, where the rules are defined, for a discussion of this point.

[3] This property is introduced by Dagan, Serrano, and Volij (1997) under the name of "supermodularity."

Order preservation under endowment variations: For each $(c, E) \in \mathcal{C}^N$, each pair $\{i, j\} \subseteq N$, and each $E' > E$, if $\sum c_k \geq E'$ and $c_i \leq c_j$, then $S_i(c, E') - S_i(c, E) \leq S_j(c, E') - S_j(c, E)$.

We would obtain an equivalent property by focusing on losses: if the endowment increases, given any two claimants, the loss incurred by the smaller one should decrease by at most as much as the loss incurred by the larger one.

For two claimants, whether a rule satisfies *order preservation under endowment variations* is easily determined by inspecting its paths of awards. To illustrate, let $N \equiv \{1, 2\}$ and $c \equiv (c_1, c_2) \in \mathbb{R}^N_+$ be such that $c_1 \leq c_2$, say. Then the property is met if the slope of its path for c is larger than or equal to 1 at each endowment at which it is well defined. The two-claimant diagrams of Chapter 2 suggest, and this is true in general, that the proportional, constrained equal awards, and constrained equal losses rules *preserve order under endowment variations*. In fact, for two claimants, of the rules that we have most frequently discussed, only the sequential priority and constrained egalitarian rules do not. For the latter, note that in Figure 2.12, the first increment in the endowment beyond the half-sum of the claims goes entirely to claimant 1, the smaller claimant.

For arbitrarily many claimants, when awards are plotted as a function of the endowment, *order preservation under endowment variations* says that, given any two claimants, the slope of the award schedule for the smaller one should be at most as large as the slope of the award schedule for the larger one at each endowment at which these slopes are well defined. Here too, the three-claimant diagrams of Chapter 2 suggest, and this is indeed the case, that most of our rules *preserve order under endowment variations* in general.

A Young rule – let $f \in \Phi$ be a representation of it – satisfies the property if and only if, for each pair $\{c_0, c'_0\} \subset \mathbb{R}_+$ such that $c_0 < c'_0$, the function $f(c_0, \cdot)$ increases everywhere at most as fast as the function $f(c'_0, \cdot)$.

All ICI and CIC rules *preserve order under endowment variations*.

∗ Relating axioms ♦ *Order preservation under endowment variations* implies *order preservation*. (Set $E = 0$ in the statement of the former property to obtain *order preservation in awards*; set $E' = \sum c_i$ to obtain *order preservation in losses*.) ♦ A rule may *preserve order under endowment variations* but violate *endowment monotonicity*. To see this, let $N \equiv \{1, 2\}$ and $c \in \mathbb{R}^N_+$ be such that $c_1 \leq c_2$. Then the path of awards for c may "bend back," resulting in a violation of *endowment monotonicity* without *order preservation under endowment variations* itself being violated. For example, consider a rule whose path of awards for $c = (2, 6)$ is bro.seg[(0, 0), (1, 2), (.5, 3.5), (2, 6)]. As the endowment increases from 3 to 4, *endowment monotonicity* is violated but the rule *preserves order under endowment variations* for c. It is easy to complete its definition so that it does so for each claims vector.

We obtain **strict order preservation under endowment variations** from *order preservation under endowment variations* by adding the requirement that whenever the inequality between the claims stated in the hypothesis is strict, the inequality appearing in the conclusion also be strict. It is met by very few of the rules of Chapter 2. The proportional rule satisfies it, however.

• Next are variants for groups of the properties just defined. If the endowment increases, given any two groups of claimants such that the aggregate claim of the first group is at most as large as the aggregate claim of the second group, the aggregate award to the first group should increase by at most as much as the aggregate award to the second group:

Group order preservation under endowment variations: For each $(c, E) \in \mathcal{C}^N$, each $E' > E$, and each pair $\{N', N''\}$ of subsets of N, if $\sum_N c_k \geq E'$ and $\sum_{N'} c_i \leq \sum_{N''} c_j$, then $\sum_{N'}[S_i(c, E') - S_i(c, E)] \leq \sum_{N''}[S_j(c, E') - S_j(c, E)]$.

Here too, this requirement could equivalently be written in terms of losses: if the endowment increases, given any two groups of claimants such that the aggregate claim of the first group is at most as large as the aggregate claim of the second group, the aggregate loss incurred by the first group should decrease by at most as much as the aggregate loss incurred by the second group.

A strict version of the property, strict group order preservation under endowment variations, says that in addition, if the inequality between the aggregate claims appearing in the hypotheses is strict, so should the inequality between the aggregate awards stated in the conclusion.

Except for two claimants of course, *group order preservation under endowment variations* is considerably more demanding than *order preservation under endowment variations*. Nevertheless it is satisfied by the proportional rule.

A characterization. As properties accumulate, the list of questions concerning their compatibility lengthens, and the answers sometimes take the form of uniqueness results. Our first theorem is a result of this type. It is a characterization of the constrained equal awards rule, the first of many that we will offer for this rule.[4]

constrained equal awards rule characterized

Theorem 4.1 *The constrained equal awards rule is the only rule satisfying* ***conditional full compensation*** *and* ***order preservation under endowment variations.***

For two claimants, the result is easily seen on Figure 3.4a, where $N \equiv \{1, 2\}$ and $c \in \mathbb{R}^N_+$ is such that $c_1 < c_2$. The first property implies that (i) the path of awards for c contains seg$[(c_1, c_1), c]$. In particular the path contains (c_1, c_1). It also contains the origin (by definition of a rule). These two points lie on a line of slope 1. The second property implies then that (ii) the path contains the segment connecting them, seg$[(0, 0), (c_1, c_1)]$. Indeed, if it contained a point x

[4] Theorem 4.1 is due to Yeh (2006).

below that segment (as is the case in Figure 3.4a), we would get a violation as the endowment increases from 0 to $\sum x_i$; if it contained a point y above the segment (as is also the case in Figure 3.4a), we would get a violation as the endowment increases from $\sum y_i$ to $2c_1$. Together, (i) and (ii) say that the path for c is that of the constrained equal awards rule.

Proof: We already know that the constrained equal awards rule satisfies the two properties listed in the theorem. Conversely, let S be a rule satisfying these properties. Let $(c, E) \in \mathcal{C}^N$ and suppose, without loss of generality, that $c_1 \leq \cdots \leq c_n$. Let $x \equiv S(c, E)$. If $E = nc_1$, then by *conditional full compensation*, $S_1(c, E) = c_1$. Now, by *order preservation in awards*, implied by *order preservation under endowment variations*, for each $i \in N \setminus \{1\}$, $S_i(c, E) = c_1$. By *order preservation in awards*, for each $0 \leq E \leq nc_1$ and each $i \in N \setminus \{1\}$, $S_1(c, E) \leq S_i(c, E)$. Since, by *order preservation under endowment variations*, $c_1 - S_1(c, nc_1) = S_1(c, nc_1) - S_1(c, E) \leq S_i(c, nc_1) - S_i(c, E) = c_1 - S_i(c, E)$, if follows that for each $0 \leq E \leq nc_1$ and each $i \in N \setminus \{1\}$, $S_1(c, E) = S_i(c, E)$. Since, by *conditional full compensation*, for each $E \leq nc_1$, $S_1(c, E) = c_1$, we can now conclude that the schedule of awards of S for claimant 1 for c is that of the constrained equal awards rule. The proof concludes by an induction argument, dealing with agents in the order of their claims. □

∗ `On the independence of axioms in Theorem 4.1.` ✦ The constrained equal losses rule satisfies *order preservation under endowment variations* but not *conditional full compensation*. ✦ Figure 3.4a shows that a rule can satisfy *conditional full compensation* but not *order preservation under endowment variations*. This is not surprising as the former property only pertains to endowments that are larger than a certain amount that depends on the claims vector.

• Next we require that if agent i's claim is at most as large as agent j's, agent i receive proportionally at least as much as agent j does (Figure 4.2a):[5]

Progressivity: For each $(c, E) \in \mathcal{C}^N$ and each pair $\{i, j\} \subseteq N$, if $0 < c_i \leq c_j$, then $\frac{S_i(c,E)}{c_i} \geq \frac{S_j(c,E)}{c_j}$.

In the context of taxation, when the issue is specifying how much each taxpayer should pay as a function of their income, it is this inequality that has usually been found most desirable. Figure 4.2b illustrates the alternative requirement that if agent i's claim is at most as large as agent j's claim, agent i receive proportionally at most as much.

Regressivity: For each $(c, E) \in \mathcal{C}^N$ and each pair $\{i, j\} \subseteq N$, if $0 < c_i \leq c_j$ then $\frac{S_i(c,E)}{c_i} \geq \frac{S_j(c,E)}{c_j}$.

[5] This terminology is inspired from public finance but it is used slightly differently.

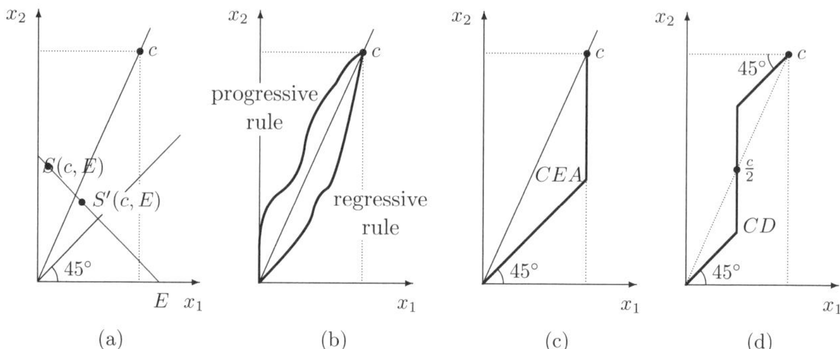

Figure 4.2: **Progressivity and regressivity.** Let $N \equiv \{1,2\}$ and $c \in \mathbb{R}^N_+$ be such that $c_1 \leq c_2$. (a) If a rule S is *progressive*, when $0 < E < \sum c_i$, $\frac{S_2(c,E)}{c_2} \geq \frac{S_1(c,E)}{c_1}$, or equivalently, $\frac{S_2(c,E)}{S_1(c,E)} \geq \frac{c_2}{c_1}$: the ray through $S(c,E)$ is steeper than the ray through c. (b) Since the inequality should hold for each value of E in that interval, the path of awards of S for c lies everywhere above or on the ray through c. If instead, the path lies everywhere above or on that ray, the rule is *progressive*. (c) The constrained equal awards rule is *regressive*. (d) A rule whose path for some claims vector c is partly above and partly below the ray through c is neither *progressive* nor *regressive*. An example is concede-and-divide.

For two claimants and measuring the smaller claim on the horizontal axis, whether a rule is *progressive* depends on whether, for each claims vector, its path of awards lies above or on the segment connecting the origin to the claims vector. This segment is the path of the proportional rule for the claims vector (Figure 4.2). Similarly, for two claimants and still measuring the smaller claim on the horizontal axis, whether a rule is *regressive* depends on whether its path of awards lies everywhere above or on that segment. For n claimants, this property should hold for each of the projections of the path onto the two-dimensional subspaces relative to pairs of claimants. The constrained equal awards rule is *regressive* (Figure 4.2c) and the constrained equal losses rule *progressive*. Concede-and-divide is neither (Figure 4.2d). **Strict regressivity** and **strict progressivity** are obtained by writing as strict inequalities the conclusions of *regressivity* and *progressivity*, except of course for $E = 0$ or $E = \sum c_i$. The proportional rule is the only rule to be both *regressive* and *progressive*.

* `Relating axioms` ♦ *Regressivity* implies *equal treatment of equals*, and so does *progressivity*.

• Next is the requirement that as the endowment increases, for each pair of claimants, successive increments be divided more and more in favor of the smaller claimant:[6]

[6] The terminology is a little dangerous because it presumes that the horizontal axis is chosen as the one on which the awards to the agent with the smaller claim is measured.

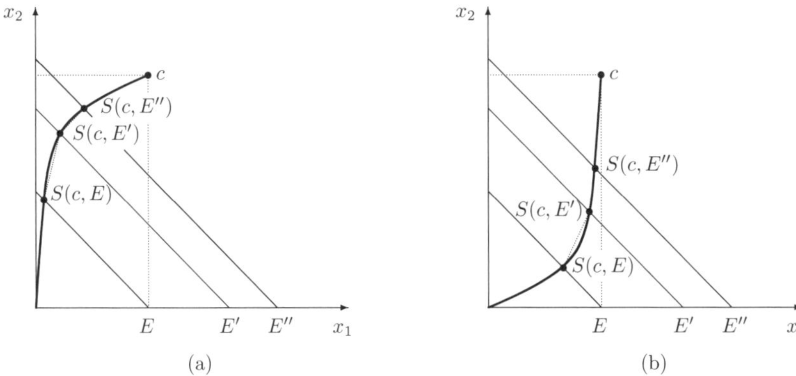

Figure 4.3: **Concavity and convexity.** Let $N \equiv \{1, 2\}$ and $c \in \mathbb{R}^N_+$ be such that $c_1 < c_2$. (a) If a rule S is *concave*, its path of awards for c is a concave curve. (b) If S is *convex*, its path for c is a convex curve.

Concavity: For each $(c, E) \in \mathcal{C}^N$, each triple $\{E, E', E''\} \subset \mathbb{R}_+$ such that $0 < E < E' < E'' \leq \sum c_k$, and each pair $\{i, j\} \subseteq N$, if $0 < c_i \leq c_j$, then

$$\frac{S_j(c, E') - S_j(c, E)}{S_i(c, E') - S_i(c, E)} \geq \frac{S_j(c, E'') - S_j(c, E')}{S_i(c, E'') - S_i(c, E')},$$

if these ratios are well defined.

Consider the two-claimant case, with $N \equiv \{1, 2\}$ say, and let $c \in \mathbb{R}^N$ be such that $0 < c_1 \leq c_2$. Then the path of awards of a *concave* rule for c is a concave curve. The property is illustrated in Figure 4.3a (by a rule that happens to violate *order preservation in losses*). For a **strictly concave** rule, the inequality written in the conclusion of *concavity* is required to be strict. The proportional and constrained equal losses rules are *concave*.

A related property is obtained by reversing the direction of the inequality. Still assuming $N \equiv \{1, 2\}$ and letting $c \in \mathbb{R}^N_+$ be such that $c_1 \leq c_2$, we refer to it as **convexity**. Using the two-claimant situation just described, the path of awards for c of a *convex* rule is a convex curve. **Strict convexity** is obtained by requiring the inequality to be strict. The property is illustrated in Figure 4.3b (by a rule that happens to violate *order preservation in awards*). Both the proportional and constrained equal awards rules are *convex*.

• A related requirement for two claimants is that each path of awards be "visible" from the origin.[7] For an observer standing there, and imagining the path to be opaque, no part of it should be hidden by some other part. Formally, each ray from the origin should meet the path at no more than one point.

[7] We use this terminology in Thomson (1998) to describe the shape of certain Pareto sets in the Edgeworth box. Alternatively we could speak of the "star-shapedness with respect to the origin" of the set of nonnegative vectors that are bounded above by the claims vector and the path of awards. "Visibility" should be understood to apply to the projections of the paths of awards onto two-dimensional subspaces.

Alternatively, the segment from the origin to a typical point on the path should lie between the path and the ray to the claims vector. This can be accomplished in two different ways: still assuming $c_1 \leq c_2$, the path may be visible "from below" (Figure 4.4) or it may be visible "from above" (Figure 4.5).

Visibility from below from the origin: For each $c \in \mathbb{R}_+^N$, each pair $\{E, E'\} \subset \mathbb{R}_+$ and each pair $\{i, j\} \subseteq N$, if $0 < E < E' \leq \sum c_k$ and $c_i \leq c_j$, then

$$\frac{S_j(c, E')}{S_i(c, E')} < \frac{S_j(c, E)}{S_i(c, E)},$$

if these ratios are well defined.

Visibility from above from the origin is obtained by simply reversing the direction of the inequality in the displayed expression.

The limit case is when a path of awards contains one or several nondegenerate segments that are lined up with the origin (Figure 4.4b). Let us refer to this property as **visibility except possibly along segments lined up with the origin**. We will see that whether there is only one such segment and this segment contains the origin is important (Section 6.1). For this reason, we define a version of the property that allows that case but only that case (Figure 4.4c):

Visibility from below from the origin except possibly for an initial segment: For each $c \in \mathbb{R}_+^N$, there is $E^* \in [0, \sum c_i[$ such that (i) for each pair $\{E, E'\} \in [0, E^*] \times [0, E^*]$,

$$\frac{S_j(c, E')}{S_i(c, E')} = \frac{S_j(c, E)}{S_i(c, E)},$$

and for each pair $\{E, E'\} \in [E^*, \sum c_i] \times [E^*, \sum c_i]$, if $0 < E < E'$ and $c_i \leq c_j$,

$$\frac{S_j(c, E')}{S_i(c, E')} < \frac{S_j(c, E)}{S_i(c, E)}.$$

Parallel definitions can of course be given when visibility is from above.

Similarly, the requirement can be formulated that, for each claims vector c, the path of awards be **visible from *c*** (Figure 4.4d).[8] Here too, visibility from a claims vector can be from below or from above.

Finally, the path for c can be *visible from below from the origin* as well as *visible from below from c* (Figure 4.4e).

Figure 4.5 illustrates the counterpart of each of the possibilities shown in Figure 4.4 when visibility is from above as opposed to from below.

If a continuous path is *visible from the origin and from the claims vector*, it can only be visible from below in both cases, or from above in both cases. We say that a path is **visible from the origin** if it is *visible from above from the origin* or *visible from below from the origin*. A path can contain a nondegenerate

[8] The two properties are also formally dual of each other (Section 7.2).

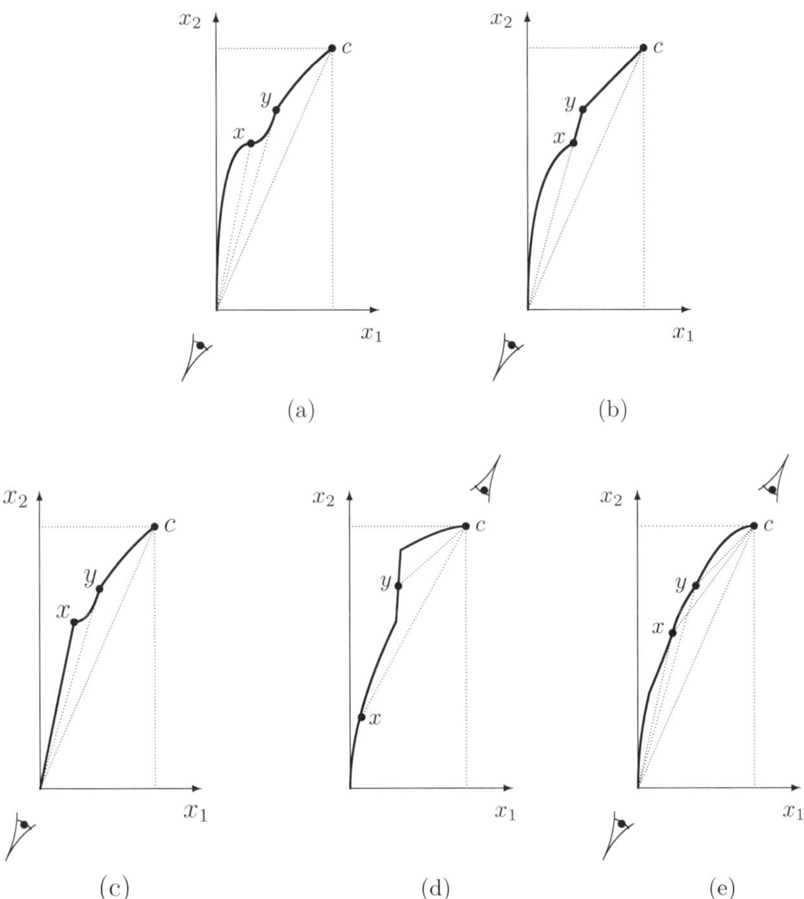

Figure 4.4: **Various notions of visibility from below.** Let $N \equiv \{1, 2\}$ and $c \in \mathbb{R}^N_+$ be such that $c_1 < c_2$. (a) If a rule is *visible from below from the origin*, an observer standing at the origin is able to see from below its entire path of awards for c. (b) This path is a limit case, as it contains a nondegenerate segment, seg$[x, y]$, that is lined up with the origin: *visibility from below from the origin except possibly along segments lined up with the origin* is satisfied. (c) This path is also a limit case. It contains a nondegenerate segment lined up with the origin but this segment contains the origin: *visibility from below from the origin except possibly for an initial segment* is satisfied. (d) This path is visible from below from c but not from the origin. (e) This path is visible from below from the origin *and* from c: each of its points, such as x and y, is visible from below, from both the origin and from c.

segment that is lined up with both the origin and the claims vector and satisfy our intermediate notion of visibility only if there is only one such segment and it actually contains either the origin or the claims vector.

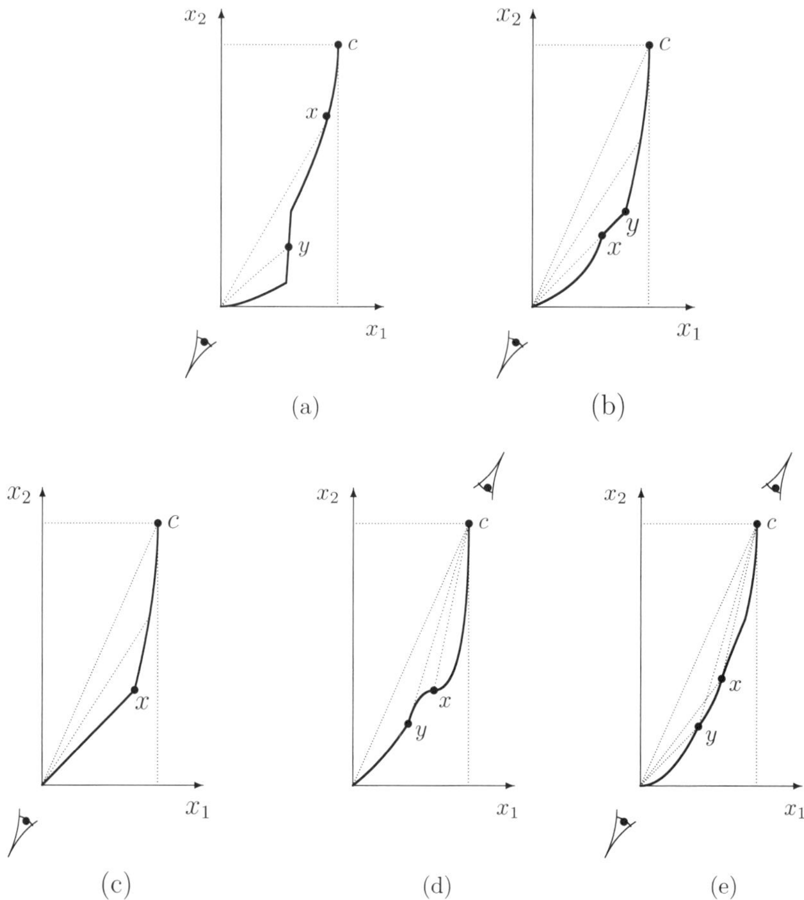

Figure 4.5: **Various notions of visibility from above.** Let $N \equiv \{1, 2\}$ and $c \in \mathbb{R}^N_+$ be such that $c_1 < c_2$. (a) If a rule is *visible from above from the origin*, an observer standing at the origin is able to see from above its entire path of awards for c. (b) This path is a limit case, as it contains a nondegenerate segment, seg$[x, y]$, that is lined up with the origin: *visibility from above from the origin except possibly along segments lined up with the origin* is satisfied. (c) This path contains a nondegenerate segment lined up with the origin that contains the origin: *visibility from above from the origin except possibly for an initial segment* is satisfied. (d) This path is visible from above from c but not from the origin. (e) This path is visible from above from the origin *and* from c: each of its points, such as x and y, is visible from above, from both the origin and from c.

`* Relating axioms` ♦ A *strictly concave* rule is *visible from below from the origin* and *visible from below from the claims vector*. A *strictly convex* rule is *visible from above from the origin* and *visible from above from the* *claims vector*. A *concave* rule satisfies *order preservation in awards*, but may violate *order preservation in losses*. The opposite holds for a *convex* rule. ♦ For each claims vector, the path of awards of a rule satisfying any of the *visibility* properties never intersects the ray to the claims vector, but the path of a rule *preserving order under endowment variations* may. ♦ If a rule is *visible from below from the origin*, or *visible from below from the claims vector*, it is *strictly progressive*. If it is *visible from above from the origin*, or *visible from above from the claims vector*, it is *strictly regressive*.

4.2 CLAIM MONOTONICITY AND RELATED PROPERTIES

In this section we formulate requirements on rules pertaining to changes in claims.

• First is the requirement that, if an agent's claim increases, they receive at least as much as initially:

Claim monotonicity: For each $(c, E) \in \mathcal{C}^N$, each $i \in N$, and each $c'_i > c_i$, we have $S_i((c'_i, c_{-i}), E) \geq S_i(c, E)$.

Figure 4.6 illustrates the property and Figure 4.7a,b shows violations of it. The property has a simple geometric description for two claimants when a rule is *endowment continuous* in addition: its paths of awards for two claims vectors that differ in only one coordinate should not cross, although they could touch

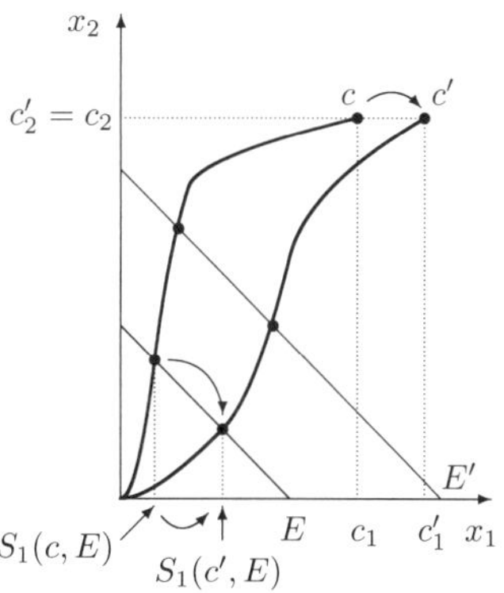

Figure 4.6: **Claim monotonicity.** Let $N \equiv \{1, 2\}$. If a rule S is *claim monotonic*, when an agent's claim increases, they receive at least as much as initially. The rule depicted here satisfies the requirement when agent 1's claim increases from c_1 to c'_1, agent 2's claim being fixed at c_2 and the endowment at E. In fact, the paths of awards of S for $c \equiv (c_1, c_2)$ and $c' \equiv (c'_1, c'_2)$, where $c'_2 \equiv c_2$, which are continuous curves, do not cross. Thus, the same conclusion holds for c_2 and any endowment as agent 1's claim increases from c_1 to c'_1.

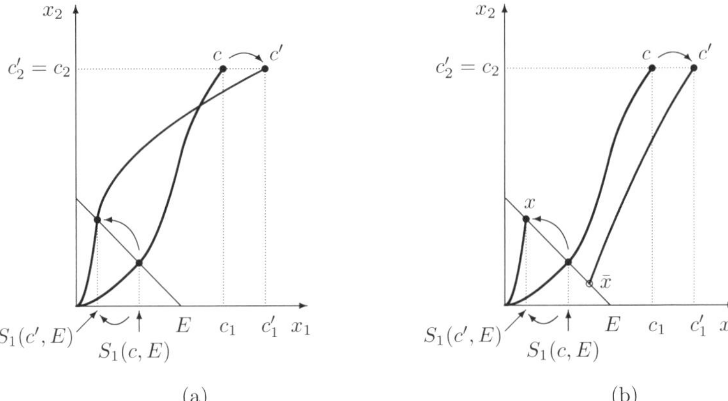

Figure 4.7: **Two violations of claim monotonicity.** (a) For the rule S depicted in this panel, the paths for c and c' cross, so *claim monotonicity* is violated, for instance, if the endowment is E. (b) Here is a discontinuous rule S whose paths for c and c' do not cross (the path for c' is in two pieces, the curvilinear segment from the origin to x, the upper endpoint x being included, and the curvilinear segment from $\bar{x}$ to c, this time the lower endpoint $\bar{x}$ being excluded), but S violates *claim monotonicity* for any endowment in $[0, E]$.

(of course, paths always meet at the origin). Figure 4.7b shows a rule violating both *endowment continuity* and *claims monotonicity*. The two paths that are drawn do not cross because one of them is discontinuous.

Most of the rules defined in Chapter 2 are *claim monotonic*. For a Young rule of representation $f \in \Phi$, the property is met if and only if the graphs of the functions $\{f(c_0, \cdot)\}_{c_0 \in \mathbb{R}_+}$ are ordered according to their argument c_0: for each pair $\{c_0, c'_0\} \subset \mathbb{R}_+$ such that $c_0 < c'_0$, the graph of $f(c_0, \cdot)$ lies everywhere on or below the graph of $f(c'_0, \cdot)$.

According to the strict version of the requirement, stated next, an agent whose claim increases always receives more than initially (except of course if $E = 0$):

Strict claim monotonicity: For each $(c, E) \in \mathcal{C}^N$ with $E > 0$, each $i \in N$, and each $c'_i > c_i$, we have $S_i((c'_i, c_{-i}), E) > S_i(c, E)$.

Among the rules of Chapter 2, the proportional rule is a rare example that satisfies this version. For a Young rule of representation $f \in \Phi$, the property holds if and only if, for each pair $\{c_0, c'_0\} \subset \mathbb{R}_+$ such that $c_0 < c'_0$, the graph of $f(c_0, \cdot)$ lies everywhere below the graph of $f(c'_0, \cdot)$ (here too, except at the left endpoint of their domain of definition, since the graphs meet there).

Similar statements can be made about Young's rules concerning other properties listed below. We will omit them, however.

• As an agent's claim increases without bound, "swamping" the other agents' claims, one could ask that they eventually be assigned the entire endowment. We will simply require that their award get arbitrarily close to the endowment:[9]

Full appropriation by unboundedly larger claimant: For each $i \in N$ and each sequence $\{(c^\nu, E^\nu)\}$ of elements of $\mathcal{C}^N$ such that $c_i^\nu \to \infty$ as $\nu \to \infty$ and for each pair $\nu, \nu' \in \mathbb{N}$, $(c_{-i}^\nu, E^\nu) = (c_{-i}^{\nu'}, E^{\nu'})$, then $S_i(c^\nu, E^\nu) \to E$ as $\nu \to \infty$.

The proportional rule satisfies this property but for a rule such as the constrained equal losses rule, for each $i \in N$, and each $(c_{-i}, E) \in \mathbb{R}_+^{N\setminus\{i\}}$, there is actually a finite value of agent i's claim beyond which agent i is assigned the entire endowment. The constrained equal awards, random arrival, and minimal overlap rules violate the property.

• *Claim monotonicity* says that an agent whose claim increases should receive at least as much as initially. However, one could argue that there is no reason why the change in the agent's award should exceed the amount by which their claim increased. Let us then require that this not be the case[10] (Figure 4.8):

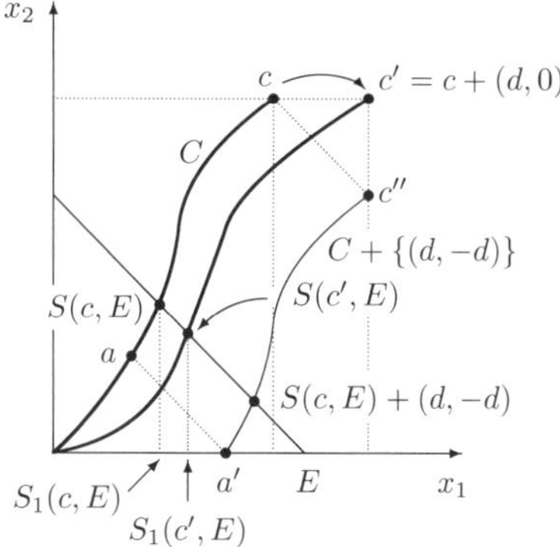

Figure 4.8: **Bounded gain from claim increase.** Let $N \equiv \{1, 2\}$ and $c \in \mathbb{R}_+^N$. A rule S satisfies *bounded gain from claim increase* if when an agent's claim increases by some amount d, their award does not increase by more than d. The curve denoted C which connects the origin to c, is the path of rule S for c. The requirement is that the path of S for $c' \equiv c + (d, 0)$ lie to the left of the translate by $(d, -d)$ of its path for c. We show only the relevant part of this translate, namely the part that lies in the nonnegative quadrant. This translation is indicated for two important points, c and a, their images being denoted c'' and a'. (They are important because they give the endpoints of this boundary curve.)

[9] Kasajima and Thomson (2011).
[10] Kasajima and Thomson (2011).

Bounded gain from claim increase: For each $(c, E) \in \mathcal{C}^N$, each $i \in N$, and each $c'_i > c_i$, we have $S_i((c'_i, c_{-i}), E) - S_i(c, E) \leq c'_i - c_i$.

A violation is illustrated in Figure 4.6 for an endowment equal to E'. Most of the rules of Chapter 2 satisfy this property. A Young rule of representation $f \in \Phi$ defined on $\mathbb{R}_+ \times \Lambda$ for some $\Lambda \subseteq \mathbb{R}$ does if for each pair $\{c_0, c'_0\} \subset \mathbb{R}_+$ such that $c_0 < c'_0$ and each $\lambda \in \Lambda$, $f(c'_0, \lambda) - f(c_0, \lambda) \leq c'_0 - c_0$.

We obtain a strict version of the property by requiring that the inequality stated in the conclusion be strict (except of course when $E = 0$).

• Under the same hypotheses as for *claims monotonicity*, but this time focusing on the agents whose claims are fixed, let us now require that each of them receive at most as much as initially. By definition, a rule is *balanced*, so this property implies *claims monotonicity*. For two claimants, the two properties are equivalent.[11]

Other-regarding claim monotonicity: For each $(c, E) \in \mathcal{C}^N$, each $i \in N$, and each $c'_i > c_i$, we have $S_{N\setminus\{i\}}((c'_i, c_{-i}), E) \leqq S_{N\setminus\{i\}}(c, E)$.

This property is satisfied by all of the central rules.

Here too, we can formulate a strict version of the property by requiring that for each claimant whose claim is positive the inequality appearing in the conclusion be strict (except of course if $E > 0$). This version clearly implies *strict claim monotonicity*. Once again, the proportional rule passes this more demanding test, but none of the other central rules does.

Instead of imagining an increase in agent i's claim, we could equivalently imagine a decrease in their claim. A special case is when agent i's claim decreases to 0. Let us call **null claim other-regarding claim monotonicity** the requirement that each of the other agents receive at least as much as initially.

• A requirement in the same family is that, if an agent's claim increases due to a transfer from some other agent, the transferee receives at least as much as initially and this other agent receive at most as much as initially:[12]

No transfer paradox: For each $(c, E) \in \mathcal{C}^N$, each pair $\{i, j\} \subseteq N$, each $c'_i > c_i$, and each $0 \leq c'_j < c_j$, if $c'_i + c'_j = c_i + c_j$, then

$$S_i((c'_i, c'_j, c_{N\setminus\{i,j\}}), E) \geq S_i(c, E) \text{ and } S_j((c'_i, c'_j, c_{N\setminus\{i,j\}}), E) \leq S_j(c, E).$$

[11] This property (Thomson, 2003) is the counterpart of a property that has been discussed in the context of classical exchange economies (Thomson, 1987). There, the issue has to do with changes in agents' private endowments.

[12] This property is first mentioned by Chun (1988a). A conceptually related property has been of particular concern to international trade theorists in their study of the Walrasian rule: we borrow the name "no-transfer paradox" from the requirement that if an agent transfers part of their private endowment to another agent, the transferring agent should end up at most as well off as if they had not done so, and the other should end up at least as well off.

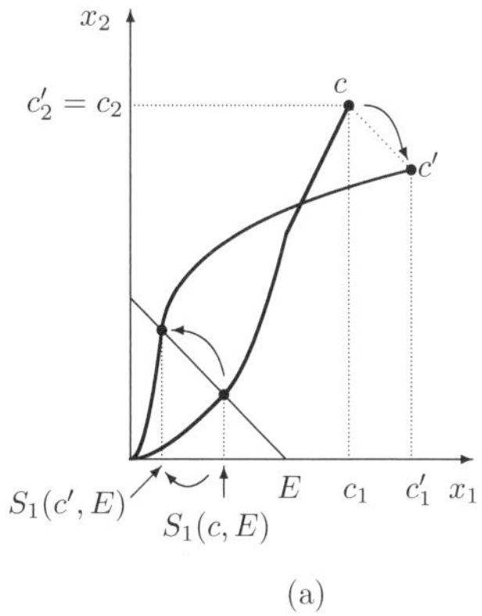

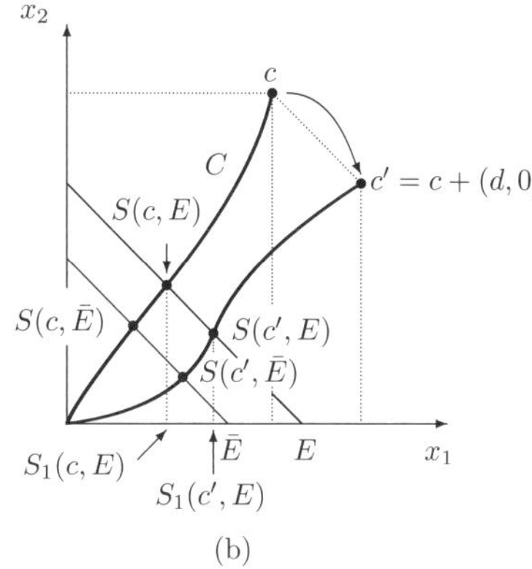

Figure 4.9: **Two properties pertaining to changes in claims.** Let $N \equiv \{1, 2\}$. (a) The rule S depicted here violates *no transfer paradox*: as a result of the claim transfer from claimant 2 to claimant 1, from $c \in \mathbb{R}^N_+$ to $c' \in \mathbb{R}^N_+$, claimant 2's award increases. (b) A rule satisfies *bounded impact of claim transfer* if, when an agent's claim increases by some amount d, their award does not increase by more than d. The curve denoted C which connects the origin to c, is the path of a rule S for c. The requirement is that its path for $c' \equiv c + (d, 0)$ lie to the left of the translate by $(d, -d)$ of its path for c. This is shown for two endowments: the differences between the abscissas of $S(c', E)$ and $S(c, E)$ and that between the abscissas of $S(c', \bar{E})$ and $S(c, \bar{E})$ are no greater than d.

Geometrically, for two claimants, and for an *endowment continuous* rule, *no transfer paradox* says that the paths of awards relative to two claims vectors located on a line of slope -1 should not cross (Figure 4.9a illustrates a violation but the property is met on Figure 4.9b). A similar statement can be made for more than two claimants about the projections of the paths of awards onto the two-dimensional subspace relative to the pair of claimants between whom a claim transfer takes place. For each endowment, and measuring the transferee's claim on the horizontal axis and the transferor's claim on the vertical axis, the projection of the vector chosen for the post-transfer claims vector lies to the southeast of the projection of the vector chosen for the initial claims vector. The sum of the coordinates of these two projections need not be equal but if the rule is *endowment continuous*, the paths traced by these projections are continuous curves that do not cross.

There are several ways of formulating strict versions of the property, depending upon whether one of the awards to the two claimants involved in the transfer is required to change, or both are.

• The next requirement limits the impact that a claim transfer has on the two claimants involved: the gain to the transferee should be at most as large as the transfer and the loss to the transferor should be at most as large as the transfer (for two claimants, the first inequality is of course equivalent to the second one) (Figure 4.9b):

Bounded impact of claim transfer: For each $(c, E) \in \mathcal{C}^N$, each pair $\{i, j\} \subseteq N$, each $c'_i > c_i$, and each $0 \leq c'_j < c_j$, if $c'_i + c'_j = c_i + c_j$, then

$$S_i((c'_i, c'_j, c_{N\setminus\{i,j\}}), E) - S_i(c, E) \leq c'_i - c_i$$

and

$$S_j(c, E) - S_j((c'_i, c'_j, c_{N\setminus\{i,j\}}), E) \leq c_j - c'_j.$$

All central rules satisfy this property. Not all of Young's rules do, however.

• If there are three claimants or more, we may be interested in the impact that a change in some agent's claim has on the relative awards to other claimants. Suppose that $|N| \geq 3$ and let $i \in N$. Let agent i's claim increase. Given any two claimants in $N \setminus \{i\}$, we require that the change in the award to the smaller one be at most as large as the change in the award to the larger one:[13]

Order preservation under claims variations: For each $(c, E) \in \mathcal{C}^N$, each $i \in N$, each $c'_i > c_i$, and each pair $\{j, k\} \subseteq N\setminus\{i\}$, if $c_j \leq c_k$, then $S_j(c, E) - S_j((c'_i, c_{-i}), E) \leq S_k(c, E) - S_k((c'_i, c_{-i}), E)$.

Once again, this requirement could equivalently be written in terms of losses. Most rules *preserve order under claims variations*. However, very few of the rules of Chapter 2 satisfy the strict version of the property – let us call it **strict order preservation under claims variations** – obtained by adding that whenever the inequality between the claims of agents j and k stated in the hypothesis is strict (and unless of course $E = 0$), the inequality between the changes in their awards stated in the conclusion also be strict.

A variant for groups of *order preservation under claims variations* can be defined. Supposing that some agent's claim increases, given two groups of claimants neither one of which containing the agent, if the aggregate claim of the first group is at most as large as the aggregate claim of the second group, the change in the aggregate award to the first group should be at most as large as the corresponding change for the second group:

Group order preservation under claims variations: For each $(c, E) \in \mathcal{C}^N$, each $i \in N$, each $c'_i > c_i$, and each pair $\{N', N''\} \subseteq N\setminus\{i\}$, if $\sum_{N'} c_j \leq \sum_{N''} c_k$, then $\sum_{N'}[S_j(c, E) - S_j((c'_i, c_{-i}), E)] \leq \sum_{N''}[S_k(c, E) - S_k((c'_i, c_{-i}), E)]$.

An equivalent formulation can be written in terms of the changes in the aggregate losses incurred by the two groups.

[13] Kasajima and Thomson (2011).

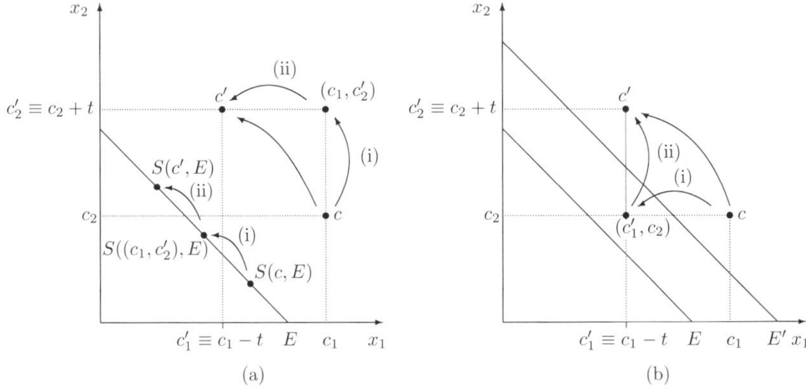

Figure 4.10: **For two claimants, claim monotonicity implies no transfer paradox**. Let $N \equiv \{1, 2\}$ and $c \in \mathbb{R}^N_+$. (a) A claim transfer of t units from agent 1 to agent 2, which takes c to $c' \equiv (c_1 - t, c_2 + t)$, can be decomposed into (i) an increase of t units in agent 2's claim, agent 1's claim being kept fixed, which takes c to (c_1, c'_2), followed by (ii) a decrease of t units in agent 1's claim, agent 2's claim being kept fixed, which takes (c_1, c'_2) to c'. If a rule S is *claim monotonic*, at each step, the awards vector it selects moves up the budget line or remains the same. (b) If we performed these operations in the reverse order (first decreasing agent 1's claim), at the intermediate stage, the endowment could exceed the sum of the claims. This would be the case here at (c'_1, c_2) for an endowment equal to E'.

Parallel order preservation requirements can be written, for individuals and for groups, when a transfer takes place between two claimants.

$*$ `Relating axioms` ♦ *Claim monotonicity* does not imply *claim continuity*. Rule 6.1 of Section 6.1 below satisfies the former property but not the latter.

♦ For two claimants, *claim monotonicity* implies *no transfer paradox*. Indeed, let $N \equiv \{1, 2\}$ say, and $(c, E) \in \mathcal{C}^N$ (Figure 4.10a). A claim transfer of $t > 0$ from agent 1 to agent 2 can be decomposed into an increase of t in agent 2's claim followed by a decrease of t in agent 1's claim. If a rule is *claim monotonic*, then after the first operation, claimant 1 receives at most as much as initially and so claimant 2 receives at least as much as initially; the second operation has the same consequences. Thus, so does the composition of the two operations. Figure 4.10b shows the importance in the proof of the order in which changes in claims are performed.

This reasoning fails for more than two claimants. In that case, however, *other-regarding claim monotonicity* does imply *no transfer paradox*. Again, this follows directly from the statements of the properties.

♦ On the other hand, *no transfer paradox* does not imply *claim monotonicity*, even for two claimants. This is shown by the next rule:

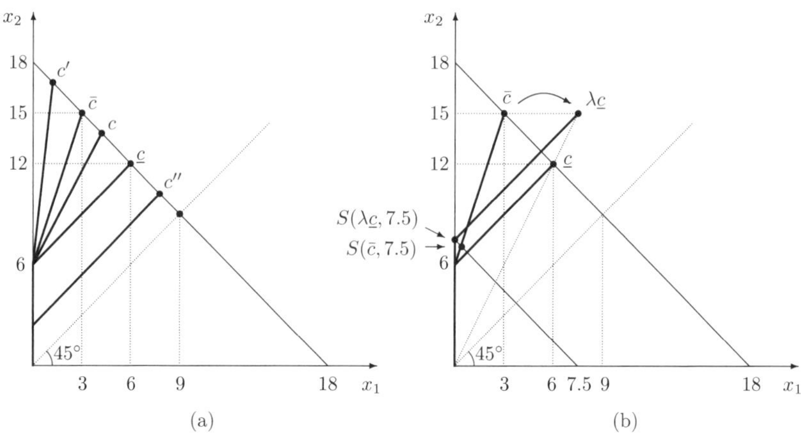

Figure 4.11: **No transfer paradox does not imply claim monotonicity.** (a) Shown are several paths of awards of Rule 4.1 called S, in particular its paths for $\underline{c} \equiv (6, 12)$ and $\bar{c} \equiv (3, 12)$. As its paths for claims vectors located on lines of slope -1 do not cross, the rule satisfies *no transfer paradox*. (b) The rule violates *claim monotonicity*. Indeed, suppose that the endowment is 7.5 and agent 2's claim is $\bar{c}_2 \equiv 15$. Then, as agent 1's claim increases from $\bar{c}_1 \equiv 3$ to $\lambda\underline{c}_1 \equiv 7.5$, where λ is such that $\lambda\underline{c}_2 = \bar{c}_2$, their award decreases.

Rule 4.1 (Figure 4.11a) Let $N \equiv \{1, 2\}$. We define the rule, denoted S, by first specifying its path of awards for each $c \in \text{seg}[(9, 9), (0, 18)]$: for each $c \in \text{seg}[(9, 9), (6, 12)]$, the path of S is that of the constrained equal losses rule; for each $c \in \text{seg}[(6, 12), (0, 18)]$, it is $\text{bro.seg}[(0, 0), (0, 6), c]$. The path for each $c \in \text{seg}[(9, 9), (18, 0)]$ is then obtained by symmetry with respect to the 45° line of the path for the symmetric image of c with respect to that line. Finally, for each $c \notin \text{seg}[(18, 0), (0, 18)]$, we identify the homothetic transformation for which the image of c belongs to that segment – let us denote this image c' – and then choose the path for c to be the inverse image under this transformation of the path for c'. These choices guarantee that S is *anonymous* and *homogeneous*.

Since the paths of awards of S are continuous curves and its paths for two claims vectors located on a line of slope -1 never cross, S satisfies *no transfer paradox*. To show that S fails *claim monotonicity*, let $\bar{c} \equiv (3, 15)$, $\underline{c} \equiv (6, 12)$, and $\lambda \in \mathbb{R}_+$ be such that $\lambda\underline{c}_2 = \bar{c}_2 = 15$ (that is, $\lambda = 1.25$) (Figure 4.11b). The path of S for $\lambda\underline{c}$ is obtained by a homothetic transformation of ratio λ from its path for $\underline{c}$: it is $\text{bro.seg}[(0, 0), (0, 7.5), \lambda\underline{c}]$. Inspection of Figure 4.11b shows that if the endowment is 7.5 (we could use any endowment in]6, 9[to make the point), and if agent 1's claim increases from $\bar{c}_1$ to $\lambda\underline{c}_1$, they receive less.

Claim monotonicity and *no-transfer paradox* specify the directions in which awards should change in response to an increase in someone's claim or in

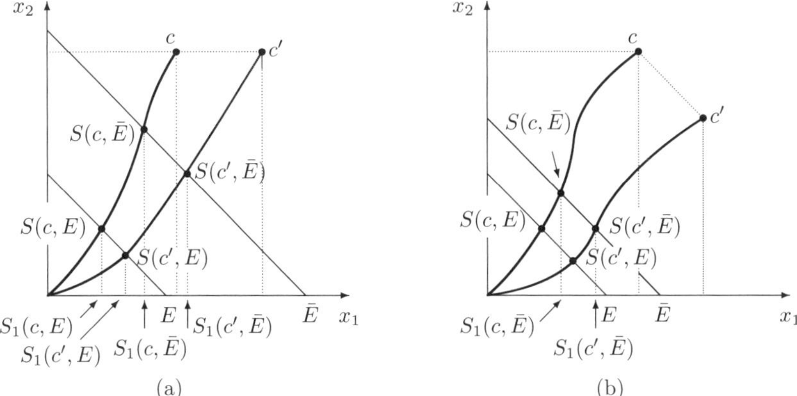

Figure 4.12: **Two endowment-monotonicity impact properties.** Let $N \equiv \{1, 2\}$. (a) If a rule S satisfies *endowment-monotone impact of claim increase*, the impact of an increase in agent 1's claim on their award is a monotone function of the endowment. (b) If it satisfies *endowment-monotone impact of claim transfer*, the impact of a claim transfer from claimant 2 to claimant 1 on their respective awards is a monotone function of the endowment.

response to a claim transfer from one claimant to another. The next two axioms tell us that these changes should be monotone functions of the endowment (Figure 4.12):

Endowment-monotonic impact of claim increase: For each pair $c, c' \in \mathbb{R}^N_+$ and each $i \in N$ such that $c_i < c'_i$ and $c_{N\setminus\{i\}} = c'_{N\setminus\{i\}}$, and each pair $\{E, \bar{E}\} \subset \mathbb{R}_+$ such that $E < \bar{E} \leq c_i + \sum_{N\setminus\{i\}} c_j$, then $S_i((c'_i, c_{-i}), E) - S_i(c, E) \leq S_i((c'_i, c_{-i}), \bar{E}) - S_i(c, \bar{E})$.

When some agent transfers some of their claim to some other agent, the difference between their awards should be a monotone function of the endowment. It is therefore maximal when the endowment is equal to the sum of the claims.

Endowment-monotonic impact of claim transfer: For each pair $\{c, c'\} \subset \mathbb{R}^N_+$, each pair $\{i, j\} \subseteq N$, and each pair $\{E, E'\} \subset \mathbb{R}_+$, if for some $t > 0$, $c'_i = c_i + t$, $c'_j = c_j - t$, and for each $k \in N \setminus \{i, j\}$, $c'_k = c_k$, and $E < \bar{E} < \sum c_i$, then $S_i(c', E) - S_i(c, E) \leq S_i(c', \bar{E}) - S_i(c, \bar{E})$ and $S_j(c, E) - S_j(c', E) \leq S_j(c, \bar{E}) - S_j(c', \bar{E})$.

A characterization. Our next main result is another characterization of the constrained equal awards rule. It differs from Theorem 4.1 only in that *order preservation under endowment variations* is replaced by *claim monotonicity*. Note that the two axioms are not directly logically related: a rule similar to Rule 4.1 can be used to show that the former does not imply the latter; the

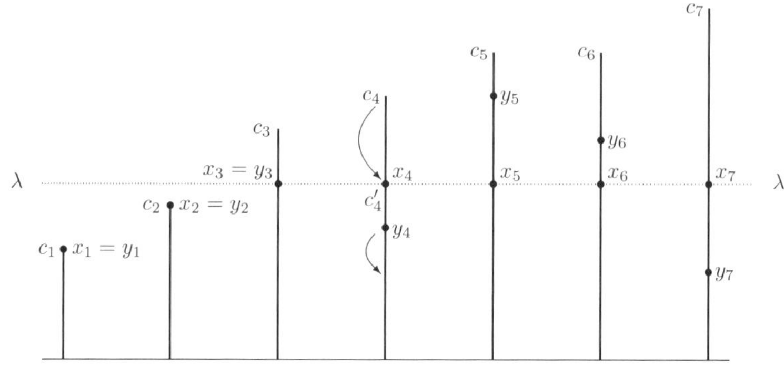

Figure 4.13: **Characterizing the constrained equal awards rule** (Theorem 4.2). The figure represents, for $N \equiv \{1, \ldots, 7\}$, a problem $(c, E) \in \mathcal{C}^N$ for which a rule satisfying the two properties listed in the theorem would choose some vector $y \neq x \equiv CEA(c, E)$. The horizontal line is placed at the height λ, where λ solves the equation giving x (see the definition of the constrained equal awards rule). By *conditional full compensation*, for each $i \in N$ such that $c_i \leq \lambda$, $y_i = x_i$. Since $x \neq y$, there is $i \in N$ for whom $y_i < \lambda \leq c_i$. Here, this double inequality holds for $i = 4$. (Note that two agents with equal claims could receive different amounts at y – this is the case for claimants 5 and 6 – and even an agent could receive less than someone whose claim is smaller than theirs – compare y_2 and y_7). Then we decrease agent 4's claim to λ. This claim becomes sustainable, so agent 4 should now be fully compensated. This is in violation of *claim monotonicity*, which implies that the new award should be at most y_4.

constrained egalitarian rule can be used to show that the latter does not imply the latter. Here is the characterization:[14]

constrained equal awards rule characterized

Theorem 4.2 *The constrained equal awards rule is the only rule satisfying conditional full compensation and claims monotonicity.*

Proof: (Figure 4.13) We already know that the constrained equal awards rule satisfies the two properties listed in the theorem. Conversely, let S be a rule satisfying these properties. Let $(c, E) \in \mathcal{C}^N$, $x \equiv CEA(c, E)$, and $y \equiv S(c, E)$. Suppose, by way of contradiction, that $y \neq x$. Let λ be the value of the parameter solving the equation giving x, namely $\sum \min\{c_i, \lambda\} = E$ and for each $i \in N$, $x_i = \min\{c_i, \lambda\}$. The claim of each $i \in N$ such that $c_i \leq \lambda$ is sustainable, so by *conditional full compensation*, $y_i = c_i = CEA_i(c, E)$. Since $x \neq y$, there is some claimant $i \in N$ whose claim is not sustainable and such that $y_i < \lambda$. Let $c' \in \mathbb{R}^N_+$ be such that $c'_i = \lambda$ and $c'_{-i} \equiv c_{-i}$. Note that $(c', E) \in \mathcal{C}^N$. Also, agent i's claim is sustainable in (c', E), and by

[14] Theorem 4.2 is due to Yeh (2004).

conditional full compensation, $S_i(c', E) = c'_i = \lambda$. Since $c'_i \leq c_i$, then by *claim monotonicity*, $S_i(c', E) \leq S_i(c, E) = y_i$. This contradicts $y_i < \lambda$. □

∗ `On the independence of axioms in Theorem 4.2.` ✦ The constrained equal losses rule satisfies *claim monotonicity*, but not *conditional full compensation*. ✦ It is more difficult to construct a rule satisfying *conditional full compensation* but not *claim monotonicity*, but here is one. Returning to Figure 3.4a, keep the same path of awards for the particular c that is shown; select c' slightly to the right of c and draw a path for c' with the same general shape (for *conditional full compensation* to hold, this path should contain the vertical segment from the intersection of the vertical line through c' with the 45° line), but make it cross the path for c. Then complete the specification of the rule so as to obtain *conditional full compensation*. This is easily done since no relational axiom is imposed. It is also clear that we could perform this operation so as to obtain a rule satisfying a number of additional properties including relational ones.

4.3 INVERSE SETS AXIOMS

Given a rule and a point in $\mathbb{R}^N_+$, we next identify all claims vectors such that the rule would choose the point for an endowment equal to the sum of its coordinates and formulate requirements having to do with the shape of the set these claims vectors constitute.

Formally, given a rule S and $x \in \mathbb{R}^N_+$, the **inverse set of S for x** is the set $S^{-1}(x) \equiv \{c \in \mathbb{R}^N_+$ **such that (i)** $(c, \sum x_i)$ **is a well-defined problem in** $\mathcal{C}^N$ **and (ii)** $x = S(c, \sum x_i)\}$.

The concept of an inverse set has been discussed in cooperative bargaining theory, and rules have been found to be usefully classified by means of the shapes of their inverse sets. Interesting shapes are convexity, star-shapedness with x as the center of the star, (which means that if $y \neq x$ belongs to the set, so does the entire segment seg$[x, y]$), cone-valuedness with x as the vertex of the cone (which means that if $y \neq x$ belongs to the set, so does the entire half-line emanating from x and passing through y), and so on.[15] Figure 4.14, which depicts the inverse sets of several rules, illustrates the wide range of the shapes they can have for our current model.[16] Some are half-lines. Some are curves that always turn their concavity towards (or always away from) the axis along which the smallest claim is measured. Some of these curves are neither convex nor concave. Instead of being curves, some inverse sets have nonempty interiors.

[15] Thomson (1996). In cooperative bargaining theory, inverse correspondences have two arguments: payoff vectors and feasible sets. Here, by *balance*, once an awards vector is specified, so is the endowment: it is the sum of the coordinates of the awards vector.

[16] They are based in part on unpublished notes by Hokari (2001). Juarez (2013) has also studied axioms of this type.

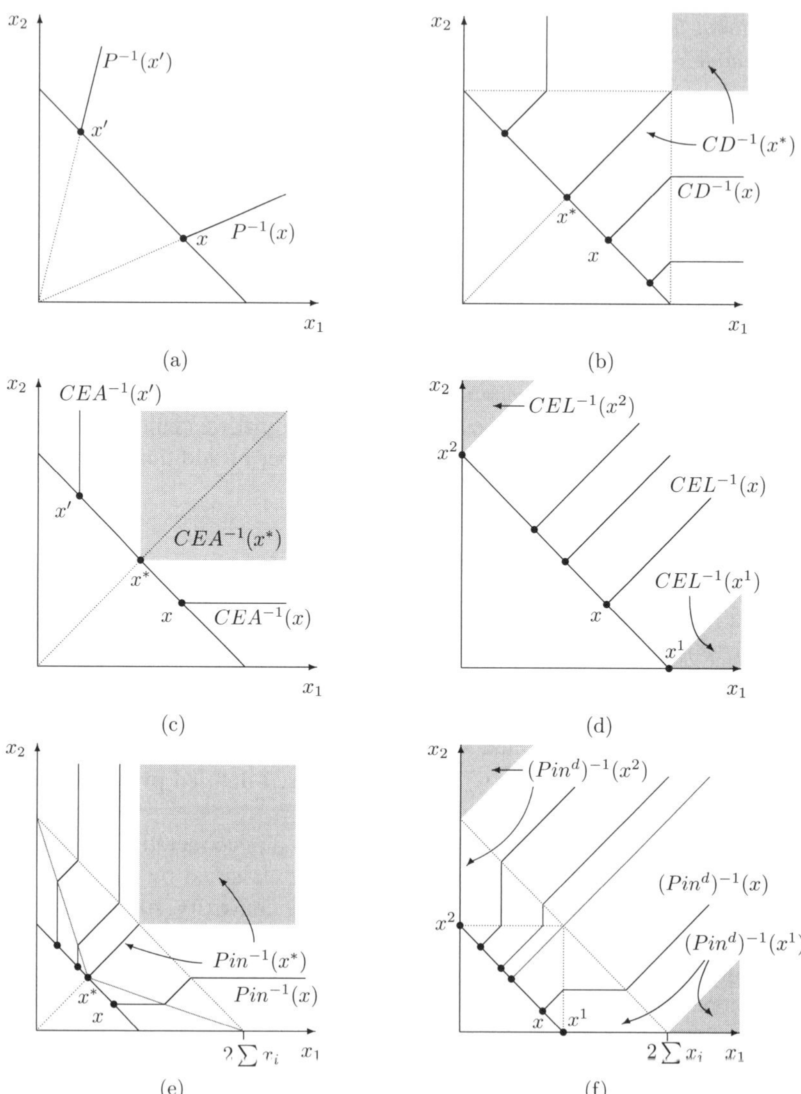

Figure 4.14: **Inverse sets for six rules.** For some rules, an inverse set may have a nonempty interior (the shaded regions). An award vector for which that is the case is denoted x^* if it has equal coordinates, x^1 or x^2 if it is on the first or on the second axis. (a) Proportional rule. (b) Concede-and-divide. (c) Constrained equal awards rule. (d) Constrained equal losses rule. (e) Piniles' rule. (f) Rule defined as Piniles' rule except that the constrained equal losses rule is substituted for the constrained equal awards in the formula.

Let us formulate as an axiom the requirement that the inverse sets of a rule all take a pre-specified shape. Examples are the following:

Convex inverse sets: For each $x \in \mathbb{R}_+^N$, $S^{-1}(x)$ is a convex set.

Star-shaped inverse sets: For each $x \in \mathbb{R}_+^N$, $S^{-1}(x)$ is a star-shaped set with x at the center of the star.

Cone-shaped inverse sets: For each $x \in \mathbb{R}_+^N$, $S^{-1}(x)$ is a cone with x as the vertex of the cone.

As we just noted, an inverse set may have a nonempty interior, and it is meaningful to require of a rule that this be the case, namely that its inverse sets be curves. Then additional requirements can be imposed on the shapes of these curves that are counterparts of the requirements we imposed on the shapes of paths of awards. Let $N \equiv \{1, 2\}$ and $c \in \mathbb{R}_+^N$ be such that $c_1 \leq c_2$. One is that for each $x \in \mathbb{R}_+^N$, the **inverse set of x be a convex curve**; another is that it **be a concave curve**. More general requirements are that it be **visible from below** or **visible from above**, either **from x** or **from the point at infinity in the direction (1, 1)**. For more than two claimants, it is on the projections of these curves onto two-dimensional subspaces that these requirements can be imposed. In Section 8.3, we will introduce invariance requirements that can be seen as members of the family. One is that the inverse set of x be star-shaped with the point at infinity in the direction $(1, 1)$ as the center of the star; the other is that it be star-shaped with the point at infinity in the direction of x as the center of the star.[17]

[17] Under the names of "uniform-increase-in-claims invariance" and "proportional increase in claims invariance," respectively.

CHAPTER 5

Claims Truncation Invariance and Minimal Rights First

A number of requirements of invariance or covariance of the awards vector chosen by a rule with respect to certain operations performed on the parameters of a problem under consideration have played a central role in the theory reviewed here. Each of these properties requires either that the awards vector the rule chooses for it be the same as the awards vector it chooses for the problem that results when subjected to such an operation, or that these two awards vectors be related in the manner in which the two problems themselves are related.

Invariance and covariance properties often reflect the idea that if two ways of looking at the situation in which people find themselves, or a change in this situation, are legitimate, they should result in the same recommendations. When two perspectives that one can take lead to different outcomes and justifications are found for both, a conflict may result. Thus, these properties are requirements of robustness to choices of equivalent, or equally valid, perspectives.

We begin their study in this chapter. We first consider the requirement on a rule that the awards vector it chooses for a problem not be affected by truncating claims at the endowment: this vector can be obtained either directly, by applying the rule to the problem, or in two steps, by first truncating claims at the endowment and then applying the rule.

Our second requirement has the same format: the awards vector chosen for a problem should be obtainable either directly, by applying the rule to it, or in two steps, by first assigning to each claimant their minimal right, revising claims and endowment accordingly, thereby obtaining a "second round" problem, and then applying the rule to this problem to calculate a second installment of awards.

The implications of each of these requirements can be described very generally. For two claimants, when imposed together and jointly with *equal treatment of equals*, we are led to concede-and-divide. For more agents, many other rules qualify, however.

5.1 CLAIMS TRUNCATION INVARIANCE

Recall that the "truncated claim of a claimant in a problem" is the minimum of the claim and the endowment. Here, we require of a rule that, for each problem, truncating claims at the endowment not affect the awards vector it chooses.

Given $(c, E) \in \mathcal{C}^N$, we have already introduced the notation $t_i(c, E) \equiv \min\{c_i, E\}$ and $t(c, E) \equiv (t_i(c, E))_{i \in N}$. Obviously, the pair $(t(c, E), E)$ is a well-defined problem.

Claims truncation invariance: For each $(c, E) \in \mathcal{C}^N$, we have $S(c, E) = S(t(c, E), E)$.

How appealing the property is depends on the context. Estate division is one in which it makes much sense: if the amount bequeathed to an heir is larger than the estate, a mistake must have been made (as was in fact suggested by some early authors in their discussion of the examples in the Talmud). In Chapter 14, we will also give an argument in favor of the property based on game-theoretic considerations (Theorem 14.3). In the context of bankruptcy, it is not as compelling, however. Consider two people who have invested in a business whose liquidation value is to be distributed. If they have both invested more than its eventual worth, shouldn't the one who has taken greater risks receive more, or at least be allowed to receive more? An implication of our invariance property together with *equal treatment of equals* is equality of their awards.[1]

Among the rules of Chapter 2, the following satisfy the property: the constrained equal awards, Talmud (and thus concede-and-divide; Figure 5.1b), random arrival, and minimal overlap rules. On the other hand, the proportional, constrained equal losses (Figure 5.1c), constrained egalitarian, and Piniles' rules violate it.

If we feel strongly that *claims truncation invariance* should be imposed, we can of course redefine the domain and only consider problems in which no claim is larger than the endowment (an interesting domain studied in Section 15.1). Equivalently, we can define a claims problem to be a pair $(c, E) \in [0, 1]^N \times \mathbb{R}_+$, where for each $i \in N$, c_i is interpreted as the percentage of the endowment claimed by agent i. Again, this restriction might be particularly meaningful in the context of estate division because wills often specify proportions of the estate that different heirs should receive, not absolute amounts.

A weak version of *claims truncation invariance* says that there is $k \geq 1$ such that for each $(c, E) \in \mathcal{C}^N$, $S(c, E) = S(t(c, kE), E)$. Let us refer to it as **weak claims truncation invariance.**[2]

[1] The idea of truncation is discussed by Aumann and Maschler (1985). *Claims truncation invariance* appears in Curiel, Maschler, and Tijs (1987), and was first proposed as a formal axiom by Dagan and Volij (1993). By analogy to a related property of solutions to the bargaining problem formulated by Nash (1950), these authors call it "independence of irrelevant claims."

[2] This property is introduced by Flores-Szwagrzak and Treibich (2016) under the name of "maximal reasonable claim."

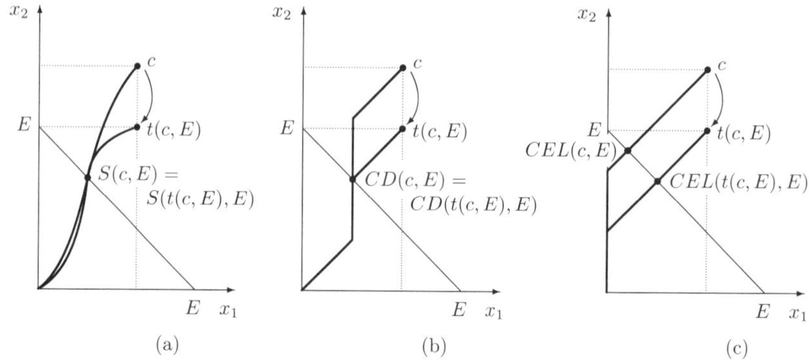

Figure 5.1: **Claims truncation invariance.** Let $N \equiv \{1, 2\}$ and $(c, E) \in \mathcal{C}^N$. (a) If a rule S is *claims truncation invariant*, and since in the problem $(c, E) \in \mathcal{C}^N$ represented here, $c_2 > E$, truncating c_2 at E does not affect the chosen awards vector. Thus, the path of awards of S for $t(c, E)$ meets its path for c on the line of equation $\sum x_i = E$, as shown. (b) Concede-and-divide satisfies the property. (c) The constrained equal losses rule violates it.

A characterization.

Figure 5.2a shows that if a two-claimant rule is *claims truncation invariant*, its paths of awards are related in a particular way; the implications of this axiom can be completely described:

family of rules characterized

Theorem 5.1 *For $|N| = 2$, say $N \equiv \{1, 2\}$. A rule S is claims truncation invariant if and only if it can be described in terms of the following networks of paths:*

(a) a path $F \subset \mathbb{R}^N_+$ that, for each $E \in \mathbb{R}_+$, meets the line of equation $x_1 + x_2 = E$ exactly once;
(b1) for each $c_2 \in \mathbb{R}_+$, a path $G^2(c_2) \subset \{x \in \mathbb{R}^N_+ \colon \sum x_i \geq c_2\}$ that, for each $E \geq c_2$, meets the line of equation $\sum x_i = E$ exactly once, and is bounded above by the line of equation $x_2 = c_2$;
(b2) for each $c_1 \in \mathbb{R}_+$, a path $G^1(c_1) \subset \{x \in \mathbb{R}^N_+ \colon \sum x_i \geq c_1\}$ that, for each $E \geq c_1$, meets the line of equation $\sum x_i = E$ exactly once, and is bounded to the right by the line of equation $x_1 = c_1$; and
(c) for each $c \in \{x \in \mathbb{R}^N_+ \colon \max\{c_i\} \leq \sum x_i \leq \sum c_i\}$ a path $H(c) \subset \mathbb{R}^N_+$ that, for each $E \in \left[\max\{c_i\}, \sum c_i\right]$, meets the line of equation $\sum x_i = E$ exactly once, and is bounded above by c,

these paths being used as follows: for each $c \in \mathbb{R}^N_+$ such that $c_1 \geq c_2$, the path for c follows F until the line of equation $\sum x_i = c_2$, then follows $G^2(c_2)$ until the line of equation $\sum x_i = c_1$, then follows $H(c)$ until c; also for each $c \in \mathbb{R}^N_+$ such that $c_1 \leq c_2$, the path for c follows F until the line of equation $\sum x_i = c_1$, follows $G^1(c_1)$ until the line of equation $\sum x_i = c_2$, then follows $H(c)$ until c.

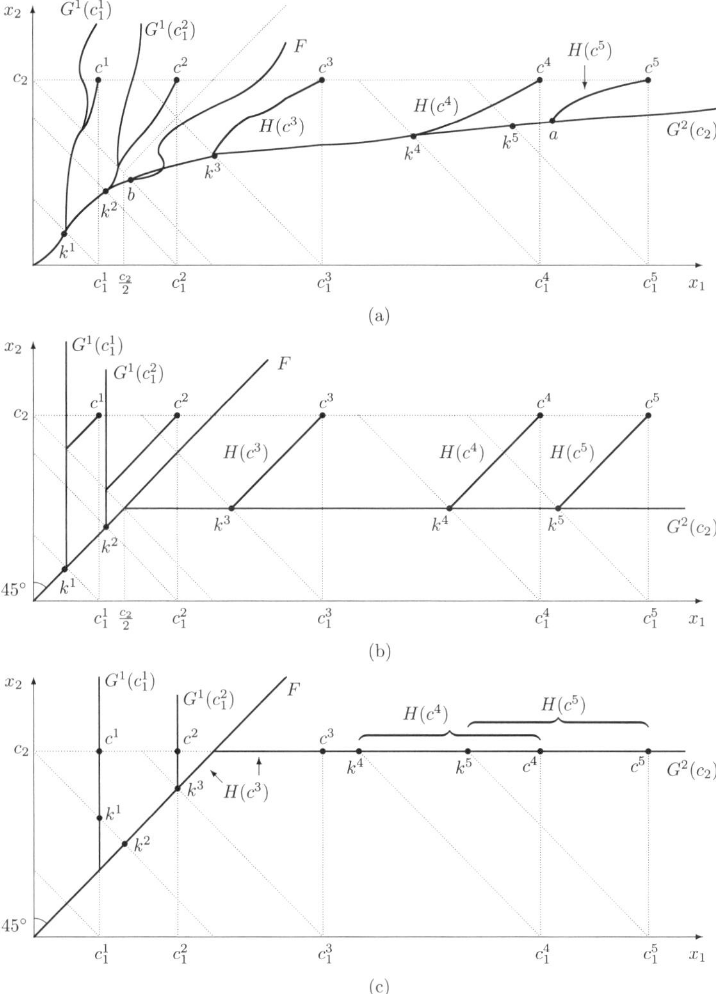

Figure 5.2: **Paths of awards of rules satisfying claims truncation invariance.** Let $N \equiv \{1, 2\}$ and agent 2's claim be fixed at c_2. (a) The path of awards of a rule S satisfying *claims truncation invariance* for a typical $c \in \mathbb{R}_+^N$ such that $c_1 > c_2$ first follows a "primary path," F, emanating from the origin, until the line of equation $x_1 + x_2 = c_2$ is reached; it then follows a "secondary path for c_2," $G^2(c_2)$, that emanates from that line and it does so up to the line of equation $x_1 + x_2 = c_1$; it ends with a "tertiary path for c," $H(c)$, a path that emanates from that line and ends at c. For example, the path for c^3 follows F from the origin to b, then $G^2(c_2)$ until k^3, and it concludes with $H(c^3)$. (b) Illustrating these definitions for concede-and-divide: its principal path F is the 45° line; given $c_2 \in \mathbb{R}_+$, its secondary path for c_2, $G^2(c_2)$, is the horizontal half-line $\{(\frac{c_2}{2}, \frac{c_2}{2}) + t(1, 0) : t \in \mathbb{R}_+\}$; given $c^3 \equiv (c_1^3, c_2)$, its tertiary path for c^3, $H(c^3)$, is seg$[k^3, c^3]$. (c) Illustrating the definitions for the constrained equal awards rule: F is also the 45° line; given $c_2 \in \mathbb{R}_+$, $G^2(c_2)$ consists of seg$[k^2, (c_2, c_2)]$ together with the horizontal half-line $\{(c_2, c_2) + t(1, 0) : t \in \mathbb{R}_+\}$; given $c^3 \equiv (c_1^3, c_2)$, $H(c^3)$ is bro.seg$[k^3, (c_2, c_2), c^3]$. For each of these three rules, we also show the secondary paths for two values of agent 1's claim, c_1^1 and c_1^2.

We call F the **primary path of** S; for each $i \in \{1, 2\}$ and each $c_i \in \mathbb{R}_+$, we call $G^i(c_i)$ the **secondary path of** S **for** c_i; for each $c \in \mathbb{R}^N_+$, we call $H(c)$ the **tertiary path of** S **for** c.

Figure 5.2a shows a generic case and Figure 5.2b,c identifies the three types of paths for concede-and-divide and the constrained equal awards rule respectively.

None of the primary, secondary, or tertiary paths need be monotone or even continuous. Also, given $i \in \{1, 2\}$ and $c_i, c'_i \in \mathbb{R}_+$, the secondary paths $G^i(c_i)$ and $G^i(c'_i)$ need not be ordered as c_i and c'_i are: $c_1 < c'_1$ does not imply that $G^1(c_1)$ is everywhere on or to the right of $G^1(c'_1)$; $c_2 < c'_2$ does not imply that $G^2(c_2)$ is everywhere on or below $G^2(c'_2)$. Similar statements can be made about tertiary paths. Also, the secondary paths need not attach to the primary path and the tertiary paths need not attach to the secondary paths. Finally, a secondary path may partly overlap with the primary path and a tertiary path may partly overlap with a secondary path (this is the case for the secondary path for c^5 in Figure 5.2a, between k^5 and a; in fact, in Figure 5.2c, tertiary paths are all entirely contained in secondary paths).

Proof: (of Theorem 5.1) It is easy to see that any rule satisfying the properties listed in the theorem satisfies *claims truncation invariance*. Conversely, let S be a rule satisfying this property. Let F be the locus of the choice made by S for the problem $((E, E), E)$ for $E \in \mathbb{R}_+$. For each $c_2 \in \mathbb{R}_+$, let $G^2(c_2)$ be the locus of the choice made by S for the problem $((c_1, c_2), c_1)$ for $c_1 \in [c_2, \infty[$, namely $G^2(c_2) \equiv \{S((c_1, c_2), c_1)\colon c_1 \in [c_2, \infty[\}$. For each $c_1 \in \mathbb{R}_+$, let $G^1(c_1)$ be defined in a similar way. It is immediate that the loci F, $\{G^1(c_1)\}_{c_1 \in \mathbb{R}_+}$, and $\{G^2(c_2)\}_{c_2 \in \mathbb{R}_+}$ have the properties required of primary and secondary paths listed in the statement in the theorem. Now, let $c \in \mathbb{R}^N_+$. For each $E \leq \min\{c_i\}$, by *claims truncation invariance* we obtain that $S(c) = S((E, E), E)$, that is, $S(c) \in F(c)$; if $\min\{c_i\} < E \leq \max\{c_i\}$, by *claims truncation invariance*, we obtain that if $c_1 < c_2$, $S(c) = S((c_1, E), E)$, that is, $S(c) \in G^1(c_1)$, and if $c_1 > c_2$, that $S(c) = S((E, c_2), E)$, that is, $S(c) \in G^2(c_2)$. If $\max\{c_i\} < E$, no restriction applies, so no constraints are placed on the tertiary path $H(c)$ except for the conditions stated under (c). □

∗ `Relating axioms` ♦ Here are the restrictions that should be imposed on the paths defined in the theorem for S to satisfy basic additional properties. For *equal treatment of equals*, F should be the 45° line. For *anonymity*, the network of paths $\{G^1(c_1)\}_{c_1 \in \mathbb{R}_+}$, $\{G^2(c_1)\}_{c_2 \in \mathbb{R}_+}$ and $\{H(c)\}_{c \in \mathbb{R}^N_+}$ should be symmetric with respect to the 45° line. For *endowment monotonicity*, these paths should be monotone curves. For *endowment continuity*, they should be continuous curves, secondary paths should attach to the primary path, and tertiary paths should attach to the secondary paths. For *claim monotonicity*, they should be ordered as claims are. ♦ If a rule is *claims truncation invariant*, it cannot be *strictly claim monotonic*. Indeed, if an agent's claim, initially larger than the endowment, increases, their award has to remain the same. ♦ *Equal treatment of equal groups* and *claims truncation invariance* are incompatible.[3] This is shown by the following example: Let $N \equiv \{1, 2, 3\}$ and $(c, E) \in \mathcal{C}^N$ be equal to $((1, 1, 2), 1)$. If a rule S satisfies *equal treatment of equal groups* then, introducing $x \equiv S(c, E)$, we have $(*)$ $x_1 + x_2 = x_3$. Note that $t(c, E) = (1, 1, 1)$. If S also satisfies *claims truncation invariance*, then $x = S((1, 1, 1), 1)$. Then by *equal treatment of equal groups* (here, *equal treatment of equals* would suffice), $x_1 = x_2 = x_3 = \frac{1}{3}$, which contradicts $(*)$.

By a simple adaptation of the proof of Theorem 5.1 one obtains a characterization of the family of rules satisfying *weak claims truncation invariance*.

5.2 MINIMAL RIGHTS FIRST

Recall that the minimal right of a claimant in a problem is what is left of the endowment after all other claimants have been fully compensated if possible; it is 0 otherwise. Awarding each claimant their minimal right is of course always feasible (Section 3.4). Our next requirement on a rule is that, for each problem, it be possible to calculate the awards vector either directly or in two steps, as follows: first, assign to each claimant their minimal right; then, after revising claims down by the minimal rights, distribute the residual endowment. The revised claims are nonnegative and their sum is at least as large as that remainder, so the problem of the second step is well defined:[4] Our notation, previously introduced, is $m_i(c, E) \equiv \max\{E - \sum_{N \setminus \{i\}} c_j, 0\}$ and $m(c, E) \equiv (m_i(c, E))_{i \in N}$.

Minimal rights first: For each $(c, E) \in \mathcal{C}^N$,

$$S(c, E) = m(c, E) + S\left(c - m(c, E), E - \sum m_i(c, E)\right).$$

An easy calculation shows that if two claimants have positive minimal rights, after being revised down, their claims are equal to the deficit.

Figure 5.3 shows a simple geometric construction that helps check whether a rule satisfies the property, and it also illustrates a violation.

Among the rules of Chapter 2, the following satisfy the property: the constrained equal losses (Figure 5.4a), Talmud (and thus, concede-and-divide), random arrival, and minimal overlap rules. The proportional and constrained equal awards (Figure 5.4b) rules do not. For the proportional rule, consider the following example. Let $N \equiv \{1, 2\}$ and $(c, E) \in \mathcal{C}^N$ be equal to $((5, 15), 12)$. We have $P(c, E) = (3, 9)$. Minimal rights are $\max\{12 - 15, 0\} = 0$ and

[3] Chambers and Thomson (2002).

[4] These facts were established in Section 3.4. Even if a rule violates the property, the vector appearing on the right-hand side of the equality is an awards vector. *Minimal rights first* is introduced by Curiel, Maschler, and Tijs (1987) under the name of the "minimal rights property." Dagan (1996) refers to it as "v-separability," and Herrero and Villar (1998) as "composition from minimal rights." The concept is adapted by Luttens (2010) to a production model in which each agent is described in terms of two parameters: skill and effort level. For another study of this model, see Giménez-Gómez and Peris (2015).

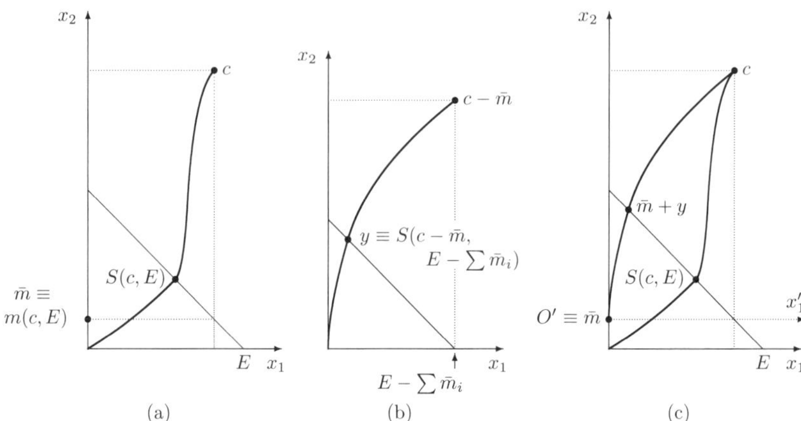

Figure 5.3: **Illustrating a violation of minimal rights first.** (a) Let $N \equiv \{1, 2\}$ and $(c, E) \in \mathcal{C}^N$ be such that $c_1 = \min\{c_i\} < E < \max\{c_i\}$. This panel shows the awards vector chosen for this problem by a rule S, $S(c, E)$, and the calculation of its vector of minimal rights, $\bar{m} \equiv m(c, E)$ (only claimant 2's minimal right is positive). (b) Depicted here is the problem derived from (c, E) by attributing minimal rights, revising claims down by these "first-round" awards, and revising the endowment down by their sum. The rule would pick y for this problem, a "second-round" awards vector. (c) Returning to (c, E), we move the origin up to $O' \equiv \bar{m}$, and we obtain above the translated axes a copy of the problem of panel (b). The line of equation $\sum x_i = E$ in the original axes is also the line of equation $\sum x_i = E - \sum m_i(c, E)$ in the translated axes. The sum of the first-round and second-round awards vectors, $\bar{m} + y$ in the original axes, differs from $S(c, E)$. Thus, S violates *minimal rights first.*

$\max\{12 - 5, 0\} = 7$. The revised claims vector is $(5, 15) - (0, 7) = (5, 8)$ and the residual endowment is $12 - (0 + 7) = 5$. Finally $P((5, 8), 5) = (\frac{25}{13}, \frac{40}{13})$. It remains to observe, focusing on agent 1's awards in the two scenarios, that $3 \neq 0 + \frac{25}{13}$.

Let $c \in \mathbb{R}^N_+$. Then for each endowment E, there is $E' \leq E$ for which the vector of minimal rights of (c, E) coincides with the awards vector the constrained equal losses rule would choose for (c, E'). Thus, and this can be seen in Figure 3.1 for two claimants, the path followed by the vector of minimal rights as the endowment increases from 0 to $\sum c_i$ coincides with the path of awards of the constrained equal losses rule for c. This observation suggests that the constrained equal losses rule satisfies *minimal rights first*, and this is indeed the case, as we already pointed out. Section 6.2 gives a proof along those lines, but for two claimants, we already saw an illustration of this fact on Figure 5.4a.[5]

[5] Another proof exploiting the relation between this property and *composition up*, defined later, is presented there.

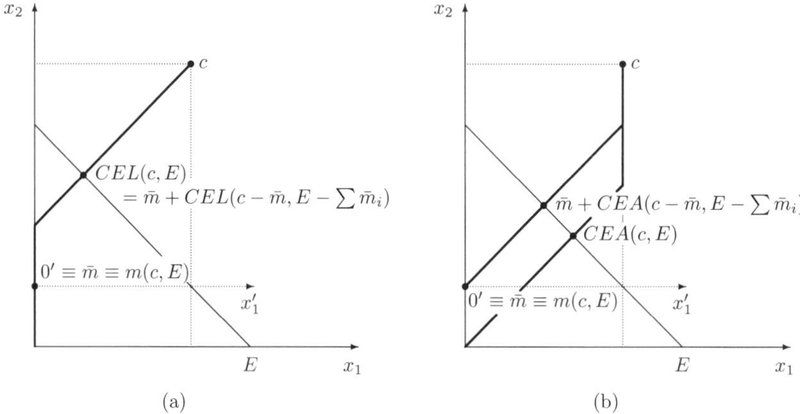

Figure 5.4: **Two rules and minimal rights first.** The notation is that of Figure 5.3. Let $N \equiv \{1, 2\}$. (a) The constrained equal losses rule satisfies *minimal rights first*. This panel represents a problem $(c, E) \in \mathcal{C}^N$ for which $CEL(c, E)$ is seen to be equal to $m(c, E) + CEL(c - m(c, E), E - \sum m_i(c, E))$. (b) The constrained equal awards rule does not. This panel shows a problem $(c, E) \in \mathcal{C}^N$ such that $CEA(c, E) \neq m(c, E) + CEA(c - m(c, E), E - \sum m_i(c, E))$.

We noted earlier that reasons why one may feel that *claims truncation invariance* should be imposed could also lead to specifying the relevant domain of problems as those for which no claim is larger than the endowment. Similarly here, on the subdomain of problems for which the sum of the $n - 1$ smallest claims is at least as large as the endowment, all minimal rights are 0, and if one feels strongly enough that *minimal rights first* should be imposed, it may be natural to limit attention to this subdomain.

A parameterized version of *minimal rights first* is obtained by applying the usual formula for a claimant's minimal right under the assumption that the endowment is only equal to a proportion $k \leq 1$ of its actual value; the statement of the axiom is otherwise unchanged. Formally, **weak minimal rights first** says that there is $k \leq 1$ such that for each $(c, E) \in \mathcal{C}^N$, $S(c, E) = m(c, kE) + S(c - m(c, kE), E - \sum m_i(c, kE))$. If k is small, not much of a step is taken in the direction of *minimal rights first*.

`* Relating axioms` ♦ *Equal treatment of equal groups* and *minimal rights first* are incompatible.[6] This is shown by the following example: Let $N \equiv \{1, 2, 3\}$ and $(c, E) \in \mathcal{C}^N$ be equal to $((1, 1, 2), 3)$. If a rule S satisfies *equal treatment of equal groups* then, introducing $x \equiv S(c, E)$, we have $(*)$ $x_1 + x_2 = x_3$. Note that $m(c, E) = (0, 0, 1)$. By *equal treatment of equal groups* (here, *equal treatment of equals* would suffice), $S((1 - 0, 1 - 0, 2 - 1), 3 - 1) =$

[6] Chambers and Thomson (2002).

$(\frac{2}{3}, \frac{2}{3}, \frac{2}{3})$. If S also satisfies *minimal rights first*, then $x = m(c, E) + S((1 - 0, 1 - 0, 2 - 1), 3 - 1) = (0, 0, 1) + (\frac{2}{3}, \frac{2}{3}, \frac{2}{3})$, which contradicts $(*)$.

Characterizations. The remainder of this chapter is devoted to characterizations. The first one involves *equal treatment of equals* and the two relational invariance properties introduced in this chapter. It highlights concede-and-divide:[7]

concede-and-divide characterized

Theorem 5.2 *For $|N| = 2$. Concede-and-divide is the only rule satisfying equal treatment of equals, claims truncation invariance, and minimal rights first.*

Proof: We already know that concede-and-divide satisfies the properties listed in the theorem. Conversely, let $N \equiv \{1, 2\}$ say, and S be a rule on $\mathcal{C}^N$ satisfying these properties. Let $(c, E) \in \mathcal{C}^N$ and, without loss of generality, suppose that $c_1 \leq c_2$.

Case 1: $E \leq c_1$ (Figure 5.5a). Truncated claims are $\min\{c_1, E\} = \min\{c_2, E\} = E$. By *claims truncation invariance*, $S(c, E) = S((E, E), E)$.

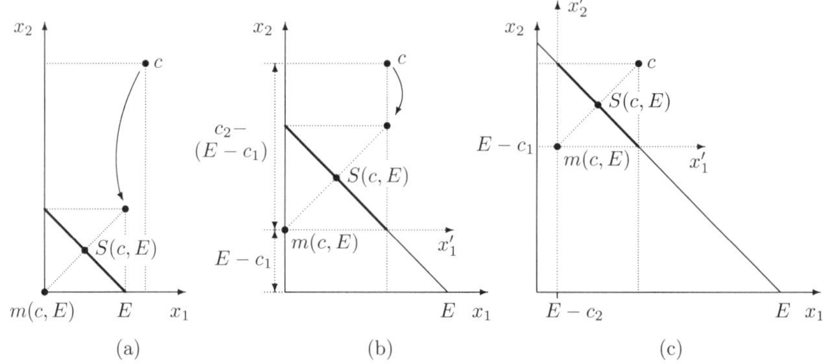

Figure 5.5: **Characterizing concede-and-divide** (Theorem 5.2). Let $N \equiv \{1, 2\}$ and $c \in \mathbb{R}^N_+$ be such that $c_1 < c_2$. We consider a rule S satisfying the properties listed in the theorem. (a) Case 1: $E \leq c_1$. Truncated claims are equal (and equal to the endowment): S chooses equal division. (b) Case 2: $c_1 < E \leq c_2$. Only agent 2's minimal right is positive. After revising this agent's down by agent 2's minimal right and truncating their revised claim, we obtain a problem in which both claims are equal (and equal to the residual endowment): S divides this remainder equally. (c) Case 3: $c_2 < E$. Both minimal rights are positive. When revised down by the minimal rights, both claims are equal (and equal to the residual endowment): S divides this remainder equally.

[7] Theorem 5.2 is due to Dagan (1996).

By *equal treatment of equals*, $S((E, E), E) = (\frac{E}{2}, \frac{E}{2}) = CD(c, E)$. Altogether, $S(c, E) = CD(c, E)$.

Case 2: $c_1 < E \leq c_2$ (Figure 5.5b). Minimal rights are $\max\{E-c_2, 0\} = 0$ and $\max\{E - c_1, 0\} = E - c_1$. Claims revised down by these quantities are c_1 and $c_2-(E-c_1)$. The residual endowment is $E-(E-c_1) = c_1$. After truncation at that amount, claims are $\min\{c_1, c_1\} = c_1$ and $\min\{c_2 - (E - c_1), c_1\} = c_1$. By *claims truncation invariance* and *equal treatment of equals*, $S((c_1, c_1), c_1) = (\frac{c_1}{2}, \frac{c_1}{2})$. By *minimal rights first*, $S(c, E) = (0, E - c_1) + (\frac{c_1}{2}, \frac{c_1}{2}) = (\frac{c_1}{2}, E - \frac{c_1}{2}) = CD(c, E)$.

Case 3: $c_2 < E$ (Figure 5.5c). Minimal rights are $\max\{E - c_2, 0\} = E - c_2$ and $\max\{E - c_1, 0\} = E - c_1$. Claims revised down by these quantities are $c_1 - (E - c_2)$ and $c_2 - (E - c_1)$. They are equal, and equal to the residual endowment, $E - (E - c_2) - (E - c_1) = c_1 + c_2 - E$. By *equal treatment of equals*, $S((c_1 + c_2 - E, c_1 + c_2 - E), c_1 + c_2 - E) = (\frac{c_1+c_2-E}{2}, \frac{c_1+c_2-E}{2})$. By *minimal rights first*, $S(c, E) = (E - c_1, E - c_2) + (\frac{c_1+c_2-E}{2}, \frac{c_1+c_2-E}{2}) = (\frac{E-c_1+c_2}{2}, \frac{E+c_1-c_2}{2}) = CD(c, E)$. □

Thus *claims truncation invariance* and *minimal rights first* are compatible but for two claimants, their conjunction is very restrictive: Theorem 5.2 says that in that case, only one rule satisfies the two properties as well as *equal treatment of equals*. In general however, a great variety of rules satisfy all three properties. For example, independently of the number of claimants, the Talmud, random arrival, and minimal overlap rules do. (This multiplicity does not contradict uniqueness for two claimants because then all three rules coincide with concede-and-divide, as we have seen.)

`* On the independence of axioms in Theorem 5.2.` ✦ The constrained equal losses rule satisfies *equal treatment of equals* and *minimal rights first* (Figure 5.4a), but not *claims truncation invariance* (Figure 5.1b). ✦ The constrained equal awards rule satisfies *equal treatment of equals* and *claims truncation invariance*, but not *minimal rights first* (Figure 5.4b). ✦ If we drop *equal treatment of equals* but add *homogeneity*, we derive a characterization of the family of weighted concede-and-divide rules (Section 3.6). This is our next theorem. We follow it by a characterization of the even wider family of rules obtained by only requiring *claims truncation invariance* and *minimal rights first*:[8]

Theorem 5.3 *For $|N| = 2$. The weighted concede-and-divide rules are the only rules satisfying homogeneity, claims truncation invariance, and minimal rights first.* weighted concede-and-divide characterized

[8] Theorem 5.3 is due to Hokari and Thomson (2003).

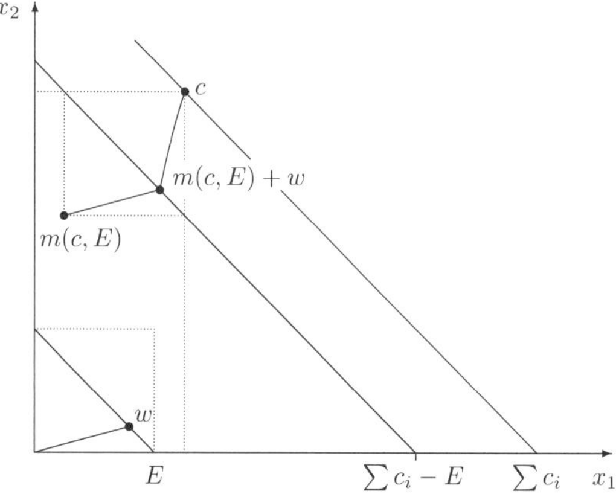

Figure 5.6: **Characterizing the family of weighted concede-and-divide rules**. Starting from Theorem 5.2, if we drop *equal treatment of equals* but add *homogeneity*, we obtain a family of rules parameterized by a point in the simplex (Theorem 5.3). To identify a rule satisfying the revised list of properties, it suffices to apply it to any problem in which the endowment is at most as large as the smaller claim. Calling w the choice made for the problem $((E, E), E)$, we deduce the choice made for any problem in which the shortfall is E: it is $m(c, E) + w$. By *homogeneity*, we conclude that the rule is the weighted concede-and-divide rule with relative weights given by the coordinates of w.

Proof: We obtain the proof by a simple adaptation of that of Theorem 5.2, so we will be a little less formal. First, we observe that all weighted concede-and-divide rules satisfy the three properties listed in the theorem. Conversely, let S be a rule satisfying the properties. Let $N \equiv \{1, 2\}$ say, $(c, E) \in \mathcal{C}^N$ and, without loss of generality, suppose that $c_1 < c_2$. The calculation of the minimal rights in (c, E) is as in the proof of Theorem 5.2. We distinguish the same three cases. In Case 1 ($E \leq c_1$), we cannot conclude that $S((E, E), E)$ is equal division anymore, so let us call w the choice S makes: $w \equiv S((E, E), E)$ (Figure 5.6). For any endowment no larger than c_1, after truncating claims, we obtain a problem that is a scale reduction or expansion of the one just solved. Thus, by *homogeneity*, S chooses the awards vector that is proportional to w. In Case 2 ($c_1 < E \leq c_2$), after attributing minimal rights and subsequently truncating claims at the revised endowment, we end up with a problem that is identical to the one obtained for the largest endowment covered under Case 1 (when $E = c_1$). In Case 3 ($c_2 < E$), after attributing minimal rights, we obtain a problem that is identical to one covered in Case 1 (the one for which the endowment is $\sum c_i - E$); no truncation is needed then. □

✦ `On the independence of axioms in Theorem 5.2` (continued). If we drop *equal treatment of equals* but do not add *homogeneity*, a characterization is still possible. The paths of awards of a rule S that is only required

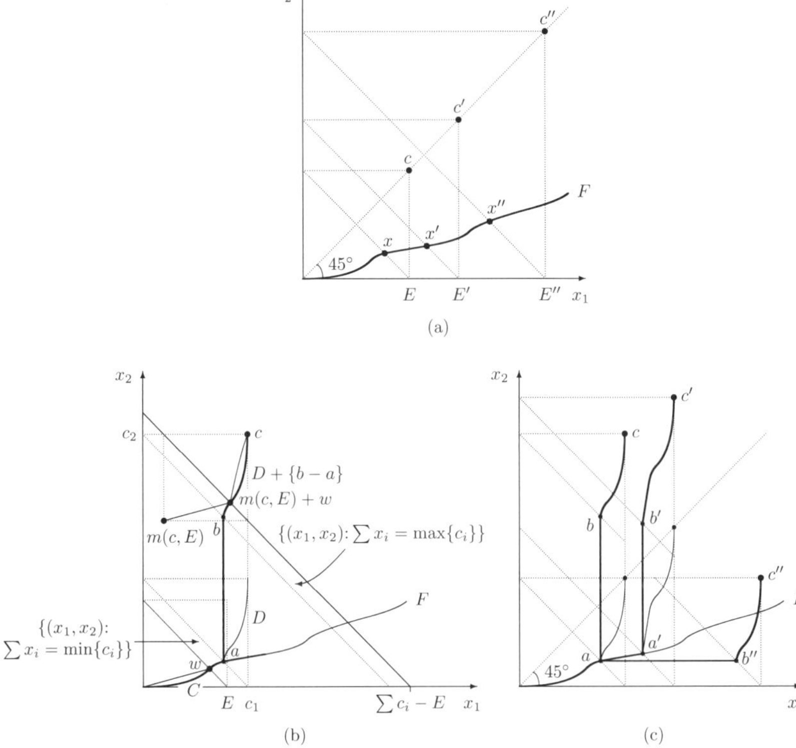

Figure 5.7: **Characterizing a family of nonhomogeneous rules generalizing concede-and-divide.** If in Theorem 5.2, we drop *equal treatment of equals*, we obtain a family of rules parameterized by an unbounded "master path" emanating from the origin. (a) We identify the master path associated with a rule in the family by solving all problems for which both claims are equal to the endowment. It is the locus F of the point chosen by the rule for such a problem as the common value of all three parameters runs from 0 to ∞. On this panel, we explicitly indicate three values, E, E', and E''. (b) Then the path of awards for a typical claims vector $c \in \mathbb{R}_+^N$, where $N \equiv \{1, 2\}$ and $c_1 < c_2$ say, consists of the union of (i) the curve C that is the part of F that lies below the line of equation $\sum x_i = c_1$, (ii) the vertical segment from the point of C that belongs to that line, the point denoted a, to the line of equation $\sum x_i = c_2$ – the highest point on that segment is denoted b – and (iii) the symmetric image of C with respect to the line of equation $\sum x_i = c_1$ (the curve D), translated vertically by $b - a = (0, c_2 - c_1)$ (the curve $D + \{b - a\}$). (c) This panel shows how to derive the paths of awards for two additional claims vectors: one above the 45° line, c', and one below the 45° line, c''. The path for c'', whose ordinate happens to be equal to the abscissa of c, contains a horizontal segment (seg$[a, b'']$) instead of a vertical segment.

to satisfy *claims truncation invariance* and *minimal rights first* are obtained as follows (Figure 5.7). Again, let $N \equiv \{1,2\}$. First, we identify the locus of the awards vector chosen by S for all problems in which both claims are equal to the endowment, and the endowment runs from 0 to ∞ (Figure 5.7a). This locus is an unbounded path – let us denote it by F – emanating from the origin. It does not have to be monotonic or even continuous, although the example depicted in the figure is monotonic and therefore continuous. The only requirement is that for each $E \in \mathbb{R}_+$, it meet the line of equation $\sum x_i = E$ exactly once. (This is as in Theorem 5.1.) Now, let $c \in \mathbb{R}^N_+$ and suppose first that $c_1 \leq c_2$. Then the path of S for c consists of (Figure 5.7b):

(i) the restriction C of F to the set of points $x \in \mathbb{R}^N_+$ satisfying $\sum x_i \leq \min\{c_i\} = c_1$. In Figure 5.7b, w designates its generic point, for a typical endowment $E < c_1$, and a is the point reached when $E = c_1$,

(ii) a vertical segment from a to the line of equation $\sum x_i = \max\{c_i\} = c_2$ – let b denote the point where the segment meets the line – and

(iii) the symmetric image of C with respect to the line of equation $\sum x_i = \min\{c_i\}$ (the curve D in Figure 5.7b) translated by $b-a$ (the curve $D+\{b-a\}$ in the figure).

Figure 5.7c shows the construction of the paths of S for two other claims vectors, c' and c''. For c'', which is below the 45° line, the vertical segment is replaced by a horizontal segment, seg$[a, b'']$ (note that $c''_2 = c_1$), defined in the same manner.

If F is the horizontal axis, the rule associated with F is $SP^{1\prec 2}$; if F is the vertical axis, we obtain $SP^{2\prec 1}$; if F is the ray in the direction $w \in \Delta^N$, we obtain CD^w; if F is the 45° line, we obtain CD itself.

The proof of the characterization is almost the same as that of Theorem 5.3. The main difference is that now the calibration of a rule requires infinitely many test problems.

CHAPTER 6

Composition Down and Composition Up

In this chapter we consider situations in which, after an awards vector has been chosen for some problem by applying some rule, the endowment changes. How should the change be handled? We propose two ways of looking at the new situation. One is simply to ignore the initial choice and to apply the rule to the new problem. The other is to take as point of departure the initial choice and to reapply the rule to take care of the difference between the initial and final endowments. Both approaches appear legitimate and we can well imagine that people will disagree about which is better depending upon the direction in which their assignments are affected. A rule that delivers the same outcome is more likely to be robust to such changes. Thus, we require that the two perspectives lead to the same awards vector.

We apply the idea to two scenarios, obtaining two invariance requirements. In one scenario, the endowment decreases; in the other, it increases.

We derive general characterizations of the families of rules satisfying one or the other of these requirements. When they are complemented with others introduced in earlier chapters, and when they are imposed jointly, additional characterizations of narrower families and of individual rules result.

6.1 COMPOSITION DOWN

Consider the following situation: a rule having been applied to divide the liquidation value of a bankrupt firm among its creditors, the firm's assets are reevaluated and found to be worth less than initially thought. Perhaps their market value has decreased, or certain assets turn out to be inaccessible. In dealing with this change, we have two options. The first one is to cancel the first division and to apply the rule to obtain awards for the revised value. The second is, using as claims the awards calculated on the basis of the original value, to reapply the rule to divide the revised value; after all, these awards are commitments that had been made but cannot be honored in the end, and it is sensible to give these commitments the status that the initial claims had. We require that both ways of proceeding result in the same awards vector, thereby

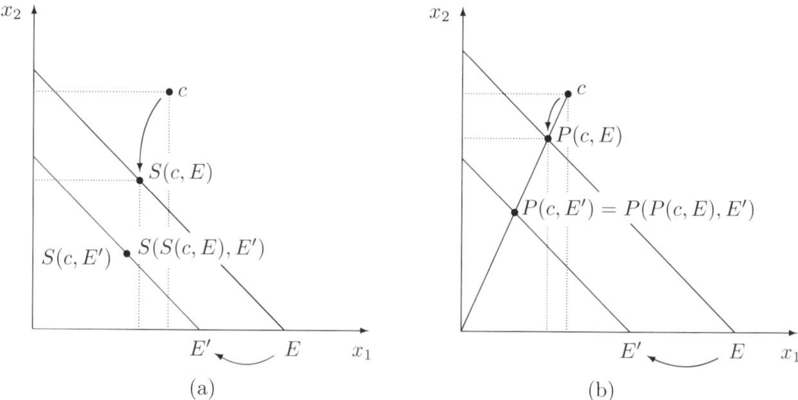

Figure 6.1: **Composition down.** (a) Let $N \equiv \{1, 2\}$ and $(c, E) \in \mathcal{C}^N$. The rule S chooses $S(c, E)$. Then the endowment decreases to E'. A first option to deal with the change is to cancel the initial division and apply S to (c, E'), thereby obtaining $S(c, E')$. A second option is to use $S(c, E)$ as claims vector in dividing E'. The resulting awards vector is $S(S(c, E), E')$. The rule S satisfies *composition down* if both ways of proceeding are equivalent: $S(c, E') = S(S(c, E), E')$. (b) The proportional rule satisfies the requirement.

circumventing any disagreement that claimants may have about which is the better approach (Figure 6.1):[1]

Composition down: For each $(c, E) \in \mathcal{C}^N$ and each $E' < E$, we have $S(c, E') = S(S(c, E), E')$.

Let S be a rule satisfying *composition down*. For each $(c, E) \in \mathcal{C}^N$, if we let the variable E' in the statement of the property vary from 0 to E, we deduce that its path of awards for $S(c, E)$ used as a claims vector is the restriction of its path for c to box$[(0, \ldots, 0), S(c, E)]$.

The proportional (Figure 6.1b), constrained equal awards, and constrained equal losses (Figure 6.2a) rules satisfy *composition down*. Interestingly and perhaps surprisingly, although the property is inherited by all weighted constrained equal awards rules and all weighted constrained equal losses rules, the weighted proportional rules with unequal weights all violate it. However, it will be convenient to wait until next section to prove this fact.

Concede-and-divide also violates *composition down* (Figure 6.2b). Since for two claimants, the minimal overlap and random arrival rules coincide with concede-and-divide, they too violate *composition down* in that case. (In fact, they violate the property for any number of claimants.)

[1] The idea is applied to surplus sharing by Moulin (1987) under the name of "path independence," and in Moulin (2000) under the name of "upper composition."

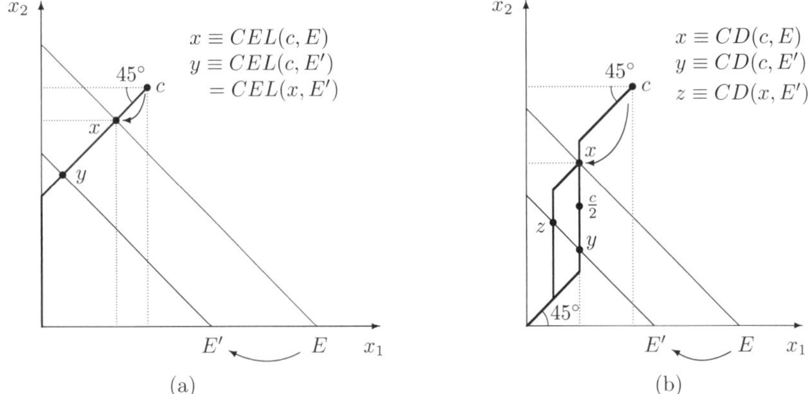

Figure 6.2: **Two rules and composition down.** Let $N \equiv \{1, 2\}$. The initial problem is $(c, E) \in \mathcal{C}^N$ and $E' < E$ is the new endowment. Using the geometry of Figure 6.1, panel (a) illustrates the fact that the constrained equal losses rule satisfies *composition down*, and panel (b) shows that concede-and-divide does not.

`* Relating axioms` ♦ *Composition down* implies *endowment monotonicity* (and therefore *endowment continuity*, which this property implies, as noted earlier). A conditional version of *composition down* can be formulated however that preserves its spirit but that is not strong enough for this implication to hold: it the requirement that the equality $S(c, E') = S(S(c, E), E')$ hold *if* $S(c, E') \leqq S(c, E)$. ♦ For two claimants, *composition down* implies *claim monotonicity*. Indeed, let $N \equiv \{1, 2\}$ say, and let c and $c' \in \mathbb{R}^N_+$ be such that, without loss of generality, $c'_1 > c_1$ and $c'_2 = c_2$. By *composition down*, the paths of awards of S for c and c' – they are continuous curves by *endowment continuity*, a property that we just established S satisfies – cannot cross (although they can touch). Thus, no part of the path for c' lies to the northwest of the path for c, which guarantees *claim monotonicity*. For more claimants, this implication fails.

Characterization. The characterization of the entire family of rules satisfying *composition down* is easy. Any such rule can be described by means of a network of monotone curves emanating from the origin, its paths of awards being subsets of these curves. Following two such curves down, if they meet, they stay together until they reach the origin. Thus, in the language of graph theory, they are the branches of a tree, which it is natural to also qualify as "monotone." Since, for each claims vector in awards space $\mathbb{R}^N_+$, there is a curve passing through it – any curve in the tree that contains the path for that claims vector does – the tree "fills" the space. The paths of awards being subsets of these curves, we call the curves **generating curves** and the tree a **generating tree**.

family of rules characterized

Theorem 6.1 *A rule satisfying composition down can be described by means of a monotone tree that fills awards space $\mathbb{R}^N_+$. For each $c \in \mathbb{R}^N_+$, the path of awards of the rule for c is the unique path in the tree from the origin to c.*

Proof: We omit the easy proof that any rule as described in the theorem satisfies *composition down*. Conversely, let S be a rule satisfying this property. We already know that *composition down* implies *endowment monotonicity*, which in turn implies *endowment continuity*. Thus, for each $c \in \mathbb{R}^N_+$, the path of awards of S is a continuous and monotone curve from the origin to c. By *composition down*, for each c' on that curve, the path of S for c' is the restriction of its path for c to box$[(0, \ldots, 0), c']$. Thus, paths of awards are subsets of a network of monotone curves emanating from the origin.

Let us follow two such curves C^1 and C^2 down to the origin. If they meet, they have to stay together until they reach the origin. Indeed, let $c^1 \in C^1$ and $c^2 \in C^2$ and consider the paths of S for these claims vectors. Let c be a point where C^1 and C^2 meet. By *composition down*, the path for c is both the restriction to box$[(0, \ldots, 0), c]$ of the path for c^1, a subset of C^1, and the restriction to box$[(0, \ldots, 0), c]$ of the path for c^2, a subset of C^2. Thus C^1 and C^2 coincide in box$[(0, \ldots, 0), c]$.

Altogether, the curves constitute a monotone tree. Since the set of claims vectors is the entire space $\mathbb{R}^N_+$, the tree is space-filling. □

Figure 6.3a shows that the branches of the trees identified in Theorem 6.1 may have a great variety of shapes, even for two claimants: although they are monotone, they may include horizontal or vertical segments, perhaps both, and they need not exhibit any convexity or even visibility properties (Section 4.1). (Notions of visibility will soon become relevant however.)

`* Relating axioms` ♦ *Composition down* does not imply *claims continuity* (although it implies *endowment monotonicity* and therefore *endowment continuity*, as we noted earlier). Indeed, consider the following rule defined on the domain of two-claimant problems: for a claims vector of equal coordinates, choose equal division; for a claims vector of unequal coordinates, give full priority to the larger claimant. This rule satisfies the former property but not the latter. It is *anonymous* and satisfies *order preservation in awards* but not *order preservation in losses*. Rule 6.1 below is a little more satisfactory in disproving the implication because it satisfies both parts of *order preservation*.

Rule 6.1 (Figures 6.3b,c) Let $N \equiv \{1, 2\}$ and S be the rule defined as follows. Let $c \in \mathbb{R}^N_+$. Then

(i) if $c_2 \leq \frac{c_1}{2}$ or $c_1 \leq \frac{c_2}{2}$, the path of awards of S is that of the constrained equal losses rule;
(ii) if $c_1 < 2c_2 < 4c_1$, the path of S is that of the proportional rule.

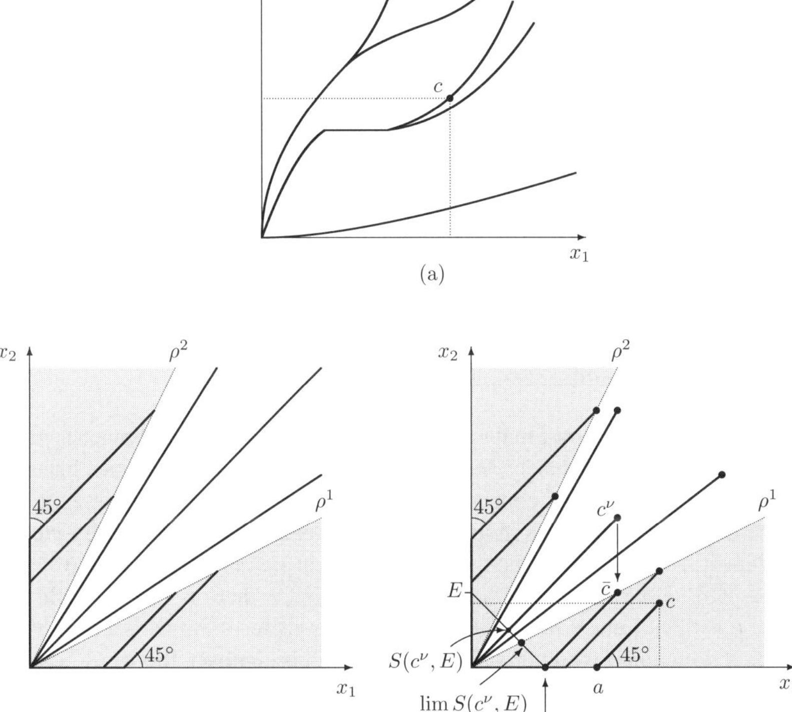

Figure 6.3: **The signature of a rule satisfying composition down is a monotone space-filling tree in awards space**. Let $N \equiv \{1, 2\}$. A rule defined on $\mathcal{C}^N$ satisfying *composition down* can be described by means of a monotone tree that fills awards space $\mathbb{R}^N_+$ and from which paths of awards are generated: for each $c \in \mathbb{R}^N_+$, its path of awards for c is the restriction to box$[(0, \ldots, 0), c]$ of any branch emanating from the origin and passing through c. (a) A few branches of such a "generating tree" for a general example. (b) The generating tree of Rule 6.1. The shaded cones contain their boundary rays. The unshaded cone does not contain its boundary rays. (c) Sample paths of awards of Rule 6.1, denoted S. The path for $\bar{c} \in \rho^1 \setminus \{0\}$ is bro.seg$[(0, 0), (\bar{c}_1 - \bar{c}_2, 0), \bar{c}]$. The rule is not *claims continuous*: $c^\nu \to \bar{c}$ but, letting $E \equiv \bar{c}_1 - \bar{c}_2$, $S(c^\nu, E)$ does not converge to $S(\bar{c}, E)$.

The generating tree of Rule 6.1 is as follows. Introducing ρ^1, the ray of equation $c_2 = \frac{c_1}{2}$, and ρ^2, the ray of equation $c_2 = 2c_1$, it consists of (i) for each $x \in \rho^1$, bro.seg$[(0, 0), (x_1 - x_2, 0), x]$, and for each $x \in \rho^2$, bro.seg$[(0, 0), (0, x_2 - x_1), x]$, and (ii) all rays between ρ^1 and ρ^2 (excluding ρ^1 and ρ^2 themselves).

To show that S is not *claims continuous*, let $\bar{c} \in \rho^1 \setminus \{0\}$, and consider the sequence $\{c^\nu\}$ of vectors in $\mathbb{R}^N_{++}$ defined, by setting, for each $\nu \in \mathbb{N}$, $c^\nu \equiv (\bar{c}_1, \bar{c}_2 + \frac{1}{\nu})$. This sequence converges to $\bar{c}$. Let $E \equiv \bar{c}_1 - \bar{c}_2$. Then for each $\nu \in \mathbb{N}$, $S(c^\nu, E) = \frac{E}{\sum c_i^\nu} c^\nu$. The sequence $\{S(c^\nu, E)\}$ converges to $\frac{E}{\sum \bar{c}_i}\bar{c}$, but $S(\bar{c}, E) = (E, 0)$.

A generating curve may be bounded above. This is the case for the generating curves of Rule 6.1 in the shaded regions of Figure 6.3b and in fact, our next result brings out this feature of generating curves as the reason for its failing *claims continuity*. This result complements Theorem 6.1: *claims continuity* forces all branches to be unbounded above:[2]

Theorem 6.2 *A rule satisfies composition down and claims continuity if and only if all branches of its generating tree (a tree whose existence is stated in Theorem 6.1), are unbounded above.*

Proof: We omit the proof that unboundedness of the generating branches guarantee *continuity*. Conversely, let S be a rule satisfying the properties listed in the theorem. Suppose by contradiction that one of its generating curves, G, is bounded above. Since G is monotone, it has a least upper bound, $\bar{c}$. By *claims continuity*, $\bar{c} \in G$. Let Δ^N be the unit simplex in $\mathbb{R}^N$ and $D \equiv \{\bar{c}\} + \Delta^N$. Let $\bar{E} \equiv \sum \bar{c}_i$. For each $i \in N$, let $A_i \equiv \{x \in \mathbb{R}^N_+ \colon$ there is $c \in D$ such that $S_i(c, \bar{E}) \leq \bar{c}_i\}$. Let $D_i \equiv \{c \in D \colon c_i = \bar{c}_i\}$. For each $i \in N$, D_i is a face of D. Since S is *continuous* and $\{x \in \mathbb{R}^N_+ \colon \sum x_i = \bar{E}\}$ is compact, the set $S^{-1}(A_i)$ is compact. Since S is *resource monotone*, this set contains D_i. Thus, the collection $(S^{-1}(A_i))_{i \in N}$ is a collection of compact subsets of D and for each $i \in N$, $S^{-1}(A_i)$ contains a face of D. By the Knaster–Kuratowsky–Mazurkiewicz lemma, there is $c \in \bigcap S^{-1}(A_i)$. Thus, for each $i \in N$, $S_i(c, \bar{E}) \leq \bar{c}_i$. Since $\sum S(c, \bar{E}) = \bar{C}$, we have that for each $i \in N$, $S_i(c, \bar{E}) = \bar{c}_i$. Thus $S(c, \bar{E}) = \bar{c}$. By *composition down*, the path for $\bar{c}$ contains the path for c. Thus, $\bar{c}$ is not the least upper bound of G after all. □

Next we add *homogeneity* to *composition down* and derive the existence of a partition of awards space into cones, each cone being spanned by one of the generating curves of the rule and its homothetic images. Since the boundary ray that two adjacent cones share may lie in the span of the generating curves of both cones, we slightly abuse common mathematical language by using the term "partition." The following theorem refers to the property of *visibility from the origin except possibly for an initial segment*, which we introduced for rules but which applies straightforwardly to generating curves (Section 4.1):

family of rules characterized

Theorem 6.3 *A rule satisfies homogeneity and composition down if and only if its generating curves (whose existence is stated in Theorem 6.1) can be*

[2] I owe the complete argument to Velez (2007).

partitioned into classes, all members of each class being related by homothetic transformations. Thus, awards space is partitioned into cones, each of which is spanned by a generating curve and its homothetic images. If $|N| = 2$, each generating curve is visible from the origin except possibly for an initial segment.

Following two monotone curves up from the origin, if they separate and meet again, we say that they have **a nontrivial intersection**.

Proof: We omit the proof that any rule as described in the theorem satisfies the properties listed there. Conversely, consider a rule S satisfying these properties. It is a direct implication of *homogeneity* that if a curve is part of the generating tree of S, each of its homothetic images is also part of the tree. *Visibility from the origin except possibly for an initial segment* for $|N| = 2$ follows from the fact that if a generating curve were to violate this property, it would have a nontrivial intersection with a homothetic image of itself, as illustrated in Figure 6.4a,b. An argument by contradiction can be used to establish the fact. Figure 6.4c shows that a curve that is visible from the origin intersects a homothetic image of itself only at the origin. Figure 6.4d shows that a curve that is visible from the origin but is not fully visible from there because it contains a nondegenerate initial segment, intersects its homothetic images along a nondegenerate segment containing the origin. The network of generating curves is a tree. □

Thus, as announced earlier, Theorem 6.3 gives us a partition of awards space into cones, each of which is spanned by a generating curve and its homothetic images. These cones need not be convex (they are for two claimants). Degenerate cones (rays) are permitted (when for each $c \in \mathbb{R}^N_+$, $E^* = \sum c_i$ in the definition of *visibility from the origin except possibly for an initial segment*). In fact, for two claimants, any boundary ray between two adjacent nondegenerate cones is a generating curve.

Using Theorems 5.1, 6.1, and 6.2 it is easy to identify the family of rules satisfying *equal treatment of equals*, *claims truncation invariance*, *composition down*, and *claims continuity* for two claimants. Let S be a rule satisfying these properties and B be a branch of the tree with which it is associated. Let (a, a) be the maximal point of B on the 45° line, Λ. Then by Theorem 5.1, either (i) B is bounded above by a horizontal line whose ordinate is $2a$, or (ii) it is bounded to the right by a vertical line whose abscissa is $2a$. For one of these statements to hold for each branch, each branch is either (iii) entirely on or below Λ, or (iv) entirely on or below Λ. Indeed, suppose that a branch that is bounded above by a horizontal line of ordinate b contains points that are above Λ. Consider such a point, x, and let $d \equiv \frac{x_1+x_2}{2}$. Since the tree is space-filling and its branches are unbounded, it admits a branch B' that has a vertical asymptote of abscissa $2d$. Thus, B' contains the segment seg$[(0, 0), (a, a)]$. Thus B, which is also infinite, and B' have a nontrivial intersection. Statements (iii) and (iv) imply that the rule satisfies *order preservation in awards*.

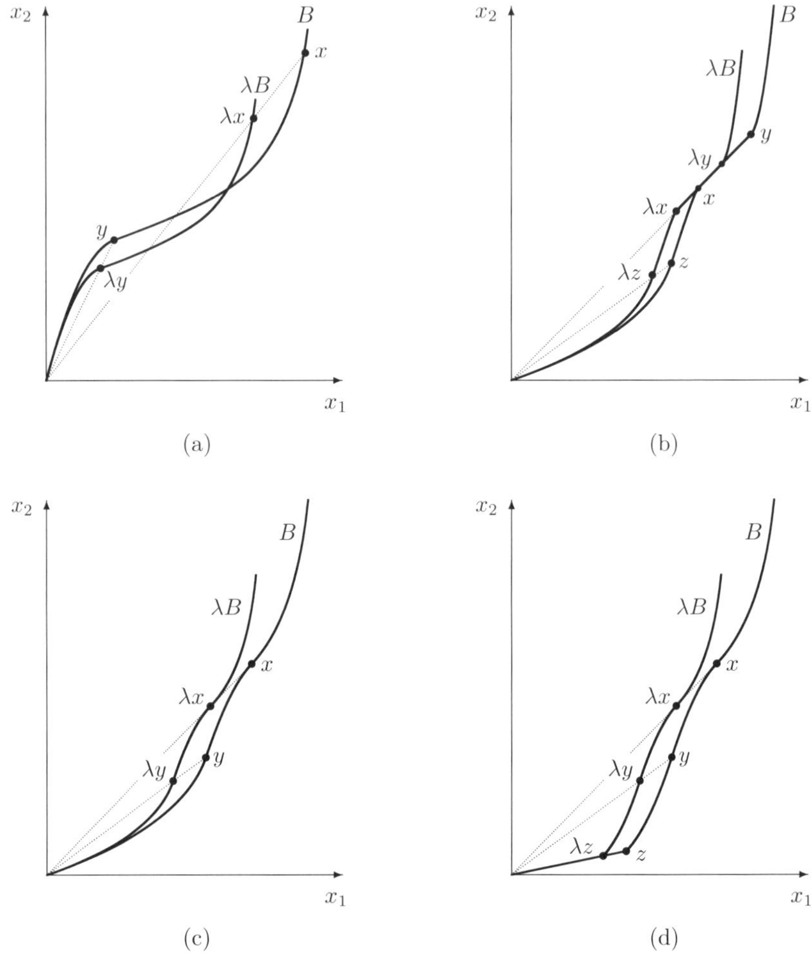

Figure 6.4: **If a rule satisfies homogeneity and composition down, its generating curves are visible from the origin except possibly for an initial segment** (Theorem 6.3). We consider a rule S satisfying the properties listed in the theorem. By *composition down*, S admits a generating tree. (a) By *homogeneity*, the tree should be globally invariant under homothetic transformations. If we impose no restrictions on the tree, a branch may have a nontrivial intersection with a homothetic image of itself, and we would not have a tree after all. This is the case here for the S-shaped branch B. (b) To prevent this, a branch should not contain a nondegenerate segment lined up with the origin but not containing the origin, such as seg$[x, y]$ here. (c) In this panel, the branch B is visible from the origin, so it intersects its homothetic images only at the origin. (d) The branch B is visible from the origin except that it contains a nondegenerate segment containing the origin, seg$[0, z]$: homothetic images of B do not have nontrivial intersection with B. Thus, *homogeneity* does not run into conflict with the required "tree-ness" of the network of curves from which paths of awards are generated.

• We conclude this section with the formulation of a strengthening of *composition down*. Starting from some initial problem (c, E), suppose that the endowment decreases. Then require that the new awards vector be obtainable in either one of the following two ways: (i) directly, or (ii) by using as claims vector each vector derived from c by replacing an arbitrary subset of its coordinates by the corresponding coordinates of the awards vector chosen for (c, E). This requirement of **strong composition down** is undoubtedly very demanding, but the constrained equal awards rule and its weighted versions satisfy it. Further generalizations of this rule, which we call **monotone path rules**, pass the test as well.[3]

For two claimants, we can easily describe all such rules, and Figure 6.5 illustrates the definition for $N \equiv \{1, 2\}$. With each continuous, monotone (not necessarily strictly so), and unbounded curve C in $\mathbb{R}^N_+$ that emanates from the origin is associated a member of the family. For each claims vector that is below C, such as c in the two panels of Figure 6.5, the path of awards consists of the part of C that extends from the origin to a point of ordinate c_2 and of the horizontal segment connecting that point to c. For each claims vector that is above C, such as c' in the two panels of Figure 6.5, the path of awards consists of the part of C that extends from the origin to a point of abscissa c'_1 together with the vertical segment connecting that point to c'.

For more agents, we obtain the path of awards of each c by traveling up along C until one claimant is fully compensated; then in the affine subspace

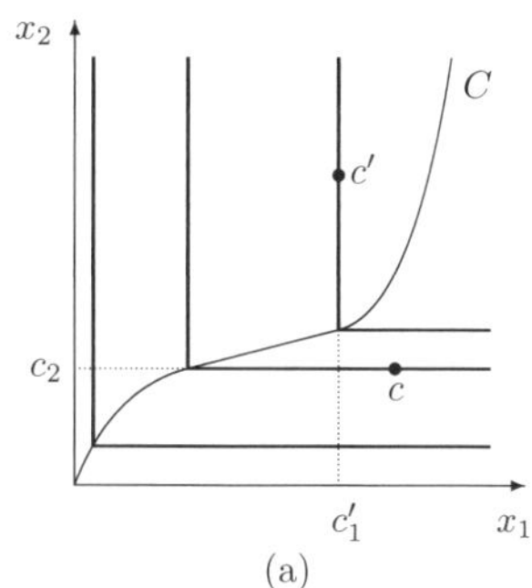

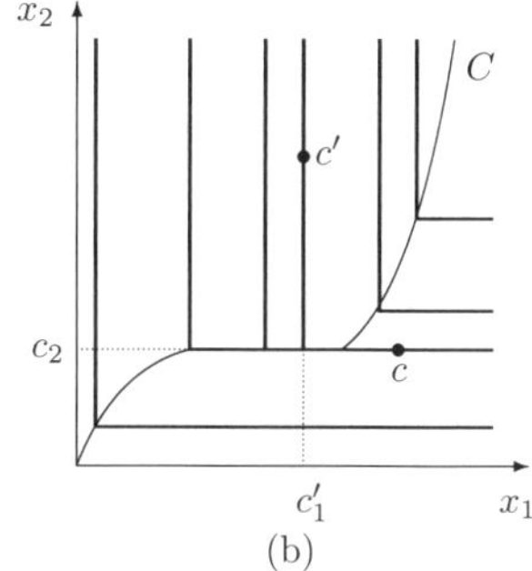

Figure 6.5: **Monotone path rules are generalizations of the constrained equal awards rule.** (a) With each curve C in awards space that emanates from the origin and is continuous, monotone, and unbounded, is associated such a rule. Its generating tree is the union of the right angles obtained by sliding the nonnegative parts of the axes along the curve. Three positions are shown here. (b) The curve C does not have to be strictly monotone. Six positions of the translated axis system are shown in this panel.

[3] Martínez (2008) proposes *strong composition down*. The monotone path rules, which he calls "fixed path rules," are analogous to the "monotone path solutions" of cooperative bargaining theory (Thomson and Myerson, 1980). They are adapted to the context of claims problems by Moulin (2002) who also refers to them as "fixed-path rules."

defined by setting the award equal to the claim, traveling up along the projection of C onto that subspace until some other claimant is fully compensated; and proceeding iteratively in this manner until we reach c. (Of course, several claimants could be fully compensated at the same time; they would drop out together.)

Given a monotone curve C in awards space satisfying the properties listed above, and each point x on C, translate the axes by the vector x; for each coordinate subspace relative to some $N' \subset N$, identify the projection of C on the affine subspace containing x; for each point y on that projected curve, translate the axes of that subspace by the vector y; proceed in this way inductively until one-dimensional subspaces are reached. The union of these axes systems constitute the monotone space-filling tree with which the rule is associated.

Note that typically neither *equal treatment of equals* nor *homogeneity* will be satisfied.

The rules constitute a family of nonsymmetric generalizations of Young's rules and they have generalized Young representations, which are described at the end of Section 10.2. The rules are characterized in Section 11.4.

6.2 COMPOSITION UP

The opposite possibility to the one that led us to formulating *composition down* is equally worthy of study, namely that the endowment increases: suppose that after the division of a firm's liquidation value among its creditors has been decided by applying some rule, the firm's assets are reevaluated, but this time, they are found to be worth more than initially thought. Their market value has increased in the meantime, or new assets have become accessible. In handling this new situation, we see two parallel options to the ones we described when we considered a possible decrease in liquidation value. The first one is to cancel the initial division and to apply the rule to divide the revised value. The second option is to let claimants keep their initial awards, revise their claims down by these awards, and reapply the rule to divide the incremental value, each claimant getting their assignment in two installments. Our next requirement is that both ways of proceeding give the same answers (Figure 6.6):[4]

Composition up: For each $(c, E) \in \mathcal{C}^N$ and each $E' > E$ such that $\sum c_i \geq E'$, we have $S(c, E') = S(c, E) + S(c - S(c, E), E' - E)$.[5]

For each $(c, E) \in \mathcal{C}^N$, if we let E' in the statement of the property vary from E to $\sum c_i$, we see that a rule S satisfies *composition up* if and only if its path of awards for $c - S(c, E)$, *using* $S(c, E)$ *as origin*, is the restriction of

[4] This property is introduced in the context of taxation by Young (1988) under the name of "composition." Moulin (2000) refers to it as "lower composition." A property in the same spirit is analyzed in the context of bargaining by Kalai (1977) under the name of "step-by-step negotiation."

[5] Note that this equality is well defined since, by definition, rules satisfy *claims boundedness*.

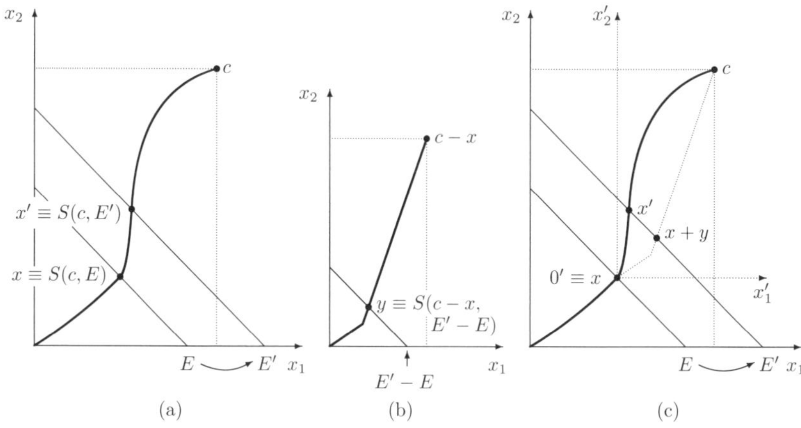

Figure 6.6: **Composition up.** Let $N \equiv \{1, 2\}$. (a) For the problem $(c, E) \in \mathcal{C}^N$, the rule S chooses $x \equiv S(c, E)$. Then the endowment increases to $E' \leq \sum c_i$. A first option to deal with the change is to cancel the initial division and apply S to (c, E'), thereby obtaining $x' \equiv S(c, E')$. (b) A second option is to let each claimant keep their component of x, and after revising c to $c - x$, to divide the increment $E' - E$. The awards vector of this second-round problem is $y \equiv S(c - x, E' - E)$. It is the point of intersection of the path of awards of S for $c - x$ with the line of equation $\sum t_i = E' - E$. In total, each claimant $i \in N$ receives $x_i + y_i$. The rule S satisfies *composition up* if both ways of proceeding are equivalent: $S(c, E') = S(c, E) + S(c - S(c, E), E' - E)$, that is, $x' = x + y$. (c) To obtain the revised claims vector, instead of moving c down by $-x$, it is more convenient to move the origin up by x. Let $0' \equiv x$ denote its new location. The line of equation $\sum t_i = E'$ in the original axes is also the line of equation $\sum t_i = E' - E$ in the axes translated to $0'$, so we only need to add to the construction the path of S for $c - x$ in these axes (dotted broken line segment copied from panel (b)). Here, $x' \neq x + y$: the property is violated.

its path for c to box$[S(c, E), c]$. The construction is similar to that illustrating *minimal rights first*, and the motivation is somewhat akin to that underlying that property. Note however that *minimal rights first* calls for the awards vector chosen for each problem to be compared to only one other awards vector, obtained by applying the rule to a derived problem. By contrast, *composition up* calls for a comparison of the awards vector chosen for each problem to the awards vectors chosen for infinitely many derived problems.

The proportional (Figure 6.7a), constrained equal awards (Figure 6.7b), and constrained equal losses rules all satisfy *composition up*. The weighted versions of these last two rules also do. Concede-and-divide does not (Figure 6.7c), and therefore neither do the minimal overlap and random arrival rules since for two claimants these rules coincide with concede-and-divide. (In fact, they violate the property for any number of claimants.)

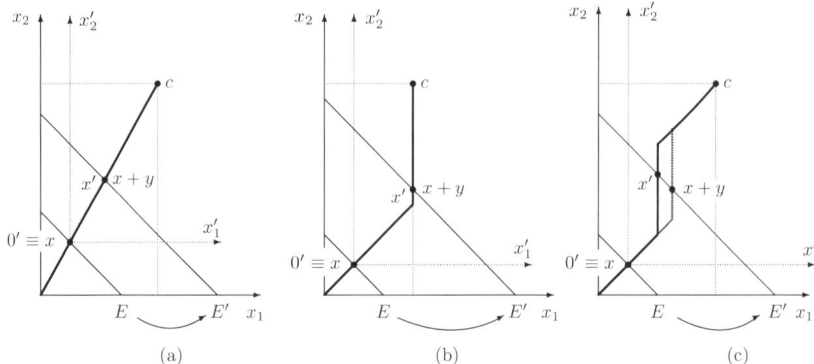

Figure 6.7: **Three rules and composition up.** The notation is that of Figure 6.6: $x \equiv S(c, E)$, $x' \equiv S(c, E')$, and $y \equiv S(c - S(c, E), E' - E)$, for $S \equiv P$, $S \equiv CEA$, and $S \equiv CD$ successively. In each case, as in Figure 6.6, the vector y is identified by using $0' \equiv x$ as origin and drawing the path of awards for $c - S(c, E)$ from that origin. (a) The proportional rule satisfies *composition up*. (b) The constrained equal awards rule does too. (c) Concede-and-divide does not.

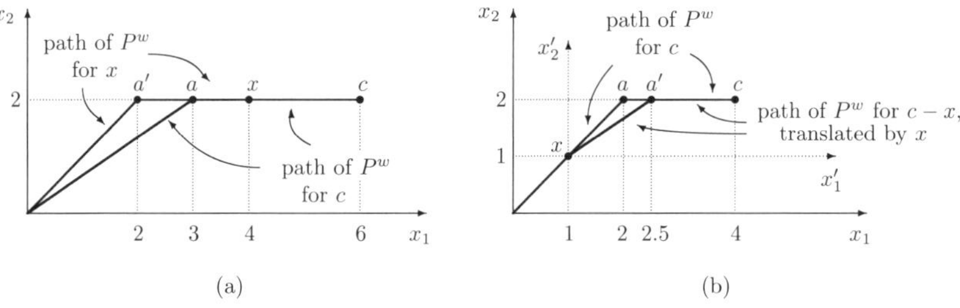

Figure 6.8: **The weighted proportional rules with unequal weights satisfy neither composition down nor composition up.** (a) Example 6.1: the path of awards of P^w for c is bro.seg$[(0, 0), a, c]$; the point x belongs to it, but the path for x, bro.seg$[(0, 0), a', x]$, is not the restriction of the path for c to box$[(0, 0), x]$. (b) Example 6.2: the path of P^w for c is bro.seg$[(0, 0), a, c]$; the point x belongs to it, but using x as origin, the path for $c - x$, bro.seg$[x, a', c]$, is not the restriction of the path for x to box$[x, c]$.

Next are two-claimant examples showing that all weighted proportional rules with unequal weights violate both *composition down* (a result announced earlier) and *composition up*. (If the weights are equal, then the proportional rule itself emerges; this rule does satisfy both properties, as we noted.)

Example 6.1 (Figure 6.8a) All weighted proportional rules with unequal weights violate *composition down*. (The example actually makes the point for a specific weight vector, but it can serve the purpose for each weight vector with unequal coordinates.) Let $N \equiv \{1, 2\}$ and $w \equiv (\frac{1}{3}, \frac{2}{3})$. Let $c \equiv (6, 2)$.

The path of awards of P^w for c is bro.seg$[(0,0), a, c]$, where $a \equiv (3,2)$. Let $x \equiv (4,2)$, a point of this path. The path of P^w for x is bro.seg$[(0,0), a', x]$, where $a' \equiv (2,2)$. It is not the restriction of the path for c to box$[(0,0), x]$, in violation of *composition down*.

Example 6.2 (Figure 6.8b) All weighted proportional rules with unequal weights violate *composition up*. (Here, too, the example, which makes the point for a specific weight vector, can serve the purpose for each weight vector with unequal coordinates.) Let $N \equiv \{1,2\}$ and $w \equiv (\frac{1}{3}, \frac{2}{3})$. Let $c \equiv (4,2)$. The path of awards of P^w for c is bro.seg$[(0,0), a, c]$, where $a \equiv (2,2)$. Let $x \equiv (1,1)$, a point of this path. The path of P^w for $c - x$ is bro.seg$[(0,0), (1.5,1), (3,1)]$. This path, translated by x, is not the restriction of the path for c to box$[x, c]$, in violation of *composition up*.

* Relating axioms ♦ A counterpart of an earlier comment about *composition down* holds: *composition up* implies *endowment monotonicity* (and therefore *endowment continuity*). Also, a conditional version of the property can be formulated according to which the equality $S(c, E') = S(c, E) + S(c - S(c, E), E' - E)$ is imposed *if* $S(c, E') \geqq S(c, E)$. This version does not imply *endowment monotonicity*. ♦ In spite of the formal similarity between *composition up* and *minimal rights first* noted above, the properties are not logically related. Indeed, the proportional rule satisfies the former but not the latter; the opposite is true for concede-and-divide.

We also recall that for each claims vector $c \in \mathbb{R}^N_+$, the locus of the vector of minimal rights obtained by varying the endowment from 0 to $\sum c_i$ is the path of awards of the constrained equal losses rule for c. From this observation and the fact that this rule also satisfies *composition up*, we deduce that it satisfies *minimal rights first*. The formal proof consists in writing the vector of minimal rights of (c, E) as

$$(\max\{E - \sum_{N\setminus\{1\}} c_i, 0\}, \max\{E - \sum_{N\setminus\{2\}} c_i, 0\}, \ldots, \max\{E - \sum_{N\setminus\{n\}} c_i, 0\}).$$

Using the notation $\Delta \equiv \sum c_i - E$, this vector is equal to

$$(\max\{c_1 - \Delta, 0\}, \max\{c_2 - \Delta, 0\}, \ldots, \max\{c_n - \Delta, 0\}),$$

which is nothing other than the constrained equal losses awards vector of (c, E') for some $E' \leq E$.

A strengthening of *composition up*, obtained similarly to the way in which we derived *strong composition down* from *composition down* – so let us call it **strong composition up** – can be formulated: in the statement of *composition up*, require invariance of the chosen awards vector with respect to the assignment to an *arbitrary subset of claimants* of their awards for the initial endowment.

Characterizations. Next are characterizations of the constrained equal awards rule on the basis of some of the properties defined so far, as well as of a family that jointly generalizes it and the constrained equal losses rule:[6]

constrained equal awards rule characterized

Theorem 6.4 *The constrained equal awards rule is the only rule satisfying equal treatment of equals, claims truncation invariance, and composition up.*

Proof: (Figure 6.9) We already know that the constrained equal awards rule satisfies the first two properties listed in the theorem, and we also observed that it satisfies *composition up* (for two claimants, see Figure 6.7b).

Conversely, let $N \equiv \{1, \ldots, n\}$ say, and S be a rule satisfying the three properties. Let $c \in \mathbb{R}^N_+$ and without loss of generality, suppose that $c_1 \leq \cdots \leq c_n$. In fact, for simplicity, suppose that $c_1 < \cdots < c_n$. We will let E increase from 0 to $\sum c_i$ and for each value of E, show that $S(c, E) = CEA(c, E)$ (a conclusion that we will not restate every time).

Case 1: $E \leq nc_1$.

Step 1: $E \leq c_1$ (Figures 6.9a,b). After truncation at E, all claims are equal. Thus, by *claims truncation invariance* and *equal treatment of equals*, S chooses equal division.

Step 2: $c_1 < E \leq c_1 + \frac{n-1}{n} c_1$ (Figure 6.9c). We first allocate an endowment equal to c_1, which, by Step 1, results in equal division. We revise all claims down by $\frac{c_1}{n}$ and the endowment down by c_1. In the resulting problem, all claims are at least as large as the endowment. Thus, by *claims truncation invariance* and *equal treatment of equals*, equal division prevails once again. In total, by *composition up*, each claimant receives $\frac{c_1}{n} + \frac{E-c_1}{n}$. Thus, S divides equally any endowment no larger than $c_1 + \frac{n-1}{n} c_1$.

Step 3: $0 \leq E < nc_1$. Iterations of this argument give us that for each $E \in [0, \lim\{c_1 + \frac{n-1}{n} c_1 + (\frac{n-1}{n})^2 c_1 + \cdots\}[$, S chooses equal division. The limit in this expression is nc_1.

Step 4: $E = nc_1$. We obtain the conclusion here by appealing to *endowment continuity*, which, as we noted earlier, *composition up* implies. At that point, each claimant receives c_1.

Case 2: $E \geq nc_1$. We invoke *composition up* and first allocate an endowment equal to nc_1. Agent 1 is then fully compensated. By *claims boundedness*, agent 1 does not partake in the division of the difference $E - nc_1$. Thus, we repeat the process described in Case 1 with the $n - 1$ other claimants. Equal division prevails among them until each of them receives c_2, at which point claimant 2 being fully compensated, does not partake in the division of any further increment, and so on.

If two agents have equal claims, in the above argument, they drop out together. □

[6] Theorem 6.4 is due to Dagan (1996).

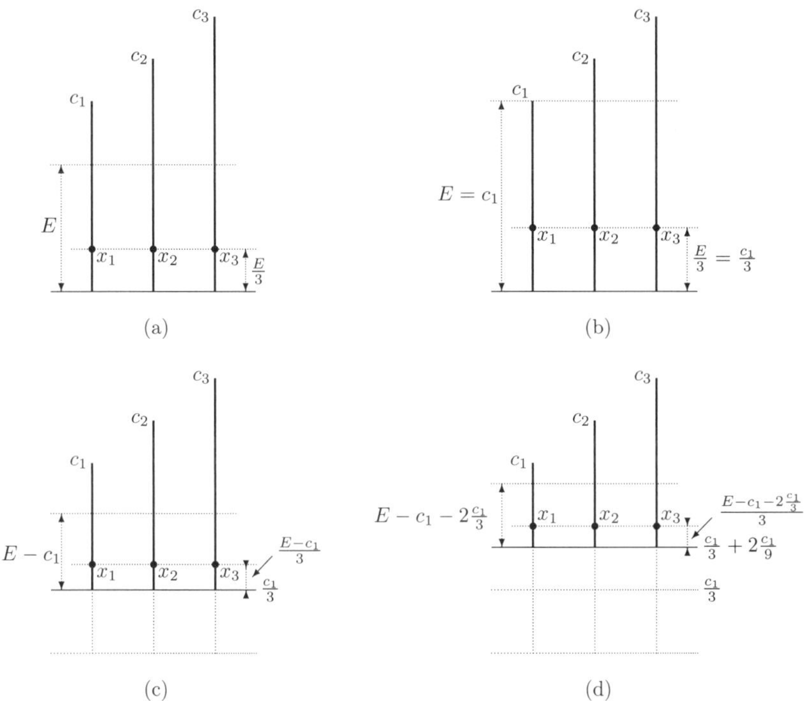

Figure 6.9: **Characterizing the constrained equal awards rule** (Theorem 6.4). Let $N \equiv \{1, 2, 3\}$ and $c \in \mathbb{R}^N_+$ be such that $c_1 < c_2 < c_3$. We consider a rule S satisfying the properties listed in the theorem. (a) By *claims truncation invariance* and *equal treatment of equals*, S divides equally any endowment no larger than the smallest claim, c_1. (b) This panel shows the case $E = c_1$; each agent receives $\frac{c_1}{3}$ then. (c) By *composition up*, if $E \in [c_1, c_1 + \frac{2}{3}c_1]$, S allocates it in two steps, first c_1, then the rest. At the second step, all revised claims are at least as large as the residual endowment (claimant 1's revised claim remains the smallest and its value is $c_1 - \frac{c_1}{n} = \frac{2}{3}c_1$), so once again, by *claims truncation invariance* and *equal treatment of equals*, we obtain equal division. Since Step 1 and Step 2 both result in equal division, we obtain equal division altogether. (d) We repeat the argument, and obtain equality of awards for each $E \in [c_1 + \frac{2}{3}c_1, c_1 + \frac{2}{3}c_1 + \frac{4}{9}c_1]$. Continuing in this way, we extend this equal division conclusion to each $E < \lim\{c_1 + \frac{2}{3}c_1 + \frac{4}{9}c_1 + \ldots\} = nc_1$. We settle the limit case $E = nc_1$ by invoking *endowment continuity*, implied by *composition up*: we still obtain equal division. If $E > nc_1$, we first allocate nc_1 then the rest. Claimant 1 being fully compensated when E reaches nc_1, their claim is reduced to 0 then, so only the others partake of the rest: they get equal shares until claimant 2 is fully compensated – this occurs when $E = nc_1 + (n-1)(c_2 - c_1)$ – and so on.

∗`On the independence of axioms in Theorem 6.4.` ✦ The weighted constrained equal awards rules with unequal weights satisfy the last two properties listed in the theorem but not *equal treatment of equals*. ✦ The proportional rule satisfies the first and last (Figure 6.7a) properties but not *claims truncation invariance* (as illustrated in Figure 9.1 below). However, replacing *claims truncation invariance* by the version we called *weak claims truncation invariance* still only leads to the constrained equal awards rule.[7] ✦ The Talmud rule satisfies the first two properties but not *composition up* (Figure 6.7c). ✦ *Equal treatment of equals* and *claim truncation invariance* together imply that if the truncated claims of two agents are equal, they should be assigned equal amounts. Requiring directly that this always be the case, written down as an axiom, together with *minimal rights first* characterize the constrained equal awards rule.[8]

constrained equal awards rule characterized

constrained equal awards rule characterized

Our next result, also a characterization of the constrained equal awards rule, is based on a lower bound requirement and *composition up*. Note that it is only for two claimants.[9] The logic of its proof is the same as that of Theorem 6.9. It relies on the fact that in both cases, the axioms imply equal division of any endowment that is sufficiently small in relation to the sum of the claims.

constrained equal awards rule characterized

Theorem 6.5 *For* $|N| = 2$. *The constrained equal awards rule is the only rule satisfying the* $\frac{1}{2}$*-truncated-claims lower bounds on awards and composition up.*

Proof: The fact that the constrained equal awards rule satisfies the $\frac{1}{2}$-*truncated-claims lower bounds on awards* is illustrated in Figure 3.3 and we already know that it satisfies *composition up*. Conversely, let $N \equiv \{1, 2\}$ and S be a rule satisfying the two properties listed in the theorem. Let $(c, E) \in \mathcal{C}^N$ be such that, without loss of generality, $c_1 \leq c_2$. By the $\frac{1}{2}$-*truncated-claims lower bounds on awards*, the path of awards of S for c contains seg$[(0, 0), (\frac{c_1}{2}, \frac{c_1}{2})]$. By *composition up*, this path contains the path of awards of S for $(\frac{c_1}{2}, c_2 - \frac{c_1}{2})$ translated by $(\frac{c_1}{2}, \frac{c_1}{2})$. By the $\frac{1}{2}$-*truncated-claims lower bounds on awards*, this second path contains seg$[(0, 0), (\frac{c_1}{4}, \frac{c_1}{4})]$. Iterating, we obtain that the path of S for c contains the union of adjacent segments of slope 1 contained in the 45° line and whose projections onto the first axis have lengths $\frac{c_1}{2}, \frac{c_1}{4}, \frac{c_1}{8}, \ldots$. Taking the limit, we conclude that the path for c contains seg$[(0, 0), (c_1, c_1)[$. By *endowment monotonicity*, implied by *composition up*, it contains seg$[(c_1, c_1), c]$. Altogether, it is the path of the constrained equal awards rule for c. □

7 Flores-Szwagrzak and Treibich (2016).

8 Yeh (2001).

9 Theorem 6.5 is due to Yeh (2008).

`* On the independence of axioms in Theorem 6.5.` ✦ Concede-and-divide satisfies the $\frac{1}{2}$*-truncated-claims lower bounds on awards* but not *composition up*. ✦ The opposite is true for the proportional rule.

Our next result is yet another characterization of the constrained equal awards rule.[10]

Theorem 6.6 *The constrained equal awards rule is the only rule satisfying conditional full compensation and composition down.* constrained equal awards rule characterized

For two claimants, we easily obtain the proof by exploiting the "tree" characterization of the family of rules satisfying *composition down* (Theorem 6.1): to each such rule is attached a monotone space-filling tree from which all of its paths of awards are derived. Let $a > 0$. Figure 3.4a shows, for $N \equiv \{1, 2\}$, that for *conditional full compensation* to hold, its path of awards for a claims vector $c \in \mathbb{R}^N_+$ such that $c_1 = a < c_2$ should contain the vertical segment from (a, a) to c. Since this observation holds for each $c_2 > a$, the tree contains the vertical half-line whose lowest point is (a, a). This is true no matter what a is. Thus, above the 45° line, the tree consists of vertical half-lines. By the same logic, below the 45° line, the tree consists of horizontal half-lines. Since the space is now filled, we have obtained the complete tree with which the rule is associated: it is the tree associated with the constrained equal awards rule. We now give the proof for arbitrarily many claimants:

Proof: (Figure 6.10) We already know that the constrained equal awards rule satisfies the two properties listed in the theorem. Conversely, let S be a rule satisfying these properties. Let $(c, E) \in \mathcal{C}^N$, $x \equiv CEA(c, E)$, and $y \equiv S(c, E)$. Suppose, by contradiction, that $y \neq x$. Without loss of generality, suppose that $c_1 \leq \cdots \leq c_n$. Let $N^s(c, E)$ be the set of agents whose claims are sustainable in (c, E) and $N^{ns}(c, E) \equiv N \backslash N^s(c, E)$ its complement. By *conditional full compensation*, for each $i \in N^s(c, E)$, $y_i = x_i = c_i$. By *balance*, there is $i \in N^{ns}(c, E)$ such that $y_i < x_i < c_i$. Let $y^{min} \equiv \min_{k \in N^{ns}(c,E)}\{y_k\}$ and $j \in N$ be such that $y_j = y^{min}$. Let $E' \equiv \sum_{\ell \in N^s(c,E)} c_\ell + |N^{ns}(c, E)| y_j$. Obviously $E' < E$. By *composition down*, $S_j(c, E') = S_j(y, E')$. By *conditional full compensation*, $S_j(y, E') = y_j$. Thus, $S_j(c, E') = y_j$. By *endowment monotonicity*, implied by *composition down*: (∗) for each $E^* \in [E', E]$, $S_j(c, E^*) = y_j$.

Since S satisfies *composition down*, S is *endowment continuous*. Note that $S_j(c, \sum c_i) = c_j$. Thus, there is $\bar{E} < \sum c_i$ such that $y_j < S_j(c, \bar{E}) < x_j$. Let $\bar{y} \equiv S(c, \bar{E})$ and $E'' \equiv \sum_{i \in N^s(c,\bar{E})} c_i + |N^{ns}(c, \bar{E})| \bar{y}_j$. By *composition down*, $S_j(c, E'') = S_j(\bar{y}, E'')$. By *conditional full compensation*, $S_j(\bar{y}, E'') = \bar{y}_j$. Thus, $S_j(c, E'') = \bar{y}_j$. Also $y_j < \bar{y}_j$, so $E' < E''$. Since $\bar{y}_j < x_j$ and

[10] Theorem 6.6 is due to Herrero and Villar (2002). Their proof involves first showing that for two claimants the axioms imply *equal treatment of equals*. Here, we follow Yeh's (2004) direct proof.

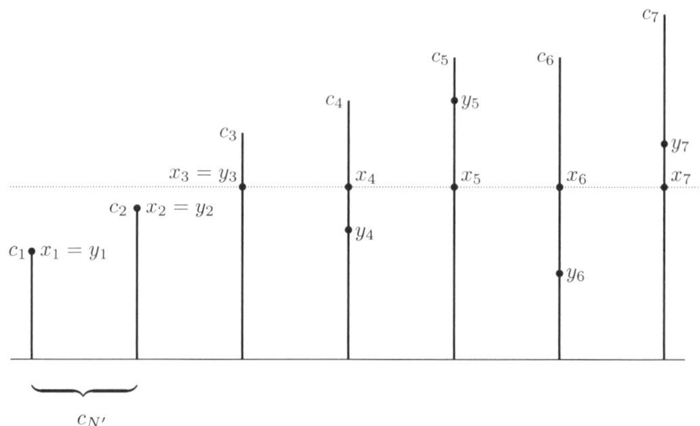

Figure 6.10: **Characterizing the constrained equal awards rule** (Theorem 6.6). Let $N \equiv \{1, \ldots, 7\}$ and $(c, E) \in \mathcal{C}^N$ be such that $c_1 \leq \cdots \leq c_7$. We call y the awards vector chosen for it by a rule S assumed to satisfy the properties listed in the theorem. The proof requires identifying a claimant who receives the least at y among all agents whose claims are not sustainable. Claimant 6 is the only such claimant here. (In general, there could be more than one.)

$E = \sum_{i \in N^s(c,E)} c_i + \sum_{i \notin N^s(c,E)} x_i$, we have $E'' < E$. Thus, $E' < E'' < E$. By the previous argument, $S_j(c, E'') = y_j$. This contradicts $(*)$. □

$*$ On the independence of axioms in Theorem 6.6. ✦ The constrained equal losses rule satisfies *composition down* but not *conditional full compensation* (Section 3.4). ✦ The entire class of rules satisfying *conditional full compensation* is easily identified. For each $(c, E) \in \mathcal{C}^N$, and still denoting by $N^s(c, E)$ the set of agents whose claims are sustainable in (c, E), it suffices to set for each $i \in N^s(c, E)$, $S_i(c, E) \equiv c_i$. To obtain slightly more interesting examples showing the independence of *composition down*, let $\bar{S}$ be some arbitrary rule. Let $j \in N$ be an agent with a maximal sustainable claim in (c, E). First, fully compensate all claimants in $N^s(c, E)$ and assign to everyone in $N^{ns}(c, E) \equiv N \setminus N^s(c, E)$ a first "installment" equal to the largest sustainable claim in (c, E). Revise claims accordingly. What remains of the endowment is $E' \equiv E - \sum_{i \in N^s(c,E)} c_i - |N^{ns}(c, E)|c_j$. Now for each $k \in N^{ns}(c, E)$, let $S_k(c, E) \equiv c_j + \bar{S}_k((0.e_{N^s(c,E)}, (c_i - c_j)_{i \in N^{ns}(c,E)}), E')$ (since the claim of each member of $N^s(c, E)$ has been revised down to 0, such a claimant receive nothing in this second round; in total, each other claimant receives c_j plus a share of E'). It is easy to guarantee that S satisfies certain additional properties by appropriately choosing $\bar{S}$. If $\bar{S}$ is the constrained equal awards rule, $S = CEA$.

We close this chapter with a characterization of the family of two-claimant rules satisfying *homogeneity* and both *composition down* and *composition up*

(Theorem 6.7).[11] We already know from Theorem 6.3 that a two-claimant rule satisfying the first two of these axioms can be described as follows: awards space is partitioned into cones, each cone being spanned by a curve that is visible from the origin except possibly for an initial segment and by its homothetic images (we called these curves "generating curves," as all paths of awards are subsets of them). We will show that *composition up* forces them to be piecewise linear in at most two pieces. But this is not enough, as revealed by Rule 6.1. It has that feature, but it violates *composition up*. To see this, and calling the rule S, let $c \equiv (1,2)$, $E \equiv \frac{1}{2}$, and $E' \equiv 2$. We have $S(c,E) = (0,\frac{1}{2})$ and $(\frac{1}{2},\frac{3}{2}) = S(c,E') \neq S(c,E)+S(c-S(c,E),E'-E) = (0,\frac{1}{2}) + S((1,\frac{3}{2}),\frac{3}{2}) = (0,\frac{1}{2}) + (\frac{3}{5},\frac{9}{10})$. The reason for the violation is that if Case (i) of the definition of the rule applies, the second segment of the typical generating curve is not parallel to a boundary ray of the cone it spans. This parallelism is an important feature of the rules defined next and characterized in Theorem 6.7:

Family $\mathcal{D}$: For $|N| = 2$. Each member of the family is associated with a monotone space-filling tree from which paths of awards are generated. This tree is as follows. Awards space $\mathbb{R}^N_+$ is partitioned into cones; for each nondegenerate cone in the partition, one boundary ray is chosen as the **first ray**, the other being the **second ray**. Each generating curve of the tree consists of a segment emanating from the origin and contained in the first ray of the cone it spans and a half-line parallel to the second ray.

We refer to a nondegenerate cone with boundary rays labeled "first" or "second" as an **oriented cone**. To describe a rule in $\mathcal{D}$, it suffices to specify a partition of awards space into cones and to orient the nondegenerate cones in the partition. The simplest case is when there is a single cone, the entire awards space; then each generating curve consists of a segment emanating from the origin and contained in one of the axes (the same one: the boundary ray that is first) and a half-line parallel to the other axis. The agent whose coordinate axis is the first boundary ray has priority over the other agent: we have a priority rule. For a nondegenerate cone that is not the entire awards space, the rule can be said to *favor agent i in the cone* if the first boundary ray lies between the ith coordinate axis and the second boundary ray.

Figure 6.11 illustrates the definition. It represents examples of partitions of awards space into oriented cones. For each nondegenerate cone, the boundary ray that is first is labeled "1" and the other is labeled "2" (we print the labels inside the cone). Given $a, b \in \Delta^N$, we denote by $\boldsymbol{C(a,b)}$ the oriented cone with first boundary ray in direction a and second boundary ray in direction b. For each claims vector $c \in \mathbb{R}^N_+$, we most conveniently obtain the path

[11] The definition of this family and Theorem 6.7 are due to Moulin (2000). The partition of awards space described in the theorem is akin to that defined by Moulin and Shenker (1999) in the context of cost allocation. Juarez (2013) characterizes the same family on the basis of different considerations.

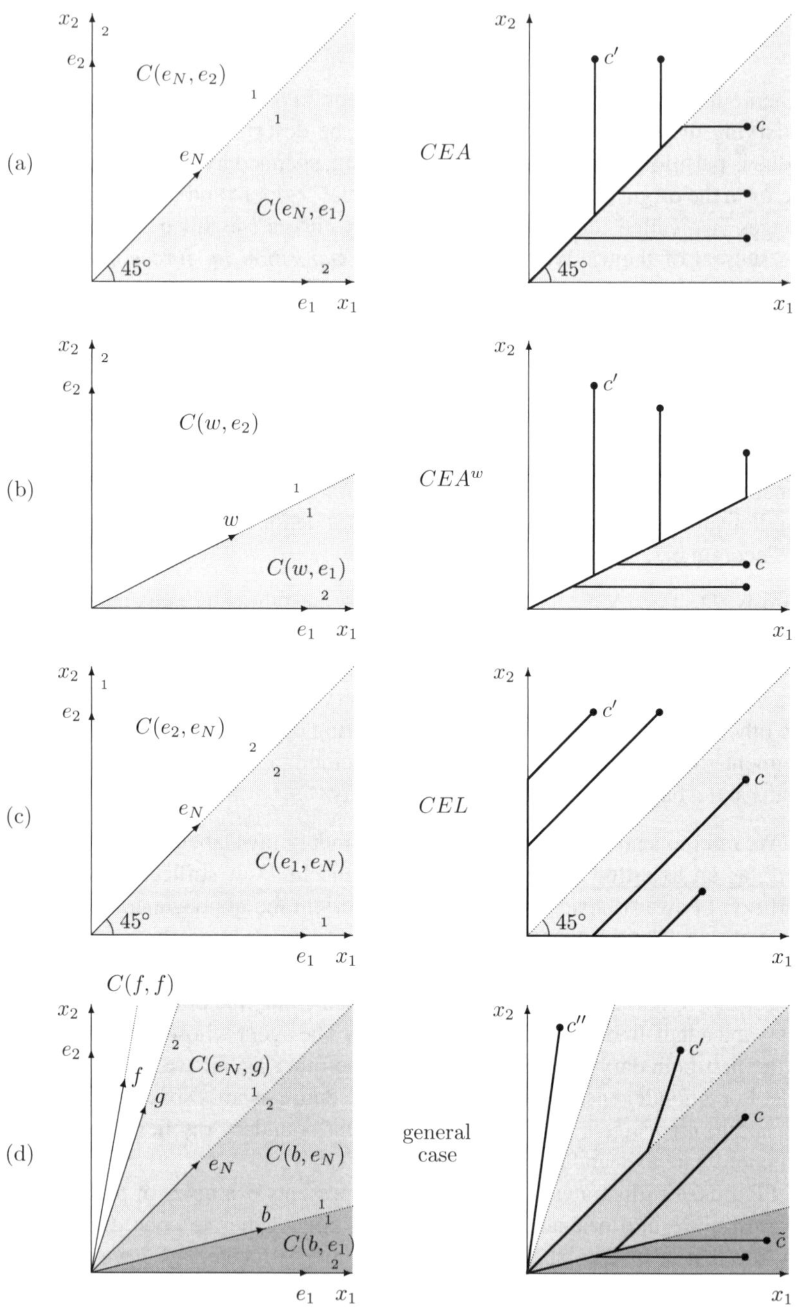

Figure 6.11: **Four members of family $\mathcal{D}$.** Let $N \equiv \{1, 2\}$. Each row concerns one rule. The left panel shows a partition of awards space into oriented cones; the right panel shows sample paths of awards of the member of $\mathcal{D}$ associated with the partition. Row (a): constrained equal awards rule. Row (b): weighted constrained equal awards rule with weights $w \in \Delta^N$. Row (c): constrained equal losses rule. Row (d): illustrating the richness of family $\mathcal{D}$. Awards space is partitioned into three nondegenerate cones (indicated by different shades of gray) and a cone of rays (unshaded).

of awards of the rule by identifying the cone to which c belongs, moving down from c along a straight line parallel to the second boundary ray of that cone until we reach its first boundary ray, then moving down this ray to the origin. If $a = b$, the resulting cone reduces to a ray and for a claims vector on the ray, the path is that of the proportional rule.

Figure 6.11a shows that the constrained equal awards rule belongs to family $\mathcal{D}$, and Figure 6.11b illustrates the fact that the weighted constrained equal awards rules also do. So do their limits as the weight vector tends to a unit vector, the sequential priority rules. The weighted constrained equal losses rules are of course included in $\mathcal{D}$. Figure 6.11c shows that this is the case for the constrained equal losses rule itself. The partition of awards space for this rule is the same as that for the constrained equal awards rule, but the labeling of each of the two nondegenerate cones of its partition is the reverse of what it is for the constrained equal awards rule. Figure 6.11d shows a more complex case, in which three cones are nondegenerate and the remainder of awards space (the unshaded part) is partitioned into an infinite union of rays. For claims vectors in that region, the paths of awards are those of the proportional rule.

For the two rules of Figure 6.12, the partition of awards space is symmetric with respect to the 45° line, and the orientations of two symmetric cones are symmetric too. Thus, the rules satisfy *anonymity* in addition to *homogeneity*, *composition down*, and *composition up*. The top row depicts a rule for which, in each of the six cones into which awards space is partitioned, the orientation favors the smaller claimant. The bottom row shows a rule with the same partition of awards space into cones, but each cone has the reverse orientation; thus, in each cone, the rule represented in this row favors the larger claimant.

Further examples of rules in $\mathcal{D}$ are the two-claimant order-preservation–constrained sequential priority rules (Section 3.7). To obtain the one of these rules that favors claimant 1 for example, it suffices in Figure 6.11a to reverse the orientation of the shaded cone.

The finer the partition of awards space into cones, the closer the resulting paths of awards are to the paths of the proportional rule. Thus, the family $\mathcal{D}$ "links" the proportional rule to the constrained equal awards, constrained equal losses, and sequential priority rules.

In light of the fact that all weighted versions of the constrained equal awards and constrained equal losses rules belong to $\mathcal{D}$ and that the proportional rule itself also does, it may be surprising that its weighted generalizations with unequal weights do not. But recall that none of these rules satisfies either *composition down* or *composition up* (Examples 6.1 and 6.2).

Theorem 6.7 *For $|N| = 2$. The members of $\mathcal{D}$ are the only rules satisfying homogeneity, composition down, and composition up.* family $\mathcal{D}$ characterized

Proof: We omit the easy proof that all members of $\mathcal{D}$ satisfy the three properties listed in the theorem. Conversely, let S be a rule satisfying these properties. We argue by contradiction. Let K be a nondegenerate cone in the partition of

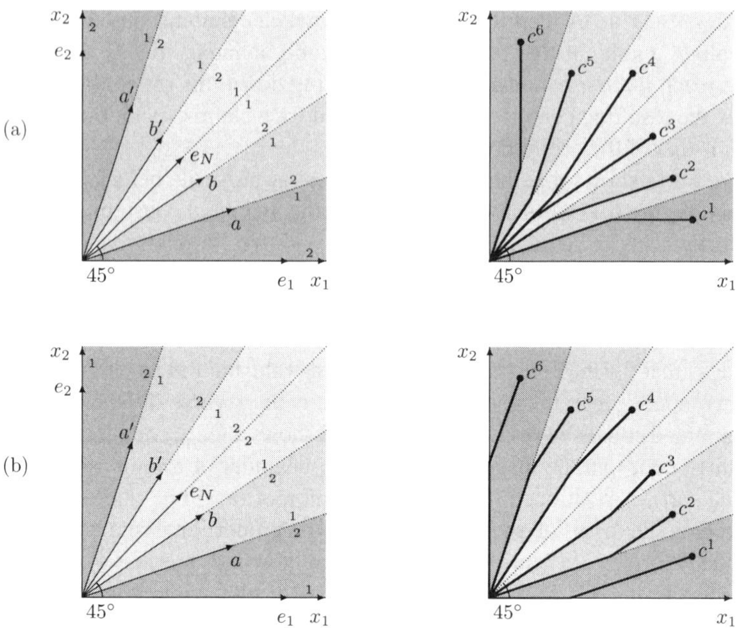

Figure 6.12: **Two members of family $\mathcal{D}$ satisfying anonymity.** Let $N \equiv \{1, 2\}$. The two panels of each row are to be interpreted as in Figure 6.11. Row (a): The vectors a and a' are symmetric of each other with respect to the 45° line, and so are the vectors b and b'. This results in a partition of awards space that also enjoys this symmetry. Moreover, the orientations of symmetric cones in the partition are symmetric. The right-hand panel shows that in each cone, paths of awards are "pulled" to the 45° line: thus, in each cone, the rule represented here favors the smaller claimant. Row (b): The partition of awards space is the same as in Row (a) but the orientation of each cone is reversed. The right-hand panel shows that each path is "pulled" to the coordinate axis that is the closest to the cone containing it: the rule represented in this row favors the larger claimant.

$\mathbb{R}^N_+$ associated with S in the manner described in Theorem 6.3. Call its boundary rays b^1 and b^2, b^1 being steeper than b^2 (Figure 6.13a). Without loss of generality, we assume that the generating curves of S in K are visible from below except possibly for some initial segment. (To deal with the case when visibility is from above, it suffices to reverse all the statements relating slopes given below.) Let $c \in K \setminus \{b^1\}$ and a be the point of intersection of b^1 with the line through c parallel to b^2. We will show that the path of awards of S for c is bro.seg$[(0, 0), a, c]$.

Step 1: The path of awards of S for c contains seg$[(0, 0), a]$ (Figure 6.13a). Suppose by contradiction that there is $E \in [0, \sum a_i]$ such that $x \equiv S(c, E) \notin$ seg$[(0, 0), a]$. Let $\bar{x}$ be the point of intersection of seg$[(0, 0), a]$ with the line of equation $\sum t_i = E$. Then $x_1 > \bar{x}_1$. By *composition up*, for each $E' > 0$

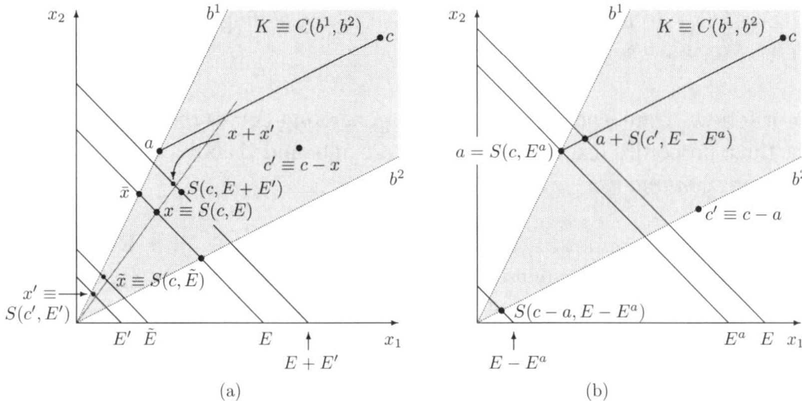

Figure 6.13: **The paths of awards of a rule satisfying homogeneity, composition down, and composition up are piecewise linear in (at most) two pieces** (Theorem 6.7). Let $N \equiv \{1, 2\}$. Given an oriented cone of the partition associated with a rule $S \in \mathcal{C}^N$, such as $K \equiv C(b^1, b^2)$ (shaded), and a claims vector $c \in K \setminus \{b^1\}$, let a be the point of b^1 such that seg$[a, c]$ is parallel to b^2. Then the path of S for c is bro.seg$[0, a, c]$. (a) Step 1: Proving that the path contains seg$[0, a]$. (b) Step 2: Proving that it contains $[a, c]$.

such that $E + E' \leq \sum c_i$, $S(c, E + E') = S(c, E) + S(c - S(c, E), E') = x + S(c - x, E')$. Since $\bar{x} \in$ seg$[(0, 0), a]$, then seg$[\bar{x}, c]$, and thus seg$[x, c]$, are steeper than seg$[a, c]$, and since seg$[a, c]$ is parallel to b^2, seg$[x, c]$ is steeper than b^2. Since the path of S for c, except possibly for an initial segment, is visible from below, seg$[x, c]$ is flatter than seg$[(0, 0), c]$, and thus flatter than b^1. Altogether, $c' \equiv c - x \in K$.

The fact that c and c' belong to the same cone of the partition of awards space associated with S, together with the *homogeneity* of S, imply that the paths of S for c and c' are subsets of two generating curves of S that are homothetic images of each other. Since each generating curve of S in K, except possibly for an initial segment, is visible from below and b^1 is a boundary ray of K, there is $\tilde{E} < E$ such that, introducing $\tilde{x} \equiv S(c, \tilde{E})$, seg$[(0, 0), \tilde{x}]$ is steeper than seg$[(0, 0), x]$. Moreover, for each $E' \leq \tilde{E}$, and introducing $x' \equiv S(c', E')$, so is seg$[(0, 0), x']$. Let $E' \leq \tilde{E}$ be chosen so that this be the case and that in addition, $E + E' \leq \sum c_i$. Since seg$[(0, 0), x']$ is steeper than seg$[(0, 0), x]$, then seg$[(0, 0), x + x']$ is steeper than seg$[(0, 0), x]$. By *composition up*, $S(c, E + E') = x + S(c', E')$. However, by *visibility from below except possibly for an initial segment*, seg$[(0, 0), S(c, E + E')]$ is at most as steep as seg$[(0, 0), x]$. We have obtained a contradiction.

Step 2: The path of awards of S for c contains seg$[a, c]$. Let $E^a \equiv \sum a_i$ and $E \in [E^a, \sum c_i]$. We will show that $S(c, E) \in$ seg$[a, c]$ (Figure 6.13b). By Step 1, $S(c, E^a) = a$. By *composition up*, $S(c, E) = S(c, E^a) + S(c - S(c, E^a), E - E^a) = a + S(c - a, E - E^a)$. Note that $c - a \in b^2$, so $S(c -$

$a, E - E^a) \in b^2$ also. Thus, we obtain $S(c, E)$ by adding to a a vector parallel to b^2: $S(c, E) \in \text{seg}[a, c]$. □

It follows from Theorem 6.7 that the generating curves of a rule satisfying the three properties listed in the theorem are unbounded above and that the rule is *claims continuous*.

*On the independence of axioms in Theorem 6.7. ✦ Rule 6.1 satisfies *homogeneity* and *composition down*, but not *composition up* (an example of a problem to make this point is provided before the definition of family $\mathcal{D}$). ✦ The rule obtained by specifying the path of awards for each $c \in \mathbb{R}^N_+$ to be the symmetric image of that of Rule 6.1 with respect to $\frac{c}{2}$ satisfies *homogeneity* and *composition up* but not *composition down*. ✦ Rules exist that satisfy the two *composition* properties but not *homogeneity*.[12] Here is the entire family for two claimants:

Family of difference rules: For $|N| = 2$. Each member of the family is defined as follows. Awards space is partitioned into cones. With each cone is associated a monotone concave or convex curve that is unbounded above and below. The asymptotic directions of this curve – there are two of them because the curve is concave or convex – are the directions of the boundary rays of the cone. Now, given $c \in \mathbb{R}^N_+$, we identify the cone to which c belongs and a pair of points $\{a(c), b(c)\}$ on the curve associated with that cone such that $b(c) - a(c) = c$. Such a pair exists. The path of awards of the rule for c is the portion of the curve lying between $a(c)$ and $b(c)$ translated by the vector $-a(c)$.

In this definition, the curve associated with each cone in the partition of awards space is not uniquely defined; any translate of it could be used instead. Moreover, even once a curve C has been chosen, the pair $\{a(c), b(c)\}$ from which the path for a typical $c \in \mathbb{R}^N_+$ is derived may not be unique either. For instance, if there are $\alpha, \beta \in \mathbb{R}^N_+$ with $\alpha \leq \beta$ such that C contains the nondegenerate segment $\text{seg}[\alpha, \beta]$, and $c = \lambda(\beta - \alpha)$ for $\lambda < 1$, infinitely many pairs will do. However, even if there is more than one pair, the path is independent of which pair we select: the rule is well defined.

Figure 6.14 illustrates the definition. The shaded area K represents a cone in the partition. We chose the curve C associated with K to pass through the origin, but as just noted, any translation of it would be just as good. We indicate the construction of the paths of awards for two claims vectors, c and $c' \in K$

[12] The family they constitute is identified by Chambers (2006). He refers to them as "difference rules." They take a particularly simple form for two claimants and he uses the expression "relative difference rules" in that case. Although rules for the general case can also be described by means of a family of curves from which paths of awards are derived, it is unclear how these curves should fit together for the existence and the uniqueness of paths of awards derived from them to be guaranteed.

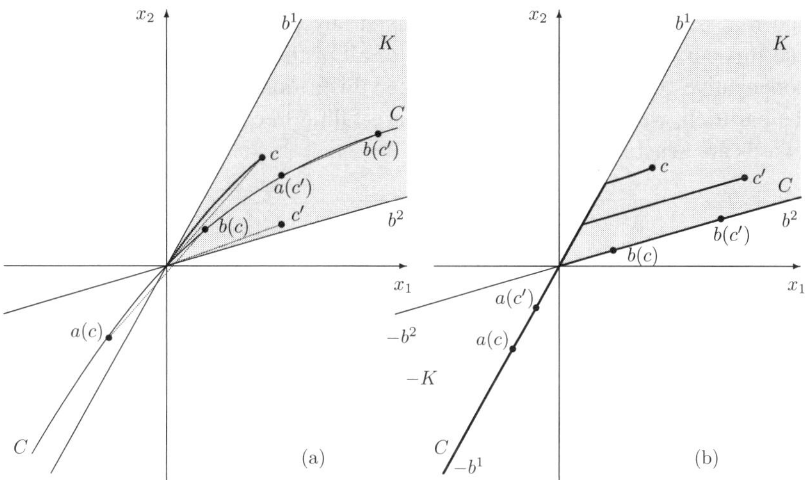

Figure 6.14: **One rule satisfying composition down and composition up, and a second one satisfying homogeneity in addition.** (a) Awards space is partitioned into cones. With each cone in the partition associated with the rule, such as the cone K (shaded), is associated a monotone concave or convex (here, concave) curve C that is unbounded above and below and whose asymptotic directions are the directions of the boundary rays of the cone. Given $c \in K$, the path of awards of the rule for c is a copy of the portion of C lying between two points of C, named $a(c)$ and $b(c)$, chosen so that $b(c) - a(c) = c$. The construction is shown here for c and a second claims vector c'. (b) The rule represented here is *homogeneous* in addition. Thus, it is in $\mathcal{D}$. For a typical cone K in the partition associated with it, we can choose the associated curve C to be the union of two rays, the steepest boundary ray of $-K$ together with the flattest boundary ray of K. The figure shows how to identify, for each of two claims vectors c and $c' \in K$, a pair of points delimiting a portion of C that, appropriately translated to the origin, yields the path of awards of the rule for that claims vector.

(the points $a(c)$ and $b(c) \in C$ are such that $b(c)-a(c) = c$ and the points $a(c')$ and $b(c') \in C$ are such that $b(c') - a(c') = c'$), but we have only drawn the path for c. If with each nondegenerate cone in the partition of awards space we associate a curve consisting of two half-lines emanating from the origin that are parallel to the two boundary rays of the cone, we obtain a member of $\mathcal{D}$ (Figure 6.14b). Then, *homogeneity* is satisfied, and in fact, within family $\mathcal{D}$, doing so for each cone in the partition is the only way in which this property can be satisfied.

An alternative way of describing a difference rule is as follows: once awards space is partitioned into cones, for each cone in the partition, specify a monotone convex or concave curve that is unbounded above and below, whose asymptotic directions are the directions of the boundary rays of the cone, and that passes through the origin. Given any point x on the curve, translate this curve by $-x$. The restrictions of all of these translated curves to the nonnegative quadrant fills the cone. When this is done for each of the cones in the partition, we obtain a monotone space-filling tree from which all paths of awards are generated.

CHAPTER 7

Duality

A claims problem can be looked at from two perspectives. The focus can be on what is available or it can be on the shortfall (the difference between the sum of the claims and the endowment). The "symmetry" in these perspectives is easily perceived in the definitions of the constrained equal awards and constrained equal losses rules, for example. It also underlies the lower and upper bounds that we proposed, the two parts of the order preservation properties, the two composition properties, and so on. We have often phrased our definitions of rules and properties so as to prepare the reader for a formal introduction of this intuitive idea, under the name of "duality." The objective of this chapter is to take that step and, in fact, to bring out the great relevance of duality to all components of our program: the concept can be applied to problems, domains of problems, rules, families of rules, properties of rules, and also to operators on the space of rules, logical relations between properties, and theorems, incompatibilities as well as characterizations. It is a major tool to structure the entire theory.

7.1 DUALITY FOR RULES

Solving a claims problem can be understood as dividing what is available or dividing what is missing, the shortfall. The two viewpoints seem to be equally worthy of study. Whether they should take us to the same awards vector is less obvious, but their possible equivalence certainly deserves consideration. In this chapter our first requirement of a rule is that it deliver awards vectors that reflect the symmetry of these viewpoints. First, say that **two problems are dual** if they have the same claims vector and the endowment of one is equal to the deficit in the other. Now require of a rule that in each problem it divide what is available in the same way as it divides the deficit in the dual problem:[1]

[1] The notion of duality for rules and the property of *self-duality* are formulated by Aumann and Maschler (1985). They note a number of passages in the Talmud where the idea of duality is implicit.

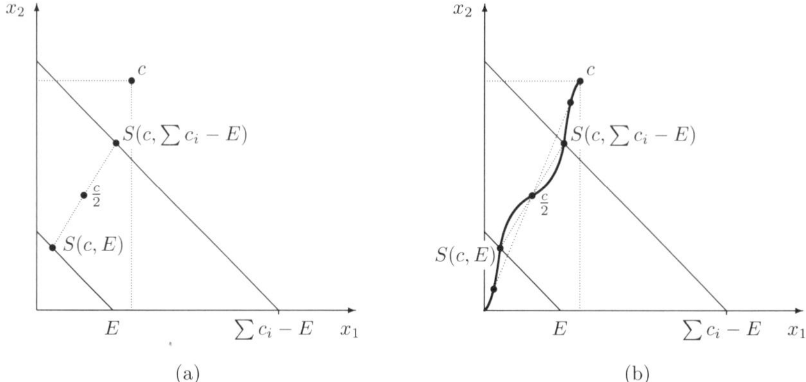

Figure 7.1: **Self-duality.** Let $N \equiv \{1, 2\}$ and $c \in \mathbb{R}^N_+$. We consider a rule S. (a) If the endowment is E, we obtain the awards vector $S(c, E)$. If we apply S to divide the shortfall instead, that is, the difference $\sum c_i - E$, the vector of losses incurred by the two claimants is $c - S(c, \sum c_i - E)$. If S is *self-dual*, these two vectors are equal. This amounts to saying that $S(c, E)$ and $S(c, \sum c_i - E)$ are symmetric of each other with respect to $\frac{c}{2}$. We indicate this symmetry by the dotted segment centered at $\frac{c}{2}$. (The lines of equation $\sum x_i = E$ and $\sum x_i = \sum c_i - E$ themselves are symmetric of each other with respect to $\frac{c}{2}$.) (b) Since such symmetry should hold for each $E \in [0, \sum c_i]$, the entire path of awards of S for c enjoys the same symmetry. This is illustrated in this panel, where we explicitly plot a second pair of symmetric points.

Self-duality: For each $(c, E) \in \mathcal{C}^N$, we have $S(c, E) = c - S(c, \sum c_i - E)$.

Geometrically, the *self-duality* of a rule means that for each $c \in \mathbb{R}^N_+$, its path of awards is symmetric with respect to $\frac{c}{2}$ (Figure 7.1b). Alternatively, for each $c \in \mathbb{R}^N_+$ and each $i \in N$, *self-duality* amounts to saying that the graph of the function giving claimant i's award as a function of the endowment (claimant i's schedule of awards) is symmetric with respect to the point $(\sum \frac{c_j}{2}, \frac{c_i}{2})$. These observations suffice to prove most of the statements listed in the following lemma:

Lemma 7.1

(a) *The proportional, Talmud, reverse Talmud, and random arrival rules are* ***self-dual****.*

(b) *A Young rule is self-dual if and only if it has a representation $f : \mathbb{R}_+ \times \Lambda \mapsto \mathbb{R}_+$, where $\Lambda \equiv [\underline{\lambda}, \bar{\lambda}] \subset \mathbb{R}$, such that for each $c_0 \in \mathbb{R}_+$, the graph of $f(c_0, \cdot)$ is symmetric with respect to $(\frac{\underline{\lambda}+\bar{\lambda}}{2}, \frac{c_0}{2})$.*

(c) *The Talmud rule is the only self-dual ICI rule. The reverse Talmud rule is the only self-dual CIC rule.*

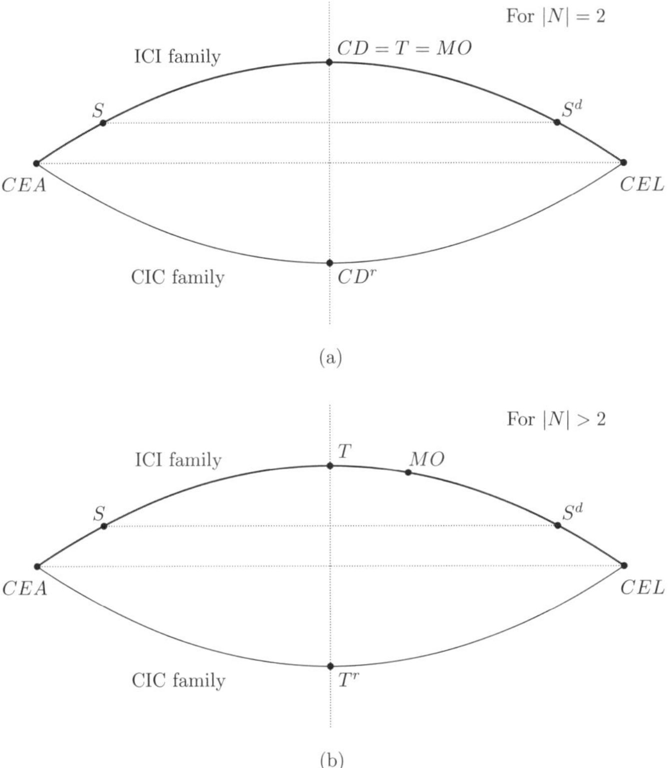

Figure 7.2: **Relating the ICI and CIC families.** These diagrams schematically represent the two families (a) for two claimants and (b) for the general case. Symmetry with respect to the vertical median line symbolizes duality. The two families have two members in common, the constrained equal awards and constrained equal losses rules. Each family contains exactly one *self-dual* rule, the Talmud rule and the reverse Talmud rule respectively (for two claimants, concede-and-divide and its reverse). Both families are closed under duality: given any rule in either family, its symmetric image with respect to the median line is also in the family. The rules S and S^d represent a typical pair of dual ICI rules. For two claimants, both the Talmud and minimal overlap rules coincide with concede-and-divide.

Several of the statements listed in Lemma 7.1 are schematically represented in Figure 7.2.[2] The symmetry in the paths of awards of a *self-dual* rule described before the statement of the Lemma is illustrated for two claimants in Figure 2.1 for the proportional rule and in Figure 2.10b for concede-and-divide (and therefore also for the Talmud and random arrival rules since then

[2] The representation of the ICI family as a strictly concave arc is to suggest that a convex combination of two members of the family is never a member of the family. The same observation applies to the CIC family.

these rules coincide with concede-and-divide). The symmetry in the schedules of awards of a *self-dual* rule can also be observed for three claimants in Figure 2.11b for the Talmud rule, in Figure 2.25b for the reverse Talmud rule, and in Figure 2.14b for the random arrival rule.

Proof: (a) The proofs for the proportional, Talmud, and reverse Talmud are direct and we omit them. They are also implied by statement (b), all three being Young rules. Thus, we only prove the statement pertaining to the random arrival rule. This proof also illustrates a useful general principle, which we will formally introduce once we have the concept of a "property being preserved by an operator."

Let then $(c, E) \in \mathcal{C}^N$. Recall the definition of the random arrival rule as the simple average of the sequential priority rules associated with all the orders in which claimants are accommodated. Now, collect these rules in pairs associated with orders that are the reverse of each other: to each order $\prec$, there indeed corresponds a reverse order, $\prec^{-1}$, and $RA(c, E)$ can be written as the simple average of expressions of the form $\frac{SP^{\prec}(c,E)+SP^{\prec^{-1}}(c,E)}{2}$. We assert that each such expression defines a *self-dual* rule. To see this, let $N \equiv \{1, \dots, n\}$ and suppose, to simplify notation, that $\prec$ is the natural order (thus $\prec^{-1}$ is the reverse of the natural order). Then, as illustrated in Figure 7.3, there is $k \in N$ such that

$$SP^{\prec}(c, E) = (c_1, \dots, c_k, E - \sum_{i=1}^{k} c_i, 0, \dots, 0),$$

and letting $E^d \equiv \sum c_j - E$, we also obtain

$$SP^{\prec^{-1}}(c, E^d) = (0, \dots, 0, E^d - \sum_{i=k+2}^{n} c_i, c_{k+2}, \dots, c_n).$$

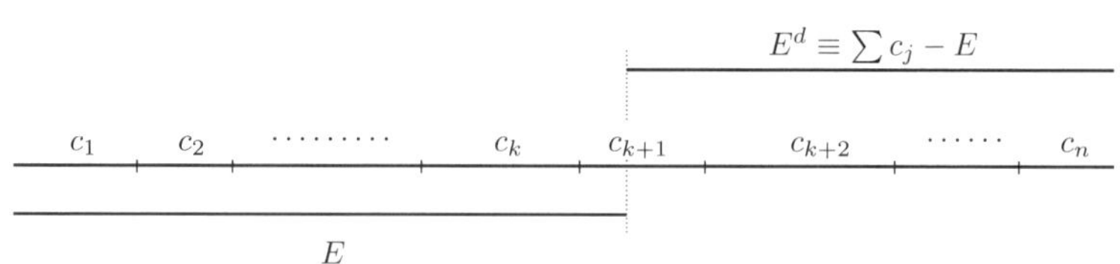

Figure 7.3: **The random arrival rule is self-dual.** Let $N \equiv \{1, \dots, n\}$ and $c \in \mathbb{R}^N_+$. If the endowment is E and claimants arrive in the order $1 \prec 2 \prec \cdots \prec n$, then under the first come, first served discipline, for some $k \in \{0, 1, \cdots, n-1\}$, the first k claimants are fully compensated, claimant $k + 1$ is partially compensated, and the remaining claimants receive nothing. If the endowment is the "dual of E relative to c," namely $E^d \equiv \sum c_j - E$, and they arrive in the reverse order, the last $n - k + 1$ claimants to arrive are fully compensated, claimant $n - k + 2$ is partially compensated (receiving the "complement" of their award for the order $1 \prec 2 \prec \cdots \prec n$, namely, the claim minus their award then), and the remaining claimants receive nothing.

It is easy to check that

$$SP^{\prec}(c, E) = c - SP^{\prec^{-1}}(c, E^d).$$

To conclude, it suffices to observe that *self-duality* is preserved under convex operations. (This is the general principle alluded to earlier and that is formally stated as Proposition 9.7 below; its proof is straightforward.)

(b) Young rules. We limit ourselves to illustrating the assertion, but we should emphasize that the symmetry of the graphs of the functions $\{f(c_0, \cdot)\}_{c_0 \in \mathbb{R}_+}$ providing a representation of a *self-dual* Young rule does not hold for an arbitrary representation of the rule. However, the following representations of several Young rules have the required symmetry to illustrate their *self-duality*: Figure 2.19 for the proportional rule; Figure 2.20 for the Talmud rule when there is an upper bound on claims and Figure 2.22a for the same rule when no upper bound on claims is imposed; Figure 2.26 for the reverse Talmud rule.

(c) ICI and CIC rules. For the ICI rule associated with the list $H \equiv (F^k, G^k)_{k=1}^{n-1} \in \mathcal{H}^N$ (list of pairs of functions satisfying the ICI relations of Subsection 2.2.3), *self-duality* requires that, focusing first on the smallest claimant, $F^1(c)$ and $\sum c_j - G^1(c)$ be equal. Since they have to satisfy the first ICI relation, $F^1(c)$ and $G^1(c)$ are uniquely determined. Turning to the second smallest claimant, and invoking the second ICI relation, we find that, in addition, $F^2(c)$ and $\sum c_j - G^2(c)$ should be equal; thus, $F^2(c)$ and $G^2(c)$ are uniquely determined too. Proceeding by induction, we establish the uniqueness of each pair $(F^k(c), G^k(c))$ for $k = 1, \ldots, n-1$. It remains to observe that the resulting list identifies the Talmud rule.

Reasoning similarly, but this time the order in which the parameters are determined is reversed, we find that only one CIC rule is *self-dual*, namely the reverse Talmud rule. □

For two claimants, and since then the minimal overlap rule coincides with concede-and-divide, we deduce that the former is *self-dual* too. But it does not have this property for any number of claimants larger than two. This is easily checked for three claimants: on Figure 2.16 the schedules of awards do not have the required symmetry that is stated before Lemma 7.1. Also, the proportional rule is the only rule to be *self-dual* and *progressive* (or *regressive*). Another straightforward observation is that, given any rule S such that $S(c, \sum \frac{c_i}{2}) = \frac{c}{2}$, there is a unique *self-dual* rule that coincides with it on the domain of problems (c, E) for which $\sum \frac{c_i}{2} \geq E$ (or on the domain of problems (c, E) for which $\sum \frac{c_i}{2} \leq E$).

Duality operator for rules

• **Definition of operator.** With each rule can be associated a unique "dual," simply the rule defined by the right-hand side of the equation appearing in the statement of *self-duality*:

Dual of rule S, S^d: For each $(c, E) \in \mathcal{C}^N$,

$$S^d(c, E) \equiv c - S(c, \sum c_i - E).$$

This definition is proper (S^d is a rule). Indeed (i) $\sum c_i \geq \sum c_i - E \geq 0$ (the pair $(c, \sum c_i - E)$ is a well-defined problem), (ii) for each $i \in N$, $0 \leq S_i^d(c, E) = c_i - S_i(c, \sum c_j - E) \leq c_i$ (*nonnegativity* of S^d follows from *claims boundedness* of S, and *claims boundedness* of S^d follows from *nonnegativity* of S), and (iii) $\sum S_i^d(c, E) = \sum c_i - (\sum c_i - E) = E$ (*balance* of S^d follows from *balance* of S). Also, as should be the case for a duality operator, the dual of the dual of any rule is the rule itself. Thus, one can speak of two rules being dual.[3] Indeed, given $(c, E) \in \mathcal{C}^N$, note that

$$S^{d\circ d}(c, E) = c - S^d(c, \sum c_i - E) = c - \left(c - S(c, \sum c_i - (\sum c_i - E))\right).$$

Thus, after canceling out terms,

$$S^{d\circ d}(c, E) = S(c, E).$$

Geometrically, for each claims vector $c \in \mathbb{R}_+^N$, the paths of awards of S and S^d are symmetric of each other with respect to $\frac{c}{2}$.

• **Examples of dual rules.** The constrained equal awards and constrained equal losses rules are dual. Given any strict order on the agent set, so are the sequential priority rules associated with that order and the reverse order. In the proof of Lemma 7.1, we exploited the fact that the simple average of two such rules is *self-dual*, but this is true for any pair of dual rules. As another illustration of this observation, the simple average of the constrained equal awards and constrained equal losses rules is *self-dual*. This average is depicted in Figure 7.4a for $N \equiv \{1, 2\}$ and $c \in \mathbb{R}_+^N$ such that $c_1 < c_2 < 3c_1$ (for $c_2 = 3c_1$, the path for c would be that of the proportional rule; for $3c_1 < c_2$, its middle segment would be a vertical segment instead of being a segment of slope 1), and in Figure 7.4b for the three-wives claims vector in the Talmud. Here is the formal definition of this rule:

***Av*:** For each $(c, E) \in \mathcal{C}^N$,

$$Av(c, E) \equiv \frac{CEA(c, E) + CEL(c, E)}{2}.$$

We just observed that the constrained equal awards and constrained equal losses rules are dual. More generally, the weighted constrained equal awards rule with weights $w \in \text{int}\{\Delta^N\}$ and the weighted constrained equal losses rule with weights proportional to $(\frac{1}{w_i})_{i \in N}$ are dual. Similarly, for two claimants, the weighted concede-and-divide rule with weights $w \in$

[3] This observation is made by Herrero (2003). It applies to each of the concepts of our theory: thus, the dual of the dual of a theorem is the theorem itself; the dual of the dual of an operator is the operator itself, and so on.

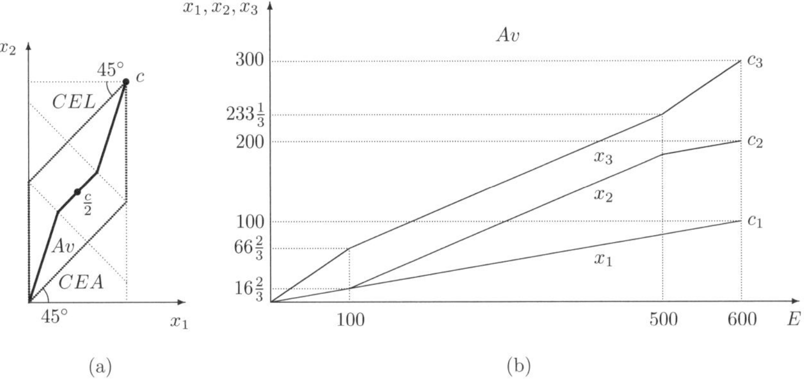

(a) (b)

Figure 7.4: **Averaging the constrained equal awards and constrained equal losses rules.** (a) Typical path of awards of this average for $N \equiv \{1, 2\}$ and $c \in \mathbb{R}^N_+$ such that $c_1 < c_2 < 3c_1$. (b) Schedules of awards for the marriage contract claims vector of the Talmud.

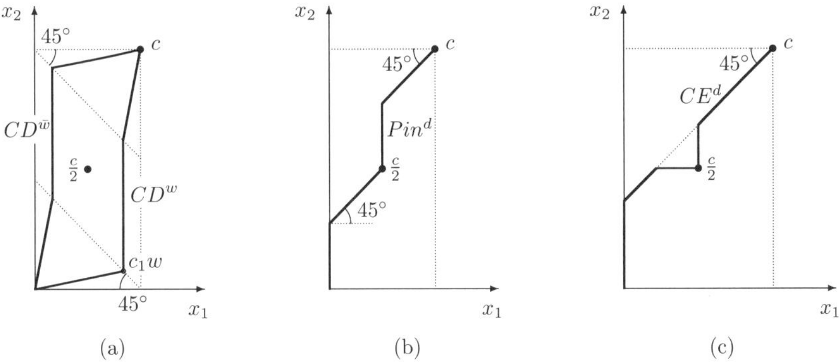

(a) (b) (c)

Figure 7.5: **Duals of a weighted concede-and-divide, Piniles', and the constrained egalitarian rules.** Let $N \equiv \{1, 2\}$ and $c \in \mathbb{R}^N_+$ be such that $c_1 < c_2$. (a) Typical paths of awards of weighted concede-and-divide relative to some weights $w \in \text{int}\{\Delta^N\}$ and of its dual, weighted concede-and-divide relative to the weights $\bar{w} \equiv (\frac{1}{w_1}, \frac{1}{w_2})$. (b) Typical path of the dual of Piniles' rule: this rule can be described as resulting from a double application of the constrained equal losses rule, using the half-claims in the formula instead of the claims themselves. (c) Typical path of the dual of the constrained egalitarian rule.

$\text{int}\{\Delta^N\}$ and the weighted concede-and-divide rule with weights proportional to $(\frac{1}{w_i})_{i \in N}$ are dual (Figure 7.5a). We had not encountered the duals of Piniles' and of the constrained egalitarian rules yet, but here are their algebraic definitions. The rules are represented in Figure 7.5b,c for two claimants.

Dual of Piniles' rule, Pin^d: For each $(c, E) \in \mathcal{C}^N$ and each $i \in N$,

$$Pin_i^d(c, E) \equiv \begin{cases} \max\{\frac{c_i}{2} - \lambda, 0\} & \text{if } E \leq \sum \frac{c_j}{2}, \\ \frac{c_i}{2} + \max\{\frac{c_i}{2} - \lambda, 0\} & \text{otherwise,} \end{cases}$$

where, in each case, $\lambda \in \mathbb{R}_+$ is chosen so as to achieve *balance*.

Dual of the constrained egalitarian rule, CE^d: For each $(c, E) \in \mathcal{C}^N$ and each $i \in N$,

$$CE_i^d(c, E) \equiv \begin{cases} \min\{\frac{c_i}{2}, \max\{c_i - \lambda, 0\}\} & \text{if } E \leq \sum \frac{c_j}{2}, \\ \max\{\frac{c_i}{2}, c_i - \lambda\} & \text{otherwise,} \end{cases}$$

where, in each case, $\lambda \in \mathbb{R}_+$ is chosen so as to achieve *balance*.

A family of rules is closed under duality if, whenever it contains a rule, it also contains its dual. We can also say that the family is **self-dual**. The next lemma identifies several such families:

Lemma 7.2 *The sequential priority, Young's, ICI, CIC, and $\mathcal{D}$ (of Theorem 6.7) families are closed under duality.*

Proof:

(a) Sequential priority family. We already noted this fact and essentially proved it when deriving the *self-duality* of the random arrival rule (Lemma 7.1a).

(b) Young's family. Let S be a member of this family, with $f \in \Phi$, defined on the product $\mathbb{R}_+ \times \Lambda$ for some interval $\Lambda \subseteq \bar{\mathbb{R}}$, being a representation of it. We show that the dual of S belongs to the family by exhibiting a Young representation of it, which we denote f^d. Let $e \in \mathbb{R}$ and for each $c_0 \in \mathbb{R}_+$, let $f^d(c_0, \cdot)$ be the function whose domain of definition is the symmetric image of Λ with respect to e and whose graph is the symmetric image of the graph of $f(c_0, \cdot)$ with respect to the point $(e, \frac{c_0}{2})$. We omit the verification that $f^d \in \Phi$ and that S^{f^d} is indeed the dual of S.

(c) ICI and CIC families (the assertion is schematically indicated in Figure 7.2). Let S be an ICI rule, associated with the list of pairs of functions $H \equiv (F^k, G^k)_{k=1}^{n-1} \in \mathcal{H}^N$ (functions satisfying the ICI relations of Subsection 2.2.3). For each $k \in \{1, \ldots, n-1\}$ and each $c \in \mathbb{R}_+^N$, let $F^{dk}(c) \equiv \sum c_i - G^k(c)$ and $G^{dk}(c) \equiv \sum c_i - F^k(c)$. It is easy to see that the functions in the list $H^d \equiv (F^{dk}, G^{dk})_{k=1}^{n-1}$ also satisfy the ICI relations, and that the ICI rule associated with H^d is indeed the dual of S. The proof for the CIC family is similar and we omit it.

(e) Family $\mathcal{D}$. The dual of a rule S in this family is the member of $\mathcal{D}$ whose partitioning of awards space into cones is the same as that associated with S, but for each cone, the orientation is reversed. (For instance, the two rules of Figure 6.12 are dual.) □

We can also say that **two families of rules are dual** if each of these families consists of all the duals of the members of the other family.

7.2 DUALITY FOR PROPERTIES

The notion of duality can be applied to properties of rules, as follows:

Two properties are dual if, whenever a rule satisfies one of them, its dual satisfies the other. **A property is self-dual** if it coincides with its dual.

A simple example of a pair of dual properties are *nonnegativity* and *claims boundedness*. To see this, let S be a rule and $c \in \mathbb{R}^N_+$. Requiring that for each $E \in [0, \sum c_i]$, $S(c, E) \geqq 0$, is equivalent to requiring that for each $E \in [0, \sum c_i]$, $c - S^d(c, \sum c_i - E) \geqq 0$. Let $F \equiv \sum c_i - E$. When E varies from 0 to $\sum c_i$, F varies from $\sum c_i$ to 0, so that for each $F \in [0, \sum c_i]$, $S^d(c, F) \leqq c$, as asserted. In the pages to follow, we will often change variables in this way but will skip the easy verification that the new variables have the required ranges.

An example of a self-dual property is *endowment monotonicity*. Indeed, let $c \in \mathbb{R}^N_+$ and note that if the path of awards of a rule for c is a monotone curve connecting the origin to c, so is its symmetric image with respect to $\frac{c}{2}$, the path of awards of the dual of the rule for c.

The dual of the *minimal rights lower bounds on awards* is the requirement that each agent receive at most the minimum of their claim and the endowment, which we called the *truncated-claims upper bounds on awards*. Indeed, let S be a rule, $(c, E) \in \mathcal{C}^N$, and $i \in N$ (and this time, omitting the quantifications), $S_i(c, E) \geq m_i(c, E) \equiv \max\{E - \sum_{N \setminus \{i\}} c_j, 0\}$ is equivalent to $c_i - S^d_i(c, \sum c_j - E) \geq \max\{E - \sum_{N \setminus \{i\}} c_j, 0\}$. Introducing $F \equiv \sum c_j - E$, we can rewrite this inequality as $c_i - \max\{-F + c_i, 0\} \geq S^d_i(c, F)$. We distinguish two cases: if $-F + c_i \geq 0$, it becomes $F \geq S^d_i(c, F)$; otherwise, it becomes $c_i \geq S^d_i(c, F)$. A compact restatement of these two conclusions is $t_i(c, F) \geq S^d_i(c, F)$, as asserted. This duality result should not be surprising since we already know that *nonnegativity*, *claims boundedness*, and *balance* together imply the *minimal rights lower bounds* (Section 3.4). Thus, the duals of these three properties together imply the dual of the *minimal rights lower bounds* (this is a special case of a general but straightforward principle formally stated as Lemma 7.3b below.) It then suffices to recall our earlier observation that *nonnegativity* and *claims boundedness* are dual properties and to note that *balance* is *self-dual*: the list itself is invariant under duality.

The two parts of *order preservation*, *in awards* and *in losses*, are also dual, as can easily be seen for two claimants as follows. Let $N \equiv \{1, 2\}$ and $c \in \mathbb{R}^N_+$. Let S be a rule. Suppose, without loss of generality, that $c_1 \leq c_2$. Then the path of awards of S for c lies everywhere on or above the 45° line if and only if the path of S^d for c lies everywhere on or below the line of slope 1 passing through c. The proof for more than two claimants is straightforward. The same observation applies to the two parts of *group order preservation, in awards* and *in losses*: they too are dual. Proving this requires some easy algebraic manipulations.

Every property has a dual. To say that a property is not *self-dual* is to say that it does not coincide with its dual.

An interesting illustration is *claim monotonicity* because its dual is a property that we had not encountered before and because in its hypotheses two parameters change, the changes being linked. Let S be a rule. Let $(c, E) \in \mathcal{C}^N$, $i \in N$, and $d > 0$. Then $S_i((c_i + d, c_{-i}), E) \geq S_i(c, E)$ is equivalent to $c_i + d - S_i^d((c_i + d, c_{-i}), \sum c_j + d - E) \geq c_i - S_i^d(c, \sum c_j - E)$. After canceling out c_i from both sides of this inequality, and letting $F \equiv \sum c_j - E$, we obtain $d \geq S_i^d((c_i + d, c_{-i}), F + d) - S_i^d(c, F)$. This says that if an agent's claim and the endowment increase by equal amounts, this claimant's award should increase by at most this amount (Figure 7.6).[4] Returning to our usual notation, here is a formal statement of the property:

Linked claim-endowment monotonicity: For each $(c, E) \in \mathcal{C}^N$, each $i \in N$, and each $d > 0$, we have $S_i((c_i + d, c_{-i}), E + d) - S_i(c, E) \leq d$.

The following proposition lists the observations made in the previous paragraphs, and it identifies other pairs of dual properties.[5]

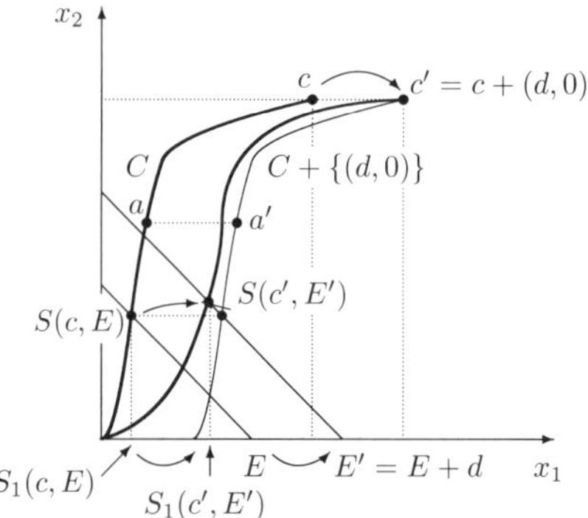

Figure 7.6: **Linked claim-endowment monotonicity.** Let $N = \{1, 2\}$ and $c \in \mathbb{R}_+^N$. A rule S satisfies *linked claim-endowment monotonicity* if, when an agent's claim (here agent 1's claim) and the endowment increase by the same amount d, the agent's award does not increase by more than d. The curve denoted C, which connects the origin to c, is the path of awards of a rule, denoted S, for c. The path of S for $c' \equiv c + (d, 0)$ lies to the left of the translate by $(d, 0)$ of C, as required. A typical point a of the path for c, and its image a' under the translation, are indicated.

[4] This property is discussed by Thomson and Yeh (2008).

[5] The statement concerning the $\frac{1}{|N|}$*-truncated-claims lower bounds on awards* and the $\frac{1}{|N|}$*-min-of-claim-and-deficit lower bounds on losses* in Proposition 7.1 is due to Moreno-Ternero and Villar (2004). Dagan (1996) shows that *claims truncation invariance* and *self-duality* imply

Proposition 7.1 *The following are pairs of dual properties:*
⋆ *positive awards and positive losses,*
⋆ *the min-of-claim-and-equal-division lower bounds on awards and the min-of-claim-and-equal-division-of-deficit lower bounds on losses,*
⋆ *the* $\frac{1}{|N|}$*-truncated-claims lower bounds on awards and the* $\frac{1}{|N|}$*-min-of-claim-and-deficit lower bounds on losses,*
⋆ *conditional full compensation and conditional null compensation,*
⋆ *order preservation in awards and order preservation in losses,*
⋆ *group order preservation in awards and group order preservation in losses,*
⋆ *progressivity and regressivity,*
⋆ *concavity and convexity,*
⋆ *claim monotonicity and linked claim-endowment monotonicity,*
⋆ *claims truncation invariance and minimal rights first,*[6]
⋆ *composition down and composition up,*
⋆ *no transfer paradox and bounded impact of claims transfers.*

Talking about two dual properties separately is justified if they are actually distinct. To prove this, for each property in the pair, this means identifying a rule satisfying the property whereas its dual does not. This can often be done by invoking standard rules, but not always. Occasionally, a rule has to be constructed to make the point. We will see several examples in the forthcoming chapters but our first illustration is here; it concerns *claim monotonicity* and its *dual*.

Proof: (of Proposition 7.1) We only give sample proofs of these assertions.

⋆ *Conditional full compensation* and *conditional null compensation*. A rule S satisfies *conditional full compensation* if and only if for each $(c, E) \in \mathcal{C}^N$ and each $i \in N$, $\sum_{j\in N} \min\{c_i, c_j\} \leq E$ implies $S_i(c, E) = c_i$. This equality holds if and only if

$$\sum_{j\in N} c_j - \sum_{j\in N} \min\{c_i, c_j\} \geq \sum_{j\in N} c_j - E \text{ implies } c_i - S_i^d(c, \sum_{j\in N} c_j - E) = c_i.$$

Since for each $j \in N$, we have $c_j - \min\{c_i, c_j\} = \max\{c_j - c_i, 0\}$, the previous implication holds if and only if

$$\sum_{j\in N} \max\{c_j - c_i, 0\} \geq \sum_{j\in N} c_j - E \text{ implies } S_i^d(c, \sum_{j\in N} c_j - E) = 0.$$

minimal rights first, a result whose proof is almost identical to the proof that *claims truncation invariance* and *minimal rights first* are dual. An explicit proof is given by Herrero and Villar (2002). Herrero and Villar (2001) prove the duality of *conditional full compensation* and *conditional null compensation*. Moulin (2000) proves the duality of the composition properties.

[6] *Weak claims truncation invariance* and *weak minimal rights first* are dual too.

Letting $F \equiv \sum_{j \in N} c_j - E$, this implication holds if and only if $\sum_{j \in N} \max\{c_j - c_i, 0\} \geq F$ implies $S_i^d(c, F) = 0$. Adding the quantifications, this is the statement that S^d satisfies *conditional null compensation*.

The constrained equal awards rule satisfies *conditional full compensation* but not *conditional null compensation* (and by *duality*, the reverse is true for the constrained equal losses rule). Thus, the properties are distinct.

⋆ *Concavity* and *convexity*. We omit the easy proof that the two properties are dual.

The constrained equal losses rule satisfies *concavity* but its dual, the constrained equal awards rule, does not. (The reverse holds for *convexity*.) Thus, the two properties are distinct.

⋆ *Claim monotonicity* and *linked claim-endowment monotonicity*. We performed the calculations before the statement of the proposition to illustrate the operation.

In Section 17.4 we construct a rule satisfying *claims monotonicity* but its dual does not. (The dual rule satisfies the opposite properties.) Thus the two properties are distinct.

⋆ *Claims truncation invariance* and *minimal rights first*. A rule S satisfies *claims truncation invariance* if and only if for each $(c, E) \in \mathcal{C}^N$, $S(c, E) = S(t(c, E), E)$. This equality holds if and only if

$$c - S^d(c, \sum c_i - E) = t(c, E) - S^d\left(t(c, E), \sum t_i(c, E) - E\right).$$

Note that for each $j \in N$, $t_j(c, E) = c_j - \max\{c_j - E, 0\} = c_j - \max\{\sum c_i - E - \sum_{N \setminus \{j\}} c_k, 0\} = c_j - m_j(c, \sum c_i - E)$. Thus, the above equality is equivalent to

$$\begin{aligned} S^d(c, \sum c_i - E) &= m(c, \sum c_i - E) \\ &\quad + S^d\left(c - m(c, \sum c_i - E), \sum c_i - \sum m_i(c, \sum c_j - E) - E\right). \end{aligned}$$

Letting $F \equiv \sum c_i - E$, and adding the quantifications, this equality holds if and only if S^d satisfies *minimal rights first*.

We saw earlier that the constrained equal awards rule satisfies *claims truncation invariance* but that its dual, the constrained equal losses rule, does not. (The reverse holds for *minimal rights first*.) Thus, the two properties are distinct.

⋆ *Composition down* and *composition up*. A rule S satisfies *composition down* if and only if for each $(c, E) \in \mathcal{C}^N$ and each $E' \in [0, E]$, $S(c, E') = S\big(S(c, E), E'\big)$. This holds if and only if

$$c - S^d(c, \sum c_i - E') = S(c, E) - S^d\left(S(c, E), \sum S_i(c, E) - E'\right).$$

Since $\sum S_i(c, E) = E$ and $S^d(c, \sum c_i - E) = c - S(c, E)$, this equality holds if and only if

$$S^d(c, \sum c_i - E') = S^d(c, \sum c_i - E) + S^d\left(c - S^d(c, \sum c_i - E), E - E'\right).$$

Letting $F \equiv \sum c_i - E'$ and $F' \equiv \sum c_i - E$, this equality holds if and only if for each $(c, F) \in \mathcal{C}^N$ and each $0 \leq F' < F$,

$$S^d(c, F) = S^d(c, F') + S^d\left(c - S^d(c, F'), F - F'\right).$$

Adding the quantifications, this is the statement that S^d satisfies *composition up*.

Just before the definition of Family $\mathcal{D}$, we used Rule 6.1 to show that a rule could satisfy *composition down* but not *composition up*. Rule 6.1 is not *claims continuous* but its definition can easily be adjusted so as to obtain a rule that satisfies this property and serve as an example of a rule satisfying *composition down* but not *composition up*. (The dual rule satisfies the opposite properties.) Thus, the two properties are distinct.

⋆ *No transfer paradox* and *bounded impact of claims transfers*. A rule S satisfies *no transfer paradox* if and only if for each $(c, E) \in \mathcal{C}^N$, each pair $\{i, j\}$, and each $0 < t \leq c_i$, if claimant i transfers t units of their claim to agent j, claimant's award does not increase and claimant j's does not decrease. We obtain its dual by replacing in the statement of this axiom $S(\tilde{c}, E)$ by the equivalent expression $\tilde{c} - S^d(\tilde{c}, \sum \tilde{c}_i - E)$ for $\tilde{c} \equiv c$ and $\tilde{c} \equiv (c'_i, c'_j, c_{N\setminus\{i,j\}})$, and simplifying the resulting inequalities. It is the property we called *bounded impact of claims transfers* (Figure 4.9b). □

Let us identify the duals of the other properties pertaining to variations in claims that we have introduced, without attempting to find names for them and omitting quantifications.

• *Bounded gain from claim increase*. Recall that this says that if an agent's claim increases by some amount, their award should increase by at most this amount (Figure 4.8). Its dual says that if an agent's claim and the endowment increase by equal amounts, their award should not decrease. Indeed, calling i the agent whose claim increases and $d > 0$ the increase in their claim, $S_i((c_i + d, c_{-i}), E) - S_i(c, E) \leq d$ is equivalent to

$$c_i + d - S^d_i((c_i + d, c_{-i}), \sum c_j + d - E) - [c_i - S^d_i(c, \sum c_j - E)] \leq d.$$

Letting $F \equiv \sum c_j - E$, we obtain $S^d_i((c_i + d, c_{-i}), F + d) - S^d_i(c, F) \geq 0$.

• *Other-regarding claims monotonicity*. This says that if an agent's claim increases, none of the other claimants' awards should increase. The hypotheses of its dual is that an agent's claim and the endowment increase by equal amounts. Its conclusion is that each of the other agents' award not decrease. Indeed, calling i the agent whose claim increases and $d > 0$ the increase in their claim, we obtain that for each $j \in N \setminus \{i\}$ and each $d > 0$, $S_j((c_i + d, c_{-i}), E + d) \geq S_j(c, E)$.

• *Order preservation under claims variations.* This says that if an agent's claim increases, given two other claimants, the smaller one should lose at most as much as the larger one. The hypotheses of its dual is that an agent's claim and the endowment increase by equal amounts. Its conclusion is that given two other claimants, the smaller one should gain at most as much as the larger one. Indeed, calling i the agent whose claim increases and $d > 0$ the increase in their claim, we obtain that for each pair $\{j, k\} \subseteq N \setminus \{i\}$ with $c_j \leq c_k$, $S_j((c_i + d, c_{-i}), E + d) - S_j(c, E) \leq S_k((c_i + d, c_{-i}), E + d) - S_k(c, E)$.

• *Group order preservation under claims variations.* This differs from the previous property only in that the comparisons of claims and awards are generalized to all pairs of groups. The dual says that if an agent's claim and the endowment increase by equal amounts, given two groups of claimants not containing the agent, if the aggregate claim of the first group is at most as large as the aggregate claim of the second group, then the increase in the aggregate award to the first group should be at most as large as the increase in the aggregate award to the second group. Indeed, calling i the agent whose claim increases and $d > 0$ the increase in their claim, for each pair $\{N', N''\} \subseteq N \setminus \{i\}$, if $\sum_{N'} c_j \leq \sum_{N''} c_k$, then

$$\sum_{N'}[c_j - S_j(c, \sum_N c_k - E) - [c_j - S_j((c_i + d, c_{-i}), \sum_N c_k + d - E)] \leq \sum_{N''}[c_j - S_j(c, \sum_N c_k - E) - [c_j - S_j((c_i + d, c_{-i}), \sum_N c_k + d - E)].$$

After canceling terms, this inequality becomes:

$$\sum_{N'}[S_j((c_i + d, c_{i-i}), \sum_N c_k + d - E) - S_j(c, \sum_N c_k - E)] \leq \sum_{N''}[S_j((c_i + d, c_{i-i}), \sum_N c_k + d - E) - S_j(c, \sum_N c_k - E)],$$

and after changing variables,

$$\sum_{N'}[S_j(c, F) - S_j((c_i + d, c_{i-i}), F + d)] \geq \sum_{N''}[S_j(c, F) - S_j((c_i + d, c_{i-i}), F + d)].$$

• **Preservation of properties. A property is preserved under duality** if, whenever a rule satisfies it, so does its dual. This is another way of saying that the property is *self-dual*. *Order preservation* and *group order preservation* are *self-dual*; indeed, as we have seen, each is the conjunction of two properties that are dual of each other. *Homogeneity*, *endowment monotonicity* (as pointed out earlier), *order preservation under endowment variations*, and the various forms of *continuity* that we have defined, as well as the strict versions of these properties when such versions exist, are all *preserved under duality*. A (non-exhaustive) list of properties that are preserved is given in the next proposition:

Proposition 7.2 *The following properties are preserved under duality:*
⋆ *equal treatment of equals,*
⋆ *minimal sharing,*

- ⋆ *order preservation,*
- ⋆ *anonymity,*
- ⋆ *equal treatment of equal groups,*
- ⋆ *group order preservation,*
- ⋆ *continuity, in its various forms,*
- ⋆ *endowment monotonicity,*
- ⋆ *order preservation under endowment variations,*
- ⋆ *homogeneity,*
- ⋆ *self-duality, and*
- ⋆ *no advantageous transfer.*

7.3 DUALITY FOR THEOREMS

Two theorems are dual if it is possible to pass from one to the other by replacing each of the concepts it involves (properties and rules) by its dual. **A theorem is self-dual** if it coincides with its dual. A characterization of any rule can be turned into a characterization of its dual by replacing each of the properties it involves by its dual. The issue of independence of the axioms can be settled in a dual way as well. The next section and chapters give many illustrations of these and related principles, which we formally state as a multipart lemma for future reference. We omit the straightforward proofs.[7]

Lemma 7.3

(a) *If a rule satisfies a certain property and is self-dual, it satisfies the dual property.*
(b) *If the properties in a list together imply some other property, the list of dual properties together imply the dual of this other property.*
(c) *If a rule is the only one satisfying a certain list of properties, its dual is the only one satisfying the list of dual properties. The principle applies to families of rules as well.*
(d) *Moreover, the properties are independent in one characterization if and only if they are independent in the other. The dual of a rule that demonstrates independence in the first characterization demonstrates independence in the other characterization.*

It is a consequence of (c) that if the properties in a list are incompatible, so is the list of dual properties. Again, the dual of a proof of the first incompatibility can be used to establish the second incompatibility. It also follows that many results can be obtained by duality from ones that we have explicitly stated so far, or that we will explicitly state. In order to save space, we have usually given only one result in a pair and either skipped or only alluded to the dual result. We have often chosen to focus on the constrained equal awards rule, and the index refers to many more characterizations of this rule as to characterizations

[7] Some of these observations are made by Herrero and Villar (2001).

of the constrained equal losses rule, but of course these characterizations come in pairs.

7.4 CHARACTERIZATIONS

Equipped with the notions of duality and of invariance under duality, we are in a position to offer several additional characterizations. We derive the first one from an earlier characterization of the constrained equal awards rule (Theorem 4.2).

constrained equal losses rule characterized

Theorem 7.1 *The constrained equal losses rule is the only rule satisfying conditional null compensation and linked claim-endowment monotonicity.*

∗ On the independence of axioms in Theorem 7.1. ✦ The constrained equal awards rule satisfies *linked claim-endowment monotonicity* but not *conditional null compensation*. ✦ We can construct rules satisfying *conditional null compensation* but not *linked claim-endowment monotonicity* in a dual manner to that in which we had constructed rules satisfying *conditional full compensation* but not *claim monotonicity*. (See the discussion of the independence of axioms in Theorem 4.2.)

The next theorem highlights the proportional rule.[8]

proportional rule characterized

Theorem 7.2 *The proportional rule is the only rule satisfying composition up and self-duality.*

Proof: (Figures 7.7–7.8). We already know that the proportional rule satisfies the two properties listed in the theorem. Conversely, let S be a rule satisfying these properties. Let $c \in \mathbb{R}^N$. By *self-duality*, $S(c, \frac{1}{2}\sum c_i) = \frac{c}{2} = P(c, \frac{1}{2}\sum c_i)$ (Figure 7.7a). For the same reason, $S(\frac{c}{2}, \frac{1}{4}\sum c_i) = \frac{c}{4}$ (Figure 7.7b). By *composition up* and using these two conclusions, since $\frac{3}{4}\sum c_i = \frac{1}{2}\sum c_i + \frac{1}{4}\sum c_i$, then $S(c, \frac{3}{4}\sum c_i) = S(c, \frac{1}{2}\sum c_i) + S(c - S(c, \frac{1}{2}\sum c_i), \frac{1}{4}\sum c_i) = S(c, \frac{1}{2}\sum c_i) + S(\frac{c}{2}, \frac{1}{4}\sum c_i) = \frac{c}{2} + \frac{c}{4} = P(c, \frac{3}{4}\sum c_i)$ (Figure 7.7c). By *self-duality*, $S(c, \frac{1}{4}\sum c_i) = \frac{c}{4} = P(c, \frac{1}{4}\sum c_i)$ (Figure 7.8a2). Iterating, we calculate that for each E of the form $\frac{k'}{2^k}\sum c_i$ where $k, k' \in \mathbb{N}$ are such that $k' \leq 2^k$, we have $S(c, E) = P(c, E)$. (The next steps of the iteration are illustrated in Figure 7.8b2–a3.) We deal with the remaining values of the endowment by appealing to *endowment continuity*, implied by *composition up*. □

∗ On the independence of axioms in Theorem 7.2. ✦ The constrained equal awards rule satisfies *composition up* (Figure 6.7b) but not *self-duality*. ✦ The Talmud rule satisfies *self-duality* (Lemma 7.1a) but not *composition up* (Figure 6.7c).

[8] Theorem 7.2 is due to Young (1988).

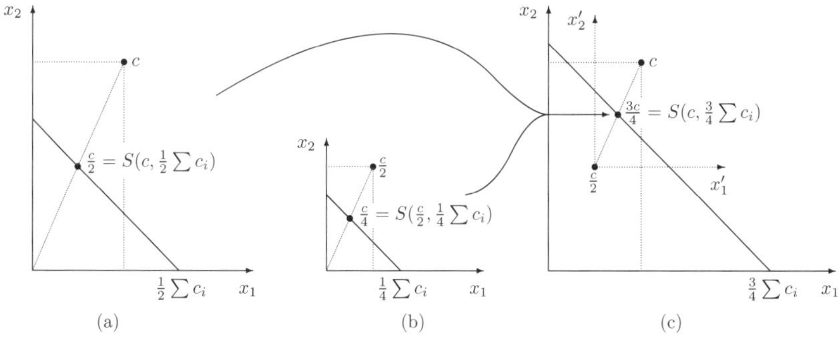

Figure 7.7: **Characterizing the proportional rule: the initial step** (Theorem 7.2). Let $N \equiv \{1, 2\}$ and $c \in \mathbb{R}^N_+$. We consider a rule S satisfying the properties listed in the theorem. (a) Here, the endowment is $\frac{1}{2}\sum c_i$. By *self-duality*, S chooses $\frac{c}{2}$, as does the proportional rule. (b) For the same reason, S chooses the proportional awards vector for the problem obtained from the one of panel (a) by halving both claims and endowment. (c) Returning to the initial claims vector, when the endowment is $\frac{3}{4}\sum c_i$, we deduce, using the conclusions illustrated in (a) and (b) and invoking *composition up*, that S chooses $\frac{c}{2} + \frac{c}{4} = \frac{3c}{4}$. Again, this is what the proportional rule does.

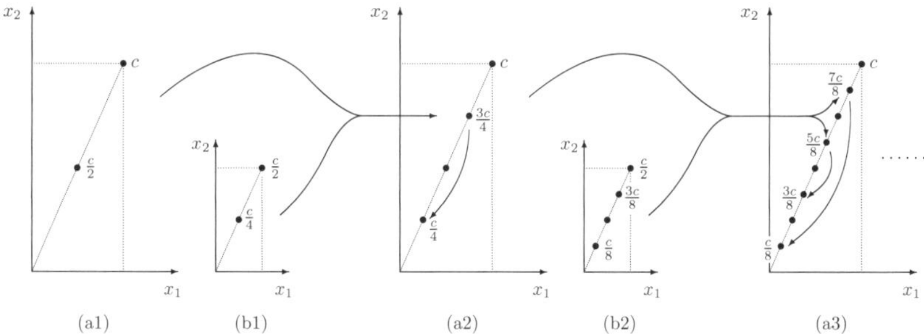

Figure 7.8: **Characterizing the proportional rule: iterating** (Theorem 7.2). Panels (a1), (b1), and (a2) reproduce in simplified form the three panels of Figure 7.7. In panel (a2), by *self-duality*, we obtain from $\frac{3c}{4}$ one more point of the path for c, namely $\frac{c}{4}$. (b2) By the same reasoning, we obtain two more points of the path for $\frac{c}{2}$, namely $\frac{3c}{8}$ and $\frac{c}{8}$. (a3) *Composition up*, together with the conclusions illustrated in (a2) and (b2), gives us two more points of the path for c, namely $\frac{5c}{8}$ and $\frac{7c}{8}$. By *self-duality*, we obtain two more points of this path, $\frac{3c}{8}$ and $\frac{c}{8}$, and so on.

Interestingly, *equal treatment of equals* is not one of the properties listed in Theorem 7.2, although the rule that is characterized satisfies it. *Self-duality* contains a very small dose of *equal treatment of equals* (when the endowment is equal to the half-sum of the claims, *self-duality* implies that two equal claimants should receive equal amounts), and *equal treatment of equals* in that special case is transferred to the whole domain by means of *composition up*.

Because of the duality between *composition down* and *composition up* (Proposition 7.1), a corollary of Theorem 7.2 is the following dual characterization of the proportional rule:

proportional rule characterized

Theorem 7.3 *The proportional rule is the only rule satisfying composition down and self-duality.*

We can also obtain a direct proof of this result by a simple adaptation of that of Theorem 7.2: we first calculate $S(c, \frac{1}{4}\sum c_i)$ by *composition down* and then $S(c, \frac{3}{4}\sum c_i)$ by *duality*; we apply the conclusions just reached to $\frac{c}{2}$ and iterate.

However, we will give another proof.[9] This one is by contradiction, by contrast to the mostly constructive proof of Theorem 7.2 (that earlier proof concluded with a continuity step). It can also be easily adapted to deliver another proof of Theorem 7.2.

Proof: (Figure 7.9) We already know that the proportional rule satisfies the two properties listed in the theorem. Conversely, let S be a rule satisfying these properties. Suppose by contradiction that there is $c \in \mathbb{R}^N_+$ such that the path of awards of S for c is not the path of P for c. By *endowment monotonicity*, implied by *composition down*, and *self-duality*, the path of S for c is a subset of box$[(0,\ldots,0), \frac{c}{2}] \cup$ box$[\frac{c}{2}, c]$. For each $E \in [0, \sum c_i]$, let $d(E)$ be the distance from $S(c, E)$ to the path of P for c.[10] Also, let E be such that $d(E) > \frac{1}{2}\sup_{E' \in [0,\sum c_i]} d(E')$, and $x \equiv S(c, E)$. By *self-duality*, we can assume that $x \geq \frac{c}{2}$. Let $E' \equiv \sum c_i - E$ and $x' \equiv S(c, E')$. By *self-duality*, (i) $x + x' = c$. By *composition down*, $x' = S(x, E')$. Let $E'' \equiv \sum x_i - E'$ and $x'' \equiv S(x, E'')$. By *composition down*, $x'' = S(c, E'')$. By *self-duality*, (ii) $x' + x'' = x$. Subtracting (ii) from (i), we obtain $x - x'' = c - x$, from which we deduce $d(E'') = 2d(E)$, which contradicts the choice of E. □

* `On the independence of axioms in Theorem 7.3.` ✦ The Talmud rule satisfies *self-duality* but not *composition down* (Figure 6.2b). ✦ The opposite is true for the constrained equal awards rule.

Our next result uses a second duality relation, that between *claims truncation invariance* and *minimal rights first* (Proposition 7.1). It is a corollary of Theorem 6.4.[11]

[9] Thomson (2016).

[10] We can use Euclidean distance to the path or distance to the path along lines of slope -1.

[11] A direct proof is given by Herrero (2003).

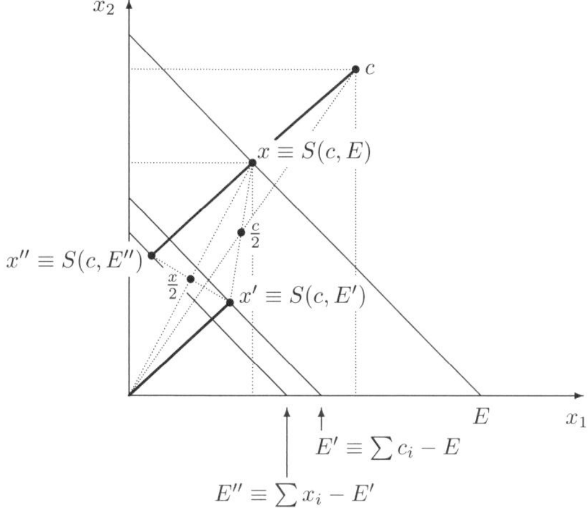

Figure 7.9: **Characterizing the proportional rule: a second proof** (Theorem 7.3). Let $N \equiv \{1, 2\}$ and $c \in \mathbb{R}^N_+$. We consider a rule S satisfying the properties listed in the theorem. We start from x, a point of its path of awards for c that is more than half as far as any other point of this path from the path of the proportional rule for c. We then identify two additional points, x' and then x'', that also belong to the path of S for c. The second point, x'', is twice as far as x from the path of the proportional rule for c. This contradicts the choice of x.

Theorem 7.4 *The constrained equal losses rule is the only rule satisfying equal treatment of equals, minimal rights first, and composition down.*

constrained equal losses rule characterized

We also give a direct proof for two claimants, working with paths of awards. The argument is very transparent then. The logic extends to three claimants or more with no difficulty, but the figures are not as helpful.

Proof: We already know that the constrained equal losses rule satisfies the three properties listed in the theorem. Conversely, let S be a rule satisfying these properties. Let $N \equiv \{1, 2\}$ and $(c, E) \in \mathcal{C}^N$. Without loss of generality, suppose $c_1 \leq c_2$.

Case 1: $E \geq c_2$. (Figure 7.10a). After attributing minimal rights and revising claims down accordingly, we obtain a problem in which claims are equal. Thus, by *equal treatment of equals* and *minimal rights first*, $S(c, E) = CEL(c, E)$. Thus, the path of awards of S for c contains seg$[c^1, c]$, where $c^1 \equiv c - \frac{1}{2}(\min\{c_1, c_2\}, \min\{c_1, c_2\}) = c - \frac{1}{2}(c_1, c_1)$.

Case 2: $c_2 > E \geq c_2 - \frac{1}{2}c_1$. Analogous reasoning tells us that the path of S for c^1 contains seg$[c^2, c^1]$, where $c^2 \equiv c^1 - \frac{1}{2}(c^1_1, c^1_1)$. By *composition down*, the path of S for c contains seg$[c^1, c] \cup$ seg$[c^2, c^1]$ (Figure 7.10b).

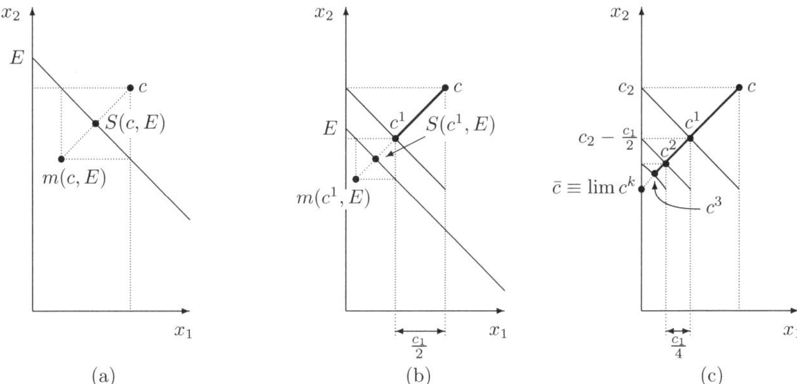

Figure 7.10: **Characterizing the constrained equal losses rule** (Theorem 7.4). Let $N \equiv \{1, 2\}$ and $c \in \mathbb{R}^N_+$ be such that $c_1 < c_2$. We consider a rule S satisfying the properties listed in the theorem. We construct its path of awards for c piece by piece. (a) We calculate the awards vector that S chooses for a typical value of $E \in [c_2, \sum c_i]$. (b) We identify the first piece, a segment of slope 1, seg$[c^1, c]$, where $c^1 \equiv c - \frac{1}{2}(c_1, c_1)$. The length of the projection of this segment on the first axis is $\frac{c_1}{2}$. Given $E \in [c_2 - \frac{c_1}{2}, c_2]$, we deduce $S(c, E)$ by invoking *composition down* and the conclusion reached for an endowment equal to c_2. (c) We obtain the second piece, a segment of slope 1, seg$[c^2, c^1]$, where $c^2 \equiv [c - (\frac{c_1}{2}, \frac{c_1}{2}) - \frac{1}{2}(\frac{c_1}{2}, \frac{c_1}{2})]$. The length of the projection of this segment on the first axis is $\frac{c_1}{4}$. Iterating, we conclude that altogether, the path contains a segment of slope 1, seg$]\bar{c}, c]$, where $\bar{c} \equiv \lim c^k$ belongs to the vertical axis. By *endowment continuity*, implied by *composition down*, $\bar{c}$ should be included. By *endowment monotonicity*, implied by *composition down*, the path should also contain seg$[(0, 0), \bar{c}]$.

Iterating: We obtain a sequence $\{c^k\}$ of points in $\mathbb{R}^N_+$ such that $c^0 \equiv c$ from which we construct a sequence of segments of slope 1 contained in the path of S for c, $\{\text{seg}[c^k, c^{k-1}]\}_{k\in\mathbb{N}}$. The projections of these segments on the first axis parallel to the second axis have lengths $\frac{c_1}{2}, \frac{c_1}{4}, \ldots, \frac{c_1}{2^k}$, and so on. Thus, $\lim c^k = \bar{c} \equiv (0, c_2 - c_1)$. By *endowment continuity*, implied by *composition down*, the path of S for c also contains $\bar{c}$ (Figure 7.10c). By *endowment monotonicity*, implied by *composition down*, it also contains seg$[(0, 0), \bar{c}]$. Altogether, it coincides with the path of the constrained equal losses rule for c. □

∗ `On the independence of axioms in Theorem 7.4.` ✦ The weighted constrained equal losses rules with unequal weights satisfy the last two properties listed in the theorem but not *equal treatment of equals*. ✦ The constrained equal awards rule satisfies the first and last properties but not *minimal rights first* (Figure 5.4b). ✦ The Talmud rule satisfies the first two but not *composition down* (Figure 6.2b).

Here is one more application of Lemma 7.3, a characterization of the constrained equal losses rule deduced from an earlier characterization of the constrained equal awards rule (Theorem 6.6).

Theorem 7.5 *The constrained equal losses rule is the only rule satisfying conditional null compensation and composition up.*

constrained equal losses rule characterized

∗ On the independence of axioms in Theorem 7.5. ✦ The constrained equal awards rule satisfies *composition up* but not *conditional null compensation*. ✦ The dual of any of the rules defined after Theorem 6.6 to show that *conditional full compensation* does not imply *composition down* can be used to show that *conditional null compensation* does not imply *composition up*.

We also offer several characterizations of concede-and-divide:[12]

Theorem 7.6 *For $|N| = 2$. (a) Concede-and-divide is the only rule satisfying the $\frac{1}{|N|}$-truncated-claims lower bound on awards and the $\frac{1}{|N|}$-min-of-claim-and-deficit lower bound on losses.*

concede-and-divide characterized

(b) It is the only rule satisfying the $\frac{1}{|N|}$-truncated-claims lower bound on awards and self-duality.

(c) It is the only rule satisfying the $\frac{1}{|N|}$-min-of-claim-and-deficit lower bound on losses and self-duality.

Proof: We already know that concede-and-divide satisfies the properties listed in the theorem.

(a) Conversely, let S be a rule satisfying the two properties listed in the hypothesis. Let $N \equiv \{1, 2\}$ and $(c, E) \in \mathcal{C}^N$ be such that, without loss of generality, $c_1 \leq c_2$. By the $\frac{1}{|N|}$*-truncated-claims lower bounds on awards*, $(*)$ the path of S for c contains seg$[(0, 0), (\frac{c_1}{2}, \frac{c_1}{2})]$ and $(**)$ the rest of it lies on or to the right of the vertical line of abscissa $\frac{c_1}{2}$. By the $\frac{1}{|N|}$*-min-of-claim-and-deficit lower bound on losses*, $(\dagger)$ it contains seg$[(\frac{c_1}{2}, c_2 - \frac{c_1}{2}), c]$ and $(\dagger\dagger)$ the rest of it lies on or to the left of the vertical line of abscissa $\frac{c_1}{2}$. $(**)$ and $(\dagger\dagger)$ together imply that it contains seg$[(\frac{c_1}{2}, \frac{c_1}{2}), (\frac{c_1}{2}, c_2 - \frac{c_1}{2})]$. Given $(*)$ and $(\dagger)$, we now conclude that it is the path of concede-and-divide.

(b) By Lemma 7.3a, the two properties in the hypothesis imply that the $\frac{1}{|N|}$*-truncated-claims lower bounds on awards* are met. We conclude by invoking (a).

(c) The same logic as in (b) applies. □

[12] Theorem 7.6 is due to Moreno-Ternero and Villar (2004). Theorem 7.7 is due to Dagan (1996).

∗ `On the independence of axioms in Theorem 7.6.` For part (a). ✦ The constrained equal awards rule satisfies the $\frac{1}{|N|}$-*truncated-claims lower bounds on awards* but not the $\frac{1}{|N|}$-*min-of-claim-and-deficit lower bounds on losses*. ✦ The opposite is true for the constrained equal losses rule. Independence for part (b). ✦ The constrained equal awards rule satisfies the $\frac{1}{|N|}$-*truncated-claims lower bounds on awards* but not *self-duality*. ✦ The opposite is true for the proportional rule. Independence for part (c). ✦ Counterexamples can be obtained by duality from those of (b).

concede-and-divide characterized

Theorem 7.7 *For* $|N| = 2$. *(a) Concede-and-divide is the only rule satisfying claims truncation invariance and self-duality.*

(b) It is the only rule satisfying minimal rights first and self-duality.

Proof: (Figure 7.11.)

(a) We already know that concede-and-divide satisfies the two properties listed in the theorem. Conversely, let S be a rule satisfying these properties. Let $N \equiv \{1, 2\}$ and $(c, E) \in \mathcal{C}^N$.

Case 1: $E = \sum \frac{c_i}{2}$. Then by *self-duality*, $S(c, E) = \frac{c}{2} = CD(c, E)$.

Suppose now, without loss of generality, that $c_1 \leq c_2$.

Case 2: $c_1 \leq E \leq c_2$. If $E \leq \frac{c_1+c_2}{2}$, let $c_2' \equiv 2E - c_1$. Note that $c_2' \geq E$. Then by *claims truncation invariance*, $S((c_1, c_2), E) = S((c_1, E), E) = S((c_1, c_2'), E)$. Since $\frac{c_1+c_2'}{2} = E$, by Case 1, $S((c_1, c_2'), E) = (\frac{c_1}{2}, \frac{c_2'}{2}) =$

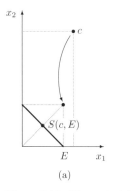

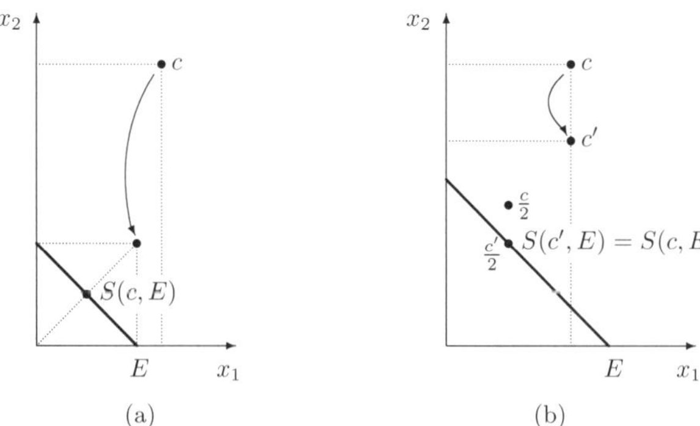

Figure 7.11: **Characterizing concede-and-divide** (Theorem 7.7). Let $N \equiv \{1, 2\}$ and $(c, E) \in \mathcal{C}^N$ be such that $c_1 \leq c_2$. We consider a rule S satisfying the properties listed in the theorem. (a) Case 1: $E \leq c_1$. By *claims truncation invariance* and *self-duality*, S chooses equal division, as concede-and-divide does. (b) Case 2: $c_1 < E \leq \frac{c_1+c_2}{2}$. We compare (c, E) to the problem in which the larger claim is such that the endowment is equal to $\frac{c_1+c_2}{2}$, and we solve that problem by *self-duality*. Invoking *claims truncation invariance* twice, we then deduce that once again, $S(c, E) = CD(c, E)$.

$(\frac{c_1}{2}, E - \frac{c_1}{2}) = CD(c, E)$. Thus, $S(c, E) = CD(c, E)$. If $E \geq \frac{c_1+c_2}{2}$, we conclude by *self-duality* (Figure 7.11b).

Case 3: $E < c_1$ or $c_2 < E$. When $E < c_1$, we obtain the awards vector by *claims truncation invariance*. When $c_2 < E$, we conclude by *self-duality*.

(b) This is because *claims truncation invariance* and *minimal rights first* are dual (Proposition 7.1), Lemma 7.3c, and (a). □

∗ On the independence of axioms in Theorem 7.7. For part (a). ✦ The constrained equal awards rule satisfies *claims truncation invariance* but not *self-duality*. ✦ It is easy to construct rules for which the reverse holds. For instance, the average of the constrained equal awards and constrained equal losses rules, Av, satisfies *self-duality* but not *claims truncation invariance*, as revealed by the following example: let $N \equiv \{1, 2\}$, and $(c, E) \in \mathcal{C}^N$ be equal to $((2, 4), 2)$. Then $Av(c, E) = \frac{(1,1)+(0,2)}{2} = (\frac{1}{2}, \frac{3}{2})$, whereas $Av(t(c, E), E) = \frac{(1,1)+(1,1)}{2} = (1, 1)$. Independence for part (b). The following examples are obtained by duality from the examples used for part (a). ✦ The constrained equal losses rule satisfies *minimal rights first* (Figure 5.4a) but not *self-duality*. ✦ The rule Av satisfies the latter property but not the former.

Theorem 7.7 does not involve *equal treatment of equals*. As was the case for Theorems 7.2 and 7.3, the small dose of *equal treatment of equals* contained in *self-duality* (for each claims vector with equal coordinates, it applies to only one endowment) is carried over to the whole domain by means of the other property required of rules.

The uniqueness results stated in Theorem 7.7 fail for more than two claimants (both the random arrival and Talmud rules satisfy the two properties listed in either part of the theorem). However, it is easily checked that for any number of claimants, the Talmud rule is the only *self-dual* rule S such that on the class of problems $(c, E) \in \mathcal{C}^N$ for which $E \leq \sum \frac{c_i}{2}$, we have $S(c, E) = CEA(\frac{c}{2}, E)$.[13]

The concept of *duality* for properties allows us to relate two negative results established earlier. First is the incompatibility of *equal treatment of equal groups* with *claims truncation invariance* (Section 5.1). Second is that of *equal treatment of equal groups* with *minimal rights first* (Section 5.2). Either result can be deduced from the other by recalling that *equal treatment of equal groups* is *self-dual* (Proposition 7.2) and that *claims truncation invariance* and *minimal rights first* are dual (Proposition 7.1).

Self-duality implies that if the endowment is equal to the half-sum of the claims, each claimant should receive their half-claim (set $E \equiv \frac{\sum c_i}{2}$ in the statement of this property), a fact that is essential in proving Theorem 7.7. There is

[13] This observation is made by Aumann and Maschler (1985).

much evidence in the Talmud for the importance of a half as a "psychological watershed."[14] We write this requirement separately:

Midpoint property: For each $(c, E) \in \mathcal{C}^N$, if $E = \sum \frac{c_i}{2}$, then $S(c, E) = \frac{c}{2}$.

`* Relating axioms` ♦ The *midpoint property* is considerably weaker than *self-duality* since for each claims vector $c \in \mathbb{R}^N_+$, it applies to *only one* value of the endowment whereas *self-duality* relates the choice made for *each* value of the endowment E to the "dual" value $\sum c_i - E$. Another way to gain insight into the relative strength of the two properties is to note that a number of interesting rules that satisfy the *midpoint property* are not *self-dual*, examples being Piniles' and the constrained egalitarian rules.[15] ♦ The midpoint property can be strengthened by adding that if the endowment exceeds the half-sum of the claims, each claimant should be assigned at least half of their claim, and that otherwise, each claimant should be assigned at most half of their claim, which could be called **domination of, or by, the midpoint**.[16]

We omit the proof of the following characterization, as it is virtually the same as that of Theorem 7.2:[17]

proportional rule characterized

Theorem 7.8 *The proportional rule is the only rule satisfying composition down, composition up, and the midpoint property.*

In Theorem 7.7, *self-duality* cannot be replaced by the *midpoint property*. If a rule satisfies *claims truncation invariance* and the *midpoint property*, we can still conclude that it coincides with concede-and-divide for each problem in which the endowment is at most the half-sum of the claims, but this conclusion does not necessarily hold for problems in which the endowment is larger than the half-sum of the claims.[18] However, in Theorem 5.2, *equal treatment of equals* can be substituted for the *midpoint property*: concede-and-divide is the only two-claimant rule satisfying *claims truncation invariance*, *minimal rights first*, and the *midpoint property*. Indeed, if the endowment is smaller than the smaller claim, then after truncation, claims are equal to the endowment, and by the *midpoint property*, equal division prevails. If the endowment is between the

[14] The expression is due to Aumann and Maschler (1985), who cite such evidence. The property is discussed by Chun, Schummer, and Thomson (2001).

[15] Also, the weighted versions of the Talmud rule obtained by thinking of it as a hybrid of the constrained equal awards and constrained equal losses rules all satisfy the *midpoint property* but not *self-duality* (Section 3.6).

[16] Again, see Aumann and Maschler (1985) who write: "it is socially unjust for different creditors to be on opposite side of this watershed [the midpoint]; for one of the creditors to get most of his claim [here, 'most of' should be understood as 'more than 1/2'] while another loses most of his" [again, "most of" should be understood as "more than 1/2]."

[17] Theorem 7.8 is due to Sakai (personal communication). The proof is essentially the same as that of that earlier theorem.

[18] Piniles' rule cannot be used to make this point because it is not *claims truncation invariant*.

two claims, then after attributing minimal rights, revising claims and endowment accordingly, and truncating revised claims at the revised endowment, claims are equal to the revised endowment, and by the *midpoint property*, equal division of it prevails. Finally, if the endowment is larger than the larger claim, after attributing minimal rights, revising claims and endowment accordingly, we obtain a problem in which claims are equal to the endowment; by the *midpoint property*, the revised endowment is divided equally. Altogether, we have obtained the path of awards of concede-and-divide.

CHAPTER 8

Other Invariance Properties

In this chapter, we present a number of additional invariance and covariance properties, some having to do with changes in claims, some with changes in the endowment, and some with changes in both claims and endowment. Several are motivated by considerations of robustness with respect to choices of perspectives in evaluating a change in the parameters of a problem. When changes are interpreted as strategic moves that agents may take, we obtain requirements of immunity to strategizing. Fairness is another motivation and, occasionally, so is mathematical simplicity.

8.1 NO ADVANTAGEOUS TRANSFER

Our first requirement of a rule is that no group of agents get more in the aggregate by transferring claims among themselves. If a group gains by a claim transfer, the complementary group loses, and the distributional properties of the rule that may have led to it being chosen will not be achieved. When the theory is interpreted in the context of taxation, fairness requires that the data pertaining to each taxpayer be truly descriptive of their circumstances (income, contribution of resources, family responsibilities) and transfers may distort the real status of each taxpayer in society. In fact, in this context, income transfers are explicitly forbidden by law. A transfer may be undertaken as a strategic move by a group and in situations in which the relevant data of a claims problem are difficult to monitor, the property is a requirement of robustness to a particular type of strategizing.[1]

[1] A property of this type is considered by Gale (1974) and Aumann and Peleg (1974) for classical exchange economies, and by Moulin (1985) for quasi-linear social choice. *No advantageous transfer* is analyzed by Chun (1988) for claims problems (under the name of "no-advantageous reallocation") together with other properties, defined below. Chun describes the implications of these properties in a model in which rules are not required to satisfy either *nonnegativity* or *claims boundedness* (see Section 15.5 for more on this issue).

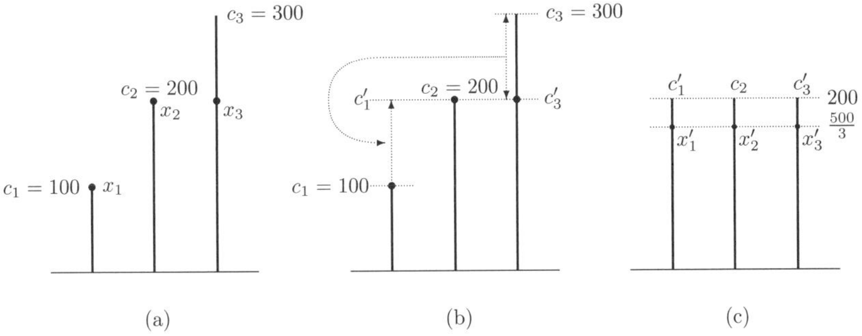

Figure 8.1: **The constrained equal awards rule violates no advantageous transfer**. (a) Let $N \equiv \{1, 2, 3\}$ and $(c, E) \in \mathcal{C}^N$ be equal to $((100, 200, 300), 500)$. At $x \equiv CEA(c, E)$, claimant 1 is fully compensated and claimants 2 and 3 receive equal amounts. (b) Claimant 3 transfers 100 units of their claim to claimant 1. (c) These agents' revised claims are $c_1' \equiv 200$ and $c_3' \equiv 200$. At $x' \equiv CEA((c_1', c_2, c_3'), E) = (\frac{500}{3}, \frac{500}{3}, \frac{500}{3})$, claimants 1 and 3 together receive more than initially: $x_1' + x_3' > x_1 + x_3$.

No advantageous transfer: For each $(c, E) \in \mathcal{C}^N$, each $N' \subset N$, and each $(c_i')_{i \in N'} \in \mathbb{R}_+^{N'}$, if $\sum_{N'} c_i' = \sum_{N'} c_i$, then $\sum_{N'} S_i(((c_i')_{i \in N'}, c_{N \setminus N'}), E) = \sum_{N'} S_i(c, E)$.

The property is *self-dual*.

Obviously, in the presence of *balance* (which is incorporated in our notion of a rule), the property is vacuously satisfied for two claimants. It is trivial to verify that the proportional rule satisfies the property and Figure 8.1 shows that the constrained equal awards rule violates it.

Our second requirement is that each claimant's award only depend on their claim, the sum of the claims of the others, and the endowment.[2] The idea here is that the only thing that should matter in deciding how much to award to a claimant is their overall position with respect to the rest of society as a whole, not with respect to each other claimant separately. This property too is vacuously met for two claimants.

Summation independence: For each $(c, E) \in \mathcal{C}^N$, each $i \in N$, and introducing $N' \equiv N \setminus \{i\}$, for each $(c_j')_{j \in N'} \in \mathbb{R}_+^{N'}$, if $\sum_{N'} c_j = \sum_{N'} c_j'$, then $S_i((c_i, (c_j')_{j \in N'}), E) = S_i(c, E)$.

The property is *self-dual*.

∗ `Relating axioms` ♦ *Summation independence* is the special case of *no advantageous transfer* obtained by considering transfers of claims among all agents but one. In fact, the implication goes in both directions. To show that *summation independence* implies *no advantageous transfer*, let $(c, E) \in \mathcal{C}^N$,

[2] This property is introduced by Moulin (1988) under the name of "decentralizability" and studied by Ching and Kakkar (2000), who refer to it as "no-arbitrage."

$c' \in \mathbb{R}^N_+$, and $N' \subset N$ be such that $\sum_{N'} c_j = \sum_{N'} c'_j$. Note that $(c', E) \in \mathcal{C}^N$. Then for each $i \in N \backslash N'$, $\sum_{N\backslash\{i\}} c_j = \sum_{N\backslash\{i\}} c'_j$, so that by *summation independence*, $S_i(c, E) = S_i(c', E)$. This equality holding for each $i \in N\backslash N'$, we deduce that $\sum_{N\backslash N'} S_i(c, E) = \sum_{N\backslash N'} S_i(c', E)$. Thus, $\sum_{N'} S_j(c, E) = \sum_{N'} S_j(c', E)$, as required by *no advantageous transfer*.

The following characterization of the proportional rule provides a strong argument in its favor.[3]

proportional rule characterized

Theorem 8.1 *For* $|N| > 2$. *The proportional rule is the only rule satisfying no advantageous transfer.*

Proof: We already know that the proportional rule satisfies *no advantageous transfer*. Conversely, let S be a rule satisfying this property. Let $F > 0$ be given and $(c, E) \in \mathcal{C}^N$ be such that $\sum_N c_i = F$. By *no advantageous transfer*, $(*)$ $S_1(c, E) + S_2(c, E) = S_1((c_1 + c_2, 0, c_3, \ldots c_n), E)$. By *no advantageous transfer*, $S_1(c, E) = S_1((c_1, 0, F - c_1, 0, \ldots, 0), E)$ and $S_2(c, E) = S_2((0, c_2, F - c_2, 0, \ldots, 0), E)$. By *no advantageous transfer*, $S_2((0, c_2, F - c_2, 0, \ldots, 0), E) = S_1((c_2, 0, F - c_2, 0, \ldots, 0), E)$. By *no advantageous transfer*, $S_1((c_1 + c_2, 0, c_3, \ldots, c_n), E) = S_1((c_1 + c_2, 0, F - c_1 - c_2, 0, \ldots, 0), E)$.

Consider the function $\psi: [0, F] \mapsto \mathbb{R}$ defined by setting, for each $t \in [0, F]$ $\psi(t) \equiv S_1((t, 0, F - t, 0, \ldots, 0), E)$. Note that $S_1(c, E) = \psi(c_1)$, $S_2(c, E) = \psi(c_2)$, and $S_1((c_1 + c_2, 0, c_3, \ldots c_n), E) = \psi(c_1 + c_2)$, and by $(*)$, $\psi(\gamma) + \psi(\gamma') = \psi(\gamma + \gamma')$.

Since (c, E) was arbitrary subject to $\sum c_i = F$, we deduce the existence of $t \in \mathbb{R}_+$ such that for each $\gamma \in [0, F]$, $\psi(\gamma) = t\gamma$ (Aczél, 1966). Given $(c, E) \in \mathcal{C}^N$ such that $\sum c_i = F$, we now obtain that for each $i \in N$, $S_i(c, E) = tc_i$. By feasibility, $t = \frac{E}{\sum c_i}$, and S is the proportional rule. □

∗`Relating axioms` ♦ Straightforward manipulations of the definitions show that *no advantageous transfer* and *claim monotonicity* together imply *no transfer paradox*. It is also a direct consequence of Theorem 8.1 and the facts that the proportional rule satisfies this property and that, if there are at least three claimants, *no advantageous transfer* by itself implies *no transfer paradox*.

8.2 CLAIMS SEPARABILITY AND VARIANTS

Our next requirement is also an independence axiom. Suppose that, when the claims of some agents change, the agents whose claims remain the same

[3] Precursors of Theorem 8.1 are due to Moulin (1985), for a model of cost allocation, and to Chun (1988) for rules that are not required to satisfy *nonnegativity* or *claims boundedness*. The proof presented here is due to Ju and Miyagawa (2002). The most general results on *no advantageous transfer* are due to Ju, Miyagawa, and Sakai (2007) as they do not limit themselves to our central domain of problems nor to our central definition of a rule.

receive the same aggregate amount as initially. Then each of them should receive the same amount as initially.

Claims separability: For each pair $\{(c, E), (\bar{c}, \bar{E})\} \subset \mathcal{C}^N$ and each $N' \subset N$, if $c_{N'} = \bar{c}_{N'}$, $E = \bar{E}$, and $\sum_{N'} S_i(c, E) = \sum_{N'} S_i(\bar{c}, \bar{E})$, then $S_{N'}(c, E) = S_{N'}(\bar{c}, \bar{E})$.

The dual says the following. Suppose that, when the claims of some agents change and the endowment changes by the aggregate change in their claims, the aggregate award to the others remains the same. Then, each of these other claimants should receive the same amount as initially.

Many rules are *claims separable*. The proportional, constrained equal awards, and constrained equal losses rules are examples. In fact, all of Young's rules are. On the other hand, the minimal overlap rule is not, as revealed by the following example. Let $N \equiv \{1, 2, 3, 4\}$ and $(c, E) \in \mathcal{C}^N$ be equal to $((12, 12, 25, 30), 35)$. Note that $\max\{c_i\} < E$. Using the notation and language introduced in Case 2 of Proposition 2.1, let t^* denote the value of the parameter solving the equation giving $MO(c, E)$. A simple calculation shows that $t^* = 20$. Then the interval that has to be covered has length $35 - 20 = 15$. Agents 3 and 4 cover it with the parts of their claims exceeding t^*, namely $25 - 20 = 5$ and $30 - 20 = 10$. We obtain the awards $x_1 \equiv \frac{12}{4}$, $x_2 \equiv \frac{12}{4}$, $x_3 \equiv \frac{12}{4} + \frac{8}{2} + 5$, and $x_4 \equiv \frac{12}{4} + \frac{8}{2} + \frac{10}{1}$. Let us now consider the problem $(c', E) \in \mathcal{C}^N$, where $c' \equiv (6, 12, 27, 30)$. Here too, $\max\{c'_i\} < E$ and Case 2 of Proposition 2.1 applies. We have $(c'_2, c'_4) = (c_2, c_4)$. The value of the parameter solving the required equation to obtain $MO(c', E)$ is $t^{*'} \equiv 22$. Here, the interval that has to be covered has length $35 - 22 = 13$. Agents 3 and 4 cover it with the parts of their claims exceeding 22, namely $27 - 22 = 5$ and $30 - 22 = 8$. The new awards are $x'_1 \equiv \frac{6}{4}$, $x'_2 \equiv \frac{6}{4} + \frac{6}{3}$, $x'_3 \equiv \frac{6}{4} + \frac{6}{3} + \frac{10}{2} + \frac{5}{1}$, and $x'_4 \equiv \frac{6}{4} + \frac{6}{3} + \frac{10}{2} + \frac{8}{1}$. Now, note that $x_2 + x_4 = x'_2 + x'_4$: the hypotheses of *claims separability* hold; yet, $x_2 \neq x'_2$.

The random arrival rule also fails *claims separability*.

In our next expression of the separability idea, we drop the assumption that the endowments are equal in the two problems under consideration. Suppose that, when the claims of some agents and the endowment change, the aggregate award to the others remains the same: then each of these other agents should receive the same amount as initially.[4]

Claims-and-endowment separability: For each pair $\{(c, E), (\bar{c}, \bar{E})\} \subset \mathcal{C}^N$, and each $N' \subset N$, if $c_{N'} = \bar{c}_{N'}$ and $\sum_{N'} S_i(c, E) = \sum_{N'} S_i(\bar{c}, \bar{E})$, then $S_{N'}(c, E) = S_{N'}(\bar{c}, \bar{E})$.

[4] Thus, *claims separability* is a weak form of *claims-and-endowment separability*, a property introduced by Chun (1999) under the name of "separability." It is inspired by a property formulated by Moulin (1987b) in the context of surplus sharing (Chapter 15) and in the context of binary social choice problems.

This property is *self-dual.*

Finally, instead of limiting ourselves to changes whose effect is unambiguously good or unambiguously bad for the entire set of claimants or some subset, as when we dealt with monotonicity requirements, we propose two axioms that accommodate both possibilities. They differ in the same way as our two versions of separability differed: in the first one, the endowment is not allowed to vary; in the second one, it is.

We first require that changes in the claims of some agents affect all agents whose claims do not change in the same direction: each of them should receive at least as much as initially, or each should receive at most as much. This uniform direction in which awards change can be interpreted as an expression of solidarity.

Claims uniformity: For each pair $\{(c, E), (\bar{c}, \bar{E})\} \subset \mathcal{C}^N$, and each $N' \subset N$, if $c_{N'} = \bar{c}_{N'}$ and $E = \bar{E}$, then either $S_{N'}(c, E) \geqq S_{N'}(\bar{c}, \bar{E})$ or $S_{N'}(c, E) \leqq S_{N'}(\bar{c}, \bar{E})$.

Next, we require that simultaneous changes in the claims of some agents and the endowment affect all agents whose claims do not change in the same direction: each of them should receive at least as much as initially, or each should receive at most as much. This requirement is an even stronger expression of solidarity.[5]

Claims-and-endowment uniformity: For each pair $\{(c, E), (\bar{c}, \bar{E})\} \subset \mathcal{C}^N$, and each $N' \subset N$, if $c_{N'} = \bar{c}_{N'}$, then either $S_{N'}(c, E) \geqq S_{N'}(\bar{c}, \bar{E})$ or $S_{N'}(c, E) \leqq S_{N'}(\bar{c}, \bar{E})$.

This property is *self-dual.*

It is clear that the properties just introduced are vacuously satisfied for two claimants.

`* Relating axioms` ♦ Each of these properties can be weakened by adding the hypothesis that the sums of the claims of the members of $N \setminus N'$ are the same in both problems.

♦ The next lemmas link the separability and uniformity ideas.

Lemma 8.1 *Claims-and-endowment uniformity implies claims-and-endowment separability.*

Proof: Let $N \in \mathcal{N}$ with $|N| \geq 3$, and S be a rule satisfying the hypothesis. Let $N' \subset N$ and $(c, E), (\bar{c}, \bar{E}) \in \mathcal{C}^N$ be such that $c_{N'} = \bar{c}_{N'}$ and $\sum_{N'} S_i(c, E) = \sum_{N'} S_i(\bar{c}, \bar{E})$. By *claims-and-endowment uniformity*, either

[5] *Claims-and-endowment uniformity* is introduced by Chun (1999) under the name of "agreement."

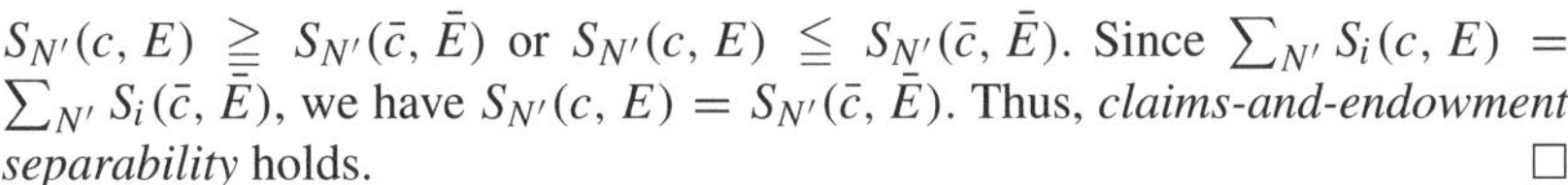

$S_{N'}(c, E) \geqq S_{N'}(\bar{c}, \bar{E})$ or $S_{N'}(c, E) \leqq S_{N'}(\bar{c}, \bar{E})$. Since $\sum_{N'} S_i(c, E) = \sum_{N'} S_i(\bar{c}, \bar{E})$, we have $S_{N'}(c, E) = S_{N'}(\bar{c}, \bar{E})$. Thus, *claims-and-endowment separability* holds. □

Lemma 8.2 *Endowment monotonicity and claims-and-endowment separability together imply claims-and-endowment uniformity.*

Proof: Let $N \in \mathcal{N}$ and S be a rule satisfying the hypotheses. Let $N' \subset N$ and $(c, E), (\bar{c}, \bar{E}) \in \mathcal{C}^N$ be such that $c_{N'} = \bar{c}_{N'}$. We assume, without loss of generality, that $\sum_{N'} S_i(c, E) \geq \sum_{N'} S_i(\bar{c}, \bar{E})$. We invoke the fact that *balance* and *endowment monotonicity* together imply *endowment continuity*. By *endowment continuity* and since $S(c, 0) = 0$, there is $E^* \in [0, E]$ such that $\sum_{N'} S_i(c, E^*) = \sum_{N'} S_i(\bar{c}, \bar{E})$. By *claims-and-endowment separability*, $S_{N'}(c, E^*) = S_{N'}(\bar{c}, \bar{E})$. By *endowment monotonicity*, $S_{N'}(c, E) \geqq S_{N'}(c, E^*) = S_{N'}(\bar{c}, \bar{E})$. Thus, *claims-and-endowment uniformity* holds. □

♦ *Claims-and-endowment uniformity* implies both *other-regarding claim monotonicity* and *endowment monotonicity*, but the conjunction of these two properties is not equivalent to *claims-and-endowment uniformity*. The reason is that the property covers situations in which simultaneous changes in the claims vector and the endowment work in opposite directions. First, if the claims of some agents decrease, by *other-regarding claim monotonicity*, each of the other claimants should receive at least as much as initially. If then the endowment decreases, by *endowment monotonicity*, each claimant should receive at most as much as they did after the change in claims. The direction of the net effect on the agents whose claims are fixed may vary from one to the other.

8.3 CONVEXITY AND ADDITIVITY PROPERTIES

The next properties have to do with convex operations on some or all of the data of claims problems, the claims vectors, the endowments, or both. They relate the choices made for a problem obtained by subjecting two problems to some operation to the choices made for these problems individually. Mathematical simplicity is part of the motivation.

• First, keeping the claims vector fixed, we require that the awards vector chosen for a convex combination of two endowments be the corresponding convex combination of the awards vectors chosen for each of the endowments:[6]

[6] This property is introduced by Chun (1988a) under the name of "linearity" for a more general notion of a rule. Theorem 8.2 is a direct corollary of one of his results.

Endowment convexity: For each $c \in \mathbb{R}^N_+$, each pair $\{E, E'\} \subset \mathbb{R}_+$ such that $\sum c_i \geq \max\{E, E'\}$, and each $\lambda \in [0, 1]$, $S(c, \lambda E + (1 - \lambda)E') = \lambda S(c, E) + (1 - \lambda)S(c, E')$.

The property is *self-dual.*

It is quite strong, as revealed by the next theorem, a characterization of the proportional rule on the basis of this sole requirement:

proportional rule characterized

Theorem 8.2 *The proportional rule is the only rule satisfying endowment convexity.*

Proof: The proportional rule obviously satisfies *endowment convexity*. Conversely, let S be a rule satisfying the property. By definition of a rule, for each $c \in \mathbb{R}^N_+$, $S(c, 0) = 0$ and $S(c, \sum c_i) = c$. Any endowment $0 \leq E \leq \sum c_i$ can be written as a convex combination of 0 and $\sum c_i$, so the conclusion follows by a direct application of *endowment convexity*. □

• Next, we consider convex combinations of claims vectors instead of endowments. Keeping the endowment fixed, let us require that the awards vector chosen then be the corresponding convex combination of the awards vectors chosen for each of the claims vectors:[7]

Claims convexity: For each pair $\{c, c'\} \subset \mathbb{R}^N_+$, each $E \in \mathbb{R}_+$ such that $\min\{\sum c_i, \sum c'_i\} \geq E$, and each $\lambda \in [0, 1]$, $S(\lambda c + (1 - \lambda)c', E) = \lambda S(c, E) + (1 - \lambda)S(c', E)$.

The property is *self-dual.*

If rules were not required to satisfy *nonnegativity*, *claims convexity* could be met, but only by making claimants' losses proportional to a fixed weight vector, a vector of ones if *equal treatment of equals* were required as well.[8] Since no such mapping satisfies *nonnegativity*, the property cannot be met by rules as we defined them.

• Observing that the domain of claims problems is closed under convex operations, we could also take convex combinations of two problems, obtaining a property that obviously implies both of the "partial" convexity properties defined above:

Full convexity: For each pair $\{(c, E), (c', E')\} \subset \mathcal{C}^N$, and each $\lambda \in [0, 1]$, $S(\lambda(c, E) + (1 - \lambda)(c', E')) = \lambda S(c, E) + (1 - \lambda)S(c', E')$.

The property is *self-dual.*

7 This property is formulated and studied by Chun and Thomson (1988) for a domain of problems whose feasible set has a boundary that is not necessarily a straight line (Section 15.7). It is also studied by Herrero, Maschler, and Villar (1999) for a domain of problems comprising all claims problems and all surplus-sharing problems (Section 15.4) under the name of "claims linearity."

8 Bergantiños and Méndez-Naya (1997).

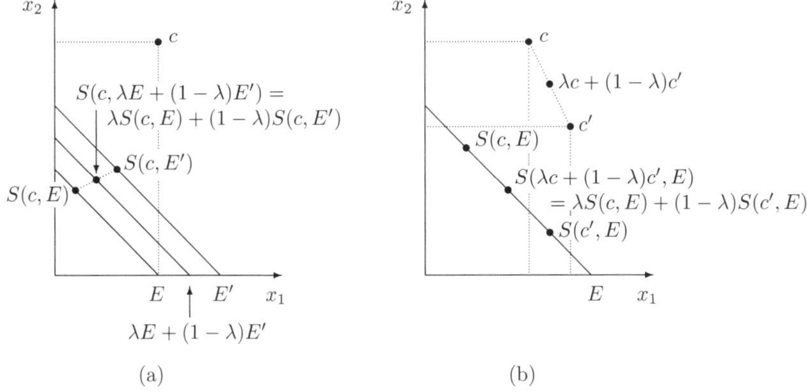

Figure 8.2: **Two convexity properties**. Let $N \equiv \{1, 2\}$. (a) A rule S satisfies *endowment convexity* if, the claims vector is being kept fixed and given two endowments, E and E', the awards vector chosen for any convex combination of E and E' is equal to the corresponding convex combination of the awards vectors chosen for each of these endowments. (b) It satisfies *claims convexity* if, the endowment is being kept fixed and given two claims vectors, c and c', the awards vector chosen for any convex combination of c and c' is equal to the corresponding convex combination of the awards vectors chosen for each of these claims vectors.

• The domain of claims problems is closed under addition, and we require next that the awards vector chosen for the sum of two problems be the sum of the awards vectors chosen for each of them (Figure 8.3a).[9]

Full additivity: For each pair $\{(c, E), (c', E')\} \subset \mathcal{C}^N$, $S(c + c', E + E') = S(c, E) + S(c', E')$.

The property is *self-dual*.

Also, in the presence of *homogeneity*, *full convexity* and *full additivity* are equivalent.

The counterpart for coalitional games (Subsection 14.1.2) of this property has played an important role in the theory of these games. In our context, it cannot be met by any rule however.

Proposition 8.1 *No rule is fully additive.*

Proof: Let $N \equiv \{1, 2\}$ and $(c, E) \in \mathcal{C}^N$ with $c > 0$ and $0 < E < \sum c_i$. Let $E', E'' \in \mathbb{R}_+$ be such that $E' + E'' = E$, $E' \leq c_1$, and $E'' \leq c_2$. Let S be a rule. By definition of a rule, $S((c_1, 0), E') = (E', 0)$ and $S((0, c_2), E'') = (0, E'')$. If S is *fully additive*, (i) $S(c, E) = (E', 0) + (0, E'')$. Let $E^*, E^{**} \in \mathbb{R}_+$ be a

[9] This property appears in Bergantiños and Méndez-Naya (2001) under the name of "additivity." Proposition 8.1 is due to them.

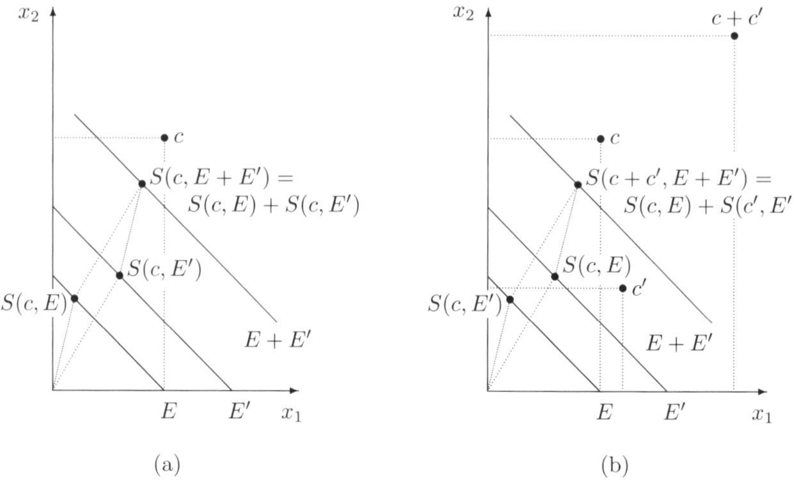

Figure 8.3: **Two additivity properties.** Let $N \equiv \{1, 2\}$. (a) A rule S satisfies *endowment additivity* if, the claims vector being kept fixed and given two endowments, E and E', the awards vector chosen for their sum is the sum of the awards vectors chosen for each of them. (b) It satisfies *full additivity* if, given two problems, the awards vector chosen for their sum (both claims vectors and endowments are added), is the sum of the awards vectors chosen for each of them.

second pair satisfying the conditions imposed on E', E''. We obtain in a similar manner that $S(c, E) = (E^*, 0) + (0, E^{**})$, which contradicts (i). □

In the paragraphs to follow we consider weakenings of *full additivity* obtained by limiting attention to subdomains of problems.

(i) A first weakening of *full additivity* involves restricting its application to problems in which claimants are ordered in the same way.[10] The minimal overlap rule satisfies this requirement.

(ii) Given $\lambda \in [0, 1]$, consider next problems in which the endowment belongs to the interval whose left endpoint is $\lambda \sum c_i - \lambda|N| \min c_i$ and whose right endpoint is $\lambda \sum c_i + (1 - \lambda)|N| \min c_i$. The left endpoint is monotone increasing in λ and the right endpoint is monotone decreasing in λ. Now, define $\mathcal{C}_0^N$ as the domain of problems for which, for each $c \in \mathbb{R}_+^N$, the endowment belongs to the interval whose left endpoint and right endpoint result when $\lambda = 1$ and $\lambda = 0$. For two claimants, this is the interval from $c_2 - c_1$ to $2c_1$. It is nonempty only if $c_2 \leq 3c_1$. Then, the *claims boundedness* constraint is not binding for the constrained equal awards rule and the *nonnegativity* constraint

[10] Bergantiños and Méndez-Naya (2001). Alcalde, Marco, and Silva (2005) consider a version of the axiom that incorporates this restriction as well as two others and base on these axioms a characterization of the minimal overlap rule.

is not binding for the constrained equal losses rule. The interval is centered at $\frac{\sum c_i}{2}$.

Let us then require[11] **full additivity on $\mathcal{C}_0^N$**. This requirement is satisfied by the reverse Talmud rule.

(iii) Another way to recover *full additivity* is to limit its application to problems in which no claim is larger than the endowment.[12] For two claimants, concede-and-divide is the only rule satisfying *equal treatment of equals*, *claims truncation invariance*, and *full additivity on the domain of problems in which each claim is at most as large as the endowment*. However, for three claimants or more, no rule satisfies *equal treatment of equals* and this conditional version of *full additivity*. concede-and-divide characterized

(iv) Our next weakening of *full additivity* involves restricting the requirement to pairs of problems that add to one whose set of award vectors is the sum of their respective sets of award vectors: for each pair $\{(c, E), (c', E')\}$ of elements of $\mathcal{C}^N$, if $X(c + c', E + E') = X(c, E) + X(c', E')$, then $S(c + c', E + E') = S(c, E) + S(c', E')$. For two claimants, this requirement is equivalent to the one stated in the previous paragraph but in general, the former implies the latter. For more than two claimants, the random arrival rule satisfies the requirement but the Talmud rule, for example, does not.

(v) A "post-application" weakening of *full additivity* is obtained by adding to the hypotheses the proviso that the component problems have equal claims vectors and that the choice made for each component be a positive vector. Let us refer to it as **equal-claims-vectors-and-positive-awards–conditional full additivity**.[13]

The next properties are obtained from *full additivity* not by limiting its scope, but by reformulating the required relationship between claims and endowment.

- First, keeping the claims vector fixed, we require that if the endowment comes in two installments, the awards vector chosen for the sum of these installments be the sum of the awards vectors chosen for each of them (Figure 8.3b).[14]

The property is discussed by Sánchez-Pérez (2018) who point out that it implies *claims truncation invariance*. Morgenstern and Dominguez (2019) show that it implies *minimal rights first*.

[11] The proposal is made by Arin, Benito, and Iñarra (2017).

[12] This paragraph is based on Salonen (2007), who introduced this property under the name of "additivity in truncated claims." He also proposed the next version of *full additivity* under the name of "efficient set additivity."

[13] This property is proposed by Flores-Szwagrzak, Garcia-Segarra, and Ginés-Vilar (2017) under the name of "restricted additivity."

[14] This property is formulated by Chun (1988a). It is discussed by Bergantiños and Vidal-Puga (2004) under the name of "additivity on E."

Endowment additivity: For each $c \in \mathbb{R}^N_+$ and each pair $\{E, E'\} \subset \mathbb{R}^2_+$ such that $\sum c_i \geq E + E'$, then $S(c, E + E') = S(c, E) + S(c, E')$.

The proportional rule satisfies this property but, as we will see, it is the only one to do so.

The dual says that if, keeping the claims vector fixed, the deficit that has to be incurred comes in two parts, the vector of losses imposed on the claimants for the sum of these deficits should be the sum of the vectors of losses imposed on them for each part.

A weaker requirement is obtained by adding the hypothesis $S(c, E + E') < c$, namely that no claimant is fully compensated for the sum problem. Let us call it **positive-losses-in-the-sum-problem–conditional endowment additivity.**[15]

The next requirements are special kinds of additivity and invariance requirements in which one of the two problems that are added takes a very simple form.

• First, we require that if all claims and the endowment increase by the same amount, each claimant's award increase by $\frac{1}{|N|}$ of that amount.[16]

Uniform-increase-in-claims-and-endowment equal incremental awards: For each $(c, E) \in \mathcal{C}^N$ and each $\delta > 0$, $S(c + \delta(1, \ldots, 1), E + \delta) = S(c, E) + (\frac{1}{|N|}, \ldots, \frac{1}{|N|})\delta$.

For a rule S satisfying *equal treatment of equals*, $S((\delta, \ldots, \delta), \delta) = \delta(\frac{1}{|N|}, \ldots, \frac{1}{|N|})$, so the requirement can be understood as a weak additivity requirement. Yet it remains a very strong requirement. Of the main rules of Chapter 2, only the minimal overlap rule satisfies it.

The dual says that if all claims increase by the same amount δ, and the endowment increases by $(|N| - 1)\delta$, each award should increase by $\frac{|N|-1}{|N|}\delta$.

• Next, increasing all claims by the same amount – this time the endowment is kept fixed – we require that the awards vector not change (Figure 8.4a). This property, as well as the next one, are requirements on inverse sets of the type introduced in Section 4.3.[17]

Uniform-increase-in-claims invariance: For each $(c, E) \in \mathcal{C}^N$ and each $\delta > 0$, $S(c + \delta(1, \ldots, 1), E) = S(c, E)$.

Here, consider the problem $((\delta, \ldots, \delta), 0)$. Any rule would select $(0, \ldots, 0)$. So, this requirement too can be understood as a weak additivity requirement.

Still, it is a very strong requirement. For two claimants, of the main rules of Chapter 2, only the constrained equal losses rule satisfies it.

[15] This property is proposed by Harless (2017a) under the name of "restricted endowment monotonicity."

[16] This property is proposed by Marchant (2008) under the name of "addition invariance 1."

[17] This property is proposed by Marchant (2008) under the name of "addition invariance 2."

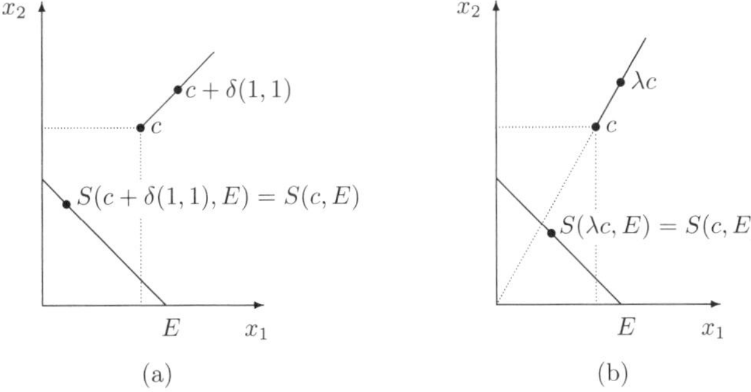

Figure 8.4: **Two invariance properties with respect to certain changes in claims vectors**. Let $N \equiv \{1, 2\}$. In both panels, the endowment is kept fixed. (a) A rule S satisfies *uniform-increase-in-claims invariance* if increasing all claims by the same positive amount does not change the chosen awards vector. (b) It satisfies *proportional-increase-in-claims invariance* if multiplying all claims by the same factor larger than one does not change the chosen awards vector.

The dual says that if all claims increase by the same amount δ and the endowment increases by $n\delta$, each award should increase by δ. This amounts to requiring additivity when to an arbitrary problem is added a trivial problem of the form $((\delta, \ldots, \delta), n\delta)$. By definition, any rule S would select $(\delta, \ldots, \delta)$.

• Instead of increasing all claims by the same positive amount one could imagine multiplying them by the same factor larger than one, and require that the chosen awards vector not change (Figure 8.4b).[18]

Proportional-increase-in-claims invariance: For each $(c, E) \in \mathcal{C}^N$ and each $\lambda > 0$, $S(\lambda c, E) = S(c, E)$.

It is clear that the proportional rule satisfies this requirement but of the main rules of Chapter 2, it is the only one to do so.

A **positive-losses–conditional** version of this property is obtained by adding to the hypotheses that $S(c, E) < c$. It is satisfied much more generally.

The dual of *proportional-increase-in-claims invariance* says that multiplying all claims by the same positive factor larger than one and increasing the endowment so that the deficit remains the same should not affect the losses incurred by the various claimants.

Characterizations. Next we present three characterizations, each based on one of the properties just defined. In each case, only one rule emerges. It is

[18] The conditional version of this property is formulated by Flores-Szwagrzak, Garcia-Segarra, and Ginés-Vilar (2017a).

indicative of the strength of these properties that none of these results implicates any other. The last two are for two claimants only but in Section 10.4 we extend their conclusions to arbitrarily many claimants by invoking a very weak variable-population requirement (Theorems 10.1–10.2).[19]

proportional rule characterized

Theorem 8.3 *The proportional rule is the only rule satisfying endowment additivity.*

Proof: We only prove the uniqueness part, but under the additional requirement of *endowment continuity*. Let S be a rule satisfying the hypotheses. Let $c \in \mathbb{R}^N_+$. Since $S(c, \sum c_i) = c$, it follows from *endowment additivity* that for each $k \in \mathbb{N}$, $S(c, \frac{\sum c_i}{k}) = \frac{c}{k} = P(c, \frac{\sum c_i}{k})$, and then that for each pair $k, k' \in \mathbb{N}$ with $k' \leq k$, $S(c, \frac{k'}{k} \sum c_i) = \frac{k'}{k} c = P(c, \frac{k'}{k} \sum c_i)$. Since, for each $E \in [0, \sum c_i]$, there are sequences $\{k^\nu\}$, $\{k'^\nu\}$ of natural numbers such that for each $\nu \in \mathbb{N}$, $k'^\nu \leq k^\nu$, and $\{\frac{k'^\nu}{k^\nu} \sum c_i\}$ converges to E, the desired conclusion follows from *endowment continuity*. □

concede-and-divide characterized

Theorem 8.4 *For* $|N| = 2$. *Concede-and-divide is the only rule satisfying uniform-increase-in-claims-and-endowment equal incremental awards .*

Proof: We only prove the uniqueness part. Let S be a rule satisfying the property named in the theorem. Let $N \equiv \{1, 2\}$ and $c \in \mathbb{R}^N_+$ be such that, without loss of generality, $c_1 \leq c_2$. We will show that the path of awards of S for c – let us call it Π – is that of concede-and-divide.

Case 1: $0 \leq E \leq c_1$ (Figure 8.5a). Let $c' \equiv (c_1 - E, c_2 - E)$ and $E' \equiv 0$. By definition of a rule, $S(c', E') = (0, 0)$. Setting $\delta = E$ in *uniform-increase-in-claims-and-endowment equal incremental awards*, we obtain $S(c, E) = (\frac{E}{2}, \frac{E}{2})$. Letting E vary in $[0, c_1]$, we conclude that Π contains seg$[(0, 0), (\frac{c_1}{2}, \frac{c_1}{2})]$.

Case 2: $c_1 \leq E \leq c_2$ (Figure 8.5b). Let $c' \equiv (0, c_2 - c_1)$ and $E' \equiv E - c_1$. By definition of a rule, $S(c', E') = (0, E - c_1)$. Setting $\delta \equiv c_1$ in *uniform-increase-in-claims-and-endowment equal incremental awards*, we obtain $S(c, E) = (\frac{c_1}{2}, E - \frac{c_1}{2})$. Letting E vary in $[c_1, c_2]$, we conclude that Π contains seg$[(\frac{c_1}{2}, \frac{c_1}{2}), (\frac{c_1}{2}, c_2 - \frac{c_1}{2})]$.

Case 3: $c_2 \leq E \leq c_1 + c_2$ (Figure 8.5c). Let $\delta \equiv \sum c_i - E$, $c' \equiv (c_1 - \delta, c_2 - \delta)$ and $E' \equiv c_1 + c_2 - 2\delta$. By definition of a rule, $S(c', E') = c'$. By *uniform-increase-in-claims-and-endowment equal incremental awards*, we obtain $S(c, E) = c' + (\frac{\delta}{2}, \frac{\delta}{2})$. Letting E vary in $[c_2, c_1 + c_2]$, we conclude that Π contains seg$[(\frac{c_1}{2}, c_2 - \frac{c_1}{2}), c]$. □

[19] Theorem 8.3 is due to Chun (1988) and Bergantiños and Vidal-Puga (2004). Theorems 8.4 and 8.5 are due to Marchant (2008).

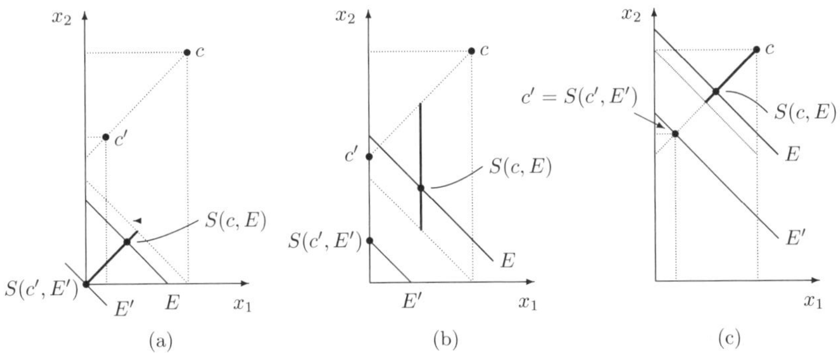

Figure 8.5: **Characterizing concede-and-divide** (Theorem 8.4). Let $N \equiv \{1, 2\}$ and $c \in \mathbb{R}^N_+$ be such that $c_1 < c_2$. We consider a rule S satisfying the property named in the theorem. (a) Showing that its path for c contains seg$[(0, 0), (\frac{c_1}{2}, \frac{c_1}{2})]$. (b) Showing that it contains seg$[(\frac{c_1}{2}, \frac{c_1}{2}), (\frac{c_1}{2}, c_2 - \frac{c_1}{2})]$. (c) Showing that it contains seg$[(\frac{c_1}{2}, c_2 - \frac{c_1}{2}), c]$.

Theorem 8.5 *For* $|N| = 2$. *The constrained equal losses rule is the only rule satisfying* ***uniform-increase-in-claims invariance****.* constrained equal losses rule characterized

Proof: We only prove the uniqueness part. Let S be a rule satisfying the property named in the theorem. Let $N \equiv \{1, 2\}$ and $(c, E) \in \mathcal{C}^N$ be such that, without loss of generality, $c_1 \leq c_2$.

Case 1: $E \leq c_2 - c_1$. By definition of a rule, $S((0, c_2 - c_1), E) = (0, E)$. We add c_1 to both claims. By *uniform-increase-in-claims invariance*, $S(c, E) = (0, E) = CEL(c, E)$.

Case 2: $c_2 - c_1 < E \leq c_1 + c_2$. Let $\delta \equiv \frac{c_1 + c_2 - E}{2}$. By definition of a rule, $S((c_1 - \delta, c_2 - \delta), E) = (c_1 - \delta, c_2 - \delta)$. We add δ to both claims. By *uniform-increase-in-claims invariance*, $S(c, E) = (c_1 - \delta, c_2 - \delta) = CEL(c, E)$. □

8.4 RATIONALIZING RULES AS MAXIMIZERS OF BINARY RELATIONS

Given a rule, we investigate here the circumstances under which a binary relation on awards space exists such that, for each problem, the choice the rule makes is given by the maximization of the relation over the set of awards vectors of the problem.[20] If yes, we say that the rule is rationalizable by the relation or, for short, that it is **rationalizable**. This question is analogous to one that has been the object of extensive literature in classical demand theory. There, the question pertains to a demand function or correspondence, and to bundles of commodities instead of awards vectors. Not surprisingly,

20 *Contraction invariance* and the adaptation of the axioms of revealed preference are due to Kıbrıs (2012, 2013), and so is Theorem 8.6.

the answers that we will provide here involve concepts of demand theory, specifically the "weak" and the "strong axioms of revealed preferences." A counterpart for claims problems of an invariance property that is part of a central justification for Nash's solution for bargaining problems will also make an appearance, as well as two earlier properties of rules having to do with their responsiveness to changes in claims: *claim monotonicity* and *other-regarding claim monotonicity*.

• Let us associate with a rule S a binary relation R^S on $\mathbb{R}^N_+$ as follows: $\boldsymbol{x}\ \boldsymbol{R^S}\ \boldsymbol{y}$ – we say that **$\boldsymbol{x}$ is revealed preferred to $\boldsymbol{y}$** – if there is a problem admitting both x and y as awards vectors and for which S chooses x. Let P^S denote the strict relation associated with R^S. *Rationalizability* is equivalent to the **Weak Axiom of Revealed Preference**, abbreviated as *WARP*, which says that if $x\ P^S\ y$, then it should not be the case that $y\ P^S\ x$: the relation P^S is asymmetric. *Rationalizability by a transitive relation* is equivalent to the **Strong Axiom of Revealed Preference**, abbreviated as *SARP*, which says that the relation P^S is acyclic. Also, a rule is **representable by a numerical function** if there is a function $\mathbb{R}^N_+ \mapsto \mathbb{R}$ such that, for each problem, the awards vector it chooses is the maximizer of the function over its set of awards vectors.

• The following requirement is a counterpart for our model of one that has played an important role in bargaining theory. It says that if a problem changes in such a way that the set of awards vectors contracts but the awards vector chosen initially remains an awards vector of the new problem, then it should still be chosen (in bargaining theory, it is the set of feasible utility vectors that is supposed to contract):

Contraction invariance: For each $(c, E) \in \mathcal{C}^N$ and each $c' \in \mathbb{R}^N_+$ such that $X(c', E) \subseteq X(c, E)$ and $S(c, E) \in X(c', E)$, then $S(c', E) = S(c, E)$.

The **dual of contraction invariance** (we do not attempt to find a name for it) is as follows. Given two claims problems, the hypotheses are that (i) the claims vector of the first one weakly dominates the claims vector of the second one, (ii) the endowment of the second one is equal to the endowment of the first one minus the difference between the sum of the coordinates of their claims vectors, and (iii) the awards vector chosen for the first one is feasible for the second one. The conclusion is that the difference between these two awards vectors is equal to the difference between the two claims vectors.

Next is the requirement that if, starting from some problem, the claims vector is replaced by any vector that it weakly dominates, and that in turn weakly dominates the awards vector that is chosen initially, then this awards vector still be chosen (Figure 8.6a):[21]

[21] Nash (1950) introduced what we call *contraction invariance*. It is usually referred to as "independence of irrelevant alternatives." What we call *claims decrease invariance* is called "contraction independence" by Kıbrıs (2012) and "independence of irrelevant alternatives" by Stovall (2014).

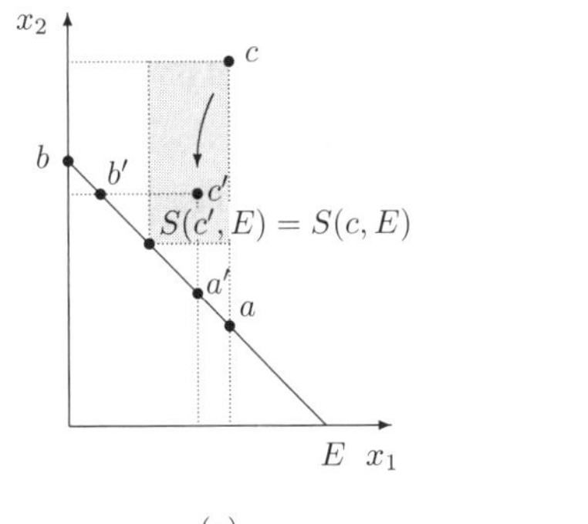

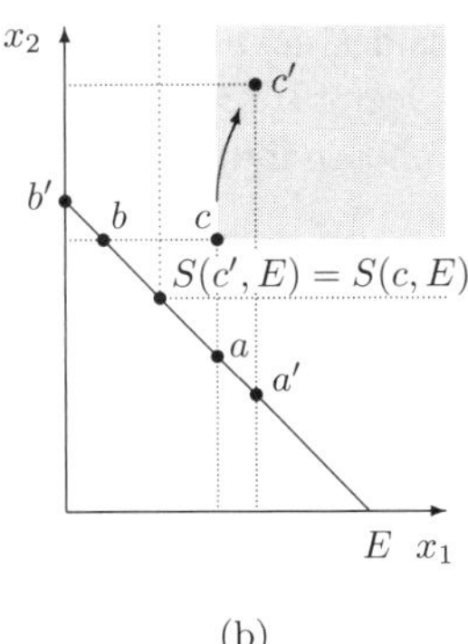

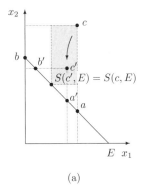

(a) (b)

Figure 8.6: **Two more invariance properties with respect to changes in the claims vector.** Let $N \equiv \{1, 2\}$ and $(c, E) \in \mathcal{C}^N$. In each panel, the shaded area indicates the region of claims vectors c' for which the choice for (c', E) is required to be the same as the choice for (c, E). (a) A rule S satisfies *claims decrease invariance* if when c changes to $c' \in \text{box}[S(c, E), c]$, the chosen awards vector remains the same (note that the set of awards vectors contracts, from seg$[a, b]$ to seg$[a', b']$). (b) It satisfies *claims increase invariance* if when c changes to $c' \geq c$, the chosen awards vector remains the same (here, the set of awards vectors expands, from seg$[a, b]$ to seg$[a', b']$).

Claims decrease invariance: For each $(c, E) \in \mathcal{C}^N$ and each $c' \in \text{box}[S(c, E), c]$, then $S(c', E) = S(c, E)$.

Contraction invariance implies *claims decrease invariance*; the reverse is not true however. Indeed, given $(c, E) \in \mathcal{C}^N$, the hypotheses $X(c', E) \subseteq X(c, E)$ may be satisfied for claims vectors c' that do not satisfy the inequality $c' \leq c$. For example, let $N \equiv \{1, 2\}$ and $(c, E) \in \mathcal{C}^N$ be equal to $((1, 2), 2)$. Suppose that $S(c, E) = (0, 2)$. Then, for each $c' \in \mathbb{R}^N_+$ such that $c'_1 \leq c_1$ and $c'_2 \geq c_2$, $X(c', E) \subseteq X(c, E)$ and $S(c, E) \in X(c', E)$. In that case, box$[S(c, E), c]$ reduces to seg$[S(c, E), c]$.

We omit the expression of the *dual* of this property.

• In bargaining theory, independence properties pertaining to expansions, as opposed to contractions, of feasible sets have been studied too. For claims problems, the most natural expression of the idea is the requirement that if a problem changes in such a way that the set of awards vectors expands (this implies that the endowment remains the same), the awards vector chosen initially still be chosen:

Expansion invariance: For each $(c, E) \in \mathcal{C}^N$ and each $c' \in \mathbb{R}_+$ such that $X(c', E) \supseteq X(c, E)$, we have $S(c', E) = S(c, E)$.

We omit the straightforward expression of the *dual* of this property.

Consider next the requirement that if, starting from some problem, the claims vector is replaced by one that dominates the initial one, then the awards vector chosen initially still be chosen (Figure 8.6b):

Claims increase invariance: For each $(c, E) \in \mathcal{C}^N$ and each $c' \geq c$, we have $S(c', E) = S(c, E)$.

Expansion invariance implies *claims increase invariance* but the reverse is not true. Indeed, the hypotheses $X(c', E) \supseteq X(c, E)$ in *expansion invariance* may be satisfied by claims vectors c' that do not satisfy the inequality $c' \geq c$. For example, let $N \equiv \{1, 2\}$ and $(c, E) \in \mathcal{C}^N$ be equal to $((1, 3), 2)$. Suppose that $S(c, E) = (1, 1)$. Then, the hypotheses of *expansion invariance* are met for each $c' \in \mathbb{R}^N_+$ such that $c'_1 \geq 1$ and $c'_2 \geq 2$, not just for each $c' \geq c$.

We omit the statement of the dual. In any case, no rule satisfies *claims increase invariance*. This is because this property implies that the inverse set of any point contains the translate to that point of the nonnegative quadrant. Given $x, y \in \mathbb{R}^N_+$ with $\sum x_i = \sum y_i \equiv E$ and $x \neq y$, let c be a point in the intersection of the translates to x and to y of the nonnegative quadrant, an intersection that is obviously nonempty (the point $(\max\{x_i, y_i\})_{i \in N}$ belongs to it for example). Applying the axiom twice, we deduce that $S(c, E) = x$ and $S(c, E) = y$, a contradiction.[22]

∗ Relating axioms ♦ *WARP* (equivalently, *rationalizability*) is equivalent to *contraction invariance*. ♦ *Contraction invariance* implies *claims truncation invariance*. ♦ *Endowment monotonicity* and *contraction invariance* together imply *composition down*. ♦ *Other-regarding claim monotonicity* and *contraction invariance* together imply **SARP**. ♦ *Continuity*, *other-regarding claim monotonicity*, and *contraction invariance* together imply *representability by a numerical function*.[23]

A characterization. Our final result in this chapter is a characterization of a family of rules, which we name **K-rules**.[24] Its members are parameterized by two objects,

(i) a function defined on the class of all problems, which associates with each problem a nonnegative vector whose coordinates add up to the endowment (we can think of such a function as a rule on which the *claims boundedness* requirement on awards vectors is not imposed), and

(ii) an "adjustment function," which associates with each such vector another one; this function is required to satisfy certain monotonicity requirements and, when applied recursively, to produce a sequence of vectors that

22 I owe this observation to Flores-Szwagrzak, Garcia-Segarra, and Ginés-Vilar (2017b).

23 The first, penultimate and last statements are due to Kıbrıs (2013). The other two are due to Stovall (2014).

24 Kıbrıs (2013) refers to them as "recursive rules." We avoid this term here because a number of other rules have been defined through recursion.

converges in $|N|$ steps to an awards vector. It is this endpoint that the rule associated with this object pair chooses.

Theorem 8.6 *The K-rules are the only rules that are claims continuous, other-regarding claims monotonic, and rationalizable.*

family of K-rules characterized

Adding *equal treatment of equals*, the only rule that still qualifies is the constrained equal awards rule (and this even if *other-regarding claims monotonicity* is dropped).

CHAPTER 9

Operators

This chapter is devoted to a study of "operators." We consider several types of operators. Our main definition refers to a mapping from the space of rules into itself. In Chapter 7, we introduced a first operator of this kind, the "duality operator." In this chapter, we base on two invariance ideas, invariance under truncation of claims at the endowment and invariance under attribution of minimal rights (Chapter 5), the definition of two more operators, the "claims truncation operator" and the "attribution of minimal rights operator." We introduce a fourth one, the "convexity operator," which exploits the convex structure of the space of rules.[1] We then undertake a systematic investigation of these operators: we uncover relations among them and identify which properties of rules each preserves, or does not preserve.

We turn next to a different type of operator, which we name "extension operators." Such an operator associates with each incompletely specified rule – we consider several ways in which a rule can be incompletely specified – a well-defined one.

The concept of an operator is extremely useful in relating rules, in deriving certain properties they have from the knowledge that certain other rules satisfy these properties, in deriving new characterizations or counterexamples from existing ones, in short, in structuring the space of rules and the entire theory.

9.1 CLAIMS TRUNCATION OPERATOR

We begin with an operator on the space of rules based on the idea that the part of a claim that exceeds the endowment could be considered irrelevant. With each rule S we associate the rule defined, for each problem, by first truncating each claim at the endowment, and then applying S:

Rule S operated from truncated claims, S^t: For each $(c, E) \in \mathcal{C}^N$,

$$S^t(c, E) \equiv S(t(c, E), E).$$

[1] Another operator from the space of rules into itself is introduced by Giménez-Gómez and Peris (2014).

We call the mapping $S \mapsto S^t$ the **claims truncation operator**.

Of course, if a rule is *claims truncation invariant*, it coincides with its image under the claims truncation operator. This is the case for the constrained equal awards rule.

Let $c \in \mathbb{R}^N_+$. As the endowment increases from zero, all truncated claims are equal at first; if S satisfies *equal treatment of equals*, S^t assigns equal amounts to all claimants. As the endowment increases further, fewer and fewer claims need to be truncated and the set of claimants who have to receive equal amounts shrinks. When the endowment is larger than the largest claim, no claim is truncated and the choices made by S^t and S coincide.

• **Examples.** Let us apply the claims truncation operator to the proportional rule, P, for two claimants, and derive the path of awards of P^t for a typical claims vector (Figure 9.1a). Let $N \equiv \{1, 2\}$ and $c \in \mathbb{R}^N_+$ be such that, without loss of generality, $c_1 < c_2$. This path is in three parts, (i) seg$[0, (\frac{c_1}{2}, \frac{c_1}{2})]$, (ii) the portion of the curve of equation $x_2 = \frac{x_1^2}{c_1 - x_1}$ that lies between the lines of equations $\sum x_i = c_1$ and $\sum x_i = c_2$ – let a be the topmost point of this arc – and (iii) seg$[a, c]$, a subset of seg$[0, c]$. Statements (i) and (iii) illustrate the observations made in the previous paragraph. To illustrate P^t for three claimants, we show its schedules of awards for the marriage contract claims vector of the Talmud (Figure 9.1b).

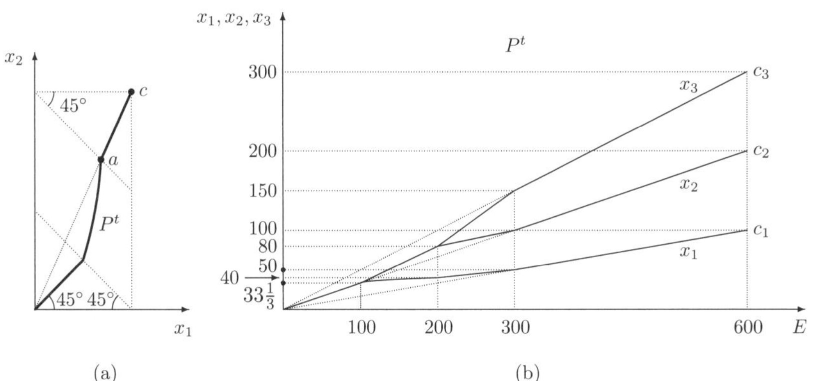

Figure 9.1: **Proportional rule operated from truncated claims.** If the endowment falls short of the smallest claim, the rule chooses equal division. If the endowment exceeds the largest claim, it chooses proportional division. (a) Typical path of award of P^t for $N \equiv \{1, 2\}$ and $c \in \mathbb{R}^N_+$ such that $c_1 < c_2$. The path is curved between the two lines of slope -1 emanating from the southeast and northwest corners of box$[0, c]$. (b) Schedules of awards of P^t for the marriage contract claims vector of the Talmud. For an endowment in the intervals $[100, 200]$ and $[200, 300]$, the schedules are curved (the curvature is too small to be noticeable).

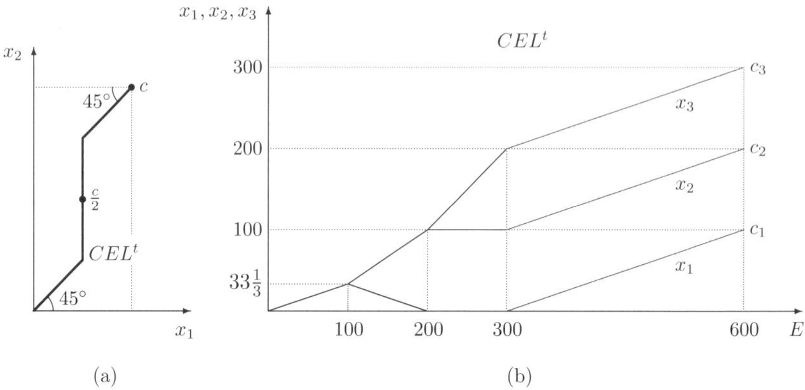

Figure 9.2: **Constrained equal losses rule operated from truncated claims.** (a) Typical path of awards of CEL^t for $N \equiv \{1, 2\}$ and $c \in \mathbb{R}^N_+$ such that $c_1 < c_2$. (b) Schedules of awards of CEL^t for the marriage contract claims vector of the Talmud.

Interestingly, for two claimants, the rule obtained by subjecting the constrained equal losses rule to the claims truncation operator coincides with concede-and-divide (Figure 9.2a). To see this, let $N \equiv \{1, 2\}$ and suppose that, without loss of generality, $c_1 < c_2$. Then if $E \leq c_1$, after truncation, both claims are equal and equal division prevails, as explained above. If $E \in [c_1, c_2]$, only agent 2's claim need to be truncated and if we keep claimant 1's award constant at $\frac{c_1}{2}$ and assign the remainder of the endowment to agent 2, both claimants incur a loss equal to $\frac{c_1}{2}$. If $E \in [c_2, \sum c_i]$, no truncation is needed, and equal division of the deficit takes place. Note that for no endowment is the nonnegativity constraint binding at the point of equal losses.

For three claimants or more, things are more complicated. An illustration for the marriage contract claims vector (100, 200, 300) of the Talmud is given in Figure 9.2b. The nonnegativity constraint is not binding at the point of equal losses from truncated claims, no matter what the estate is, but barely ("barely" because for each estate between 200 and 300, claimant 1 receives 0). Here is an example for which the constraint is binding: let $N \equiv \{1, 2, 3\}$ and $(c, E) \in \mathcal{C}^N$ be equal to ((1, 20, 20), 10). Then, at the point of equal losses from truncated claims, claimant 1 would receive $1 - \frac{11}{3}$, a negative amount.

9.2 ATTRIBUTION OF MINIMAL RIGHTS OPERATOR

We based the definition of the two-claimant rule we call concede-and-divide on the idea that for each $(c, E) \in \mathcal{C}^N$ and each $i \in N$, claimant i can be understood as conceding the difference $E - c_i$ to the other claimant (or 0 if this difference is negative). First attributing to each claimant the amount conceded to them by the other – switching perspectives, we called this amount the "minimal right" in Section 3.4 – and in a second step, taking care of the residual endowment, is an appealing way to break down a problem into components about which one may have stronger intuition. Two variants of the idea can be formulated depending upon whether or not claims are revised down prior to the second step, but it seems most natural to carry out this revision, and we did so. Thus, we propose to associate with each rule S the rule obtained by the following two-step process, which we now define for an arbitrary number of claimants: for each problem, first assign to each claimant their minimal right; revise claims down by these first-round awards, and divide the residual endowment by applying S.[2]

Rule S operated from minimal rights, S^m: For each $(c, E) \in \mathcal{C}^N$,

$$S^m(c, E) \equiv m(c, E) + S\left(c - m(c, E), E - \sum m_i(c, E)\right).$$

We call the mapping $S \mapsto S^m$ the **attribution of minimal rights operator**.

Of course, if a rule satisfies *minimal rights first*, it is invariant under this operator. This is the case for the constrained equal losses rule.

Note that if a claimant's minimal right is positive, after being revised down by this amount, their claim is equal to the deficit. Indeed, if $m_i(c, E) \equiv \max\{E - \sum_{N\setminus\{i\}} c_j, 0\} > 0$, then $c_i - m_i(c, E) = \sum c_j - E$. Thus, any two claims that are revised down are equal after the revision. Also, these revisions do not affect how claims are ordered: if $c_i \leq c_j$, then $c_i - m_i(c, E) \leq c_j - m_j(c, E)$, or equivalently:

$$(*) \quad c_i - \max\{E - \sum_{N\setminus\{i\}} c_k, 0\} \leq c_j - \max\{E - \sum_{N\setminus\{j\}} c_k, 0\}.$$

To prove $(*)$, note first that since $c_i \leq c_j$, then $\sum_{N\setminus\{i\}} c_k \geq \sum_{N\setminus\{j\}} c_k$. We distinguish three cases:

Case 1: $E \leq \sum_{N\setminus\{j\}} c_k$. Then $(*)$ becomes $c_i \leq c_j$, which is true by hypothesis.

Case 2: $\sum_{N\setminus\{j\}} c_k < E \leq \sum_{N\setminus\{i\}} c_k$. Then $(*)$ becomes $c_i \leq c_j - [E - \sum_{N\setminus\{j\}} c_k)$, or $E \leq \sum_{N\setminus\{i\}} c_k$, which is true by hypothesis.

Case 3: $\sum_{N\setminus\{i\}} c_k < E$. Then $(*)$ becomes $\sum_N c_k - E \leq \sum_N c_k - E$.

• **Examples.** Our first application of the attribution of minimal rights operator is to the proportional rule. The resulting rule is illustrated in Figure 9.3.

If, instead, we start from the constrained equal awards rule, we obtain the rule illustrated in Figure 9.4. For two claimants, this rule coincides with

[2] We proved in Section 3.4 that the revised problem is well defined. If claims were not revised after the attribution of the minimal rights, we would obtain the vector $m(c, E) + S\left(c, E - \sum m_i(c, E)\right)$, which would not necessarily be an awards vector of (c, E): indeed, an agent could receive more than their claim.

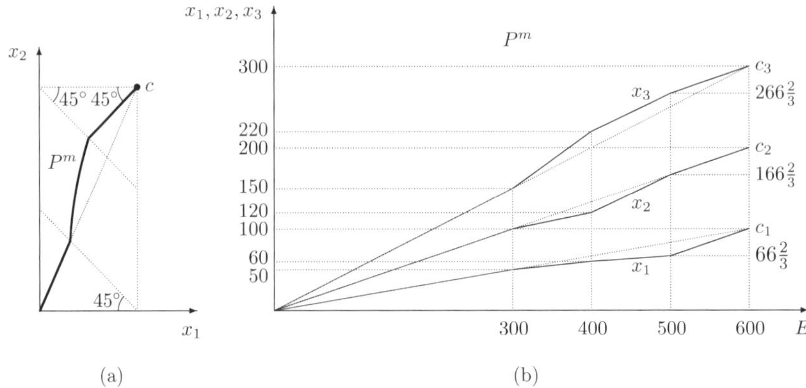

Figure 9.3: **Proportional rule operated from minimal rights.** If the endowment falls short of the smallest claim, the rule chooses proportional division. If the endowment exceeds the largest claim, it chooses equal division. (a) Typical path of awards for $N \equiv \{1, 2\}$ and $c \in \mathbb{R}^N_+$ such that $c_1 < c_2$. The path is curved between the two lines of slope -1 emanating from the southeast and northwest corners of box$[0, c]$. (b) Schedules of awards of P^m for the marriage contract claims vector of the Talmud. For an endowment in the intervals $[300, 400]$ and $[400, 500]$, the schedules are curved (the curvature is too small to be noticeable).

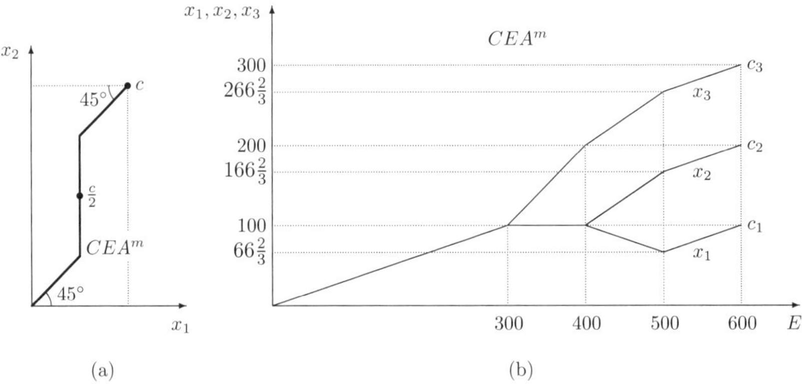

Figure 9.4: **Constrained equal awards rule operated from minimal rights.** (a) Typical path of awards of CEA^m for $N \equiv \{1, 2\}$ and $c \in \mathbb{R}^N_+$ such that $c_1 < c_2$. (b) Schedules of awards of CEA^m for the marriage contract claims vector of the Talmud.

concede-and-divide (Figure 9.4a) as easily seen. Note that for the marriage contract problem of the Talmud, when the estate lies in the interval $[300, 400]$, the constraint that claimant 1 not be assigned more than their claim is met as an equality, claimant 1 being fully compensated (Figure 9.4b).

9.3 CONVEXITY OPERATOR

We introduce here the operator that associates a new rule with each ordered list of rules and each ordered list of nonnegative weights adding up to one, one weight for each rule. This new rule is intended to provide a compromise between them.[3]

• **Definition of operator.** The idea of averaging as a means of compromising is a recurrent theme in game theory and the theory of resource allocation. Taking convex combinations of rules is particularly tempting here because the set of awards vectors of each problem is convex. In many situations, averaging corresponds to operating some random device (flipping a coin; drawing from a deck of cards), and it allows reconciling objectives that are perceived as skewed in opposite directions.[4] The non-convexity of efficient sets, for instance in bargaining theory or in classical resource allocation theory, often denies us the benefits of randomization, but in the present context, we face no such difficulty.

In contrast with the operators previously defined, the operator we introduce here takes pairs of lists as arguments. Let K be a finite set:[5]

Weighted average of $(S^k)_{k\in K}$ with weights $(\lambda^k)_{k\in K} \in \Delta^K$, $w((S^k)_{k\in K}, (\lambda^k)_{k\in K})$: For each $(c, E) \in \mathcal{C}^N$,

$$w((S^k)_{k\in K}, (\lambda^k)_{k\in K})(c, E) \equiv \sum_{k\in K} \lambda^k S^k(c, E).$$

We call the mapping $((S^k)_{k\in K}, (\lambda^k)_{k\in K}) \mapsto \sum_{k\in K} \lambda^k S^k(c, E)$ a **convexity operator**. Note that for each problem, averaging occurs along budget lines.

• **Examples.** We have already encountered the rule defined as the average of the constrained equal awards and constrained equal losses rules (Section 7.1). This averaging gives us a compromise between the somewhat extreme (subject to *order preservation*) and opposite ways in which these two rules treat the smaller claimants in relation to the larger claimants. More generally, we could place unequal weights on the two rules. For two claimants and a fixed claims vector, Figure 9.5 shows paths of awards for several weight vectors.

The random arrival rule can be seen as the result of compromising among the extreme ways in which the sequential priority rules treat claimants (here there are no constraints).

[3] Thomson and Yeh (2001).

[4] Note that the resolution given in the Talmud for the contested garment problem is the average of the divisions (100, 100) and (0, 200) that are the most advantageous to each of the two claimants.

[5] We require finiteness for mathematical simplicity. Ju and Moreno-Ternero (2007) fix a rule $\bar{S}$, and for each $\lambda \in [0, 1]$, work with the operator that associates with each rule S the convex combination of S and $\bar{S}$ with weights λ and $1 - \lambda$. Thus, their operator is indexed by a pair $(\bar{S}, \lambda)$ of a rule and a point in the unit interval.

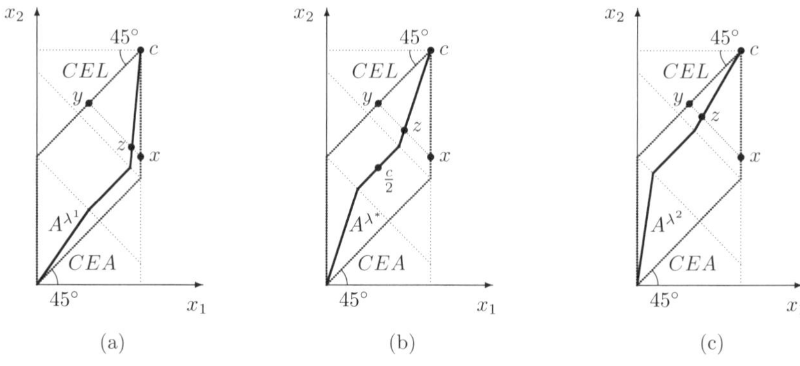

Figure 9.5: **Three weighted averages of the constrained equal awards and constrained equal losses rules.** For each problem, we average along the budget line the recommendations made by the constrained equal awards and constrained equal losses rules. When the endowment is allowed to vary in $[0, \sum c_i]$, we obtain the average of their paths of awards along lines of slope -1. In each panel, a budget line is shown together with the two awards vectors, x and y, selected by these two rules along that budget line. Their average is denoted z. (a) Here, a larger weight is placed on the constrained equal awards rule than on the constrained equal losses rule: $\lambda^1 \equiv (\frac{4}{5}, \frac{1}{5})$. (b) Here, equal weights are placed on both rules: $\lambda^* \equiv (\frac{1}{2}, \frac{1}{2})$. (c) Now, a larger weight is placed on the constrained equal losses rule than on the constrained equal awards rule: $\lambda^2 \equiv (\frac{1}{4}, \frac{3}{4})$.

9.4 RELATING AND COMPOSING THE OPERATORS

In this section, we establish a number of links between the operators we have defined.[6] Given a rule S, we denote the rule obtained by subjecting it to the operator p and then to the operator p', namely $(S^p)^{p'}$, by $S^{p' \circ p}$.

We first describe the result of the composition with itself of each of the duality, claims truncation, and attribution of minimal rights operators. We have already made these observations, but we collect them here for convenience.

composing each operator with itself

Theorem 9.1 *For each rule S, we have $S^{t \circ t} = S^t$, $S^{m \circ m} = S^m$, and $S^{d \circ d} = S$.*

Proof: The first assertion is trivial. The second one was presented as Lemma 3.1. The last one was proved when the duality operator was introduced. □

Our next theorem relates the duality operator to the claims truncation and attribution of minimal rights operators (Figure 9.6).

[6] The results of this chapter are due to Thomson and Yeh (2001, 2008).

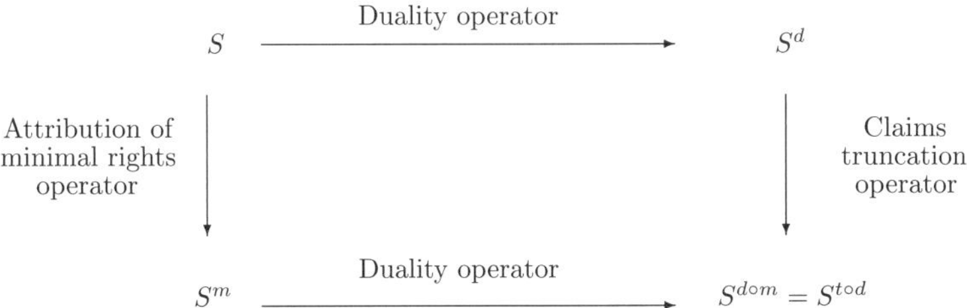

Figure 9.6: **The duality operator relates the claims truncation and minimal rights operators** (Theorem 9.2). Commutative diagram indicating how the duality of two rules is preserved if one of them is subjected to the claims truncation operator and the other to the attribution of minimal rights operator.

Theorem 9.2 *Consider a pair of dual rules. Then subjecting one of them to the attribution of minimal rights operator and the other to the claims truncation operator yields two rules that are dual too. Formally, for each pair of dual rules, S and R, S^m and R^t are dual too.* operators that commute

The duality between the constrained equal awards rule subjected to the attribution of minimal rights operator and the constrained equal losses rule subjected to the claims truncation operator, obtained as an application of the theorem – indeed, these rules are dual – can be seen for two claimants by comparing Figures 9.2a and 9.4a (in either case, we obtain concede-and-divide, a *self-dual* rule), and for three claimants by comparing Figures 9.2b and 9.4b.

For two claimants, the proof of Theorem 9.2 is an easy exercise. It suffices to consider each of the three possibilities, $E \leq \min\{c_i\}$, $\min\{c_i\} < E \leq \max\{c_i\}$, and $\max\{c_i\} < E$. Here is the argument for the general case:

Proof: Let $(c, E) \in \mathcal{C}^N$. By definition of the claims truncation and attribution of minimal rights operators, showing that

$$S^m(c, E) = R^{dot}(c, E) \equiv c - R^t(c, \sum_N c_i - E)$$

is equivalent to showing that

$$(*) \quad m(c, E) + S\left(c - m(c, E), E - \sum_N m_i(c, E)\right)$$

$$= c - R\left(t(c, \sum_N c_i - E), \sum_N c_i - E\right).$$

Since S is dual to R,

$$S\left(c - m(c,E), E - \sum_N m_i(c,E)\right)$$
$$= c - m(c,E) - R\left(c - m(c,E), \sum_N (c_i - m_i(c,E)) - (E - \sum_N m_i(c,E)\right),$$

Substituting in $(*)$, our task becomes that of showing that

$$R\left(c - m(c,E), \sum_N c_i - E\right) = R\left(t(c, \sum_N c_i - E), \sum_N c_i - E\right).$$

We prove this equality by showing that for each $i \in N$, $c_i - m_i(c,E) = t_i(c, \sum_N c_j - E)$, that is:[7]

$$(**) \quad c_i - \max\{E - \sum_{N\setminus\{i\}} c_j, 0\} = \min\{c_i, \sum_N c_j - E\}.$$

Indeed, for each $i \in N$, $c_i - \max\{E - \sum_{N\setminus\{i\}} c_j, 0\} = c_i + \min\{\sum_{N\setminus\{i\}} c_j - E, 0\} = \min\{\sum c_j - E, c_i\}$. □

Here is another (double) illustration of Theorem 9.2 for two claimants. Panel (b) of Figure 9.7 shows Piniles' rule, and panel (a) the rule obtained by subjecting it to the attribution of minimal rights operator. Panel (e) shows the dual of Piniles' rule, and panel (d) the rule obtained by subjecting it to the claims truncation operator. Since the rule of panel (a) is *self-dual*, we could have anticipated the same rule in panel (d). Also, panel (c) shows Piniles' rule subjected to the claims truncation operator, and panel (f) its dual, when subjected to the attribution of minimal rights operator. We can easily check on the figures the symmetry with respect to the half-claims vector of the paths of awards that is asserted in Theorem 9.2.

Define the **duality of two operators** as follows: if two rules are dual, the rule obtained by subjecting one of them to one of the operators and the rule obtained by subjecting the other to the other operator are dual too. According to Theorem 9.2, the claims truncation and attribution of minimal rights operators are dual.

Another way of defining new rules from existing ones is to compose the attribution of minimal rights and claims truncation operators. Let S be a rule. To solve a problem, we first attribute to each claimant their minimal right, and revise their claim down by this "first-round award" and the endowment

[7] This identity can be used to prove that if $c_i \geq c_j$, then $c_i - m_i(c,E) \geq c_j - m_j(c,E)$, as shown in Section 5.2.

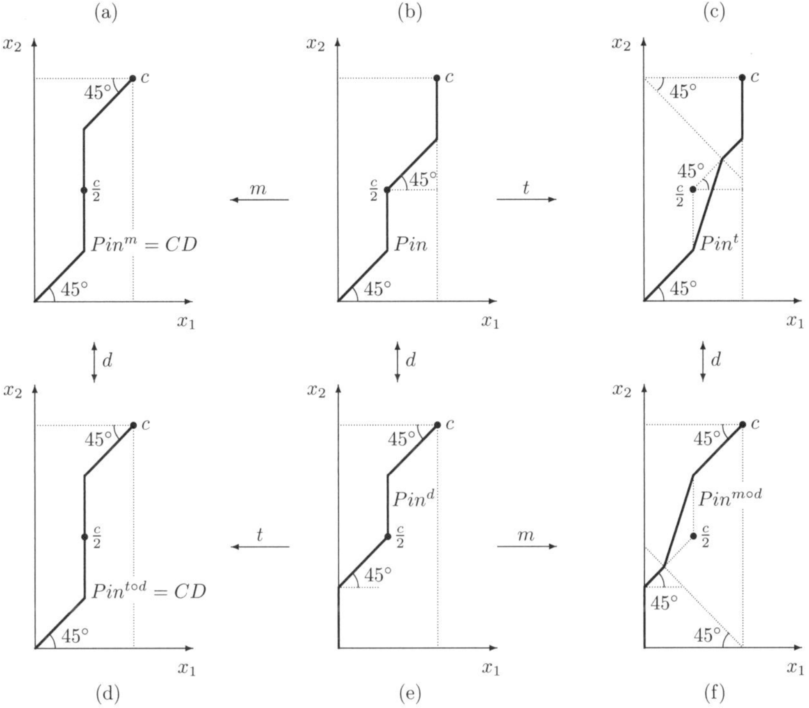

Figure 9.7: **Relating the claim truncation and attribution of minimal rights operators through duality: an application** (illustrating Theorem 9.2). Top row: (b) Piniles' rule, subjected to (a) the attribution of minimal rights operator, and (c) the claims truncation operator. Bottom row: (e) the dual of Piniles' rule, subjected to (d) the claims truncation operator, and (f) the attribution of minimal rights operator. The dual of each rule depicted in the top row is the rule depicted below it.

down by the sum of these awards. We then truncate revised claims at the residual endowment. Now, we apply S, each agent getting their award in two installments:

Rule *S* operated from minimal rights and truncated claims, S^{tom}: For each $(c, E) \in \mathcal{C}^N$,

$$S^{tom}(c, E) \equiv m(c, E) + S\Big(t\Big(c - m(c, E), E - \sum m_i(c, E)\Big), \\ E - \sum m_i(c, E)\Big).$$

We refer to the rule obtained in this way when the point of departure is the proportional rule as the **adjusted proportional rule**:[8]

[8] The rule is defined and studied by Curiel, Maschler, and Tijs (1988). This paper is the source of several of the results concerning the properties of this rule noted in this book.

For two claimants, it turns out that the adjusted proportional rule coincides with concede-and-divide. In fact, Theorem 9.3 below states that concede-and-divide is the outcome not only when it is the proportional rule that is subjected to the composition of the attribution of minimal rights and claims truncation operators, but in fact whenever we start from a rule satisfying *equal treatment of equals*.

It appears just as natural to apply the two operators in the reverse order. How does this reversal affect the final result? Theorem 9.3 also states that once again, the end result is concede-and-divide.

composing claims truncation and minimal rights operators

Theorem 9.3 *For $|N| = 2$. Consider a rule satisfying equal treatment of equals. Then the rule obtained by first subjecting it to the attribution of minimal rights operator and second to the claims truncation operator (truncation of the revised claims is at the residual endowment) coincides with concede-and-divide. The same conclusion holds if these operators are applied in the reverse order. Altogether, for each S satisfying equal treatment of equals, $S^{tom} = S^{mot} = CD$.*

concede-and-divide characterized

Proof: Let $N \equiv \{1, 2\}$, say. Let $(c, E) \in \mathcal{C}^N$ and, without loss of generality, suppose $c_1 \leq c_2$. We distinguish three cases:

Case 1: $E \leq c_1$. Minimal rights are both 0. Thus, first-round awards are 0 and no revision of claims or endowment takes place. After truncation at E, both claims are equal to E. In the second round, by *equal treatment of equals*, S chooses equal division.

Case 2: $c_1 < E \leq c_2$. Claimant 1's minimal right is 0 and claimant 2's minimal right is $E - c_1$. We revise claims down to c_1 and $c_2 - (E - c_1)$ (a nonnegative number); the residual endowment is c_1. After truncation at c_1, both claims are equal to c_1. In the second round, by *equal treatment of equals*, S chooses equal division of the residual endowment, namely $\frac{c_1}{2}$ for each claimant. Altogether, claimant 1 receives $\frac{c_1}{2}$ and claimant 2 receives $E - \frac{c_1}{2}$.

Case 3: $c_2 < E$. Claimant 1's minimal right is $E - c_2$ and claimant 2's minimal right is $E - c_1$. We revise claims down to $c_1 - (E - c_2)$ and $c_2 - (E - c_1)$ (again, these are nonnegative numbers); the residual endowment is $E - \sum(E - c_i)$. After truncation at the residual endowment, claims are equal. In the second round, by *equal treatment of equals*, S chooses equal division.

It is easy to see that in each case, we obtain the awards vector chosen by concede-and-divide, and that the same conclusion holds if the two operators are composed in the reverse order. □

It so happens that the order independence stated as part of Theorem 9.3 does not require that the point of departure be a rule S satisfying *equal treatment of equals*. Uniqueness of the resulting rule is lost if this property is dropped, but if S is *homogeneous*, what comes out are the weighted concede-and-divide

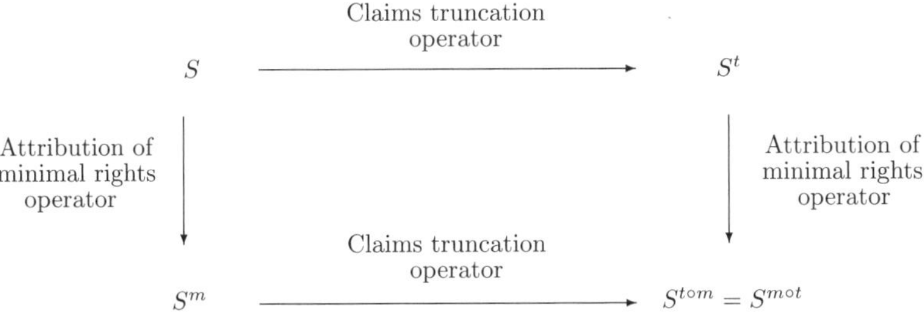

Figure 9.8: **The attribution of minimal rights operator and the claims truncation operator commute.** We represent the first operator by top-to-bottom arrows and the second operator by left-to-right arrows.

rules defined in Section 3.6; otherwise, we obtain the generalizations of these rules introduced there (see the discussion of the independence of the axioms of Theorem 5.2).

In the general n-claimant case, we also lose uniqueness but we still have order independence:

Theorem 9.4 *Given any rule, the rule obtained by first subjecting it to the attribution of minimal rights operator and then to the claims truncation operator coincides with the rule obtained by applying these operators in the reverse order. Formally, for each S,* $S^{tom} = S^{mot}$.

composing claims truncation and minimal rights operators

Proof: Let $(c, E) \in \mathcal{C}^N$ be given. The proof is in three steps.

Step 1: $m(c, E) = m(t(c, E), E)$.
We write out the obvious proof for completeness. Let $i \in N$.

Case 1: there is $j \in N\backslash\{i\}$ such that $c_j \geq E$. Then $m_i(c, E) = 0$. Also, $t_j(c, E) = E$, so $m_i(t(c, E), E) = 0$. Thus, $m_i(c, E) = m_i(t(c, E), E)$.

Case 2: for each $j \in N\backslash\{i\}$, $c_j < E$. Then for each $j \in N\backslash\{i\}$, $t_j(c, E) = c_j$, and thus, $m_i(t(c, E), E) \equiv \max\{E - \sum_{N\backslash\{i\}} t_j(c, E), 0\} = \max\{E - \sum_{N\backslash\{i\}} c_j, 0\} \equiv m_i(c, E)$.

Step 2: $t\left(c - m(c, E), E - \sum m_i(c, E)\right) = t(c, E) - m(t(c, E), E)$.
Without loss of generality, we assume $c_1 \leq \cdots \leq c_n$. Note that $\sum_{N\backslash\{n\}} c_i \leq \sum_{N\backslash\{n-1\}} c_i \leq \cdots \leq \sum_{N\backslash\{1\}} c_i$. By Step 1, we only need to show that for each $i \in N$,

$$t_i\left(c - m(c, E), E - \sum m_j(c, E)\right) = t_i(c, E) - m_i(c, E) \quad (\dagger).$$

By Step 1 and the definitions of functions $t(\cdot, \cdot)$ and $m(\cdot, \cdot)$, we need to show that for each $i \in N$,

$\min\{c_i - \max\{E - \sum_{N\setminus\{i\}} c_j, 0\}, E - \sum_{h\in N} \max\{E - \sum_{N\setminus\{h\}} c_j, 0\}\} = \min\{c_i, E\} - \max\{E - \sum_{N\setminus\{i\}} c_j, 0\}$.

Adding $\max\{E - \sum_{N\setminus\{i\}} c_j, 0\}$ to both sides, we need to show that

$$\min\{c_i, E - \sum_{h\in N\setminus\{i\}} \max\{E - \sum_{N\setminus\{h\}} c_j, 0\}\} = \min\{c_i, E\} \quad (*).$$

Case 1: for each $h \in N \setminus \{i\}$, $E - \sum_{N\setminus\{h\}} c_j \leq 0$. Then $(*)$ holds directly.

Case 2: for some $h^* \in N \setminus \{i\}$, $E - \sum_{N\setminus\{h^*\}} c_j > 0$. Then $c_i < E$ and

$$\begin{aligned} &E - \sum_{h\in N\setminus\{i\}} \max\{E - \sum_{N\setminus\{h\}} c_j, 0\} \\ &= E - (E - \sum_{N\setminus\{h^*\}} c_j) - \sum_{h\in N\setminus\{i,h^*\}} \max\{E - \sum_{N\setminus\{h\}} c_j, 0\} \\ &= c_i + \sum_{j\in N\setminus\{i,h^*\}} c_j - \sum_{h\in N\setminus\{i,h^*\}} \max\{E - \sum_{N\setminus\{h\}} c_j, 0\} \\ &= c_i + \sum_{h\in N\setminus\{i,h^*\}} \min\{\sum_N c_j - E, c_h\} \\ &\geq c_i. \end{aligned}$$

Hence, both left- and right-hand sides of $(*)$ are equal to c_i.

Step 3: Conclusion. Using Step 2 and then Step 1, we obtain,

$$\begin{aligned} S^{tom}(c, E) &= m(c, E) + S(t(c - m(c, E), \\ &\qquad E - \sum m_i(c, E)), E - \sum m_i(c, E)) \\ &= m(c, E) + S(t(c, E) - m(t(c, E), E), E - \sum m_i(c, E)). \\ &= m(t(c, E), E) + S(t(c, E) - m(t(c, E), E), \\ &\qquad E - \sum m_i(t(c, E), E)) \\ &= S^{mot}(c, E). \end{aligned}$$

□

Starting from some problem, let us assign to each claimant their minimal right, revise their claim down by this quantity and the endowment down by the sum of the minimal rights. We have already noted that in the well-defined problem that results, namely $(c - m(c, E), E - \sum m_j(c, E))$, minimal rights are all 0 (Lemma 3.1). Now, let us consider the problem obtained from it by truncating claims at the endowment. In this new problem, we assert that minimal rights are still all 0:

Proposition 9.1 *For each* $(c, E) \in \mathcal{C}^N$, *consider the problem* (c', E') *obtained from it by attributing minimal rights, revising claims and endowment accordingly, and then truncating revised claims at the residual endowment, namely*

$$(c', E') \equiv \left(t\left(c - m(c, E), E - \sum m_j(c, E)\right), E - \sum m_j(c, E)\right).$$

In this problem, minimal rights are all 0.

Proof: We need to show that

$$\begin{aligned} m_i(c', E') &\equiv \max\{E' - \sum_{N\backslash\{i\}} c'_j, 0\} \\ &= \max\{E' - \sum_{N\backslash\{i\}} t_j(c - m(c, E), E'), 0\} \\ &= 0. \end{aligned}$$

Replacing E' by its value, this is equivalent to showing that

$$E - \sum m_j(c, E) \leq \sum_{N\backslash\{i\}} t_j\left(c - m(c, E), E - \sum m_k(c, E)\right),$$

and using the following equality (Relation † established in proving Theorem 9.4, but written for claimant j),

$$t_j\left(c - m(c, E), E - \sum m_k(c, E)\right) = t_j(c, E) - m_j(c, E),$$

that

$$E - m_i(c, E) \leq \sum_{N\backslash\{i\}} t_j(c, E),$$

equivalently, that

$$(*) \quad E - \sum_{N\backslash\{i\}} t_j(c, E) \leq m_i(c, E).$$

To prove $(*)$, we distinguish two cases:

Case 1: there is $j \in N\backslash\{i\}$ such that $c_j \geq E$. Then the left-hand side of $(*)$ is at most equal to 0, whereas the right-hand side is 0. Thus, $(*)$ holds.

Case 2: there is no such j. Then the left-hand side of $(*)$ is equal to $E - \sum_{N\backslash\{i\}} c_j$ and the right-hand side is the maximum of that same quantity and 0. Once again, $(*)$ holds. □

Parallel statements hold when we apply the two operators in the reverse order.

Next, we relate the convexity operator to the other three:

convexity operator distributive

Theorem 9.5 *The convexity operator is distributive with respect to the claims truncation, minimal right, and duality operators. Formally, for each pair of lists* $(S^k)_{k\in K}, (\lambda^k)_{k\in K} \in \Delta^K$,

$$\left(w((S^k)_{k\in K}, (\lambda^k)_{k\in K})\right)^t = w\left(((S^k)^t)_{k\in K}, (\lambda^k)_{k\in K}\right),$$

similar statements holding with either the attribution of minimal rights or duality operator replacing the claims truncation operator.

Proof: We only prove that the convexity operator is distributive with respect to the attribution of minimal rights operator. A similar argument can be made for the other two operators. Let $(c, E) \in \mathcal{C}^N$, K a finite index set, $\left(S^k\right)_{k\in K}$ a list of rules indexed by $k \in K$, and $\left(\lambda^k\right)_{k\in K} \in \Delta^K$ be given. Let $R^m(c, E) \equiv \left(w\left(\left(S^k\right)_{k\in K}, \left(\lambda^k\right)_{k\in K}\right)\right)^m (c, E)$. We assert that

$$R^m(c, E) \equiv \left(w\left(\left(S^k\right)_{k\in K}, \left(\lambda^k\right)_{k\in K}\right)\right)^m (c, E) = \sum_{k\in K} \lambda^k \left(S^k\right)^m (c, E).$$

Indeed

$$\begin{aligned} R^m(c, E) &\equiv m(c, E) + R\left(c - m(c, E), E - \sum m_i(c, E)\right) \\ &= \sum_{k\in K} \lambda^k m(c, E) + \sum_{k\in K} \lambda^k S^k\left(c - m(c, E), E - \sum m_i(c, E)\right) \\ &= \sum_{k\in K} \lambda^k \left(m(c, E) + S^k\left(c - m(c, E), E - \sum m_i(c, E)\right)\right) \\ &= \sum_{k\in K} \lambda^k \left(S^k\right)^m (c, E). \end{aligned}$$

□

9.5 PRESERVATION OF PROPERTIES UNDER OPERATORS

We take each of the four operators in turn and identify which properties it preserves and which ones it does not preserve. The proofs of the positive results are usually straightforward and we omit most of them. For the proofs of the negative results, we need counterexamples. We can often invoke a standard rule for that purpose, but on a number of occasions we have to construct a rule to make the point. Table 16.2 collects all of our conclusions.[9]

[9] Unfortunately, logical relations among properties do not necessarily facilitate the task. Given two properties, A and B, such that A implies B, knowing that A is preserved (or not preserved) under a certain operator on rules does not allow us to deduce that B is also preserved (or not preserved) under this operator. However, if we have proved that B is not preserved under the operator by exhibiting a rule that happens to satisfy A (instead of just B), then we have also proved that A is not preserved either.

We already addressed the issue of which properties are preserved under duality in Chapter 7.

The following proposition allows one to deduce which properties are preserved under attribution of minimal rights from the knowledge of which ones are preserved under claims truncation, or conversely. By appealing to it, we can derive Propositions 9.4 and 9.5 below from Propositions 9.2 and 9.3 respectively. Of course, implications in the opposite direction hold too.

Lemma 9.1 *A property is preserved under claims truncation if and only if its dual is preserved under attribution of minimal rights.*

Proof: Let A be a property preserved under claims truncation, A^d its dual, and S be a rule satisfying A^d. We need to show that S^m satisfies A^d. Since A is dual to A^d, S^d satisfies A. Since A is preserved under claims truncation, $S^{t \circ d}$ satisfies A. Since A^d is dual to A, $S^{d \circ t \circ d}$ satisfies A^d.

We now assert that $S^{d \circ t \circ d} = S^m$. To prove this, first recall that according to Theorem 9.2, if R is the dual of S, then R^t is the dual of S^m. Thus $R^{d \circ t} = S^m$. Since $R = S^d$, then $S^{d \circ t \circ d} = S^m$.

Since $S^{d \circ t \circ d}$ satisfies A^d, so does S^m. This proves the statement in one direction. The other direction is virtually identical. □

9.5.1 Properties Preserved under Claims Truncation

We say that a **property is preserved under claims truncation** if whenever a rule satisfies it, so does the rule obtained by subjecting it to the claims truncation operator.

Certain properties are obviously preserved under claims truncation, examples being *equal treatment of equals*, *order preservation*, and of course *claims truncation invariance*. Equally obvious is that *concavity* or *convexity* are not. A little less clear is that a property as basic as *endowment monotonicity* is not preserved, but that is the situation.

The next two propositions give lists of properties that are preserved under the claims truncation operator and of properties that are not preserved, and in the latter case, a few representative proofs.

Proposition 9.2 *The following properties are preserved under claims truncation:*

⋆ *the $\frac{1}{|N|}$-truncated-claims lower bounds on awards and the $\frac{1}{|N|}$-min-of-claim-and-deficit lower bounds on losses,*

⋆ *equal treatment of equals,*

⋆ *order preservation in awards and order preservation in losses,*

⋆ *anonymity,*

⋆ *continuity,*

⋆ *claim monotonicity,*

⋆ *homogeneity, and*
⋆ *claims truncation invariance and minimal rights first.*

Proposition 9.3 *The following properties are not preserved under claims truncation:*
⋆ *conditional full compensation and conditional null compensation,*
⋆ *equal treatment of equal groups,*
⋆ *group order preservation in awards and group order preservation in losses,*
⋆ *regressivity and progressivity,*
⋆ *endowment monotonicity,*
⋆ *linked claims-endowment monotonicity,*
⋆ *composition down and composition up,*
⋆ *self-duality,*
⋆ *the midpoint property, and*
⋆ *no advantageous transfer (for $|N| \geq 3$).*

Proof: We give selected proofs of these assertions.

⋆ *Group order preservation in awards.* The proportional rule satisfies the property (Section 3.7) but P^t does not. To see this, let $N \equiv \{1, 2, 3, 4\}$ and $(c, E) \in \mathcal{C}^N$ be equal to $((\frac{1}{2}, 3, 3, 9), 3)$. Then $x \equiv P^t(c, E) = (\frac{3}{19}, \frac{18}{19}, \frac{18}{19}, \frac{18}{19})$. Now, note that $c_1 + c_4 > c_2 + c_3$ but $x_1 + x_4 < x_2 + x_3$, in violation of *group order preservation in awards.*[10]

For *group order preservation in losses*, the same rule can be used. This also follows from Proposition 9.1

⋆ *Endowment monotonicity.* The constrained equal losses rule satisfies the property but CEL^t does not. This can be seen by inspection of Figure 9.2b, which shows the schedules of awards of this rule for $N \equiv \{1, 2, 3\}$ and $(c, E) \in \mathcal{C}^N$ equal to $((100, 200, 300), 100)$. We calculate that $CEL^t(c, E) = (\frac{100}{3}, \frac{100}{3}, \frac{100}{3})$. However, for $E' \equiv 200$, we obtain $CEL^t(c, E') = (0, 100, 100)$: claimant 1 receives less after the increase in the endowment. This negative result for this rule requires an example with at least three claimants since for two claimants, CEL^t coincides with concede-and-divide, which is *endowment monotonic* (Figure 9.2a). However, the property is not preserved for two claimants either. Here is an example that makes the point:

Rule 9.1 (Figure 9.9) Let $N \equiv \{1, 2\}$. Let S be a rule whose path of awards for $c \equiv (4, 7)$ is bro.seg$[(0, 0), (3.5, 3.5), c]$ and whose path for $c' \equiv (4, 6)$ is bro.seg$[(0, 0), (2, 4), c']$. Both of these paths are monotone, and for S to be *endowment monotonic*, it suffices to choose its paths for all other

[10] We could have given an example with three claimants, but our four-claimant example is slightly more interesting as it shows that preservation fails also for the weaker property obtained by requiring that only groups of equal sizes be compared.

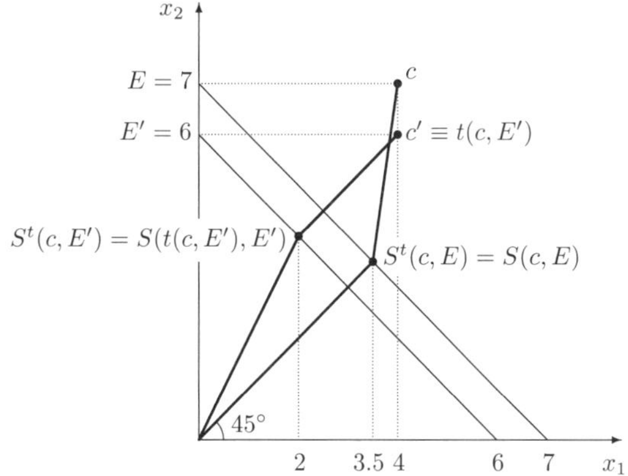

Figure 9.9: **Endowment monotonicity is not preserved under claims truncation, even for two claimants** (Proposition 9.3e). Paths of awards of Rule 9.1, called S, for $c \equiv (4, 7)$ and $c' \equiv (4, 6)$. For c, when S^t is applied, as the endowment decreases from $E = 7$ to $E' = 6$, claimant 2 receives more (4 instead of 3.5).

claims vectors to be monotone curves. This is easily done and we will not do so explicitly. The definition of S can in fact be completed in such a way that S satisfies additional basic properties such as *anonymity*, *continuity*, *order preservation*, and so on.

Now, let $E \equiv 7$ and $E' \equiv 6$. We have $S^t(c, E) = S(c, E) = (3.5, 3.5)$ but $S^t(c, E') = S(t(c, E'), E') = S(c', E') = (2, 4)$. Rule S^t assigns less to claimant 2 when the endowment is E than when it is E', in violation of *endowment monotonicity*.

⋆ *Composition down*. The proportional rule satisfies the property (Section 6.1) but P^t does not. To see this, let $N \equiv \{1, 2\}$ and $(c, E) \in \mathcal{C}^N$ be equal to $((1, 3), 1)$, and let $E' \equiv 3$. Then $P^t(c, E) = (\frac{1}{2}, \frac{1}{2}) \neq P^t(P^t(c, E'), E) = (\frac{3}{7}, \frac{4}{7})$. In Figure 9.1, the path for a, a point of the path for c, terminates with a nondegenerate subset of seg$[0, a]$ instead of with a curve.

For *composition up*, we use the same example. We calculate that $P^t(c, E') = (\frac{3}{4}, \frac{9}{4}) \neq P^t(c, E) + P^t(c - P^t(c, E), E' - E) = (\frac{1}{2}, \frac{1}{2}) + (\frac{2}{5}, \frac{8}{5})$. The result also follows from Proposition 9.1.

⋆ *Self-duality* and the *midpoint property*. Again, we can use the proportional rule but this time we omit the proof.

⋆ *No advantageous transfer* (for $|N| \geq 3$). The proportional rule is the only rule satisfying *no advantageous transfer* (Theorem 8.1) and therefore P^t violates the property. This can also be easily verified directly. □

9.5.2 Properties Preserved under Attribution of Minimal Rights Operator

We say that **a property is preserved under attribution of minimal rights** if whenever a rule satisfies it, so does the rule obtained by subjecting it to the attribution of minimal rights operator.

Quite a few properties are preserved under attribution of minimal rights. Examples are *equal treatment of equals* and *claims truncation invariance*, and of course *minimal rights first*. Clearly *concavity* and *convexity* are not preserved. A less obvious example is *endowment monotonicity*, but this can be seen in Figure 9.4b.

Direct proofs of the assertions made in the propositions below can be obtained in a parallel way to the way Propositions 9.2–9.3 were proved. We give only one:

Proposition 9.4 *The following properties are preserved under attribution of minimal rights:*
⋆ *the* $\frac{1}{|N|}$*-truncated-claims lower bounds on awards and the* $\frac{1}{|N|}$*-min-of-claim-and-deficit lower bounds on losses,*
⋆ *equal treatment of equals,*
⋆ *order preservation in awards and order preservation in losses,*
⋆ *anonymity,*
⋆ *continuity,*
⋆ *linked claims-endowment monotonicity,*
⋆ *homogeneity, and*
⋆ *claims truncation invariance and minimal rights first.*

Proof: ⋆ *Order preservation in awards*. It suffices to recall that if $c_i \leq c_j$, then (i) $m_i(c, E) \leq m_j(c, E)$, but also (ii) $c_i - m_i(c, E) \leq c_j - m_j(c, E)$ (Section 5.2). Thus, if S satisfies *order preservation in awards*, and using (ii), we obtain

$$S_i\left(c - m(c, E), E - \sum m_k(c, E)\right) \leq S_j\left(c - m(c, E), E - \sum m_k(c, E)\right),$$

which, added to (i), gives,

$$\begin{aligned} &m_i(c, E) + S_i\left(c - m(c, E), E - \sum m_k(c, E)\right) \\ \leq\ &m_j(c, E) + S_j\left(c - m(c, E), E - \sum m_k(c, E)\right), \end{aligned}$$

or, equivalently, $S_i^m(c, E) \leq S_j^m(c, E)$. □

Proposition 9.5 *The following properties are not preserved under attribution of minimal rights:*
⋆ *conditional full compensation and conditional null compensation,*
⋆ *equal treatment of equal groups,*
⋆ *group order preservation in awards and group order preservation in losses,*

⋆ *endowment monotonicity,*
⋆ *regressivity and progressivity,*
⋆ *claims monotonicity,*
⋆ *composition down and composition up,*
⋆ *self-duality,*
⋆ *the midpoint property, and*
⋆ *no advantageous transfer (for* $|N| \geq 3$*).*

Proof: We give a few sample proofs.

⋆ *Conditional full compensation*. The constrained equal awards rule satisfies the property, but $CEA^m = CD$ does not (Section 3.4).

⋆ *Endowment monotonicity*. The constrained equal awards rule satisfies the property, but CEA^m does not. Figure 9.4 shows that for the claims vector $(100, 200, 300)$ of the marriage contract claims vector of the Talmud, as the endowment increases from 400 to 500, claimant 1's award decreases. As was the case for the proof that *endowment monotonicity* is not preserved under claims truncation, this negative result for this rule requires more than two claimants. Indeed, for two claimants, preservation takes place, as CEA^m coincides with concede-and-divide then, a rule that is *endowment monotonic*. For two claimants, a rule similar to Rule 9.1 can be constructed to make the point however.

⋆ *Claim monotonicity*. The proof that this property is not preserved under attribution of minimal rights is relegated to the appendix (Section 17.5).

⋆ *Composition down*. The proportional rule satisfies the property but P^m does not.

For *composition up*, the proportional rule can also be used. □

9.5.3 Properties Preserved under the Composition of the Claims Truncation and Attribution of Minimal Rights Operators

We say that **a property is preserved under the composition of claims truncation and attribution of minimal rights** (alternatively, according to Theorem 9.4, we could compose the operators in the reverse order), if whenever a rule satisfies the property, the rule obtained by subjecting it to this sequence of operators also does. The following theorem relates the duality operator to the composition of the claims truncation and attribution of minimal rights operators.

claims truncation and minimal rights operators commute

Theorem 9.6 *Consider a pair of dual rules. Then the rules obtained by subjecting them to the claim truncation operator and then to the attribution of minimal rights operator are dual too. A parallel result holds if the two operators are applied in the reverse order. Formally, if S and R are dual, so are S^{tom} and R^{tom}, and so are S^{mot} and R^{mot}.*

Proof: By Theorem 9.2, S^t and R^m are dual. By Theorem 9.2 applied to these two rules, S^{mot} and R^{tom} are dual. By Theorem 9.4, $R^{tom} = R^{mot}$. Thus, S^{mot} and R^{mot} are dual (and of course, so are S^{tom} and R^{tom}). □

If a property is preserved under the claims truncation operator as well as under the attribution of minimal rights operator, then of course it is preserved under their composition. However, a property may be preserved under neither operator and yet be preserved under their composition. An example is *self-duality*. This result, formally stated next, is a corollary of Theorem 9.6.[11]

Corollary 9.1 *Self-duality is preserved under the composition of the claims truncation and attribution of minimal rights operators, in either order.*

The order independence that is part of the statement of the corollary is also a consequence of Theorem 9.4.

The *midpoint property* is another property that is not preserved under either the claims truncation or attribution of minimal rights operators, but is preserved under their composition:

Proposition 9.6 *The midpoint property is preserved under the composition of the claims truncation and attribution of minimal rights operators.*

Proof: Let S be rule satisfying the *midpoint property*. Let $(c, E) \in \mathcal{C}^N$ be given with $E = \frac{1}{2}\sum c_i$. We need to show that $S^{mot}(c, E) = \frac{c}{2}$. By definition of the operators, $S^{mot}(c, E) = m(t(c, E), E) + S(t(c, E) - m(t(c, E), E), E - \sum m_i(t(c, E), E))$. Using the equality $m(t(c, E), E) = m(c, E)$ (Step 1 of the proof of Theorem 9.4), this equality simplifies to $S^{mot}(c, E) = m(c, E) + S(t(c, E) - m(c, E), E - \sum m_i(c, E))$. Now, we assert that $(*)$ for each $i \in N$, $t_i(c, E) + m_i(c, E) = c_i$. In the proof, we use the fact that, since $E = \frac{1}{2}\sum c_i$, then $E - \sum_{j \in N\setminus\{i\}} c_j = c_i - E$. Now, $t_i(c, E) + m_i(c, E) = \min\{c_i, E\} + \max\{E - \sum_{j \in N\setminus\{i\}} c_j, 0\} = \min\{c_i, E\} + \max\{c_i - E, 0\}$. We distinguish two cases, $c_i \leq E$ and $c_i > E$. In each case, the assertion follows directly.

We now assert that $E - \sum m_i(c, E) = \frac{1}{2}[\sum t_i(c, E) - \sum m_i(c, E)]$. Indeed, this equality can be rewritten as $E = \frac{1}{2}[\sum t_i(c, E) + \sum m_i(c, E)]$, which is true because of $(*)$ and the hypothesis $E = \frac{1}{2}\sum c_i$. Thus, in the problem $(t(c, E) - m(c, E), E - \sum m_i(c, E))$, the endowment is equal to the half-sum of the claims. Since S satisfies the *midpoint property*, $S(t(c, E) - m(c, E), E - \sum m_i(c, E)) = \frac{1}{2}[t(c, E) - m(c, E)]$.

We can now write $S^{mot}(c, E) = m(c, E) + \frac{1}{2}[t(c, E) - m(c, E)] = \frac{1}{2}[t(c, E) + m(c, E)]$, and appealing to $(*)$ again, $S^{mot}(c, E) = \frac{c}{2}$. □

[11] Curiel, Maschler, and Tijs (1987) show that the adjusted proportional rule is *self-dual*. This result follows from Corollary 9.1.

We have seen a number of properties that are preserved under neither the claims truncation nor the attribution of minimal rights operators. Among those, only *self-duality* and the *midpoint property* are preserved under the composition of these operators. For example, consider *endowment monotonicity*. The constrained equal awards rule is *endowment monotonic*. However, for three claimants or more, the rule obtained by subjecting it to the attribution of minimal rights operator, CEA^m, is not (as noted previously, for the example depicted in Figure 9.4, as the endowment increases from 400 to 500, claimant 1 receives less), and thus neither is CEA^{tom} (for two claimants, we obtain concede-and-divide, which is *endowment monotonic*).

Another example is *composition down*. The proportional rule satisfies *composition down* but P^{tom} does not (for two claimants, by Theorem 9.3, we obtain concede-and-divide, which violates the property). If a property is not preserved under the composition of the claims truncation and attribution of minimal rights operators, neither is its dual, and since the proportional rule is *self-dual*, we conclude that *composition up* is not preserved under this composition either.

9.5.4 Properties Preserved under Convexity

Next are lists of properties that are preserved under convexity and of properties that are not so preserved. Few are not preserved. First we note the following:

Lemma 9.2 *If a property is preserved under convexity, so is its dual.*

We omit the proof of this lemma as well as that of the next proposition.

Proposition 9.7 *The following properties are preserved under convexity:*
⋆ *the* $\frac{1}{|N|}$*-truncated-claims lower bounds on awards and the* $\frac{1}{|N|}$*-min-of-claim-and-deficit lower bounds on losses;*
⋆ *conditional full compensation and conditional null compensation,*
⋆ *equal treatment of equals,*
⋆ *order preservation in awards and order preservation in losses,*
⋆ *anonymity,*
⋆ *equal treatment of equal groups,*
⋆ *group order preservation in awards and group order preservation in losses,*
⋆ *endowment monotonicity,*
⋆ *order preservation under endowment variations,*
⋆ *progressivity and regressivity,*
⋆ *continuity,*
⋆ *claim monotonicity and linked claim-endowment monotonicity,*
⋆ *homogeneity,*
⋆ *claims truncation invariance and minimal rights first,*
⋆ *self-duality,*

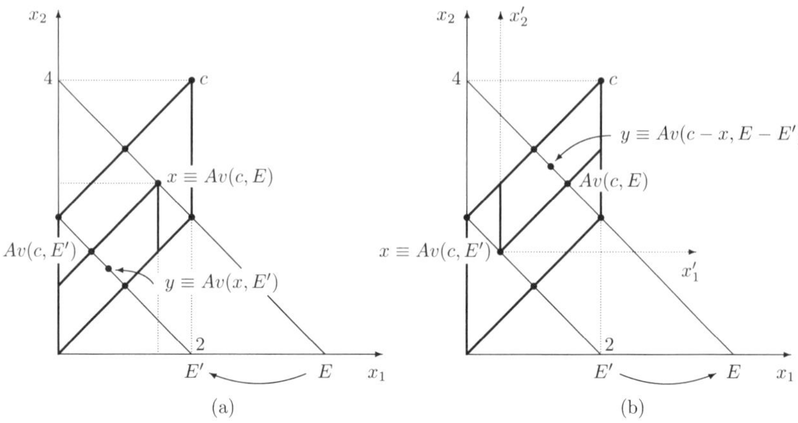

Figure 9.10: **Neither composition down nor composition up is preserved under convexity** (Proposition 9.8). (a) *Composition down* is not preserved under convexity, as shown by the average of the constrained equal awards and constrained equal losses rules. (b) Neither is *composition up*, as shown by the same rule.

⋆ *the midpoint property, and*
⋆ *no advantageous transfer.*

Proposition 9.8 *The following properties are not preserved under convexity:*
⋆ *composition down and* ***composition up****.*

Proof: ⋆ *Composition down.* Both the constrained equal awards and constrained equal losses rules satisfy the property, but their simple average $\frac{CEA+CEL}{2}$ does not: indeed, let $N \equiv \{1, 2\}$ and $(c, E) \in \mathcal{C}^N$ be equal to $((2, 4), 4)$ (Figure 9.10a). Also, let $E' \equiv 2$. Then $Av(c, E) = \frac{CEA(c,E)+CEL(c,E)}{2} = \frac{(2,2)+(1,3)}{2} = (\frac{3}{2}, \frac{5}{2})$, and $Av((\frac{3}{2}, \frac{5}{2}), E') = \frac{(1,1)+(\frac{1}{2},\frac{3}{2})}{2} = (\frac{3}{4}, \frac{5}{4}) \neq (\frac{1}{2}, \frac{3}{2}) = \frac{(1,1)+(0,2)}{2} = Av(c, E')$.

Composition up. This follows from the fact just proved and Lemma 9.2. Here is a direct proof that uses the same example (Figure 9.10b). We have $Av(c, E') = (\frac{1}{2}, \frac{3}{2})$, $Av((\frac{3}{2}, \frac{5}{2}), E - E') = \frac{(1,1)+(\frac{1}{2},\frac{3}{2})}{2} = (\frac{3}{4}, \frac{5}{4})$, so that $Av(c, E') + Av(c - Av(c, E'), E - E') = (\frac{1}{2}, \frac{3}{2}) + (\frac{3}{4}, \frac{5}{4}) \neq \frac{(2,2)+(1,3)}{2} = Av(c, E)$. □

9.6 EXTENSION OPERATORS

Each of the operators studied in the foregoing sections associates with each rule some other rule. Another type of operators have been proposed, to extend incompletely specified rules, that is, rules defined on a subdomain of problems, so as to deliver rules defined on the entire domain of problems. In this section, we introduce several operators of this type.

(a) First, we may have a rule defined on the domain of two-claimant problems and want to extend it to problems involving arbitrarily many claimants. It would be premature to go into details here as the required definitions rely on concepts not introduced yet, but a preview should be useful to illustrate the wide range of these operators.

(i) Section 10.2 introduces a property of "consistency" that often allows us to perform such extensions.
(ii) Section 10.7 defines a weaker property of "average consistency" that almost always allows us to do so.
(iii) Section 12.3 suggests "merging claims" as the basis for the definition of a number of additional operators to extend two-claimant rules.

(b) Alternatively, we may have a rule defined only for problems in which claims and endowment satisfy certain restrictions, and want to extend it to problems that are free of these restrictions.

(i) An interesting starting point is a rule defined on the domain of problems in which the endowment is at most as large as the largest claim, $\mathcal{C}^N_{E \leq \max\{c_i\}}$. Rabad's proposal (Subsection 2.1.9) is an example. In Subsection 2.1.9, variant (iii), we extended Rabad's proposal by means of a repeated application of it involving endowment truncation and claims revision (another extension we defined led us to the minimal overlap rule). We did not have the notion of a general operator then, but equipped with such a definition, we can now ask: if the starting point were a rule defined on this domain other than Rabad's proposal, what would happen?

For a precise statement of this question, let S be a rule defined on $\mathcal{C}^N_{E \leq \max\{c_i\}}$. Given a problem (c, E) for which $E > \max\{c_i\}$, let us successively apply S to divide an amount equal to the largest claim, each time revising claims down by the awards made, until the residual endowment is at most as large as the largest claim, in which case we apply S one last time. The endowment is exhausted then and we let each claimant keep the successive amounts awarded to them along the way. This defines a rule since the *nonnegativity* and *claims boundedness* requirements will obviously be met. Here is the formal definition of this process, illustrated in Figure 9.11 for a rule satisfying *order preservation in awards* (so that the way claimants are ordered remains the same along the way):

Completion of a rule S defined on $\mathcal{C}^N_{E \leq \max\{c_i\}}$ by recursive endowment truncation and claims revision, S^*: Let $(c, E) \in \mathcal{C}^N$.

If $\sum c_i = E$ or $\max\{c_i\} \geq E$, let $S^*(c, E) \equiv S(c, E)$.

If $\max\{c_i\} < E$, we consider the sequences $\{(c^t, E^t)\}$ and $\{x^t\}$ defined by

$(c^1, E^1) \equiv (c, \max\{c_i\})$ and $x^1 \equiv S(c^1, E^1)$,

$(c^2, E^2) \equiv (c^1 - x^1, \max\{c^1_i - x^1_i\})$ and $x^2 \equiv S(c^2, E^2)$,

and more generally and until a step T such that $E^T \leq \max\{c^T_i\}$ has been reached,

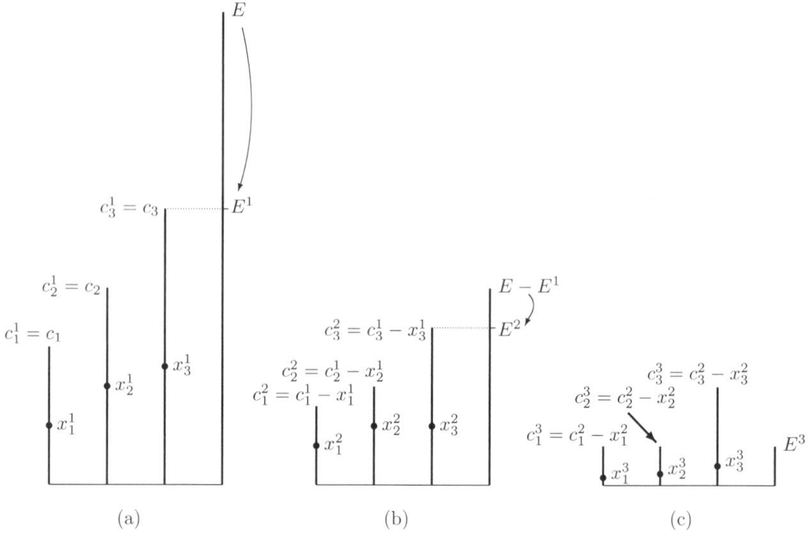

Figure 9.11: **Operator to extend to the entire domain a rule S defined on the domain of problems in which the endowment is at most as large as the largest claim.** Let $N \equiv \{1, 2, 3\}$ and $(c, E) \in \mathcal{C}^N_{E>\max\{c_i\}}$. (a) Step 1: let $c^1 \equiv c$. Since E exceeds the largest claim, $\max\{c_i^1\}$, S is applied to divide an amount E^1 equal to this largest claim, using c^1 as claims vector. Let $x^1 \equiv S(c^1, E^1)$. (b) Step 2: let $c^2 \equiv c^1 - x^1$. Since the residual endowment, $E - E^1$, exceeds the largest revised claim, $\max\{c_i^2\}$, S is applied to divide an amount E^2 equal to this largest revised claim, using c^2 as claims vector. Let $x^2 \equiv S(c^2, E^2)$. (c) Step 3: let $c^3 \equiv c^2 - x^2$. The residual endowment at this point, $E^3 \equiv E - E^1 - E^2$, falls short of the largest twice-revised claim, $\max\{c_i^3\}$, so S is applied to divide this remainder, using c^3 as claims vector. We select as awards vector for (c, E) the sum of the awards vectors of each step: $S^*(c, E) \equiv \sum_{k=1}^{k=3} S(c^k, E^k)$.

$(c^t, E^t) \equiv (c^{t-1} - x^{t-1}, \max\{c_i^{t-1} - x_i^{t-1}\})$, and $x^t \equiv S(c^t, E^t)$.

Then let $S^*(c, E) \equiv \sum_{t=1}^{t=T} x^t$.

We call the mapping $S \mapsto S^*$ the **recursive–endowment-truncation-and-claims-revision completion operator**.

The question of course is whether this operator is well defined. The next theorem says that it is: no matter what rule S defined on $\mathcal{C}^N_{E\leq\max\{c_i\}}$ is applied, when the sum of the claims exceeds the endowment, a finite step T does exist at which the residual endowment is at most as large as the largest claim of that step, so that after one final application of S, the endowment is exhausted:[12]

[12] The proof of Theorem 9.7 is due to Miyagawa (personal communication). To see that convergence may not be finite when $\sum c_i = E$, consider the trivial problem $((1, 2), 3)$ and apply the proportional rule. The recursion idea is used by Bergantiños and Méndez-Naya (2001) to obtain

Theorem 9.7 *The recursive–endowment-truncation-and-claims-revision completion operator is well defined.*

recursive–endowment-truncation-and-claims-revision completion operator well defined

Proof: We need to show that for each rule S defined on $\mathcal{C}^N_{E \leq \max\{c_i\}}$ and each $(c, E) \in \mathcal{C}^N$ such that $\sum c_i > E$, there is $t \in \mathbb{N}$ such that $\max\{c_i^1\} + \cdots + \max\{c_i^t\} \geq E$. The proof is by contradiction. For each $t \in \mathbb{N}$, let $e^t \equiv \max\{c_i^t\}$ be the amount distributed at Step t, and $E^t \equiv e^1 + \cdots + e^t$ be the amount distributed up to and including Step t. Suppose then that for each $t \in \mathbb{N}$, $E^t < E$. Note that for each $i \in N$ and each $t \in \mathbb{N}$, $c_i^t \leq e^t$. Also, for each $t \in \mathbb{N}$, $\sum c_i^t = \sum c_i - E^{t-1}$ and $E^t = E^{t-1} + e^t$. Thus, $|N|e^t \geq \sum c_i^t = \sum c_i - E^t + e^t$, which, using our hypothesis $E^t < E$, simplifies to $(|N| - 1)e^t \geq \sum c_i - E$. Now, since $\{e^t\}$ is a nowhere-decreasing sequence, which implies that for each $t \in \mathbb{N}$, $E^t \geq te^t$, we deduce $E^t \geq t\frac{\sum c_i - E}{|N|-1}$. Thus, for t large enough, $E^t > E$, which contradicts our hypothesis. □

When applied to Rabad's proposal, this theorem delivers a rule to which we refer as the **recursive–endowment-truncation-and-claims-revision completion of Rabad's proposal**.

(ii) Alternatively, let us suppose that we have a rule S defined on the domain of problems in which the endowment is at least as large as the largest claim, $\boldsymbol{\mathcal{C}^N_{E \geq \max\{c_i\}}}$ (we return to this domain in Section 15.1). How should we extend S to the entire domain $\mathcal{C}^N$?

(ii1) Let $(c, E) \in \mathcal{C}^N_{E < \max\{c_i\}}$. To solve this problem, we imagine that instead, the endowment were equal to the largest claim and we apply S (Figure 9.12). The amounts awarded then add up to more than the actual endowment E, so let us think of them as revised claims on E. If E is still smaller than the largest revised claim, we imagine that the endowment is equal to that claim and we reapply S. We repeat. This process defines a sequence of claims vectors. If at some stage T, the endowment is at least as large as the largest claim, we apply S one last time. We propose to extend S by choosing $S(c^T, E)$ for (c, E).

Completion of a rule S defined on $\mathcal{C}^N_{E \geq \max\{c_i\}}$ by recursive application of composition down, S^{**}: Let $(c, E) \in \mathcal{C}^N$.

If $E \geq \max\{c_i\}$, let $S^{**}(c, E) \equiv S(c, E)$.

If $E < \max\{c_i\}$, we consider the sequence $\{c^t, E^t\}$ defined by
$(c^1, E^1) \equiv (c, \max\{c_i\})$ and $x^1 \equiv S(c^1, E^1)$,

a completion of Rabad's proposal, under the name of "extended Ibn Ezra rule." They establish convergence in a finite number of steps for this application, a special case of Theorem 9.7. See also Alcalde, Marco, and Silva (2005). Bergantiños and Méndez-Naya (2001) characterize the rule on the basis of *equal treatment of equals*, *claims truncation invariance*, and conditional forms of *composition up* and *full additivity* (claims should be ordered in the same way in the component problems).

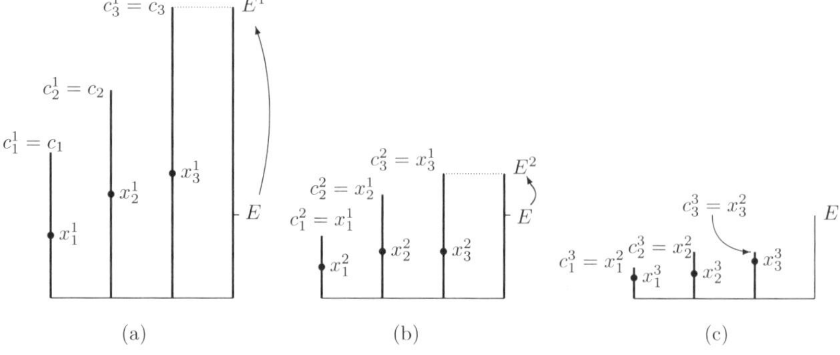

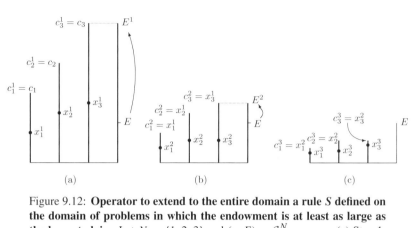

Figure 9.12: **Operator to extend to the entire domain a rule S defined on the domain of problems in which the endowment is at least as large as the largest claim.** Let $N \equiv \{1, 2, 3\}$ and $(c, E) \in \mathcal{C}^N_{E<\max\{c_i\}}$. (a) Step 1: Let $c^1 \equiv c$. Since E falls short of the largest claim, $\max\{c_i^1\}$, S is applied to divide an amount E^1 equal to $\max\{c_i^1\}$, using c^1 as claims vector. Let $x^1 \equiv S(c^1, E^1)$. (b) Step 2: Let $c^2 \equiv S(c^1, E^1)$. Since E falls short of the largest revised claim, $\max\{c_i^2\}$, S is applied to divide an amount E^2 equal to $\max\{c_i^2\}$, using c^2 as claims vector. Let $x^2 \equiv S(c^2, E^2)$. (c) Step 3: Let $c^3 \equiv S(c^2, E^2)$. Now, E exceeds the largest twice-revised claim, $\max\{c_i^3\}$, so S is applied to divide E, using c^3 as claims vector: we set $S^{**}(c, E) \equiv S(c^3, E)$ $(= x^3$ in the figure).

$(c^2, E^2) \equiv (x^1, \max\{x_i^1\})$ and $x^2 \equiv S(c^2, E^2)$,

and more generally $(c^t, E^t) \equiv (x^{t-1}, \max\{x_i^{t-1}\})$ and $x^t \equiv S(c^t, E^t)$.

If for some $T \in \mathbb{N}$, $\max\{c_i^T\} \leq E$, let $S^{**}(c, E) = S(c^T, E)$.

We call the mapping $S \mapsto S^{**}$ the **recursive–composition-down completion operator**.

We should not expect to be able to complete every rule in this manner. For instance, if a rule assigns the entire endowment to the largest claimant, the first revision delivers a problem in which all claims except the largest one are revised to 0 and the largest one is not revised. Thus, the endowment itself is not revised at the next round, so in fact the next problem is the same.

(ii2) Here is another way to extend a rule S defined on $\mathcal{C}^N_{E\geq\max\{c_i\}}$ to the whole domain of claims problems. Given $(c, E) \in \mathcal{C}^N_{E<\max\{c_i\}}$, for each $i \in N$ such that $c_i > E$, let $k_i \in \mathbb{N}$ be such that $0 < c_i - k_i E < E$, and let claimant i be "represented" by $k_i + 1$ claimants, k_i of them having a claim equal to E and the last one having a claim equal to $c_i - k_i E$. Keep as is the claims of all other claimants. Apply S to the resulting problem, and assign to each claimant in the first category the sum of the awards to their representatives.

(ii3) The third extension method we propose is as follows. Given $(c, E) \in \mathcal{C}^N_{E<\max\{c_i\}}$, for each $i \in N$, find the smallest $k_i \in \mathbb{N}$ such that $\frac{c_i}{k_i} \leq E$ and let claimant i be represented by k_i claimants each having a claim equal to that fraction. Apply S to the resulting problem, and again, assign to claimant i the sum of the awards to their representatives. (Note that even if S is *continuous*, its image under this operator is not.)

Instead of thinking of the operators we just defined as completion operators, one can think of each of them as an operator from a subdomain to the complementary subdomain: given S defined on $\mathcal{C}^N_{E \geq \max\{c_i\}}$, we obtain a rule defined on the complement by applying an operator of the first type, and given a rule defined on $\mathcal{C}^N_{E \leq \max\{c_i\}}$, we obtain a rule defined on the complement by applying an operator of the second type. The question can then be asked: "What are the fixed points of the composition of these two operators?" The proportional rule is one for the recursive–endowment-truncation-and-claim-revision and recursive–composition-down operators. Are there others?

Another interesting question concerning any operator is "Which properties of rules does it preserve?" We know the answers concerning the four operators whose analysis forms the bulk of this chapter with much generality, as we have seen. The opposite is true for our completion operators.

Theorem 3.2 can also be used to generate rules. The point of departure is a lower bound function, which can be seen as a rule on which *balance* is not imposed, and the end-result is a well-defined rule. Questions about preservation of properties can also be asked about this kind of an operator. Indeed, most of the properties of rules can be meaningfully rewritten for lower bound functions. Consider *claim monotonicity* for example: a lower bound function is *claim monotonic* if, when an agent's claim increases, their lower bound does not decrease. Now, we can ask: if a lower bound function is *claim monotonic*, is the rule obtained by subjecting it to the recursion operator of Subsection 3.4.2 also *claim monotonic*? We only know some of the answers to this type of questions: *order preservation* is preserved but neither part of this two-part requirement is. Neither *claim monotonicity* nor *endowment monotonicity* is preserved, but *claims truncation invariance* is.[13]

9.7 SUMMARIZING

Table 16.2 summarizes what we have learned about the preservation of properties by operators. It reveals that of the four main operators, the convexity operator preserves the largest number of commonly studied properties of rules. The duality operator preserves slightly more properties than either the claims truncation or attribution of minimal rights operators. These last two operators, being dual, exhibit symmetric patterns of property preservation. Their composition is a little better behaved than either since it preserves a few properties that neither one of the two preserves.

[13] Dominguez (2013).

Few properties are preserved by all operators, and only basic properties have that feature. The surprise here is perhaps that some of these properties, such as monotonicity properties, are not preserved more generally than is the case.

Another way in which the concepts introduced in the foregoing pages can be useful is in determining whether certain rules satisfy certain properties. To illustrate, let us ask whether the random arrival rule satisfies *minimal rights first*. The answer is yes and a direct proof can certainly be obtained. Although it still exploits the fact that *minimal rights first* is preserved under convexity, it involves tedious algebraic calculations. However, this result can be derived very easily from the following observations:

(i) the random arrival rule is *claims truncation invariant* (this is an implication of the fact that each sequential priority rule satisfies the property and that the property is preserved under convexity);
(ii) when taken in pairs corresponding to reverse orders, two sequential priority rules average to a *self-dual* rule;
(iii) the random arrival rule is *self-dual*, being the average of such pairs of sequential priority rules and *self-duality* being preserved under convexity (Proposition 9.7); and finally,
(iv) if a rule satisfies a property, its dual (which is itself if it is *self-dual*) satisfies the dual property. Here, we invoke the duality of *claims truncation invariance* and *minimal rights first* (Proposition 7.1).

CHAPTER 10

Variable-Population Model: Consistency and Related Properties

In this chapter and the next two, we consider the possibility that the population of claimants changes and we formulate and study a variety of requirements designed to guarantee the good behavior of division rules in such circumstances. One would expect that the ways in which one solves problems involving different populations of claimants would be, or should be, related. For instance, using the proportional formula when the number of claimants is even and the constrained equal awards formula otherwise would likely appear strange. Central to this chapter is an invariance requirement called "consistency," according to which the choice made for a problem by a rule should be "confirmed" in each of the "reduced" problems that results when some claimants have received their awards and left. Another important property is a "converse" of consistency, which says the following: suppose that an awards vector for a problem is such that, for each two-claimant subset of the claimants it involves, it chooses the restriction of the vector to that population for the associated reduced problem this population faces; then the requirement is that it be chosen for the initial problem. We also define weaker variants of these properties, in particular a version of consistency for which all but two claimants leave the scene, "bilateral consistency," and versions in which the departing agents are assigned nothing or are fully compensated.

We begin with a number of logical relations and structural results concerning these properties and previously introduced ones. An important lemma, the Elevator Lemma, states that if two rules agree for two claimants, one of them being bilaterally consistent and the other conversely consistent, they agree in general. We introduce the notion of "lifting" a property by means of consistency: this allows us to deduce that if a property is satisfied by a rule for two claimants and the rule is consistent, then, in fact, it is satisfied for arbitrarily many claimants.

We continue with characterizations involving consistency, its converse, or variants of these properties, together with one or several of the properties introduced for the fixed-population version of our model. A central result is a characterization of Young's family. We close with a notion of consistency "on average," which preserves much of the spirit of consistency but is satisfied significantly more broadly.

10.1 THE VARIABLE-POPULATION MODEL

Obviously, to be able to test how well rules respond to changes in populations, they have to be defined over domains of problems in which the claimant set is not fixed. For that purpose, we generalize the model of the previous chapters. It will be most convenient to imagine that there is an infinite set of "potential" claimants, indexed by the natural numbers, $\mathbb{N}$.[1] In each given claims problem, however, only a finite number of them will be present. Let $\mathcal{N}$ be the class of finite subsets of $\mathbb{N}$. A **claims problem** is defined by specifying some population $N \in \mathcal{N}$, then a pair $(c, E) \in \mathbb{R}^N_+ \times \mathbb{R}_+$ such that $\sum_N c_i \geq E$. With $\mathcal{C}^N$ still designating the domain of all problems with claimant set N, we set $\mathcal{C} \equiv \bigcup_{N \in \mathcal{N}} \mathcal{C}^N$. A division rule here, or simply a **rule**, is a function defined over $\mathcal{C}$ that associates with each $N \in \mathcal{N}$ and each $(c, E) \in \mathcal{C}^N$ an awards vector of (c, E). Given $N \in \mathcal{N}$, we denote by $S|_{\mathcal{C}^N}$ the restriction of a rule S to the subdomain of problems with claimant set N.

The next two chapters offer a number of characterizations involving variable-population axioms as well as some of the axioms introduced in Chapters 3–8 for fixed populations. The latter should therefore be reformulated so as to apply to the more general concept of a rule under examination here. To that end, it suffices to rewrite them *for each* population $N \in \mathcal{N}$. To save space, we will not do so explicitly but simply warn the reader that henceforth our earlier axioms should be understood to include this additional quantification. For instance, *equal treatment of equals* now reads:

Equal treatment of equals: For each $N \in \mathcal{N}$, each $(c, E) \in \mathcal{C}^N$, and each pair $\{i, j\} \subseteq N$, if $c_i = c_j$, then $S_i(c, E) = S_j(c, E)$.

The case of *anonymity* is a little more subtle because now the property also covers situations in which the claimant set changes without its cardinality changing: in addition to requiring invariance of a rule with respect to relabeling of claimants within each fixed group $N \in \mathcal{N}$, it requires invariance with respect to relabeling across groups of the same size. Writing out all the quantifications gives us: "for each pair of groups of the same size, for each pair of problems faced by the two groups, for each bijection from the first group to the second (this is the renaming operation), if the claim of each member of the first group in the problem it faces is equal to the claim of that member's image under that bijection for the problem the second group faces, then the member's award in the first problem should be equal to the award to the image in this member's second problem." If the groups are the same, we obtain the property that we

[1] We will also occasionally comment on the case when the population of potential claimants is finite.

considered under the name of *anonymity* in the fixed-population version of the model. A slightly different formal statement for the variable-population model is as follows:

Anonymity: For each pair $\{N, N'\} \subset \mathcal{N}$ such that $|N| = |N'|$, each $(c, E) \in \mathcal{C}^N$, each bijection π from N to N', and each $i \in N$, $S_{\pi(i)}((c_{\pi(i)})_{i \in N}, E) = S_i(c, E)$.

Similarly, we redefine rules originally introduced in the context of a fixed population in the obvious way so as to accommodate variable populations. For example, by the "constrained equal awards rule," we now mean the rule that coincides, for each population of claimants, with the rule to which we referred by that name in the previous chapters.

10.2 CONSISTENCY AND RELATED PROPERTIES

One of the central properties of a rule in the context of a variable population is an invariance property. It expresses the robustness of the choice it makes under the departure of some agents with their assignments. The principle underlying this requirement has been the object of considerable attention in the recent literature on the design of allocation rules.[2]

In this paragraph, we begin with a formulation that extends much beyond claims problems. This is reflected in the language that we use. Consider some domain of allocation problems and a rule defined on this domain. Given a problem in the domain, apply the rule to it. Then imagine that some agents receive their assignments and leave. The principle says that if the situation is reevaluated at that point from the viewpoint of the remaining claimants, the rule should assign to each of them the same thing as initially.

The issue arises in each application of the principle of how to define the problem faced by the remaining agents. Whereas in some contexts several definitions make sense, here one stands out as most natural: when some claimants leave, they leave with their awards; in the reduction, we simply keep the claims of the remaining claimants at their initial values and we define the endowment as what is left. Equivalently, because of *balance*, we can define the endowment in the reduced problem as the sum of the amounts initially assigned to the remaining claimants.

• For a formal statement, let N designate the initial population of claimants, $(c, E) \in \mathcal{C}^N$ the problem they face, and x the awards vector the rule under consideration chooses for (c, E). Let some claimants leave with their awards, $N' \subset N$ designating the population of remaining claimants. Since by definition of a rule, for each $i \in N$, $x_i \in [0, c_i]$, the sum of the claims of the remaining claimants, $\sum_{N'} c_i$, is at least as large as the residual endowment, $E - \sum_{N \setminus N'} x_i = \sum_{N'} x_i$. Thus, the pair $(c_{N'}, \sum_{N'} x_i)$ is a well-defined

[2] The many applications that have been made of it are surveyed by Thomson (2011, 2018a).

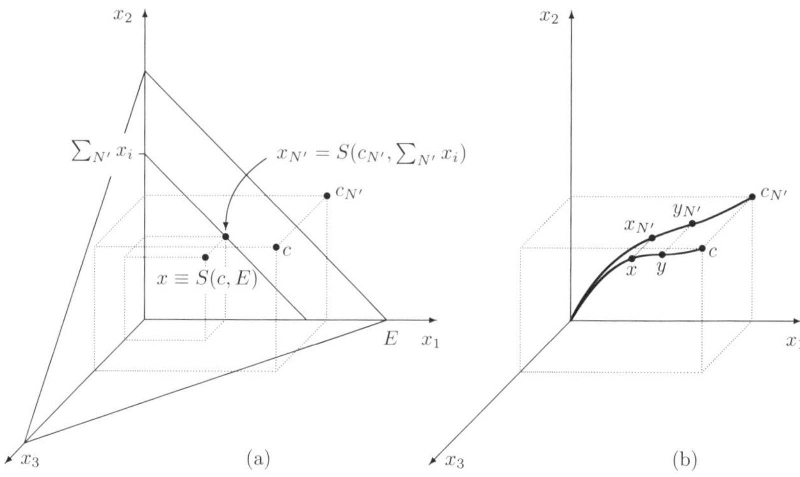

Figure 10.1: **Consistency.** We consider a rule S. Let $N \equiv \{1,2,3\}$ and $(c, E) \in \mathcal{C}^N$. (a) We first apply S to (c, E), obtaining $x \equiv S(c, E)$. Then we imagine claimant 3 leaving the scene with their award, x_3. What remains of the endowment for the group $N' \equiv \{1, 2\}$ of remaining claimants is $E - x_3$, equivalently $\sum_{N'} x_i$. We regard $(c_{N'}, \sum_{N'} x_i)$ as the problem that N' faces at this point. *Consistency* of S says that when applied to it, S chooses the same award for each member of N' as initially: $S(c_{N'}, \sum_{N'} x_i) = x_{N'}$. Thus, if a vector x belongs to its path of awards for c, its projection onto $\mathbb{R}^{N'}$ belongs to its path for $c_{N'}$. (b) This should be true for each $E \in [0, \sum_N c_i]$, so the projection onto $\mathbb{R}^{N'}$ of the path of S for c should be a subset of its path for $c_{N'}$. This panel also shows two points of the former, x and y, and their projections onto $\mathbb{R}^{N'}$, $x_{N'}$ and $y_{N'}$, which are two points of the latter. If S is *continuous*, this inclusion is in fact an equality.

claims problem.[3] It is the **reduced problem of (c, E) with respect to the subgroup N' of N and the awards vector x of (c, E)**. We require that in this problem, the rule assign to each $i \in N'$ the same amount as initially, namely x_i (Figure 10.1):[4]

Consistency: For each $N \in \mathcal{N}$, each $(c, E) \in \mathcal{C}^N$, and each $N' \subset N$, if $x \equiv S(c, E)$, then $S(c_{N'}, \sum_{N'} x_i) = x_{N'}$.

The weaker version of the property obtained when all but two claimants leave is called **bilateral consistency**.[5]

It follows directly from its definition that the proportional rule is *consistent*: for each problem, if awards are chosen proportional to claims, awards to the

[3] We can say that the domain of claims problems is "closed under the reduction operation."

[4] A more complex reduction operation, proposed by Albizuri Leroux, and Zarzuelo (2010), involves a revision of claims.

[5] Bilateral versions of the variants of *consistency* introduced below can also be defined.

members of any subgroup of claimants are proportional to their own claims. (These awards obviously satisfy the *balance* requirement in the reduced problem they face.) The constrained equal awards rule also satisfies the property. Indeed, for each problem, if a value of the parameter that solves the equation giving its constrained equal awards vector has been found and some claimants leave with their awards, the same value solves the corresponding equation for the reduced problem the remaining claimants face. The same argument applies to the constrained equal losses rule. As for the Talmud rule, its *consistency* can be deduced from the *consistency* of the constrained equal awards and constrained equal losses rules and the specific way in which these rules are modified (half-claims are used instead of claims themselves) and combined to yield it.

On the other hand, the random arrival rule is not *consistent*. To prove this, let us once again use the marriage contract problem in the Talmud $((100, 200, 300), 200)$ for which the calculations are illustrated in Table 2.1 of Subsection 2.1.8 where the rule is defined. They produce the awards vector $(33\frac{1}{3}, 83\frac{1}{3}, 83\frac{1}{3})$. Suppose now that claimant 3 leaves with their award. Then claimants 1 and 2, whose claims are 100 and 200, face the problem of dividing $200 - 83\frac{1}{3} = 116\frac{2}{3}$. They can be ordered in two ways, $1 \prec 2$ and $2 \prec 1$, to which correspond the awards vectors $(100, 16\frac{2}{3})$ and $(0, 116\frac{2}{3})$ respectively. The random arrival rule chooses the average of these vectors, namely $(50, 66\frac{2}{3})$. These awards differ from the amounts it had awarded to these claimants initially.

The minimal overlap rule is another important rule that fails *consistency*. Let $N \equiv \{1, 2, 3\}$ and $(c, E) \in \mathcal{C}^N$ be equal to $((3, 6, 6), 7)$ (Figure 10.2).

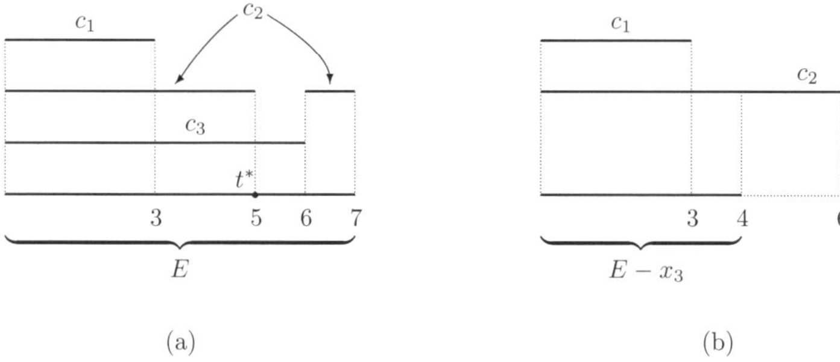

Figure 10.2: **The minimal overlap rule is not consistent**. (a) Let $N \equiv \{1, 2, 3\}$ and $(c, E) \in \mathcal{C}^N$ be equal to $((3, 6, 6), 7)$. The critical value t^* of the parameter for which we obtain minimal overlap (Case 2 of Proposition 2.1 applies) is 5, resulting in the awards vector $(1, 3, 3)$. (b) If claimant 3 leaves with their award of 3, the set of remaining claimants is $N' \equiv \{1, 2\}$ and the reduced problem they face is $((3, 6), 4) \in \mathcal{C}^{N'}$. In this problem, agent 2's claim is larger than the residual endowment. The minimal overlap rule selects $(1.5, 2.5)$ (Case 1 of Proposition 2.1 applies). This vector is not the restriction of $(1, 3, 3)$ to the population $\{1, 2\}$.

Then $MO(c, E) = (1, 3, 3)$. Suppose now that claimant 3 leaves with their award. Then, claimants 1 and 2, whose claims are 3 and 6, face the problem of dividing $7 - 3 = 4$. For this problem, the minimal overlap rule chooses $(1.5, 2.5)$.

Concerning Young's rules, we have the following positive result, from which several of the observations made earlier follow directly because they are Young rules:

Lemma 10.1 *Young's rules are consistent.*

The straightforward proof is illustrated in Figure 10.3.

Several other rules introduced in Chapter 2, such as Piniles' and the constrained egalitarian rules, are *consistent* too. This can be seen directly from their definitions but it is also a consequence of Lemma 10.1 and the fact that they are Young rules. This argument also applies to the duals of Piniles' and of the constrained egalitarian rules because Young's family is closed under duality (Lemma 7.2). It also follows from Proposition 10.4 below, according to which, if a rule is *consistent*, so is its dual.

Turning now to the weighted versions of the *consistent* rules just identified (Section 3.6), we find that *consistency* is preserved provided the weights are chosen in what can naturally be referred to as a "consistent" manner, as explained next. In the context of a variable population, when defining weighted

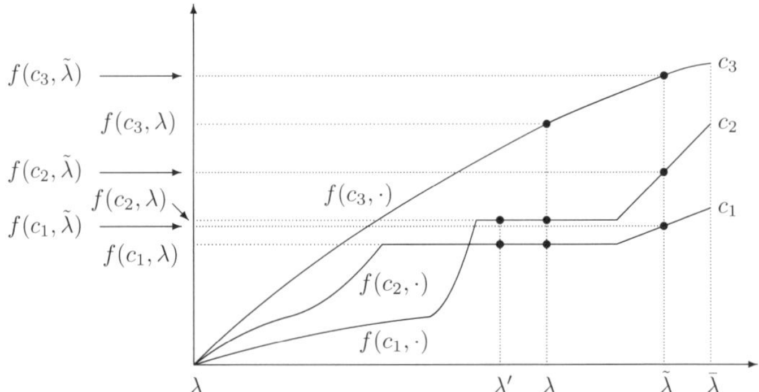

Figure 10.3: **Young's rules are consistent**. Let $N \equiv \{1, 2, 3\}$ and $(c, E) \in \mathcal{C}^N$. The choice made for (c, E) by a Young rule admitting the representation $f \in \Phi$ – we show the graphs of the function $f(c_0, \cdot)$ for the three relevant values of c_0, the three coordinates of c – is obtained by identifying λ such that $f(c_1, \lambda) + f(c_2, \lambda) + f(c_3, \lambda) = E$: the rule chooses the awards vector $(f(c_i, \lambda))_{i \in N}$. Now, we imagine claimant 3 leaving with their award. For the problem of dividing $E' \equiv E - f(c_3, \lambda) = f(c_1, \lambda) + f(c_2, \lambda)$ between claimants 1 and 2, λ also solves the equation in μ, $f(c_1, \mu) + f(c_2, \mu) = E'$: claimants 1 and 2 still receive $f(c_1, \lambda)$ and $f(c_2, \lambda)$ respectively. (There could be other solutions to this equation, λ' being an example here, but the awards vectors associated with them would be the same.)

rules, we can in principle choose a weight vector for each group of claimants separately, and when solving problems involving a particular group, use the vector chosen for the group. However, one can guess that for *consistency* to hold, these vectors should be related in some fashion. This is indeed the case. Starting from some problem, what is needed is that if some claimants leave, the weight vector used for the population of remaining claimants when solving the reduced problem they face be proportional to the restriction to that population of the weight vector used when solving the initial problem. One way to achieve this proportionality in general is to choose an infinite list of positive "reference" weights, one for each potential claimant; then, when solving any problem, to use the restriction of this reference list to the population of agents involved in the problem. It is easy to show that the generalizations of the fixed-population versions of the weighted constrained equal awards and weighted constrained equal losses rules obtained in this manner are *consistent.*

In order to give full priority to particular claimants over others, if desired, we partition the set of potential claimants into reference priority classes, as in Section 3.6. For each class and each member of the class, we specify a positive weight. When solving a problem, we handle in succession the classes the reference partition induces, using for the members of each induced class the weights assigned to them in the reference class that contains it. Partitioning "insulates" groups of claimants from one another. If, for each class, we use the restriction of a *consistent* rule, *consistency* will hold overall. The various rules that we attach to each component of the partition do not have to be related in any particular way.

Consistent versions of the monotone path rules, which we proposed as nonhomogeneous generalizations of the constrained equal awards rule (Section 6.1), are defined as follows (Figure 10.4). Let $\Lambda \equiv [\underline{\lambda}, \bar{\lambda}[$ and for each $i \in \mathbb{N}$, let $F_i : \Lambda \mapsto \mathbb{R}_+$ be a continuous, nowhere decreasing, and unbounded function such that $F_i(\underline{\lambda}) = 0$. Let $F \equiv (F_i)_{i \in \mathbb{N}}$ and let $\mathcal{F}$ be the class of all such lists. Given $F \in \mathcal{F}$, for each $i \in N$ and each $c_i \geq 0$, let $f_i(c_i, \cdot)\colon \Lambda \mapsto \mathbb{R}_+$ be the function whose graph follows that of F_i until a point of ordinate c_i is reached and continues horizontally from then on. Then, for each $N \in \mathcal{N}$ and each $(c, E) \in \mathcal{C}^N$, the **monotone path rule associated with $\boldsymbol{F} \in \boldsymbol{\mathcal{F}}$** chooses the vector $x \in X(c, E)$ such that for some $\lambda \in \Lambda$ and each $i \in N$, $x_i = f_i(c_i, \lambda)$. We can think of f as a generalization of what we called a "representation" of a Young rule. For such a rule, all the f_is are equal. Here they may differ across agents. On the other hand, they take a very simple form and, in fact, if all the F_is are equal – then all the f_is are equal too – the resulting rule is the constrained equal awards rule.

Figure 10.4 illustrates the definition for $N \equiv \{1, 2\}$. Given $F \in \mathcal{F}$, panel (a) shows F_1 and F_2 as well as the graphs of $f_1(c_0, \cdot)$ for three values of c_0 called a, c_1, and c_1', and the graphs of $f_2(c_0, \cdot)$ for three values of c_0 called b, c_2, and c_2'. Panel (b) shows the locus G of the point $(F_1(\lambda), F_2(\lambda))$ as λ varies in Λ. It also shows the paths of awards of the rule associated with F for two claims vectors, $c \equiv (c_1, c_2)$ and $c' \equiv (c_1', c_2')$. A typical path follows G until

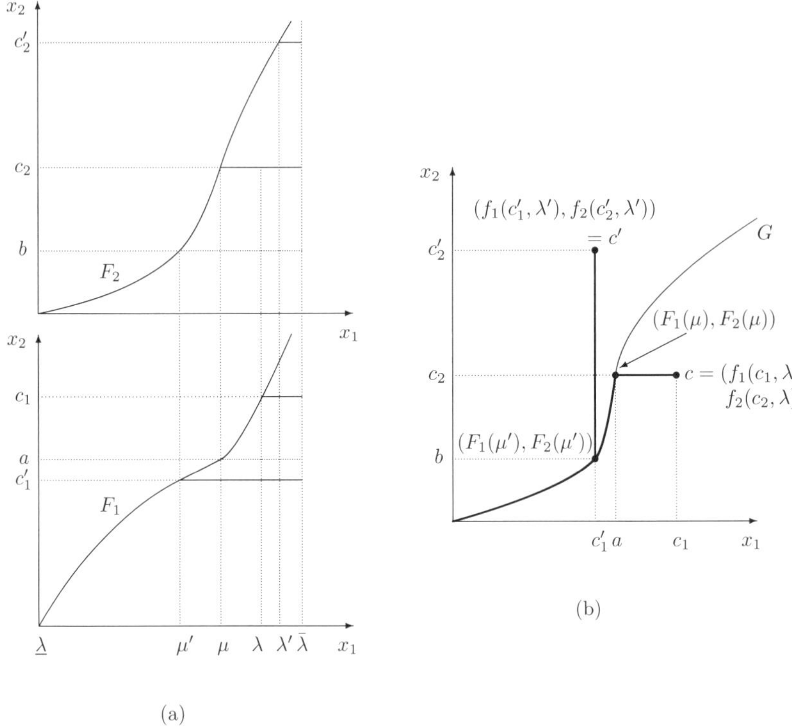

Figure 10.4: **A generalized Young representation of a monotone path rule**. (a) We specify an interval $\Lambda \equiv [\underline{\lambda}, \bar{\lambda}[$ of real numbers (here, $\underline{\lambda} = 0$). For each agent $i \in \mathbb{N}$, we specify a function $F_i : \Lambda \mapsto \mathbb{R}_+$ satisfying certain properties. Shown are F_1 and F_2. For each $i \in \mathbb{N}$ and each $c_0 \geq 0$, we call $f_i(c_0, \cdot)$ the function whose graph follows that of F_i until a point of ordinate c_0 is reached, and continues horizontally from then on. Given $N \in \mathcal{N}$ and $(c, E) \in \mathcal{C}^N$, the monotone path rule associated with $(F_i)_{i \in \mathbb{N}}$ chooses the awards vector $(f_i(c_i, \tilde{\lambda}))_{i \in N}$, where $\tilde{\lambda}$ is such that $\sum f_i(c_i, \tilde{\lambda}) = E$. (b) For $N \equiv \{1, 2\}$, this panel shows the paths of awards of the rule for two claims vectors, c and c' in $\mathbb{R}^N_+$. The parameters λ and λ' are the smallest values of $\tilde{\lambda}$ for which $(f_1(c_1, \tilde{\lambda}), f_2(c_2, \tilde{\lambda})) = c$ and $(f_1(c_1, \tilde{\lambda}), f_2(c_2, \tilde{\lambda})) = c'$.

one claimant is fully compensated, then it continues to the claims vector, horizontally if it is claimant 2 who is fully compensated first, as is the case for c, and vertically if it is claimant 1 who is fully compensated first, as is the case for c'.[6]

• Apart from *bilateral consistency*, another weaker form of *consistency* can be formulated for situations in which some claims are 0. By definition of a

[6] It follows from our assumptions that the projection of G onto each coordinate axis is unbounded. One could accommodate the possibility of an unbounded G having a bounded projection on some axis at the cost of some technical complications.

rule, their holders are assigned 0; if they leave, we require that in the resulting reduced problem, each remaining claimant be assigned the same amount as initially.[7]

Null claims consistency: For each $N \in \mathcal{N}$, each $(c, E) \in \mathcal{C}^N$, and each $N' \subset N$, if $c_{N \setminus N'} = 0$, then $S_{N'}(c, E) = S(c_{N'}, E)$.

An important way in which this requirement differs from *consistency* is that the rule is not used in defining the problem faced by the smaller population; there is no change in the endowment because, by definition of a rule, any claimant whose claim is 0 is assigned 0. Many rules that violate *consistency* satisfy this weaker property. This is the case for the random arrival and minimal overlap rules. The proof for the former requires some algebraic manipulation of the combinatorial coefficients appearing in its definition. The proof for the latter is obvious once we remember how to arrange claims so as to solve the exercise underlying its definition.

We should also note that equivalently, instead of removing agents whose claims are 0, we could add such agents, and require that the awards to the agents initially present not be affected.

• Next are two requirements of intermediate strength between *consistency* and *null claims consistency*. First, if some claimants are assigned 0, and whether or not their claims are 0, and they leave, in the resulting reduced problem each remaining claimant should receive the same amount as initially:[8]

Null compensation consistency: For each $N \in \mathcal{N}$, each $(c, E) \in \mathcal{C}^N$, and each $N' \subset N$, if $S_{N \setminus N'}(c, E) = 0$, then $S_{N'}(c, E) = S(c_{N'}, E)$.

Examples of rules satisfying *null compensation consistency* but not *consistency* are once again the random arrival and minimal overlap rules. Indeed, for either rule, the only circumstance in which someone is assigned nothing is when either the endowment is 0, in which case there is nothing to check, or their claim is 0, and the property amounts to *null claims consistency*, a property satisfied by both rules, as we just saw.

Second, if some claimants are fully compensated, and they leave with their awards, in the resulting reduced problem, each remaining claimant should receive the same amount as initially:

[7] The requirement that the award to an agent whose claim is 0 be 0 corresponds to the property known in the theory of coalitional games as the "dummy property." The property is considered by Chun (1988) in the present context, although he does not impose *nonnegativity* on rules. It is automatically satisfied by rules as we defined them. What we call *null claims consistency* is what Dagan and Volij (1993) call "zero out," Chun (1999) "dummy," Moulin (2000) "independence of null demands," and Ju (2003) "null consistency."

[8] Moulin (2000) uses the expression "zero consistency." Ju and Moreno-Ternero (2014) refer to the two properties as "zero-award-out-consistency" and "full-award-out-consistency" respectively.

Full compensation consistency: For each $N \in \mathcal{N}$, each $(c, E) \in \mathcal{C}^N$, and each $N' \subset N$, if $S_{N \setminus N'}(c, E) = c_{N \setminus N'}$, then $S_{N'}(c, E) = S(c_{N'}, E - \sum_{N \setminus N'} c_i)$.

Again, both the random arrival and minimal overlap rules can be used to make the point that this property is weaker than *consistency*. The hypotheses are satisfied only in trivial cases.[9]

Consistency and the variants just defined can also be written for correspondences: a correspondence S defined on $\mathcal{C}$ is *consistent* if for each problem, *each* awards vector it chooses for this problem (note this additional quantification), and each subgroup of the agents involved in the problem, the restriction of the awards vector to the subgroup is *one* of the choices S makes for the associated reduced problem. Formally, for each $N \in \mathcal{N}$, each $(c, E) \in \mathcal{C}^N$, *each* $x \in S(c, E)$, and each $N' \subset N$, $x_{N'} \in S(c_{N'}, E - \sum_{N \setminus N'} x_i)$.

The following lemma collects some observations about some of the mappings introduced in early chapters.

Lemma 10.2 *(a) The correspondences that associate with each problem (i) its set of awards vectors, or (ii) its set of awards vectors satisfying the order preservation inequalities, or (iii) its set of awards vectors satisfying the group order preservation inequalities, are consistent.*

(b) The correspondences that associate with each problem (i) its set of awards vectors satisfying the $\frac{1}{|N|}$*-truncated-claims lower bounds, or (ii) its set of awards vectors satisfying the min-of-claim-and-equal-division lower bounds, are not null-claims consistent.*

Proof: (a) We omit the trivial proof.

(b) For (i), let $N \equiv \{1, 2, 3\}$, $(c, E) \in \mathcal{C}^N$ be equal to $((0, 2, 3), 3)$. The $\frac{1}{|N|}$-truncated-claims lower bounds are $(0, \frac{2}{3}, 1)$. The awards vector $x \equiv (0, 2, 1)$ satisfies the bounds. If claimant 1 leaves with an award of 0, claimants 2 and 3 face the reduced problem $((2, 3), 3)$ in which the bounds are $(1, 1.5)$. It is not true that $x_{\{2,3\}} = (2, 1) \geqq (1, 1.5)$.

For (ii), using the same example, we find that the min-of-claim-and-equal-division lower bounds are $(0, 1, 1)$, which the awards vector $x \equiv (0, 1, 2)$ satisfies. If claimant 1 leaves with their award of 0, claimants 2 and 3 face the reduced problem $((2, 3), 3)$ in which the bounds are $(1.5, 1.5)$. It is not true that $x_{\{2,3\}} = (1, 2) \geqq (1.5, 1.5)$. □

[9] For other classes of problems in which payoffs can be ordered, another weakening of *consistency* has been considered in which only the agent with the smallest payoff is allowed to leave. Alternatively, it could be the agent with the largest payoff who is so allowed. These versions strengthen *null compensation consistency* and *full compensation consistency*.

10.3 CONVERSE CONSISTENCY

• The next property is based on a thought experiment that is "symmetric" to that underlying *consistency*: given some problem, it allows us to deduce the desirability of a proposed awards vector for it from the desirability of its restriction to each two-claimant subgroup for the reduced problem they face after the members of the complementary subgroup have left with their awards. Specifically, suppose that an awards vector x for some problem has the following property: for each two-claimant subgroup of the claimants involved in this problem, the rule chooses the restriction of x to the subgroup for the associated reduced problem they face. Then the rule should choose x for the initial problem:

Converse consistency: For each $N \in \mathcal{N}$, each $(c, E) \in \mathcal{C}^N$, and each $x \in X(c, E)$, if for each $N' \subset N$ with $|N'| = 2$, we have $x_{N'} = S(c_{N'}, \sum_{N'} x_i)$, then $x = S(c, E)$.[10]

Note that, for each $x \in X(c, E)$ and each $N' \subset N$, the pair $(c_{N'}, \sum_{N'} x_i)$ is a well-defined problem. Obviously, if some x exists satisfying the hypotheses of the property, and S is *conversely consistent*, x uniquely satisfies these hypotheses; otherwise, S would choose several awards vectors for (c, E). In any case, if S is *endowment monotonic for two claimants*, there can be at most one x satisfying the hypotheses (the same logic underlies Proposition 10.1).

To illustrate the property, consider the proportional rule. Let $N \in \mathcal{N}$ and $(c, E) \in \mathcal{C}^N$. Let $x \in X(c, E)$ be such that for each two-claimant subgroup N' of N, the restriction of x to N' is the awards vector the proportional rule chooses for $(c_{N'}, \sum_{N'} x_i)$. This implies that for each $N' \subset N$ with $|N'| = 2$, there is $\lambda^{N'} \in \mathbb{R}_+$ such that $x_{N'} = \lambda^{N'} c_{N'}$. Since these subgroups overlap, it is immediate that the coefficients of proportionality $\{\lambda^{N'}\}_{N' \subset N; |N'|=2}$ are all equal, so that in fact $x = P(c, E)$. Thus, the proportional rule is *conversely consistent*.[11] It is equally easy to check that the constrained equal awards, constrained equal losses, and Talmud rules are *conversely consistent*. In fact, we have:

Lemma 10.3 *Young's rules are conversely consistent.*

Proof: Let S be a Young rule, admitting the representation $f : \mathbb{R}_+ \times \Lambda \mapsto \mathbb{R}_+$, where $\Lambda = [\underline{\lambda}, \bar{\lambda}] \subseteq \bar{\mathbb{R}}$. Let $N \in \mathcal{N}$, $(c, E) \in \mathcal{C}^N$, and $x \in X(c, E)$ be such that for each $N' \subset N$ with $|N'| = 2$, $x_{N'} = S(c_{N'}, \sum_{N'} x_k)$. For each $i \in N$, let $\Lambda_i \equiv \{\lambda \in \Lambda : f(c_i, \lambda) = x_i\}$. Note that for each $i \in N$, Λ_i is a closed

[10] We could have equivalently written "for each $x \in \mathbb{R}^N$ such that $\sum x_i = E$."

[11] This suggests the formulation of a stronger version of *converse consistency* in which the hypotheses are only written for a list of subgroups of the initial group defining a connected graph containing all members of N. See Thomson (1994b) for a discussion.

interval. By hypothesis, for each $\{i, j\} \subset N$, $\Lambda_i \cap \Lambda_j \neq \emptyset$. We prove by induction on the number of claimants in N – let us use the notation $n \equiv |N|$ – that the intervals $(\Lambda_i)_{i \in N}$ have at least one point in common. If $n = 2$, there is nothing to prove. Let $n \geq 3$ and suppose the result is true up to $n - 1$, and without loss of generality, let $N \equiv \{1, \ldots, n\}$. Let $\Lambda^* \equiv \bigcap_{k=1}^{n-1} \Lambda_k \subset \Lambda$. By the induction hypothesis, $\Lambda^* \neq \emptyset$. Suppose by contradiction that $\Lambda^* \cap \Lambda_n = \emptyset$ and, without loss of generality and introducing $\underline{\mu} \equiv \min\{\lambda\colon \lambda \in \Lambda^*\}$, that $\Lambda_n \subset [\underline{\lambda}, \underline{\mu}[$. For each $i < n$, let $\lambda_i \in \Lambda_i \cap \Lambda_n$, $\lambda^* \equiv \max_{i=1,\ldots,n-1}\{\lambda_i\}$, and i^* be such that $\lambda_{i^*} = \lambda^*$. Since for each $i < n$, $\lambda_i \in \Lambda_i$, then $\lambda^* \in \Lambda^*$. Since λ^* is obtained for the group $\{i^*, n\}$, then $\lambda^* \in \Lambda_n$, a contradiction.

By choosing $\lambda \in \bigcap_N \Lambda_i$, we deduce that $x \in S(c, E)$. □

On the other hand, neither the random arrival rule nor the minimal overlap rule is *conversely consistent*. To see this for the former, let $N \equiv \{1, 2, 3\}$ and $(c, E) \in \mathcal{C}^N$ be equal to $((2, 4, 5), 5)$. Let $x \equiv (1, 2, 2)$. We note that $(x_1, x_2) = RA((c_1, c_2), x_1 + x_2)$, two similar statements holding for the groups $\{1, 3\}$ and $\{2, 3\}$. However, $RA(c, E) = (\frac{5}{6}, \frac{11}{6}, \frac{14}{6}) \neq x$. Since for two claimants, the minimal overlap rule coincides with the random arrival rule, the awards vector x also satisfies the hypotheses of *converse consistency* for the minimal overlap rule (in each of the three two-claimant groups to consider, the largest claim is at least as large as the endowment, so Case 1 of Proposition 2.1 applies). However, $MO(c, E) = (\frac{2}{3}, \frac{2}{3} + \frac{2}{2}, \frac{2}{3} + \frac{2}{2} + \frac{1}{1}) \neq x$ (here too, the largest claim is at least as large as the endowment, so Case 1 of Proposition 2.1 still applies).

Let us call **weak converse consistency** the version of *converse consistency* obtained by writing the hypothesis *for each proper subgroup* of the entire set of claimants (instead of for each subgroup of two claimants). The random arrival and minimal overlap rules do not satisfy this property either and Lemma 10.4 below provides an explanation why.

• A rule could in principle be *conversely consistent* because there is never any awards vector for which the hypotheses of the property are all met (except for $E = 0$ or $E = \sum c_i$, in which case they have to hold, but then, by definition of a rule, the conclusion holds too). Thus, another version of the property is obtained by requiring that for each problem, there should be such a vector. If there is one, it is of course unique if we require that it be chosen by the rule for the problem. Alternatively, we could simply demand that the rule select from the set they constitute. Let S be a rule. For each $N \in \mathcal{N}$ and each $(c, E) \in \mathcal{C}^N$, let us introduce a notation for the set of awards vectors of (c, E) satisfying the hypotheses of *converse consistency* for (c, E) and S:[12]

cv.cs(*c*, *E*; *S*)$\equiv \{x \in X(c, E)\colon$ for each $N' \subset N$ with $|N'| = 2, x_{N'} = S(c_{N'}, \sum_{N'} x_i)\}$

[12] This property is introduced by Chun (1999) under the name of "converse consistency."

Strong converse consistency: For each $N \in \mathcal{N}$ and each $(c, E) \in \mathcal{C}^N$, $\{\text{cv.cs}(c, E; S)\} = S(c, E)$.

Strong converse consistency implies that for each $N \in \mathcal{N}$ and each $(c, E) \in \mathcal{C}^N$, $\{\text{cv.cs}(c, E; S)\}$ is a singleton. We have already noted that if S is *endowment monotonic for two claimants*, this set contains at most one point.

Converse consistency and its strong version can of course also be written for correspondences.

10.4 OTHER LOGICAL RELATIONS BETWEEN CONSISTENCY, ITS CONVERSE, AND OTHER PROPERTIES

We now investigate the logical relations between *consistency*, *converse consistency*, the variants of these properties we defined, and other properties that we introduced in previous chapters.

♦ It turns out that *weak converse consistency* is only apparently weaker than *converse consistency*:[13]

Lemma 10.4 *Converse consistency and weak converse consistency are equivalent.*

Proof: Let S be a rule satisfying *weak converse consistency*. We assert that S satisfies *converse consistency* itself. We show, by recursive application of *weak converse consistency*, that if an awards vector of some problem satisfies the hypotheses of *converse consistency* for S, then in fact, it satisfies the hypotheses of *weak converse consistency* for S. Indeed, let $N \in \mathcal{N}$, $(c, E) \in \mathcal{C}^N$, and $x \in X(c, E)$ be such that for each $N' \subset N$ with $|N'| = 2$, $x_{N'} = S(c_{N'}, \sum x_i)$. Let $\bar{N} \subset N$ with $|\bar{N}| = 3$, and note that the hypotheses on x just stated imply that for each $N' \subset \bar{N}$, $x_{N'} = S(c_{N'}, \sum_{N'} x_i)$. By *weak converse consistency*, $x_{\bar{N}} = S(c_{\bar{N}}, \sum_{\bar{N}} x_i)$. This conclusion holds for each $\bar{N} \subset N$ with $|\bar{N}| = 3$. Next, let $\tilde{N} \subset N$ with $|\tilde{N}| = 4$. At this point, we know that for each $N' \subset \tilde{N}$, $x_{N'} = S(c_{N'}, \sum_{N'} c_i)$. Again, by *weak converse consistency*, $x_{\tilde{N}} = S(c_{\tilde{N}}, \sum_{\tilde{N}} c_i)$. The induction continues in this manner until the entire set of claimants is reached. One final application of *weak converse consistency* delivers the desired conclusion. □

♦ Next, we show that the very mild property of *endowment monotonicity* and *bilateral consistency* together imply *strong converse consistency*. Also, *strong converse consistency* implies *consistency*.[14]

[13] This equivalence holds for most resource allocation problems (Thomson, 1998, 2011, 2017a).

[14] Lemmas 10.5 and 10.6 are due to Chun (1999). On other domains, the counterparts of *consistency* and *converse consistency* are not usually logically related. For instance, for bargaining

Lemma 10.5 *Endowment monotonicity and bilateral consistency together imply strong converse consistency.*

Proof: Let S be a rule satisfying the hypotheses of the lemma. To show that S is *strongly conversely consistent*, we show that for each $N \in \mathcal{N}$ and each $(c, E) \in \mathcal{C}^N$, (i) cv.cs$(c, E; S) \neq \emptyset$ and then (ii) in fact, $|$cv.cs$(c, E; S)| = 1$.

Let $x \equiv S(c, E)$. By *bilateral consistency*, for each $N' \subset N$ such that $|N'| = 2$, $S(c_{N'}, \sum_{N'} x_i) = x_{N'}$. Thus, cv.cs$(c, E; S) \neq \emptyset$.

To show that for each $N \in \mathcal{N}$ and each $(c, E) \in \mathcal{C}^N$, $|$cv.cs$(c, E; S)| = 1$, suppose, by way of contradiction, that there are $(c, E) \in \mathcal{C}^N$ and $y \in \mathbb{R}^N_+$ such that $y \neq x$ and $y \in$ cv.cs$(c, E; S)$. Since $y \neq x$, there is $N' \subseteq N$ such that $\sum_{N'} y_i \neq \sum_{N'} x_i$. Without loss of generality, suppose that $\sum_{N'} y_i > \sum_{N'} x_i$. By *endowment monotonicity* applied to $(c_{N'}, \sum_{N'} y_i)$ and $(c_{N'}, \sum_{N'} x_i)$, we obtain $y_{N'} \geq x_{N'}$. Let $i^* \in N$ be such that $y_{i^*} > x_{i^*}$.

Now, let $N'' \subseteq N$ be such that $|N''| = 2$ and $i^* \in N''$. By *endowment monotonicity* applied to $(c_{N''}, \sum_{N''} y_i)$ and $(c_{N''}, \sum_{N''} x_i)$, and since $y_{i^*} > x_{i^*}$, we obtain $y_j \geq x_j$ for each $j \neq i^*$, so that $\sum_N y_i > \sum_N x_i$. However, by *balance*, $\sum_N y_i = \sum_N x_i = E$, a contradiction. □

Since Young's rules satisfy the hypotheses of Lemma 10.5, the logical relation it states can also be used to give an indirect proof of Lemma 10.3.

Lemma 10.6 *Strong converse consistency implies consistency.*

Proof: Let S be a rule satisfying the hypothesis of the lemma. Let $N \in \mathcal{N}$ and $(c, E) \in \mathcal{C}^N$. By *strong converse consistency*, there is $x \in \mathbb{R}^N_+$ such that $\{x\} =$ cv.cs$(c, E; S)$ and $x = S(c, E)$. To show that S is *consistent,* we need to show that for each $N' \subset N$, $x_{N'} = S(c_{N'}, \sum_{N'} x_i)$. By *claims boundedness*, the pair $(c_{N'}, \sum_{N'} x_i)$ is a well-defined problem in $\mathcal{C}^{N'}$. Since $x \in$ cv.cs$(c, E; S)$, then for each $N'' \subset N$ such that $|N''| = 2$, $x_{N''} = S(c_{N''}, \sum_{N''} x_i)$. Thus, by *strong converse consistency*, $x_{N'} = S(c_{N'}, \sum_{N'} x_i)$. Thus, *consistency* holds. □

It follows from Lemmas 10.5–10.6 that *endowment monotonicity* and *bilateral consistency* together imply *consistency.*[15]

♦ Does *converse consistency* itself imply *consistency*? It may be natural to conjecture such an implication because, among the rules that we have encountered so far, if a rule satisfies the former property it also satisfies the latter. However, the implication does not hold. Here is in fact a way to construct infinitely many rules that are *conversely consistent* but not *consistent.*

problems, the Nash solution is *consistent* but not *conversely consistent* whereas the egalitarian solution is *conversely consistent* but not *consistent.* For details, see Thomson (2018a). Otten, Peters, and Volij (1996) prove a result very similar to Lemma 10.5 for the problem of fully allocating a social endowment of a single commodity when preferences are single-peaked (Subsection 2.1.7).

[15] This is proved in a different way by Dagan, Serrano, and Volij (1997).

Let S be a two-claimant rule that is *endowment monotonic*. We noted earlier that by *endowment monotonicity*, for each $N \in \mathcal{N}$ such that $|N| = 2$, and each $(c, E) \in \mathcal{C}^N$, the set $\text{cv.cs}(c, E) \equiv \{x \in X(c, E)\colon \text{ for each } N' \subset N \text{ with} |N'| = 2, x_{N'} = S(c_{N'}, \sum_{N'} x_i)\}$ contains at most one point. Now, let $\bar{S} \equiv S$ on the subdomain of two-claimant problems, and for each $N \in \mathcal{N}$ with $|N| > 2$, and each $(c, E) \in \mathcal{C}^N$, let $\bar{S}(c, E)$ be the unique point of $\text{cv.cs}(c, E)$ if this set is nonempty and an arbitrary awards vector of (c, E) otherwise. Each such rule $\bar{S}$ is *conversely consistent*, but accidentally *consistent*.

The rule $\bar{S}$ just defined is unlikely to satisfy any desirable properties but other examples can be constructed to serve the same purpose that are quite well behaved. To prove this, we will find it most convenient to wait for the introduction of the concept of *average consistency* however (Section 10.7).

♦ The next lemma reveals a very useful monotonicity implication of *bilateral consistency*, when imposed in conjunction with two basic properties.[16]

Lemma 10.7 *Equal treatment of equals, endowment continuity, and bilateral consistency together imply endowment monotonicity.*

Proof: Let S be a rule satisfying the hypothesis of the lemma. To see that it is *endowment monotonic*, assume by contradiction that there are $N \in \mathcal{N}$, $(c, E) \in \mathcal{C}^N$, $E' > E$ with $\sum c_i \geq E'$, and $i \in N$ such that $x_i \equiv S_i(c, E) < S_i(c, E') \equiv x'_i$. By feasibility, there is $j \in N$ such that $x_j \equiv S_j(c, E) > S_j(c, E') \equiv x'_j$. By *bilateral consistency*, $(x_i, x_j) = S((c_i, c_j), x_i + x_j)$ and $(x'_i, x'_j) = S((c_i, c_j), x'_i + x'_j)$. Suppose without loss of generality that $x_i + x_j \leq x'_i + x'_j$. Let $n \in \mathbb{N}$ be sufficiently large that $x_i + nx_j > x'_i + nx'_j$. Let $N' \in \mathcal{N}$ be a group of $n + 1$ claimants containing $\{i, j\}$, and let $(c', F) \in \mathcal{C}^{N'}$ be such that for each $k \in N' \backslash \{i\}$, $c'_k = c_j$. Let $w(F) \equiv S_i(c', F) + S_j(c', F)$. By *endowment continuity*, the function w is continuous. Also, $w(0) = 0$ and $w(c_i + nc_j) = c_i + c_j$. Thus, there is $F' \in \mathbb{R}_+$ such that $w(F') = x'_i + x'_j$. By *bilateral consistency* and *equal treatment of equals*, $S(c', F') = (x'_i, x'_j, \ldots, x'_j)$. Thus, $F' = x'_i + nx'_j$.

We repeat the argument: since $w(0) = 0 \leq x_i + x_j \leq w(F')$, there is $F \in \mathbb{R}_+$ such that $0 \leq F \leq F'$ and $w(F) = x_i + x_j$. By *equal treatment of equals*, $S(c', F) = (x_i, x_j, \ldots, x_j)$, so that $F = x_i + nx_j$. The choice of n implies that $F > F'$, which contradicts the earlier inequality $F \leq F'$. □

The following is also of interest:[17]

Proposition 10.1 *Given a rule defined on the domain of two-claimant problems that is endowment monotonic, there is at most one bilaterally consistent rule that, for two claimants, coincides with it.*

[16] Lemma 10.7 is due to Young (1987).

[17] Proposition 10.1 is due to Aumann and Maschler (1985).

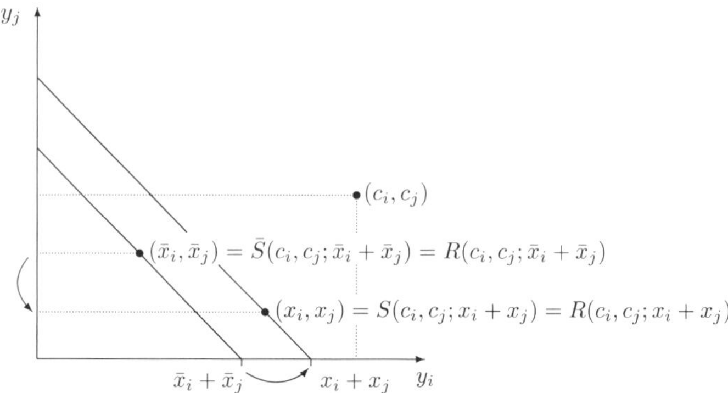

Figure 10.5: **There is at most one bilaterally consistent rule that coincides for two claimants with a prespecified endowment monotonic rule** (Proposition 10.1). If the endowment increases from $\bar{x}_i + \bar{x}_j$ to $x_i + x_j$, claimant j receives less.

Proof: (Figure 10.5) Let R be a rule defined on the domain of two-claimant problems. We argue by contraposition and suppose that there are two distinct *bilaterally consistent* rules S and $\bar{S}$ that, for two claimants, coincide with R. We will show that R fails *endowment monotonicity*. Since $S \neq \bar{S}$, there are $N \in \mathcal{N}$ with $|N| \geq 3$ and $(c, E) \in \mathcal{C}^N$ such that $x \equiv S(c, E) \neq \bar{S}(c, E) \equiv \bar{x}$. Thus, by *balance*, there is $\{i, j\} \subset N$ such that $(*)$ $x_i > \bar{x}_i$ and $x_j < \bar{x}_j$. Suppose, without loss of generality, that $x_i + x_j \geq \bar{x}_i + \bar{x}_j$. Since S is *bilaterally consistent* and, for two claimants, S coincides with R, we obtain $(x_i, x_j) = S((c_i, c_j), x_i + x_j) = R((c_i, c_j), x_i + x_j)$. Similarly, since $\bar{S}$ is *bilaterally consistent* and, for two claimants, $\bar{S}$ coincides with R, we obtain $(\bar{x}_i, \bar{x}_j) = S((c_i, c_j), \bar{x}_i + \bar{x}_j) = R((c_i, c_j), \bar{x}_i + \bar{x}_j)$. Thus, as the endowment increases from $\bar{x}_i + \bar{x}_j$ to $x_i + x_j$, R assigns less to claimant j (second inequality in $(*)$), in violation of *endowment monotonicity*. □

♦ The following lemma holds very generally, much beyond the scope of the model under study here, and it has proved extremely useful in a wide range of studies. It says that given two rules, if one of them is *bilaterally consistent*, the other *conversely consistent*, and they coincide for two claimants, then they coincide in general. We refer to it as the Elevator Lemma, using the following visual metaphor. We partition the domain of all problems into subdomains according to how many claimants are involved, and stack these subdomains like the floors of a building. We start from some arbitrary problem involving at least three claimants and apply the first rule to it, thereby obtaining some awards vector x. Since this rule is *bilaterally consistent*, the restriction of x to each two-claimant group is the choice it makes for the reduced problem relative to that group and x (we press the "down" button of the elevator to reach the second floor). Because for two claimants, the two rules coincide, we derive a parallel list of statements concerning x for the second rule. This list constitutes

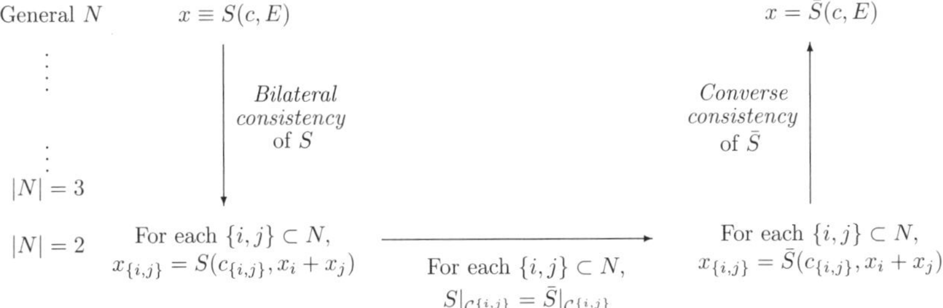

Figure 10.6: **Elevator Lemma:** if a *bilaterally consistent* rule S coincides with a *conversely consistent* rule $\bar{S}$ for two claimants, then S coincides with $\bar{S}$ in general. In this illustration, groups of claimants are stacked up according to their cardinality like the floors of a building. The point of departure is some problem $(c, E) \in \mathcal{C}^N$ for some $N \in \mathcal{N}$ such that $|N| > 2$ (top left). We call x the choice S makes for (c, E). To see that x is also the choice $\bar{S}$ makes for (c, E) (top right), follow the arrows.

the hypotheses of *converse consistency* for x and that rule. Since the rule is *conversely consistent*, we go back up (we press the "up" button) to conclude that x is the awards vector it chooses for the initial problem.

Lemma 10.8 (Elevator Lemma) *If a rule is bilaterally consistent, another conversely consistent, and they coincide for two claimants, then they coincide for any number of claimants.*[18]

Proof: (Figure 10.6). Let S be a *bilaterally consistent* rule, $\bar{S}$ a *conversely consistent* rule, and suppose that S and $\bar{S}$ coincide on the subdomain of two-claimant problems. Let $N \in \mathcal{N}$ with $|N| > 2$, $(c, E) \in \mathcal{C}^N$, and $x \equiv S(c, E)$. We need to show that $x = \bar{S}(c, E)$. Since S is *bilaterally consistent*, for each $N' \subset N$ with $|N'| = 2$, $x_{N'} = S(c_{N'}, \sum_{N'} x_i)$. Since $S = \bar{S}$ on the subdomain of two-claimant problems, for each $N' \subset N$ with $|N'| = 2$, $x_{N'} = \bar{S}(c_{N'}, \sum_{N'} x_i)$. Since $\bar{S}$ is *conversely consistent*, $x = \bar{S}(c, E)$. □

When thinking about how to handle a class of problems that may involve arbitrarily many agents, whether they are claims problems or some other type of problems, it is quite natural to first decide how to deal with two agents, that is, to select a two-claimant rule; then to extend in some fashion to arbitrary populations the conclusions reached for that case. One natural requirement on the rule that emerges is that it be *bilaterally consistent*. The rule can then be said to be a **bilaterally consistent extension** of the two-claimant rule that was the point of departure. The Elevator Lemma shows how to take advantage of *converse consistency* to derive such extensions.

[18] For a general presentation of the Elevator Lemma and many of its applications, see Thomson, (2011, 2017a).

The Elevator Lemma takes a slightly different form for correspondences. It asserts that if a correspondence is *bilaterally consistent*, another *conversely consistent*, and the former is a subcorrespondence of the latter for two agents, then the inclusion holds for any number of agents. It is not true however that if, in addition, equality holds for two claimants, it holds in general. To see this, choose the first correspondence to be the one that selects, for each two-claimant problem, its entire set of awards vectors and for more than two claimants, selects the proportional awards vector; for the second correspondence, choose the one that always selects the entire set of awards vectors.

♦ Next, we show how certain fixed-population properties can be strengthened by *consistency*. First is *equal treatment of equals*, which is strengthened to *anonymity*.[19] Next is *equal-division–conditional full compensation*, which is strengthened to *conditional full compensation*.[20]

Lemma 10.9 *Equal treatment of equals and consistency together imply anonymity.*

Proof: Let S be a rule satisfying the hypotheses. Let $N, N' \in \mathcal{N}$ be such that $|N| = |N'|$, and $\pi : N \mapsto N'$ be a bijection. Let $(c, E) \in \mathcal{C}^N$. We show that for each $i \in N$, $S_{\pi(i)}((c_{\pi(i)})_{i \in N}, E) = S_i(c, E)$.

Case 1: $N \cap N' = \emptyset$. Let $\bar{c} \in \mathbb{R}^{N \cup N'}$ be defined by $\bar{c}_N \equiv c$, and for each $i \in N'$, $\bar{c}_{\pi(i)} \equiv c_i$. By *equal treatment of equals*, for each $i \in N$, $S_i(\bar{c}, 2E) = S_{\pi(i)}(\bar{c}, 2E)$. Thus, $\sum_N S_j(\bar{c}, 2E) = \sum_{N'} S_j(\bar{c}, 2E) = E$. Applying *consistency* twice, for each $i \in N$, $S_{\pi(i)}((c_{\pi(i)})_{i \in N}, E) = S_{\pi(i)}(\bar{c}, 2E) = S_i(\bar{c}, 2E) = S_i(c, E)$.

Case 2: $N \cap N' \neq \emptyset$. Let $N'' \subset \mathbb{N} \backslash (N \cup N')$ be such that $|N''| = |N|$. Let $\pi'\colon N \mapsto N''$ and $\pi''\colon N'' \mapsto N'$ be bijections such that $\pi = \pi'' \circ \pi'$. We consider $((c_{\pi'(i)})_{i \in N}, E) \in \mathcal{C}^{N''}$. By the previous paragraph, $S_{\pi(i)}((c_{\pi(i)})_{i \in N}, E) = S_{\pi''(\pi'(i))}(((c_{\pi''(\pi''(i))})_{i \in N}), E) = S_{\pi'(i)}((c_{\pi'(i)})_{i \in N}, E) = S_i(c, E)$. □

Lemma 10.10 *Equal-division–conditional full compensation and consistency together imply conditional full compensation.*

Proof: Let S be a rule satisfying the hypotheses of the lemma. Let $N \in \mathcal{N}$ and $(c, E) \in \mathcal{C}^N$ be such that without loss of generality, $N \equiv \{1, \cdots, n\}$ and $c_1 \leq \cdots \leq c_n$. Suppose that at least one claim in (c, E) is sustainable and let $j \in N$ be such that c_j is the highest such claim. We will show that for each $k \leq j$, $S_k(c, E) = c_k$.

[19] Lemma 10.9 is due to Chambers and Thomson (2002).

[20] Lemma 10.10 is due to Yeh (2006).

Case 1: $k = 1$. Since $\sum_{i\in N} \min\{c_j, c_i\} \leq E$, then $\sum_{k=1}^{k=j-1} c_k+(n-j+1)c_j \leq E$. Since $c_1 \leq \cdots \leq c_j \leq \cdots \leq c_n$, then $nc_1 \leq E$. By *equal-division-conditional full compensation*, $S_1(c, E) = c_1$.

Case 2: $k > 1$. The induction hypotheses is that for each $t < j$ and each $k \in \{1, \ldots, t\}$, $S_k(c, E) = c_k$. We show that $S_{t+1}(c, E) = c_{t+1}$. Let $N' \equiv \{t + 1, \ldots, n\}$. Since $\sum_{k=1}^{k=j-1} c_k + (n - j + 1)c_j \leq E$ and $c_{t+1} \leq \cdots \leq c_j \leq \cdots \leq c_n$, then $c_{t+1} \leq \frac{E-\sum_{k=1}^{t} c_k}{n-1}$. By *equal-division-conditional full compensation*, $S_{t+1}(c_{N'}, E - \sum_{k=1}^{t} c_k) = c_{t+1}$. By the induction hypothesis, for each $k \in \{1, \ldots, t\}$, $S_k(c, E) = c_k$. By *consistency*, $S_{t+1}(c_{N'}, E - \sum_{k+1}^{t} c_k) = S_{t+1}(c, E)$. Thus, $S_{t+1}(c, E) = c_{t+1}$. □

Operators

We conclude this section with a discussion of the extent to which *consistency* and its *converse* are preserved under our four main operators. Table 16.2 summarizes the findings of Propositions 10.2, 10.3, and 10.4 below. We omit the easy proof of Proposition 10.2.

Proposition 10.2 *The following properties are preserved under convexity, claims truncation, and attribution of minimal rights:*
⋆ *Null claims consistency, and*
⋆ *null compensation consistency and full compensation consistency.*

Proposition 10.3 ⋆ *Neither consistency nor converse consistency is preserved under convexity.*
⋆ *Neither is preserved under claims truncation.*
⋆ *Neither is preserved under attribution of minimal rights.*
⋆ *Neither is preserved under the composition of the claims truncation and attribution of minimal rights operators.*

Proof: ⋆ Convexity operator. The constrained equal awards and constrained equal losses rules are *consistent* but their simple average, the rule Av, is not.[21] To see this, let $N \equiv \{1, 2, 3\}$ and $(c, E) \in \mathcal{C}^N$ be equal to $((100, 200, 300), 240)$. Then $Av(c, E) = \frac{(80,80,80)+(0,70,170)}{2} = (40, 75, 125)$. Now, let $N' \equiv \{1, 2\}$ and note that $Av((100, 200), 40 + 75) = \frac{(57.5,57.5)+(7.5,107.5)}{2} \neq (40, 75) = Av_{N'}(c, E)$.

To prove the result for *converse consistency*, we can use the same rule.

⋆ Claims truncation operator. The proportional rule is *consistent*, but when operated from truncated claims, it is not. Indeed, let $N \equiv \{1, 2, 3\}$ and

[21] Note that the rule is *continuous*, *anonymous*, and *self-dual* (being the average of two rules that are dual of each other). It is not *strictly endowment monotonic*. (It does enjoy the property for two claimants for some of the configurations of claims of Figure 16.2, but violations would occur if the larger claim were larger than three times the smaller claim.)

$(c, E) \in \mathcal{C}^N$ be equal to $((1, 1, 3), 3)$. Then $x \equiv P^t(c, E) = (\frac{3}{5}, \frac{3}{5}, \frac{9}{5})$ (note that no truncation is actually needed here). Now, let $N' \equiv \{1, 3\}$ and note that after claimant 2 leaves with $\frac{3}{5}$, we obtain $P^t((c_1, c_3), x_1 + x_3) = P^t((1, 3), \frac{12}{5}) = P((1, \frac{12}{5}), \frac{12}{5}) \neq (\frac{3}{5}, \frac{9}{5}) = P_{N'}(c, E)$.

Also, the proportional rule is *conversely consistent*, but when operated from truncated claims, it is not. Indeed, let $N \equiv \{1, 2, 3\}$ and $(c, E) \in \mathcal{C}^N$ be equal to $((2, 4, 6), 3)$. Let $x \equiv (1, 1, 1)$. We have $(x_1, x_2) = P^t((2, 4), 1 + 1) = P((2, 2), 2)$; $(x_1, x_3) = P^t((2, 6), 1 + 1) = P((2, 2), 2)$; and $(x_2, x_2) = P^t((4, 6), 1 + 1) = P((2, 2), 2)$. Yet, $x \neq P^t((2, 4, 6), 3) = P((2, 3, 3), 3) = (\frac{3}{4}, \frac{9}{8}, \frac{9}{8})$.

⋆ Attribution of minimal rights operator. The constrained equal awards rule is *consistent* but when operated from minimal rights, it is not. Indeed, let $N \equiv \{1, 2, 3\}$ and $(c, E) \in \mathcal{C}^N$ be equal to $((1, 2, 3), 4)$. Then $x \equiv CEA^m(c, E) = (1, 1, 2)$, but after claimant 3 leaves with 2, we obtain $CEA^m((c_1, c_2), x_1 + x_2) = CEA^m((1, 2), 3) = (.5, 1.5) \neq (1, 1) = CEA_{N'}(c, E)$.

⋆ Composition of the claims truncation and attribution of minimal rights operators. We just used the constrained equal awards rule to show that *consistency* is not preserved under the minimal rights operator. Now, note that the rule is *claims truncation invariant*, so $CEA^{m \circ t} = CEA^m$. □

We can apply the reasoning used in proving the last statement of the proposition more generally. Consider a property that we have shown not to be preserved under the minimal rights operator by exhibiting a rule that satisfies *claims truncation invariance*. Then the property is not preserved under the composition of the claims truncation and attribution of minimal rights operators. Also, consider a property that we have shown not to be preserved under claims truncation by exhibiting a rule that satisfies *minimal rights first*. Then the property is not preserved under the composition of the claims truncation and attribution of minimal rights operators.

Next, we turn to the duality operator.

Proposition 10.4 *The following properties are preserved under duality:*
⋆ *null claims consistency,*
⋆ *bilateral consistency and consistency, and*
⋆ *converse consistency.*

Proof: ⋆ Let S be a rule satisfying *null claims consistency*. Let $N \in \mathcal{N}$ and $(c, E) \in \mathcal{C}^N$ and suppose that there is $N' \subset N$ such that $c_{N \setminus N'} = 0$. The equality $S_{N'}(c, E) = S(c_{N'}, E)$ is equivalent to $c_{N'} - S^d_{N'}(c, \sum_N c_j - E) = c_{N'} - S^d(c_{N'}, \sum_{N'} c_j - E)$. We cancel $c_{N'}$ from both sides, note that $\sum_N c_j = \sum_{N'} c_j$, and letting $F \equiv \sum_{N'} c_j - E$, we obtain $S^d_{N'}(c, F) = S^d(c_{N'}, F)$. Thus S^d satisfies *null claims consistency*.

⋆ Let S be a *consistent* rule. Let $N \in \mathcal{N}$ and $(c, E) \in \mathcal{C}^N$. Let $N' \subset N$. We need to show that $S^d_{N'}(c, E) = S^d(c_{N'}, \sum_{N'} S^d_j(c, E))$. This is equivalent to showing that

$$c_{N'} - S_{N'}(c, \sum_N c_i - E) = c_{N'} - S(c_{N'}, \sum_{N'} c_j - \sum_{N'} (c_j - S_j(c, \sum_N c_i - E))$$

or

$$S_{N'}(c, \sum_N c_i - E) = S(c_{N'}, \sum_{N'} S_j(c, \sum_N c_i - E)),$$

and letting $F \equiv \sum_N c_i - E$,

$$S_{N'}(c, F) = S(c_{N'}, \sum_{N'} S_j(c, F)),$$

which holds, by *consistency* of S.

To prove the assertion concerning *bilateral consistency*, it suffices to add the restriction $|N'| = 2$ to the foregoing argument.

⋆ Let S be a *conversely consistent* rule. Let $N \in \mathcal{N}$, $(c, E) \in \mathcal{C}^N$, and $x \in X(c, E)$. Suppose that for each $N' \subset N$ with $|N'| = 2$, $x_{N'} = S^d(c_{N'}, \sum_{N'} x_i)$. We need to show that $x = S^d(c, E)$. By definition of S^d, our hypothesis can be written a follows: for each $N' \subset N$ with $|N'| = 2$, $x_{N'} = c_{N'} - S(c_{N'}, \sum_{N'} c_i - \sum_{N'} x_i)$, or equivalently: for each $N' \subset N$ with $|N'| = 2$, $(c - x)_{N'} = S(c_{N'}, \sum_{N'}(c_i - x_i))$. The vector $c - x$ satisfies the hypotheses of *converse consistency* for S and the well-defined problem $(c, \sum_N (c_i - x_i))$. Since S is *conversely consistent*, $c - x = S(c, \sum_N (c_i - x_i))$, so that $x = c - S(c, \sum_N c_i - \sum_N x_i) = c - S(c, \sum_N c_i - E) = S^d(c, E)$. Thus S^d is *conversely consistent.* □

Lemma 10.11 *Null compensation consistency and full compensation consistency are dual properties.*

Proof: Let S be a rule satisfying *null compensation consistency*. Let $N \in \mathcal{N}$, $(c, E) \in \mathcal{C}^N$, and $N' \subset N$. Writing that if $S_{N \setminus N'}(c, E) = 0$, then $S_{N'}(c, E) = S(c_{N'}, E)$ is equivalent to writing that if $c_{N \setminus N'} - S^d_{N \setminus N'}(c, \sum_N c_j - E) = 0$, then $c_{N'} - S^d_{N'}(c, \sum_N c_j - E) = c_{N'} - S^d(c_{N'}, \sum_{N'} c_j - E)$. We cancel $c_{N'}$ from both sides of this equality, and note that $\sum_N c_j = \sum_{N'} c_j + \sum_{N \setminus N'} c_j$. Letting $F \equiv \sum_N c_j - E$, we obtain that if $c_{N \setminus N'} - S^d_{N \setminus N'}(c, F) = 0$, then $S^d_{N'}(c, F) = S^d(c_{N'}, F - \sum_{N \setminus N'} c_j)$. Thus, S^d satisfies *full compensation consistency.* □

10.5 LIFTING OF PROPERTIES BY BILATERAL CONSISTENCY

It sometimes happens that knowing that a property is satisfied by a rule for two claimants and that the rule is *bilaterally consistent*, allows us to conclude that the property is satisfied by the rule for any number of claimants. Returning to our elevator metaphor (Lemma 10.8), we say that **the property is lifted** from the two-claimant case to the general case by *bilateral consistency*.

When a property is not lifted directly, we may ask whether lifting occurs for a rule satisfying additional properties. If that is the case, we say that **the property is lifted with the assistance of these properties**.

The following lemmas list such results. They are gathered according to the auxiliary properties involved.

It will help to have available the following general structural result relating lifting and duality. We omit its proof:

Lemma 10.12 *If a property is lifted by bilateral consistency from the two-claimant case to the general case with the assistance of certain properties, then the dual of the property is lifted with the assistance of the duals of these properties.*

We start with a list of properties that are lifted without any assistance.[22]

Lemma 10.13 *(Lifting Lemma) The following properties are lifted by bilateral consistency from the two-claimant case to the general case:*
⋆ *equal treatment of equals,*
⋆ *the* $\frac{1}{|N|}$*-truncated-claims lower bounds on awards and the* $\frac{1}{|N|}$*-min-of-claim-and-deficit lower bounds on losses,*[23]
⋆ *order preservation in awards and order preservation in losses,*
⋆ *endowment monotonicity, and*
⋆ *composition down and composition up.*

Proof: We omit the proofs concerning *equal treatment of equals* and the *order preservation* properties, which are trivial.[24]

⋆ *The* $\frac{1}{|N|}$*-truncated-claims lower bounds on awards.* Let $N \in \mathcal{N}$ with $|N| \geq 3$, $(c, E) \in \mathcal{C}^N$, and $x \equiv S(c, E)$. Suppose by contradiction, that there is $i \in N$ such that $x_i < \frac{1}{|N|}\min\{c_i, E\}$, which implies that (i) $x_i < \frac{c_i}{2}$ and (ii) $x_i < \frac{1}{|N|}E$. By *balance*, there is $j \in N$ such that $x_j > \frac{1}{|N|}E$. Using (ii), we deduce $x_i < x_j$, which we write as (iii) $x_i < \frac{x_i+x_j}{2}$. Let $N' \equiv \{i, j\}$. By *bilateral consistency*, $(x_i, x_j) = S((c_i, c_j), x_i + x_j)$. Since S meets the $\frac{1}{|N|}$*-truncated-claims lower bounds on awards for two claimants*, $x_i \geq \frac{1}{2}\min\{c_i, x_i + x_j\}$. This is incompatible with (i) and (iii).

[22] The statements concerning *equal treatment of equals*, the *order preservation* properties, and the *composition* properties are in Hokari and Thomson (2008). The statement concerning *endowment monotonicity* is in Dagan, Serrano, and Volij (1997) and Hokari and Thomson (2008). Lemmas 10.14 and 10.15 are due to Hokari and Thomson (2008).

[23] The *min-of-claim-and-equal-division lower bounds on awards* is trivially lifted (and so is its dual). Indeed, for two claimants, only one rule satisfies it, the constrained equal awards rule (Section 3.4). Moreover, this rule is the only *bilaterally consistent* extension of its two-claimant version, and it satisfies the property for any number of claimants.

[24] Obviously, their generalizations to groups are not lifted since, for two claimants, they coincide with their individual versions.

The assertion concerning the $\frac{1}{|N|}$*-min-of-claim-and-deficit lower bounds on losses* follows from the statement just proved, the fact that this property is dual to the $\frac{1}{|N|}$*-truncated-claims lower bounds on awards* (Proposition 7.1), and Lemma 10.12.

⋆ *Endowment monotonicity.* Let $N \in \mathcal{N}$ with $|N| \geq 3$, $(c, E) \in \mathcal{C}^N$, and $\bar{E} > E$ be such that $\bar{E} \leq \sum c_i$. Let $x \equiv S(c, E)$ and $\bar{x} \equiv S(c, \bar{E})$. Suppose by contradiction that there is $i \in N$ such that $\bar{x}_i < x_i$. Then by *balance* there is $j \in N$ such that $\bar{x}_j > x_j$. By *bilateral consistency*, $(x_i, x_j) = S((c_i, c_j), x_i + x_j)$ and $(\bar{x}_i, \bar{x}_j) = S((c_i, c_j), \bar{x}_i + \bar{x}_j)$. The problems $((c_i, c_j), x_i + x_j)$ and $((c_i, c_j), \bar{x}_i + \bar{x}_j)$ differ only in their endowments, so that by *endowment monotonicity for two claimants*, either $(\bar{x}_i, \bar{x}_j) \geqq (x_i, x_j)$ or $(\bar{x}_i, \bar{x}_j) \leqq (x_i, x_j)$, which we know not to be true.

⋆ *Composition down.* Let $N \in \mathcal{N}$ with $|N| \geq 3$, $(c, E) \in \mathcal{C}^N$ and $E' < E$. Let $x \equiv S(c, E)$, $y \equiv S(c, E')$, and $z \equiv S(x, E')$. We need to show that $y = z$. We argue by contradiction. Suppose that $y \neq z$. Then by *balance* there is $\{i, j\} \subset N$ such that $y_i < z_i$ and $y_j > z_j$. By *bilateral consistency*, $(x_i, x_j) = S((c_i, c_j), x_i + x_j)$, $(y_i, y_j) = S((c_i, c_j), y_i + y_j)$, and $(z_i, z_j) = S((x_i, x_j), z_i + z_j)$.

Case 1: $x_i + x_j \leq y_i + y_j$. By *endowment monotonicity for two claimants* (implied by *composition down for two claimants*) applied to $((c_i, c_j), x_i + x_j)$ and $((c_i, c_j), y_i + y_j)$, and using the fact that $x_i \geq z_i$ (recall that $z \equiv S(x, E')$), we obtain $y_i \geq x_i \geq z_i$, which contradicts $y_i < z_i$.

Case 2: $x_i + x_j > y_i + y_j$. By *composition down for two claimants*, $(y_i, y_j) = S((x_i, x_j), y_i + y_j)$. By *endowment monotonicity for two claimants* applied to $((x_i, x_j), y_i + y_j)$ and $((x_i, x_j), z_i + z_j)$, we obtain that either $(y_i, y_j) \geqq (z_i, z_j)$ or $(y_i, y_j) \leqq (z_i, z_j)$, which we know not to be true.

The assertion concerning *composition up* follows from the statement just proved, the fact that this property is dual to *composition down* (Proposition 7.1), and Lemma 10.12. □

Next we identify several properties that are not lifted. Neither *endowment continuity* nor *self-duality* is. We establish these two negative conclusions by means of a single example: a rule satisfying both properties for two claimants and is *bilaterally consistent* may satisfy neither for more than two claimants. Similarly, a rule can be constructed that satisfies *endowment continuity* and *anonymity* for two claimants as well as *bilateral consistency*, but satisfies neither *endowment continuity* nor *anonymity* for more than two claimants.

Lemma 10.14 ⋆ *A rule satisfying endowment continuity for two claimants, self-duality for two claimants, and bilateral consistency may satisfy neither endowment continuity nor self-duality in general.*

⋆ *A rule satisfying endowment continuity for two claimants, anonymity for two claimants, and bilateral consistency may satisfy neither endowment continuity nor anonymity in general.*

The proof of the first statement is relegated to an appendix (Section 17.6). The rule that we construct for that purpose is not *endowment monotonic*, but this should be expected since this property implies *endowment continuity* and it is lifted (Lemma 10.13). Thus, a rule that can be used to show that *endowment continuity* is not lifted necessarily violates *endowment monotonicity*. We omit the proof of the second statement.

A property that provides enough assistance for the lifting of several others is *endowment monotonicity for two claimants*:

Lemma 10.15 *(Assisted Lifting Lemma) The following properties are lifted by bilateral consistency from the two-claimant case to the general case with the assistance of endowment monotonicity for two claimants:*
⋆ *anonymity,*
⋆ *order preservation under endowment variations,*
⋆ *self-duality,*
⋆ *conditional full compensation and conditional null compensation,*
⋆ *claim monotonicity and linked claim-endowment monotonicity, and*
⋆ *claims truncation invariance and minimal rights first.*

Proof: For each of these assertions, let S be a rule satisfying the hypotheses.
⋆ *Anonymity.* Let $N, \bar{N} \in \mathcal{N}$ with $|N| = |\bar{N}| \geq 3$, $(c, E) \in \mathcal{C}^N$, and $\bar{c} \in \mathbb{R}^{\bar{N}}$ be such that for some bijection $\pi : N \mapsto \bar{N}$, and for each $i \in N$, $\bar{c}_i = c_{\pi(i)}$. We argue by contradiction. Suppose that $x \equiv S(c, E) \neq S(\bar{c}, E) \equiv \bar{x}$. Then there is $\{i, j\} \subset N$ such that $x_i > \bar{x}_{\pi(i)}$ and $x_j < \bar{x}_{\pi(j)}$. By *bilateral consistency*, $(x_i, x_j) = S((c_i, c_j), x_i + x_j)$ and $(\bar{x}_{\pi(i)}, \bar{x}_{\pi(j)}) = S((c_{\pi(i)}, c_{\pi(i)}), \bar{x}_{\pi(i)} + \bar{x}_{\pi(j)})$. By *anonymity for two claimants*, $(\bar{x}_{\pi(i)}, \bar{x}_{\pi(j)}) = S((c_i, c_j), \bar{x}_{\pi(i)} + \bar{x}_{\pi(j)})$. The problems $((c_i, c_j), x_i + x_j)$ and $((c_i, c_j), \bar{x}_{\pi(i)} + \bar{x}_{\pi(j)})$ differ only in their endowments, so that by *endowment monotonicity for two claimants*, either $(x_i, x_j) \geqq (\bar{x}_{\pi(i)}, \bar{x}_{\pi(j)})$ or $(x_i, x_j) \leqq (\bar{x}_{\pi(i)}, \bar{x}_{\pi(j)})$, which we know not to be true.

⋆ *Order preservation under endowment variations.* Let $N \in \mathcal{N}$ with $|N| \geq 3$, $(c, E) \in \mathcal{C}^N$, and $E' \in \mathbb{R}_+$ be such that $\sum c_i \geq E' > E$. Note that $(c, E') \in \mathcal{C}^N$. Let $\{i, j\} \subset N$ be such that $c_j \geq c_i$. Let $x \equiv S(c, E)$ and $x' \equiv S(c, E')$. We need to show that $x'_j - x_j \geq x'_i - x_i$. By *endowment monotonicity for two claimants* and Lemma 10.13, for each $k \in N$, $x'_k \geq x_k$, so $x_i + x_j \leq x'_i + x'_j$. By *bilateral consistency*, $(x_i, x_j) = S((c_i, c_j), x_i + x_j)$ and $(x'_i, x'_j) = S((c_i, c_j), x'_i + x'_j)$. By *order preservation under endowment variations for two claimants*, $x'_j - x_j \geq x'_i - x_i$.

⋆ *Self-duality.* Let $N \in \mathcal{N}$ with $|N| \geq 3$ and $(c, E) \in \mathcal{C}^N$. Let $x \equiv S(c, E)$ and $y \equiv S^d(c, E)$. We need to show that $x = y$. We argue by contradiction. Suppose that there is $i \in N$ such that $x_i < y_i$. Then there is $j \in N \setminus \{i\}$ such that $x_j > y_j$. By Proposition 10.4, S^d is *bilaterally consistent*. Then, since S and S^d coincide for two claimants, $(x_i, x_j) = S((c_i, c_j), x_i + x_j)$ and $(y_i, y_j) = S^d((c_i, c_j), y_i + y_j) = S((c_i, c_j), y_i + y_j)$. The problems $((c_i, c_j), x_i + x_j)$ and $((c_i, c_j), y_i + y_j)$ differ only in their endowments, so that by *endowment monotonicity for two claimants*, either $(x_i, x_j) \geqq (y_i, y_j)$ or $(x_i, x_j) \leqq (y_i, y_j)$, which we know not to be true.

⋆ *Conditional full compensation*. Let $N \in \mathcal{N}$ with $|N| \geq 3$, $(c, E) \in \mathcal{C}^N$, and $x \equiv S(c, E)$. Let $i \in N$ be such that $\sum_{j \in N} \min\{c_j, c_i\} \leq E$. We need to show that $x_i = c_i$. We argue by contradiction. Suppose that $x_i < c_i$.

First, we claim that there is $j \in N \setminus \{i\}$ such that $x_j > c_i$. Indeed, if for each $k \in N \setminus \{i\}$, $x_k \leq c_i$, then $E = x_i + \sum_{k \in N \setminus \{i\}} x_k < \sum_{j \in N} \min\{c_j, c_i\} \leq E$, a contradiction.

By *bilateral consistency*, $(x_i, x_j) = S((c_i, c_j), x_i + x_j)$. Since $c_i < x_j \leq c_j$, then $((c_i, c_j), 2c_i) \in \mathcal{C}^{\{i,j\}}$. Moreover, by *conditional full compensation for two claimants*, $S((c_i, c_j), 2c_i) = (c_i, c_i)$. The problems $((c_i, c_j), x_i + x_j)$ and $((c_i, c_j), 2c_i)$ differ only in their endowments, so that by *endowment monotonicity for two claimants*, either $(x_i, x_j) \geqq (c_i, c_i)$ or $(x_i, x_j) \leqq (c_i, c_i)$, which we know not to be true.

The proof for *conditional null compensation* follows from the statement just proved, the facts that this property is dual to *conditional full compensation* (Proposition 7.1) and that *endowment monotonicity* is a *self-dual* property, and Lemma 10.12.

⋆ *Claim monotonicity*. Let $N \in \mathcal{N}$ with $|N| \geq 3$ and $(c, E) \in \mathcal{C}^N$. Let $i \in N$ and $\bar{c} \in \mathbb{R}^N_+$ be such that $\bar{c}_i > c_i$ and for each $j \in N \setminus \{i\}$, $\bar{c}_j = c_j$. Let $x \equiv S(c, E)$ and $\bar{x} \equiv S(\bar{c}, E)$. We need to show that $\bar{x}_i \geq x_i$. We argue by contradiction. Suppose that $\bar{x}_i < x_i$ (Figure 10.7a).

Let $j \in N \setminus \{i\}$. We assert that $\bar{x}_i + \bar{x}_j < x_i + x_j$. Suppose by contradiction that $\bar{x}_i + \bar{x}_j \geq x_i + x_j$ (Figure 10.7b). By *bilateral consistency*, $(x_i, x_j) = S((c_i, c_j), x_i + x_j)$ and $(\bar{x}_i, \bar{x}_j) = S((\bar{c}_i, c_j), \bar{x}_i + \bar{x}_j)$. By *endowment monotonicity for two claimants*, $S_i((\bar{c}_i, c_j), x_i + x_j) \leq S_i((\bar{c}_i, c_j), \bar{x}_i + \bar{x}_j)$. By *claims monotonicity for two claimants*, $S_i((c_i, c_j), x_i + x_j) \leq S_i((\bar{c}_i, c_j), x_i + x_j)$. Thus $x_i = S_i((c_i, c_j), x_i + x_j) \leq S_i((\bar{c}_i, c_j), \bar{x}_i + \bar{x}_j) = \bar{x}_i < x_i$, a contradiction.

Since $\bar{x}_i < x_i$, there is $j \in N$ such that $\bar{x}_j > x_j$. Then, by *endowment monotonicity for two claimants*, $S_j((\bar{c}_i, c_j), \bar{x}_i + \bar{x}_j) \leq S_j((\bar{c}_i, c_j), x_i + x_j)$ and by *claims monotonicity for two claimants*, $S_j((\bar{c}_i, c_j), x_i + x_j) \leq S_j((c_i, c_j), x_i + x_j)$. Hence, $\bar{x}_j = S_j((\bar{c}_i, c_j), \bar{x}_i + \bar{x}_j) \leq S_j((c_i, c_j), x_i + x_j) = x_j$, a contradiction.

The proof for *linked claim-endowment monotonicity* follows from the statement just proved, the facts that this property is dual to *claim monotonicity* (Proposition 7.1) and that *endowment monotonicity* is a *self-dual* property (Proposition 7.2), and Lemma 10.12.

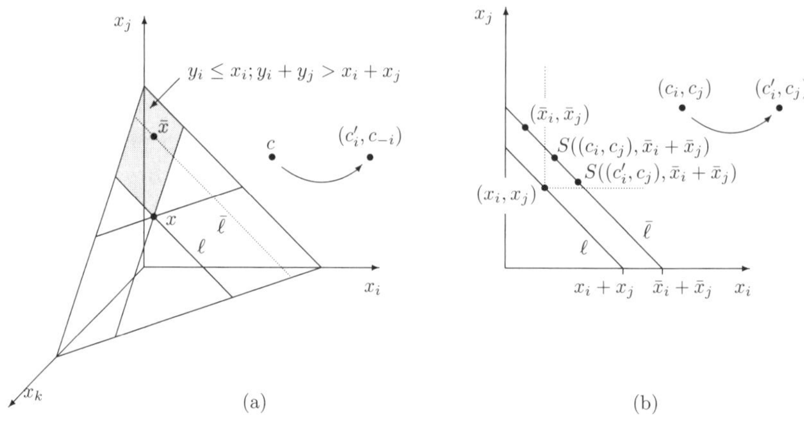

Figure 10.7: **Lifting of claim monotonicity with the assistance of endowment monotonicity** (Lemma 10.15). (a) The proof is by contradiction. This figure represents a pair of three-claimant problems, (c, E) and $((c'_i, c_{-i}), E)$, that differ only in agent i's claim and for which *claim monotonicity* is violated. (b) Two-claimant problems $((c_i, c_j), x_i + x_j)$ and $((c'_i, c_j), \bar{x}_i + \bar{x}_j)$ obtained by reducing the three-claimant problems of panel (a) with respect to $\{i, j\}$ and x on the one hand, and $\bar{x}$ on the other.

$\star$ *Claims truncation invariance*. Let $N \in \mathcal{N}$ with $|N| \geq 3$ and $(c, E) \in \mathcal{C}^N$. Let $x \equiv S(c, E)$. We need to show that $x = S(t(c, E), E)$. Let $\{i, j\} \subset N$. By *bilateral consistency*, $(x_i, x_j) = S((c_i, c_j), x_i + x_j)$. By *claims truncation invariance for two claimants*, $(x_i, x_j) = S((t_i(c, x_i + x_j), t_j(c, x_i + x_j)), x_i + x_j)$. Since $x_i + x_j \leq E$, we have $t_i((c_i, c_j), x_i + x_j) \leq t_i(c, E)$. Similarly, $t_j((c_i, c_j), x_i + x_j) \leq t_j(c, E)$. Now, we assert that $(x_i, x_j) = S_{\{i,j\}}(t_i(c, E), t_j(c, E), E)$. Indeed, if $c_i \geq x_i + x_j$, we have $t_i((c_i, c_j), x_i + x_j) = x_i + x_j$, but then, for each $c'_i \geq x_i + x_j$, we obtain $t_i((c'_i, c_j), x_i + x_j) = x_i + x_j$, and by *claims truncation invariance for two claimants*, $S((c'_i, c_j), x_i + x_j) = S((c_i, c_j), x_i + x_j)$. This conclusion holding for each pair $\{i, j\} \subset N$, we deduce by *converse consistency*, which holds by Lemma 10.5, that $x = S(t(c, E), E)$.

The proof for *minimal rights first* follows from the statement just proved, the facts that this property is dual to *claims truncation invariance* (Proposition 7.1) and that *converse consistency* is a *self-dual* property (Proposition 10.4), and Lemma 10.12. □

The next lemma involves two auxiliary properties.[25] For the benefit of being able to collect our lifting results in one place, we invoke the conclusion of a theorem to be presented shortly (Theorem 10.9):

[25] Lemmas 10.16 and 10.17 are due to Chun, Schummer, and Thomson (2001).

Lemma 10.16 *The midpoint property for two claimants is lifted by consistency from the two-claimant case to the general case with the assistance of continuity and equal treatment of equals.*

Proof: Let S be a rule satisfying the properties listed in the lemma. Then, by Theorem 10.9 below, it is a Young rule. Let $f : \mathbb{R}_+ \times [\underline{\lambda}, \bar{\lambda}] \mapsto \mathbb{R}$ be a Young representation of it. For each $c_0 \in \mathbb{R}_+$, and since $f(c_0, \cdot)$ is continuous and nowhere decreasing, there is a (unique) closed interval $I_0 \subset [\underline{\lambda}, \bar{\lambda}]$ where it takes the value $\frac{c_0}{2}$. By the *midpoint property for two claimants*, for each pair $\{c_0, c_0'\} \subset \mathbb{R}_+$, we have $I_0 \cap I_0' \neq \emptyset$. We then deduce, by an argument similar to that used to prove Lemma 10.3, that for each $N \in \mathcal{N}$ with $|N| \geq 3$ and each $(c, E) \in \mathcal{C}^N$ with $E = \sum_N \frac{c_i}{2}$, we have $\bigcap_N I_i \neq \emptyset$. By choosing $\lambda \in \bigcap_N I_i$, we obtain $S(c, E)$: it is the awards vector at which each agent's award is their half-claim. □

Lemma 10.17 *Converse consistency and the midpoint property for two claimants together imply the midpoint property in general.*

Proof: Let S be a rule satisfying the hypotheses of the theorem. Let $N \in \mathcal{N}$ with $|N| \geq 3$, $(c, E) \in \mathcal{C}^N$ be such that $E = \sum \frac{c_i}{2}$, and $x \equiv \frac{c}{2}$. By the *midpoint property for two claimants*, for each $N' \subset N$ with $|N'| = 2$, $x_{N'} = S(c_{N'}, \sum_{N'} x_i)$. By *converse consistency*, $x = S(c, E)$. □

10.6 CHARACTERIZATIONS

This section is devoted to characterizations. We start with characterizations involving *null claims consistency* and *full compensation consistency*. In Section 8.3, for two claimants, we characterized concede-and-divide and the constrained equal losses rule on the basis of additivity and invariance properties (Theorems 8.4 and 8.5) and in Section 6.2, also for two claimants, we characterized the constrained equal awards rule on the basis of a lower bound and a composition property (Theorem 6.5). All three uniqueness results extend to our variable-population model if *null claims consistency* is added, delivering the minimal overlap, constrained equal awards, and constrained equal losses rules respectively. Since the latter two rules are in fact *consistent*, much of the interest of the uniqueness parts of Theorems 10.2 and 10.3 stems from the fact that *null claims consistency* is significantly weaker than *consistency*.[26]

Theorem 10.1 *The minimal overlap rule is the only rule satisfying uniform-increase-in-claims-and-endowment equal incremental awards and null claims consistency.*

minimal overlap rule characterized

[26] Theorems 10.1 and 10.2 are due to Marchant (2008), Theorem 10.3 to Yeh (2008).

constrained equal losses rule characterized

Theorem 10.2 *The constrained equal losses rule is the only rule satisfying uniform-increase-in-claims invariance and null claims consistency.*

Proof: We already know that the constrained equal losses rule satisfies the properties listed in the theorem. Conversely, let S be a rule satisfying these properties. Let $(c, E) \in \mathcal{C}^N$ be such that, without loss of generality, $c_1 \leq \cdots \leq c_n$. As in Theorem 8.5, we obtain that for each $\delta \in [0, \min\{c_1, \frac{\sum c_i - E}{|N|}\}]$, $S(c, E) = S(d - \delta e_N)$, so in particular, $S(c, E) = S(d - \min\{c_1, \frac{\sum c_i - E}{|N|}\} e_N)$.

Case 1: $E \geq \sum c_i - |N| c_1$. Then for each $i \in N$, $S_i(c, E) = c_i - \frac{\sum c_i - E}{|N|}$.

Case 2: $E < \sum c_i - |N| c_1$. For each $i \in N$, $S_i(c, E) = S_i(c - c_1 e_n, E)$. Let $N' \equiv \{i \in N : c_i > c_1\}$. For each $i \in N$ such that $c_i = c_1$, by definition of a rule, $S_i(c, E) = 0$. By *null claims consistency*, $S_{N'}(c, E) = S(c_{N'} - c_1 e_{N'}, E)$. We then repeat the argument with the members of N'. □

constrained equal awards rule characterized

Theorem 10.3 *The constrained equal awards rule is the only rule satisfying the $\frac{1}{|N|}$-truncated-claims lower bounds on awards, composition up, and null claims consistency.*

The proof is given by a simple induction argument letting, for each problem, the endowment grow from 0 to the sum of the claims.

We also have the following extension of a characterization of the two-claimant constrained equal awards rule. This time it is *full compensation consistency* that permits the extension although once again, this rule satisfies *consistency* itself. In fact, for two claimants, the constrained equal awards rule is the only rule satisfying the *min-of-claim-and-equal-division lower bounds on awards*, so an application of the Elevator Lemma would deliver the constrained equal awards rule directly if *consistency* were imposed.[27]

constrained equal awards rule characterized

Theorem 10.4 *The constrained equal awards rule is the only rule satisfying the min-of-claim-and-equal-division lower bounds on awards and full compensation consistency.*

Proof: We already know that the constrained equal awards rule satisfies the *min-of-claim-and-equal-division lower bounds on awards* and because it is *consistent*, it satisfies *full compensation consistency*, which is a weaker property. Conversely, let S be a rule satisfying the two properties listed in

[27] Theorem 10.4 is closely related to Moulin (2002)'s characterization of the constrained equal awards rule on the basis of *min-of-claim-and-equal-division lower bounds on awards*, *composition up*, and *null claims consistency*.

the theorem, $N \in \mathcal{N}$, and $(c, E) \in \mathcal{C}^N$. To simplify notation, suppose that $N = \{1, \ldots, n\}$ and that $c_1 \leq \cdots \leq c_n$. If $E \leq nc_1$, then by the *min-of-claim-and-equal-division lower bounds on awards*, $S(c, E) = (\frac{E}{n}, \ldots, \frac{E}{n}) = CEA(c, E)$. If $nc_1 < E \leq c_1 + (n-1)c_2$, then by the *min-of-claim-and-equal-division lower bounds on awards*, $S_1(c, E) = c_1$. By *full compensation consistency*, $S_{N\setminus\{1\}}(c, E) = S((c_2, \ldots, c_n), E - c_1)$, which, by the *min-of-claim-and-equal-division lower bounds on awards*, is equal to $(\frac{E-c_1}{n-1}, \ldots, \frac{E-c_1}{n-1})$. Altogether, $S(c, E) = CEA(C, E)$. We consider next the case $c_1 + (n-1)c_2 < E \leq c_1 + c_2 + (n-2)c_3$, to conclude that $S = CEA$, and iterate. □

The next two results describe situations in which the choice of a certain rule for two claimants plus the insistence on *bilateral consistency* imply a unique way of solving all problems. They are obtained by applying the Elevator Lemma.[28]

Proposition 10.5 *The proportional rule is the only rule to agree with the two-claimant version of this rule for two claimants, and to be bilaterally consistent – alternatively, conversely consistent.*

proportional rule characterized

Proof: We already know that the proportional rule is *consistent*. For the uniqueness part, it suffices to observe that it is also *conversely consistent*. the result follows then from the Elevator Lemma. The characterization involving *converse consistency* is obtained in a similar manner, exploiting the fact that the proportional rule is *consistent*. □

Proposition 10.6 *The Talmud rule is the only rule to agree with concede-and-divide for two claimants and to be bilaterally consistent – alternatively, conversely consistent.*

A parallel statement can be made about each Young rule because such a rule is *consistent* and *conversely consistent*, but Proposition 10.6 is particularly interesting because we already have characterizations of concede-and-divide involving properties that happen to be satisfied by the Talmud rule for arbitrary populations of claimants.[29] These previous results allow us to derive the following full characterizations of the Talmud rule:

[28] Proposition 10.6 is due to Aumann and Maschler (1985). Similarly, Albizuri Leroux, and Zarzuelo (2010) assert that on the domain of problems in which no claim exceeds the endowment, the random arrival rule is the unique rule to coincide with concede-and-divide for two claimants and to be *bilaterally consistent* in their sense (footnote 4). A correction is by Hwang and Wang (2009).

[29] If they were not, we would still have a characterization, but we would have to limit the scope of some fixed-population properties to the two-claimant case, which would be awkward.

Talmud rule characterized

Theorem 10.5 *The Talmud rule is the only rule satisfying*

(a) *equal treatment of equals, claims truncation invariance, minimal rights first, and bilateral consistency – alternatively, converse consistency.*
(b) *the $\frac{1}{|N|}$-truncated-claims lower bounds on awards, self-duality, and bilateral consistency – alternatively, converse consistency. Here, either the $\frac{1}{|N|}$-truncated-claims lower bounds on awards or self-duality can be replaced by the $\frac{1}{|N|}$-min-of-claim-and-deficit lower bounds on losses.*
(c) *claims truncation invariance, self-duality, and bilateral consistency – alternatively, converse consistency. Here, claims truncation invariance can be replaced by minimal rights first.*

Proof: We already know that the Talmud rule satisfies the properties listed in these assertions, so for each of them in turn, let us consider a rule satisfying the properties it refers to.

(a) Uniqueness is a consequence of Theorem 5.2 and Proposition 10.6 together.
(b) Uniqueness is a consequence of Theorem 7.6 and Proposition 10.6 together.
(c) Uniqueness is a consequence of Theorem 7.7. □

Next are characterizations of the constrained equal awards rule:[30]

constrained equal awards rule characterized

Theorem 10.6 *The constrained equal awards rule is the only rule satisfying*

(a) *equal-division–conditional full compensation, composition down, and bilateral consistency – alternatively, converse consistency;*
(b) *equal-division–conditional full compensation, order preservation in awards, and bilateral consistency – alternatively, converse consistency.*
(c) *equal-division–conditional full compensation, claim monotonicity, and bilateral consistency – alternatively, converse consistency.*

Proof: We already know that the constrained equal awards rule satisfies the properties listed in these assertions, so for each of them in turn, let us consider a rule S satisfying the properties.

(a) For two claimants, *equal-division–conditional full compensation* is equivalent to *conditional full compensation*. Thus, by Theorem 6.6, S is the constrained equal awards rule. The constrained equal awards rule is *conversely consistent*. We conclude by invoking the Elevator Lemma. The characterization involving *converse consistency* is obtained in a similar manner.
(b) Again, we show that for two claimants, $S = CEA$. Without loss of generality, let $N \equiv \{1, 2\}$, and $(c, E) \in \mathcal{C}^N$ be such that $c_1 \leq c_2$.

[30] Theorem 10.6a is due to Herrero and Villar (2002). Parts (b) and (c) are due to Yeh (2006).

Case 1: $E \geq 2c_1$. Then, *equal-division conditional full compensation* directly implies that $S_1(c, E) = c_1 = CEA_1(c, E)$ and therefore that $S(c, E) = CEA(c, E)$.

Case 2: $E < 2c_1$. We introduce agent 3 with claim $c_3 \equiv \frac{E}{2}$ and augment the endowment by that amount. Let $E' \equiv 3\frac{E}{2}$. The pair $((c, c_3), E')$ is a well-defined problem, and since $c_3 = \frac{E'}{3}$, by *equal-division conditional full compensation*, $(*)$ $S_3((c, c_3), E') = c_3$. Since $E < 2c_1$, then $c_3 \leq c_1 \leq c_2$. Given $(*)$, *order preservation in awards* gives us $\frac{E'}{3} = S_3((c, c_3), E') \leq S_1((c, c_3), E') \leq S_2((c, c_3), E')$, so that in fact $S_1((c, c_3), E') = S_2((c, c_3), E') = \frac{E'}{3}$. We now observe that the reduced problem of $((c, c_3), E')$ with respect to N and $S((c, c_3), E')$ is (c, E). By *bilateral consistency*, $S(c, E) = (\frac{E'}{3}, \frac{E'}{3}) = (\frac{E}{2}, \frac{E}{2}) = CEA(c, E)$.

The conclusion $S = CEA$ for more than two claimants follows then by the Elevator Lemma.[31]

(c) This follows from Theorem 4.2 and Lemma 10.10. □

We also have the following characterization of the reverse Talmud rule:[32]

Theorem 10.7 *The reverse Talmud rule is the only rule satisfying weak conditional null compensation, weak conditional full compensation, order preservation under endowment variations, and bilateral consistency – alternatively converse consistency.* reverse Talmud rule characterized

Proof: We already know that the reverse Talmud rule satisfies the properties listed in the theorem. Conversely, let S be a rule satisfying these properties. We first show that for two claimants, S is the reverse Talmud rule. Let $N \equiv \{1, 2\}$, say, and $c \in \mathbb{R}^N_+$ be such that, without loss of generality, $c_1 \leq c_2$. *Weak*

[31] Uniqueness can also be proved with *order preservation under endowment variations* replacing *order preservation in awards* because the former implies the latter. The proof would be obtained in the same manner as the proof of (c), invoking the characterization of the constrained equal awards rule on the basis of *conditional full compensation* and *order preservation under endowment variations* (Theorem 4.1).

[32] Theorem 10.7 is due to van den Brink, Funaki, and van der Laan (2013). The same logic gives us that for each $\alpha \in [0, 1]$, the reverse TAL rule of parameter α, U^α (Subsection 2.2.3) is the only rule satisfying *α-conditional full compensation*, *$(1-\alpha)$-conditional null compensation*, *order preservation under endowment variations*, and *bilateral consistency*. Indeed, the first two axioms imply that for $|N| = 2$, say $N \equiv \{1, 2\}$, and for each $c \in \mathbb{R}^N_+$ such that, without loss of generality, $c_1 \leq c_2$, (i) the path of awards for c should contain a vertical segment containing the origin and a vertical segment containing c. The point of maximal ordinate of the first segment and the point of minimal ordinate of the second segment belong to a line of slope 1. Thus, by *order preservation under endowment variations* (ii) the path for c should also contain the segment connecting these two points. The path for c is now determined, and it is that of U^α. Once again, the proof concludes by noting that on $\bigcup_{N \in \mathcal{N}} \mathcal{C}^N$, U^α is *conversely consistent*, and invoking the Elevator Lemma. The argument with *converse consistency* is the same.

conditional null compensation says that the path of awards of S for c should contain seg$[(0,0), (0, \frac{c_2-c_1}{2})]$, and *weak conditional full compensation* that it should contain seg$[(c_1, \frac{c_1+c_2}{2}), c]$. Since the point of maximal ordinate of the first segment and the point of minimal ordinate of the second segment belong to a line of slope 1, *order preservation under endowment variations* implies that the path contains the segment connecting these two points. (This is as in the proof of Theorem 4.1.) Altogether, the path is that of the reverse Talmud rule, as we asserted. The proof concludes by noting that this rule is *conversely consistent* and invoking the Elevator Lemma. The characterization involving *converse consistency* is obtained by simply replacing in the last sentence the statement that the Talmud rule is *conversely consistent* by the statement that it is *consistent*. □

Another characterization of the reverse Talmud rule is obtained as a corollary of the following characterization of the reverse TAL family. We omit the proof. In Section 8.3 we proposed to weaken *full additivity* by restricting its application to a domain we called $\mathcal{C}_0^N$. Let us generalize the property to our variable-population model by writing it for the domain $\mathcal{C}_0 \equiv \bigcup \mathcal{C}_0^N$, under the name of **full additivity on $\mathcal{C}_0$**:[33]

reverse TAL rules characterized

Theorem 10.8 *The reverse TAL rules are the only rules satisfying full additivity on $\mathcal{C}_0$ and consistency.*

Adding the *midpoint property* to the axioms of Theorem 10.8, we single out the reverse Talmud rule, as announced:

reverse Talmud rule characterized

Corollary 10.1 *The reverse Talmud rule is the only rule satisfying the midpoint property, full additivity on $\mathcal{C}_0^N$, and consistency.*

proportional rule characterized

Theorem 8.1 tells us that for each $N \in \mathcal{N}$ such that $|N| > 2$ the proportional rule is the only rule defined on $\mathcal{C}^N$ satisfying *no advantageous transfer*. In our variable-population framework, it follows that this rule is the only rule on $\mathcal{C}$ satisfying *no advantageous transfer* and *consistency*. Theorem 8.1 did not cover the two-claimant case because then, *no advantageous transfer* is vacuously satisfied by all rules. *Consistency* allows the conclusion to be extended to that case.

The implications of *consistency* have been described very completely for the problem of adjudicating conflicting claims, with few auxiliary properties.[34] To derive the main results on this issue, the critical concept is that of a Young rule. The following characterization is fundamental. Step 1 of the proof states that a rule satisfying the hypotheses is *endowment monotonicity*,

[33] Theorem 10.8 and Corollary 10.1 are due to Arin, Benito, and Iñarra (2017).

[34] Theorems 10.9 and 10.10 are due to Young (1987a). Kaminski (2000, 2006) proves very general versions of this theorem in which agents are described in terms of "types" that belong to separable topological spaces.

but for simplicity, we continue under the assumption that the strict form of this property holds.

Theorem 10.9 *Young's rules are the only rules satisfying equal treatment of equals, endowment continuity, and consistency.*

Young's rules characterized

Proof: We already know that Young's rules satisfy the three properties listed in the theorem. (For *consistency*, see Lemma 10.1.) Conversely, let S be a rule satisfying these properties.

Step 1: S is endowment monotonic. This follows from Lemma 10.7.

Step 2: Completion of the proof under the assumption that S is strictly endowment monotonic. Let $N \equiv \{1,2\}$ and $c_1 > 0$. For each $\lambda \in [0,1]$, consider the equation in t, $(t, \lambda) = S((c_1, 1), t + \lambda)$. By *continuity* and *strict endowment monotonicity*, this equation has a unique solution, which we write as $t = f(c_1, \lambda)$; moreover, f is continuous and strictly monotonic in λ. By *anonymity*, implied by *equal treatment of equals* and *consistency* (Lemma 10.9), the same function f would have been obtained starting from any pair $\{i, j\}$ instead of $\{1, 2\}$.

We will prove that f is a Young representation of S. Let $N \in \mathcal{N}$ and $(c, E) \in \mathcal{C}^N$ be such that $c > 0$, and let $x \equiv S(c, E)$. Let N' be a group containing N and one additional claimant, claimant m, whose claim c_m we set equal to 1. Let $c' \in \mathbb{R}^{N'}_+$ be defined by $c' \equiv (c, c_m)$. Let $\{i, j\} \subset N$. By *continuity*, there is $F \in \mathbb{R}_+$ such that $S_i(c', F) + S_j(c', F) = x_i + x_j$. By *bilateral consistency*, in (c', F), claimants i and j receive x_i and x_j respectively. Similarly, there is $F' \in \mathbb{R}_+$ such that $S_i(c', F') + S_k(c', F') = x_i + x_k$. By *bilateral consistency*, in (c', F'), claimants i and k receive x_i and x_k respectively. Since claimant i receives the same amounts in (c', F) and (c', F'), by *strict endowment monotonicity*, $F = F'$. Repeating this reasoning, we deduce that there are $E^* \in \mathbb{R}$ and $\lambda^* \in \mathbb{R}$ such that $S(c', E^*) = (x, \lambda^*)$. By *bilateral consistency*, for each $i \in N$, $(x_i, \lambda^*) = S((c_i, 1), x_i + \lambda^*)$, so that by definition of f, for each $i \in N$, $x_i = f(c_i, \lambda^*)$.

Conversely, suppose that there are $x \in X(c, E)$ and $\lambda \in \mathbb{R}$ such that for each $i \in N$, $f(c_i, \lambda) = x_i$. Let $E \equiv \sum x_i$ and $x' \equiv S(c, E)$. By the above reasoning, there is $\lambda' \in \mathbb{R}$ such that for each $i \in N$, $f(c_i, \lambda') = x'_i$ and $\sum x'_i = \sum x_i = E$. Since f is strictly monotonic with respect to its second argument, for each $i \in N$, $x'_i = x_i$. Thus, f is a Young representation of S. □

∗ `On the independence of axioms in Theorem 10.9.` ✦ Section 3.6 describes generalizations of Young's rules that fail *equal treatment of equals*, but are *continuous* and *consistent*, and, in fact, *endowment monotonic* too. However, other rules enjoy these properties.[35] ✦ Without *consistency*, of

[35] Stovall (2014a) gives an example. He also proposes additional properties of rules in the presence of which the asymmetric generalizations of Young's rules of Section 3.6 become the only

course, many rules become admissible since we can now solve problems in a manner that depends arbitrarily on the population of claimants present.

It can also be shown but we omit the proof, that any rule satisfying the properties listed in Theorem 10.9 is equivalently defined by maximizing a separable additive objective function:[36]

Young's rules characterized

Theorem 10.10 *A rule satisfies equal treatment of equals, endowment continuity, and consistency if and only if there is a function* $H : \mathbb{R}_+ \times \mathbb{R}_+ \mapsto \mathbb{R}$ *such that* (i) *the function associating with each* $x \in \mathbb{R}^N_+$ *the expression* $\sum H(c_i, x_i)$ *is continuous, increasing, and strictly convex with respect to* x, *and* (ii) *for each* $N \in \mathcal{N}$ *and each* $(c, E) \in \mathcal{C}^N$ *with* $c > 0$, *the rule chooses the maximizer of* $\sum H(c_i, x_i)$ *with respect to* x *satisfying* $\sum x_i = E$.

Our next theorem is a characterization of the equal-sacrifice family, a subfamily of Young's family.[37]

equal-sacrifice rules characterized

Theorem 10.11 *On the domain of problems with positive claims, the equal-sacrifice rules are the only rules satisfying continuity, strict endowment monotonicity, strict order preservation in awards, composition down, and consistency.*

The proof is relegated to an appendix (Section 17.7).

`*On the independence of axioms in Theorem 10.11.` ✦ The implications of dropping in turn each of the axioms of the theorem are not fully understood. However, we do have a characterization of the class of rules satisfying *continuity*, *equal treatment of equals*, *composition down*, and *consistency*. These rules are generalizations of the equal-sacrifice rules which, when interpreted in the context of taxation, allow the accommodation of "poverty lines."[38] ✦ If *composition down* is dropped, it follows from Theorem 10.9 that any of Young's rules having a representation f that is strictly monotonic with respect to its second argument and such that, for each pair $\{c_0, c'_0\} \subset \mathbb{R}_+$ with $c_0 < c'_0$, the graph of $f(c_0, \cdot)$ lies everywhere on or below the graph of $f(c'_0, \cdot)$, except of course at the left endpoint of their domain of definition since they both take the value 0 at that point, is admissible. ✦ If *consistency* is dropped, we can choose a different equal-sacrifice rule for each population of claimants, but there are other options, and here, too, a characterization is possible. Indeed, we already have a characterization of the family of rules satisfying *composition down*: any such rule can be described by means of a monotone

acceptable ones. One is a continuity requirement and the other is another expression of the consistency idea.

[36] Again, see Young (1987a).

[37] Theorems 10.11 and 10.12 are due to Young (1988).

[38] The characterization is due to Chambers and Moreno-Ternero (2017).

space-filling tree (Theorem 6.1). For *claims continuity* to hold, all branches should be infinite (Theorem 6.2). Then, in fact, joint *continuity* holds. For *strict endowment monotonicity* to hold, all branches should be strictly monotone. In each coordinate subspace, strict monotonicity in that subspace should hold too. For *strict order preservation in awards*, the branches should meet only at the origin. These conditions are sufficient.

A characterization of the duals of the equal-sacrifice rules follows by duality from Theorem 10.11. The next result is another corollary of this theorem, obtained by adding *homogeneity*. It identifies a very narrow subfamily of the equal-sacrifice rules:

two equal-sacrifice rules characterized

Theorem 10.12 *If in addition to the requirements of Theorem 10.11, homogeneity is imposed, then the only acceptable rules are the equal-sacrifice rules relative to a function u such that either* $u(x) \equiv ln(x)$ *or* $u(x) \equiv -x^p$ *for* $p < 0$.

In the context of taxation, the first case corresponds to proportional taxation (also called "flat taxation"), and the second case to the Young rule for which, for each $i \in N$, $x_i \equiv c_i - [c_i^p + \lambda^p]^{\frac{1}{p}}$ for $\lambda \in [0, \infty]$, where $p < 0$.

Piniles' rule characterized

As noted earlier, Piniles' rule is *consistent*. A characterization of this rule is obtained if we impose the following property of **composition up from midpoint**: it should make no difference whether the endowment is allocated (i) in one step, or (ii) in two steps, as follows: first, allocate whichever is smaller, the endowment or the half-sum of the claims, and in the latter case, allocate the residual endowment after dividing claims by two.[39]

Theorem 12.5 below states that the proportional rule is the only rule satisfying *claims continuity*, *equal treatment of equal groups*, and a variable-population property that follows from *equal treatment of equals* and *consistency*, "replication invariance" (Lemma 12.3a). Since its proof relies on the population of potential claimants being unbounded, so does this characterization. It turns out however that if it is bounded, uniqueness still holds, but a different kind of argument is required. It is given next. Let $\mathcal{I} \subset \mathbb{N}$ denote the set of potential claimants.[40]

proportional rule characterized

Theorem 10.13 *Suppose* $|\mathcal{I}| \geq 3$. *The proportional rule is the only rule satisfying claims continuity, equal treatment of equal groups, and bilateral consistency.*

[39] Formally, the property is as follows: for each $N \in \mathcal{N}$ and each $(c, E) \in \mathcal{C}^N$, $S(c, E) = S(c, \min\{E, \frac{1}{2}\sum c_i\}) + S(c, \max\{E - \frac{1}{2}\sum c_i, 0\})$.

[40] Theorem 10.13 is due to Chambers and Thomson (2002).

Proof: We already know that the proportional rule satisfies the three properties listed in the theorem. Conversely, let S be a rule satisfying these properties. We show that $S = P$ in two steps. Step 1 is for two claimants. Step 2 is for the remaining cases.

Step 1: For two claimants, S coincides with P.

Without loss of generality, let $N \equiv \{1, 2\}$ and $(c, E) \in \mathcal{C}^N$.

Substep 1-1: If for some $m \in \mathbb{N}$, $c_1 = mc_2$, then $S_1(c, E) = mS_2(c, E)$.

We prove this assertion by induction on m (Figure 10.8a). If $m = 1$, it follows from *equal treatment of equal groups* (here, *equal treatment of equals* would suffice).

Now, let $n \geq 2$, and suppose that for each $m \in \mathbb{N}$ such that $m < n$, the assertion is true. We will show that it is true for $m = n$. Suppose then that $c_1 = nc_2$. Let $\ell \in \mathbb{N}\backslash\{1, 2\}$ (such an ℓ exists since $|\mathcal{I}| \geq 3$), and to simplify notation suppose that $\ell = 3$. Let $N' \equiv \{1, 2, 3\}$ and $(c', E') \in \mathcal{C}^{N'}$ be defined by setting $c'_1 \equiv c_1$, $c'_2 \equiv c_2$, $c'_3 \equiv (n-1)c_3$, and $E' \equiv E + \frac{n-1}{n+1}E$. Let $y \equiv S(c', E')$.

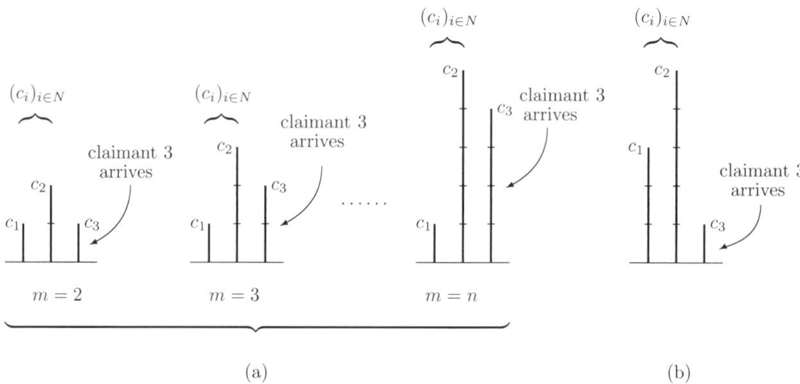

Figure 10.8: **Characterizing the proportional rule** (Theorem 10.13). (a) Uniqueness for $N \equiv \{1, 2\}$ is illustrated here for $c \in \mathbb{R}^N_+$ such that $c_1 \leq c_2$. We first assume that c_2 is an integer multiple of c_1 and we proceed by induction on this integer, called m. For $m = 1$ (case not represented), it suffices to appeal to *equal treatment of equals*. For $m = 2$ (first case represented), we introduce a third agent, agent 3, set $c_3 \equiv c_1$, and augment the endowment by $\frac{E}{3}$. We apply *equal treatment of equal groups* to $\{2\}$ and $\{1, 3\}$, and invoke *bilateral consistency* and the conclusion just reached for $m = 1$ to claimants 1 and 3. For $m = n$, we introduce a third agent, agent 3, set $c_3 \equiv (n-1)c_1$, and augment the endowment by $\frac{n-1}{n+1}E$. We invoke *bilateral consistency* and apply *equal treatment of equal groups* to $\{2\}$ and $\{1, 3\}$, and the conclusion just reached for $m = n-1$ to claimants 1 and 3. (b) If the larger claim is not an integer multiple of the smaller claim but they are both integer multiples of the same number, we introduce a third agent, agent 3, and set their claim equal to that number. We invoke *bilateral consistency* and apply the previous conclusion to the pair $\{\{1\}, \{3\}\}$ and then to the pair $\{\{2\}, \{3\}\}$.

Since $c'_1 = c'_2 + c'_3$, by *equal treatment of equal groups*, $y_1 = y_2 + y_3$. By *bilateral consistency* and the induction hypothesis, $y_3 = (n-1)y_2$. These last two equalities give $y_1 = ny_2$. By *balance*, we then have $y = (n, 1, n-1)\frac{E}{n+1}$. By *bilateral consistency*, $(y_1, y_2) = S(c'_N, y_1 + y_2)$, and since $(c'_N, y_1 + y_2) = (c, E)$, we obtain $S_1(c, E) = nS_2(c, E)$, as asserted.

Substep 1-2: If for some $q \in \mathbb{Q}$, $c_1 = qc_2$, then $S_1(c, E) = qS_2(c, E)$.
We have $c_1 = \frac{r}{m}c_2$ for some $r, m \in \mathbb{N}$ (Figure 10.8b). Let $\ell \in \mathcal{I}\backslash\{1, 2\}$ (since $|\mathcal{I}| \geq 3$, such an ℓ exists), and again for simplicity, set $\ell = 3$. Let $N' \equiv \{1, 2, 3\}$. Let $(c', E') \in \mathcal{C}^{N'}$ be defined by setting $c'_1 \equiv c_1$, $c'_2 \equiv c_2$, $c'_3 \equiv \frac{1}{m}c_2$, and $E' \equiv E + \frac{1}{r+m}E$. Let $y \equiv S(c', E')$. By *bilateral consistency* and Substep 1-1, $y_1 = ry_3$ and $y_2 = my_3$. By *balance*, we then have $y = (r, m, 1)\frac{E}{r+m}$. By *bilateral consistency*, $(y_1, y_2) = S(c'_N, y_1 + y_2)$, and since $(c'_N, y_1 + y_2) = (c, E)$, we obtain $S_1(c, E) = qS_2(c, E)$, as asserted.

Substep 1-3: For each $(c, E) \in \mathcal{C}^N$, $S(c, E) = P(c, E)$.
The result follows from Substep 1-2 and *claims continuity*.

Step 2: For one claimant and for three claimants or more, S coincides with P.
The assertion is obvious for one claimant. For three claimants or more, it follows from Step 1 by an application of the Elevator Lemma, using the facts that P is *conversely consistent* and that S is *bilaterally consistent*. □

We know that for each N with $|N| \geq 3$, the proportional rule is the only rule on $\mathcal{C}^N$ satisfying *no advantageous transfer* (Theorem 8.1). Since the proportional rule satisfies *group order preservation*, we can say that *no advantageous transfer* "almost" implies *group order preservation*. "Almost" because *no advantageous transfer* says nothing about two-claimant problems, and although *group order preservation* has little power then, as it reduces to *order preservation*, it is not vacuous. The converse statement, "*group order preservation* implies *no advantageous transfer*," is of course not true: indeed, if the population of claimants is fixed, *group order preservation* only implies certain inequalities between the coordinates of the awards vector chosen for each problem. (We described these inequalities in Section 3.7 when we introduced the property.) We can choose awards vectors satisfying the required inequalities independently population by population.

We conclude this section by inquiring about the implications of *claims truncation invariance* for Young's rules. The Talmud rule is a member of the family of rules that satisfy this property. There are infinitely many others, however. They constitute a complex subfamily.[41]

[41] Hokari and Thomson (2010).

10.7 AVERAGE CONSISTENCY

We propose here a weakening of *consistency* and base on this notion the definition of an operator that will allow us to extend virtually all two-claimant rules to arbitrary populations.

(a) Suppose a rule is not *consistent*. Then there is at least one group of claimants, one problem involving this group, one subgroup, and one claimant in the subgroup such that, when applied to the reduced problem associated with the subgroup and the choice the rule makes for the problem – let us call this choice x – the rule assigns to this claimant an amount that differs from their component of x. Under *balance*, this means that in this reduced problem, the rule assigns to at least one claimant less, and to at least one claimant more, than at x. Of course, a claimant who receives less than at x in the reduced problem associated with x and some subgroup to which the claimant belongs may receive more than at x in the reduced problem associated with x and some other such subgroup. Suppose however that *on average*, when all the reduced problems associated with x and the subgroups to which the claimant belongs are considered, the claimant does receive the component of x. In fact, suppose that a similar statement can be made about each claimant. Then we may be satisfied with x after all for the problem under consideration. If this is true for each problem, and to the extent that the formation of subgroups is often a thought experiment anyway, this weaker notion than *consistency* may be quite acceptable.

For both conceptual and computational reasons, two-claimant problems are a natural point of departure, and the variant of the idea obtained by limiting the averaging to groups of size two is particularly appealing. We focus on it in the remainder of our discussion.[42] Here is the formal statement of this variant. Let S be a rule.

Average consistency: For each $N \in \mathcal{N}$, each $(c, E) \in \mathcal{C}^N$, and each $i \in N$, and introducing $x \equiv S(c, E)$, $x_i = \frac{1}{|N|-1} \sum_{j \in N \setminus \{i\}} S_i((c_i, c_j), x_i + x_j)$.

The property is illustrated on Figure 10.9.[43] It shows, for $N \equiv \{1, 2, 3\}$ and a problem $(c, E) \in \mathcal{C}^N$, the awards vector x chosen by a rule S to be such that x_1 is the average of the amounts that S awards to claimant 1 in the two reduced problems associated with x and the two-claimant subgroups of N to which claimant 1 belongs, $\{1, 2\}$ and $\{1, 3\}$. Similar equalities hold for claimants 2 and 3. So, x would be judged satisfactory.

Average consistency is self-dual.

42 This property is studied by Dagan and Volij (1997), to whom Theorem 10.14 is due. It is inspired by an idea introduced in a study of a certain class of coalitional games with nontransferable utility, the class of "hyperplane games," by Maschler and Owen (1989).

43 If all subgroups are considered, the requirement becomes $x_i = \frac{1}{2^{|N|-2}} \sum_{N' \subset N, i \in N'} S_i(c_{N'}, \sum_{N'} x_j)$.

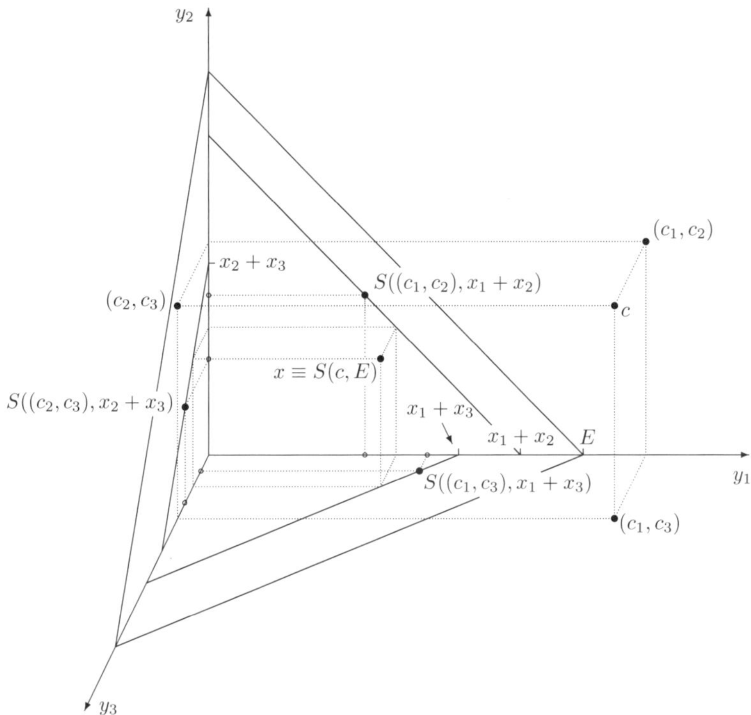

Figure 10.9: **Average consistency**. We consider a rule S. Let $N \equiv \{1, 2, 3\}$ and $(c, E) \in \mathcal{C}^N$. The restriction of $x \equiv S(c, E)$ to the group $\{1, 2\}$ is not the choice made by S for the reduced problem $((c_1, c_2), x_1 + x_2)$. This is in violation of *consistency*. However, the average of the amounts assigned to claimant 1 by S in the two two-claimant reduced problems associated with x in which claimant 1 is involved, $((c_1, c_2), x_1 + x_2)$ and $((c_1, c_3), x_1 + x_3)$ (these amounts are indicated by the two little open circles on the first axis), is equal to x_1, and similar equalities hold for claimants 2 and 3, as required by *average consistency*.

Average consistency is not preserved under convex operations. To prove this, let us consider the constrained equal awards and constrained equal losses rules. We used them to show that *consistency* itself is not preserved under such operations. Since they are *consistent*, they are of course *average consistent*, and thus the issue is whether their average is *average consistent*. The answer is no, as can be shown by means of simple examples.[44]

(b) The idea underlying *average consistency* can be exploited to define a procedure to extend an arbitrary two-claimant rule to any number of claimants. Let S be such a rule: given $N \in \mathcal{N}$ and $(c, E) \in \mathcal{C}^N$, we propose to select $x \in \mathbb{R}^N_+$ such that $\sum_N x_i = E$ and for each $i \in N$,

[44] The fact that the two rules are dual of each other does not help.

$x_i = \frac{1}{|N|-1} \sum_{j \in N \setminus \{i\}} S_i((c_i, c_j), x_i + x_j)$. (Note that if the equality holds for $|N| - 1$ claimants, it holds for the last one.) Questions of course are whether such an x exists, and if it does, whether it is unique. The following theorem states that as soon as S is *endowment monotonic*, both answers are positive:

average consistent extension well-defined

Theorem 10.14 *Let S be an* **endowment monotonic** *two-claimant rule. Then, for each $N \in \mathcal{N}$ and each $(c, E) \in \mathcal{C}^N$, there is a unique $x \in \mathbb{R}^N_+$ such that $\sum x_i = E$ and for each $i \in N$, $x_i = \frac{1}{|N|-1} \sum_{j \in N \setminus \{i\}} S_i((c_i, c_j), x_i + x_j)$.*

The proof is relegated to an appendix (Section 17.7).

Theorem 10.14 provides the basis for calling the mapping that coincides with S for two claimants and associates with each $N \in \mathcal{N}$ such that $|N| > 2$ and each $(c, E) \in \mathcal{C}^N$ the vector x identified in the theorem the average consistent extension of S.

In searching for extensions to general populations of two-claimant rules whose components (indexed by the two-claimant groups) are weighted versions of concede-and-divide, we will encounter difficulties in achieving *consistency* (Theorem 11.7). Also, in searching for extensions of two-claimant rules whose components (again, these are indexed by the two-claimant groups) are members of family $\mathcal{D}$ (characterized in Theorem 6.7), we will find that *consistency* places severe restrictions (Theorem 11.8). No such difficulty occurs if we are satisfied with *average consistency*. Indeed, the hypotheses of Theorem 10.14 do not include *equal treatment of equals*, a property that the members of the families just mentioned do not generally satisfy. Its only hypothesis on the two-claimant mapping that serves as point of departure is *endowment monotonicity*, a very mild property that all weighted concede-and-divide rules as well as all members of $\mathcal{D}$ satisfy. Thus, *average consistency* offers significantly broader opportunities than *consistency* for extending to general populations rules that have been found desirable for two claimants.

This is in particular so because many properties a two-claimant rule enjoys are inherited by its *average consistent* extension. *Anonymity* and *endowment monotonicity* are examples of such properties. The proof of this fact involves calculations similar to those used in the proof of Theorem 10.14 itself and we omit it.[45]

(c) The notion of *average consistency* also provides a tool to answer the question whether a prespecified two-claimant *endowment monotonic* rule has a *consistent* extension. The argument is as follows: given such a rule, S, (i) find its *average consistent* extension R, (whose existence and uniqueness follows from Theorem 10.14); then (ii) when no *consistent* extension exists, R is not *consistent*, which can be shown by means of an example; otherwise, R is the sought-after extension.[46]

[45] It is given by Dagan and Volij (1997).

[46] This argument is developed by Dagan and Volij (1997).

This approach is somewhat roundabout however, whereas the geometric method developed in Chapter 11 below is direct. The main difficulty is that Step (i) may be rather involved, as is readily apparent even when the point of departure are two-claimant rules that are quite simple. Also, the issue may not be to only determine whether a particular *anonymous* way of solving two-claimant problems can be extended in a *consistent* way. Indeed *anonymity* is not always desirable, as we have already argued. If *anonymity* is not imposed, the question may be instead whether, for each two-claimant population, it is possible to select one rule from a family of two-claimant rules that have been found desirable for that population in such a way that the collection of these mappings has a *consistent* extension to general populations, a question of the type examined here. (We will see several other examples in Chapter 11.) Then the calculations may be even more prohibitive.

∗ `Relating axioms` ♦ We asserted in Section 10.4 that *converse consistency* does not imply *consistency*, and announced that to make the point, it would be most convenient to invoke the concept of *average consistency*. Here is an argument that delivers an infinite family of examples. Take any two-claimant *endowment monotonic* rule S. By Theorem 10.14, it has a well-defined *average consistent* extension R, and whenever an awards vector satisfies the hypotheses of *converse consistency* for some problem, R chooses it. Thus, R is *conversely consistent*. However, an arbitrary *endowment monotonic* rule S does not necessarily have a *consistent* extension. We asserted earlier that the operator that associates with each two-claimant rule its *average consistent* extension preserves a number of interesting properties that hold for two claimants. Thus, the rule R we just constructed to establish that *converse consistency* does not imply *consistency* can be guaranteed to be well behaved from a number of respects.

CHAPTER 11

Constructing Consistent Extensions of Two-Claimant Rules

The Elevator Lemma (Lemma 10.8) is a powerful tool to check whether a two-claimant rule can be extended to general populations in a *consistent* way. A difficulty in applying it, however, is that we have to guess what the extension is. In some cases, the definition of the rule for two claimants is suggestive of what the extension has to be. The two-claimant proportional rule certainly falls in that category. In other cases, the two-claimant rule has several natural extensions to general populations; however, if one is *consistent*, this extension is easily singled out. Here, an example is concede-and-divide, with which we know that several rules coincide for two claimants (the random arrival, minimal overlap, and Talmud rules being the main ones), but among them, only one is *consistent*, the Talmud rule. Difficult cases are when a two-claimant rule has no obvious extension to general populations, or when a definition seems natural but fails *consistency*. How should we go about finding a *consistent* extension if one exists, or prove that none does if that is the situation? In this chapter, we develop a geometric technique that often helps resolve these issues.

We proceed by means of a series of examples of increasing complexity (Section 11.1).[1] The technique is particularly simple for *strictly endowment monotonic* rules and we present it in this case first (Example 11.1). Next, we consider rules that are *endowment monotonic* but not *strictly* so, distinguishing two subcases. For one of them, the lack of *strict monotonicity* turns out to be immaterial (Example 11.2). For the other, it creates complications; we identify the circumstances when these complications occur (Example 11.3) and show how to handle them. To gain further familiarity with the technique, we then apply it to two examples for which we already know the answer to the extension question. The first one is a weighted constrained equal awards rule in the two-claimant case. Provided the weights chosen for the various two-claimant populations are what can only be called "consistent" as well, a *consistent* extension exists. We show how to recover it (Example 11.4).

[1] The general technique is described in Thomson (2007a).

We then use the technique to explain how someone unaware of the Talmud rule would be able to rediscover it as the *consistent* extension of concede-and-divide (Example 11.5). The geometry is more subtle, but its logic is the same.

In Section 11.2, we address a number of additional and more delicate questions. Initially, we search for extensions of two-claimant rules satisfying *equal treatment of equals* and ask:

1: Do the two-claimant weighted averages of the constrained equal awards and constrained equal losses rules have *consistent* extensions?
2: Does the two-claimant claims-truncated proportional rule have a *consistent* extension?
3: Does the two-claimant DT rule have a *consistent* extension?
4. Do the ICI and CIC families have *consistent* members?

In Section 11.3 we establish two other results exploiting our geometric technique. We do not impose *equal treatment of equals* there, which creates additional difficulties. We show how they can be overcome.

1. One pertains to our earlier search for weighted generalizations of the two-claimant Talmud rule (Theorems 11.7 and 17.1).
2. We also settle the question of whether there are *consistent* extensions of the two-claimant rules satisfying *homogeneity*, *composition down*, and *composition up* (these rules are described in Theorem 6.7). There are. We identify when and what these rules are.

In all but one of these various applications, paths of awards are piecewise linear, which is of much help in carrying out the required construction.

11.1 A GENERAL EXTENSION TECHNIQUE

Consistency of a rule says that for each population $N \in \mathcal{N}$ and each claims vector $c \in \mathbb{R}^N_+$, the path of awards of the rule for c, when projected onto the coordinate subspace relative to each $N' \subset N$, is a subset of its path for $c_{N'}$ (Figure 10.1).

Conversely, supposing that the paths of awards of a *consistent* rule are given for two claimants, can one construct its paths for larger populations? The answer is often yes. For simplicity, let us limit our attention to situations in which there are only three potential claimants. Let $N \equiv \{1, 2, 3\}$ and $c \in \mathbb{R}^N_+$. Given are Π_3, the path for $c_{\{1,2\}}$, Π_2, the path for $c_{\{1,3\}}$, and Π_1, the path for $c_{\{2,3\}}$. To construct the path for c, Π, let for each $t \in [0, c_1]$, $H(t)$ denote the plane parallel to the subspace $\mathbb{R}^{\{2,3\}}$ of equation $x_1 = t$. We identify the points of intersections of $H(t)$ with Π_3 and Π_2, and the set A of point(s) of $\mathbb{R}^N$ whose projections on $\mathbb{R}^{\{1,2\}}$ and $\mathbb{R}^{\{1,3\}}$ are these points. For the projections of Π on $\mathbb{R}^{\{1,2\}}$ and $\mathbb{R}^{\{1,3\}}$ to be Π_3 and Π_2, the path Π has to include a subset of A. When this reasoning is applied to each $t \in [0, c_1]$, and depending on the monotonicity properties of these two paths, Π may or may not be determined at this stage. If not, we turn to the projection of Π onto $\mathbb{R}^{\{2,3\}}$. This projection should be Π_1.

Note that in the process just described, the three coordinates do not play symmetric roles, but instead of considering a plane moving parallel to the subspace $\mathbb{R}^{\{2,3\}}$ (the plane $H(t)$) we could just as well have chosen to work with a plane moving parallel to the subspace $\mathbb{R}^{\{1,3\}}$ or with a plane moving parallel to the subspace $\mathbb{R}^{\{1,2\}}$.

We will be looking for *bilateral consistent* extensions of two-claimant rules, and in all of our applications, the two-claimant rule that is our point of departure is *endowment monotonic*. If a rule is *endowment monotonic for two claimants* and *bilaterally consistent*, it is in fact *consistent*, so in such a case, we could equivalently be looking for a *consistent* extension. In stating our positive results and to emphasize that *consistency* is met, we list *consistency* as our variable population axiom. In stating our negative results, which holds even if *bilateral consistency* is imposed, it is that weaker version that we list.

Example 11.1 (Figure 11.1) The paths Π_3 and Π_2 are strictly monotonic. For that reason, they suffice to construct Π. Figure 11.1b shows the plane $H(t)$ and its points of intersections with these paths for two values of $t \in [0, c_1]$, called t^1 and t^2. For $t = t^1$, they are k^1 and ℓ^1. We denote m^1 the point in $\mathbb{R}^N$ whose projections on $\mathbb{R}^{\{1,2\}}$ and $\mathbb{R}^{\{1,3\}}$ are k^1 and ℓ^1. It belongs to Π. The plane $H(t^1)$ should contain no other point of Π. For $t = t^2$, we obtain the points k^2 and ℓ^2, and then m^2. It too belongs to Π and again, the plane $H(t^2)$ should contain no other point of Π. As t ranges from 0 to c_1, we trace out the whole of Π. Figure 11.1c shows that the projection of Π onto $\mathbb{R}^{\{2,3\}}$ is Π_1. Figure 11.1d shows the path for c and its three projections.

Example 11.2 (Figure 11.2) The path Π_3 is not strictly monotonic: for some $t \in [0, c_1]$, the intersection of $H(t)$ with Π_3 contains a nondegenerate segment parallel to $\mathbb{R}^{\{2\}}$, seg$[k^1, k^2]$. However, since the intersection of $H(t)$ with Π_2 is a singleton, called ℓ, and Π_3 and Π_2 are otherwise strictly monotonic, we can still construct Π uniquely. There has to be a segment in Π parallel to $\mathbb{R}^{\{2\}}$ – seg$[m^1, m^2]$ in the figure, m^1 being obtained by matching k^1 and ℓ, and m^2 being obtained by matching k^2 and ℓ – and the projection of Π onto $\mathbb{R}^{\{2,3\}}$ contains a segment parallel to $\mathbb{R}^{\{2\}}$ – seg$[n^1, n^2]$ in the figure. (Then both Π and Π_1 also fail to be strictly monotonic.)

Example 11.3 (Figure 11.3) There is $t \in \mathbb{R}_+$ such that the intersections of $H(t)$ with the paths Π_3 and Π_2 contain segments, seg$[k^1, k^2]$ and seg$[\ell^1, \ell^2]$ respectively. Then Π can be any monotonic curve in $H(t)$ connecting m^1 and m^2, and still satisfy the projection requirements on $\mathbb{R}^{\{1,2\}}$ and $\mathbb{R}^{\{1,3\}}$. By *endowment monotonicity* (by Lemma 10.13, this property, which is satisfied here for two claimants, also holds for three claimants), the curve should be a monotone curve in the shaded rectangle in that plane. To pin it down, we use

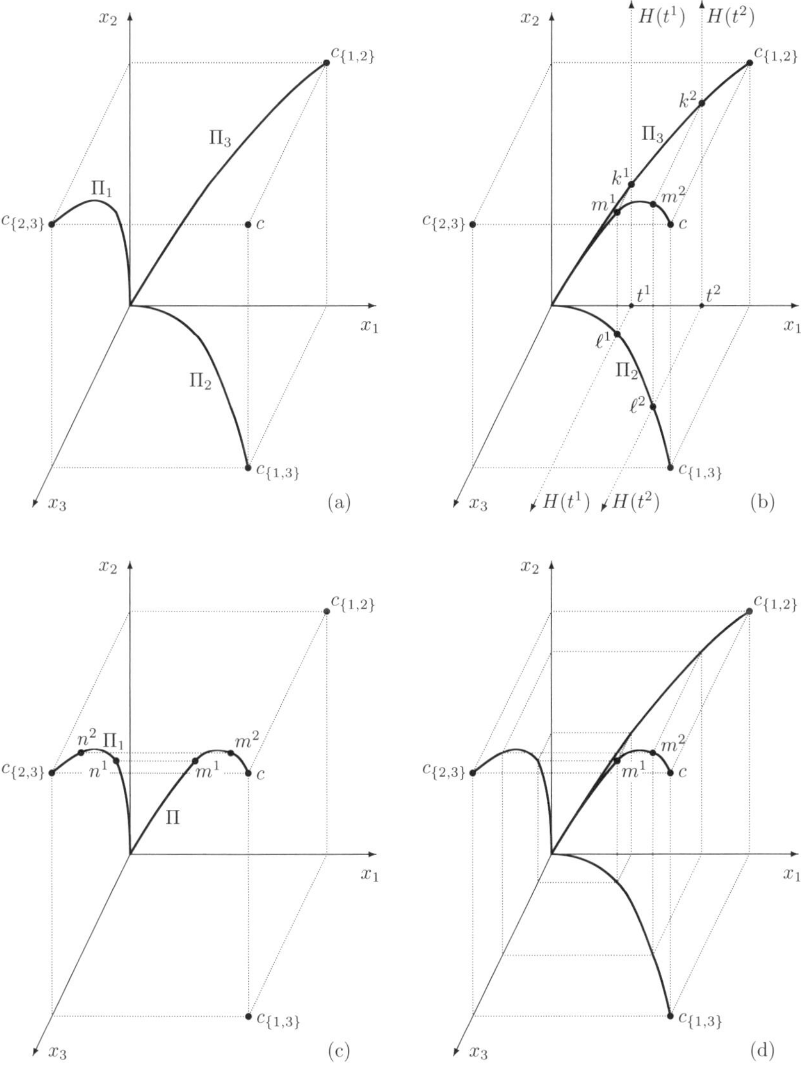

Figure 11.1: **Constructing the consistent extension of a strictly endowment monotonic two-claimant rule** (Example 11.1). (a) The paths Π_3, Π_2, and Π_1, from which we have to construct the three-dimensional path for c, Π. (b) The plane $H(t^1)$ (indicated by its lines of intersections with $\mathbb{R}^{\{1,2\}}$ and $\mathbb{R}^{\{1,3\}}$) intersects Π_3 at k^1 and Π_2 at ℓ^1. We denote m^1 the point in $\mathbb{R}^N_+$ whose projection onto $\mathbb{R}^{\{1,2\}}$ is k^1 and whose projection onto $\mathbb{R}^{\{1,3\}}$ is ℓ^1. It has to be a point of Π. By considering the plane $H(t^2)$, we define in a similar way k^2 and ℓ^2, and then m^2. (c) If the rule is *consistent*, the projections n^1 and n^2 on $\mathbb{R}^{\{2,3\}}$ of m^1 and m^2 belong to Π_1. (d) The paths for c and its projections.

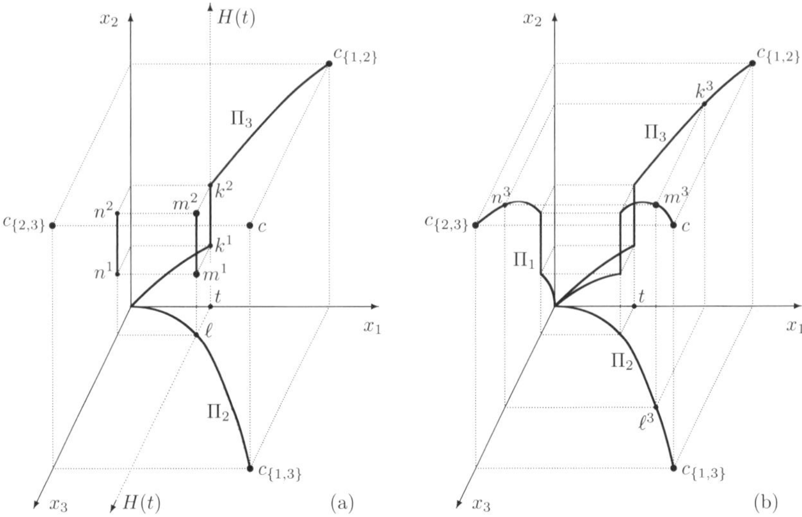

Figure 11.2: **Constructing the consistent extension, if it exists, of an endowment monotonic (but not strictly so) two-claimant rule** (Example 11.2). (a) Here, there is $t \in [0, c_1]$ such that the intersection of $H(t)$ with Π_3 contains a segment parallel to $\mathbb{R}^2$, seg$[k^1, k^2]$, but the intersection of $H(t)$ with Π_2 is a singleton, ℓ. We deduce that Π contains a segment parallel to $\mathbb{R}^2$, seg$[m^1, m^2]$. (b) We uniquely deduce the whole of Π from Π_3 and Π_2 since, except for Π_3 in $H(t^1)$, Π_3 and Π_2 are strictly monotonic. Once we have obtained Π, we project it onto $\mathbb{R}^{\{2,3\}}$; this projection should be Π_1.

the fact that its projection onto $\mathbb{R}^{\{2,3\}}$ has to be Π_1. Since Π_3 and Π_2 violate strict monotonicity only in $H(t)$, the construction of Π is otherwise uniquely defined (as in Example 11.1 of Figure 11.1).

The case of rules whose paths of awards are piecewise linear is particularly interesting because it occurs frequently, and we will see several important examples. To illustrate, and still supposing that $N \equiv \{1, 2, 3\}$, let $c \in \mathbb{R}^N_+$. If the path for $c_{\{1,2\}}$ has n_3 kinks and the path for $c_{\{1,3\}}$ has n_2 kinks, the path for c has at most $n_3 + n_2$ kinks, and by projection on $\mathbb{R}^{\{2,3\}}$, so does the path for $c_{\{2,3\}}$. If the paths were in general position, the number of kinks in Π would be $n_3 + n_2$, and so would the number of kinks in its projection on $\mathbb{R}^{\{2,3\}}$. However, there are two reasons why this sum need not be reached; it is only an upper bound. First, a kink in Π_3 and a kink in Π_2 may have equal first coordinates. Second, the projections of the first two kinks of Π onto $\mathbb{R}^{\{2,3\}}$ may be lined up with the origin, or the projections of three of its successive kinks may be lined up. These possibilities are illustrated by the next two examples.

When extending the definitions of the weighted constrained equal awards with positive weights and weighted constrained equal losses rules with positive weights to the variable-population case, we need to specify for each $N \in \mathcal{N}$ a

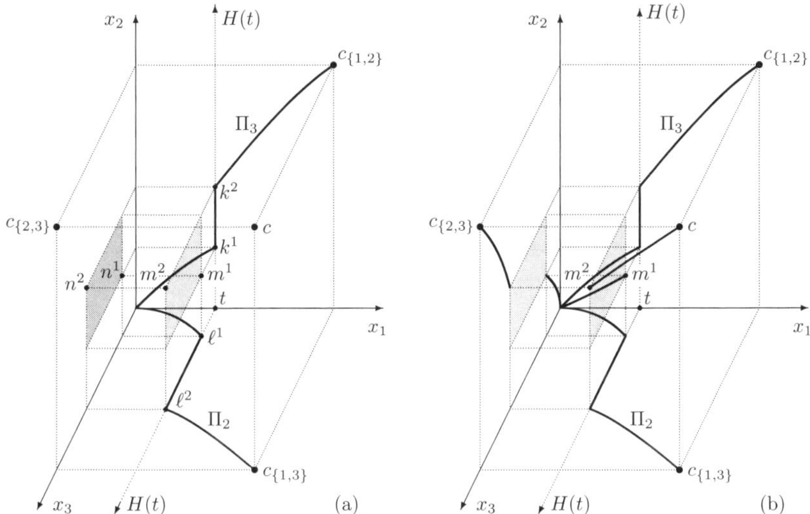

Figure 11.3: **Constructing the consistent extension, if it exists, of an endowment monotonic (but not strictly so) two-claimant rule (continued)** (Example 11.3). (a) Here, there is $t \in [0, c_1]$ such that the intersection of $H(t)$ with Π_3 contains a segment parallel to $\mathbb{R}^{\{2\}}$, seg$[k^1, k^2]$, and its intersection with Π_2 contains a segment parallel to $\mathbb{R}^{\{3\}}$, seg$[\ell^1, \ell^2]$. Thus, Π could be any weakly monotonic curve in the shaded rectangle in $H(t)$ connecting m^1 to m^2. The projection of that curve onto $\mathbb{R}^{\{2,3\}}$ is contained in the shaded rectangle in $\mathbb{R}^{\{2,3\}}$. This projection connects n^1 to n^2, the projections of m^1 and m^2. (b) To complete Π in the shaded rectangle in $H(t)$, we have to use the fact that its projection on $\mathbb{R}^{\{2,3\}}$ is Π_1. The sought-after completion is simply a translate of the part of Π_1 that lies in the shaded rectangle in $\mathbb{R}^{\{2,3\}}$ (this part of Π_1 is not represented).

weight vector to be used to solve problems in $\mathcal{C}^N$. The relative weights attached to two claimants who are both members of two different groups could in principle depend on the identity of their fellow claimants. However, if *consistency* is imposed, given two claimants and two groups related by inclusion and containing both, the relative weights attached to these two claimants as members of the two groups should be equal. One way to achieve this equality is to attach a positive reference weight to each potential claimant, before that claimant is implicated in any problem, so to speak, and for each actual problem, to attach to the claimants who are present weights proportional to their reference weights. Since all reference weights are positive, the generalizations of the constrained equal awards and constrained equal losses rules so obtained are well defined, and they are *consistent*. So are the weighted generalizations of the hybrid rules (Figure 3.7).[2] The consistency of the weights is brought out by our construction.

[2] They also all admit representations of a type that slightly generalizes the definition given in Chapter 2 (Young, 1987a).

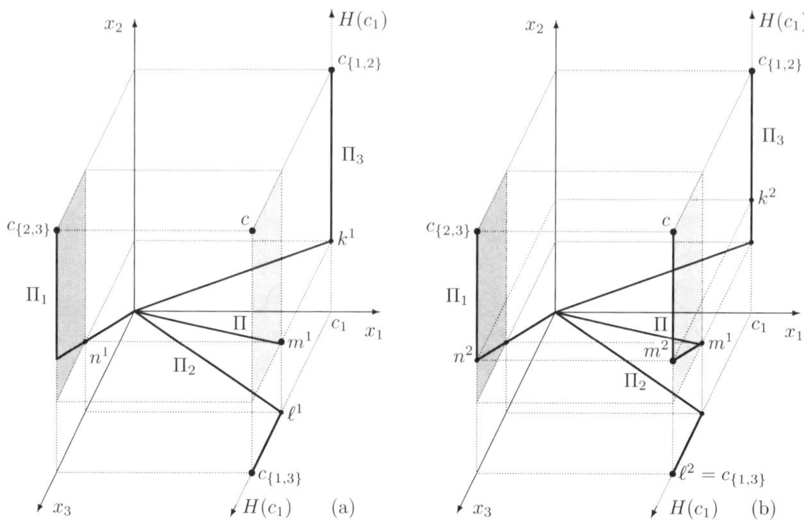

Figure 11.4: **Constructing the consistent extension of a two-claimant weighted constrained equal awards rule** (Example 11.4). (a) We obtain the path Π from the origin to the point m^1 at which it reaches $H(c_1)$ from its projections onto $\mathbb{R}^{\{1,2\}}$ and $\mathbb{R}^{\{1,3\}}$, seg$[(0,0), k^1]$ and seg$[(0,0), \ell^1]$. (b) From m^1, it could continue to c in some arbitrary fashion in the shaded rectangle in $H(c_1)$: its projections onto $\mathbb{R}^{\{1,2\}}$ and $\mathbb{R}^{\{1,3\}}$ are guaranteed then to be what they are supposed to be, namely seg$[k^1, c_{\{1,2\}}]$ and seg$[\ell^1, c_{\{1,3\}}]$. However, the requirement that its projection onto $\mathbb{R}^{\{2,3\}}$ be Π_1 determines the continuation uniquely, namely bro.seg$[m^1, m^2, c]$.

Example 11.4 (Figure 11.4) A two-claimant weighted constrained equal awards rule. The slope of the first segment of Π_3, seg$[(0,0), k^1]$, is given by the weights attached to claimants 1 and 2 in solving problems in $\mathcal{C}^{\{1,2\}}$. The slope of the first segment of Π_2, seg$[(0,0), \ell^1]$, is given by the weights attached to claimants 1 and 3 in solving problems in $\mathcal{C}^{\{1,3\}}$. The point m^1 is the point of Π whose projections onto $\mathbb{R}^{\{1,2\}}$ and $\mathbb{R}^{\{1,3\}}$ are k^1 and ℓ^1. Since its projection onto $\mathbb{R}^{\{2,3\}}$, n^1, should be a point of Π_1, we deduce the weights attached to claimants 2 and 3 in solving problems in $\mathcal{C}^{\{2,3\}}$: they have to be consistent with the weights chosen for the two-claimant populations $\{1,2\}$ and $\{1,3\}$. We determine the continuation of Π in box$[m^1, c]$ from the knowledge that its projection on $\mathbb{R}^{\{2,3\}}$ is Π_1.

Example 11.5 (Figure 11.5) Concede-and-divide. Let $c \in \mathbb{R}^N$ be such that $c_1 < c_2 < c_3$. By examining its projections on $\mathbb{R}^{\{1,2\}}$, we construct the path Π until the point m^1 where it reaches $H(\frac{c_1}{2})$. We determine its continuation from its projection on $\mathbb{R}^{\{2,3\}}$, which should be Π_1. In the figure, we only indicate its construction up to $\frac{c}{2}$.

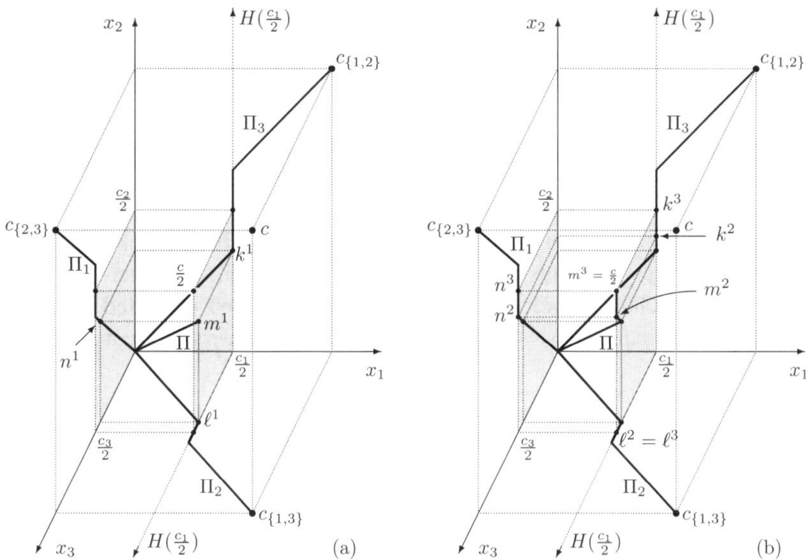

Figure 11.5: **Constructing the consistent extension of concede-and-divide** (Example 11.5). The figure illustrates, for $c \in \mathbb{R}_+^{\{1,2,3\}}$ such that $c_1 < c_2 < c_3$, the construction of Π from the origin to $\frac{c}{2}$. (a) We obtain its initial segment, seg$[(0,0,0), m^1]$, from its projections Π_3 and Π_2 onto $\mathbb{R}^{\{1,2\}}$ and $\mathbb{R}^{\{1,3\}}$. (b) We determine the continuation of Π in the shaded rectangle in $H(\frac{c_1}{2})$ from its projection Π_1 onto $\mathbb{R}^{\{2,3\}}$. The result is the Talmud rule.

11.2 CONSISTENT EXTENSIONS OF TWO-CLAIMANT RULES SATISFYING EQUAL TREATMENT OF EQUALS

Having illustrated our technique for constructing *consistent* extensions of two-claimant rules for various configurations of their paths and showed that these configurations occur for central rules, we now apply it to answer a number of additional questions: we consider (i) weighted averages of the constrained equal awards and constrained equal losses rules, (ii) the truncated proportional rule and the DT rule, and (iii) members of the ICI and CIC families.

11.2.1 Consistent Extension of Weighted Averages of the Two-Claimant Constrained Equal Awards and Constrained Equal Losses Rules

Our first question is whether weighted averages of the two-claimant constrained equal awards and constrained equal losses rules have *consistent* extensions. The answer is generally no. We have used such an average to show that *consistency* is not preserved under convex operations (Proposition 10.3), but this does not imply that the two-claimant version of such a rule does not have a *consistent* extension. However, we show below that indeed no *consistent* extension exists. Moreover, allowing for each two-claimant population the weight to depend on the identity of its two members does not help. For each $N \in \mathcal{N}$ with $|N| = 2$, let $\lambda^N \in [0, 1]$ be the weight placed on the constrained equal awards rule for that population (and therefore $1 - \lambda^N$ is the weight placed on the constrained equal losses rule). Note that unless all the λ^N's are equal, *anonymity* is violated across two-claimant populations, but the property still holds within each such population. We refer to a collection of two-claimant rules so defined as a **generalized weighted average** of the two-claimant constrained equal awards and constrained equal losses rules.[3]

consistent extensions of weighted average of constrained equal awards, constrained equal losses rules

Theorem 11.1 *A generalized weighted average of the two-claimant constrained equal awards and constrained equal losses rules has a bilaterally consistent extension if and only if one of the following two cases occurs:*

(i) for each two-claimant population, all the weight is placed on the former, that is, the constrained equal awards rule is used; then the extension to arbitrary populations is the constrained equal awards rule;
(ii) for each two-claimant population, all the weight is placed on the latter, that is, the constrained equal losses rule is used; then the extension to arbitrary populations is the constrained equal losses rule.

Proof: For each $N \in \mathcal{N}$ with $|N| = 2$, let $\lambda^N \in [0, 1]$. Let us suppose that there is a *consistent* rule S such that for each $N \in \mathcal{N}$ with $|N| = 2$, $S = A^{\lambda^N}$. We will show that this is possible only if either for each $N \in \mathcal{N}$ with $|N| = 2$, $\lambda^N = 1$, or for each $N \in \mathcal{N}$ with $|N| = 2$, $\lambda^N = 0$. We will do so by considering the population of claimants $N \equiv \{1, 2, 3\}$ when their claims are $c \equiv (2, 4, 6)$.

Since, for each $N \in \mathcal{N}$ with $|N| = 2$, $S = A^{\lambda^N}$, we know the paths of awards of S for (c_1, c_2), (c_1, c_3), and (c_2, c_3). They are illustrated in Figure 11.6 for $\lambda^{\{1,2\}} = \lambda^{\{1,3\}} = \lambda^{\{2,3\}} = 0.8$. Using notation that reflects their dependence on these weights, they are:

- $\Pi_3(\lambda^{\{1,2\}}) = \text{bro.seg}[(0,0), a(\lambda^{\{1,2\}}), b(\lambda^{\{1,2\}}), (c_1, c_2)]$
- $\Pi_2(\lambda^{\{1,3\}}) = \text{bro.seg}[(0,0), d(\lambda^{\{1,3\}}), (c_1, c_3)]$
- $\Pi_1(\lambda^{\{2,3\}}) = \text{bro.seg}[(0,0), e(\lambda^{\{2,3\}}), f(\lambda^{\{2,3\}}), (c_2, c_3)]$

the coordinates of the points $a(\lambda^{\{1,2\}})$, $b(\lambda^{\{1,2\}})$, $d(\lambda^{\{1,3\}})$, $e(\lambda^{\{2,3\}})$, and $f(\lambda^{\{2,3\}})$ being indicated on the figures.

Let us call Π the path of awards of S for c, and Π'_1 its projection onto $\mathbb{R}^{\{2,3\}}$. We distinguish four cases:

[3] Theorem 11.1 is due to Thomson (2007a).

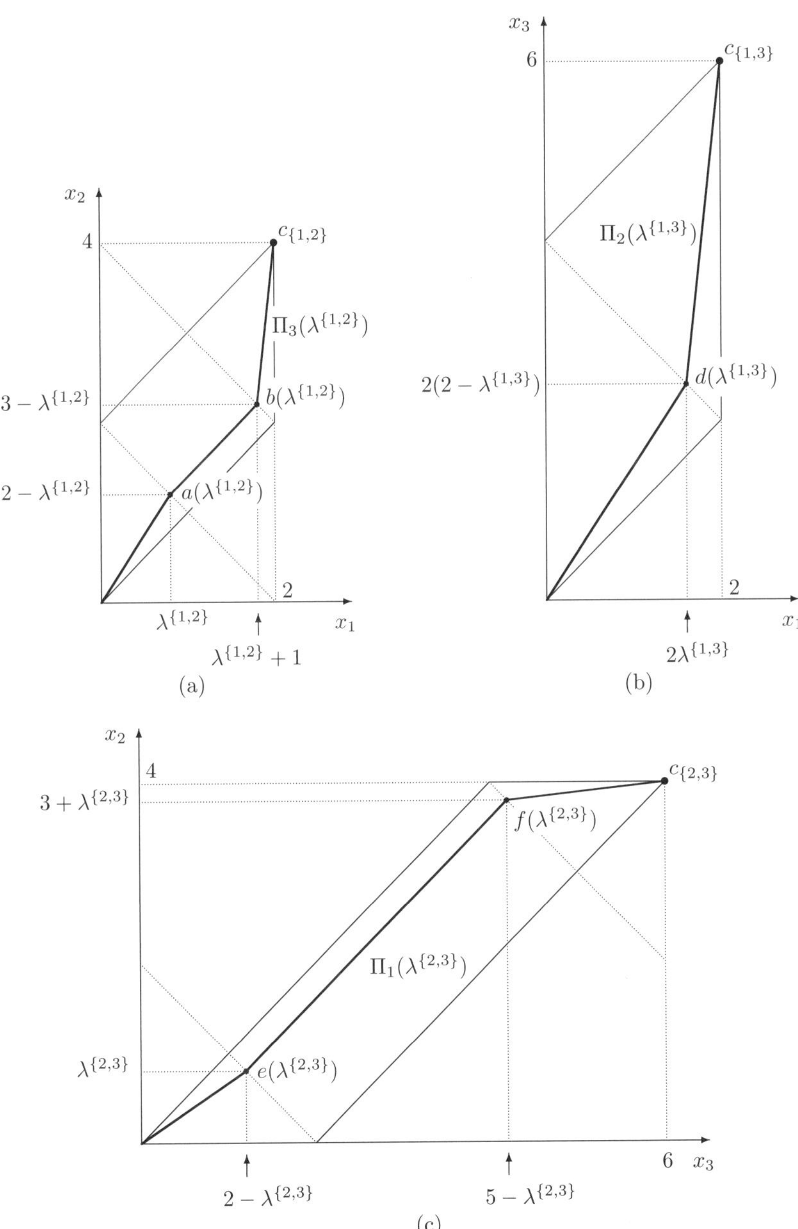

Figure 11.6: **Proof of Theorem 11.1: constructing the paths of awards for $c_{\{1,2\}}$, $c_{\{1,3\}}$, and $c_{\{2,3\}}$.** In these illustrations, $\lambda^{\{1,2\}} = \lambda^{\{1,3\}} = \lambda^{\{2,3\}} = 0.8$. (a) Path of $A^{\lambda^{\{1,2\}}}$ for $c_{\{1,2\}}$. (b) Path of $A^{\lambda^{\{1,3\}}}$ for $c_{\{1,3\}}$. (c) Path of $A^{\lambda^{\{2,3\}}}$ for $c_{\{2,3\}}$.

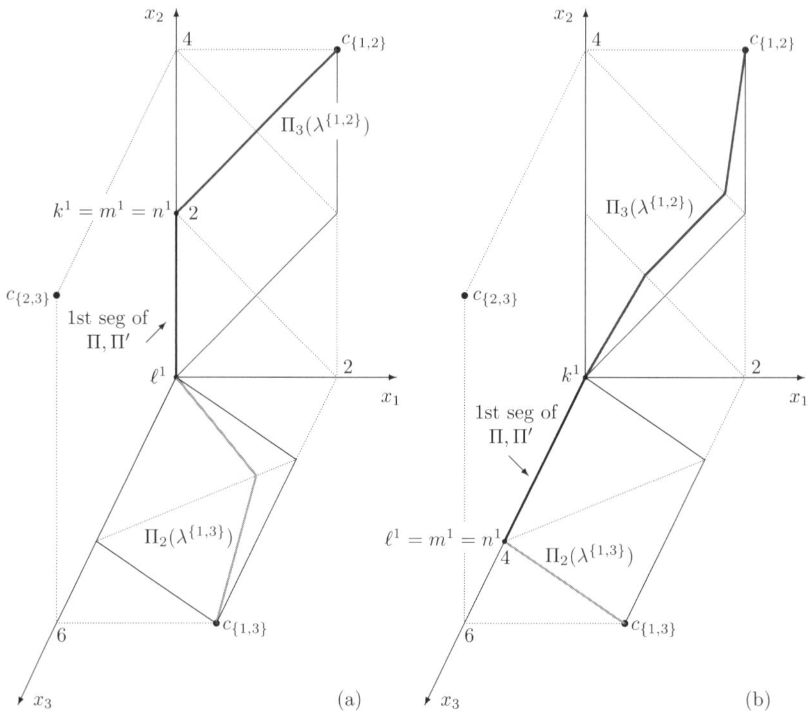

Figure 11.7: **Proof of Theorem 11.1: constructing the first segment of Π.** (a) Here, $\lambda^{\{1,2\}} = 0$ and $\lambda^{\{1,3\}} > 0$. (b) Here, $\lambda^{\{1,2\}} > 0$ and $\lambda^{\{1,3\}} = 0$.

Case 1: $\lambda^{\{1,2\}} = 0$ and $\lambda^{\{1,3\}} > 0$. The plane $H(0) = \mathbb{R}^{\{1,2\}}$ contains seg[(0, 0), (0, 2)], the first segment of the path for (c_1, c_2), and it intersects the path for (c_1, c_3) only at the origin. Thus, the path for c starts with seg[(0, 0, 0), (0, 2, 0)] and its projection onto $\mathbb{R}^{\{2,3\}}$ starts with seg[(0, 0), (2, 0)] (in Figure 11.7a, the three segments just mentioned coincide, and in our previous notation, $k^1 = m^1 = n^1$). This is in violation of what we know of the path for (c_2, c_3) (the situation is similar to that encountered in Example 11.2).

Case 2: $\lambda^{\{1,2\}} > 0$ and $\lambda^{\{1,3\}} = 0$. The plane $H(0) = \mathbb{R}^{\{1,2\}}$ intersects the path for (c_1, c_2) only at the origin, and it contains seg[(0, 0), (0, 4)], the first segment of the path for (c_1, c_3). Thus, the path for c starts with seg[(0, 0, 0), (0, 0, 4)] and its projection onto $\mathbb{R}^{\{2,3\}}$ starts with seg[(0, 0), (0, 4)] (in Figure 11.7b, these three segments coincide, and in our previous notation, $\ell^1 = m^1 = n^1$). This is in violation of what we know of the path for (c_2, c_3).

Case 3: $\lambda^{\{1,2\}} = \lambda^{\{1,3\}} = 0$. This assumption means that $S = CEL$ for problems involving either {1, 2} or {1, 3}. Analysis similar to that of Example 11.4 leads us to the conclusion $S = CEL$.

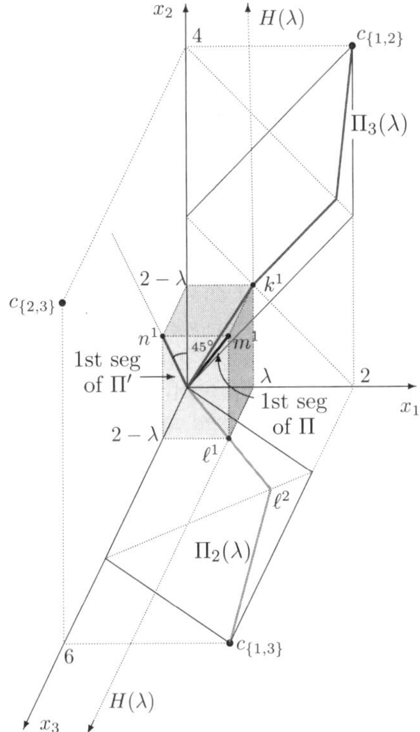

Figure 11.8: **Proof of Theorem 11.1: constructing the first segment of Π (continued).** This figure shows the construction if $\lambda^{\{1,2\}} = \lambda^{\{1,3\}} > 0$ (both of these numbers are denoted λ in the figure). The projection of the first segment of Π onto $\mathbb{R}^{\{2,3\}}$ differs from the first segment of $\Pi_1(\lambda^{\{2,3\}})$ (not represented).

Case 4: $\lambda^{\{1,2\}} > 0$ and $\lambda^{\{1,3\}} > 0$. Figure 11.8a shows the case when $\lambda^{\{1,3\}} = \lambda^{\{1,2\}}$, so that the kink reached first by $H(t)$, as t increases from 0, belongs to $\Pi_3(\lambda^{\{1,2\}})$. For $\lambda^{\{1,3\}}$ sufficiently small in relation to $\lambda^{\{1,2\}}$, the kink reached first would be in $\Pi_2(\lambda^{\{1,3\}})$. As t increases from 0, the plane $H(t)$ intersects $\Pi_3(\lambda^{\{1,2\}})$ and $\Pi_2(\lambda^{\{1,3\}})$ at points that first belong to seg$[0, k^1]$ and seg$[0, \ell^2]$ in Figure 11.8a. Since $\lambda^{\{1,2\}} = \lambda^{\{1,3\}}$, Π begins with a segment that lies in the plane of equation $x_2 = x_3$ (it is seg$[(0,0,0), m^1]$ in the figure), and its projection onto $\mathbb{R}^{\{2,3\}}$ also begins with a segment of slope 1.

If $\lambda^{\{1,2\}} < \lambda^{\{1,3\}}$, this projection lies between the 45° line in $\mathbb{R}^{\{2,3\}}$ and the second axis, but is not contained in the 45° line. This cannot be so because, as $c_3 > c_2$, the first segment of the path of S for (c_2, c_3) lies between the 45° line in $\mathbb{R}^{\{2,3\}}$ and the third axis. Thus, $\lambda^{\{1,2\}} \geq \lambda^{\{1,3\}}$. Figure 11.8b shows how the slope of the first segment of the projection of Π onto $\mathbb{R}^{\{2,3\}}$ has moved in the right direction by choosing $\lambda^{\{1,2\}} \geq \lambda^{\{1,3\}}$. By considering the claims vector $(2, 6, 4)$, we conclude in a similar way that $\lambda^{\{1,2\}} \leq \lambda^{\{1,3\}}$. Thus, $\lambda^{\{1,2\}} =$

$\lambda^{\{1,3\}}$. Then, as already noted, Π begins with a segment in the plane of equation $x_2 = x_3$ and its projection on $\mathbb{R}^{\{2,3\}}$ has slope 1. This implies that the first segment of the path for (c_2, c_3) has slope 1. This is possible only if $\lambda^{\{2,3\}} = 1$. We can apply this argument to deduce that $\lambda^N = 1$ for each other $N \in \mathcal{N}$ with $|N| = 2$. Indeed, all three weights are positive, and any two of them being positive implies that the third one is 1. Now, we can invoke the analysis of Example 11.4 to conclude that $S = CEA$. □

Similar questions can be asked about the existence of *consistent* extensions of two-claimant averages of the proportional and constrained equal awards rules. The answer is that here, too, and even if the weight is allowed to depend on the claims vector (as before, let us speak of "generalized averages"), all the weight should always be placed on the proportional rule, or all of the weight should always be placed on the constrained equal awards rule. Parallel results are obtained when the point of departure are two-claimant averages of the proportional and constrained equal losses rules:[4]

consistent extensions of weighted average of proportional, constrained equal awards rules

Theorem 11.2 *A generalized weighted average of the two-claimant proportional and constrained equal awards rules has a bilaterally consistent extension if and only if one of the following two cases occurs:*

(i) for each two-claimant population, all the weight is placed on the former, that is, the proportional rule is used; then the extension to arbitrary populations is the proportional rule;
(ii) for each two-claimant population, all the weight is placed on the latter, that is, the constrained equal awards rule is used; then the extension to arbitrary populations is the constrained equal awards rule.

11.2.2 Two-Claimant Rules that Have No Consistent Extension

In each of the examples just analyzed, paths of awards are piecewise linear, which has helped, but we can sometimes apply the technique we developed to solve the extension question for two-claimant rules whose paths exhibit some curvature. For instance, consider the rule obtained from the proportional rule by subjecting it to the claims truncation operator (Figure 9.1). It is easy to show that this rule is not *consistent* (we gave an example earlier), but does its two-claimant version have a *bilaterally consistent* extension? The answer is no:[5]

[4] Thomson (2015c).

[5] Dagan and Volij (1997) show that if a two-claimant rule has a *bilateral consistent* extension, then to each problem, a certain binary relation associated with each awards vector for this problem is transitive. To prove that the two-claimant claims-truncated proportional rule has no *consistent* extension, they give an example of this sort for which transitivity is violated. The proof that we present here, due to Thomson (2008a), is constructive.

Theorem 11.3 *The two-claimant claims-truncated proportional rule has no bilaterally consistent extension.*

two-claimant claims-truncated proportional rule has no bilaterally consistent extension

The proof is relegated to an appendix (Section 17.9).

By duality, we deduce from Theorem 11.3 that the two-claimant version of the rule obtained by subjecting the proportional rule to the attribution of minimal rights operator has no *bilaterally consistent* extension either. However, the rule obtained by subjecting the two-claimant proportional rule to the composition of the claims truncation and attribution of minimal rights operators (in either order) is concede-and-divide, which we know has a *consistent* extension, namely the Talmud rule.

Our next result pertains to the rule defined by the recursive application of the $\frac{1}{|N|}$-truncated-claims lower bounds on awards, the DT rule of Subsection 3.4.2. It is not *bilaterally consistent* either, as is easy to see, but does its two-claimant version have a *bilaterally consistent* extension? Here, too, the answer is no.[6]

Theorem 11.4 *The two-claimant DT rule has no bilaterally consistent extension.*

two-claimant DT rule has no bilaterally consistent extension

We omit the proof, which follows the same logic as that of Theorem 11.3.

11.2.3 Consistent ICI and CIC Rules

We return to the ICI family and search for its *consistent* members. In the variable-population framework, an ICI rule is defined by selecting, for each $N \in \mathcal{N}$, a pair of list of functions $H^N \equiv (F^N, G^N) \in \mathcal{H}^N$, and applying the definition of Chapter 2 (we are adding the superscript N, which was not necessary then). Naturally, if these functions are chosen independently as N varies in $\mathcal{N}$, there is no reason to expect *consistency* to be met.

However, the family does have *consistent* members, the constrained equal awards, constrained equal losses, and Talmud rules being examples. Are there others? The answer is yes. For a complete description of the subfamily that these rules constitute – our next theorem – we need to introduce the class $\mathbf{\Gamma}$ of functions $\gamma\colon \mathbb{R}_+ \mapsto \mathbb{R}_+$ that are (i) nowhere decreasing, and such that (ii) for each $c_0 \in \mathbb{R}_+$, $\gamma(c_0) \leq c_0$, and (iii) the function $c_0 \mapsto c_0 - \gamma(c_0)$ is also nowhere decreasing. (These requirements together imply that γ is continuous.) With each $\gamma \in \Gamma$ we associate an ICI rule as follows; given $N \in \mathcal{N}$ and $c \in \mathbb{R}^N_+$, let $n \equiv |N|$ and $\tilde{c}$ be the vector in $\mathbb{R}^n_+$ obtained from c by writing its coordinates in increasing order:

ICI* rule associated with $\boldsymbol{\gamma \in \Gamma}$, $\boldsymbol{ICI^\gamma}$: For each $N \in \mathcal{N}$ and each $c \in \mathbb{R}^N_+$, ICI^γ is the ICI rule whose component relative to N is associated with the

[6] Theorem 11.4 is due to Dominguez and Thomson (2006).

list $(F^k(c), G^k(c))_{k=1}^{n-1}$ defined by setting, for each $k = 1, \ldots, n$, $F^k(c) \equiv (n\gamma(\tilde{c}_1), \gamma(\tilde{c}_1)+(n-1)\gamma(\tilde{c}_2), \ldots, \gamma(\tilde{c}_1)+\gamma(\tilde{c}_2)+\cdots+\gamma(\tilde{c}_{n-2})+2\gamma(\tilde{c}_{n-1}))$, the list $(G^k(c))_{k=1}^{n-1}$ being obtained from the list $(F^k(c))_{k=1}^{n-1}$ by means of the ICI relations.

If $\gamma = e$ (recall that e is the identity function), $ICI^\gamma = CEA$; if $\gamma = 0$, $ICI^\gamma = CEL$; and if $\gamma = \frac{e}{2}$, $ICI^\gamma = T$.

The ICI* rules are Young rules. They have to because they satisfy the properties listed in Theorem 10.9, a characterization of Young's family. Given $\gamma \in \Gamma$, Figure 11.9a shows a representation f^γ of ICI^γ. Let $\underline{\lambda} = 0$, $\bar{\lambda} > 0$, and $\lambda^* \in]\underline{\lambda}, \bar{\lambda}[$. Let A be the graph of a continuous and increasing function $g\colon [0, \lambda^*[\mapsto \mathbb{R}_+$ such that $g(0) = 0$ and $g(\lambda) \to \infty$ as $\lambda \to \lambda^*$. Let B be the graph of a continuous and increasing function $h\colon]\lambda^*, \bar{\lambda}] \mapsto \mathbb{R}_-$ such that $h(\lambda) \to -\infty$ as $\lambda \to \lambda^*$, and $h(\bar{\lambda}) = 0$. Now, for each $c_0 \in \mathbb{R}_+$, let $f^\gamma(c_0, \cdot)\colon [\underline{\lambda}, \bar{\lambda}] \mapsto \mathbb{R}_+$ be the function whose graph follows A from $(0, 0)$ until the point of ordinate $\gamma(c_0)$ – let λ_0 denote the abscissa of this point – continues horizontally until it meets the curve $B + \{0, c_0\}$ – let μ_0 denote the abscissa of the meeting point – and then follows this curve to $(\bar{\lambda}, c_0)$. It is easy to verify that the function $f^\gamma\colon \mathbb{R}_+ \times [\underline{\lambda}, \bar{\lambda}] \mapsto \mathbb{R}_+$ satisfies the required properties to be a Young representation of a Young rule.

To see that indeed f^γ is a Young representation of ICI^γ, it is enough to consider the two-claimant case, the logic being the same for arbitrarily many

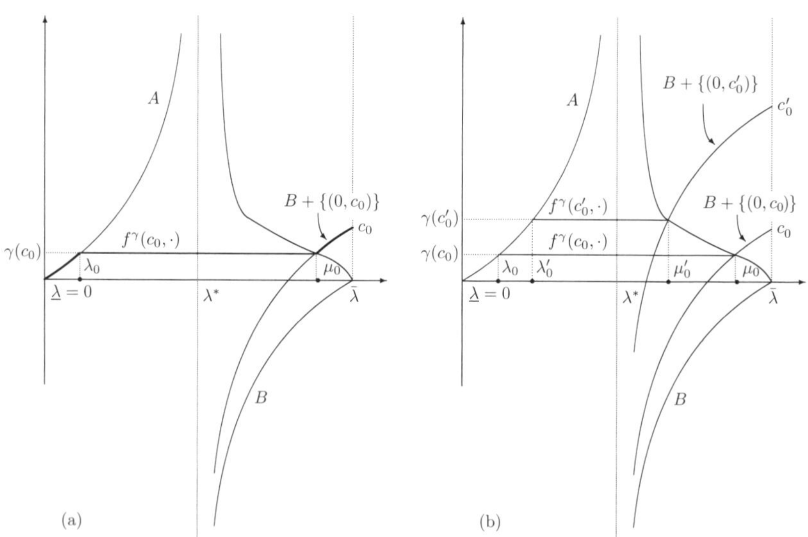

Figure 11.9: **Young representation of the ICI* rule associated with some $\gamma \in \Gamma$, ICI^γ.** (a) Constructing the schedule $f^\gamma(c_0, \cdot)$ of ICI^γ for a typical $c_0 \in \mathbb{R}_+$. (b) Showing the schedules $f^\gamma(c_0, \cdot)$ and $f^\gamma(c'_0, \cdot)$ of ICI^γ for claims c_0 and c'_0. These schedules are used to determine the path of ICI^γ for (c_0, c'_0).

claimants. Let $N \equiv \{1, 2\}$ say, $c_0, c'_0 \in \mathbb{R}_+$ be such that $c_0 < c'_0$, and suppose that agent 1's claim is c_0 and agent 2's claim is c'_0. The graphs of $f^\gamma(c_0, \cdot)$ and $f^\gamma(c'_0, \cdot)$ are plotted in Figure 11.9b, λ'_0 and μ'_0 being associated with c'_0 in the manner λ_0 and μ_0 were associated with c_0. Properties (ii) and (iii) of γ imply that $\lambda_0 \leq \lambda'_0 < \mu'_0 \leq \mu_0$. As the endowment E increases from 0 to $c_0 + c'_0$, the value of λ for which $f^\gamma(c_0, \lambda) + f^\gamma(c'_0, \lambda) = E$ increases from $\underline{\lambda}$ to $\bar{\lambda}$. Initially, as both graphs follow A, equal division of E prevails. At $\lambda = \lambda_0$, the graph of $f^\gamma(c_0, \cdot)$ becomes horizontal whereas that of $f^\gamma(c'_0, \cdot)$ is still rising, so claimant 2 receives the totality of each increment in E for a while. At $\lambda = \lambda'_0$, claimant 2's graph also becomes horizontal and remains so until $\lambda = \mu'_0$ whereas claimant 1's graph remains horizontal until $\lambda = \mu_0 > \mu'_0$. We have a "dead interval" $[\lambda'_0, \mu'_0]$ of values of λ in which both awards are constant. At $\lambda = \mu'_0$ the graph of $f^\gamma(c'_0, \cdot)$ starts rising again whereas that of $f^\gamma(c_0, \cdot)$ remains horizontal. Thus, once again, claimant 2 receives the totality of each increment in E and does so for a while. At $\lambda = \mu_0$, claimant 1's graph starts rising too. Since the parts of the two graphs that we now follow are vertical translates of the same curve (the curve B), both claimants receive equal shares of each increment in E. This goes on until both are fully compensated. Altogether, we have traced out the path of ICI^γ for (c_0, c'_0).

If $\gamma = e$, the horizontal segment in the schedule for c_0 meets the curve $B + \{(0, c_0)\}$ at $(\bar{\lambda}, c_0)$, so B is actually not used in determining the schedule for c_0 (the graph of $f^e(c_0, \cdot)$); then $ICI^\gamma = CEA$. If $\gamma = 0$, the horizontal segment in the schedule for c_0 (the graph of $f^0(c_0, \cdot)$) is contained in the horizontal axis; now, it is A that is not used and $ICI^\gamma = CEL$. If $\gamma = \frac{e}{2}$, the locus of the point of intersection of the horizontal segment of the schedule for c_0 (the graph of $f^{\frac{e}{2}}(c_0, \cdot)$) with $B + \{(0, c_0)\}$ as c_0 varies is the symmetric image of B with respect to the horizontal axis. For each $\theta \in [0, 1[$, if $\gamma \equiv \theta e$, then this locus is the symmetric image with respect to the horizontal axis of the curve obtained from B by a vertical homothetic transformation of ratio $\frac{\theta}{1-\theta}$; then $ICI^\gamma = T^\theta$ (the TAL rule of parameter θ defined in Subsection 2.2.3).

The family Γ is a convex family of functions, but the ICI* family itself is not a convex family of rules. However, it is closed under duality.

We are now ready for a characterization of the *consistent* ICI rules.[7]

Theorem 11.5 *The ICI* rules are the only ICI rules satisfying consistency.* identifying consistent ICI rules

Proof: Each ICI* rule is by definition an ICI rule. It is *consistent* because it is a Young rule and all such rules are.[8]

[7] Theorems 11.5 and 11.6 are due to Thomson (2008b).

[8] A direct proof of the *consistency* of the ICI* rules is as follows. Let $\gamma \in \Gamma$ and consider ICI^γ. Let $N \in \mathcal{N}$ and $(c, E) \in \mathcal{C}^N$. Suppose first that $E \leq \sum_N \gamma(c_i)$. Then there is $k \in \{0, \ldots, |N|\}$ such that each claimant $i \in N$ whose claim is one of the k smallest claims in c receives $\gamma(c_i)$ and all others receive equal amounts. Let $\tilde{N}$ be the first of these two sets. Let $N' \subset N$ and $\tilde{N}' \equiv N' \cap \tilde{N}$. The members of $\tilde{N}'$ have the smallest claims in N'. Let us assign to each $i \in \tilde{N}'$

Conversely, let S be a *consistent* ICI rule.

Step 1: There is a function $\gamma\colon \mathbb{R}_+ \mapsto \mathbb{R}_+$ such that the following holds. Let $N \in \mathcal{N}$ with $|N| = 2$ and $c \in \mathbb{R}^N_{++}$ have unequal coordinates. Then the common value of the coordinates of the lowest endpoint of the middle segment in the path of S for c is $\gamma(\min c_i)$.

Let $N \equiv \{1, 2, 3\}$ and $c \in \mathbb{R}^N_+$ be such that $0 < c_1 < c_2 < c_3$. Let Π_1, Π_2, and Π_3 be the paths of awards of S for (c_2, c_3), (c_1, c_3), and (c_1, c_2) respectively. By the projection implication of *consistency*, the projections of the path of S for c, Π, on each of the two-dimensional subspaces $\mathbb{R}^{\{1,2\}}$, $\mathbb{R}^{\{1,3\}}$, and $\mathbb{R}^{\{2,3\}}$, are Π_3, Π_2, and Π_1 respectively.

By definition of an ICI rule and since $0 < c_1 < c_2$, Π_3 contains a segment parallel to $\mathbb{R}^{\{2\}}$ – let us denote its endpoints k^1 and k^2, with $k^1 \leq k^2$ – and since $0 < c_1 < c_3$, Π_2 contains a segment parallel to $\mathbb{R}^{\{3\}}$ (Figure 11.10a). Let a_1 and b_1 be the first coordinates of these segments. We will show that $a_1 = b_1$.

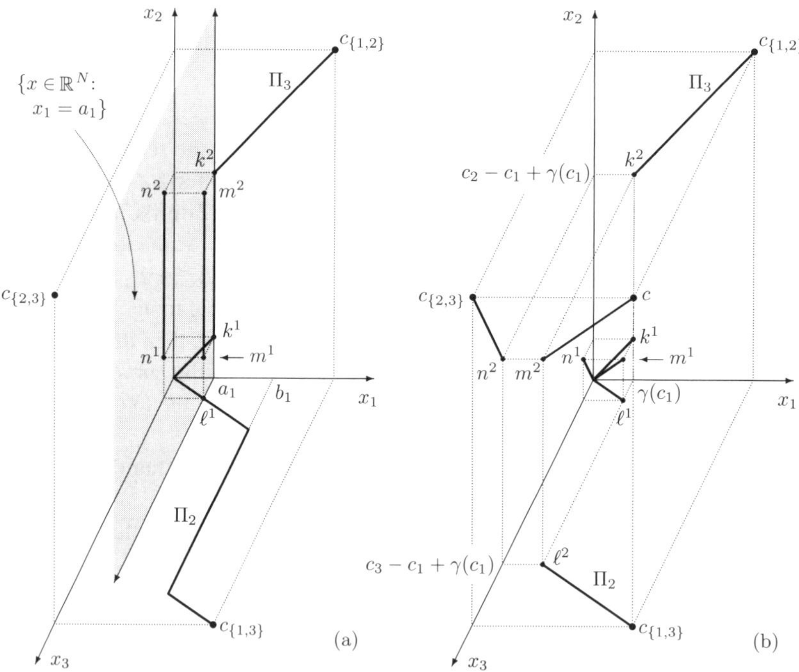

Figure 11.10: **Proof of Theorem 11.5.** (a) Step 1: deriving the existence of the function $\gamma\colon \mathbb{R}_+ \mapsto \mathbb{R}_+$. (b) Step 3: γ is nowhere decreasing, and so is $e - \gamma$.

the amount $\gamma(c_i)$ and to the others equal shares of what is left. The claimants in $N' \setminus \tilde{N}$ are the claimants in $N \setminus \tilde{N}$ and this common amount is what they had been assigned initially. The case $E > \sum \gamma(c_i)$ can be analyzed similarly.

Suppose by contradiction that $a_1 \neq b_1$. Consider the plane in $\mathbb{R}^N$ of equation $x_1 = a_1$. Its intersection with Π_3 is seg$[k^1, k^2]$ (Figure 11.10a) and its intersection with Π_2 is a singleton, denoted ℓ^1. (Figure 11.10a shows the case $a_1 < b_1$ but the argument is independent of whether $a_1 < b_1$ or $a_1 > b_1$.) Thus, Π contains the segment whose projection onto $\mathbb{R}^{\{1,2\}}$ is seg$[k^1, k^2]$ and whose projection onto $\mathbb{R}^{\{1,3\}}$ is ℓ^1. It is seg$[(a_1, k_2^1, \ell_3^1), (a_1, k_2^2, \ell_3^1)] \subset \mathbb{R}^N$ (seg$[m^1, m^2]$ in the figure). The projection of this segment onto $\mathbb{R}^{\{2,3\}}$ is a segment parallel to $\mathbb{R}^{\{2\}}$, seg$[(0, k_2^1, \ell_3^1), (0, k_2^2, \ell_3^1)]$ (seg$[n^1, n^2]$ in the figure). This segment has to belong to the path of S for (c_2, c_3). However, since $0 < c_2 < c_3$, the path of an ICI rule for (c_2, c_3) does not contain a segment parallel to $\mathbb{R}^{\{2\}}$. Thus, $a_1 = b_1$, as we asserted.

The ICI rules satisfy *equal treatment of equals* and S is *consistent*. Thus, by Lemma 10.9, S is *anonymous*. We now deduce the following. Let $N \in \mathcal{N}$ with $|N| = 2$, and $c \in \mathbb{R}^N_{++}$ have unequal coordinates. Then the common value of the coordinates of the lowest endpoint of the middle segment in the path of S for c is independent of who the larger claimant is (above, the larger claimant in (c_1, c_2) is claimant 2 and the larger claimant in (c_1, c_3) is claimant 3). Also, this common value is independent of who the smaller claimant is (there, for both (c_1, c_2) and (c_1, c_3), the smaller claimant is claimant 1). We have now established Step 1, which asserts the existence of a function $\gamma\colon \mathbb{R}_{++} \mapsto \mathbb{R}_+$ satisfying certain properties.

If one coordinate of c is 0 or both are 0, the path of S for c is degenerate. To cover this case, it suffices to extend the domain of definition of γ to the whole of $\mathbb{R}_+$ by setting $\gamma(0) \equiv 0$.

Step 2: The functions γ and $e - \gamma$ are nowhere decreasing. Also, $\gamma \leq e$. First, we show that γ is nowhere decreasing. Let $a, b \in \mathbb{R}_{++}$ be such $a < b$. Let $c \in \mathbb{R}^N_+$ be such that $c_1 = a$, $c_2 = b$, and $c_3 > c_2$. To show that $\gamma(a) \leq \gamma(b)$, we consider the claims vector $c \equiv (c_1, c_2, c_3)$ (Figure 11.10b). By Step 1, the path of S for (c_1, c_2) contains seg$[(0, 0), (\gamma(c_1), \gamma(c_1))]$ ($=$ seg$[(0, 0), k^1]$ on the figure) and its path for (c_1, c_3) contains seg$[(0, 0), (\gamma(c_1), \gamma(c_1))]$ ($=$ seg$[(0, 0), \ell^1]$). Thus, its path for c contains seg$[(0, 0, 0), (\gamma(c_1), \gamma(c_1), \gamma(c_1))]$ ($=$ seg$[(0, 0, 0), m^1]$), and thus, projecting onto $\mathbb{R}^{\{2,3\}}$, its path for (c_2, c_3) contains seg$[(0, 0), (\gamma(c_1), \gamma(c_1))]$ ($=$ seg$[(0, 0), n^1]$). By Step 1, and since $c_2 < c_3$, the path of S for (c_2, c_3) contains seg$[(0, 0), (\gamma(c_2), \gamma(c_2))]$ and it has a kink at $(\gamma(c_2), \gamma(c_2))$. These two conclusions can hold together only if $\gamma(c_2) \geq \gamma(c_1)$.

Next, we show that $e - \gamma$ is nowhere decreasing. The argument is similar to the one just made. The path of S for (c_1, c_2) contains seg$[(\gamma(c_1), c_2 - c_1 + \gamma(c_1)), (c_1, c_2)]$ ($=$ seg$[k^2, c_{\{1,2\}}]$ on the figure) and its path for (c_1, c_3) contains seg$[(\gamma(c_1), c_3 - c_1 + \gamma(c_1)), (c_1, c_3)]$ ($=$ seg$[\ell^2, c_{\{1,3\}}]$). Thus, its path for c contains seg$[(\gamma(c_1), c_2 - c_1 + \gamma(c_1), c_3 - c_1 + \gamma(c_1)), c]$ ($=$ seg$[m^2, c]$), and projecting onto $\mathbb{R}^{\{2,3\}}$, its path for (c_2, c_3) contains seg$[(c_2 - c_1 + \gamma(c_1), c_3 - c_1 + \gamma(c_1)), (c_2, c_3)]$ ($=$ seg$[n^2, c_{\{2,3\}}]$). By Step 1, and since $c_2 < c_3$, the path of S for (c_2, c_3) contains seg$[(\gamma(c_2), c_3 - c_2 + \gamma(c_2)), (c_2, c_3)]$

and it has a kink at $(\gamma(c_2), c_3 - c_2 + \gamma(c_2))$. These two conclusions can hold together only if $c_2 - \gamma(c_2) \geq c_1 - \gamma(c_1)$.

Step 3: Concluding. Steps 1 and 2 together imply that there is $\gamma \in \Gamma$ such that on the domain of two-claimant problems in which claims are unequal, $S = ICI^\gamma$. Since the ICI rules satisfy *equal treatment of equals*, this equality holds trivially for two-claimant problems in which claims are equal. By hypothesis, S is *consistent*, and since ICI^γ is *consistent* and *endowment monotonic*, it is *conversely consistent* (Lemma 10.5). Thus, by the Elevator Lemma (Lemma 10.8), $S = ICI^\gamma$ for any number of claimants. □

The TAL family is obtained if *homogeneity* is added to the requirements of Theorem 11.5.

A theorem parallel to Theorem 11.5 describes the implications of *consistency* for the CIC rules. Let $N \in \mathcal{N}$ and $c \in \mathbb{R}^N_+$. Again, we use the notation $n \equiv |N|$ and designate the vector in $\mathbb{R}^n_+$ obtained from c by listing its components in increasing order by $\tilde{c}$. The rules that emerge are indexed by the same object as the *consistent* ICI rules, namely a function in the class we denoted Γ (refer to the definition of the ICI* rules):

CIC* rule associated with $\gamma \in \Gamma$, CIC^γ: For each $N \in \mathcal{N}$ and each $c \in \mathbb{R}^N_+$, CIC^γ is the CIC rule whose component relative to N has parameters $(F^k(c), G^k(c))_{k=1}^{n-1}$ defined by $(F^k(c))_{k=1}^{n-1} \equiv (\gamma(\tilde{c}_n) - \gamma(\tilde{c}_{n-1}), \gamma(\tilde{c}_n) + \gamma(\tilde{c}_{n-1}) - 2\gamma(\tilde{c}_{n-2}), \ldots, \gamma(\tilde{c}_n) + \gamma(\tilde{c}_{n-1}) + \cdots + \gamma(\tilde{c}_2) - (n-1)\gamma(\tilde{c}_{n-1}))$, $(G^k(c))_{k=1}^{n-1}$ being obtained from $(F^k(c))_{k=1}^{n-1}$ by means of the CIC relations.

If $\gamma = 0$, $CIC^\gamma = CEA$; if $\gamma = e$, $CIC^\gamma = CEL$; and if $\gamma = \frac{e}{2}$, $CIC^\gamma = T^r$ (the reverse Talmud rule).

We have the following characterization, whose proof we omit:

identifying consistent CIC rules

Theorem 11.6 *The CIC* rules are the only CIC rules satisfying consistency.*

Adding *homogeneity* to the requirements of Theorem 11.6, we obtain the reverse TAL family. Figure 17.13 of Section 17.10 shows Young representations of a typical CIC* rule and of a *homogeneous* CIC* rule *(a reverse TAL rule).

11.2.4 Other Consistent Families

The issue of identifying, within a family of two-claimant rules, the ones that admit *consistent* extensions, and of describing these extensions, has been asked in other contexts. For instance, we have discussed averaging as a way of reaching compromises between different viewpoints. The proportional and constrained equal awards rules represent focal positions between which one may be interested in reaching such a compromise. The question then arises of whether and how this can be done in a way that is compatible with *consistency*.

There is not a single way of averaging, however. We have already encountered the one that consists in averaging, for each endowment, the awards vectors chosen by two rules. An alternative is as follows. Let $N \in \mathcal{N}$ with $|N| = 2$, and let $c \in \mathbb{R}^N_+$ be such that $c_1 < c_2$ say. Let $0 \leq x_1 \leq c_1$. A question we can ask about a rule is this: suppose that we have decided to assign x_1 to claimant 1. What award for agent 2 would "go" or "fit" with x_1? For someone who favors proportionality, the answer is $\frac{c_2}{c_1}x_1$. For someone who favors equality, the answer is $x_2 = x_1$ unless $x_1 = c_1$, in which case such a person would accept that claimant 2 be awarded more than claimant 1; in fact, any amount between x_1 and c_2 would have to be acceptable for someone holding this opinion. The compromise that we now propose is to average between the answers just described. Geometrically, and because $c_1 < c_2$, this amount to choosing as path of awards for c the vertical average of the paths of awards of the proportional and constrained equal awards rules. Of course, for $c_1 > c_2$, we would perform a horizontal average.[9]

An attractive compromise is one that is simple but flexible enough to accommodate the variability in opinions about the weights to place on one or the other of several viewpoints. Averaging is certainly simple and, for flexibility, we let the weights vary with the claims vector and depend on the identity of the two claimants. Let this be our point of departure, then, namely a family of two-claimant rules defined for each claims vector as averages of the proportional and constrained equal awards rules parallel to the axis along which the larger claim is measured, with the weights possibly depending on the claims vector. Now, what about extending this proposal to three claimants or more? To do so, we invoke *consistency*. The projection technique illustrated in the previous subsection can be invoked to answer this question but it turns out that a very small family of rules satisfies these properties.[10]

11.3 CONSISTENT EXTENSIONS OF TWO-CLAIMANT RULES THAT MAY NOT SATISFY EQUAL TREATMENT OF EQUALS

Here, we apply the technique developed in Section 11.1 to identify *consistent* extensions of two-claimant rules that may not satisfy *equal treatment of equals*. In particular, we ask when and how the weighted versions of concede-and-divide we encountered in Section 3.6 and characterized in Theorem 5.3 can be extended to more than two claimants. We also ask when and how a family of rules we characterized on the basis of *homogeneity* and the two main composition properties (Theorem 6.7) have such extensions. In each case, we find the existence of extensions to impose serious restrictions on the two-claimant rules we start from. We describe these restrictions and identify the resulting rules.

9 The discussion is taken from Moreno-Ternero and Thomson (2017) who propose yet other ways of defining compromises between two rules.

10 Thomson (2015b) identifies the subfamilies satisfying additional properties.

11.3.1 Generalizing the Talmud Rule by Not Insisting on Equal Treatment of Equals

We turn to the question raised in Section 3.6 of how to define generalizations of the Talmud rule that do not necessarily satisfy *equal treatment of equals*. We propose two approaches.

A first approach. We start from the requirement on the sought-after generalization that its two-claimant components coincide with weighted concede-and-divide rules (Figure 3.6). Indeed, as we argued earlier, these rules can be seen as legitimate generalizations of the two-claimant components of the Talmud rule that do not necessarily satisfy *equal treatment of equals*.[11] These generalizations are characterized in Theorem 5.3. We identify the only *consistent* rules satisfying the requirement other than the Talmud rule. We start with an informal description of a typical rule in the family they constitute.

First, we partition the population of potential claimants into reference ordered priority classes. We describe this partition by means of a binary relation on this population, each indifference class of the relation corresponding to a priority class. Second, for each component of the reference partition containing only two agents, we attach positive weights to them. These two objects, the partition and the list of weights, constitute the signature of the rule.

For each specific problem to be solved, the reference partition induces an ordered partition of the set of claimants who are actually present. We handle the components of this induced partition in succession, as discussed in Section 3.6. When the turn comes of a component of the induced partition that has two members and this component is actually a component of the reference partition, we apply the weighted concede-and-divide rule relative to the weights chosen for these claimants. However, when the turn comes of any other component of the induced partition, we apply the Talmud rule itself: this means that in fact we always treat symmetrically any two agents belonging to a component of the reference partition that has three claimants or more. This symmetric treatment conclusion applies in particular if the component of the induced partition has only two claimants but it is induced from a component of the reference partition that has more than two members. An example illustrating what to do is schematically represented in Figure 11.11. This conclusion highlights a serious limitation on what can be done to accommodate differences between claimants other than their claims if we have to respect *consistency*.

Here are the formal definitions. Let $\precsim$ be a complete and transitive binary relation on the set of potential claimants $\mathbb{N}$. For each $i \in \mathbb{N}$ who belongs to a

[11] The developments described in the following section are due to Hokari and Thomson (2003). They should be compared to results due to Orshan (1994) and Hokari (2000, 2005) pertaining to coalitional games (Chapter 14). These authors uncovered serious limitations in generalizing the prenucleolus so as to allow for a differential treatment of symmetric players and preserve a form of *consistency* formulated for that model on the basis of which this solution had been characterized.

	$w \in \text{int}\{\Delta^{\{8,10\}}\}$					
ref partition	… 7, 5, 3, 1}	{2, 4, 6}	{8, 10}	{12}	{14, 16, 18}	{20, 22, 24, …
induced partition	{5, 3, 1}	{2}	{8, 10}	{12}	{14, 16}	{20, 22, 24}
formula	T	X	CD^w	X	T	T

Figure 11.11: **A member of family $\mathcal{T}^1$.** Above the horizontal line are the data defining the rule. The reference partition of the set of potential claimants is just above the line, with the left-to-right order indicating decreasing priority. For each two-claimant component N of the partition, a vector $w \in \text{int}\{\Delta^N\}$ is specified. Below the line, we show how to apply the rule to a problem faced by the population $N \equiv \{1, 2, 3, 5, 8, 10, 12, 14, 16, 20, 22\}$. First, we calculate the partition of N induced by the reference partition: it is shown just below the line. We handle its components from left to right. The first one is $\{1, 3, 5\}$, (obviously) induced from a component of the reference partition with more than three claimants: we apply the Talmud rule. The second one is $\{2\}$, and for this trivial one-claimant population, there is only one rule, indicated by X (it is the rule that chooses the unique awards vector of each problem). Next is $\{8, 10\}$, induced from a two-claimant component of the reference partition: weights $w \in \text{int}\{\Delta^{\{8,10\}}\}$ have been specified for that class, so we apply the weighted concede-and-divide rule CD^w. Finally are $\{14, 16\}$ and $\{20, 22, 24\}$, both of which are induced from components of the reference partition containing at least three claimants: we apply the Talmud rule in both cases.

two-claimant indifference class of this relation, let $w_i > 0$ be a weight and let w be the list of the weights attached to all such claimants. Let $\mathcal{P}^1$ be the set of all pairs $(\preccurlyeq, w)$ obtained in this manner. In the example of Figure 11.11, only one component of the reference partition consists of exactly two claimants so the list w has only two coordinates.

Family $\mathcal{T}^1$ of sequential Talmud rules: [12] With each pair $(\preccurlyeq, w) \in \mathcal{P}^1$ is associated a member of the family, denoted $\boldsymbol{ST}^{\preccurlyeq, w}$, as follows. Given $N \in \mathcal{N}$ and $(c, E) \in \mathcal{N}$, the relation $\preccurlyeq$ is used to induce an ordered partition of N into classes to be handled in succession, nothing being given to any member of a class until all members of the previous class are fully compensated. Awards are calculated in one of three ways:

- One-claimant class: there is only one way to perform the division;
- Two-claimant class $\{i, j\}$ induced from a two-claimant component of the reference partition: the weighted concede-and-divide rule relative to the weights (w_i, w_j) specified for these two claimants is applied;
- Any other class (including any two-claimant class induced from a component of the reference partition with more than two claimants; also, any three-claimants-or-more induced class): the Talmud rule is applied.

[12] Note that our formal phrasing is a little different from our informal description. A third one could be given that involves lexicographic systems of weights.

The family $\mathcal{T}^1$ is closed under duality. We offer the following characterization:

sequential Talmud rules characterized

Theorem 11.7 *Suppose that S is a rule such that*

(∗) *for each pair* $\{i, j\} \in \mathcal{N}$, *there is a vector of weights* $(\alpha_{ij}, \alpha_{ji}) \in \Delta^{\{i,j\}}$ *such that* $S|_{\mathcal{C}^{\{i,j\}}} = CD^{(\alpha_{ij},\alpha_{ji})}$,

and that satisfies bilateral consistency. Then there is a reference ordered partition of the set of potential claimants – let $\preccurlyeq$ *be the complete and transitive binary relation on that set that describes it – such that for each pair* $\{i, j\} \in \mathcal{N}$,

(i) $(\alpha_{ij}, \alpha_{ji}) = (1, 0)$ *if and only if* $i \prec j$;
(ii) $(\alpha_{ij}, \alpha_{ji}) \in int\{\Delta^{\{i,j\}}\}$ *if and only if* $i \sim j$;
(iii) *if there is* $k \in \mathbb{N}\backslash\{i, j\}$ *such that* $i \sim j \sim k$, *then* $\alpha_{ij} = \alpha_{ji}$.

Moreover, $S = ST^{\preccurlyeq,w}$, *where for each two-claimant component of the partition induced by* $\preccurlyeq$, *and calling its two members i and j,* $(w_i, w_j) = (\alpha_{ij}, \alpha_{ji})$.

Conversely, for each $(\preccurlyeq, w) \in \mathcal{P}^1$, *the sequential Talmud rule* $ST^{\preccurlyeq,w} \in \mathcal{T}^1$ *satisfies condition* (∗) *and bilateral consistency. Here, for each pair* $\{i, j\} \in \mathcal{N}$, *the weights* $(\alpha_{ij}, \alpha_{ji})$ *are constructed from* $(\preccurlyeq, w)$ *by the formula*

$$(\alpha_{ij}, \alpha_{ji}) \equiv \begin{cases} (1, 0) & \text{if } i \prec j, \\ \left(\frac{w_i}{w_i+w_j}, \frac{w_j}{w_i+w_j}\right) & \text{if } i \sim j. \end{cases}$$

To prove Theorem 11.7, we establish four lemmas (Lemmas 11.1–11.4).

It is clear that each member of family $\mathcal{T}^1$ satisfies condition (∗). Next, we establish its *consistency*.

Lemma 11.1 *Each member of family* $\mathcal{T}^1$ *is consistent.*

Proof: Let $(\preccurlyeq, w) \in \mathcal{P}^1$. Let $N \in \mathcal{N}$, $(c, E) \in \mathcal{C}^N$, and $x \equiv ST^{\preccurlyeq,w}(c, E)$. We show that for each $N' \subset N$, $x_{N'} = ST^{\preccurlyeq,w}\left(c_{N'}, E - \sum_{N\backslash N'} x_i\right)$. By the definition of *consistency*, it is enough to suppose that $N' \equiv N\backslash\{j\}$ for some $j \in N$.

Let $(N^1, N^2, \ldots, N^K)$ be the ordered partition of N induced by $\preccurlyeq$. Let $\ell \in \{1, 2, \ldots, K\}$ be such that $j \in N^\ell$. For each $k \in \{1, 2, \ldots, K\}$, let E^k be the amount available to the members of N^k when its turn comes. For each $k \in \{1, 2, \ldots, K\}$ with $k \neq \ell$, let E'^k be the amount available to the members of N^k in $(c_{N'}, E - x_j)$. Also, if $N^\ell\backslash\{j\} \neq \emptyset$, let E'^ℓ be the corresponding amount for $N^\ell\backslash\{j\}$ in $(c_{N'}, E - x_j)$.

Clearly, for each $k < \ell$, $E'^k = E^k$. Thus, for each $k < \ell$, $x_{N^k} = ST^{\preccurlyeq,w}_{N^k}(c_{N'}, E - x_j)$.

First, suppose that $N^\ell = \{j\}$. Then $x_j = E^\ell$ and

$$E'^{(\ell+1)} = \min\left\{E - x_j - \left(\sum_{k=1}^{\ell} E^k - E^\ell\right), \sum_{i \in N^{\ell+1}} c_i\right\} = E^{\ell+1}.$$

Similarly, for each $k \geq \ell + 1$, $E'^k = E^k$. Thus, for each $k > \ell$, $x_{N^k} = ST^{\preccurlyeq,w}_{N^k}(c_{N'}, E - x_j)$.

Next, suppose that $|N^\ell| \geq 2$. By definition,

$$E'^\ell = \begin{cases} \min\{E - x_j, \sum_{i \in N^\ell \setminus \{j\}} c_i\} & \text{if } \ell = 1, \\ \min\{E - x_j - \sum_{k=1}^{\ell-1} E^k, \sum_{i \in N^\ell \setminus \{j\}} c_i\} & \text{if } \ell > 1. \end{cases}$$

Case 1: $x_j = c_j$. Then $E'^\ell = E^\ell - x_j$ and

$$E'^{(\ell+1)} = \min\left\{E - x_j - \left(\sum_{k=1}^{\ell} E^k - x_j\right), \sum_{i \in N^{\ell+1}} c_i\right\} = E^{\ell+1}.$$

Similarly, for each $k \geq \ell + 1$, $E'^k = E^k$.

Case 2: $x_j < c_j$. Then

$$E^\ell = \begin{cases} E & \text{if } \ell = 1, \\ E - \sum_{k=1}^{\ell-1} E^k & \text{if } \ell > 1. \end{cases}$$

Also, for each $k > \ell$, $E^k = 0$. Recall that for each $i \in N$, $x_i \leq c_i$. Thus,

$$\sum_{i \in N^\ell \setminus \{j\}} c_i \geq \sum_{i \in N^\ell \setminus \{j\}} x_i = E^\ell - x_j = \begin{cases} E - x_j & \text{if } \ell = 1, \\ E - x_j - \sum_{k=1}^{\ell-1} E^k & \text{if } \ell > 1. \end{cases}$$

This implies that $E'^\ell = E^\ell - x_j \leq \sum_{i \in N_\ell \setminus \{j\}} c_i$, and hence, for each $k > \ell$, $E'^k = E^k = 0$.

In both cases, $E'^\ell = E^\ell - x_j$ and for each $k > \ell$, $E'^k = E^k$. If $|N^\ell| \geq 3$, then by *consistency* of the Talmud rule, for each $i \in N^\ell \setminus \{j\}$, $x_i = T_i(c_{N^\ell}, E^\ell) = T_i(c_{N^\ell \setminus \{j\}}, E^\ell - x_j) = ST_i^{\preccurlyeq,w}(c_{N'}, E - x_j)$. If $N^\ell = \{i, j\}$, then $x_i = E^\ell - x_j = ST_i^{\preccurlyeq,w}(c_{N'}, E - x_j)$. Finally, for each $k > \ell$, since $E'^k = E^k$, we have $x_{N^k} = ST^{\preccurlyeq,w}_{N^k}(c_{N'}, E - x_j)$. □

The weighted concede-and-divide rules are *endowment monotonic*. Moreover, if a rule is *endowment monotonic for two claimants* and *bilaterally consistent*, it is *endowment monotonic* in general (Lifting Lemma 10.13). Thus, if a rule satisfies condition (∗) of Theorem 11.7 and *bilateral consistency*, it is *endowment monotonic*.

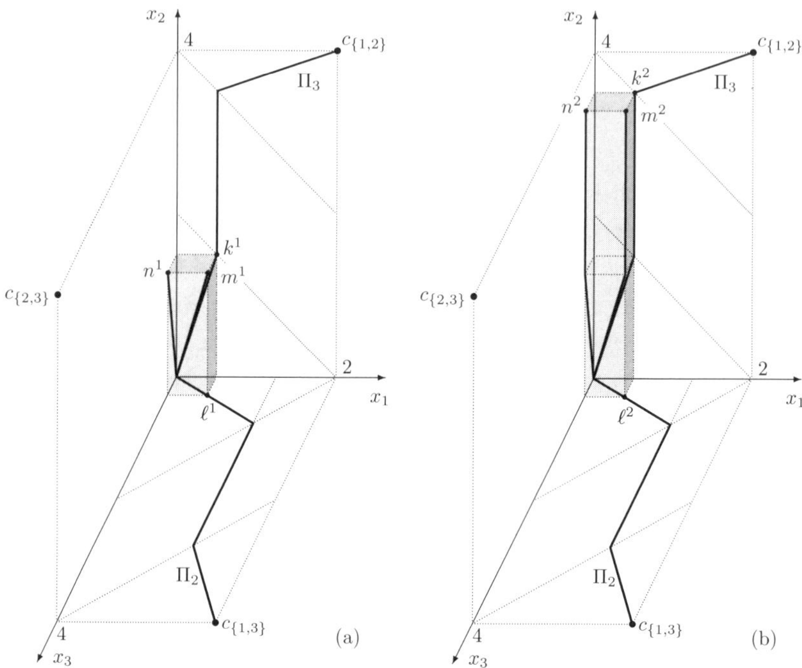

Figure 11.12: **Proof of Lemma 11.2(i); construction of Π.** These two panels show the construction of the first two segments of Π. (The path consists of five segments.)

Lemma 11.2 *Let S be a rule satisfying condition* $(*)$ *of Theorem 11.7 and bilateral consistency. Let* $N \equiv \{i, j, k\}$. *Then the weight vectors appearing in condition* $(*)$ *are such that:*

(i) *If* $\alpha_{ji}, \alpha_{jk} \notin \{0, 1\}$, *then* $\alpha_{ji} = \alpha_{jk}$.
(ii) *If* $\alpha_{ji} < 1$ *and* $\alpha_{jk} = 1$, *then* $\alpha_{ik} = 1$.

Proof:

(i) The proof is illustrated in Figure 11.12. for $N \equiv \{1, 2, 3\}$ and $c \in \mathbb{R}^N_+$ equal to $(2, 4, 4)$. The paths of awards of S for $c_{\{1,2\}}$ and $c_{\{1,3\}}$ are denoted Π_3 and Π_2. We assume by contradiction that the common value of the first coordinates of the two kinks of Π_3 is not equal to the common value of the first coordinates of the two kinks of Π_2. The two panels show how to construct the first two segments of the path for c of the unique (if there is one) *consistent* rule whose paths for $c_{\{1,2\}}$ and $c_{\{1,3\}}$ are Π_3 and Π_2. The three-dimensional path (not represented) has four kinks and so does its projection onto $\mathbb{R}^{\{2,3\}}$. This contradicts what we know of paths of awards in that space: they too have at most two kinks.
(ii) Suppose that $\alpha_{ji} < 1$ and $\alpha_{jk} = 1$, and to simplify notation, that $N = \{1, 2, 3\}$ so that $i = 1$, $j = 2$, and $k = 3$. Let $(c_1, c_2, c_3) \equiv$

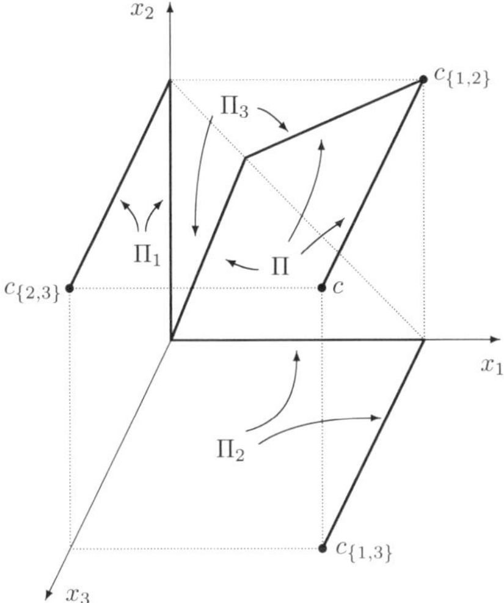

Figure 11.13: **Proof of Lemma 11.2(ii); relating the claimants' weights.**

$(1, 1, 1)$. Since $S(c, E)$ is nowhere decreasing and continuous in E, for some $E_1 > 0$, $S_1(c, E_1) + S_2(c, E_1) = 1$. By *bilateral consistency* and condition $(*)$, $\big(S_1(c, E_1), S_2(c, E_1)\big) = S((c_1, c_2), 1) = (\alpha_{12}, \alpha_{21})$. By *bilateral consistency*, $\big(S_2(c, E_1), S_3(c, E_1)\big) \in \Pi_1$. Thus, as indicated in Figure 11.13, $S_3(c, E_1) = 0$. By *bilateral consistency*, $(\alpha_{12}, 0) = (S_1(c, E_1), S_3(c, E_1)) \in \Pi_2$. Since $\alpha_{12} > 0$ and invoking condition $(*)$, we deduce that $\alpha_{13} = 1$. □

Lemma 11.2 essentially implies the existence of a weak order on $\mathbb{N}$ that is used in the definition of each sequential Talmud rule in $\mathcal{T}^1$.

Lemma 11.3 *Let S be a rule satisfying condition $(*)$ of Theorem 11.7 and bilateral consistency. Let $\preccurlyeq$ be the binary relation on $\mathbb{N}$ defined as follows: for each pair $\{i, j\} \in \mathcal{N}$, $i \preccurlyeq j$ if and only if $\alpha_{ij} > 0$. This relation satisfies the following two properties:*

(i) *$\preccurlyeq$ is complete and transitive.*
(ii) *If $i, j, k \in \mathbb{N}$ are distinct and $i \sim j \sim k$, then*

$$\alpha_{ij} = \alpha_{ji} = \alpha_{ik} = \alpha_{ki} = \alpha_{jk} = \alpha_{kj} = \frac{1}{2}.$$

Proof: We omit the obvious proof that $\preccurlyeq$ is complete, and only show that $\preccurlyeq$ is transitive. Let $i, j, k \in \mathbb{N}$ be such that $i \preccurlyeq j$ and $j \preccurlyeq k$. Then $\alpha_{ij} > 0$ and $\alpha_{jk} > 0$. We want to show that $\alpha_{ik} > 0$. Suppose, by contradiction, that $\alpha_{ik} = 0$. Then $\alpha_{ki} = 1$. By condition (ii) of Lemma 11.2, $\alpha_{kj} < 1$ and $\alpha_{ki} = 1$ imply $\alpha_{ji} = 1$, which contradicts $\alpha_{ij} > 0$. Thus, $\alpha_{ik} > 0$.

Next, let $i, j, k \in \mathbb{N}$ be distinct and such that $i \sim j \sim k$. Then, by the definition of $\preccurlyeq$,

$$\alpha_{ij}, \alpha_{ji}, \alpha_{ik}, \alpha_{ki}, \alpha_{jk}, \alpha_{kj} \notin \{0, 1\}.$$

By condition (i) of Lemma 11.2,

$$\alpha_{ij} = \alpha_{ji} = \alpha_{ik} = \alpha_{ki} = \alpha_{jk} = \alpha_{kj} = \frac{1}{2}. \qquad \square$$

At this point, we know that if a rule satisfies condition $(*)$ and *bilateral consistency*, then for two claimants, it coincides with a sequential Talmud rule in $\mathcal{T}^1$.

Lemma 11.4 *Each member of $\mathcal{T}^1$ is conversely consistent.*

Proof: Let $S \in \mathcal{T}^1$. Clearly, S satisfies condition $(*)$. By Lemma 11.1, S is *bilaterally consistent.* As mentioned just before Lemma 11.2, condition $(*)$ and *bilateral consistency* together imply *endowment monotonicity*. *Endowment monotonicity* and *bilateral consistency* together imply *converse consistency* (Lemma 10.5). $\square$

We are now ready to complete the proof of Theorem 11.7.

Proof: (of Theorem 11.7) We already know that for each $(\preccurlyeq, w) \in \mathcal{P}^1$, $ST^{\preccurlyeq, w}$ satisfies condition $(*)$ and *bilateral consistency*.

Conversely, let S be a rule satisfying these requirements. Let $\preccurlyeq$ denote the weak order defined in Lemma 11.3. For each $i \in \mathbb{N}$, let

$$w_i \equiv \begin{cases} \alpha_{ij} & \text{if there is } j \in \mathbb{N} \setminus \{i\} \text{ such that } \{h \in \mathbb{N} \mid h \sim i\} = \{i, j\}, \\ 1 & \text{otherwise.} \end{cases}$$

Then, by Lemma 11.3, S coincides with $ST^{\preccurlyeq, w}$ for two claimants. We conclude by invoking the Elevator Lemma. $\square$

Since each rule in $\mathcal{T}^1$ satisfies *homogeneity*, *claims truncation invariance*, and *minimal rights first*, we obtain the following corollary of Theorems 5.3 and 11.7.

Corollary 11.1 *The members of $\mathcal{T}^1$ are the only rules satisfying homogeneity, claims truncation invariance, minimal rights first, and consistency.*

A second approach. At the beginning of this section, we announced two approaches to the problem of defining generalizations of the Talmud rule that do not necessarily satisfy *equal treatment of equals*. We now turn to the second one. It is based on a different way of thinking of concede-and-divide, and of the asymmetric generalizations of this rule that we called "hybrid rules." The rules are illustrated in Figure 3.7. We have already discussed how to generalize the weighted constrained equal awards and constrained equal losses rules themselves so as to obtain *consistency* when the weights are positive. To allow for an extreme asymmetric treatment of claimants, we partition the population of potential claimants into priority classes and proceed as we did in our first approach.

If the starting point is the constrained equal awards rule, we apply the weighted constrained equal awards rule with weights proportional to the reference weights attached to the members of the class until each of them is fully compensated. If the starting point is the constrained equal losses rule, we proceed similarly. If the starting point is the hybrid of the two rules, we refer to the components of the reference partition of the set of potential claimants as "half-priority classes." For each problem, once again, we identify the partition of the set of claimants actually present induced by the reference partition. We start with the class with the highest half-priority and apply the weighted hybrid rule with weights proportional to the reference weights attached to its members until each of them receives half of their claim. Then we turn to the component of the induced partition that has the next highest half-priority, and apply the weighted hybrid rule with weights proportional to the reference weights attached to its members until each of them receives half of their claim, and so on. When each claimant has received half of their claim, we revisit each component of the partition, in the same order, and return to the corresponding hybrid rule – the rule with weights proportional to the reference weights attached to its members – and we do so until each of them is fully compensated. The formal definitions are given in Appendix 17.11.

The rules we identify admit generalized Young representations, as defined at the end of Section 3.6. We explained there how to construct such representations for weighted constrained equal awards rules, choosing for their domain of definition the entire set of nonnegative reals. We would instead look for a representation defined on a compact interval $[a, b]$. We would similarly construct generalized Young representations of weighted constrained equal losses rules, choosing as domain of definition a compact interval $[d, e]$ with $b = d$. Finally, we would piece these representations together, choosing as domain of definition of the combined function the interval $[a, e]$.

Consistent extensions of the weighted versions of Piniles' rule can be defined following the approach we just described.

11.3.2 Consistent Extensions of Two-Claimant Rules Satisfying Homogeneity, Composition Down, and Composition Up

In Section 6.2, we looked for two-claimant rules satisfying *homogeneity*, *composition down*, and *composition up*, but not necessarily *equal treatment of equals*. We uncovered a large family, which we denoted $\mathcal{D}$ (Theorem 6.7). In our present framework, in which the claimant set is variable, the implication of this theorem is that if a rule satisfies these axioms, then for each two-claimant population, it coincides with a member of $\mathcal{D}$. Thus, our starting point is a list

labels	P	weighted CEA	$S \in \mathcal{D}^{\{8,10\}}$		weighted CEL	weighted CEA
ref weights		$w_2\ w_4\ w_6$			$w_{14}\ w_{16}\ w_{18}$	$w_{20}\ w_{22}\ w_{24}\ \ldots$
ref partition	$\ldots\ 7,\ 5,\ 3,\ 1\}$	$\{2,\ 4,\ 6\}$	$\{8,\ 10\}$	$\{12\}$	$\{14,\ 16,\ 18\}$	$\{20,\ 22,\ 24,\ \ldots$
induced partition	$\{5,\ 3,\ 1\}$	$\{2\}$	$\{8,\ 10\}$	$\{12\}$	$\{14,\ 16\}$	$\{20,\ 22\}$
formula	P	X	S	X	CEL^{α}	CEA^{β}

Figure 11.14: **A member of family $\mathcal{M}$.** Above the horizontal line are the data defining the rule. The reference partition of the set of potential claimants is shown just above the line, with the left-to-right order indicating decreasing priority. To each two-claimant component N of this partition, a member of $\mathcal{D}^N$ is attached; to each component with more than two claimants, one of three labels is attached, P, weighted CEA, or weighted CEL; to each claimant who belongs to one of these components that is labeled either weighted CEA or weighted CEL, a positive weight is attached. We now show how to apply the rule to a problem faced by the population $N \equiv \{1, 2, 3, 5, 8, 10, 12, 14, 16, 20, 22\}$. First we calculate the partition of N induced by the reference partition; it is shown just below the line. We handle its components from left to right. The first one is $\{1, 3, 5\}$, induced from a component of the reference partition labeled "P": we apply the proportional rule. The second one is $\{2\}$, and for a one-claimant population, there is only one rule, indicated by X (it is the rule that chooses the unique awards vector of each problem). Next is $\{8, 10\}$, induced from a two-claimant component of the reference partition: we apply the two-claimant rule $S \in \mathcal{D}^{\{8,10\}}$ attached to that group. Next is $\{14, 16\}$, induced from a three-claimant component of the reference partition labeled "weighted CEL": we apply the weighted constrained equal losses rule with weights $\alpha \equiv (\frac{w_{14}}{w_{14}+w_{16}}, \frac{w_{16}}{w_{14}+w_{16}})$. Finally is $\{20, 22\}$, induced from a component of the reference partition labeled "weighted CEA": we apply the weighted constrained equal awards rule with weights $\beta \equiv (\frac{w_{20}}{w_{20}+w_{22}}, \frac{w_{22}}{w_{20}+w_{22}})$.

of members of $\mathcal{D}$ indexed by the two-claimant subsets of the set of potential claimants, and we now address two questions. What restrictions should such a list satisfy for it to have a *consistent* extension to general populations? When an extension exists, we know by Proposition 10.1 that it is unique because all members of $\mathcal{D}$ are *endowment monotonic*. But what is it? Theorem 11.8 below provides the answers. It identifies the lists of members of $\mathcal{D}$ that have *consistent* extensions, and for each such list, it describes the extension. The rules we obtain constitute the following family, a member of which being represented in Figure 11.14:[13]

Family $\mathcal{M}$: *Each member of this family is defined as follows. There is a reference ordered partition of the set of potential claimants into priority classes. To each two-claimant class is attached a member of $\mathcal{D}$. To each class with three or more claimants is attached one of the following three labels: (i) "P,"*

[13] Theorem 11.8 is due to Moulin (2000). The proof below follows Thomson (2013b).

(ii) "weighted CEA," a positive weight being specified for each member of the class, or (iii) "weighted CEL," again a positive weight being specified for each member of the class.

For each claims problem, the reference partition induces an ordered partition of the set of claimants involved in it. The components of this partition are handled in succession. Trivially, if the component coincides with a one-claimant class, there is only one way to allocate the endowment. If the component coincides with a two-claimant reference class, the two-claimant rule in $\mathcal{D}$ attached to that class is applied. If the component is induced from a three-or-more-claimants reference class, there are three cases, depending upon the label attached to the class:

- *Label is "P": the proportional rule is applied;*
- *Label is "weighted CEA": the weighted constrained equal awards rule with weights proportional to the weights attached to the claimants who are present is applied;*
- *Label is "weighted CEL": the weighted constrained equal losses rule with weights proportional to the weights attached to the claimants who are present is applied.*

The family $\mathcal{M}$ is closed under duality. This can be seen directly. It is also a consequence of the fact that it is characterized by a list of axioms that is invariant under duality.

Theorem 11.8 *The members of family $\mathcal{M}$ are the only rules satisfying homogeneity, composition down, composition up, and consistency.* consistent extensions of members of $\mathcal{D}$ characterized

The proof consists of another application of the technique developed in Section 11.1. Its structure is more involved than has been the case so far, but the logic of each step is similar. Consider a rule satisfying the axioms of the theorem. Let $N \in \mathcal{N}$ with $|N| = 3$, say $N \equiv \{1, 2, 3\}$ (the argument is the same for more agents), and let $c \in \mathbb{R}^N_+$. For most claims vectors c, we can uniquely determine the path of awards of the rule for c by exploiting the projection implication of *consistency* on only two two-dimensional subspaces, say $\mathbb{R}^{\{1,2\}}$ and $\mathbb{R}^{\{1,3\}}$. Projecting the path for c onto the third two-dimensional subspace, $\mathbb{R}^{\{2,3\}}$, should yield the path for the projection of c onto that subspace, $c_{\{2,3\}}$. Recalling that to each member of $\mathcal{D}$ is associated an oriented partition of award space, we identify those profiles of partitions of the awards spaces $\mathbb{R}^{\{1,2\}}$, $\mathbb{R}^{\{1,3\}}$, and $\mathbb{R}^{\{2,3\}}$ that allow a *consistent* extension to exist. We uncover the forbidden profiles of partitions by forcing two kinds of contradiction:

1. When the projection on $\mathbb{R}^{\{2,3\}}$ of the path for c is piecewise linear in two segments, these two segments "reveal" the directions of the boundary rays of a nondegenerate cone in the $\{2, 3\}$-partition. By performing the operation for some $c' \neq c$, we sometimes obtain a second cone that overlaps with the first cone. We then have an "overlap contradiction."

2. The path for c may have two kinks, neither one of which is lost in the projection onto $\mathbb{R}^{\{2,3\}}$. Since, for the members of family $\mathcal{D}$, a path can have at most one kink, we have a "two-kink contradiction."

Proof: (of Theorem 11.8) We omit the easy proof that the members of $\mathcal{M}$ satisfy the four properties listed in the theorem. (For the composition properties, this can be seen directly. It is also a consequence of the fact that they can are satisfied for two claimants and that, according to Lemma 10-13, they are lifted.) Conversely, let S be a rule satisfying these properties. The proof that $S \in \mathcal{M}$ is in four lemmas.

Lemma 11.5 *(Part 1 of the proof of Theorem 11.8) The population of potential agents is partitioned into priority classes to be handled in succession.*

Proof: Given $i, j \in \mathbb{N}$, we say that ***i* has priority over *j*** (for S), written as $i \prec j$, if for each $c \in \mathbb{R}_+^{\{i,j\}}$, the path of awards of S for c is bro.seg$[(0,0), (c_i, 0), c]$. If neither $i \prec j$ nor $j \prec i$, we write $i \sim j$. If either $i \prec j$ or $i \sim j$, we write $i \preceq j$.

Step 1: The relation $\preceq$ is complete and transitive. Completeness is trivial. For transitivity, it suffices to show that if $i \prec j$ and $j \preceq k$, then $i \prec k$. To fix the ideas, suppose that $i = 2$, $j = 1$, and $k = 3$. We need to show that $2 \prec 3$. Let $(c_2, c_3) \in \mathbb{R}_+^{\{2,3\}}$.

Case 1: 1 $\prec$ 3 (Figure 11.15a). Let $N \equiv \{1, 2, 3\}$. Let $c_1 > 0$ and $c \equiv (c_1, c_2, c_3)$. Then $\Pi_3 =$ bro.seg$[(0,0), (0, c_2), (c_1, c_2)]$ and $\Pi_2 =$

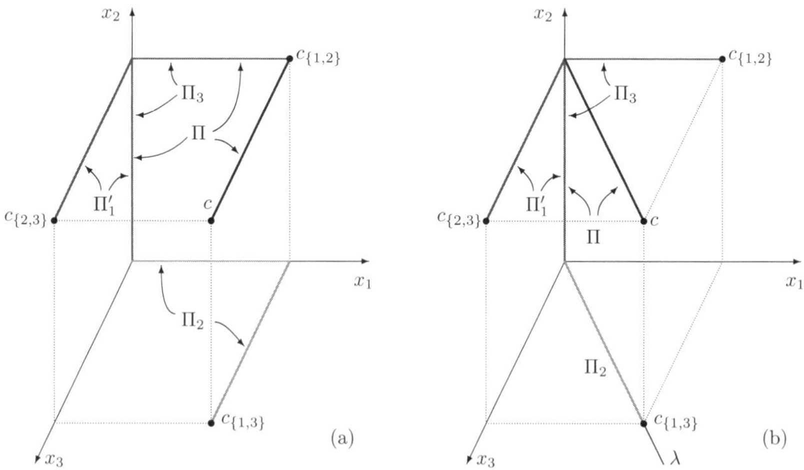

Figure 11.15: **Lemma 11.5: Partitioning the set of potential claimants into priority classes.** If agent 2 has priority over agent 1 and agent 3 does not have priority over agent 1, then agent 2 has priority over agent 3. In panel (a), agent 1 has priority over agent 3. In panel (b), agent 1 does not have priority (agents 1 and 3 are in the same priority class).

bro.seg$[(0,0),(c_1,0),(c_1,c_3)]$. Inspection of the figure reveals that the only path in $\mathbb{R}^N$ whose projections onto $\mathbb{R}^{\{1,2\}}$ and $\mathbb{R}^{\{1,3\}}$ are Π_3 and Π_2 respectively is bro.seg$[(0,0,0),(0,c_2,0),(c_1,c_2,0),c]$: by *bilateral consistency*, Π is this path.

Case 2: $1 \sim 3$ (Figure 11.15b). Since $1 \sim 3$, the $\{1,3\}$-partition contains at least one interior ray λ, and there is $c_1 \in \mathbb{R}_+$ such that $(c_1,c_3) \in \lambda$. Let $c \equiv (c_1,c_2,c_3)$. Thus, $\Pi_3 =$ bro.seg$[(0,0),(0,c_2),(c_1,c_2)]$ and $\Pi_2 =$ seg$[(0,0),(c_1,c_3)]$. Inspection of the figure reveals that the only path in $\mathbb{R}^N$ whose projections onto $\mathbb{R}^{\{1,2\}}$ and $\mathbb{R}^{\{1,3\}}$ are Π_3 and Π_2 respectively is bro.seg$[(0,0,0),(0,c_2,0),c]$: by *bilateral consistency*, Π is this path.

In either case, the projection Π'_1 of Π onto $\mathbb{R}^{\{2,3\}}$ is bro.seg$[(0,0),(c_2,0),(c_2,c_3)]$, which is the path of $SP^{2\prec 3}$ for (c_2,c_3). By *bilateral consistency*, $\Pi_1 = \Pi'_1$. This conclusion holds for each $(c_2,c_3) \in \mathbb{R}^{\{2,3\}}_+$. Thus, $2 \prec 3$.

Step 2: For each $N \in \mathcal{N}$, the components of the ordered partition of N induced by $\preceq$ should be handled in succession. To see this, suppose that there are $N \in \mathcal{N}$, $i, j \in N$, and $(c,E) \in \mathcal{C}^N$ such that $(*)$ $x_i < c_i$ and $x_j > 0$, where $x \equiv S(c,E)$. Let $N' \equiv \{i,j\}$. By *bilateral consistency*, $x_{N'} = S(c_{N'}, \sum_{N'} x_k)$. By $(*)$, it is not the case that $i \prec j$. □

Having partitioned the population of potential agents into priority classes, we now study each class separately. Obviously, there is only one rule for a one-claimant class. For that reason, for a two-claimant class, *consistency* has no bite; only the fixed-population axioms do and by Theorem 6.7 we know that we have to apply a member of family $\mathcal{D}$. Next, let $\tilde{N}$ be a class with three or more claimants. In fact, let us assume that $|\tilde{N}| = 3$ because, if $|\tilde{N}| > 3$, our conclusions extend by induction. Also, to simplify notation, we set $\tilde{N} \equiv \{1,2,3\}$. We identify the restrictions on the partitions associated with the two-claimant subsets of $\tilde{N}$ that are needed for the axioms to be satisfied.

Given a ray $\rho \in \mathbb{R}^{\{1,2\}}_+$ of direction (α_1,α_2) and a ray $\lambda \in \mathbb{R}^{\{1,3\}}_+$ of direction (β_1,β_3) such that $\alpha_2\beta_3 > 0$ and $\alpha_1\beta_1 > 0$, we designate by $\boldsymbol{d(\rho,\lambda)}$ the ray in $\mathbb{R}^{\{2,3\}}_+$ of direction $(\alpha_2\beta_1, \alpha_1\beta_3)$. (This is the ray obtained by projection onto $\mathbb{R}^{\{2,3\}}_+$ of the unique ray in $\mathbb{R}^N_+$ whose projections onto $\mathbb{R}^{\{1,2\}}$ and $\mathbb{R}^{\{1,3\}}$ are ρ and λ.) Recall that the notation $C(a,b)$ designates the oriented cone in which ray a is first and ray b is second.

We now return to the proof of Theorem 11.8. There are two possibilities, an easy one covered by Lemma 11.6 and a more complex one covered by Lemmas 11.7–11.8.

Lemma 11.6 *(Part 2 of the proof of Theorem 11.8) If, for each pair of claimants in $\tilde{N}$, the partition of their award space consists entirely of rays, then on $\bigcup_{N\subseteq\tilde{N}} \mathcal{C}^N$, $S = P$.*

Proof: The hypothesis is that $S = P$ on the subdomain of two-claimant problems. It follows directly from the *bilateral consistency* of S and the Elevator Lemma that S coincides with P on $\bigcup_{N\subseteq\tilde{N}} \mathcal{C}^N$. □

We relegate the proofs of the next two lemmas to an appendix (Section 17.12).

Lemma 11.7 *(Part 3 of the proof of Theorem 11.8) If there is a two-claimant group $\bar{N} \subset \tilde{N}$ such that the $\bar{N}$-partition contains a nondegenerate cone K, then, for each two-claimant group $N \subset \tilde{N}$ (including $\bar{N}$), the N-partition consists of exactly two nondegenerate cones and their boundary rays.*

The two nondegenerate cones of the partition of a two-dimensional awards space have a common boundary ray, which we call the **central direction** of the space.

Lemma 11.8 *(Part 4 of the proof of Theorem 11.8) Either (i) the central direction of each two-dimensional awards space is first for both cones, or (ii) it is second for both. Also, (iii) the central directions of the various two-dimensional awards spaces are consistent (they are all defined by projection of a single direction in the three-dimensional space).*

Concluding the proof of Theorem 11.8. Case (i) of Lemma 11.8 amounts to saying that for each two-claimant group $N \subset \tilde{N}$, S coincides on $\mathcal{C}^N$ with a weighted constrained equal awards rule, and (iii) implies that the weights attached to the two claimants in these groups are consistent (in the sense that they are derived from a single set of reference weights for the members of $\tilde{N}$). An application of the Elevator Lemma delivers a weighted constrained equal awards rule for $\tilde{N}$ relative to the weights just identified. Case (ii) of Lemma 11.8 together with (iii) leads to a weighted constrained equal losses rule instead. □

The order-preservation–constrained sequential priority rules introduced in the context of a fixed population are most naturally generalized to the variable-population case by using for each population the order induced by a single reference order on the set of potential claimants. It is easy to see that none of these rules is *consistent*. We had pointed out that their two-claimant versions belong to $\mathcal{M}$, and it follows from Theorem 11.8 that none of these two-claimant rules has a *consistent* extension.

11.4 FURTHER CHARACTERIZATIONS INVOLVING CONSISTENCY AND OTHER AXIOMS BUT NOT EQUAL TREATMENT OF EQUALS

In this section, we present other characterizations in which *consistency* plays a central role. They all involve additional invariance properties but *equal treatment of equals* is not imposed. In each of these characterizations, the axioms are independent but we will skip the verification of this fact.

(a) **Adding claims truncation invariance and composition up.** Our first theorem differs from Theorem 11.8 is that *composition down* and *homogeneity* are dropped but *claims truncation invariance* added. As was the case then, no symmetry requirement is imposed, and once again, the rules that come out are based on specifying an ordered partition of the set of potential claimants, and for each component of the partition, a rule for which no agent is given priority over any other agent. (This does not mean that the members of a class are put on the same level, however.) When each component consists of a single agent, we obtain a sequential priority rule. For a component that has more than one member, a weighted constrained equal awards formula has to be applied. That is the entire family.[14]

The proof does not have the structure of the proofs presented in the previous sections, in which the implications for two claimants of a list of axioms that do not involve *consistency* are first derived, the questions addressed in a second step being whether *consistent* extensions of these two-claimant rules exist, and if yes, what these extensions look like. Here, *consistency* is invoked throughout.

Important notation: We use the symbol $*$ to indicate the composite nature of the rules characterized in the theorems of this section.

Family of sequential-priority$*$weighted-constrained-equal-awards composites: *Each member of this family is defined as follows. There is a reference ordered partition of the set of potential claimants into priority classes. For each claimant who is not the single member of a priority class, a positive weight is specified.*

For each claims problem, the reference partition induces an ordered partition of the set of claimants involved in it. The components of this partition are handled in succession. For each component, the weighted constrained equal awards rule relative to the weights attached to its members is applied.

Theorem 11.9 *The sequential-priority$*$weighted-constrained-equal-awards composites are the only rules satisfying claims truncation invariance, composition up, and bilateral consistency.* sequential-priority$*$weighted constrained equal awards composites characterized

(b) **Adding contraction invariance.** In addition to *bilateral consistency*, what unites the next three theorems is the imposition of *contraction invariance*.[15] The first one is a characterization of the monotone path rules introduced in Section 6.1 for fixed populations and generalized in Section 10.2 to variable populations:

[14] Theorem 11.9 is due to Flores-Szwagrzak (2015). In this theorem, weakening *claims truncation invariance* to *weak claims truncation invariance* does not affect the conclusion (Flores-Szwagrzak and Treibich, 2016).

[15] Theorems 11.10–11.12 are due to Stovall (2014b). Because of the alternative representation, stated after Theorem 11.10, of a monotone path rule as resulting from the maximization of an objective function satisfying certain properties, he calls them "collectively rational additively separable rules." For another characterization, see Martínez (2008). Further results are due to Stovall (2018).

monotone path rules characterized

Theorem 11.10 *The monotone path rules are the only rules satisfying endowment monotonicity, contraction invariance, and bilateral consistency.*

A counterpart of Theorem 10.10 holds. It says that a monotone path rule can be equivalently defined as follows: for each $i \in \mathbb{N}$, there is a function $U_i : \mathbb{R}_+ \mapsto \mathbb{R}$ that is continuous and strictly concave, and such that for each $N \in \mathcal{N}$ and each $(c, E) \in \mathcal{C}^N$, the choice made for (c, E) is obtained by maximizing the expression $\sum_{i \in N} U_i(x_i)$ over the set of awards vectors $x \equiv (x_i)_{i \in N}$ of (c, E). We noted earlier that these rules have generalized Young representations.

In the next theorem, we add the *dual of contraction invariance* to the axioms of Theorem 11.10. Only the sequential priority rules survive:

sequential priority rules characterized

Theorem 11.11 *The sequential priority rules are the only rules satisfying endowment monotonicity, contraction invariance, its dual, and bilateral consistency.*

If instead, we add *equal treatment of equals* to the axioms of Theorem 11.10, the constrained equal awards rule emerges and nothing else:

constrained equal awards rule characterized

Theorem 11.12 *The constrained equal awards rule is the only rule satisfying equal treatment of equals, endowment monotonicity, contraction invariance, and bilateral consistency.*

(c) **Adding a conditional form of endowment additivity.** A central axiom in the next three theorems is the conditional form of *endowment additivity* obtained by limiting its applications to situations in which each claimant experiences a positive loss for the sum problem. In Section 8.3 we referred to it as *positive-losses-in-the-sum-problem–conditional endowment additivity*.

To describe the result, we need to define a family of rules that generalize both the weighted constrained equal awards rules and the weighted proportional rules. Given $u : \mathbb{R}^N_+ \mapsto \mathbb{R}^N_+$ such that for each $i \in N$, $u_i(c) = 0$ only if $c_i = 0$, the **directional rule associated with *u*** is the rule defined as follows: given $c \in \mathbb{R}^N_+ \setminus \{0\}$, the path of awards for c is obtained by moving (in a straight line) in the direction $u(c)$ until some claimant is fully compensated, then moving in the subspace that does not include that claimant in the direction of the projection of $u(c)$ onto that subspace until someone else is fully compensated, and so on. If more than one claimant reach full compensation at the same time, they drop out together.

A subfamily is obtained by requiring that the function that is applied to determine the direction of movement be separable. This requirement can be expressed by specifying, for each $i \in \mathbb{N}$, a function $u_i : \mathbb{R}_+ \mapsto \mathbb{R}_+$ that is strictly positive on $\mathbb{R}_{++}$, and setting, for each $(c, E) \in \mathcal{C}^N$, $u(c) \equiv$

$(u_i(c_i))_{i \in \mathbb{N}}$. Let us refer to this subfamily as the **separable directional rules.**[16]

When all the u_is are equal, the resulting rule satisfies *equal treatment of equals*. when they are linear, we obtain a weighted proportional rule; when they are equal to the identity function, the proportional rule; when they are constant, a weighted constrained equal awards rule; when these constants are equal, the constrained equal awards rule.

The generalizations of the separable directional rules to our variable-population model defined next involve partitioning the population of potential claimants into priority classes, and within each class, applying a separable directional rule.

Family of sequential-priority∗separable-directional composite rules: *Each member of this family is defined as follows. There is a reference ordered partition of the set of potential claimants into priority classes. For each claimant who is not the single member of a priority class, a function defined on* $\mathbb{R}_+$ *and taking its values in* $\mathbb{R}_+$ *but is strictly positive on* $\mathbb{R}_{++}$ *is specified.*

For each claims problem, the reference partition induces an ordered partition of the set of claimants involved in it. The components of this partition are handled in succession. For each component, the separable directional rule relative to the functions associated with its members is applied.

Theorem 11.13 *The sequential-priority∗separable-directional composite rules are the only rules satisfying endowment continuity, positive-losses-in-the-sum-problem–conditional endowment additivity, and consistency.* sequential-priority∗ separable-directional composites

Weakening *consistency* to *full compensation consistency* in Theorem 11.13 enlarges the family of acceptable rules significantly but a characterization is still possible. We omit the description of the additional rules that qualify. composites characterized

Moving in the opposite direction, let us instead add to the axioms of Theorem 11.13 *minimal sharing* (recall that this is the requirement that if two agents have positive claims, neither claimant be fully compensated if the other receives nothing). Then the only rules that remain acceptable are those for which all claimants belong to a single priority class.

Alternatively, let us add *equal treatment of equals* and *claims truncation invariance*. Only one rule survives, even if *endowment continuity* is dropped:

Theorem 11.14 *The constrained equal awards rule is the only rule satisfying equal treatment of equals, positive-losses-in-the-sum-problem–conditional endowment additivity, claims truncation invariance, and consistency.* constrained equal awards rule characterized

[16] The subfamily is introduced by Harless (2017a) under the name of "weighted proportional rule." Theorems 11.13–11.15 are due to him. It bears some similarity to a family of population monotonic bargaining solutions defined by Thomson (1996), a family that simultaneously generalizes the egalitarian and Kalai–Smorodinsky solutions.

The final results involving *positive-losses-in-the-sum-problem–conditional endowment additivity* are two characterizations of the proportional rule.

proportional rule characterized

Theorem 11.15 *The proportional rule is the only rule satisfying*

(i) positive-losses-in-the-sum-problem–conditional endowment additivity, self-duality, and null claims consistency;
(ii) minimal sharing, positive-losses-in-the-sum-problem–conditional endowment additivity, and null claims consistency.

(d) **Adding one or the other of two conditional forms of full additivity.** Our last theorems in this chapter involve conditional forms of *full additivity*. The first one is a characterization of the family of rules obtained by first specifying an ordered partition of the set of potential claimants and for each component of the partition in turn, operating the proportional rule. Thus, within each class, *equal treatment of equals* is satisfied. This is almost as in Theorem 11.7, which states that a certain list of axioms that does not include *equal treatment of equals* can be satisfied only if extreme violations of this axiom occur, as reflected in the partitioning of the set of potential claimants into priority classes, but that within each class induced from a reference class with at least three claimants, the axiom is in fact satisfied. Thus, the only nontrivial and non-extreme violations of the axiom are for classes in the induced partition that coincide with reference classes consisting of exactly two claimants. Here is the formal definition of the rules:

Family of sequential-priority∗proportional composite rules: *Each member of this family is defined as follows. There is a reference ordered partition of the set of potential claimants into priority classes.*

For each claims problem, the reference partition induces an ordered partition of the set of claimants involved in it. The components of this partition are handled in succession. For each component, the proportional rule is applied.

We remind the reader that the positive-losses–conditional qualification attached to the invariance property listed in the next theorem refers to the requirement that the awards vector chosen for the initial problem appearing in the hypotheses be strictly dominated by the claims vector.[17]

sequential-priority∗proportional composites characterized

Theorem 11.16 *The sequential-priority∗proportional composite rules are the only rules satisfying continuity, positive-losses–conditional proportional-increase-in-claims invariance, equal-claims-vectors-and-positive-awards–conditio full additivity, and bilateral consistency.*

These rules are almost universally used in practice, but this theorem is the only characterization they have been given.

[17] Theorem 11.16 is due to Flores-Szwagrzak, Garcia-Segarra, and Ginés-Vilar (2017a).

Our last theorem is a characterization of the following family:

Family of sequential-priority∗weighted-constrained-equal-losses composite rules: *Each member of this family is defined as follows. There is a reference ordered partition of the set of potential claimants into priority classes. For each claimant who is not the single member of a priority class a positive weight is specified.*

For each claims problem, the reference partition induces an ordered partition of the set of claimants involved in it. The components of this partition are handled in succession. For each component, the weighted constrained equal losses rule relative to the weights attached to its members is applied.

The characterization is based on another conditional form of *full additivity*, the conditioning being on the awards vectors chosen for the problems that are added being positive vectors. We designate it by adding the positive-awards–conditional qualification to *full additivity*.[18]

Theorem 11.17 *The sequential-priority∗weighted-constrained-equal-losses composite rules are the only rules satisfying endowment monotonicity, (alternatively continuity), positive-awards–conditional full additivity, and bilateral consistency.*

sequential-priority∗ weighted constrained equal losses composites characterized

Only one of the axioms in this theorem is not *self-dual*, *positive-losses–conditional full additivity*. Its dual requires additivity only if the vectors of losses of the component problems are both positive. The dual of the theorem says that the sequential-priority∗weighted-constrained equal awards composite rules are the only rules satisfying *endowment monotonicity* (alternatively *continuity*), *positive-losses–conditional full additivity*, and *bilateral consistency*.

[18] Theorem 11.17 is due to Flores-Szwagrzak, Garcia-Segarra, and Ginés-Vilar (2017b).

CHAPTER 12

Variable-Population Model: Other Properties

In this chapter, we complete the analysis of the variable-population version of our model and study a range of monotonicity and invariance properties of rules in this context. We start with a monotonicity requirement pertaining to variations in populations, which is motivated by solidarity considerations. We continue with invariance requirements with respect to merging claims on the one hand and with respect to splitting claims on the other hand. Their underpinnings are mainly strategic and they would also fit well in the chapter devoted to the game-theoretic analysis of claims problems (Chapter 14), but as they involve changes in the set of active agents, they also have a natural place in the current chapter. The next requirement involves replicating problems – it is an invariance requirement with respect to such operations – and it gives insights into the behavior of rules when there are a large number of claimants whose claims are small in relation to aggregate claim. We close with the formulation of several properties having to do with simultaneous variations in several parameters of a claims problem. These too emerge out of solidarity considerations.

12.1 POPULATION MONOTONICITY AND RELATED PROPERTIES

• The monotonicity requirement that is most relevant in the context of a variable population is that if new claimants arrive whose claims are determined to be just as valid as those of the claimants initially present, each of the latter receive at most as much as initially. Equivalently, if some claimants leave but there still is not enough to honor all of the remaining claims, each remaining claimant should receive at least as much as initially (Figure 12.1):[1]

Population monotonicity: For each $N \in \mathcal{N}$, each $(c, E) \in \mathcal{C}^N$, and each $N' \subset N$, if $\sum_{N'} c_i \geq E$, then $S(c_{N'}, E) \geqq S_{N'}(c, E)$.

[1] The first axiomatizations based on this property, in the context of bargaining, are due to Thomson (1983a,b). For a survey of the literature devoted to its study, see Thomson (1995a).

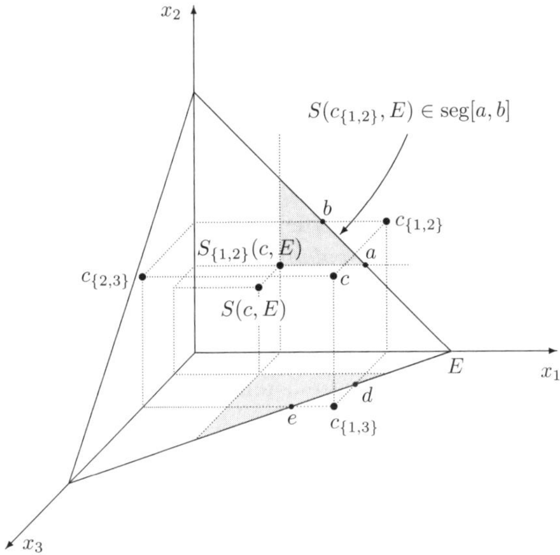

Figure 12.1: **Population monotonicity.** We consider a rule S. Let $N \equiv \{1, 2, 3\}$ and $(c, E) \in \mathcal{C}^N$. *Population monotonicity* requires that S assign to each member of $\{1, 2\}$ at least as much in $(c_{\{1,2\}}, E)$, the problem obtained from (c, E) by removing claimant 3, as it does in (c, E): $S(c_{\{1,2\}}, E) \geqq S_{\{1,2\}}(c, E)$. Thus, $S(c_{\{1,2\}}, E)$ should be in the shaded triangle in $\mathbb{R}^{\{1,2\}}$. To obtain an awards vector, the choice is further limited to seg$[a, b]$. Now, imagine instead that claimant 2 were removed. Then, for the problem $(c_{\{1,3\}}, E)$, S should choose an awards vector confined to the shaded triangle in $\mathbb{R}^{\{1,3\}}$, and then to seg$[e, d]$. Finally, if claimant 1 were removed, the endowment would be sufficient to honor the claims of agents 2 and 3, so nothing would be required of the projection of $S(c, E)$ onto $\mathbb{R}^{\{2,3\}}$. (The pair $(c_{\{2,3\}}, E)$ is not a claims problem.)

Comparing the choices made for (c, E) and $(c_{N'}, E)$ is possible only if the pair $(c_{N'}, E)$ is a well-defined problem, namely if $\sum_{N'} c_i \geq E$, which is the reason for this proviso in the statement of the property. Figure 12.1 illustrates the possibility that it may not be, when the initial population is $\{1, 2, 3\}$ and agent 1's claim is removed: indeed, the projection of c onto $\mathbb{R}^{\{2,3\}}$ is below the line of equation $x_2 + x_3 = E$.

* `Relating axioms` ♦ If some agents have claims equal to 0, by the *nonnegativity* of a rule, they receive 0. If they leave, *population monotonicity* and *balance* together imply that each of these claimants should receive the same amount as initially. This is also the requirement that we introduced earlier under the name of *null claims consistency*.[2] ♦ *Null claims*

[2] Thus, this property could also be called "null claims population monotonicity," but we will not use this expression.

other-regarding claim monotonicity and *null claims consistency* together imply *population monotonicity*. Indeed, let $N \in \mathcal{N}$, $(c, E) \in \mathcal{C}^N$, and $N' \subset N$. Then $S(c_{N'}, E) = S_{N'}((c_{N'}, 0_{N \setminus N'}), E) \geqq S_{N'}(c, E)$, where the first equality is by *null claims consistency* and the second one by *null claims other-regarding claim monotonicity*. This is the inequality required by *population monotonicity*.

Like all of the monotonicity properties that we formulated for the fixed-population version of the model, *population monotonicity* is very weak: most of the rules that have been studied in the literature satisfy it. It is the case of all of Young's rules, as well of the random arrival and minimal overlap rules. Some rules of interest do not, however. For instance, the rule defined by operating the constrained equal awards rule from minimal rights fails the test. Indeed, consider the marriage contract problem of the Talmud, in which $N \equiv \{1, 2, 3\}$ and $c \equiv (100, 200, 300)$, when the endowment is 300. Figure 9.4b shows that claimant 1 is fully compensated then. But if claimant 2 were not present, the problem to be solved would be $((100, 300), 300) \in \mathcal{C}^{\{1,3\}}$, for which the rule chooses $(50, 250)$ (for two claimants, the rule coincides with concede-and-divide, and when the endowment is larger than the half-sum of the claims, which would be the case then, it imposes equal losses on both claimants). Claimant 1's award would be smaller than in the initial three-claimant problem.

Next, we inquire whether our operators preserve *population monotonicity*. Our first result, which concerns the duality operator, is negative.[3]

Proposition 12.1 *Population monotonicity is not preserved under duality.*

The proof is relegated to an appendix (Section 17.13). We exhibit there a rule that is *population monotonic* whereas its dual is not. The rule is *anonymous*, *homogeneous*, and *endowment monotonic*. Since *endowment monotonicity* implies *endowment continuity,* it is also *endowment continuous* (in fact, it is fully *continuous*). Thus, these properties do not help the duality operator preserve *population monotonicity*.

The dual of *population monotonicity* is the requirement that if new claimants arrive and the endowment increases by the sum of their claims, then each claimant initially present receive at least as much as initially. Indeed, in the notation used in the definition of *population monotonicity*, the statement that for each $i \in N'$ and each $E \in [0, \sum_{N'} c_i]$, we have $S_i(c_{N'}, E) \geq S_i(c, E)$, is equivalent to the statement that for each $i \in N'$ and each $E \in [0, \sum_{N'} c_j]$, we have $c_i - S_i^d(c_{N'}, \sum_{N'} c_j - E) \geq c_i - S_i^d(c, \sum_N c_j - E)$. Canceling out c_i from both sides and letting $F \equiv \sum_{N'} c_j - E$, we derive that for each $i \in N'$ and each $F \in [0, \sum_{N'} c_j]$, we have $S_i^d(c_{N'}, F) \leq S_i^d(c, F +$

[3] Proposition 12.1 is due to Thomson and Yeh (2008).

$\sum_{N \setminus N'} c_j$). Let us introduce the property formally, returning to our usual notation:[4]

Linked endowment-population monotonicity: For each $N \in \mathcal{N}$, each $(c, E) \in \mathcal{C}^N$, and each $N' \subset N$, if $\sum_{N'} c_i \geq E$, we have $S(c_{N'}, E) \leqq S_{N'}(c, E + \sum_{N \setminus N'} c_j)$.

• A strict version of *population monotonicity*, parallel to the ones we offered for other monotonicity requirements, says that, in addition, if the claim of at least one departing claimant is positive and so is the endowment, each of the remaining claimants whose claim is positive should receive more:

Strict population monotonicity: For each $N \in \mathcal{N}$, each $(c, E) \in \mathcal{C}^N$, and each $N' \subset N$, if $\sum_{N'} c_j \geq E$, then $S(c_{N'}, E) \geqq S_{N'}(c, E)$ and if $\sum_N c_j > \sum_{N'} c_j$, then for each $i \in N'$ such that $c_i > 0$, $S_i(c_{N'}, E) > S_i(c, E)$.

This implies that at least one of the departing agents is assigned a positive amount in the initial problem. A conditional variant of this property is obtained by writing its conclusion only *if* that is the case.

Like many of the strict versions of our previous monotonicity properties, *strict population monotonicity* is considerably more demanding than *population monotonicity* itself. Obviously, the proportional rule satisfies it, however. So does the minimal overlap rule, an assertion whose proof we omit.

On the other hand, the Talmud rule, which is *population monotonic*, is not *strictly* so. To see this, let $N \equiv \{1, 2, 3\}$ and $(c, E) \in \mathcal{C}^N$ be equal to $((20, 100, 200), 125)$. Then $T(c, E) = (10, 50, 65)$. Let $N' \equiv \{2, 3\}$. We have $T(c_{N'}, E) = (50, 75)$: claimant 2's award is unaffected by the departure of claimant 1. Note that claimant 1's initial award is positive, so the conditional variant of the property is not met either.

• Since there is no way in which someone who is fully compensated could get more after the departure of some claimants, another conditional variant of *strict population monotonicity* is obtained by applying its conclusion only to agents whose initial awards are not equal to their claims (this implies of course that any such agent has a positive claim). This property is satisfied much more generally. For example, the constrained equal awards rule passes this test of intermediate strength between *population monotonicity* and *strict population monotonicity*. However, the example just given to show that the Talmud rule is not *strictly population monotonic* also shows that it violates the variant just defined.

∗ Relating axioms ♦ The following observation relates *consistency* and two properties involving changes in the endowment, in the population, and in both: If a rule is *endowment monotonic* and *consistent*, it is *population*

[4] It appears in Thomson and Yeh (2001, 2008) and Grahn and Voorneveld (2002).

monotonic and *linked endowment-population monotonic*. Each of these two implications is easily obtained directly. Also, each of them can be derived from the other by noting that the two properties imposed as hypothesis are preserved under duality, and that *population monotonicity* and *linked endowment-population monotonicity* are dual properties.

Concerning the other operators, we offer two positive results and two negative ones:

Proposition 12.2 *Population monotonicity is preserved by the claims truncation and convexity operators. It is not preserved by the attribution of minimal rights operator nor is it preserved by the composition of the claims truncation and attribution of minimal rights operators.*

Proof: We omit the straightforward proofs of the first two assertions. For the attribution of minimal rights operator, we use the constrained equal awards rule, and note that, soon after the formal introduction of *population monotonicity*, we use the constrained equal awards rule operated from minimal rights to illustrate a violation of *population monotonicity*. This rule is *claims truncation invariant*. To establish the remaining assertion, the constrained equal awards rule can also be used. □

By duality, it follows from Proposition 12.2 that *linked endowment-population monotonicity* is preserved by both the attribution of minimal rights and the convexity operators, but not by the claims truncation operator nor by the composition of the claims truncation and attribution of minimal rights operators.

We continue with further expressions of the order preservation idea, this time in response to variations in populations. First, when population decreases, of two remaining claimants, the award to the smaller claimant should increase by at most as much as the award to the larger claimant (this is equivalent to a similar inequality about the losses they incur):

Order preservation under population variations: For each $N \in \mathcal{N}$, each $(c, E) \in \mathcal{C}^N$, each $N' \subset N$, and each pair $\{i, j\} \subseteq N'$, if $\sum_{N'} c_k \geq E$ and $c_i \leq c_j$, then $S_i(c_{N'}, E) - S_i(c, E) \leq S_j(c_{N'}, E) - S_j(c, E)$.

A more demanding variant of the property, **strict order preservation under population variations**, is obtained by requiring in addition that if $c_i < c_j$ (and of course if $E > 0$), then the inequality appearing in the conclusion be strict as well.

The dual of *order preservation under population variations* says that if an increase in the population of claimants is accompanied by an increase in the endowment equal to the sum of the claims of the new claimants, then given two claimants initially present, the award to the smaller one should increase by at most as much as the award to the larger one.

Versions for groups of these properties can be defined. For instance, when population decreases, of two groups of remaining claimants, the aggregate award to the group with the smaller aggregate claim should increase by at most as much as the aggregate award to the group with the larger aggregate claim. This is equivalent to writing a parallel inequality on the aggregate losses incurred by the two groups. (We omit the strict form of the property.)

Group order preservation under population variations: For each $N \in \mathcal{N}$, each $(c, E) \in \mathcal{C}^N$, each $N' \subset N$, and each pair $\{N'', N'''\} \subseteq N'$, if $\sum_{N''} c_i \leq \sum_{N'''} c_i$, then $\sum_{N''}[S_j(c_{N'}, E) - S_j(c, E)] \leq \sum_{N'''}[S_j(c_{N'}, E) - S_j(c, E)]$.

The dual says that if an increase in the population of claimants is accompanied by an increase in the endowment equal to the sum of the claims of the new claimants, then, given two groups of claimants initially present, the aggregate award to the group with the smaller aggregate claim should increase by at most as much as the aggregate award to the group with the larger aggregate claim.

We conclude this section with the requirement that the impact of an increase in population on any initial claimant be a monotone function of the endowment. It is a counterpart of two earlier properties having to do with claim increases and claim transfers (Section 4.2).

Endowment-monotonic impact of population variations: For each pair $\{N, N'\} \in \mathcal{N}$ such that $N' \subset N$, each $c \in \mathbb{R}^N_+$, each $i \in N$, each pair $\{E, E'\} \subset \mathbb{R}_+$ such that $E < E' < \sum_{N'} c_k$, then $S_i(c, E) - S_i(c', E) \leq S_i(c, E') - S_i(c', E')$.

12.2 GUARANTEE STRUCTURES

If a rule is *population monotonic*, starting from some initial problem, the arrival of new claimants will have a negative impact on each of the claimants initially present, but how much of an impact? A claimant may well accept contributing to honoring new claims if this impact is limited but object to it if it is too large. How should this impact be measured? A natural measure, especially for a *homogeneous* rule, is the ratio of a claimant's final to initial assignments. Of course, this ratio will depend on the parameters of the initial and final problems and in particular their sizes. We propose to summarize the behavior of the rule by the smallest value it takes. Seen positively, this number can be interpreted as a guarantee that, as population increases, the claimant will get at least a certain percentage of their initial award. A rule that offers high guarantees should be more robust to changes in the circumstances in which claimants find themselves.

We will work with *anonymous* rules so the identity of the members of the initial and incoming groups will not have to be taken into consideration.

Now, calculating a guarantee when *all* parameters are allowed to vary is likely to yield very low guarantees and not to be very informative, so we will do the calculations for each pair of population sizes, the size of the initial population and the size of the incoming population. We will identify the worst-case scenario as a function of these two parameters. We call the list of the smallest ratios the "guarantee structure of the rule." The parameterization by the sizes of the initial and newly arrived groups will give us a fine description of the behavior of the rule.

We then calculate the guarantee structures of the leading rules, hoping to be able to compare rules on that basis. We will say that a rule dominates another if its guarantee structures vectorially dominates that of the second rule. By contrast to real-valued criteria, the vector-valued criteria that we define only provide a partial ranking of rules. Thus, one should not expect to be able to rank rules very generally. Surprisingly, the notion of a guarantee structure allows comparing rules in broad families.

The basic notion we propose focuses on individual claimants, but definitions can also be given that concern groups of claimants. This takes us to the notion of a collective guarantee structure.

We will also study how the guarantee structures of a rule are affected by operators. Finally, we will look for rules offering maximal guarantees within classes of rules. Here are the formal definitions.[5]

Individual guarantee of S for populations of size $n, m \in \mathbb{N}$, $ig^S(n, m)$: $ig^S(n,m) \equiv \inf_{N,M\in\mathcal{N},\, N\cap M=\emptyset,\, |N|=n,\, |M|=m, i\in N,\, (c_N,E)\in\mathcal{C}^N,\, c_M\in\mathbb{R}^M} \left\{ \frac{S_i(c_{N\cup M},E)}{S_i(c_N,E)} \right\}$

Next, we measure the average impact that the arrival of new claimants has on the claimants who are initially present.

Average guarantee of S for populations of size $n, m \in \mathbb{N}$, $ag^S(n, m)$: $ag^S(n,m) \equiv \inf_{N,M\in\mathcal{N},\, N\cap M=\emptyset,\, |N|=n,\, |M|=m, (c_N,E)\in\mathcal{C}^N,\, c_M\in\mathbb{R}^M} \left\{ \frac{1}{|N|} \sum_{i\in N} \frac{S_i(c_{N\cup M},E)}{S_i(c_N,E)} \right\}$.

Finally, we calculate the overall impact on the initial population of the arrival of new claimants.

Collective guarantee of S for populations of size $n, m \in \mathbb{N}$, $cg^S(n, m)$: $cg^S(n,m) \equiv \inf_{N,M\in\mathcal{N},\, N\cap M=\emptyset,\, |N|=n,\, |M|=m, (c_N,E)\in\mathcal{C}^N,\, c_M\in\mathbb{R}^M} \left\{ \frac{1}{E} \sum_{i\in N} S_i(c_{N\cup M}, E) \right\}$.

The **individual guarantee structure of S** is the double list $\alpha^S \equiv (\alpha^S(m,n))_{m,n\in\mathbb{N}}$. Similarly, the **average guarantee structure of S** and its

[5] This section is inspired by Thomson and Lensberg (1983), Thomson (1983c), and Chun and Thomson (1989), who developed the definitions of individual and collective guarantees in the context of the theory of bargaining, and derived characterizations of the Kalai–Smorodinsky, egalitarian, and Nash solution on the basis of these definitions. The results of this section are due to Harless (2017b,c).

collective guarantee structure are obtained by collecting all the numbers calculated for each pair n, m when n and m are given arbitrary values in $\mathbb{N}$.

For an *endowment monotonic* and *consistent* rule, individual and collective guarantees coincide.

We have the following characterization, in which the main substantial requirement is *consistency*.

Theorem 12.1 *The constrained equal awards rule is the only rule satisfying endowment continuity, consistency, and to offer maximal average guarantees.* constrained equal awards rule characterized

We relegate the proof to an appendix (Section 17.14).

An interesting question is how guarantees are affected by operators. The answer is that for each of the notions we have defined, the guarantees offered by a weighted average of two rules dominates the average of the guarantees offered by the two rules individually. For the other operators, the answers we offer involve additional properties of rules.

Proposition 12.3 *Let S be a rule.*

Concerning the claims truncation operator,

(a1) $ig^S \leq ig^{S^t}$, $ag^S \leq ag^{S^t}$, *and* $cg^S \leq cg^{S^t}$.

(a2) If S satisfies order preservation, then for each $m \in \mathbb{N}$, $ig^{S^t}(1, m) = ag^{S^t}(1, m) = cg^{S^t}(1, m) = \frac{1}{1+m}$.

(a3) If S is a Young rule satisfying order preservation and claims truncation invariance, then for each $m \in \mathbb{N}$, $ig^S(\cdot, m) = ig^{S^t}(\cdot, m) = \frac{1}{1+m}$, *and* $cg^S(\cdot, m) = cg^{S^t}(\cdot, m) = \frac{1}{1+m}$;

Concerning the attribution of minimal rights operator,

(b1) for each $m \in \mathbb{N}$, $ig^{S^m}(1, m) = ag^{S^m}(1, m) = cg^S(1, m) = ig^S(1, m)$, *and*

(b2) If S satisfies other-regarding claim monotonicity, then $ig^{S^m} \leq ig^S$, $ag^{S^m} = ag^S$, *and* $cg^{S^m} = cg^S$.

12.3 MERGING AND SPLITTING CLAIMS; MANIPULATION ISSUES AND EXTENSION OPERATORS

Here, we consider the merging of the claims of two or several agents into one and the splitting of the claim of an agent into several claims. We investigate the strategic implications of such operations. We also use the merging of claims as the basis for the definition of operators to extend two-claimant rules to arbitrarily many claimants.

12.3.1 No Advantageous Merging or Splitting and Variants

• We imagine a group of claimants transferring their claims to one of them who will represent them and dropping out; their representative shows up with a claim equal to the sum of the claims of the members of the group, including that of the representative. Can the representative be assigned more than what they would be assigned together without the transfer? We require that this never be the case.

Conversely, a claimant could distribute their claim among a group of agents not initially involved, perhaps keeping some of it. Can that claimant and these new agents be assigned more together than what the claimant would be assigned otherwise? Again, we require that this never be the case.[6]

When manipulations of this kind cannot be monitored and prevented, the following property addresses the concerns that one may have about their impact on the distributional objectives embodied in the rule. It is an invariance requirement:

No advantageous merging or splitting: For each pair $\{N, N'\}$ of elements of $\mathcal{N}$ such that $N' \subset N$, each $(c, E) \in \mathcal{C}^N$, and each $c' \in \mathbb{R}_+^{N'}$, if there is $i \in N'$ such that $c'_i = c_i + \sum_{N \setminus N'} c_j$ and for each $k \in N' \setminus \{i\}$, $c'_k = c_k$, then $S_i(c', E) = S_i(c, E) + \sum_{N \setminus N'} S_j(c, E)$.

The property is satisfied by the proportional rule but not by any of the other rules that we have seen. For the proportional rule, for each problem, there is $\lambda \in [0, 100]$ such that each agent receives $\lambda\%$ of their claim and, therefore, the sum of the awards to a group of agents is $\lambda\%$ the sum of their claims. Suppose the group selects one of its members as representative, all of its members transferring their claims to that member. In the resulting problem, the proportion of their claim that each agent receives is still λ. Thus, the representative claimant receives $\lambda\%$ of their new claim: the representative's award is equal to the sum of the initial awards to the claimants represented and the representative.

Legal or practical constraints may make it difficult or impossible to merge claims, and in others, it is splitting claims that may not be an option. Hence the interest of rules that satisfy **no advantageous merging** (if two or more claimants are replaced by one of them whose claim is equal to the sum of theirs, this claimant should receive at most as much as what together they received initially), and of rules that satisfy **no advantageous splitting** (if an agent transfers some of their claim to one or more new agents, then what the transferring agent and the new agents receive together should be at most as much as what the transferring agent received initially).

Since the constrained equal awards rule favors the relatively smaller claimants, one can guess that it is manipulable by splitting and not manipulable

[6] It is first considered in the present context by O'Neill (1982). Banker (1981) discusses it in the general context of cost allocation.

by merging. This is indeed the case. As the constrained equal losses rule favors the relatively larger claimants, it is equally intuitive that it exhibits a symmetric pattern of manipulability. Each member of the TAL family $\{T^\theta\}_{\theta\in[0,1]}$ behaves like the constrained equal awards rule for low values of the endowment and like the constrained equal losses rule for high values, where "low" and "high" are defined in relation to the parameter θ, and therefore inherits some immunity to merging from the constrained equal awards rule and some immunity to splitting from the constrained equal losses rule, depending upon the value of the endowment in relation to the sum of the claims, but it is not fully immune to either one of these types of operations.[7]

• **Other-regarding merging-or-splitting invariance.** A strengthening of *no advantageous merging* is obtained by focusing on the agents not involved in the merging or splitting operations, and to require that each of them receive the same amount as initially.[8]

• **No advantageous multilateral merging** pertains to the following operation. Starting from some problem, we imagine a group of agents redistributing their claims among the members of some second group and leaving: the requirement is that in the problem that results, the second group be assigned in total at most as much as what the two groups were initially assigned in total.

No advantageous uniformity-preserving multilateral merging is obtained from the previous requirement by adding to the hypotheses that (i) the claims of the members of the two groups involved in the merging operation are equal and that (ii) after this operation, so are the claims of the members of the second group.

`* Relating axioms` ♦ *No advantageous merging* and *no advantageous splitting* are dual.[9] To see this, let $N \in \mathcal{N}$ and $(c, E) \in \mathcal{C}^N$ be given. Let $N' \subset N$ and $i \in N'$. Let $\bar{c} \in \mathbb{R}^{(N\setminus N')\cup\{i\}}$ be such that $\bar{c}_{N\setminus N'} = c_{N\setminus N'}$, and $\bar{c}_i = \sum_{N'} c_j$. *No advantageous merging* says that $S_i(\bar{c}, E) \leq \sum_{N'} S_j(c, E)$. This inequality is equivalent to $\bar{c}_i - S^d_i(\bar{c}, \sum_N \bar{c}_k - E) \leq \sum_{N'}[c_j - S^d_j(c, \sum_N c_k - E)]$.

We cancel the claims terms on both sides, and change variables, replacing $\sum_N c_k - E$ by E, to obtain $S^d_i(\bar{c}, E) \geq S^d_i(c, E) + \sum_{N'\setminus\{i\}} S^d_j(c, E)$, which is nothing other than the statement of *no advantageous splitting*.

♦ Fixed-population versions of *no advantageous splitting* and *no advantageous merging* can be formulated for which, in the first case, an agent splits part

[7] This intuition is made formal by Moreno-Ternero (2007), who identifies, for each $\theta \in [0, 1]$, the domain of problems for which the ratio of the endowment to the sum of the claims is at least θ as the domain on which the TAL rule of parameter θ is *splitting-proof* for example. He also defines "a rule as being more manipulable than some other rule" if, for each problem and each group of claimants, the gain these claimants can achieve by appearing as a single claimant over appearing separately is at least as large for the first rule as it is for the second rule, and shows that two TAL rules can be compared in this way according to their parameters.

[8] This formulation is proposed by Curiel, Maschler, and Tijs (1987) under the name of the "additivity of claims property," and further explored by Moreno-Ternero (2006) under the name of "strong non-manipulability."

[9] De Frutos (1999).

of their claim among agents whose initial claims are 0; and for which, in the second case, the agent whose claims are merged remain but their claims are set equal to 0. Each of the variable-population splitting and merging axioms implies its fixed-population counterpart. Each of the fixed-population splitting and merging axioms together with *null claims consistency* implies its variable-population counterpart. Also, each of the variable-population splitting and merging axioms implies *null claims consistency*. In fact, the following is true:

Lemma 12.1

(a) No advantageous merging implies null compensation consistency.
(b) No advantageous splitting implies full compensation consistency.

Proof: (a) Let S be a rule satisfying the hypothesis. let $N \in \mathcal{N}$, $(c, E) \in \mathcal{C}^N$, and $N' \subset N$, and suppose that $c_{N \backslash N'} = 0$. Let $x \equiv S(c, E)$ and $y \equiv S(c_{N'}, E)$. Let $i \in N'$. We will show that $x_i = y_i$. Indeed, note that we can pass from (c, E) to $(c_{N'}, E)$ by having all of the members of $N \backslash N'$ transfer their claims to agent i. By *no advantageous merging*, in the resulting problem, the award to the composite claimant representing the group $(N \backslash N') \cup \{i\}$ should be equal to the sum of the initial awards to the agents whom the composite claimant represents. By definition of a rule, for each $j \in N \setminus N'$, $x_j = 0$, and this sum is equal to $x_i + |N \backslash N'| \times 0 = x_i$. Since this conclusion holds for each $i \in N$, we obtain that for each $i \in N$, $y_i \leq x_i$. Since $E = \sum y_i \leq \sum x_i = E$, we deduce that in fact, for each $i \in N'$, $x_i = y_i$, as required by *null claims consistency*.

(b) This follows by duality. □

♦ *No advantageous merging or splitting* implies *no advantageous transfer*. Indeed, let $N \in \mathcal{N}$, and let (c, E) and $(\bar{c}, \bar{E})$ be two problems in $\mathcal{C}^N$ that differ only in the claims of some members of some group $N' \subset N$, these claims adding up to the same quantity in both. By *no advantageous merging or splitting*, the sum of what the members of N' receive in (c, E) is equal to what a member of N' representing them – let us name the representative agent agent k – would receive in the problem $(\tilde{c}, E)$ with agent set $(N \backslash N') \cup \{k\}$ and claims $\tilde{c}_{N \backslash N'} \equiv c_{N \backslash N'}$ and $\tilde{c}_k \equiv \sum_{N'} c_i$. The problem $(\bar{c}, \bar{E})$ can also be "collapsed" to $(\tilde{c}, E)$. Thus, $\sum_{N'} S_i(c, E) = S_k(\tilde{c}, E) = \sum_{N'} S_i(\bar{c}, \bar{E})$, as announced.

♦ It follows directly from the definitions that *other-regarding merging-or-splitting invariance* implies *no advantageous merging or splitting* but in fact the two properties are equivalent.[10]

♦ *Equal treatment of equal groups* and *consistency* together imply *no advantageous merging or splitting*.[11]

[10] Moreno-Ternero (2006).

[11] Chambers and Thomson (2002).

♦ It is indicative of the strength of *no advantageous multilateral merging* that this axiom together with *consistency* imply *no advantageous splitting*.[12] It is of course not true that *no advantageous merging* and *consistency* together imply *no advantageous splitting*; the constrained equal awards rule satisfies the first two properties but not the last one.

♦ A Young rule is *progressive* if and only if it satisfies *no advantageous merging* and *no advantageous uniformity-preserving multilateral merging*.

The following theorem identifies those of Young's rules that satisfy either *no advantageous merging* or *no advantageous splitting*.[13]

Theorem 12.2

(a) *A Young rule of representation $f \in \Phi$ with domain $\mathbb{R}_+ \times \Lambda$, where $\Lambda \subseteq \bar{\mathbb{R}}$, satisfies no advantageous splitting if and only if for each $\lambda \in \Lambda$, $f(\cdot, \lambda)$ is super-additive in its first argument.* subfamily of Young's family characterized

(b) *Instead, it satisfies no advantageous merging if and only if for each $\lambda \in \Lambda$, $f(\cdot, \lambda)$ is sub-additive in its first argument.*

Proof: (a) We omit the proof that a rule as described in the theorem satisfies *no advantageous splitting*. Conversely, let S be a Young rule with representation $f \in \Phi$ with domain $\mathbb{R}_+ \times \Lambda$ where $\Lambda \subseteq \bar{\mathbb{R}}$. It suffices to show that S is immune to one agent splitting their claim into two parts. Suppose that f is not super-additive in its first argument. This means that there are $\lambda \in \Lambda$ and $c_0, c_0' \in \mathbb{R}_+$ such that

$$(*) \quad f(c_0 + c_0', \lambda) < f(c_0, \lambda) + f(c_0', \lambda).$$

Let $N \equiv \{1, 2\}$ and $(c_1, c_2) = (c_0, c_0')$. For each $i \in N$, since $f(c_i, \cdot)$ is continuous and nowhere decreasing, there is a closed interval containing λ where it takes the value $f(c_i, \lambda)$. For each $i \in N$, the left endpoint of this interval is no greater than λ. Without loss of generality, suppose that the left endpoint of claimant 1's interval is at least as large as the left endpoint of claimant 2's interval. Let us denote it $\hat{\lambda}$. Then, (i) for each $i \in N$, $f(c_i, \hat{\lambda}) = f(c_i, \lambda)$ and (ii) for each $\lambda' < \hat{\lambda}$, $f(c_1, \lambda') < f(c_1, \hat{\lambda})$.

Let $\hat{c}_1 \equiv c_1 + c_2$, and let us introduce claimant 3 with claim $\hat{c}_3 \equiv c_1$. Let $\hat{c} \equiv (\hat{c}_1, \hat{c}_3)$ and $\hat{E} \equiv f(\hat{c}_1, \hat{\lambda}) + f(\hat{c}_3, \hat{\lambda})$. Consider the two-claimant problem with agent set $\{1, 3\}$, $((\hat{c}_1, \hat{c}_3), \hat{E})$. Clearly, $S((\hat{c}_1, \hat{c}_3), \hat{E}) = (f(\hat{c}_1, \hat{\lambda}), f(\hat{c}_3, \hat{\lambda}))$.

[12] Ju and Moreno-Ternero (2011).

[13] It answers a question first addressed by de Frutos (1999) who asserts that concavity of the representations with respect to the first argument is necessary and sufficient for *no advantageous merging*, and similarly that convexity is necessary and sufficient for *no advantageous splitting*. These properties of the representations are sufficient but not necessary. Theorem 12.2 is due to Ju (2003). Other results in the same spirit are developed by Ju and Moreno-Ternero (2006, 2011).

Let $\hat{c}' \in \mathbb{R}_+^{N\cup\{3\}}$ be defined by setting $\hat{c}'_N \equiv (c_1, c_2)$ and $\hat{c}'_3 \equiv \hat{c}_3$. We have that $(\hat{c}', \hat{E}) \in \mathcal{C}^{N\cup\{3\}}$. Now, by (∗) applied to $(c_1, c_2) = (c_0, c'_0)$ and since $\hat{\lambda} \leq \lambda$ and (i) and (ii),

$$\begin{aligned} f(\hat{c}_1, \hat{\lambda}) + f(\hat{c}_3, \hat{\lambda}) &= f(c_1 + c_2, \hat{\lambda}) + f(\hat{c}_3, \hat{\lambda}) \\ &\leq f(c_1 + c_2, \lambda) + f(\hat{c}_3, \lambda) \\ &< f(c_1, \lambda) + f(c_2, \lambda) + f(\hat{c}_3, \lambda) \\ &= f(c_1, \hat{\lambda}) + f(c_2, \hat{\lambda}) + f(\hat{c}_3, \hat{\lambda}) \\ &= f(\hat{c}'_1, \hat{\lambda}) + f(\hat{c}'_2, \hat{\lambda}) + f(\hat{c}'_3, \hat{\lambda}). \end{aligned}$$

Hence, $f(\hat{c}'_1, \hat{\lambda}) + f(\hat{c}'_2, \hat{\lambda}) + f(\hat{c}'_3, \hat{\lambda}) > \hat{E}$. Let $\lambda' \in [\underline{\lambda}, \bar{\lambda}]$ be such that $f(\hat{c}'_1, \lambda') + f(\hat{c}'_2, \lambda') + f(\hat{c}'_3, \lambda') = \hat{E}$. Then $\lambda' < \hat{\lambda}$. Now, by (ii), $f(\hat{c}'_3, \lambda') = f(c_1, \lambda') < f(c_1, \hat{\lambda}) = f(\hat{c}_3, \hat{\lambda})$. Therefore, $S_3(\hat{c}', \hat{E}) < S_3(\hat{c}, \hat{E})$. So, $S_1(\hat{c}', \hat{E}) + S_2(\hat{c}', \hat{E}) > S_1(\hat{c}, \hat{E})$. Since $\hat{c}_1 = c_1 + c_2 = \hat{c}'_1 + \hat{c}'_2$, S violates *no advantageous splitting*.

(b) The proof is analogous to the proof of part (a). It also follows from duality. □

As a corollary of Theorem 8.1 (which states that if there are at least three claimants, the proportional rule is the only rule satisfying *no advantageous transfer*), we obtain the following alternative characterization of this rule.[14]

proportional rule characterized

Theorem 12.3 *The proportional rule is the only rule satisfying no advantageous merging or splitting.*

Proof: We already know that the proportional rule satisfies *no advantageous merging or splitting*. Uniqueness for three claimants or more is a consequence of Theorem 8.1 and the fact that *no advantageous merging or splitting* implies *no advantageous transfer*, as just established. Uniqueness for two claimants is a direct consequence of uniqueness for three claimants or more and *no advantageous merging or splitting*. □

12.3.2 Extension Operators Based on the Merging of Claims

Given a rule that is defined only for two-claimant problems, we exploit here the possibility of merging claims to extend it to arbitrary populations. We start with

[14] These logical relations are stated in Chun (1988). Precursors of Theorem 12.3 are due to O'Neill (1982) and Chun (1988). O'Neill imposes *dummy* and *null claims consistency*, both of which are shown to be redundant by Chun. Chun's result concerns generalized rules, that is, rules that do not necessarily satisfy *nonnegativity* nor *claims boundedness* (Section 15.5). He obtains the result as a corollary of a characterization of the proportional rule on the basis of *no advantageous transfer*. De Frutos (1999) gives a direct proof for a concept of a rule that does not include *claims boundedness*. Ju and Miyagawa (2002) consider rules as we define this term, and derive Theorem 12.3 as a corollary of a characterization of the proportional rule on the basis of *no advantageous transfer* alone (Theorem 8.1). Also, see Banker (1981). Curiel, Maschler, and Tijs (1987) characterize the adjusted proportional rule along similar lines.

a process that turns out to provide a rationalization for the Talmud rule. We then generalize this process in various ways and obtain a number of operators achieving such extensions.

(i) **Merging claims and the Talmud rule: the Aumann–Maschler step-by-step merging process.** We begin with concede-and-divide and a scenario involving a merging of claims that reduces a problem involving arbitrarily many claimants to a sequence of two-claimant problems. The end-result is the awards vector recommended by the Talmud rule for the initial problem.[15]

Here is formal description of the process. Let $N \equiv \{1, \ldots, n\}$ and $c \in \mathbb{R}^N_+$ be such that $c_1 \leq \cdots \leq c_n$. At Step 1, we apply concede-and-divide to the two-claimant problem in which claimant 1 faces a composite agent whose claim is $c_2 + \cdots + c_n$. The award to the composite claimant is intended to be distributed to the represented agents as the process runs its course. Claimant 1 leaves with their award unless either (i) that award is larger than $\frac{1}{|N|-1}$ of the award to the composite claimant (otherwise, claimant 1 would get more than the $|N| - 1$ other claimants would get on average, and this would cause a violation of *order preservation in awards*), and in this case we choose equal division among all n agents and we are done, or (ii) claimant 1's loss is larger than their average loss, in which case we choose equal division of the deficit among all n agents; (otherwise, claimant 1's loss would be greater than the loss the $|N| - 1$ other claimants would incur on average, and this would cause a violation of *order preservation in losses*), and in this case we choose equal division of the deficit among all n agents, and we are done.

At Step 2, we apply concede-and-divide to the two-claimant problem in which claimant 2 faces a composite agent whose claim is $c_3 + \cdots + c_n$ and the endowment is what the first composite agent received at Step 1. Claimant 2 leaves with their award unless either (i) that award is larger than the average award for the group $N \setminus \{1\}$, in which case we choose equal division of what the first composite claimant has been assigned among these $n - 1$ agents and we are done (for similar order preservation reasons), or (ii) claimant 2's loss is larger than the average loss for the group $N \setminus \{1\}$, in which case we choose equal division of the deficit that they face among these $n - 1$ agents, and we are done (again, for order preservation reasons).

We continue in this way until claimants $n - 1$ and n are the only ones left. We apply concede-and-divide one last time.

We refer to the process just described as the **Aumann–Maschler step-by-step merging-solving process.**[16]

[15] This argument, and Theorem 12.4, are due to Aumann and Maschler (1985).

[16] The following example illustrates the possibility of a violation of the order preservation inequalities appearing in the process: if $(c, E) = ((100, 200, 300), 100)$, at the first step, we obtain $x_1 = 50$ and the composite claimant that claimant 1 faces obtains 50. Thus on average, claimants 2 and 3, whom the composite claimant represents, would obtain less than claimant 1, so we do equal division among all three. For $E = 500$,

We omit the proof of the following theorem:

Aumann–Maschler merging-solving process

Theorem 12.4 *For each problem, the endpoint of the Aumann–Maschler step-by-step merging-solving process is the Talmud awards vector.*

(ii) **Generalizing the Aumann–Maschler process to obtain a general extension operator.** The Aumann–Maschler process can serve as a point of departure to define a general operator to associate with any two-claimant rule a rule that is defined for arbitrary populations. Indeed, we could use a rule other than concede-and-divide to solve the successive two-claimant problems that appear along the Aumann–Maschler process. For instance, if the point of departure is the two-person TAL rule of parameter θ (Subsection 2.2.3; recall that this is a subfamily of the ICI family), the endpoint is T^{θ}.[17]

(iii) **Other extension operators.** Other ways can be considered of collapsing an arbitrary problem to one with only two claimants. It is indeed not clear why at each step, it should be the smallest claimant who faces everyone else. An alternative is to have the largest claimant do so, for example.

Another formulation is obtained by specifying ahead of time an order on the claimant set; having the first claimant face a representative of the others; applying the chosen two-claimant rule to the resulting two-claimant problem; having the first claimant in that order leave with their assignment; repeating with the second claimant in the resulting reduced problem; and so on until only two claimants are left – one final application of the rule delivering an awards vector for the problem under consideration – finally, taking the average of the awards vectors associated with the various orders on the claimant set.[18] If we take as point of departure an arbitrary two-claimant rule and associate with it a rule for arbitrary populations in this manner, we define a general operator. In Chapter 11, we used *consistency* to extend two-claimant rules to arbitrary populations. Here, it is not a property that provides the basis for the extension of a two-claimant rule, but a mixed operation involving merging claims and averaging awards vectors:

we would obtain $x_1 = 50$, and the composite claimant obtains 450. Here on average, claimants 2 and 3, whom the composite claimant represents, would incur a smaller loss than claimant 1, so we divide the deficit equally among the three claimants, obtaining (66.6, 166.6, 266, 6). If $(c, E) = ((100, 200, 300, 400, 500), 510)$, the process assigns 50 to claimant 1 and 460 to the composite claimant $\{2, \ldots 5\}$; it then assigns 100 to claimant 2 and 360 to the composite claimant $\{3, \ldots, 5\}$; at the next step, we would obtain 150 for claimant 3 and 210 for the composite claimant $\{4, 5\}$ and no matter how this amount would be divided, claimant 1 would obtain more than at least one of claimants 4 and 5, so we divide 360 equally among claimants 3, 4, and 5. Altogether, we obtain (50, 100, 120, 120, 120).

[17] Moreno-Ternero (2011a).

[18] This suggestion is made by Quant, Borm, and Maaten (2005). It is developed by Quant and Borm (2011). They use the expression "random conjugate of a rule" for what we call its "merging-solving-averaging extension."

Merging-solving-averaging extension operator: Let S be a two-claimant rule. Let $N \in \mathcal{N}$ with $|N| > 2$, $\pi \in \Pi^N$ be an order on the claimant set, and $i_1, i_2, \ldots, i_n$ be the resulting ordered list of claimants. Given $(c, E) \in \mathcal{C}^N$, let $x^\pi_{i_1} \equiv S((c_{i_1}, \sum_{N\setminus\{i_1\}} c_j), E)$, $x^\pi_{i_2} \equiv S((c_{i_2}, \sum_{N\setminus\{i_1,i_2\}} c_j), E - x^\pi_{i_1})$, and so on. Let x^π be the resulting awards vector. Finally, let $S^{merg-solv-av}(c, E) \equiv \frac{1}{|N|!}\sum_{\pi\in\Pi^N} x^\pi$. The rule $\boldsymbol{S^{merg-solv-av}}$ is the **merg–solv–av extension** of S.

Whereas, as we saw, not all two-claimant rules have *consistent* extensions, here no such difficulty arises. Indeed, at each step, when an agent is served, they receive a nonnegative amount that is bounded above by their claim. These properties of awards are preserved by averaging. Thus, $S^{merg-solv-av}$ is indeed a well-defined rule. It is interesting to ask which properties of S are inherited by $S^{merg-solv-av}$, or what adjustments in the process are needed to obtain certain properties.[19] Each of the following properties is inherited by the merg–solv–av extension of a two-claimant rule satisfying it: *homogeneity*, *endowment monotonicity*, *claims truncation invariance*, *minimal rights first*, and *self-duality*.[20] Some properties are not inherited, an example being *composition down*.

(iv) **Further generalizations.** The following further generalization appears worth exploring. The goal is still to define an operator to extend a two-claimant rule S so as to solve problems involving arbitrarily many claimants, but instead of imagining that at each step, a single claimant is pitted against everyone else, it involves partitioning the claimant set into two components, and having these two components be claimants in a derived problem. The most natural way to do so is to add up the claims of the members of each component as we have done already. We apply S to the resulting two-claimant problem. This determines an award for each component, which we partition in turn into two subcomponents and, after adding up the claims of the members of each subcomponent, we apply S once again. We proceed in this manner until each agent has been involved in a two-claimant problem as a singleton.

The successive partitioning of the claimant set can be described as a tree. To make the outcome not depend on which particular tree is chosen, we take the average of the awards vectors obtained for all possible trees. It is this vector that we choose as final awards vector.

Again, an interesting question is what properties of the two-claimant rule that is the point of departure are inherited by the mapping on the domain of

[19] We could also use the term "lifted" here, but we prefer avoiding it as the meaning would differ from the meaning we gave to it when we spoke of a property being lifted by *bilateral consistency*.

[20] The proof for *claims truncation invariance* relies on a recursive formula for the operator. The proof for *self-duality* involves showing that for each $(c, E) \in \mathcal{C}^N$, and each order in which claimants may arrive, in the calculation of $S^{merg-solv-av}(c, E)$, the terms relative to that order and the reverse order add up to c. *Order preservation* is inherited if the two-claimant rule satisfies certain additional but mild properties.

problems of arbitrary size that is defined in this way, or what adjustments in the process would help achieving certain properties.

12.4 REPLICATION AND DIVISION: INVARIANCE AND LIMIT RESULTS

The next property we study involves a replication operation of a type that is often considered in order to model exchange economies in which each agent is "small" in relation to the entire market, so that taking prices as given when solving for the most preferred bundle in the agent's budget set is justified. Here, we will use it to model situations with a large number of small claimants, as in a class action suit for example. We formulate an axiom of invariance under replications as well as an axiom of invariance "under divisions" and relates these axioms to previously introduced ones. We also ask whether anything interesting can be said about the manner in which a rule may fail to be replication invariant. The answer is yes, and it will take us to results stating the approximate equivalence of certain rules for problems with many small claimants.

• Let $N \in \mathcal{N}$ and $k \in \mathbb{N}$. **A k-replica of a problem with claimant set N** is a problem in which the claimant set contains N and each member of N has $k-1$ clones – these agents have claims equal to that member – and in which the endowment is k times what it is initially. We formulate the requirement that the awards vector chosen for it be a k-replica of the awards vector chosen for the model problem (the problem that is replicated).

Formally, given $(c, E) \in \mathcal{C}^N$, and designating by N' the claimant set in the replica problem and (c', E') the replica problem, we have $N' \supset N$, $|N'| = k|N|$, and there is a partition $(N^i)_{i \in N}$ of N' into $|N|$ groups of k agents each, $(N^i)_{i \in N}$, such that for each $i \in N$ and each $j \in N^i$, $c'_j = c_i$; finally $E' = kE$ (Figure 12.2).[21]

Replication invariance: For each $N \in \mathcal{N}$, each $(c, E) \in \mathcal{C}^N$, each $N' \supset N$, and each $(c', E') \in \mathcal{C}^{N'}$, if (c', E') is a k-replica of (c, E), with associated partition $(N^i)_{i \in N}$, then for each $i \in N$ and each $j \in N^i$, $S_j(c', E') = S_i(c, E)$.

The property is *self-dual*.

We use the symbol $*$ to indicate replications. For instance, $k*(c, E)$ denotes a k-replica of (c, E) and if x is an awards vector for (c, E), $k * x$ denotes the corresponding replica awards vector for $k * (c, E)$. Using this notation, *replication invariance* can be given the shorthand expression "if $x = S(c, E)$, then $k * x = S(k * (c, E))$." There is a slight abuse of notation here, since there is not a unique k replica of a problem: two k-replicas of a given problem may

[21] The terminology is a little unclear, as by a k-replica economy, it can be understood that the model economy is replicated $k-1$ times, so that they are k copies of it at the end; but it can also be understood that the model economy is replicated k times.

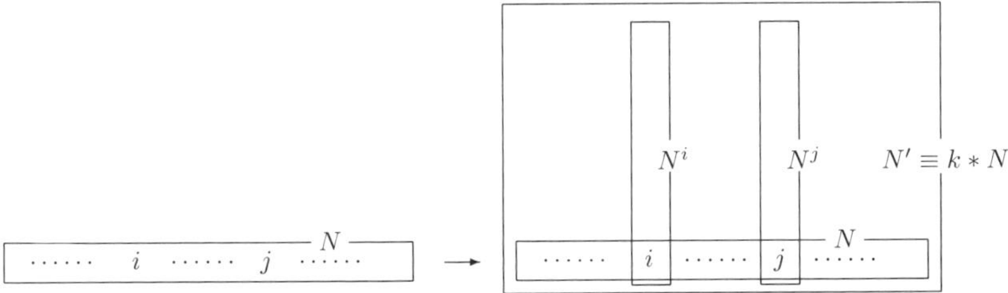

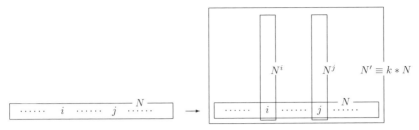

Figure 12.2: **Who's who in a replica problem.** Starting from the claimant set N, to define a k-replica of $(c, E) \in \mathcal{C}^N$, we introduce $k-1$ clones of each of them (agents with equal claims). In the replica problem, N^i designates the set consisting of claimant i and associated clones, and $N' \equiv k * N$ is the total population. The endowment is kE.

differ in the identities of the clones of each of the claimants involved in the initial problem. *Replication invariance* amounts to saying that how they are specified does not matter.

$*$ `Relating axioms` ♦ For the situation under consideration here, in which the population of potential claimants is infinite, *replication invariance* implies *equal treatment of equals*. Indeed, when two agents have equal claims in some problem, a replica of that problem involves new agents who can be thought of as clones of either one of them. This reasoning fails, however, if the population of potential claimants is finite. Then two agents with equal claims may be part of a problem that cannot be replicated because there are not enough claimants for that, and one cannot appeal to *replication invariance* to relate their awards.

It is straightforward to verify that Young's rules are *replication invariant*. On the other hand, none of the random arrival, minimal overlap, or DT rule is. Indeed, let $N \equiv \{1, 2\}$ and $(c, E) \in \mathcal{C}^N$ be defined by $(c, E) = ((2, 4), 2)$. Then $RA(c, E) = (1, 1)$. Now, let $N' \equiv \{1, \ldots, 4\}$ and $(c', E') \equiv ((2, 4, 2, 4), 4) \in \mathcal{C}^{N'}$. Then $RA(c', E') = (\frac{2}{3}, \frac{4}{3}, \frac{2}{3}, \frac{4}{3})$. Claimants 1 and 2 are not getting the same amounts in (c, E) and in (c', E'), which is a $2*$replica of (c, E). Also, $MO(c, E) = (1, 1)$ and $MO(c', E') = (\frac{1}{2}, \frac{3}{2}, \frac{1}{2}, \frac{3}{2})$, so the same negative conclusion applies to the minimal overlap rule. It is easy to construct examples to make the same point for the DT rule.

Given any problem (c, E) with $E > 0$, there is k large enough such that in a k-replica of (c, E), the endowment is larger than each agent's claim, and the minimal right of each agent is 0. Thus, for claims problems obtained by replicating some model problem sufficiently many times, there is no difference between a rule S, its variant obtained by truncating claims first, S^t, (Section 5.1), and its variant obtained by attributing minimal rights first, S^m (Section 5.2).

• A stronger variant of *replication invariance* is obtained by allowing the order of replication to be claimant dependent, as follows. Let $N \in \mathcal{N}$, $(c, E) \in$

$\mathcal{C}^N$, and x be the choice made for (c, E) by a rule S. Imagine new agents coming in, each of whom has a claim equal to the claim of one of the members of N, and at the same time, the endowment increasing so that it is possible to assign to each new claimant the amount initially assigned to the agent in N whose claim is equal to that of the new agent. Require that in the augmented problem, S assign to each initial claimant the amount assigned to them initially, and to each new claimant an amount equal to that initially assigned to the agent in N whose claim is equal to that of the new claimant:

Claimant-wise-replication invariance: For each $N \in \mathcal{N}$, each $(c, E) \in \mathcal{C}^N$, each $N' \in \mathcal{N}$ with $N' \cap N = \emptyset$, each $(\bar{c}, \bar{E}) \in \mathcal{C}^{N \cup N'}$, if $\bar{c}_N = c$ and there is $N'' \subset N$ and a correspondence $b\colon N'' \mapsto N'$ such that for each $i \in N''$, and each $j \in b(i)$, $c_j = c_i$, and $\bar{E} = E + \sum_{i \in N''} |b(i)| S_i(c, E)$, then $S_N(\bar{c}, \bar{E}) = S(c, E)$ and for each $i \in N''$ and each $j \in b(i)$, $S_j(\bar{c}, \bar{E}) = S_i(c, E)$.

The property is *self-dual*.

Young's rules satisfy this property. On the other hand, neither the random arrival nor the minimal overlap does since neither is even *replication invariant* as we saw above.

We could conceive of alternative ways of modeling situations in which each claimant is "small." For instance, we could consider sequences of problems obtained by drawing claims from a distribution with bounded support and whose endowment per capita has a limit. We will not explore such a formulation. A difficulty here is that by definition of a problem, the sum of the claims should be at least as large as the endowment. Alternatively, we could model the set of agents as a continuum.[22]

• Here is a formulation of a sort of converse of *replication invariance* of a rule. Consider a claims problem that happens to be a replica of some model problem.[23] If the rule chooses for it an awards vector that happens to be a replica (of the same order) of an awards vector for the model problem, then this model awards vector should be the choice the rule makes for the model problem:[24]

Division invariance: For each $N \in \mathcal{N}$, each $(c, E) \in \mathcal{C}^N$, each $N' \supset N$, and each $(c', E') \in \mathcal{C}^{N'}$, if (c', E') is a k-replica of (c, E), with associated partition $(N^i)_{i \in N}$, and $S(c', E')$ is a replica of some awards vector $x \in X(c, E)$ associated with the same partition, then $S(c, E) = x$.

The property is *self-dual*.

`* Relating axioms` ♦ Obviously, *replication invariance* implies *division invariance*. The next lemma is a partial converse:

[22] Section 15.3.

[23] The two properties are not dual in the formal sense of Chapter 7, which is why we chose the term "converse."

[24] This is the counterpart of a property formulated by Thomson (1988) for exchange economies.

Lemma 12.2 *Equal treatment of equals and division invariance together imply replication invariance.*

Proof: Let S be a rule satisfying the hypotheses. Let $N \in \mathcal{N}$, $(c, E) \in \mathcal{C}^N$ and $k \in \mathbb{N}$. Let $N' \in \mathcal{N}$, and $(c', E') \in \mathcal{C}^{N'}$ be a k-replica of (c, E). By *equal treatment of equals*, all clones of each member of N receive equal amounts at $S(c', E')$. Thus, the hypothesis of *division invariance* applies, and $S(c', E') = k * S(c, E)$, as required by *replication invariance*. □

♦ The reason why *replication invariance* and *division invariance* are not equivalent is that a rule may trivially be *division invariant* since the hypotheses of the property are never met (except of course in the trivial case when $E = 0$ when they have to be). Such a rule has no reason to be *replication invariant*. Specifically, consider a rule that chooses for each replica problem an awards vector at which at least two claimants with equal claims do not receive equal amounts (this is possible if $E > 0$). Any such rule is *division invariant*. Yet, it violates *replication invariance*.

♦ Our next lemma relates *consistency* and *converse consistency* to *division invariance* and *replication invariance*.[25]

Lemma 12.3

(a) *Equal treatment of equals and consistency together imply replication invariance and division invariance.*
(b) *Anonymity and converse consistency together imply invariance under replication of two-claimant problems.*

Proof: For each implication, let S be a rule satisfying the hypotheses.

(a) Let $N \in \mathcal{N}$ and $(c, E) \in \mathcal{C}^N$. Let $k \in \mathbb{N}$ and (c', E') be a k-replica of (c, E), with agent set N'. By *equal treatment of equals*, all clones of each member of N receive equal amounts at $S(c', E')$, so that $S(c', E') = k * x$ for some x that is balanced for (c, E). By *consistency*, $x = S(c, E)$. So, $S(c', E') = k * S(c, E)$.
(b) (Figure 12.3) Let $N \in \mathcal{N}$ be such that $|N| = 2$ and $(c, E) \in \mathcal{C}^N$. Let $k \in \mathbb{N}$ and (c', E') be a k-replica of (c, E), with agent set N'. We need to show that $S(c', E') = k * S(c, E) \equiv y$. Let $\bar{N} \subset N'$ with $|\bar{N}| = 2$, say $\bar{N} \equiv \{\ell, \ell'\}$. There are two cases.

Case 1: $\bar{N}$ contains a clone of each of the claimants in N, as illustrated by N^1 on the figure. Then, by *anonymity*, $(y_\ell, y_{\ell'}) = S((c_\ell, c_{\ell'}), y_\ell + y_{\ell'})$.

Case 2: $\bar{N}$ consists of two clones of some claimant in N, as illustrated by N^2 on the figure. Then $y_\ell = y_{\ell'}$, so that by *equal treatment of equals*, implied by *anonymity*, $(y_\ell, y_{\ell'}) = S((c_\ell, c_{\ell'}), y_\ell + y_{\ell'})$.

[25] Lemma 12.3 is due to Chambers and Thomson (2002).

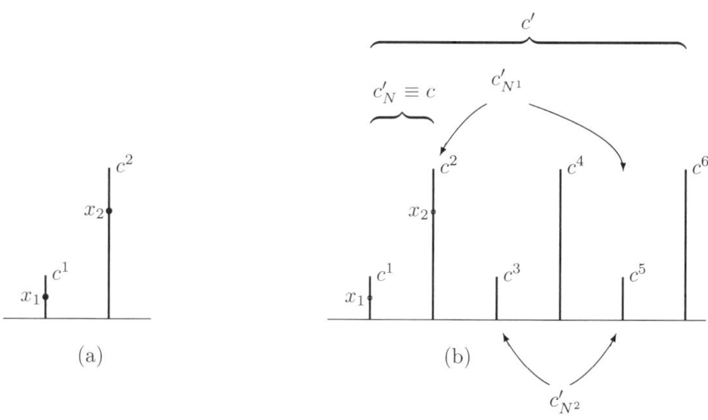

Figure 12.3: **Showing that anonymity and converse consistency together imply invariance under replication for two-claimant problems** (Lemma 12.3b). We consider a rule S satisfying *anonymity* and *converse consistency*. (a) We start from $N \equiv \{1, 2\}$ and $(c, E) \in \mathcal{C}^N$, a problem for which S chooses an awards vector we call x. (b) This panel represents a k-replica c' of c (here, $k = 3$ and the enlarged agent set is $\{1, \ldots, 6\}$, agents 3 and 5 having claims equal to that of claimant 1 and agents 4 and 6 having claims equal to that of claimant 2). We show that the hypotheses of *converse consistency* apply to the corresponding k-replica of x for (c', kE). First, the group $N^1 \equiv \{2, 5\}$ is a copy of N, so by *anonymity* the awards vector that S chooses for $(c'_{N^1}, x_1 + x_2)$ is a copy of x with x_2 assigned to claimant 2 and x_5 assigned to claimant 5. Also, the group $N^2 \equiv \{3, 5\}$ consists of two claimants with equal claims (both are clones of claimant 1), so by *equal treatment of equals*, implied by *anonymity*, the awards vector that S chooses for $(c'_{N^2}, x_1 + x_1)$ is (x_1, x_1). Similar reasoning applies to the other two-claimant groups. By *converse consistency*, the awards vector that S chooses for (c', kE) is a k-replica of x.

Thus, y satisfies the hypotheses of *converse consistency* for S and (c', E'). Since S satisfies this property, $y = k * S(c, E) = S(c', E')$. □

Characterizations. We close this section with characterizations of the proportional rule. When introducing *group order preservation*, we noted that for each problem, the inequalities it states are satisfied by a nonempty polygonal region of awards vectors. Thus, many rules satisfy this punctual property. However, if *claims continuity* and *replication invariance* are imposed as well, only the proportional rule qualifies:[26]

proportional rule characterized

Theorem 12.5 *The proportional rule is the only rule satisfying claims continuity, equal treatment of equal groups, and replication invariance.*

[26] Theorem 12.5, first established by Ching and Kakkar (2000), is independently discovered by Chambers and Thomson (2002). The discussion of the independence of the properties is taken from these two papers.

Proof: We already know that the proportional rule satisfies the three properties listed in the theorem. Conversely, let S be a rule satisfying these properties. Let $N \in \mathcal{N}$ and $(c, E) \in \mathcal{C}^N$.

Case 1: there are $a > 0$ and $\nu \in \mathbb{N}^N$ for which $c = \nu a$. Let $\lambda \in \mathbb{R}_+$ be such that $P(c, E) = \lambda c$. Also, let n be a common multiple of the ν_i's, when i runs over N.

Let $(\bar{c}, \bar{E})$ be an n-replica of (c, E), and $y \equiv S(\bar{c}, \bar{E})$. For each $\{i, j\} \subseteq N$, there is a subset N' of the claimant set of the replica problem containing ν_j clones of claimant i and ν_i clones of claimant j. Let N^i consists of all the members of N' who are clones of claimant i and N^j consists of all the members of N' who are clones of claimant j. Then $\sum_{\ell \in N^i} c_\ell = \sum_{\ell \in N^j} c_\ell$, so that by *equal treatment of equal groups*, $\sum_{\ell \in N^i} y_\ell = \sum_{\ell \in N^j} y_\ell$. By *equal treatment of equals*, implied by *equal treatment of equal groups*, we have that for each pair $\{\ell, m\} \subseteq N^i$, $y_\ell = y_m$, and for each pair $\{\ell, m\} \subseteq N^j$, $y_\ell = y_m$. It follows that for some $k \in \mathbb{N}$, $y_{N^i \cup N^j} = k(c_{N^i}, c_{N^j})$. Since this conclusion is independent of the identities of the clones of claimant i and of the clones of claimant j that are chosen to compose N^i and N^j, and since the argument applies for each $\{i, j\} \subseteq N$, we deduce that in fact there is $\lambda \in \mathbb{R}$ such that in $(\bar{c}, \bar{E})$, for each $i \in N$, each clone of claimant i receives λc_i. By *replication invariance*, $S(c, E) = \lambda c$.

Case 2: otherwise. Here, we conclude by an approximation argument, invoking *claims continuity*. □

∗ `On the independence of axioms in Theorem 12.5.` ✦ Rules other than the proportional rule exist that satisfy the last two properties of the theorem but not *claims continuity*.[27] If we drop *claims continuity* but strengthen *equal treatment of equals groups* to *group order preservation*, once again, the proportional rule is the only admissible rule. ✦ Young's rules satisfy *claims continuity* and *replication invariance* but not necessarily *equal treatment of equal groups*. ✦ Consider a rule that chooses in a *claims continuous* manner from the set of awards vectors that respect the *group order preservation* inequalities. Such a rule satisfies this property and *claims continuity*. As the claims vector varies, the region to choose from changes shape and defining *claims continuous* selections requires care. Choosing the point x maximizing $\prod x_i$ over it is an example of a selection method that works.

proportional rule characterized

The following additional characterizations of the proportional rule hold.

Theorem 12.6 *The proportional rule is the only rule satisfying*

proportional rule characterized

(a) *claims continuity, equal treatment of equal groups, and division invariance.*
(b) *claims continuity, equal treatment of equal groups, anonymity, and converse consistency.*

27 Ching and Kakkar (2000) give an example.

Proof: We already know that the proportional rule satisfies the properties listed in both parts of the theorem.

(a) Uniqueness is a consequence of Lemma 12.2 and Theorem 12.5.
(b) For uniqueness, let S be a rule satisfying the properties. Theorem 12.5 and Lemma 12.3b together imply that $S = P$ for two claimants. Since P is *bilaterally consistent* and S *conversely consistent*, by the Elevator Lemma, $S = P$ in general. □

12.4.1 Convergence of Rules under Replication

If a rule is not *replication invariant*, it is natural to ask whether anything interesting can nevertheless be said about the awards vector it chooses for a replica of some initial problem as a function of the awards vector it chooses for the model problem as the order of replication increases.[28] Our next theorems answer this question in the affirmative for three rules. Theorem 12.7 concerns the minimal overlap rule, for which we already gave an example showing that it is not *replication invariant*. The theorem can be interpreted as saying that for problems with a large number of claimants whose claims are small in relation to the endowment, the rule essentially behaves like the constrained equal losses rule. Theorem 12.8 pertains to the random arrival rule and Theorem 12.9 to the DT rule. They relate these rules in a similar manner to the proportional rule.

In preparation for Theorem 12.7, let us start with a two-claimant problem. Let $N \equiv \{1, 2\}$ and $(c, E) \in \mathcal{C}^N$ be such that $c_1 \leq c_2$. Since the minimal overlap rule satisfies *equal treatment of equals*, it follows that for each $k \in \mathbb{N}$, the awards vector it chooses for $k * (c, E)$ is the k-replica of an awards vector of (c, E). Thus, we can conveniently represent the minimal overlap awards vector of $k * (c, E)$ by means of its projection on $\mathbb{R}^N$, the awards space of the original two-claimant population.

For each $k \in \mathbb{N}$, there is an interval of values of E for which $MO(k * (c, E)) = CEL(k * (c, E)) = k * CEL(c, E)$ (this last equality is because the constrained equal losses rule is *replication invariant*). For $k = 1$, this interval is $[c_2, c_1 + c_2]$. Indeed, the path of awards of the minimal overlap rule for c coincides with that of the constrained equal losses rule for c when E is restricted to the interval $[c_2, c_1 + c_2]$. Under replication, this coincidence is

[28] As a means of studying the behavior of allocation rules in exchange economies with many "small" participants, researchers have found it to be a useful technique to follow the allocations they recommend along sequences of replicated economies. Certain rules that differ in finite economies have been found to become asymptotically equivalent in large economies, providing insightful links between them. An important result along those lines for classical exchange economies is the convergence of the core to the set of Walrasian outcomes. Other mathematical formulations of largeness have also been studied.

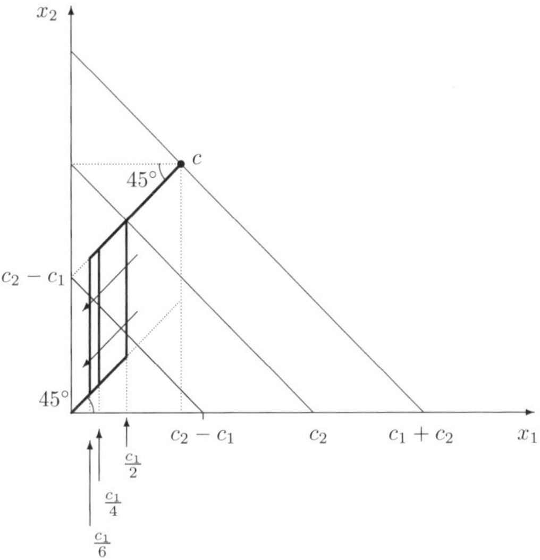

Figure 12.4: **Convergence of the minimal overlap rule to the constrained equal losses rule under replication of a two-claimant example.** We show the projections onto $\mathbb{R}^{\{1,2\}}$ of the paths of awards of the minimal overlap rule for the k-replica, for $k = 1, 2, 3$, of a claims vector $c \in \mathbb{R}_+^{\{1,2\}}$ such that $c_1 < c_2$. This projection consists of a segment contained in the 45° line, a vertical segment to the line of slope 1 passing through c, and a segment to c contained in that line. The vertical segments for $k = 1, 2, 3$ have abscissas $\frac{c_1}{2}$, $\frac{c_1}{4}$, and $\frac{c_1}{6}$. The northeast-to-southwest arrows indicate how the path evolves as k increases. When k is large, the segment containing the origin is negligible, the vertical segment is close to seg$[(0, 0), (0, c_2 - c_1)]$, and the third segment is a segment of slope 1 that extends to c from a point that is close to $(0, c_2 - c_1)$. Thus, the path is close to that of the constrained equal losses rule for c.

preserved. As k increases, the interval of values of E in which coincidence occurs enlarges, and at the limit, it is $[c_2 - c_1, c_1 + c_2]$.

Figure 12.4 shows the paths of awards of the minimal overlap rule for the k-replicas of c, when $k = 1, 2$, and 3, projected onto $\mathbb{R}^N$. For a generic $k \in \mathbb{N}$, the path consists of a segment lying in the 45° line (seg$[(0, 0), (\frac{c_1}{2k}, \frac{c_1}{2k})]$), a vertical segment of length $c_2 - c_1$ of abscissa $\frac{c_1}{2k}$, and a segment of slope 1 to c. For each $E \in]c_2 - c_1, c_1 + c_2]$, there is $k \in \mathbb{N}$ such that for each $k' \geq k$, $MO_N(k' * (c, E)) = CEL(c, E)$. For each $E \in [0, c_2 - c_1]$, there is no finite k after which coincidence with the awards vector chosen by the constrained equal losses rule occurs.

Turning now to the replication of a problem with more than two claimants, it is of interest that for each $N \in \mathcal{N}$, each $c \in \mathbb{R}_+^N$, and each $k \in \mathbb{N}$, the path of awards of the minimal overlap rule for the k-replica of c, when projected onto $\mathbb{R}_+^N$, is the path of an ICI rule for c. In fact, one can calculate the breakpoints in the schedule giving the award to each claimant of a given type as a function of the endowment, and show that each breakpoint converges to a breakpoint of the schedule for the constrained equal losses rule for c.[29]

under replication, minimal overlap rule converges to constrained equal losses rule

Theorem 12.7 *Consider a problem and replicate it. The minimal overlap awards vector of the replica problem is the replica of an awards vector of the initial problem that, as the order of replication increases, converges to the constrained equal losses awards vector of that problem.*

Proof: Let $N \in \mathcal{N}$ and $(c, E) \in \mathcal{C}^N$. Let $k \in \mathbb{N}$. In the calculation of its minimal overlap awards vector, two cases have to be distinguished depending upon whether the largest claim is larger than the endowment (Proposition 2.1). Since the largest claim in any replica of (c, E) is equal to the largest claim in (c, E) whereas the endowment increases without bound in the replication (except in the trivial case when it is initially 0), it follows that for each k larger than some critical value $\bar{k}$, no claim is larger than the endowment, kE. To simplify notation and without loss of generality, let us assume that the inequality $\max c_i \leq E$ holds for (c, E) itself, and also that $N \equiv \{1, \ldots, n\}$ with $c_1 \leq \cdots \leq c_n$. Then, recalling Proposition 2.1, we obtain $MO(c, E)$ by identifying $t \in \mathbb{R}$ such that $\sum_N \max\{c_i - t, 0\} = E - t$. Let t^k be the solution to the corresponding equation in the k-replica of (c, E), namely $k \sum_N \max\{c_i - t^k, 0\} = kE - t^k$.

We assert that $\{t^k\}$ is a decreasing sequence. Indeed, in the passage from a k-replica of (c, E) to a $(k+1)$-replica, and using the language introduced when we defined the rule (Subsection 2.1.9), the amount to be covered increases by E, but if we set $t^{k+1} = t^k$, the additional parts of claims made available by the arrival of an additional replica of N to cover the increase in the endowment would be $\sum_N \max\{c_i - t^k, 0\} = E - \frac{t^k}{k} < E$. Let $\bar{t} \equiv \lim t^k$ and $\bar{i} \equiv \max\{i \in N \colon c_i \leq \bar{t}\}$. For each $i \in N$, let $N^i(k)$ be the set of claimants who are clones of claimant i in the k-replica of (c, E). Now, there is $i^k \in N$ such that what each agent $j \in k * N$ receives can be expressed as

$$x_j \equiv \begin{cases} \frac{c_1}{nk} & \text{if} \quad j \in N^1(k) \\ \frac{c_1}{nk} + \frac{c_2 - c_1}{(n-1)k} & \text{if} \quad j \in N^2(k) \\ \quad \vdots \quad + \quad \vdots & \quad \vdots \\ \frac{c_1}{nk} + \frac{c_2 - c_1}{(n-1)k} + \cdots + \frac{c_{i^k} - c_{i^k - 1}}{(n - i^k + 1)k} & \text{if} \quad j \in N^{i^k}(k) \\ \frac{c_1}{nk} + \frac{c_2 - c_1}{(n-1)k} + \cdots + \frac{c_{i^k} - c_{i^k - 1}}{(n - i^k + 1)k} & \text{if } j \in N^i(k) \text{ for each } i \geq i^k \\ \quad + \frac{t^k - c_{i^k}}{n - i^k} + c_i - t^k & \end{cases}$$

As $k \to \infty$, each of the ratios goes to 0. Thus at the limit, for each $i < \bar{i}$, each agent j who is a clone of agent i receives 0, and for each $i \geq \bar{i}$, each

[29] Theorem 12.7 is due to Chun and Thomson (2005).

agent j who is a clone of agent i receives $c_j - \bar{t}$. Thus, the limit awards vector is the one chosen by the constrained equal losses rule. □

The next theorem gives a limit result for the random arrival rule. This time, replication takes us to the proportional rule.[30]

Theorem 12.8 *Consider a problem and replicate it. The random arrival awards vector of the replica problem is the replica of an awards vector of the initial problem that, as the order of replication increases, converges to the proportional awards vector of that problem.*

under replication, random arrival rule converges to proportional rule

We relegate the proof to an appendix (Section 17.15).

Theorem 12.8 extends to situations in which the claimant population is enlarged in a more general manner than through replication.[31]

Our third convergence result pertains to the DT rule, which, as is easily shown, is not *replication invariant*. The result has the same format as Theorems 12.7–12.8. As was the case for the random arrival rule, the proportional rule is the limit.[32]

Theorem 12.9 *Consider a problem and replicate it. The DT awards vector of the replica problem is the replica of an awards vector of the initial problem that, as the order of replication increases, converges to the proportional awards vector of that problem.*

under replication, DT rule converges to proportional rule

Proof: Let $N \in \mathcal{N}$ and $(c, E) \in \mathcal{C}^N$ be given. If $E = 0$, there is nothing to prove, so let us assume that $E > 0$. Again, let $k * (c, E)$ be a problem obtained by replicating k-times the problem (c, E). For k large enough, for each $i \in N$, $kE > c_i$, and at the first round, each agent $i \in k * N$ receives $\frac{1}{k|N|} c_i$. (The total distributed is $\frac{k}{|N|} \frac{1}{k} \sum_{j \in N} c_j = \frac{1}{|N|} \sum_{j \in N} c_j$.) Revised claims are proportional to original claims. At the second round, if the residual endowment is larger than the largest revised claim, proportional division to the revised claims prevails. Thus, total awards so far are still proportional to original claims. This goes on until a stage $\bar{k}(k)$ at which the endowment is smaller than the largest claim revised $\bar{k}(k)$ times. This remainder is divided among $k|N|$ claimants. Each replica of the original population receives in total at most $\frac{\max c_j}{k|N|}$, so the sum of the partial terms received by each member of each copy goes to zero as $k \to \infty$. □

A final and obvious result concerns the adjusted proportional rule. Since in any problem replicated sufficiently many times, minimal rights are all zero and

under replication, adjusted proportional rule converges to proportional rule

[30] Theorem 12.8 is due to Chun and Thomson (2005).

[31] Chun and Lee (2007).

[32] Theorem 12.9 is due to Dominguez and Thomson (2006).

no claim exceeds the endowment, under replication this rule behaves like the proportional rule.

12.5 BALANCED IMPACT AND POTENTIAL

The requirements considered in this section are unlike any other that we have seen so far. First, given some problem with agent set N and given two claimants in N, i and j, we calculate the impact on agent i's award of agent j departing with an award equal to agent j's own claim if possible, and the entire endowment otherwise (for a residual endowment of $\max\{E-c_j, 0\}$), and symmetrically we calculate the impact on agent j's award of agent i departing with agent i's own claim if possible and the entire endowment otherwise. We require these two calculations to deliver the same number.[33]

Balanced impact: For each $N \in \mathcal{N}$, each $(c, E) \in \mathcal{C}^N$, and each $\{i, j\} \subseteq N$,

$$S_i(c, E) - S_i\left(c_{-j}, \max\{E - c_j, 0\}\right) = S_j(c, E) - S_j\left(c_{-i}, \max\{E - c_i, 0\}\right).$$

Note that because (c, E) is a well-defined problem, so are $(c_j, \max\{E - c_j, 0\})$ and $(c_j, \max\{E - c_j, 0\})$.

The dual of *balanced impact* says that the impact on agent i's award of agent j's withdrawing and the endowment being replaced by the maximum of its initial value and the sum of everyone's claim except for agent j's claim is equal to the impact on agent j's award of agent i's withdrawing under symmetric terms.

random arrival rule characterized

Theorem 12.10 *The random arrival rule is the only rule satisfying balanced impact.*

Proof: The fact that the random arrival rule satisfies *balanced impact* is most easily established by exploiting a certain correspondence between this rule and the solution to coalitional games with transferable utility known as the Shapley value (Theorem 14.2a). The relevant definitions are given in Subsection 14.1.2.

Conversely, let S^1 and S^2 be two rules satisfying *balanced impact*. The proof that $S^1 = S^2$ is by induction on the number of claimants. If there is only one claimant, the result is trivial. Suppose then that the result is true up to $n - 1$ claimants. Let $N \in \mathcal{N}$ be a population of size n, and $(c, E) \in \mathcal{C}^N$. Let $\{i, j\} \subset N$. We have

[33] This is a natural adaptation to the present context of a requirement introduced in the theory of coalitional games by Myerson (1980) (see also Hart and Mas-Colell, 1989). It appears in Bergantiños and Méndez-Naya (1997), under the name of "balanced contributions," to whom Theorem 12.10 is due. A version of it for the domain of "multi-issue" claims problems (Section 15.7) is established by Lorenzo-Freire, Alsonso-Meijide, Casas-Mendez, and Hendrickx (2007). The proof of Theorem 12.10 is closely patterned after the proof of the characterization of the Shapley value developed by Myerson (1980). Albizuri and Santos (2014) generalize the approach.

$$\begin{aligned} S_i^1(c,E) - S_j^1(c,E) &= S_i^1\left(c_{-j}, \max\{E-c_j,0\}\right) \\ &\quad - S_j^1\left(c_{-i}, \max\{E-c_i,0\}\right) \\ &= S_i^2\left(c_{-j}, \max\{E-c_j,0\}\right) \\ &\quad - S_j^2\left(c_{-i}, \max\{E-c_i,0\}\right) \\ &= S_i^2(c,E) - S_j^2(c,E), \end{aligned}$$

where the first and third equalities are by *balanced impact* and the second one is by the induction hypothesis.

Since $\sum_N S_k^1(c,E) = \sum_N S_k^2(c,E) = E$, we conclude that $S^1(c,E) = S^2(c,E)$. □

We conclude this section by introducing the notion of a **potential**: this is a real-valued function Pot defined on the domain $\bigcup_{N\in\mathcal{N}} \mathcal{C}^N$ augmented for convenience by the "empty" problem (the problem whose claimant set is empty) such that for each $N \in \mathcal{N}$ and each $(c,E) \in \mathcal{C}^N$, $\sum_N[Pot(c,E) - Pot(c_{N\setminus\{i\}}, \max\{E-c_i,0\})] = E$, where by convention, the value of the potential for the empty problem is 0. We call the i-th difference appearing in this expression claimant i's **contribution** to the potential.[34] Our final result is another characterization of the random arrival rule:

Theorem 12.11 *There is a unique potential. For each problem, the random arrival awards vector is the profile of the claimants' contributions to the potential.* random arrival rule characterized

12.6 MULTIPLE PARAMETER CHANGES; LOGICAL RELATIONS AND CHARACTERIZATIONS

Although we have so far mainly considered changes in only one parameter of a problem at a time, several of them could change simultaneously. We allowed this possibility on a few occasions in previous chapters (Section 8.2), and duality considerations confirmed the relevance of properties pertaining to simultaneous changes in two parameters (*linked claim-endowment monotonicity* and *linked endowment-population monotonicity*). An interesting feature of these simultaneous changes was that they were related. We begin this section by formulating a property in which variations in two parameters occur but these changes are not related, as in Section 8.2.[35]

We consider simultaneous replacements of endowment and population, and require that each claimant who is present before and after the change (these are the relevant agents here) receive at least as much as initially, or that each receive at most as much as initially:

[34] The notion of a potential is proposed by Hart and Mas-Colell (1989). Theorem 12.11 is due to Hwang (2015). See also Albizuri and Santos (2014).

[35] *Endowment-and-population uniformity* is introduced by Chun (1999) under the name of "population-and resource monotonicity." Lemmas 12.4–12.9, are due to him.

Endowment-and-population uniformity: For each $N \in \mathcal{N}$, each $N' \subset N$, each $(c, E) \in \mathcal{C}^N$, and each $(c', E') \in \mathcal{C}^{N'}$, if $c_{N'} = c'$, then either $S_{N'}(c, E) \geqq S(c', E')$ or $S_{N'}(c, E) \leqq S(c', E')$.

This property is *self-dual*.

Obviously, in the light of *balance*, it implies both *endowment monotonicity* and *population monotonicity*, but the converse is not true. As was the case for the properties introduced in Section 8.2, the reason is that the change in the endowment and the change in the population may work in opposite directions. Consider, for instance, increases in both. By *endowment monotonicity*, as the endowment increases, each claimant should receive at least as much as initially. If the population increases, by *population monotonicity*, each claimant initially present should receive at most as much as they did after the change in the endowment. For these agents, the conjunction of these two uniform changes (uniform in direction) may not be uniform itself; altogether, some of them may receive more and others less. The random arrival rule illustrates the possibility.

Next, we investigate logical relations among the properties defined in Section 8.2 and the property just introduced. All results come in pairs relating two properties. A first property implies a second one. The second property, in conjunction with a mild auxiliary property (either *endowment monotonicity* or *null claims consistency*) implies the first one.[36] The lemmas and the theorem closing this chapter all involve at least one variable-population property and they pertain to rules defined on $\mathcal{C} \equiv \bigcup_{N \in \mathcal{N}} \mathcal{C}^N$.

Lemma 12.4 *Endowment-and-population uniformity implies consistency.*

Proof: Let S be a rule satisfying the hypothesis. Let $N \in \mathcal{N}$, $(c, E) \in \mathcal{C}^N$, and $N' \subset N$. Let $x \equiv S(c, E)$. By *claims boundedness*, $(c_{N'}, \sum_{N'} x_i) \in \mathcal{C}^{N'}$. Let $y \equiv S(c_{N'}, \sum_{N'} x_i)$. By *endowment-and-population uniformity*, either (i) $y \geqq x_{N'}$ or (ii) $y \leqq x_{N'}$. By *balance*, $\sum_{N'} y_i = \sum_{N'} x_i$. Thus, from either (i) or (ii), we obtain $y = x_{N'}$. Thus, *consistency* holds. □

Lemma 12.5 *Endowment monotonicity and consistency together imply endowment-and-population uniformity.*

Proof: Let S be a rule satisfying the hypotheses. Let $N \in \mathcal{N}$, $(c, E) \in \mathcal{C}^N$, $N' \subset N$, and $(c', E') \in \mathcal{C}^{N'}$ be such that $c_{N'} = c'$. Let $x \equiv S(c, E)$. By *consistency*, $x_{N'} = S(c_{N'}, \sum_{N'} x_i) = S(c', \sum_{N'} x_i)$.

By *endowment monotonicity*, (i) if $E' \geq \sum_{N'} x_i$, then $S(c', E') \geqq S(c', \sum_{N'} x_i) = x_{N'} = S_{N'}(c, E)$, and (ii) if $E' \leq \sum_{N'} x_i$, then $S(c', E') \leqq$

[36] Although most of the properties formulated above have counterparts for other domains such as the classical exchange economies, or economies with single-peaked preferences, the logical relations uncovered below do not all extend to these domains.

$S(c', \sum_{N'} x_i) = x_{N'} = S_{N'}(c, E)$. Thus, *endowment-and-population uniformity* holds. □

Our next pair of lemmas relate *endowment-and-population uniformity* and *claims-and-endowment uniformity*.

Lemma 12.6 *Endowment-and-population uniformity implies claims-and-endowment uniformity.*

Proof: Let S be a rule satisfying the hypothesis. By Lemma 12.4, S is *consistent*. Let $N \in \mathcal{N}$, $N' \subset N$, and $(c, E), (\bar{c}, \bar{E}) \in \mathcal{C}^N$ be such that $c_{N'} = \bar{c}_{N'}$. Let $x \equiv S(c, E)$. By *consistency*, $S(c_{N'}, \sum_{N'} x_i) = x_{N'}$. By *endowment-and-population uniformity*, either $S_{N'}(\bar{c}, \bar{E}) \geqq x_{N'}$ or $S_{N'}(\bar{c}, \bar{E}) \leqq x_{N'}$. Thus, *claims-and-endowment uniformity* holds. □

Lemma 12.7 *Null claims consistency and claims-and-endowment uniformity together imply endowment-and-population uniformity.*

Proof: Let S be a rule satisfying the hypotheses. Let $N \in \mathcal{N}$, $N' \subset N$, $(c, E) \in \mathcal{C}^{N'}$, and $(\bar{c}, \bar{E}) \in \mathcal{C}^N$ be such that $c_{N'} = \bar{c}_{N'}$. Let $x \equiv S(c, E)$. Let $(c'', E) \in \mathcal{C}^N$ be such that for each $i \in N'$, $c''_i \equiv c_i$, and for each $i \in N \backslash N'$, $c''_i \equiv 0$. By *null claims consistency*, $S_{N'}(c'', E) = S_{N'}(c, E) = x$. By *claims-and-endowment uniformity* applied to (c'', E) and $(\bar{c}, \bar{E})$, either $S_{N'}(\bar{c}, \bar{E}) \geqq S_{N'}(c'', E) = x_{N'}$ or $S_{N'}(\bar{c}, \bar{E}) \leqq S_{N'}(c'', E) = x_{N'}$. Thus, *endowment-and-population uniformity* holds. □

Our final pair of lemmas relate *consistency*, *null claims consistency*, and *claims-and-endowment separability*.

Lemma 12.8 *Consistency implies claims-and-endowment separability.*

Proof: Let S be a rule satisfying the hypothesis. Let $N \in \mathcal{N}$, $N' \subset N$, and $(c, E), (\bar{c}, \bar{E}) \in \mathcal{C}^N$ be such that $c_{N'} = \bar{c}_{N'}$ and $\sum_{N'} S_i(c, E) = \sum_{N'} S_i(\bar{c}, \bar{E})$. By *consistency*, $S_{N'}(c, E) = S(c_{N'}, \sum_{N'} S_i(c, E))$ and $S_{N'}(\bar{c}, \bar{E}) = S(\bar{c}_{N'}, \sum_{N'} S_i(\bar{c}, \bar{E}))$. Since $c_{N'} = \bar{c}_{N'}$ and $\sum_{N'} S_i(c, E) = \sum_{N'} S_i(\bar{c}, \bar{E})$, we obtain $S(c_{N'}, \sum_{N'} S_i(c, E)) = S(\bar{c}_{N'}, \sum_{N'} S_i(\bar{c}, \bar{E}))$, which implies $S_{N'}(c, E) = S_{N'}(\bar{c}, \bar{E})$. Thus, *claims-and-endowment separability* holds. □

Lemma 12.9 *Null claims consistency and claims-and-endowment separability together imply consistency.*

Proof: Let S be a rule satisfying the hypotheses. Let $N \in \mathcal{N}$ and $N' \subset N$, and $(c, E) \in \mathcal{C}^N$. Let $x \equiv S(c, E)$. We need to show that $x_{N'} = S(c_{N'}, \sum_{N'} x_i)$. Let $(\bar{c}, \bar{E}) \in \mathcal{C}^N$ be defined by $\bar{c}_{N'} \equiv c_{N'}$, $\bar{c}_{N \backslash N'} \equiv 0$, and

$\bar{E} \equiv \sum_{N'} x_i$. By *balance*, $\sum_{N'} S_i(\bar{c}, \bar{E}) = \bar{E}$. Since $\bar{c}_{N'} = c_{N'}$ and $\sum_{N'} S_i(\bar{c}, \bar{E}) = \sum_{N'} S_i(c, E)$, then by *claims-and-endowment separability*, $S_{N'}(\bar{c}, \bar{E}) = S_{N'}(c, E) = x_{N'}$. By *null claims consistency* again, $S(c_{N'}, \sum_{N'} x_i) = S_{N'}(\bar{c}, \bar{E}) = x_{N'}$. Thus, *consistency* holds. □

The following characterizations are direct consequences of Theorem 10.9 and of the logical relations just established:

Young's family characterized

Theorem 12.12 *Consider the class of rules satisfying equal treatment of equals and endowment continuity. Among those, Young's rules are the only ones to satisfy*

(a) *endowment-and-population uniformity, or*
(b) *null claims consistency and claims-and-endowment uniformity, or*
(c) *null claims consistency and claims-and-endowment separability.*

CHAPTER 13

Ranking Awards Vectors and Ranking Rules

In this chapter, we propose to rank rules on the basis of how evenly they distribute the endowment. In the theory concerning the measurement of income inequality, a number of criteria have been developed to compare income distributions, and these criteria are just as natural here.

Since rules are more complex objects than income distributions, however, one should not expect to be able to compare any two rules very generally. The comparisons are likely to depend on the specific values of the claims, of the endowment, of the number of claimants, and even on their identities. In fact, for each particular problem, the awards vectors chosen by two rules may not be comparable at all. Nevertheless, one may hope that within specific classes of rules, comparisons would be possible. The main results of this chapter more than fulfill this hope. In fact, they concern families of rules that are sufficiently wide as to contain all of the rules that have been most often discussed in the literature. Some also exploit the fact that the space of rules can be structured in various ways by operators (Chapter 9).

The main criterion that we consider is the "Lorenz criterion," but we also offer some results pertaining to two other notions: given a claims problem and an awards vector for it, we measure how differently claimants are treated at this awards vector by the gap between the largest and smallest amounts any two claimants receive. We also use the variance of the amounts claimants receive.

The Lorenz order is a partial order in n-dimensional Euclidean space. We base on it the definition of a partial order on the space of rules. For each problem, the orders on the set of awards vectors induced by the gap and variance measures of each particular problem are complete but they too only induce partial orders on the space of rules.

We leave it to the reader's judgment how differences in claims should be reflected in awards vectors. Our goal in this chapter is simply to provide tools to help in this evaluation. These tools happen to allow comparisons of rules within broad families.

13.1 ORDERS BASED ON THE LORENZ CRITERION

In this chapter, and apart from Section 13.3, the population of claimants is a fixed set N.

We begin by defining a ranking of vectors that is standard in the literature on the evaluation of income distributions. Given a problem and two awards vectors for it, we say that the former "Lorenz-dominates the latter" if its smallest coordinate is at least as large as the smallest coordinate of the second vector, the sum of its two smallest coordinates is at least as large as the corresponding sum for the second vector, and so on. Strict Lorenz domination holds if at least one of these inequalities is strict. For a formal statement, given $x \in \mathbb{R}^N_+$, we denote by $\tilde{x}$ the vector obtained from x by rewriting its coordinates in increasing order. Now, given x and $y \in \mathbb{R}^N_+$ with $\sum x_i = \sum y_i$, we say that **x Lorenz-dominates y**, which we write as $x \succsim_L y$, if $\tilde{x}_1 \geq \tilde{y}_1$, $\tilde{x}_1 + \tilde{x}_2 \geq \tilde{y}_1 + \tilde{y}_2$, $\tilde{x}_1 + \tilde{x}_2 + \tilde{x}_3 \geq \tilde{y}_1 + \tilde{y}_2 + \tilde{y}_3$, and so on. **Strict Lorenz domination** holds if at least one of these inequalities is strict. We write $x \succ_L y$ if $x \succsim_L y$ but not $y \succsim_L x$. Given two rules S and S', we say that **S Lorenz-dominates S'** if, for each $(c, E) \in \mathcal{C}^N$, $S(c, E) \succeq_L S'(c, E)$. We write $S \succ_L S'$ if in addition, there is $(c, E) \in \mathcal{C}^N$ for which $S(c, E) \succ_L S'(c, E)$. A passage from x to y is **Lorenz improving** if y Lorenz-dominates x.

Parallel rankings can be based on the ordered vectors of losses. We can speak of a loss vector Lorenz-dominating some other loss vector, and a rule Lorenz-dominating some other rule in terms of losses.

13.1.1 Maximality and Minimality Results

The following is an obvious characterization of the constrained equal awards rule as being maximal from the viewpoint of the Lorenz order.[1]

constrained equal awards rule characterized

Theorem 13.1 *For each problem, the constrained equal awards vector is the only one to maximize the Lorenz order among all awards vectors.*

Proof: Let $(c, E) \in \mathcal{C}^N$. Suppose, to simplify notation, that $c_1 \leq \cdots \leq c_n$. Let $x \equiv CEA(c, E)$ with λ such that for each $i \in N$, $x_i = \min\{c_i, \lambda\}$. If $y \in X(c, E)$ differs from x, there is $i \in N$ such that $y_i < c_i \leq \lambda$ and $j \in N$ with $x_j \leq \lambda < y_j$. Let $\delta \leq \min\{c_i - x_i, y_j - \lambda\}$ and $z \in X(c, E)$ be obtained from y by transferring δ from claimant j to claimant i. This transfer is a Lorenz-improving transfer, so y is not Lorenz-maximal in $X(c, E)$. □

We also have:

[1] The first explicit statement of Theorem 13.1 is in Moulin (1988). See also Hougaard and Thorlund-Peterson (2001) and Bosmans and Lauwers (2011). Theorem 13.2 is due to Bosmans and Lauwers (2011). Theorem 13.3 is due to Chun, Schummer, and Thomson (2001).

Theorem 13.2 *For each problem, the constrained equal losses awards vector is the only one to minimize the Lorenz order among all awards vectors satisfying the order preservation inequalities.* constrained equal losses rule characterized

By duality, we deduce from Theorem 13.1 that for each problem, the constrained equal losses awards vector is the only awards vector to minimize the Lorenz order for losses among all awards vectors. It also follows from Theorem 13.2 that for each problem, the constrained equal awards awards vector is the only awards vector to maximize the Lorenz order for losses among all awards vectors satisfying the *order preservation* inequalities.

The next theorem describes the awards vector chosen for each problem by the constrained egalitarian rule as maximal in the Lorenz order among all awards vectors for that problem chosen by rules satisfying two very mild requirements:

Theorem 13.3 *Consider the class of rules satisfying endowment monotonicity and the midpoint property. In that class, the constrained egalitarian rule chooses for each problem the awards vector that maximizes the Lorenz order.* constrained egalitarian rule characterized

Proof: Let S be a rule satisfying the two axioms of the theorem. Let $(c, E) \in \mathcal{C}^N$. Invoking these axioms, either $S(c, E) \leqq \frac{c}{2}$ or $S(c, E) \geqq \frac{c}{2}$.

Case 1: $E \leq \sum \frac{c_i}{2}$. Then $S(c, E) \leqq \frac{c}{2}$. Let $Y(c, E) \equiv \{x \in \mathbb{R}^N_+ : 0 \leqq x \leqq \frac{c}{2} \text{ and } \sum x_i = E\}$. Since $Y(c, E)$ is compact, and the Lorenz order is acyclic and lower continuous, it can be maximized over $Y(c, E)$. Let $x \in Y(c, E)$ be a maximizer. Suppose by contradiction that $x \neq CE(c, E)$.

Let $x^{max} \equiv \max\{x_j\}$. Since $x \neq CE(c, E)$, there is $i \in N$ such that $x_i < x^{max}$ and $x_i < \frac{c_i}{2}$. Let $\delta \equiv \min\{\frac{c_i}{2}, x^{max}\} - x_i$. Let $N' \equiv \{j \in N : x_j = x^{max}\}$.

Define $y \in \mathbb{R}^N$ as follows: $y_i \equiv x_i + \frac{\delta}{2}$; for each $j \in N'$, $y_j \equiv x_j - \frac{\delta}{2|N'|}$; and for each $k \notin N' \cup \{i\}$, $y_k \equiv x_k$. It is straightforward to check that $y \in Y(c, E)$ and that y Lorenz-dominates x, contradicting our choice of x.

Case 2: $E > \sum \frac{c_i}{2}$. A similar argument can be developed for this case. □

The following are characterizations of Piniles' and minimal overlap rules. We omit the proofs.[2]

Theorem 13.4

(a) *Consider the class of rules satisfying order preservation, the midpoint property, endowment monotonicity, and composition up from midpoint. In that class, Piniles' rule is, uniquely, Lorenz-maximal.* Piniles' rule characterized

[2] Theorem 13.4(a) is due to Schummer and Thomson (1997), and Theorem 13.4(b) to Bosmans and Lauwers (2011). Theorem 13.5 to Bosmans and Lauwers (2011).

Piniles' rule characterized

(b) Consider the class of rules satisfying order preservation in awards, the midpoint property, endowment monotonicity, and order preservation under endowment variations. In that class, Piniles' rule is, uniquely, Lorenz-maximal.

Corollary 13.1 *Piniles's rule Lorenz-dominates the proportional, Talmud, random arrival, and adjusted proportional rule.*

minimal overlap rule characterized

Theorem 13.5 *Consider the class of rules satisfying order preservation, the $\frac{1}{|N|}$-truncated-claims lower bounds on awards, order preservation under claims variations, and null claims consistency. In that class, the minimal overlap rule is, uniquely, Lorenz-minimal.*

Corollary 13.2 *The Talmud, random arrival, and adjusted proportional rules Lorenz-dominate the minimal overlap rule.*

The proof consists in checking that the Talmud rule indeed satisfies the properties listed in Theorem 13.5.

13.1.2 A Criterion for Lorenz-Domination within the ICI Family

Our next theorem identifies a sufficient condition relating the parameters defining two ICI rules for one of them to Lorenz-dominate the other.[3]

for ICI rules, criterion for Lorenz-domination

Theorem 13.6 *Let S and S' be two ICI rules, associated with $H \equiv (F, G)$ and $H' \equiv (F', G') \in \mathcal{H}^N$ respectively. If for each $k \in \{1, \ldots, |N|-1\}$, $F^k \leq F'^k$, then $S' \succcurlyeq_L S$.*

Let x and $x' \in \mathbb{R}^N_+$ be such that $\sum x_i = \sum x'_i$. We will exploit the fact that $x' \succeq_L x$ if and only if we can obtain x' from x by means of a sequence of Lorenz-improving transfers. The transfers are from one (or several) claimant(s) to one (or several) claimant(s).

Let $c \in \mathbb{R}^N_+$. Lemma 13.1 pertains to the special case when for some $k \in \{1, \ldots, n\}$, only F^k increases, or slightly more generally, for some $k \in \{1, \ldots, n\}$ and some $\bar{k} \in \{0, \ldots, n-k-1\}$, $\bar{k}$ successive values of F^ℓ are equal and increase together, all other F^ℓ's remaining the same.

Lemma 13.2 states that the passage from H to H' described in the hypotheses of Theorem 13.6 can be written as the composition of elementary increases as described in Lemma 13.1.

For the proof of Lemma 13.1, we recall that an ICI rule is defined, for each claims vector, and letting the endowment increase from 0 to the sum of the claims, as follows: carry out equal division first among the members of groups of decreasing sizes, then among the members of the same groups

[3] Theorem 13.6 is due to Thomson (2012a).

considered in the reverse order. We will speak of agents "entering" or "leaving" the distribution.

Lemma 13.1 *Let S and S' be two ICI rules, associated with $H \equiv (F, G)$ and $H' \equiv (F', G') \in \mathcal{H}^N$ respectively. If there are $k \in \{1, \ldots, n\}$ and $\bar{k} \in \{0, \ldots, n-k-1\}$ such that $F^k = \cdots = F^{k+\bar{k}} < F'^k = \cdots = F'^{k+\bar{k}}$ and for each $\ell \notin \{k, \ldots k+\bar{k}\}$, $F^\ell = F'^\ell$, then for each $(c, E) \in \mathcal{C}^N$, $S'(c, E)$ Lorenz-dominates $S(c, E)$.*

Proof: In the light of the calculations following the introduction of the ICI relations, we know that the ICI rule associated with the pair $(F, G) \in \mathcal{H}^N$ is defined, for each $c \in \mathbb{R}^N_+$, by the location within $[0, \sum c_i]$, of nested subintervals, $I^1(c) \equiv [F^1(c), G^1(c)]$, $I^2(c) \equiv [F^2(c), G^2(c)]$, ..., $I^{n-1}(c) \equiv [F^{n-1}(c), G^{n-1}(c)]$, of successive lengths $\delta^1(c)$, $\delta^2(c)$,..., $\delta^{n-1}(c)$, these lengths being the same for all members of the ICI family. Since the calculations are performed for each claims vector separately, let us omit c from the notation (and write F^k instead of $F^k(c)$ for instance).

First, let us suppose that no two claims are equal, which means that $\bar{k} = 0$ in the statement of the lemma. Let $k \in \{1, \ldots, n-1\}$, and consider the passage from F^k to $F'^k > F^k$. We show that for each $E \in [0, \sum c_i]$, $x' \equiv S'(c, E)$ is obtained from $x \equiv S(c, E)$ by means of Lorenz-improving transfers (Figure 13.1).

Case 1: $E \in [0, F^k]$. Then $x' = x$ and the conclusion holds trivially.

Case 2: $E \in [F^k, F'^k]$. (This means that claimant k leaves the distribution later for S' than for S.) Let $\Delta \equiv E - F^k$. Rule S distributes this difference equally among claimants $k+1, \ldots, n$. Rule S' distributes it equally among claimants $k, \ldots, n$, claimants $1, \ldots, k-1$'s awards remaining at the values they are given by both rules when $E = F^k$. The differences between the successive partial sums for S' and S are: $0, \ldots, 0$ (this last 0 being the $(n-k+1)$-th term), $\frac{\Delta}{n-k+1}$, $(1 - \frac{1}{n-k})\frac{\Delta}{n-k+1}, \ldots, (1 - \frac{n-k}{n-k})\frac{\Delta}{n-k+1}$. The maximal values of these differences are obtained for $\Delta^* \equiv F^k - F'^k$.

Case 3: $E \in [F'^k, G^k]$. As E increases in that interval, both rules distribute each increment in the same fashion. Thus, the differences between the successive partial sums remain what they are under Case 2 for the largest value of the endowment covered under that case, namely $E = F'^k$.

Case 4: $E \in [G^k, G'^k]$. (This means that claimant k reenters the distribution later for S' than for S.) Let $\bar{\Delta} \equiv E - G'^k$. Rule S distributes this difference equally among claimants $k, \ldots, n$. Rule S' distributes it equally among claimants $k+1, \ldots, n$. We obtain the differences between the successive partial sums for S' and S by adding to what they are at the end of Case 2, for $E = F'^k$, the following sequence: $0, \ldots, 0$ (this last zero being the $(n-k+1)$-th term), $-\frac{\Delta}{n-k+1}$, $-(1 - \frac{1}{n-k})\frac{\Delta}{n-k+1}, \ldots, -(1 - \frac{n-k}{n-k})\frac{\Delta}{n-k+1}$. When $E = G^k$, $\bar{\Delta} = G^k - G'^k$, and since $G'^k - G^k = F'^k - F^k$, the second sequence is the

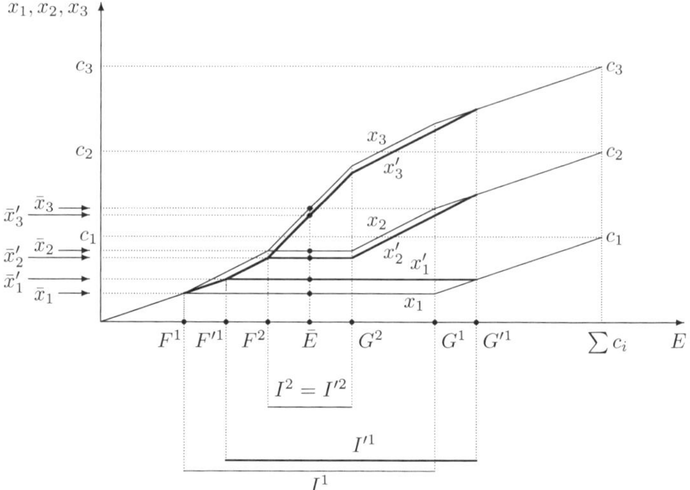

Figure 13.1: **A criterion for Lorenz domination within the ICI family** (illustrating Lemma 13.1). Let $N \equiv \{1, 2, 3\}$ and $c \in \mathbb{R}^N_+$. In this example, and starting from the two intervals $I^1 \equiv [F^1, G^1]$ and $I^2 \equiv [F^2, G^2]$ defining an ICI rule, we move I^1 to the right, obtaining $I'^1 \equiv [F'^1, G'^1]$. For values of the endowment E in either the interval $[0, F^1]$ or the interval $[G'^1, \sum c_i]$, this does not affect awards. As E increases from F^1 to F'^1, its distribution becomes more favorable to claimant 1 at the expense of claimants 2 and 3, and the reverse occurs as it increases from G^1 to G'^1. The differences between the two distributions remain the same for each endowment in the interval $[F'^1, G^1]$. We call $\bar{x}$ and $\bar{x}'$ the two distributions obtained for a typical $\bar{E}$ in that interval.

negative of the first sequence, and the successive partial sums for S' and S are equal.

Case 5: $E \in [G'^k, \sum c_i]$. The successive partial sums remain equal until E reaches $\sum c_i$.

When two claims are equal, two adjacent parameters are equal for all ICI rules. Then to pass from one to the other, we have to adjust adjacent parameters together. This requires a straightforward adaptation of the calculations just made. If exactly $\bar{k}$ successive parameters are equal, starting with E^k, the transfer is from claimants $k, \ldots, k + \ell$ to claimants $k + \bar{k}, \ldots, n$ for initial values of the endowment, and later, from claimants $k + \bar{k} + 1, \ldots, n$ to claimants $k, \ldots, k + \bar{k}$. □

Lemma 13.2 *Let S and S' be two ICI rules, associated with H and $H' \in \mathcal{H}^N$ respectively, with H and H' satisfying the hypotheses of Theorem 13.6. Then one can pass from H to H' by a succession of adjustments as described in Lemma 13.1.*

We will illustrate the proof by means of examples, supposing first that no two claims are equal. Again, we drop c from the notation. If $F \leq F'$, then each interval for S lies to the left of the corresponding interval for S'. For two claimants, there is a single interval, and there are no nesting constraints: we can pass from I^1 to I'^1 in one step.

If $n \geq 3$, we may need more than one step. Suppose $n = 3$. Then there are two intervals, I^1 and I^2.

In each of the examples, $F^1 = F^2 = 0$ (thus, $S = CEL$) and $G'^1 = G'^2 = \sum c_i$ (thus, $S' = CEA$). This is the case for which the required movements are the largest, and they give us an upper bound on the number of steps. To preserve nesting, we move I^1 to the right, then I^2, then I^1 again, and so on.

Example 13.1 (Figure 13.2a): Let $N \equiv \{1, 2, 3\}$ and $c \equiv (4, 5, 6)$. Then $\delta_1 = 3$ and $\delta_2 = 1$. We label "0" the initial positions of the two intervals $[F^1, G^1]$ and $[F^2, G^2]$. Since their left endpoints are equal, we can only move the upper one. The difference $\delta^1 - \delta^2$ of their lengths is equal to 2. It is the maximal amount by which we can move the upper interval. We label "1" the result of this first move. Once this is done, we can move the lower interval, and the maximal amount of this move is also $\delta^1 - \delta^2 = 2$. We label "2" the result of this second move. We now return to the higher interval. Once again, we can move it by the same amount. We label "3" the result of this third move. We continue in this manner until the right endpoints of both intervals are $\sum c_i$. Altogether, for the example, we need 13 steps. (The successive values of the left endpoints of the two intervals are (0, 0), (0, 2), (2, 2), (2, 4), (4, 4), (4, 6), (6, 6), (6, 8), (8, 8), (8, 10), (10, 10), (10, 12), (12, 12), (12, 13).)

Example 13.2 (Figure 13.2b): Let $N \equiv \{1, 2, 3\}$ and $c \equiv (1, 2, 12)$. Then $\delta^1 = 12$ and $\delta^2 = 10$. The sum of the claims is the same as in Example 1 but we need fewer steps to pass from the constrained equal losses rule to the constrained equal awards rule. The difference $\delta^1 - \delta^2$ is still equal to 2, but since δ^1 is close to $\sum c_i$, there is less ground to cover. (The five successive values of the left endpoints of the two intervals are (0, 0), (0, 2), (2, 2), (2, 4), (3, 4), (3, 5).)

Example 13.3 (Figure 13.2c): Let $N \equiv \{1, 2, 3\}$ and $c \equiv (1, 6, 8)$. Then $\delta^1 = 12$ and $\delta^2 = 2$. The higher interval has much to move but because the difference $\delta^1 - \delta^2$ is large, at each step, we can move it by a larger amount. (The three successive values of the left endpoints of the two intervals are (0, 0), (0, 10), (3, 10), (3, 13).)

These examples show that when claims are different, we can move each interval by the difference between the lengths of two successive intervals. Since the distance by which we have to move any interval is finite, we can do so in finitely many steps.

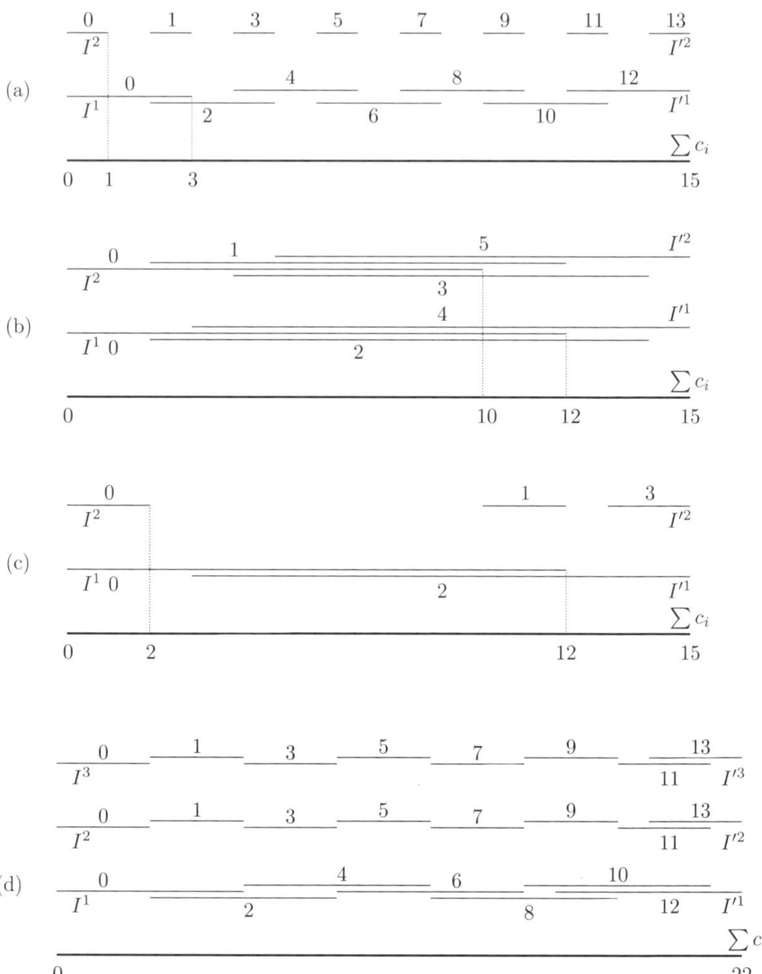

Figure 13.2: **Passing from one ICI rule to the other** (illustrating Lemma 13.2.) (a) Example 13.1. (b) Example 13.2. (c) Example 13.3. We represent the intervals I^1 and I^2 as horizontal segments at several heights. We number their successive positions, starting with "0." At Step 1, the higher interval moves to the right, its new position being labeled "1." At Step 2, the lower interval moves, its new position being labeled "2," and so on. (d) For Example 13.4, there are three intervals I^1, I^2, and I^3. Since $c_2 = c_3$, I^2 and I^3 have equal lengths, and they have to move together.

Example 13.4 (Figure 13.2d): Let $N \equiv \{1, 2, 3, 4\}$ and $c \equiv (4, 5, 5, 8)$. Then $\delta^1 = 6$ and $\delta^2 = \delta^3 = 3$. Here, two intervals are equal, so they have to move together. (The 13 successive values of the left endpoints of the three intervals are (0, 0, 0), (0, 3, 3), (3, 3, 3), (3, 6, 6), (6, 6, 6), (6, 9, 9), (9, 9, 9),

(9, 12, 12), (12, 12, 12), (12, 15, 15), (15, 15, 15), (15, 18, 18), (16, 18, 18), (16, 19, 19).)

Proof: (of Lemma 13.2). The proof is by induction on the number of claimants. The assertion is true for two claimants. Indeed, there is only one interval then and we can move it to its required position in one step. Suppose the assertion is true for $n-1$ claimants. We prove it for n claimants. We carry out a sequence of moves of intervals to the right. Suppose first that all claims are distinct. We move I^{n-1} and I^{n-2} in turn. Moving I^{n-2} by any amount may require moving I^{n-3}, ..., I^1 first, but by the induction hypothesis, this requires finitely many steps. If at any step, one of the intervals I^k reaches the position I'^k, we stop for that interval, and the exercise splits into two parts: one of them involves all claimants $\ell > k$ and the other involves all claimants $\ell < k$. We proceed with each group separately, but for each of them, by the induction hypothesis, the number of required steps is finite.

The sum of the maximal movements of I^{n-1} and I^{n-2} during the first two steps is given by the difference $\delta^{n-2} - \delta^{n-1} = 2(c_{n-1} - c_{n-2}) > 0$. At each of the next steps, we can move either one of these intervals by this difference. As the distance by which each has to move is finite, we need finitely many steps. Altogether, we can therefore move all intervals from their initial to their final positions in finitely many steps.

If some claims are equal, we have to move some intervals together, but this can only decrease the number of steps we need. □

Proof: (of Theorem 13.6). It is a direct consequence of Lemmas 13.1 and 13.2. □

We offer two interesting Lorenz comparisons of rules as a corollary of Theorem 13.6:[4]

Corollary 13.3

(a) *The Talmud rule Lorenz-dominates the minimal overlap rule.*
(b) *For each pair* $\{\theta^1, \theta^2\}$ *of elements of* $[0,1]$, *if* $\theta^1 < \theta^2$, *then* T^{θ^2} *Lorenz-dominates* T^{θ^1}.

Proof: Let $N \equiv \{1, \ldots, n\}$ and $c \in \mathbb{R}^N_+$ be such $c_1 \leq \cdots \leq c_n$. (a) The proof consists in noting that the sequence of parameters associated with the Talmud rule and the sequence of parameters associated with the minimal overlap rule satisfy the inequalities stated in Theorem 13.6. They are $(F^{Tk})_{k=1}^{n-1} = (n\frac{c_1}{2}, \frac{c_1}{2} + (n-1)\frac{c_2}{2}, \ldots, \frac{c_1}{2} + \frac{c_2}{2} + \cdots + (n-k+1)\frac{c_k}{2}, \ldots, \frac{c_1}{2} + \frac{c_2}{2} + \cdots + \frac{c_{n-1}}{2} + 2\frac{c_{n-1}}{2})$ and $(F^{MOk})_{k=1}^{n-1} = (c_1, c_2, \ldots, c_{n-1})$ (Lemma 2.2). Ignoring the case $n = 1$ for which the conclusion holds trivially, observe that

[4] Part (a) was derived by different means earlier and stated as Corollary 13.2. A direct proof of (b) is given by Moreno-Ternero and Villar (2006b).

$$\begin{array}{lllllllll}
n\frac{c_1}{2} & & & & & & & \geq & c_1 \\
\frac{c_1}{2} & + & (n-1)\frac{c_2}{2} & & & & & \geq & c_2 \\
\cdots & & & & & & & \geq & \cdots \\
\frac{c_1}{2} & + & \frac{c_2}{2} & + & \cdots & + & (n-k+1)\frac{c_k}{2} & \geq & c_k \\
\cdots & & & & & & & \geq & \cdots \\
\frac{c_1}{2} & + & \frac{c_2}{2} & + & \cdots & + & \cdots \quad + \; 2\frac{c_{n-1}}{2} & \geq & c_{n-1}
\end{array}$$

The first inequality is obviously satisfied. The remaining ones can be written, for each $k = 2, \ldots, n-1$, as $\sum_{\ell=1}^{k-1} c_\ell + (n-k+1)c_k \geq 0$.

(b) Given $\theta \in [0, 1]$, we have $F^{T^\theta} = (n\theta c_1, \theta c_1 + \theta(n-1)c_2, \ldots, \theta c_1 + \theta c_2 + \cdots + \theta(n-k+1)c_k, \ldots, \theta c_1 + \theta c_2 + \cdots + 3\theta c_{n-1} + 2\theta c_{n-1})$. The functions $F^{T^{\theta^1}}$ and $F^{T^{\theta^2}}$ are proportional, thus they trivially satisfy the hypotheses of the theorem. □

A parallel conclusion to that of Theorem 13.6 holds for the CIC family. The proof is parallel too, and we omit it. The only difference is that the transfer is from one claimant to several others instead of from several claimants to one of them. Also, a counterpart of Corollary 13.3 holds for the family $\{U^\theta\}_{\theta \in [0,1]}$.

The form taken for the ICI* rules (Subsection 11.2.3) by the sufficiency criterion of Theorem 13.6 is particularly simple. Moreover, it becomes necessary.

for ICI* rules, criterion for Lorenz-domination

Theorem 13.7 *Let S and S' be two ICI* rules, associated with γ and $\gamma' \in \Gamma$. Then S^γ Lorenz-dominates $S^{\gamma'}$ if and only if $\gamma \geq \gamma'$.*

Proof: The fact that if $\gamma \geq \gamma'$, then S^γ Lorenz-dominates $S^{\gamma'}$, is a consequence of Theorem 13.6. Conversely, suppose that there is $c_0 \in \mathbb{R}_+$ such that $\gamma(c_0) < \gamma'(c_0)$. Let $N \equiv \{1, 2\}$ and $c \in \mathbb{R}^N_+$ such that $c_1 = c_0$ and $c_2 > c_0$. It is easy to see that the path of S^γ for c lies to the northwest of the path of $S^{\gamma'}$ for c, so in fact, for each $E \in [0, \sum c_i]$, $S^{\gamma'}(c, E) \succeq_L S^\gamma(c, E)$. Also, for some E (in fact, for each E in an entire interval), $S^{\gamma'}(c, E) \succ_L S^\gamma(c, E)$. □

A counterpart of Theorem 13.7 can also be established for the CIC* family.

13.2 PRESERVATION OF ORDERS BY OPERATORS

Recall that, given an operator p and a rule S, S^p designates the rule obtained by subjecting S to p. Let $\succeq$ be an order on the space of rules. **Operator p preserves the order $\succeq$** if for each pair of rules S and S' such that $S \succeq S'$, we have $S^p \succeq S'^p$. Similarly, the **convexity operator preserves the order $\succeq$** if for each rule S, each finite index set K, each list $(S^k)_{k \in K}$ such that for each $k \in K$, $S^k \succeq S$, and each list $(\lambda^k)_{k \in K} \in \Delta^K$, we have $\sum \lambda^k S^k \succeq S$.

The following theorem pertains to our four central operators.[5]

Theorem 13.8

Lorenz order preserved or reversed

(a) The claims truncation operator preserves the Lorenz order.
(b) The attribution of minimal rights operator preserves the Lorenz order for any two rules satisfying order preservation in awards.
(c) The duality operator reverses the Lorenz order for any two rules satisfying order preservation.
(d) The convexity operator preserves the Lorenz order within the class of rules satisfying order preservation in awards.

Proof: Let S and S' be two rules such that $S \succeq_L S'$.

(a) Let $N \in \mathcal{N}$ and $(c, E) \in \mathcal{C}^N$. Then $S^t(c, E) = S(t(c, E), E) \succeq_L S'(t(c, E), E) = S'^t(c, E)$.

(b) Let $N \equiv \{1, \ldots, n\}$ and $c \in \mathbb{R}^N_+$ be such that $c_1 \leq \cdots \leq c_n$. We need to compare $S^m(c, E) \equiv m(c, E) + S(c - m(c, E), E - \sum m_i(c, E))$ and $S'^m(c, E) \equiv m(c, E) + S'(c - m(c, E), E - \sum m_i(c, E))$. Obviously, $m_1(c, E) \leq \cdots \leq m_n(c, E)$ and a simple calculation shows that $c_1 - m_1(c, E) \leq \cdots \leq c_n - m_n(c, E)$ (Section 9.2). Thus, since S and S' satisfy *order preservation in awards*, $S_1(c - m(c, E), E - \sum m_i(c, E)) \leq \cdots \leq S_n(c - m(c, E), E - \sum m_i(c, E))$ and $S'_1(c - m(c, E), E - \sum m_i(c, E)) \leq \cdots \leq S'_n(c - m(c, E), E - \sum m_i(c, E))$. Altogether

$$m_1(c, E) + S_1(c - m(c, E), E - \sum m_i(c, E)) \leq \cdots \leq m_n(c, E) + S_n(c - m(c, E), E - \sum m_i(c, E))$$

and similarly,

$$m_1(c, E) + S'_1(c - m(c, E), E - \sum m_i(c, E)) \leq \cdots \leq m_n(c, E) + S'_n(c - m(c, E), E - \sum m_i(c, E)).$$

Since $S \succeq_L S'$, then for each $k = 1, \ldots, n$,

$$\sum_{i=1}^{k} S_i(c - m(c, E), E - \sum m_i(c, E)) \geq \sum_{i=1}^{k} S'_k(c - m(c, E), E - \sum m_i(c, E)).$$

[5] Theorems 13.8 and 13.9 are due to Thomson (2012a). Part (c) of Theorem 13.8 is also in Bosmans and Lauwers (2011). It fails without *order preservation*. To see this, let $N \equiv \{1, 2\}$ and $c \equiv (1, 2) \in \mathbb{R}^N_+$. Let S be a rule whose path of awards for c is bro.seg$[(0, 0), (0, \frac{3}{2}), c]$ and whose path coincides with that of CEL for each other claims vector. (This rule is discontinuous but we can easily adapt it to satisfy this property too.) Clearly $CEL \succeq_L S$, but it is not true that $S^d \succeq_L CEL^d = CEA$. Indeed, the path of S^d for c is bro.seg$[(0, 0), (1, \frac{1}{2}), c]$. Note that S violates *order preservation in losses* but satisfies *order preservation in awards.* We can establish the relevance of *order preservation in awards* by means of the same example: $CEA \succeq_L S^d$, but it is not true that $(S^d)^d \succeq_L CEA^d = CEL$.

For each $k = 1, \ldots, n$, we obtain the kth partial sums for $S^m(c, E)$ and $S'^m(c, E)$ from the partial sums just calculated by adding the same quantity $\sum_{i=1}^k m_i(c, E)$. Thus, the inequalities between them are preserved and $S^m \succeq_L S'^m$.

(c) Suppose S and S' satisfy *order preservation*. We need to show that $S'^d \succeq_L S^d$. Let $N \equiv \{1, \ldots, n\}$ and $c \in \mathbb{R}_+^N$ be such that $c_1 \leq \cdots \leq c_n$. By definition of the duality operator, $S'^d(c, E) \succeq_L S^d(c, E)$ means that $[c - S'(c, \sum c_i - E)] \succeq_L [c - S(c, \sum c_i - E)]$. Let $\bar{E} \equiv \sum c_i - E$. Since S and S' satisfy *order preservation in losses*, $c_1 - S_1(c, \bar{E}) \leq \cdots \leq c_n - S_n(c, \bar{E})$ and $c_1 - S'_1(c, \bar{E}) \leq \cdots \leq c_n - S'_n(c, \bar{E})$. Thus, we need to show that for each $k = 1, \ldots, n$, $\sum_{i=1}^k [c_i - S'_i(c, \bar{E})] \geq \sum_{i=1}^k [c_i - S_i(c, \bar{E})]$. For each $k = 1, \ldots, n$, and after canceling from both sides of the kth inequality in this list the partial sum $\sum_{i=1}^k c_i$, we obtain $\sum_{i=1}^k S_i(c, \bar{E}) \geq \sum_{i=1}^k S'_i(c, \bar{E})$, which holds because S and S' satisfy *order preservation in awards*. Thus, $S \succeq_L S'$.

(d) We omit the easy proof. □

Given any rule, we now ask whether it can be Lorenz-compared to the rule obtained by subjecting it to a particular operator. The next theorem provides two answers to this question. Recall that *other-regarding claims monotonicity* says that whenever an agent's claim decreases, each of the other agents should receive at least as much as initially.

Theorem 13.9

on Lorenz-domination

(a) Let S be a rule satisfying order preservation in awards and other-regarding claim monotonicity. Then S is Lorenz-dominated by the rule obtained by subjecting S to the claims truncation operator.

(b) Let S be a rule satisfying order preservation and the dual of other-regarding claim monotonicity. Then S Lorenz-dominates the rule obtained by subjecting S to the attribution of minimal rights operator.

Proof: (a) Let S be a rule satisfying the hypotheses. Let $N \in \mathcal{N}$, $(c, E) \in \mathcal{C}^N$ with $c_1 \leq \cdots \leq c_n$, $x \equiv S(c, E)$, and $N' \equiv \{i \in N : c_i > E\}$. In the problem $(t(c, E), E)$, the claim of each agent $i \in N'$ is truncated at E. Let $y \equiv S(t(c, E), E)$. By *order preservation in awards*, $x_1 \leq \cdots \leq x_n$. Also, the order of claims is not affected by the truncation. By *order preservation in awards*, $y_1 \leq \cdots \leq y_n$. Thus, the successive sums of ordered coordinates of x and y involve the same successive sets of claimants. If $N' = \emptyset$, there is nothing to prove, so let us assume otherwise, and let $i \in N$ be the agent with the smallest index in N'. By *other-regarding claim monotonicity*, for each $j < i$ (there may be no such j), $y_j \geq x_j$. Thus $\frac{\sum_{k \geq i} y_k}{|N'|} \geq \frac{\sum_{k \geq i} x_k}{|N'|}$. By *equal treatment of equals*, which *order preservation in awards* implies, for each pair $\{k, k'\} \subseteq N'$, $y_k = y_{k'} \equiv a$. Thus, there is $k \in N'$ such that for each $k' \in N'$ with $k' \leq k$, $y_{k'} = a \geq x_{k'}$, and for each $k' > k$, $y_{k'} = a \leq x_{k'}$. Altogether, for each $k' \leq k$, $y_{k'} > x_{k'}$, and for each $k' > k$, $y_{k'} \leq x_{k'}$. Then an easy calculation shows that $y \succeq_L x$.

(b) This statement follows from (a) by dual reasoning. It exploits the fact that after attribution of minimal rights, the revised claims of all agents whose minimal rights are positive are equal. □

13.3 LIFTING OF ORDERS BY BILATERAL CONSISTENCY

The idea of lifting developed in Section 10.5 can be applied to orders on the space of rules. We return to the variable-population version of our model. Say that an **order $\succeq$ is lifted** if whenever two rules S and S' defined on $\bigcup_{N \in \mathcal{N}} \mathcal{C}^N$ are such that $S \succeq S'$ for two claimants, and both rules are *bilaterally consistent*, then $S \succeq S'$ for arbitrarily many claimants. As we did for properties, we can also speak of **an order being lifted with the assistance of particular properties**. Just as was the case there, *endowment monotonicity* is quite helpful in this regard. This is revealed by the following lifting result. It will allow us to Lorenz-compare important rules, exploiting their *consistency* and the fact that we can easily Lorenz-compare them for two claimants.[6]

Lemma 13.3 *let S and S' be two rules satisfying order preservation in awards for two claimants, endowment monotonicity for two claimants, and bilateral consistency. If S Lorenz-dominates S' for two claimants, then S Lorenz-dominates S' in general.*

Proof: Let $N \in \mathcal{N}$ and $(c, E) \in \mathcal{C}^N$. Let $x \equiv S(c, E)$ and $x' \equiv S'(c, E)$. To simplify notation, suppose $N \equiv \{1, \ldots, n\}$ and $c_1 \leq \cdots \leq c_n$. Since S and S' satisfy *order preservation in awards for two claimants*, a property that is lifted (Lemma 10.13c), $x_1 \leq \cdots \leq x_n$ and $x'_1 \leq \cdots \leq x'_n$. Suppose that x does not Lorenz-dominate x'. Then there is $\bar{i} \in N$ such that $\sum_{\ell=1}^{\bar{i}} x'_\ell > \sum_{\ell=1}^{\bar{i}} x_\ell$. Let i be the smallest index for which this is the case. Obviously, $x'_i > x_i$. Also, $\sum_N x_k = \sum_N x'_k$, and thus, there is $j \in N$ with $i < j$ such that $x'_j < x_j$. Let $N' \equiv \{i, j\}$. Since S is *bilaterally consistent*, $(x_i, x_j) = S((c_i, c_j), x_i + x_j)$. Since S' is *bilaterally consistent*, $(x'_i, x'_j) = S'((c_i, c_j), x'_i + x'_j)$. Let $y \equiv S'((c_i, c_j), x_i + x_j)$. If $x'_i + x'_j \leq x_i + x_j$, then since S' is *endowment monotonic for two claimants*, $y_i \geq x'_i > x_i$. If $x'_i + x'_j > x_i + x_j$, then since S' is *endowment monotonic for two claimants*, $y_j \leq x'_j < x_j$. Since S and S' satisfy *order preservation in awards*, $x_i \leq x_j$ and $y_i \leq y_j$. In either case, we conclude that (y_i, y_j) Lorenz-dominates (x_i, x_j). Thus, it is not true that $S \succeq_L S'$ for two claimants. □

[6] Lemma 13.3 is due to Thomson (2012a). Some of the comparisons stated in Corollary 13.4 are also proved by Bosmans and Lauwers (2011). Their approach is to identify Lorenz-minimal or Lorenz-maximal elements among families of rules satisfying certain properties.

Corollary 13.4 *The constrained equal awards rule Lorenz-dominates the constrained egalitarian rule, which Lorenz-dominates Piniles' rule, which Lorenz-dominates the proportional rule and the Talmud rule, both of which Lorenz-dominate the constrained equal losses rule.*

Proof: The fact that all of these rules satisfy the first two axioms of Lemma 13.3 is direct. We have established their *bilateral consistency* in Chapter 10. We can easily check the Lorenz-domination statements for two claimants by inspecting their paths of awards. (Figures 16.1 and 16.2 can be consulted for that purpose.) □

13.4 OTHER PROPERTIES OF RULES PERTAINING TO ORDERS

We consider here the requirement on a rule that possible inequalities in claims be diminished by its application.[7] We formulate the property for the Lorenz order, but it could be written for any order. The same comment applies to the property introduced below.

Lorenz-inequality reduction: For each $(c, E) \in \mathcal{C}^N$, $[c - S(c, E)] \succeq_L c$.

We first state several interesting logical relations between several properties that we have seen.[8]

Lemma 13.4

(a) *Order preservation in losses and progressivity together imply Lorenz-inequality reduction.*
(b) *Lorenz-inequality reduction and consistency together imply progressivity.*
(c) *Lorenz-inequality reduction, endowment continuity (or endowment monotonicity), and consistency together imply order preservation in losses.*

We continue with a characterization of a subfamily of Young's family.

on Lorenz inequality reduction

Theorem 13.10 *A rule satisfies Lorenz inequality reduction, endowment continuity, and consistency if and only if (i) it is a Young rule whose representations are superhomogeneous*[9] *in claims. In addition, (ii)* $f: \mathbb{R}_+ \times \Lambda \mapsto \mathbb{R}$ *being any such representation, for each* $\lambda \in \Lambda$, *the function* $c_0 \in \mathbb{R}_+ \mapsto c_0 - f(\lambda, c_0)$ *is nowhere decreasing.*

[7] This property is studied by Ju and Moreno-Ternero (2006).

[8] Lemma 13.4 and Theorem 13.10 are due to Ju and Moreno-Ternero (2008).

[9] A function is "superhomogeneous" if the value it takes when its argument is multiplied by $\lambda > 0$ is always at least as large as λ times the value it takes for the argument.

We also address the question of whether *Lorenz inequality reduction* is preserved by operators.[10]

Proposition 13.1 *The convexity operator preserves Lorenz inequality reduction. So does the attribution of minimal rights operator.*

Given two claims problems with equal aggregate claims and equal endowments, we ask next that a possible Lorenz rankings of their claims vectors be reflected in either the awards vector chosen by the rule or in the implied losses vector, or in both. The idea is that a rule should not have too much of an impact on the distribution of wealth in society. Given that claimants will not receive what they are entitled to, some impact is unavoidable, but limiting it might contribute to the stability of society:[11]

Let $E > 0$ and c and $c' \in \mathbb{R}^N_+$ be such that $\sum c_i = \sum c'_i \leq E$. Supposing that $c \succeq_L c'$, we require that the awards vectors $S(c, E)$ and $S(c', E)$ be comparable in the order $\succeq_L$ and that they be Lorenz-ordered in the same way, and that so be the corresponding vectors of losses:

Lorenz rankings preservation: For each pair $\{(c, E), (c', E')\} \subset \mathcal{C}^N$ such that $\sum c_i = \sum c'_i$, $E = E'$, and $c \succeq_L c'$, then $S(c, E) \succeq_L S(c', E')$ and $[c - S(c, E)] \succeq_L [c' - S(c', E')]$.

We refer to the first part of this property as **Lorenz rankings preservation in awards** and to the second part as **Lorenz rankings preservation in losses**. These axioms are dual.

Proposition 13.2 *The constrained equal awards rule preserves Lorenz rankings in awards. The constrained equal losses rule preserves Lorenz rankings in losses. The proportional rule preserves Lorenz rankings.*

How restrictive is *Lorenz ranking preservation*? For two claimants, it is not restrictive at all, and all of the rules that are commonly discussed satisfy it. For three claimants, infinitely many rules do too, but among the standard rules, only the proportional rule passes the test. If there are at least four claimants, the following uniqueness result holds:[12]

Theorem 13.11 *For $|N| \geq 4$. The proportional rule is the only rule that preserves order and preserves Lorenz rankings.* proportional rule characterized

[10] Proposition 13.1 is due to Ju and Moreno-Ternero (2008).

[11] These properties are formulated by Hougaard and Thorlund-Peterson (2001) to whom Proposition 13.2 is due. Kasajima and Velez (2010, 2011) refer to them as "claims-inequality preservation in gains" and "claims-inequality preservation in losses."

[12] The question is asked by Hougaard and Østerdal (2005), who assert that if there are at least three agents, only the proportional rule qualifies. In fact, this is true only if there are at least four claimants, as established by Kasajima and Velez (2011). These authors also settle the case of two claimants and the case of three claimants for *continuous* rules (2010). The latter is considerably more complex.

We omit the difficult proof.

13.5 ORDERS BASED ON GAP AND VARIANCE

A ranking of rules alternative to the Lorenz ranking can be based on the difference, for each problem, between the largest amount any claimant receives and the smallest amount any claimant receives. For each $(c, E) \in \mathcal{C}^N$ and each $x \in X(c, E)$, let $g(x) \equiv \max\{x_i\} - \min\{x_i\}$ be the **gap at *x***.

A third ranking can be based on the variance, for each problem, of the amounts all agents receive. For each $(c, E) \in \mathcal{C}^N$ and each $x \in X(c, E)$, let $\mathrm{v}(x) \equiv \frac{1}{n} \sum_N (x_i - \frac{E}{n})^2$ be the **variance at *x***.

In general, an awards vector that maximizes the Lorenz order may not minimize the difference between the largest and smallest amounts any two claimants receive. To see this, compare the awards vectors $x \equiv (4, 9, 10)$ and $y \equiv (5, 6, 12)$. Note that $\sum x_i = \sum y_i = 23$, $g(x) = 6$, $g(y) = 7$, but x does not Lorenz-dominate y. However, for two claimants, the two exercises coincide. Also, if a rule is the only one minimizing the gap (or the variance), it does not follow that it is the only one maximizing the Lorenz order.

The next theorems identify maximal elements for the orders based on gap or variance:[13]

constrained equal awards rule characterized

Theorem 13.12 *For each claims problem, the awards vector chosen by the constrained equal awards rule is the only one at which the difference between the largest amount received by any claimant and the smallest such amount is minimized.*

Proof: (Figure 13.3). Let $(c, E) \in \mathcal{C}^N$. Recall that $X(c, E) \equiv \{x \in \mathbb{R}^N_+ : 0 \leqq x \leqq c$ and $\sum x_i = E\}$ and for each $x \in \mathbb{R}^N_+$, $g(x) \equiv \max\{x_i\} - \min\{x_i\}$. Since $X(c, E)$ is compact and g is continuous, there is a minimizer of g over $X(c, E)$. Let $x \in \operatorname{argmin}_{y \in X(c,E)} g(y)$. Suppose by contradiction that $x \neq CEA(c, E)$.

Let $x^{max} \equiv \max\{x_j\}$. Since $x \neq CEA(c, E)$, there is $i \in N$ such that $x_i < x^{max}$ and $x_i < c_i$. Let $\delta \equiv \min\{c_i, x^{max}\} - x_i$ and $N' \equiv \{j \in N : x_j = x^{max}\}$.

Define $y \in \mathbb{R}^N$ as follows: $y_i \equiv x_i + \frac{\delta}{2}$; for each $j \in N'$, $y_j \equiv x_j - \frac{\delta}{2|N'|}$; and for each $k \notin N' \cup \{i\}$, $y_k \equiv x_k$. It is easy to check that $y \in X(c, E)$ and $g(y) < g(x)$, contradicting our choice of x. (In the figure, after the transfer, claimants 4 and 5 are still the ones receiving the largest amount but this need not be the case. Also, agent 1's award is unchanged but it could have increased, this resulting in the gap decreasing from both ends.) □

[13] Theorems 13.12 and 13.13 are due to Schummer and Thomson (1997). These results parallel their characterizations of an important rule to the problem of allocation when preferences are single-peaked (discussed in Subsection 2.1.7), the uniform rule (defined in that subsection).

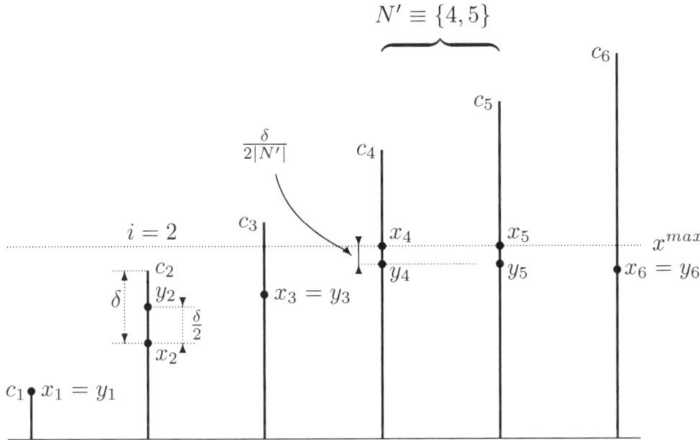

Figure 13.3: **Characterizing the constrained equal awards rule as gap minimizer** (Theorem 13.12). The proof is by contradiction. Let $N \equiv \{1, \ldots, 6\}$. A rule S satisfying the properties of the theorem chooses for some $(c, E) \in \mathcal{C}^N$ an awards vector $x \neq CEA(c, E)$. Claimant 2 is one who at x receives less than their claim, although someone else receives more than them (claimant 3 is also in that position). Claimant 2 is claimant i in the proof. Claimants 4 and 5 are the ones who at x receive the largest amount among all claimants. They constitute the group N' in the proof.

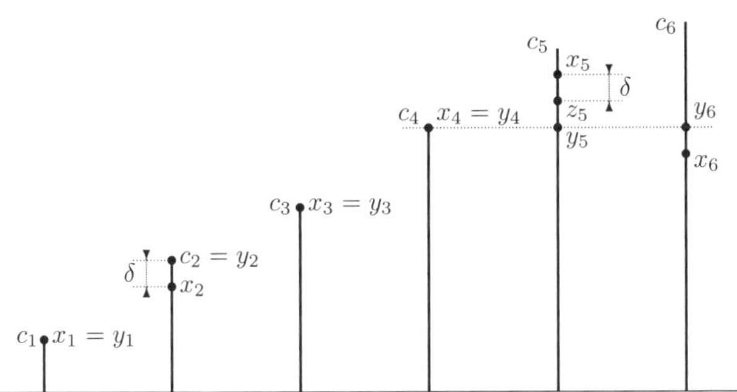

Figure 13.4: **Characterizing the constrained equal awards rule as variance minimizer** (Theorem 13.13). The proof is by contradiction. Let $N \equiv \{1, \ldots, 6\}$. A rule S satisfying the properties of the theorem chooses for some $(c, E) \in \mathcal{C}^N$ an awards vector $x \neq CEA(c, E)$. Claimant 2 is one who at x receives less than the constrained equal awards rule would assign to them. Claimant 2 is claimant i in the proof. Claimant 5 is one who at x receives more than the constrained equal awards rule would assign to them. Claimant 5 is claimant j in the proof.

Theorem 13.13 *For each claims problem, the awards vector chosen by the constrained equal awards rule is the only one at which the variance of the amounts received by all of the claimants is minimized.*

constrained equal awards rule characterized

Proof: Let $(c, E) \in \mathcal{C}^N$, and for each $x \in \mathbb{R}^N_+$, recall that $v(x) \equiv \frac{1}{n} \sum_N (x_i - \frac{E}{n})^2$. Since $X(c, E)$ is compact and v is continuous, there is a minimizer of v over $X(c, E)$. Let $x \in \text{argmin}_{y \in X(c,E)} v(y)$. Suppose $x \neq y \equiv CEA(c, E)$. Then there is $\{i, j\} \subseteq N$ such that $x_i < y_i$ and $x_j > y_j$. By definition of the constrained equal awards rule, $x_i < y_i \leq y_j < x_j$.

Let $\delta \equiv \min\{y_i - x_i, x_j - y_j\}$. Note that $\delta > 0$. Let $z \in \mathbb{R}^N$ be defined as follows: $z_i \equiv x_i + \delta$; $z_j \equiv x_j - \delta$; and for each $k \notin N \backslash \{i, j\}$, $z_k \equiv x_k$. Since $x \in X(c, E)$, $z_i \leq y_i$, $z_j \leq x_j$, and $\sum z_k = E$, then $z \in X(c, E)$. Letting $e \equiv \frac{E}{|N|}$, we have

$$\begin{aligned}
n \cdot v(x) - n \cdot v(z) &= (x_i - e)^2 + (x_j - e)^2 - (z_i - e)^2 - (z_j - e)^2 \\
&= \{(x_i - e)^2 - (z_i - e)^2\} + \{(x_j - e)^2 - (z_j - e)^2\} \\
&= (x_i - 2e + z_i)(x_i - z_i) + (x_j - 2e + z_j)(x_j - z_j) \\
&= (2x_i + \delta - 2e)(-\delta) + (2x_j - \delta - 2e)\delta \\
&= \delta(-2x_i + 2x_j - 2\delta) \\
&> 2\delta(x_j - x_i - (x_j - x_i)) \\
&= 0,
\end{aligned}$$

the inequality coming from the fact that $x_i < y_i \leq y_j < x_j$. This contradicts our choice of x. □

The constrained equal losses rule can be characterized in dual fashion to each of the ways in which the constrained equal awards rule is characterized in Theorems 13.12 and 13.13; it suffices to replace gains by losses. We can obtain the proofs by duality from the proofs of these results:

constrained equal losses rule characterized

Theorem 13.14 *For each claims problem, the awards vector chosen by the constrained equal losses rule is the only one at which the difference between the largest loss incurred by any claimant and the smallest loss incurred by any claimant is minimized.*

constrained equal losses rule characterized

Theorem 13.15 *For each claims problem, the awards vector chosen by the constrained equal losses rule is the only one at which the variance of the losses incurred by all of the claimants is minimized.*

Given the similarities in the definitions of the constrained equal awards and constrained egalitarian rules, it is natural to wonder whether counterparts of the characterizations of the former as being most egalitarian subject to certain constraints can be stated for the latter by simply modifying the constraints. The answer is yes: this rule is most egalitarian among all rules satisfying *endowment monotonicity* and the *midpoint property*:

constrained egalitarian rule characterized

Theorem 13.16 *For each claims problem, the difference between the largest amount received by any claimant and the smallest such amount is at* *most as large at the awards vector chosen by the constrained egalitarian rule as the corresponding difference at the awards vector chosen by each other rule satisfying* **endowment monotonicity** *and the* **midpoint property**. *For two claimants, the constrained egalitarian rule is the only rule to so behave.*

We omit the proof, which is similar to that of Theorem 13.12. The uniqueness result for two claimants does not hold for more than two claimants, but a result parallel to Theorem 13.13 is true in general. We also omit its proof.[14]

Theorem 13.17 *For each claims problem, the variance of the amounts received by the various claimants is at most as large at the awards vector chosen by the constrained egalitarian rule as the corresponding variance at the awards vector chosen by any other rule satisfying endowment monotonicity and the midpoint property.* constrained egalitarian rule characterized

We conclude with some results pertaining to preservation by operators of the orders based on gap and variance.

Proposition 13.3

gap dominance, variance dominance preserved by operators

(a) *The claims truncation operator preserves gap dominance.*
(b) *So does the minimal rights operator.*
(c) *The duality operator reverses it.*
(d) *Parallel statements hold for the order based on variance.*

Figure 13.5 summarizes our results on Lorenz comparisons for the main rules. The relations it indicates can be justified as follows. For the string

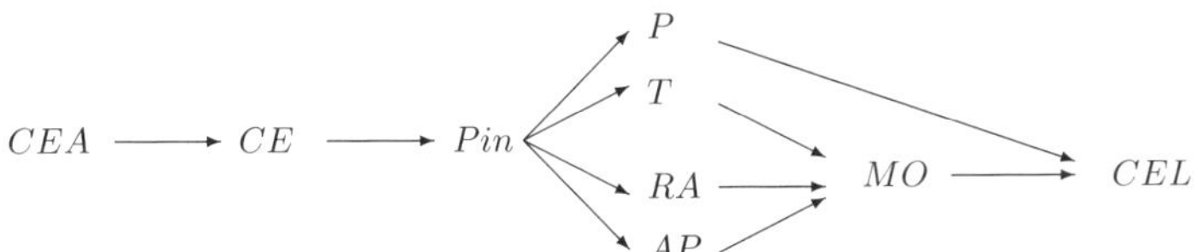

Figure 13.5: **Summarizing Lorenz rankings.** An arrow from a rule S to a rule S' indicates that $S \succeq_L S'$. The notation CE refers to the constrained egalitarian rule and the notation AP to the adjusted proportional rule.

[14] Theorem 13.17 is due to Chun, Schummer, and Thomson (2001). It is worth noting that the characterization of the uniform rule for rationing problem with single-peaked preferences on which it is based is obtained by considering one rationing problem at a time, whereas the characterization proposed here is defined for rules defined on the whole domain of claims problems. The *midpoint property* pertains to a small subdomain of the domain of claims problems, and it is a punctual requirement, whereas *endowment monotonicity* is a relational requirement.

$CEA \succ_L CE \succ_L Pin \succ_L \{P, T\} \succ_L CEL$, see Corollary 13.4. The fact that $\{T, RA, AP\} \succ_L MO$ is stated as Corollary 13.2. The fact that $Pin \succ_L \{P, T, RA, AP\}$ is stated as Corollary 13.1.

The figure suggests that T, RA, AP, and MO are not Lorenz comparable. They coincide for two claimants, so of course, they are Lorenz indistinguishable then, so let us suppose that there are more than two claimants. Fix the claims vector. When the endowment is equal to the half-sum of the claims, all four rules select equal division. Because the first three are *self-dual*, if a Lorenz ranking of the awards vectors selected by any two of the three is possible for some endowment E, a Lorenz ranking is also possible for the dual endowment, but it will go in the opposite direction. Thus one should not expect a uniform ranking over all endowments. However, a ranking for endowments that are no greater than the half-sum of the claims (and the reverse ranking for endowments that are no smaller than the half-sum of the claims) is possible: in the lower range of the endowment, $P \succ_L AP \succ_L T$. However, P and RA are not Lorenz comparable in either the lower range of the endowment or in its upper range; RA and AP are not Lorenz comparable in either range; and P and MO are not Lorenz comparable in the lower range.[15]

[15] These results are due to Bosmans and Lauwers (2011).

CHAPTER 14

Modeling Claims Problems as Games

Here, we borrow concepts, techniques, and results from game theory to solve claims problems. Proceeding in this manner has proved very successful in many branches of economic theory: the economies under study are converted into games, the games are solved, and the allocations generating the solution payoff vectors are chosen as outcomes for the economies. We draw upon both the cooperative and the noncooperative branches of the game theory literature. We will see that this approach provides additional support for several of the rules to which the axiomatic approach had led us.[1]

14.1 MODELING CLAIMS PROBLEMS AS COOPERATIVE GAMES

For the theory of cooperative games to be applicable to solve claims problems, we first have to formally associate with each claims problem a cooperative game. Two important classes of such games are bargaining games and coalitional games with transferable utility. We propose two definitions, one for each class.

14.1.1 Bargaining Games

Here, we show the relevance of concepts of the cooperative theory of bargaining to the analysis of claims problems.

(i) **Bargaining games and solutions to bargaining games.** We need the following definitions, which we introduce in the context of a fixed population. They can be generalized to variable populations in the usual way.[2] Let $N \in$ be a set of agents, called **players**. A **bargaining game** is a pair (B, d),

[1] A related approach is followed by Tejada and Álvarez-Mozos (2016). They explore correspondences between claims problems and so-called "multi-sided Böhm-Bawerk assignment games."

[2] For an exposition, see Thomson (1996).

where B is a subset of $\mathbb{R}^N$ and d is a point of B. The set B, called the **feasible set**, is interpreted as the set of utility vectors available to the group N by unanimous agreement, and d, called the **disagreement point**, is interpreted as the utility vector that the group obtains if its members fail to reach an agreement. The set B is most commonly assumed to be a convex and compact subset of $\mathbb{R}^N$, and the pair (B, d) to be non-degenerate in the sense that there is $x \in B$ with $x > d$. Let $\mathcal{B}^N$ be the domain of all bargaining games.

A **bargaining solution on $\mathcal{B}^N$** is a function that associates with each game in $\mathcal{B}^N$ a unique point in its feasible set. This point is called the **solution outcome** of the game. Our generic notation for bargaining solutions is the letter φ. The following are important solutions.

The **Nash solution** outcome of $(B, d) \in \mathcal{B}^N$ is the unique vector at which the "Nash product" $\prod_N (x_i - d_i)$ is maximized in $\{x \in B : x \geqq d\}$. For the **weighted Nash solution with weights $(\alpha_i)_{i \in N} \in$ int$\{\Delta^N\}$**, the solution outcome is obtained by maximizing the "weighted Nash product" $\prod_N (x_i - d_i)^{\alpha_i}$ subject to the same constraint instead. The **egalitarian solution** chooses the maximal point of B of equal utility gains from d. The **lexicographic egalitarian solution** chooses the point of B at which utility gains from d are maximized in a lexicographic way, starting with the smallest gain.[3] The **Kalai–Smorodinsky solution** chooses the maximal point of B on the segment from d to the **ideal point of (B, d)**, denoted $a(B, d)$, where for each $i \in N$, $a_i(B, d)$ is the maximal utility for agent i in $\{x \in B : x \geqq d\}$. The **extended equal losses solution** chooses the maximal point of B at which the losses from the ideal point of all players whose utility gains are positive are equal and the utilities of the others are equal to their disagreement utilities, and the number of players in the first set is maximal. The definition of the **Perles–Maschler solution** is somewhat more involved, and because the result that we cite for this solution is limited to the two-claimant case when the undominated boundary of $\{x \in B : x \geqq d\}$ is a segment, we only give it for that case: then the solution chooses the middle of the segment. Also for two players, the **equal area solution** chooses the undominated point y of $\{x \in B : x \geqq d\}$ for which the area of the part of $\{x \in B : x \geqq d\}$ to the right of the vertical line through y is equal to the area of the part of $\{x \in B : x \geqq d\}$ above the horizontal line through y.[4]

[3] Given $x, y \in \mathbb{R}^\ell$, we say that "x is larger than y in the lexicographic (maximin) order" if, designating by $\tilde{x}$ and $\tilde{y}$ the vectors obtained from x and y by rewriting their coordinates in increasing order, we have either $\tilde{x}_1 > \tilde{y}_1$ or $[\tilde{x}_1 = \tilde{y}_1$ and $\tilde{x}_2 > \tilde{y}_2]$, or $[\tilde{x}_1 = \tilde{y}_1, \tilde{x}_2 = \tilde{y}_2$, and $\tilde{x}_3 > \tilde{y}_3]$, and so on.

[4] The Nash solution is defined by Nash (1950), the weighted Nash solutions by Harsanyi and Selten (1972), the Kalai–Smorodinsky solution by Kalai and Smorodinsky (1975), the lexicographic egalitarian solution by Imai (1983), and the extended equal losses solution by Bossert (1993), in a contribution building on the equal losses solution of Chun (1988b). The Perles–Maschler solution is defined by Perles and Maschler (1981). The equal area solution

(i) **Mapping claims problems into bargaining games.** In order to apply bargaining solutions to solve claims problems, we first need a procedure to convert each claims problem into a bargaining game. A natural choice is to take the set of all nonnegative distributions of the endowment dominated by the claims vector as feasible set, and the origin as disagreement point. This is the formulation we adopt. It makes sense since we have always required that no claimant ever receive more than their claim. However, rules satisfying this requirement could be responsive to changes in claims that do not affect the associated bargaining game as just defined (the proportional rule is an example), and one could argue that too much information is lost in this passage from claims problems to bargaining games. Another model is possible however, in which the claims vector remains as separate data. The relevant concept is then the generalization of the notion of a bargaining game obtained by adding to it a claims vector (Section 15.7).

Summarizing, given a claims problem $(c, E) \in \mathcal{C}^N$, its **associated bargaining game** is the game whose feasible set $\boldsymbol{B(c, E)}$ is $\{x \in \mathbb{R}^N : \sum x_i \leq E$ and $0 \leqq x \leqq c\}$, and whose disagreement point is the origin.[5]

We illustrate this definition in Figure 14.1 for two problems, one with two claimants and the other with three claimants. We show two important bargaining solutions there. We reproduce the problems in Figure 14.2, and show another bargaining solution.

In classical bargaining theory, the feasible set is allowed to be an arbitrary compact and convex set, but here, we have the special case of a feasible set whose undominated boundary is a certain kind of polygonal subset of a hyperplane normal to a vector of ones.

(i) **Correspondences between division rules and solutions to bargaining games.** If for each claims problem, the choice made by a given division rule coincides with the choice made by a given bargaining solution when applied to the associated bargaining game, we say that **the rule corresponds to the solution**. This amounts to saying that the diagram of Figure 14.3 commutes. The next theorem describes a number of such correspondences. They involve several central rules and all of the best-known bargaining solutions.

Theorem 14.1 *The following correspondences between division rules and bargaining solutions hold:*[6] correspondence division rules bargaining solutions

(a) *The constrained equal awards rule and the Nash bargaining solution*;

is discussed by Anbarci (1993). The various ways to extend it to more than two players are discussed in Thomson (1996).

[5] This amounts to assuming that agents have utility functions that are linear in money and normalized so that the utility of 0 is 0.

[6] Statements (a), (c), and (d) can be found in Dagan and Volij (1993); Statements (b) and (e) in Thomson (2003). A related contribution is by Giménez-Gómez, Osório, and Peris (2015).

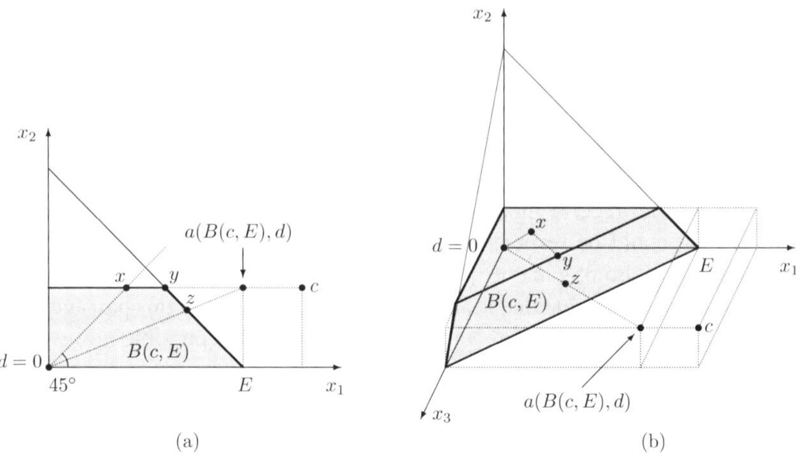

Figure 14.1: **Claims problems and their associated bargaining games, and two bargaining solutions.** Let $N \equiv \{1, 2\}$ and $(c, E) \in \mathcal{C}^N$. The shaded area represents the set of feasible vectors that are dominated by c. We take it as the feasible set of the bargaining game associated with (c, E). We denote this set $B(c, E)$. We take the origin as disagreement point ($d = 0$). The egalitarian solution outcome of $B(c, E)$ is the maximal feasible vector x at which gains from d are equal. (a) Here, at x, the sum of the agents' payoffs is smaller than the endowment. We recover efficiency by a lexicographic operation. The point that results, y, is the constrained equal awards vector of (c, E). We denote z the Kalai–Smorodinsky solution outcome of $B(c, E)$; it is the maximal feasible point proportional to its ideal point. It is also the awards vector the proportional rule operated from truncated claims chooses for (c, E). (b) Here, $N \equiv \{1, 2, 3\}$ and $(c, E) \in \mathcal{C}^N$. The notation is as in panel (a).

(b) *The constrained equal awards rule and the lexicographic egalitarian solution;*
(c) *The proportional rule and the weighted Nash solution with weights equal to claims;*[7]
(d) *The proportional rule operated from truncated claims and the Kalai–Smorodinsky solution;*
(e) *The constrained equal losses rule operated from truncated claims and the extended equal losses bargaining solution;*
(f) *For $|N| = 2$. Concede-and-divide and the Perles–Maschler solution.*

Proof: We only prove (a) as the other statements follow directly from the definitions. Let $(c, E) \in \mathcal{C}^N$ and x be the maximizer of the Nash product over $B(c, E)$. We will show that any agent who receives less than their claim receives at least as much as anybody else. Let $i \in N$ be such an agent and

[7] Note that the bargaining solution depends on the problem through the claims vector.

suppose by contradiction that there is $j \in N$ such that $x_i < x_j$. Let x' be the awards vector defined by $x'_i \equiv \frac{x_i+x_j}{2}$, $x'_j \equiv x'_i$, and for each $k \in N \setminus \{i, j\}$, $x'_k \equiv x_k$. The vector x' satisfies the required constraints to be an awards vector of (c, E) and it achieves a higher Nash product than x.

It now follows that we can partition the player set into two groups, one group of players who receive their claims (this set could be empty), the other group consisting of the others, who receive equal amounts. The only awards vector of (c, E) satisfying all of these conditions is its constrained equal awards vector.

(b) and (d) are illustrated in Figure 14.1 for two examples. (e) is illustrated in Figure 14.2 for the same examples. □

Concerning (e), and since for two claimants, concede-and-divide coincides with the constrained equal losses rule operated from truncated claims, and the

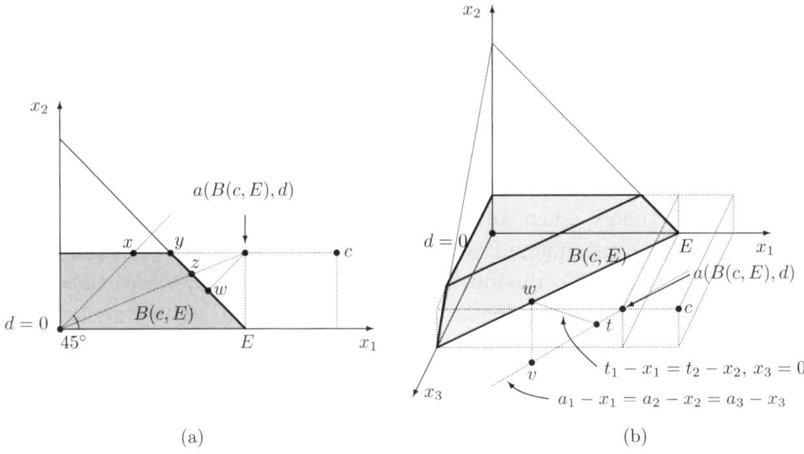

Figure 14.2: **The extended equal losses bargaining solution.** This solution chooses the maximal point w of $B(c, E)$ at which losses from the ideal point are as equal as possible, subject to no one receiving a negative amount. (a) Let $N \equiv \{1, 2\}$ and $(c, E) \in \mathcal{C}^N$. For two claimants, there is an awards vector at which the two agents incur equal losses from the ideal point of $(B(c, E), d)$, denoted $a(B(c, E), d)$. (b) Here, $N \equiv \{1, 2, 3\}$ and $(c, E) \in \mathcal{C}^N$. For more than two claimants, there may be no point of equal losses: the line of equation $a_1 - x_1 = a_2 - x_2 = a_3 - x_3$ does not meet $B(c, E)$. Then w is the point at which the losses of all agents receiving a positive payoff are equal, and the others receive 0. We can obtain it in two different ways. (i) We first follow a line of equal losses from a, until some agent's payoff is 0. In the example, this occurs at t, for claimant 2. We continue along a line of equal losses in the plane of equation $x_2 = 0$, and reach the boundary of $B(c, E)$ at w. (ii) We follow the line of equal losses from a until we reach the comprehensive hull of $B(c, E)$, at the point v; then we move up to reach a point of $B(c, E)$; again, w is the outcome.

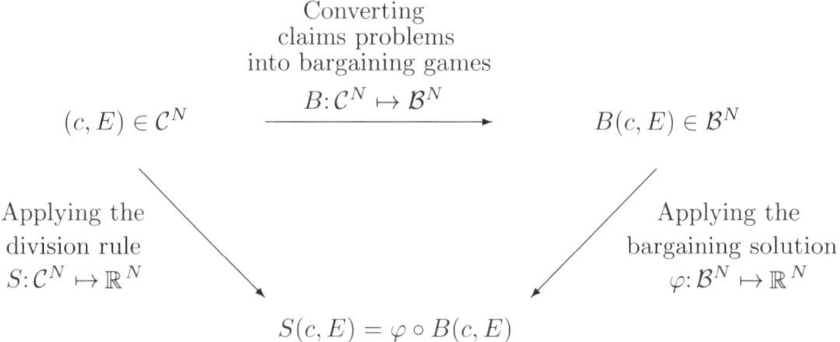

Figure 14.3: **What it means for a division rule to correspond to a solution to bargaining games.** Starting from a claims problem $(c, E) \in \mathcal{C}^N$, we can either apply to it a given division rule S, thereby obtaining the awards vector $S(c, E)$; or we can first convert it into a bargaining game – this is the operation denoted B, the resulting game being $B(c, E) \in \mathcal{B}^N$ – and then apply to this game a given bargaining solution φ, obtaining the awards vector $\varphi \circ B(c, E)$. The rule S and the solution φ "correspond" if, for each (c, E), the diagram commutes: $S = \varphi \circ B$.

extended equal losses solution simply consists in equating losses from the ideal point, we can say that concede-and-divide corresponds to what can be called then the "equal losses solution."

For two claimants, when we apply the equal area solution, we obtain a rule that we have not encountered yet.[8] The rule – let us call it the **equal area rule** and denote it EA – obviously satisfies *claims truncation invariance*, so Theorem 5.1, a characterization of all rules satisfying this axiom, applies. Let us describe EA using the terminology of that theorem. First, because it satisfies *equal treatment of equals* as well, its "primary path" F is the 45° line. Second, for each $c_2 \in \mathbb{R}_+$, its "secondary path for c_2," $G^2(c_2)$, is a concave curve (as stated in Theorem 5.1, for each $E \geq c_2$, this curve meets the line of equation $\sum x_i = E$ exactly once and it is bounded above by the line of equation $x_2 = c_2$). Third, for each $c \in \mathbb{R}^N_+$, its "tertiary path for c," $H(c)$, is also a concave curve (this curve emanates from the line of equation $\sum x_i = c_1$, and for each $c_1 \leq E \leq c_1 + c_2$, it meets the line of equation $\sum x_i = E$ exactly once and is bounded above by c). Now for each $c \in \mathbb{R}^N_+$ such that $c_1 \geq c_2$ say, the path for c follows the primary path F up to the line of equation $\sum x_i = c_2$, then follows the secondary path $G^2(c_2)$ up to the line of equation $\sum x_i = c_1$, and concludes by following the tertiary path for c, $H(c)$. We omit the equations of $G^2(c_2)$ and $H(c)$ (they are quadratic expressions).

As we noted earlier, there are multiple ways of extending the equal area solution of bargaining theory to games involving more than two players.

[8] The proposal is made by Ortells and Santos (2011) under the name of "pseudo-average rule," and further studied by Thomson (2018b), who proves the nonexistence of a *consistent* extension of this two-claimant definition.

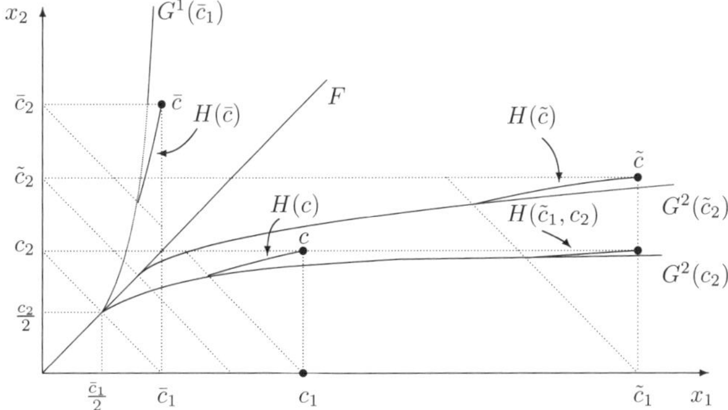

Figure 14.4: **Generating the paths of awards of the equal area rule.** Let $N \equiv \{1, 2\}$. We show the "primary path" of EA, F, which is the 45° line, three "secondary paths," $G^1(\bar{c}_1)$, $G^2(c_2)$, and $G^2(\tilde{c}_2)$, and four "tertiary paths," $H(c)$, $H(\tilde{c}_1, c_2)$, $H(\tilde{c})$, and $H(\bar{c})$. Since $c_1 > c_2$, the path of EA for $c \equiv (c_1, c_2)$ consists of some initial segment in F, seg$[(0,0), (\frac{c_2}{2}, \frac{c_2}{2})]$, the part of $G^2(c_2)$ that lies between the lines of equations $x_1 + x_2 = c_2$ and $x_1 + x_2 = c_1$, and the curve $H(c)$.

With each of these definitions would be associated a different rule for claims problems with more than two claimants. Alternatively, one could look for a *consistent* extension of the two-claimant definition, as in Chapter 11. However, no such extension exists.

(iv) **A variant and a comment on consistency.** An alternative specification of the disagreement point is possible: it is the vector of minimal rights. For two players, consider a solution for bargaining games that is efficient, respects the possible symmetry of problems, and only depends on the part of the feasible set that dominates the disagreement point. Then it is easy to see that when used to solve claims problems, the solution delivers concede-and-divide. For arbitrary populations, we obtain a correspondence between the adjusted proportional rule and the Kalai–Smorodinsky solution.[9]

The similarity in the logic underlying the conditions under which two-claimant rules have *consistent* extensions and the search for generalizations of the egalitarian solution is instructive. A **monotone path bargaining solution** is defined by means of a continuous and monotone path in $\mathbb{R}^N_+$, originating at 0 and unbounded above. The path is fixed in advance, and the solution chooses, for each game, the intersection of its undominated boundary with the path.[10] In the variable-population context, a monotone path should be selected for each population of players in the utility space of that population. An interesting question concerns the conditions that these paths should

[9] Dagan and Volij (1993).

[10] Thomson and Myerson (1980).

satisfy for the counterparts for bargaining games of *population-monotonicity* and *consistency* to hold.[11] The answer is that for each population $N \in \mathcal{N}$ and each subpopulation $N' \subset N$, the projection of the path for N onto the utility space pertaining to N' should be a subset of the path for N'. This is the requirement that guarantees the *consistency* of our rules to solve claims problems.

If a rule is *endowment monotonic for two claimants* and *consistent*, then it is *endowment monotonic* for any number of claimants (Lifting Lemma 10.13): if its paths of awards are monotone for two claimants, they are monotone for any population of claimants. Then, for each list of claims, one claim for each potential claimant, the list of all the paths of awards for the claims vectors obtained by restricting this list to finite subpopulations of the set of potential claimants, almost defines a monotone path bargaining solution. We write "almost" because there are two differences. First, in the present context, paths are not unbounded: instead, since by definition, for each problem, the endowment is never larger than the sum of the claims, the path for each claims vector is bounded above by this vector. Second, if the endowment is equal to the sum of the claims, each claimant should be fully compensated. This implies that if, in addition, the rule is *endowment monotonic*, then the projection of its path relative to each population onto the subspace relative to each subpopulation *coincides* with its path for that subpopulation, as opposed to being a subset.

(v) **An evaluation of the derivation of rules through the theory of bargaining games.** Theorem 14.1 establishes useful links between the theory developed here for the adjudication of conflicting claims and the theory of bargaining. However, it is important to understand that, since the class of bargaining games associated with claims problems constitutes a very narrow subclass of the class of bargaining games traditionally studied, bargaining solutions that give different answers in general often coincide on this subclass. A striking illustration of this phenomenon is the fact that the constrained equal awards rule corresponds to solutions as different as the Nash and lexicographic egalitarian solutions.[12]

[11] A bargaining solution is *consistent* if, for each population of players N, each game G this population may face, and each subpopulation N' of N, the payoff vector it chooses for the reduced game associated with N' and the payoff vector chosen for G is the restriction to that subpopulation of that payoff vector (if this reduced game is in the domain). See Thomson and Lensberg (1989) for details.

[12] It is indeed puzzling that a solution that is scale invariant (invariant under linear transformations, independent agent by agent, of their utilities), such as the Nash solution, coincides with a solution that involves utility comparisons, such as the lexicographic egalitarian solution. The solution to this puzzle is simply that the subclass of bargaining games associated with claims problems is not rich enough for scale transformations in which the scale coefficients differ across agents to ever be applicable.

14.1.2 Coalitional Games

We now turn to a class of games that is richer than the class of bargaining games because their specification includes what each group of players can achieve. In this context, groups are referred to as **coalitions**.

(i) **Coalitional games and solutions to coalitional games.** We need the following concepts. As before, let N be a fixed set of **players**. A (transferable utility) **coalitional game** is a list $v \equiv (v(N'))_{N' \subseteq N} \in \mathbb{R}^{2^{|N|}-1}$, where for each **coalition** $\emptyset \neq N' \subseteq N$, $v(N')$ is the **worth of N'**. This number is usually interpreted as a measure of what the coalition can achieve on its own, but calculating it requires that assumptions be made concerning the behavior of the complementary coalition. Several choices are often plausible however. This is certainly the case in the context of claims problems.

Let $\mathcal{V}^N$ be a class of coalitional games with player set N. A (feasible) **payoff vector for $v \in \mathcal{V}^N$** is a vector in $\mathbb{R}^N$ whose coordinates add up to no more than $v(N)$. A **solution on $\mathcal{V}^N$** is a correspondence that associates with each $v \in \mathcal{V}^N$ a nonempty set of payoff vectors for v whose coordinates add up to $v(N)$, a property we call **efficiency**. One of the most important solutions is the one that chooses for each game $v \in \mathcal{V}^N$ all of the efficient payoff vectors that no coalition can improve upon: the **core of $v \in \mathcal{V}^N$, $C(v)$,** is the set of payoff vectors $x \in \mathbb{R}^N$ such that $\sum_N x_i = v(N)$ and for each $\emptyset \neq N' \subseteq N$, $\sum_{N'} x_i \geq v(N')$. The core may consist of several points or of a single point, and it may be empty.

The solutions presented next are well-defined *single-valued* mappings. First is the **Shapley value.**[13] Imagine players arriving one at a time. For each player, calculate the impact of their arrival on the worth of the coalition consisting of all the players who arrived before them. We call this difference the "contribution" of the player to the coalition. If a player is the first to arrive, that player's contribution is simply defined to be their own worth (equivalently, the difference between their own worth and the worth of the empty coalition, which we set equal to 0). Finally, choose each player's payoff to be the average of their contributions when all orders of arrival are equally likely. For a formal expression, recall that $\mathcal{O}^N$ is the set of strict orders on N. Let $v \in \mathcal{V}^N$. Then for each $i \in N$, we obtain the payoff $\frac{1}{|N|!} \sum_{\prec \in \mathcal{O}^N} [v(\{j \in N | j \prec i\} \cup \{i\}) - v(\{j \in N | j \prec i\})]$. Collecting terms, the following is an alternative and more familiar expression for the **Shapley value of player i in $v \in \mathcal{V}^N$**:

$$Sh_i(v) \equiv \sum_{N' \subseteq N, i \in N'} \frac{(|N'|-1)!(|N|-|N'|)!}{|N|!} [v(N') - v(N' \backslash \{i\})].$$

The next solution is defined by means of an operation analogous to the one underlying the lexicographic egalitarian solution to bargaining games. Given

[13] Shapley (1953).

$N' \subset N$ and $x \in \mathbb{R}^N$, the larger the difference $v(N') - \sum_{N'} x_i$, the less well coalition N' is treated at x, so we call it the **dissatisfaction of N' at x**. (Note that a payoff vector belongs to the core if all of these differences are non-positive.) The **kernel of $v \in \mathcal{V}^N$** is the set of payoff vectors such that for each pair $\{i, j\} \subseteq N$, the maximal dissatisfaction of all coalitions not containing player i is equal to the maximal dissatisfaction of all coalitions not containing player j. The **prenucleolus of $v \in \mathcal{V}^N$, $PreNu(v)$,** is the set of payoff vectors at which the vector of dissatisfactions $(v(N') - \sum_{N'} x_i)_{N' \subseteq N}$ is minimized in the lexicographic (maximin) order among all efficient payoff vectors.[14] For the **nucleolus**, the minimization is carried out among the set of efficient payoff vectors at which each player gets at least what they could get on their own. Although it is defined as a set, the prenucleolus is actually a singleton. The **per capita prenucleolus** and **per capita nucleolus** are defined as the prenucleolus and nucleolus respectively except that the per capita dissatisfactions are used instead of the dissatisfactions themselves in the minimization exercise.

Our next definition is based on the Lorenz order, already encountered in Chapter 13. We will state the special form it takes for an important class of games, namely games exhibiting strongly increasing "returns to size." Informally, a game is **convex** if, for each player, and for each pair of coalitions ordered by inclusion and such that the player does not belong to the larger one, their contribution to that coalition is at least as large as their contribution to the smaller one: formally, for each $i \in N$ and each pair $\{N', N''\}$ of subsets of N such that $N' \subset N''$ and $i \notin N''$, $v(N'' \cup \{i\}) - v(N'') \geq v(N' \cup \{i\}) - v(N')$. The **Dutta–Ray solution outcome of a convex game $v \in \mathcal{V}^N$, $DR(v)$,** is the payoff vector in the core of v (the core of a convex game is nonempty) that Lorenz-dominates each other core payoff vector.

An equivalent definition (still for the class of convex games), which will be very useful in proving Theorem 14.2 below is the following:[15]

$$DR(v) \equiv \text{argmin}_{x \in C(v)} \sum_N \left[x_i - \frac{v(N)}{n} \right]^2.$$

Finally is a solution in the spirit of the Kalai–Smorodinsky solution to bargaining games, the **τ-value**. We obtain it by first identifying natural minimal and maximal payoffs for each player; then by choosing the efficient point on the segment connecting the vector of minimal payoffs to the vector of maximal payoffs. Formally, for each $i \in N$, let $M_i(v) \equiv v(N) - v(N \setminus \{i\})$ and $m_i(v) \equiv \max_{N' \subseteq N, i \in N'} (v(N') - \sum_{j \in N' \setminus \{i\}} M_j(v))$. The **$\tau$-outcome of $v \in \mathcal{V}^N$** is given by the following formula:

[14] See Schmeidler (1969), to whom the definition of the prenucleolus, as well as its basic properties listed below, are due.

[15] This formula is due to Hokari (2000).

$$\tau(v) \equiv \lambda M(v) + (1 - \lambda)m(v),$$

where $\lambda \in \mathbb{R}$ is chosen so that $\sum \tau_i(v) = v(N)$.[16]

(ii) **Mapping claims problems into coalitional games.** In order to be able to use solutions to coalitional games to generate rules for claims problems, we need to define a procedure to associate with each claims problem a coalitional game. Here is the one that has been mostly studied.

Given $(c, E) \in \mathcal{C}^N$, define the worth of each coalition $N' \subseteq N$ to be the difference between the endowment and the sum of the claims of the members of the complementary coalition if this difference is nonnegative and 0 otherwise. Using earlier language, this amount is "conceded" by the complementary coalition. It is certainly what N' can secure without going to court. As so defined, the worth of a coalition is a rather pessimistic assessment of what it can achieve. However, the bias being systematic across coalitions, we might still expect the resulting game to appropriately summarize the actual situation. Altogether, given a claims problem $(c, E) \in \mathcal{C}^N$, its **associated coalitional game** is the game $\boldsymbol{v(c, E)} \in \mathcal{V}^N$ defined by setting, for each $\emptyset \neq N' \subseteq N$, $v(c, E)(N') \equiv \max\{E - \sum_{N \setminus N'} c_i, 0\}$.[17] Clearly, $v(c, E)(N) = E$.

Note that the core of the game $v(c, E)$ and the core of the game derived in a similar way after truncating claims at the endowment are the same.

The core of the game $v(c, E)$ is nonempty and we can easily describe it:

Lemma 14.1 *For each claims problem, the core of its associated coalitional game is its set of awards vectors.*[18]

Proof: Let $(c, E) \in \mathcal{C}^N$. Let $x \in X(c, E)$ and $N' \subseteq N$. For each $j \in N \setminus N'$, $x_j \leq c_j$, so that $E - \sum_{N \setminus N'} x_j \geq E - \sum_{N \setminus N'} c_j$. Thus, $\sum_{N'} x_i = E - \sum_{N \setminus N'} x_j \geq E - \sum_{N \setminus N'} c_j$. In addition, for each $i \in N'$, $x_i \geq 0$, so $\sum_{N'} x_i \geq 0$. Altogether, $\sum_{N'} x_i \geq \max\{E - \sum_{N \setminus N'} c_j, 0\} = v(N')$: N' cannot improve upon x. Since this conclusion holds for each $N' \subseteq N$, $x \in C(v(c, E))$.

Conversely, let $x \in C(v(c, E))$, and $i \in N$. Since $\{i\}$ cannot improve upon x, then $x_i \geq v(c, E)(\{i\}) = \max\{E - \sum_{N \setminus \{i\}} c_j, 0\} \geq 0$. Also, since $N \setminus \{i\}$ cannot improve upon x, then $\sum_{N \setminus \{i\}} x_j \geq v(c, E)(N \setminus \{i\}) = \max\{E - c_i, 0\}$. Thus, $\sum_{N \setminus \{i\}} x_j \geq E - c_i$. Adding x_i to both sides of this inequality and remembering that $v(c, E)(N) = E$, so that $\sum_N x_j = E$, we obtain $c_i \geq x_i$. Thus, for each $i \in N$, $0 \leq x_i \leq c_i$. Altogether, $x \in X(c, E)$. □

[16] For a convex game v, $M(v)$ dominates $m(v)$. Minimal and maximal payoffs can certainly be defined in other ways.

[17] The procedure is proposed by O'Neill (1982). Later, we consider a different formulation, due to Driessen (1998), which corresponds to an optimistic assessment of what a coalition can achieve. Driessen shows that the results are not affected by this alternative specification.

[18] Recall that these are the efficient vectors $x \in \mathbb{R}^N$ satisfying $\sum x_i = E$ and $0 \leqq x \leqq c$.

A consequence of Lemma 14.1 is that, for each $k \in \mathbb{N}$, the core of $v(k * (c, E))$ is simply the replica of the core of $v(c, E)$. This invariance property is to be contrasted with what happens on classical exchange economies, where the core shrinks under replication.

Our next observation is that the game $v(c, E)$ is convex.[19]

Proposition 14.1 *For each claims problem, the coalitional game associated with it is convex.*

We relegate the proof to an appendix (Section 17.16).

The importance of this result stems from the fact that on the domain of convex games, solutions tend to behave better than they do in general. For example, when a game is convex, its Shapley value payoff vector belongs to its core. In fact, the vertices of the core (the core is a polyhedron, being defined by a system of inequalities), are the payoff vectors whose average defines the Shapley value payoff vector.[20] Moreover, its kernel and prenucleolus coincide.[21]

For three claimants, and representing the set of feasible vectors as the points of a two-dimensional simplex, we can easily identify the core, the Shapley value, and the kernel. Figure 14.5 illustrates these definitions for $N \equiv \{1, 2, 3\}$ and $c \equiv (2, 4, 8)$, when E is given four successive values, 5, 9, 11, and 13. Let us do the calculations for $E \equiv 13$ (panel (d)). To simplify notation, we drop the dependence on (c, E) of the coordinates of $v(c, E)$, and we omit the curly brackets around sets of players when describing coalitions, obtaining
$v(1) = \max\{13 - 4 - 8, 0\} = 1,$
$v(2) = \max\{13 - 2 - 8, 0\} = 3,$
$v(3) = \max\{13 - 2 - 4, 0\} = 7,$
$v(12) = \max\{13 - 8, 0\} = 5,$

19 This is noted by Curiel, Maschler, and Tijs (1987). These authors also identify conditions on a three-player convex game v under which there is a claims problem whose associated coalitional game is v. Not surprisingly, given that many more parameters are needed to define a TU game than a claims problem, they are very restrictive. Quant, Borm, Reijnierse, and van Velzen (2005) show that a coalitional game is convex and satisfies a property they call "compromise stability" if and only if it is "strategically equivalent" to the coalitional game associated with a claims problem. (Two games are strategically equivalent if one can pass from one to the other by multiplication of its coordinates by a positive constant and adding to the worth of each coalition the sum over the members of the coalition of the coordinates of a fixed vector.) A contribution in the same spirit is by Potters, Poos, Muto, and Tijs (1989). Driessen (1997) identifies conditions under which a claims problem can be seen as a certain kind of cost allocation problem. Driessen (1988) provides further insights on duality.

20 Shapley (1971).

21 Curiel, Maschler, and Tijs (1987) prove that the sum of the minimal rights in each problem $(c, E) \in \mathcal{C}^N$ is at most equal to E by using the convexity of the game $v(c, E)$, which implies its "superadditivity," which says that for each coalition and each partition of it, the sum of the worths of the components of the partition is at most as large as the worth of that coalition. Thus, applying this property to the partition of the entire set of claimants into singleton coalitions, we obtain $\sum m_i(c, E) \equiv \sum v(c, E)(\{i\}) \leq v(c, E)(N) \equiv E$.

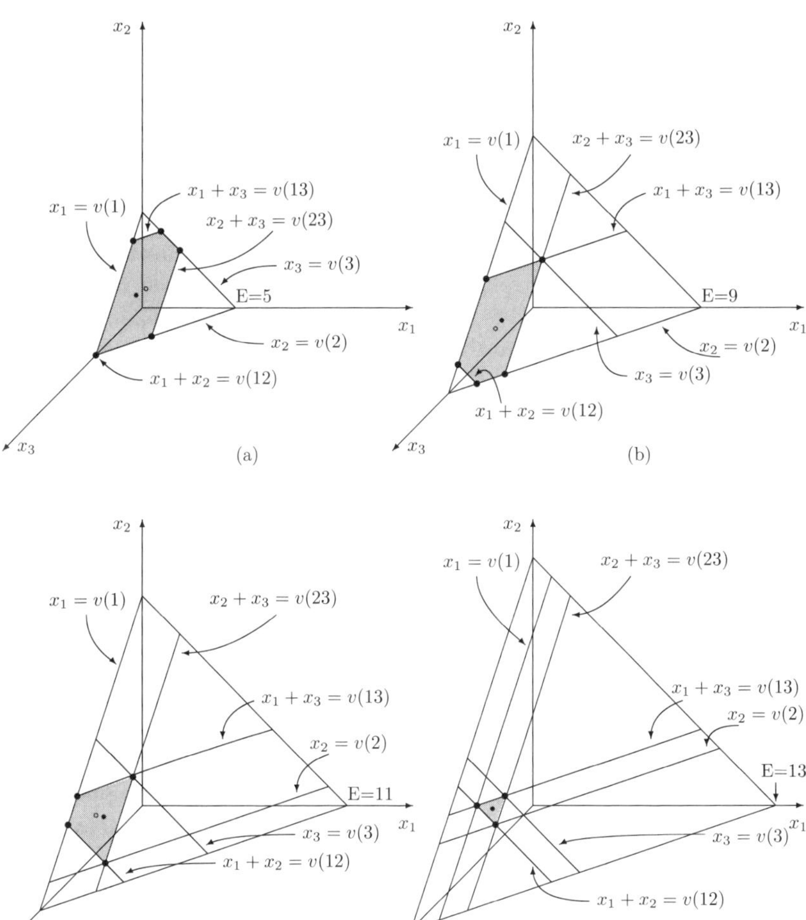

Figure 14.5: **Core of the coalitional game associated with a claims problem.** Let $N \equiv \{1, 2, 3\}$. Identifying the cores of the coalitional games associated with the problems in which claims are $(2, 4, 8)$ and the endowment takes four successive values, 5 (panel a), 9 (panel b), 11 (panel c), and 13 (panel d). They are the shaded polygonal areas. Each of the binding constraints defining the core is a binding constraint for the set of awards vectors. The average of the vertices of the core, some of which count several times, is the Shapley value payoff vector. We indicate this payoff vector by a smaller dot. The nucleolus is the open circle. In panel (d), they coincide.

$v(13) = \max\{13 - 4, 0\} = 9,$
$v(23) = \max\{13 - 2, 0\} = 11,$ and
$v(N) = 13.$

The payoff vectors corresponding to the orders of arrival $1 \prec 2 \prec 3$ and $1 \prec 3 \prec 2$ are both $(1, 4, 8)$; for the orders $2 \prec 1 \prec 3$ and $2 \prec 3 \prec 1$, we obtain

(2, 3, 8), and for the orders $3 \prec 1 \prec 2$ and $3 \prec 2 \prec 1$, we obtain (2, 4, 7). These three payoff vectors are the vertices of the small triangle defining the core in Figure 14.5d. It will help understand Theorem 14.2 below to note that each of them corresponds to the awards vector calculated by imagining agents arriving one at a time, in *reverse order*, and being fully compensated until money runs out.[22]

(iii) **Correspondences between division rules and solutions to TU coalitional games.** If for each claims problem, the choice made by a given division rule coincides with the choice made by a given solution to coalitional games when applied to the associated coalitional game, we say that **the rule corresponds to the solution**. This amounts to saying that the diagram of Figure 14.6 commutes. Just as we saw for bargaining solutions, a number of correspondences exist between division rules and solutions to coalitional games. Theorem 14.2 below gives a list.[23] Incidentally, our earlier Lemma 14.1 can be understood as stating a result of this type for multi-valued mappings.

The first correspondence is between the random arrival rule and the Shapley value. Although the Shapley value is best known for its combinatorial expression, it also has a random arrival interpretation, which we used to introduce it as the interpretation helps see the connection. We exploit this connection in the proof of the correspondence. There is also a formal relationship between the Talmud rule and both the kernel and the nucleolus (again, they coincide for the games under consideration). The constrained equal awards rule is not left out since it corresponds to the Dutta–Ray solution. The rule obtained from the proportional rule by subjecting it to the attribution of minimal rights and claims truncation operators (the "adjusted proportional rule") corresponds to the τ-value.

One rule will come out that we have not encountered yet. The ***HBRK* rule**, which we name after its inventors,[24] is an ICI rule. Like all such rules, it can be understood as a hybrid of modified versions of the constrained equal awards and constrained equal losses rules. For each claims vector, the constrained equal awards rule is applied to a problem in which claims are adjusted down in a particular fashion, as the endowment runs from 0 to the sum of the adjusted claims; claims are revised down by these amounts and the constrained equal losses rule is applied for all larger values of the endowment. Specifically, given $c \in \mathbb{R}^N_+$ such that $c_1 \leq \cdots \leq c_n$ and $i \in N$, let $\delta_i(c)$ be defined recursively as

[22] They are also the awards vector obtained by imagining that the first claimants to arrive absorb the deficit until it has been reduced to 0; the agents who come next being fully compensated.

[23] For an in-depth study of various solutions to coalitional games and how they relate to rules for claims problems, see Quant, Borm, Reijnierse, and van Velzen (2005).

[24] Huijink, Borm, Reijnierse, and Kleppe (2015).

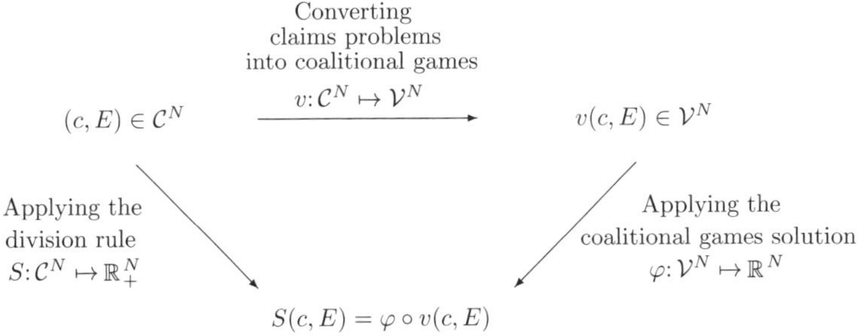

Figure 14.6: **What it means for a division rule to correspond to a solution to coalitional games.** Starting from a claims problem $(c, E) \in \mathcal{C}^N$, we can either apply to it a given division rule S, thereby obtaining the awards vector $S(c, E)$; or we can first convert it into a coalitional game – this is the operation denoted v, the resulting game being $v(c, E) \in \mathcal{V}^N$ – and then apply to this game a given solution to coalitional games φ, obtaining the awards vector $\varphi \circ v(c, E)$. The rule S and the solution φ "correspond" if, for each $(c, E) \in \mathcal{C}^N$, the diagram commutes: $S = \varphi \circ v$.

$$\delta_i(c) \equiv \max_{j \in \{1,\ldots,i\}} \{\frac{1}{n+j-1}(jc_i - (n-1)\sum_{1}^{j-1} \delta_\ell(s))\},$$

and let $\delta(c) \equiv (\delta_i(c))_{i \in N}$.

Now, for each $(c, E) \in \mathcal{C}^N$, let

$$HBRK(c, E) \equiv \begin{cases} CEA(\delta(c), E) & \text{if } E \in [0, \sum \delta_i(c)], \\ \delta(c) + CEL(c - \delta(c), E - \sum \delta_i(c)) & \text{otherwise.} \end{cases}$$

Theorem 14.2 *The following correspondences between division rules and solutions to coalitional games hold:*[25]

correspondence between division rules solutions to TU games

(a) *The random arrival rule and the Shapley value*;
(b) *The Talmud rule and the kernel (and the nucleolus)*;
(c) *The constrained equal awards rule and the Dutta–Ray solution*;
(d) *The adjusted proportional rule and the τ-value;*
(e) *The HBRK rule and the per-capita nucleolus.*

To prove several of these assertions, it will be convenient to invoke a property of these solutions that is a counterpart of what we called *consistency* for

[25] Statement (a) is due to O'Neill (1982), Statement (b) to Aumann and Maschler (1985), Statement (c) to Dutta and Ray (1989), Statement (d) to Curiel, Maschler, and Tijs (1987), and Statement (e) to Huijink, Borm, Reijnierse, and Kleppe (2015), who establish a number of the properties of the HBRK rule: for two claimants, it coincides with concede-and-divide; it satisfies *endowment monotonicity*, *claim monotonicity* and *linked claim-endowment monotonicity*, *claims truncation invariance* and *minimal rights first*. It violates *composition down* and *composition up*, *no advantageous transfer*, *null claims consistency*, *converse consistency*, *population monotonicity* and *linked endowment-population monotonicity*.

division rules. We describe it next.[26] Given $N \in \mathcal{N}$, $v \in \mathcal{V}^N$, $x \in \mathbb{R}^N$, and $N' \subset N$, we define the worth of each coalition $N'' \subseteq N'$ in the **max reduced game associated with N' and x, $\rho^x_{N'}(v)$,** as follows: the worth of N' itself, $\rho^x_{N'}(v)(N')$, is the difference between the worth of the grand coalition in v and the sum of the payoffs of the members of $N \setminus N'$ at x; if $N'' \subset N'$, the worth of N'' is the maximal surplus N'' can obtain when it "gets together" with a subset M of the complementary group $N \backslash N'$ – this yields $v(N'' \cup M)$ – and pays the members of M their components of x, the maximization being carried over all $M \subseteq N \backslash N'$. Thus, $\rho^x_{N'}(v)(N'') \equiv \max\{v(N'' \cup M) - \sum_M x_i : M \subseteq N \backslash N'\}$. A *single-valued* solution φ is **max consistent** if, when the reduction is performed with respect to the choice x it makes for v, in the reduced game, it assigns to each of the players involved in it their component of x: formally, for each $N \in \mathcal{N}$, each $v \in \mathcal{V}^N$, and each $N' \subset N$, and introducing $x \equiv \varphi(v)$, we have $\varphi(\rho^x_{N'}(v)) = x_{N'}$.

Proof: We only prove the first three statements. Let $(c, E) \in \mathcal{C}^N$.

(a) **Random arrival rule.** To show that the random arrival division rule corresponds to the Shapley value, fix an order of arrival of the claimants. For each $i \in N$, let N' be the set of claimants who arrive before claimant i. Then according to the first come, first served procedure underlying the rule, claimant i receives

$$x_i \equiv \begin{cases} c_i & \text{if } E - \sum_{N'} c_j \geq c_i; \\ E - \sum_{N'} c_j & \text{if } c_i > E - \sum_{N'} c_j \geq 0; \\ 0 & \text{if } 0 > E - \sum_{N'} c_j. \end{cases}$$

We will show that x_i is a component of claimant i's Shapley value payoff in the coalitional game $v(c, E)$, namely the component pertaining to the reverse order of arrival. Indeed, for that order, the set of claimants who arrive before claimant i is $N'' \equiv N \backslash (N' \cup \{i\})$ and claimant i's contribution to N'' in $v(c, E)$ is $y_i \equiv v(N'' \cup \{i\}) - v(N'') = \max\{E - \sum_{N'} c_j, 0\} - \max\{E - \sum_{N' \cup \{i\}} c_j, 0\}$. Again, we distinguish three cases, to obtain

$$y_i = \begin{cases} E - \sum_{N'} c_j - (E - \sum_{N' \cup \{i\}} c_j) & \text{if } E \geq \sum_{N' \cup \{i\}} c_j; \\ E - \sum_{N'} c_j - 0 & \text{if } \sum_{N' \cup \{i\}} c_j > E \geq \sum_{N'} c_j; \\ 0 - 0 & \text{if } 0 > E - \sum_{N'} c_j. \end{cases}$$

After rearranging terms, we see that these three cases coincide with the three cases identified in the expression giving x_i; thus $x_i = y_i$.

The random arrival rule assigns to claimant $i \in N$ the average of the x_is when all orders of arrival are chosen with equal probabilities, and the Shapley value of player i is the same average of these same numbers, establishing the announced correspondence.

[26] This definition is due to Davis and Maschler (1965). We follow the terminology of Thomson (2011, 2017a).

(b) **Talmud rule.** The proof that the Talmud division rule corresponds to the nucleolus (kernel) is relegated to an appendix (Section 17.17).

(b) **Constrained equal awards rule.** Again, see appendix (Section 17.17). □

Of course, not all division rules correspond to some solution to coalitional games. The following theorem identifies *claims truncation invariance* as the critical property for this to be the case.[27] It explains in particular why neither the proportional rule nor the constrained equal losses rule appear in Theorem 14.2:

Theorem 14.3 *A rule corresponds to some solution to coalitional games if and only if it is* ***claims truncation invariant****.*

Proof: Since for each $(c, E) \in \mathcal{C}^N$, $v(c, E) = v(t(c, E), E)$, the result is clear in one direction. Conversely, let S be a rule satisfying *claims truncation invariance*. Let $\varphi\colon \mathcal{V}^N \mapsto \mathbb{R}^N$ be the solution for coalitional games defined by setting, for each $v \in \mathcal{V}^N$, $\varphi(v) \equiv S((c_i(v))_{iinN}, E(v))$ where, for each $i \in N$, $c_i(v) \equiv v(N) - v(N \setminus \{i\}) + \frac{v(N) - \sum[v(N) - v(N\setminus\{j\})]}{|N|}$ and $E(v) \equiv v(N)$. Now, for each $(c, E) \in \mathcal{C}^N$, it remains to observe that $\varphi(v(c, E)) = S(t(c, E), E) = S(c, E)$. □

Figure 14.7 shows how the formula that converts claims problems into coalitional games relates the reduction operations for these two classes of objects. Let $N \in \mathcal{N}$, $(c, E) \in \mathcal{C}^N$, and $x \in X(c, E)$. Now, let $N' \subset N$ and

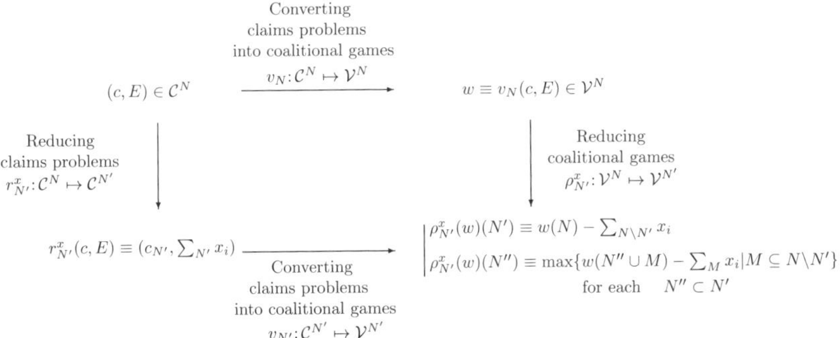

Figure 14.7: **Commutative diagram.** Horizontal arrows indicate the operation consisting in converting a claims problem $(c, E) \in \mathcal{C}^N$, for $N \in \mathcal{N}$, into a coalitional game $v \in \mathcal{V}^N$. The vertical arrow on the left shows how to reduce (c, E) with respect to $N' \subset N$ and $x \in X(c, E)$. The vertical arrow on the right shows how to reduce v with respect to N' and x, which is also an efficient vector of v. The diagram commutes: $v_{N'} \circ r^x_{N'} = \rho^x_{N'} \circ v_N$.

[27] Theorem 14.3 is due to Curiel, Maschler, and Tijs (1987).

consider the reduced problem of (c, E) with respect to N' and x, $r^x_{N'}(c, E) \equiv (c_{N'}, \sum_{N'} x_i)$, and the coalitional game associated with this reduced problem, $v_{N'}(c_{N'}, \sum_{N'} x_i)$. Alternatively, calculate the coalitional game associated with (c, E), $v_N(c, E)$, and the reduced game of v_N with respect to N' and x, $\rho^x_{N'}(v(c, E))$.[28] The composition of these two operations takes us to the same game, that is, the diagram of Figure 14.7 commutes: $v_{N'} \circ r^x_{N'} = \rho^x_{N'} \circ v_N$.

(iv) **Variants.** The formula we used to convert claims problems into coalitional games is plausible but it is not the only one that one could imagine, as the assessment of the worth of a coalition may be considered too pessimistic. To describe the alternative proposals that have been made, let $(c, E) \in \mathcal{C}^N$.

- **An optimistic assessment of the worth of a coalition.** An alternative definition of the worth of a coalition is the minimum of the endowment and the sum of the claims of its members. This time, one can argue that the worth of a coalition is assessed in too optimistic a way. However, it turns out that when applying the standard solutions for TU games to the resulting game, we obtain the same answers as when we apply them to the coalitional games associated with claims problems in the manner defined earlier.

  The idea of duality can be applied to coalitional games, and for each problem the optimistic coalitional game associated with it is dual to the pessimistic one. The Shapley values of the two games coincide. So do their nucleoli.

- **Averaging the pessimistic and optimistic assessments of the worth of a coalition.** The space of games is a convex space and a compromise between the pessimistic and optimistic formulas that we have discussed can be obtained by averaging. Since the Shapley value is a linear function on the space of games, and for each problem, the Shapley values of the optimistic and pessimistic games associated with it coincide, it follows that the Shapley value of any average of the two games associated with each claims problem also delivers the same awards vectors.[29]

- **Yet another formula to assess the worth of a coalition.** Next, we define the worth of a coalition $S \subset N$ as either the largest claim of any of its members, or the endowment if that largest claim is larger, namely $v(S) \equiv \min\{E, \max_{i \in S} c_i\}$ if $S \subset N$, and $v(N) = E$.[30] When we apply the Shapley value to the coalitional games associated in this manner with the various examples discussed in the Talmud, we obtain most of the recommendations made there. (We do not obtain the recommendations made for all of the marriage contract problems presented in Subsection 2.1.6, but instead other recommendations given elsewhere in the Talmud.)

[28] The following discussion follows Aumann and Maschler (1985).

[29] Driessen (1998).

[30] This proposal is made by Aumann (2010). Guiasu (2011) is a two-step attempt at generating the recommendations made in the Talmud and by Ibn Ezra. It involves mapping claims problems into coalitional games in a different way and applying the Shapley value. See de Mesnard (2015) for an assessment.

This formula is difficult to justify, however. It is the one that has been used to convert "airport problems" into games,[31] and it is tempting to exploit the fact that an airport problem appears to be a claims problem in which the endowment is equal to the largest claim. Proceeding in this way raises conceptual issues though, because an airport problem has a public good character that a claims problem lacks. This difference is reflected in the specification of the core constraints. For an airport problem, each group of agents should contribute at most what it would have to pay on its own, but this is not how we defined the core of a claims problem. Another issue is that the rule we just obtained violates *claims boundedness*, a basic requirement.

• **Deriving the worth of a coalition from the equilibria of a strategic game.** Another way of mapping a coalitional game into a claims problem $(c, E) \in \mathcal{C}^N$ is as follows. Let $N' \subset N$, and consider the following two-player constant-sum strategic game in which the two players are N' and its complement $N \backslash N'$; a strategy for N' consists in claiming a specific part of the endowment of size equal to the minimum of the endowment and the sum of the claims of its members, a strategy for $N \backslash N'$ being similarly defined; finally, the payoff function is defined by dividing each part of the endowment equally among the players claiming it. This game is analyzed in Subsection 14.2.1 below. Its value defines the worth of N' and when the calculation is done for each $N' \subset N$, we obtain a coalitional game.[32]

This game has the advantage over the other coalitional games that we have discussed of not suffering from what we described earlier as the extreme pessimism embodied in O'Neill's formula, nor from the extreme optimism embodied in the dual formula.

However, its core may be empty. To see this, consider the following example: $N \equiv \{1, 2, 3\}$ and $(c, E) \in \mathcal{C}^N$ is equal to $((50, 50, 50), 100)$. Then in the two-player strategic game opposing $N' \equiv \{1, 2\}$ and $N \setminus N' = \{3\}$, a dominant strategy for N' is to cover the whole endowment with its aggregate claim of 100. Then no matter what agent 3 claims, N' obtains $50 + \frac{50}{2}$. For x to be in the core, N' should get at least that much. Two similar inequalities hold for the other two strategic games opposing a two-claimant coalition as one player to the remaining claimant as the other player. But the three inequalities cannot jointly hold since the endowment is only 100.

[31] An airport problem with agent set N (Littlechild and Owen, 1973; for a survey of the literature, see Thomson, 2007b) is defined as follows: there is a group N of agents who share a facility but have different needs for it; each agent $i \in N$ is characterized by the cost $c_i \in \mathbb{R}_+$ of the facility of a size that the agent needs. The facility, when built at a particular level, accommodates at no extra cost any agent who needs it at a lower level. The facility has to be built so as to accommodate everyone. Thus, the eventual cost is the cost of accommodating the agent with the greatest need. Altogether, it is a pair $(c, E) \in \mathbb{R}^{|N|+1}$ with $E = \max\{c_i\}$. The issue is how much each agent should contribute. As for claims problems, we are looking for $x \in \mathbb{R}^N_+$ such that $\sum x_i = E$.

[32] This is the standard way of making the conversion (von Neumann and Morgenstern, 1994). This game is proposed by O'Neill (1982).

An interesting question is whether the awards vectors obtained by applying the various solutions that we have considered coincide with the awards vectors obtained by applying these solutions to the other games we have proposed to model claims problems.

• **Associating a coalitional game with a pair of claims problems.** Another way of using the theory of coalitional games to solve claims problems involves associating such a game with each *pair* of problems that differ only in their endowments. Let us call such a game a "transition game." Axioms can be formulated that specify how rules should (implicitly) deal with it.[33]

recursive–claim-truncation-and-endowment-revision completion of Rabad's proposal characterized

Recall the recursive–claim-truncation-and-endowment-revision completion of Rabad's proposal and Theorem 9.7, which generalized it. It turns out that this rule is the only one to satisfy *anonymity*, *claims truncation invariance*, a property in the spirit of the well-known "dummy" requirement in the theory of coalitional games, and a form of *composition up* based on transition games.

minimal overlap rule characterized

The minimal overlap rule was proposed as another way of completing Rabad's proposal and it has been characterized along similar lines: it is the only rule to satisfy the following three axioms. The first two, which apply directly to rules, are *anonymity* and *claims truncation invariance*. The third one says that given two problems that differ only in their endowments, if the core of the transition game associated with the pair is not empty, the difference between the awards vectors chosen for the two problems by the rule should belong to it.[34]

(v) **An evaluation of the derivation of rules through the theory of coalition form games.** We conclude this section with a discussion of the significance of the results described in this section. Invoking the tools of game theory to solve allocation problems is worthwhile, but the approach is fraught with conceptual and technical difficulties that one should be aware of. These difficulties extend beyond the class of claims problems and in our discussion, we will use general language.

The first task when proceeding in this manner is converting the allocation problems under study into games. It is rarely the case that there is a unique way of doing so, however. Even if one has decided on which particular game-theoretic solution to use, the composition of the two mappings will deliver a rule that generally will depend on the conversion formula.

The second issue is what solution to operate. We may be tempted to use a solution that has been given an attractive characterization but the image of the domain of allocation problems in which we are interested may constitute but a small domain of coalitional games. This image may not be sufficiently rich for the characterization to hold. For some solutions, "minimal richness" results for characterizations are available and the image may pass one or the other of these minimality tests. For example, it is well understood how rich a domain

[33] The proposal and the characterization are due to Alcalde, Marco, and Silva (2005).

[34] Alcalde, Marco, and Silva (2008).

of coalitional games should be for various characterizations of the Shapley value to go through. On the other hand, we know little about the corresponding question for the nucleolus.

Returning to our model, note that only $n+1$ numbers are needed to specify an n-agent claims problem. Thus, converting such a problem into a coalitional game entails a considerable enlargement of the dimensionality of the space in which one is operating (from $n+1$ to 2^n-1). As a result, the image of the entire domain of claims problems (whether under O'Neill's conversion formula, the formula that has been most commonly considered, or any of the alternatives that we have discussed) is indeed a very small and highly structured subdomain of the entire domain of coalitional games, a subdomain on which the behavior of solutions for coalitional games is likely to be quite different from what it is in general. This is an important reason why the Talmud rule emerges as the composition of this conversion formula with the nucleolus. The nucleolus is in general quite difficult to calculate, as is well known, and in fact, for many classes of games, no closed-form expression is available, but here it can be described by an explicit formula. It is certainly not obvious that the formula would be the one that gives the Talmud rule, but some light is certainly thrown on this nucleolus–Talmud connection by observing that the nucleolus attempts to choose a sort of "middle" of the core and that the Talmud rule can also be understood as choosing a central compromise in the set of awards vectors. This is not the whole story of course. Indeed, although rules such as the constrained equal awards or constrained equal losses rules certainly cannot be described in this way, the random arrival rule can. Yet, it does not lead to the Talmud rule.

Third, because coalitional games are complex objects, the axioms on which characterizations are based in the theory of coalitional games are not always as straightforward expressions of the general principles that constitute the conceptual foundations of the axiomatic program as is the case for simpler classes of allocation problems. This is particularly true for the consistency ideas on the basis of which the nucleolus has been derived (see the reduction operation illustrated in Figure 14.7). Multiple expressions of the consistency principle have been formulated for coalitional games, and their comparative evaluation is not straightforward.[35] By contrast, it has a very clear and uncontroversial expression in the context of claims problems, as we have seen. This is in part because claims problems are among the simplest types of allocation problems. One could even argue that it is for these problems that its expression is the most compelling. Thus, priority should be given to understanding the implications of consistency requirements directly, in the natural space to which claims problems belong. In fact, we do have very general (the auxiliary axioms are very mild) theorems describing these implications (for example, Theorem 10.9). These theorems can help us avoid the somewhat awkward

[35] The various applications of the consistency principle are reviewed in Thomson (2011, 2018a).

process of transporting problems into a space of considerably higher dimensionality in which requirements of good behavior of solutions do not always have transparent expressions.

14.2 MODELING CLAIMS PROBLEMS AS STRATEGIC GAMES

In this section, we present a variety of strategic games associated with a claims problem, and show that several of the awards vectors chosen by rules that we had derived axiomatically arise as (noncooperative) equilibrium outcomes of the games.

14.2.1 Game of Stakes

Let $(c, E) \in \mathcal{C}^N$. We associate with (c, E) a normal form game defined as follows, thinking of E not as an abstract number but as an entity made up of specific parts (as when we defined the minimal overlap rule). Each agent's strategy consists of parts of the endowment adding up to their claim. An agent is allowed to stake the same part of the endowment more than once. Somewhat more precisely, a strategy for a player $i \in N$ is a partition of $[0, E]$ into intervals and for each interval an integer interpreted as the number of times the agent stakes that interval. These choices should be such that the sum over the intervals of the product of the length of that interval with the number of times agent i claims it is equal to c_i. Without loss of generality, we can assume that all the partitions are the same across claimants. Each part of the endowment is divided proportionately to the number of agents claiming it, taking into account possible multiplicities. So, for example, if a given interval is claimed three times by one claimant and five times by some other claimant, and is not claimed by anyone else, it is divided in the proportion 3 to 5 among the first two claimants, and none of the other claimants get any of it. A claimant's payoff is the sum of the various compensations the claimant gets for the various intervals the claimant claimed.

Games of this type have been considered in game theory under the name of "Colonel Blotto games." They are notoriously difficult to solve. Nevertheless, a complete description of the equilibria of our game, let us call it a **game of stakes** and denote it $\Gamma^{stake}(c, E)$, can be given.[36]

[36] This game is formulated by O'Neill (1982), to whom Theorem 14.4 is due. Ashlagi, Karagözoğlu, and Klaus (2012) consider a simple version of Nash's (1953) game of demands, when the feasible set consists of all the vectors whose coordinates add up to some given endowment, as in Subsection 14.1.1. When demands are incompatible they are interpreted as claims and instead of assigning to each agent a disagreement utility, as Nash has suggested, the agent is awarded what some prespecified division rule would assign them in the resulting claims problem. They require the rule to satisfy some basic properties and identify general conditions under which equal division is the only equilibrium outcome.

Proportional division to the number of times the various agents have staked each particular unit is the formula that we consider, but other formulas make sense too. "Winner takes all" is an alternative one, although it does seem rather extreme. (If there are ties in the number of agents who claim a unit the maximal number of times, and calling k this maximal number, equal division between all the agents who have indeed claimed it k times and assigning nothing to the others is a plausible complement to the formula.)

For each part of the endowment, the larger the number of other claimants have claimed it, the less a given claimant receives. This is as in the definition of the minimal overlap rule but here, the parts of the endowment claimed by an agent are the result of a strategic choice the agent makes as opposed to being specified for the agent by a benevolent planner intent on social harmony and whose conception of social harmony is embodied in a particular way of viewing possible overlaps in claims.

Our first theorem, illustrated in Figure 14.8 for a three-claimant example, pertains to the case when no claim exceeds the endowment.

Theorem 14.4 *For each claims problem $(c, E) \in \mathcal{C}^N$ in which no claim is larger than the endowment, the game $\Gamma^{stake}(c, E)$ has at least one Nash equilibrium at which no agent claims any part of the endowment more than once. Such an equilibrium is characterized by the property that the part of the endowment that is claimed by all claimants is minimized; subject to that, the part that is claimed by exactly $n - 1$ claimants is minimized, and so on.* equilibria of game of stakes

The arrangement of claims described in the theorem is "dual" (not in a formal sense) of the one defining the minimal overlap rule. We had suggested it in Subsection 2.1.9 as another way of implementing the goal of minimizing conflict among claims. Focusing instead on the part of the endowment that the fewest agents claim and making that part as large as possible in a recursive way

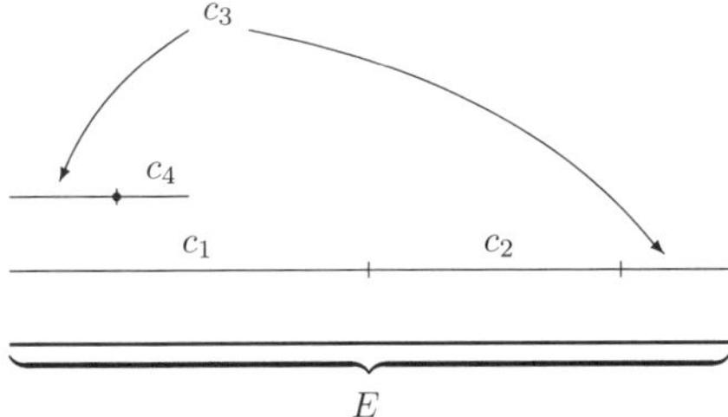

Figure 14.8: **Game in which strategies are claims on specific parts of the endowment**. Let $N \equiv \{1, 2, 3, 4\}$ and $(c, E) \in \mathcal{C}^N$. Each horizontal segment represents a part of the endowment that is claimed by a particular agent. Each agent claims an amount equal to their claim. Note that each of agents 1, 2, and 4 claims a single interval, whereas agent 3 claims two.

gave us that rule. Focusing on the part that the most agents claim and making that part as small as possible in a recursive way did not produce a well-defined rule, however. This phenomenon is reflected here in the multiplicity of the equilibrium awards vectors of the game $\Gamma^{stake}(c, E)$.

The two-claimant case is particularly simple. Indeed, up to inessential relabeling of part of the endowment, there is then a unique Nash equilibrium, which we obtain by a minimal overlap of the claims, and the resulting awards vector is the one chosen by the minimal overlap rule (and therefore concede-and-divide).

Proof: We assert that at equilibrium, there is $k \in \mathbb{N}$ such that each part of E is claimed by either k or $k + 1$ agents. Suppose otherwise, namely that for some $k \in \mathbb{N}$, the part of E that k agents claim, E^k, is positive and that so is the part of E that k' agents claim, $E^{k'}$, with $k' - k \geq 2$. Then any of the agents claiming a positive part of $E^{k'}$ would gain by transferring some of its claim to E^k.

The proof that this condition is sufficient for equilibrium is clear. By transferring some of their claim from a part of E that is claimed by k agents to a part of E that is claimed by $k - 1$ agents, an agent does not change their payoff. By transferring part of their claim from a part of E that is claimed by $k - 1$ agents to a part of E that is claimed by k agents, the transferring agent decreases it. □

Even if no claim exceeds the estate, there may be equilibria in which some agents claim the same part of the endowment more than once, a possibility that we excluded in Theorem 14.4.[37] Here is a complete description.

Theorem 14.5 *Let $(c, E) \in \mathcal{C}^N$ be a problem in which no claim exceeds the estate. Let $K \in \mathbb{N}$ and $R \in \mathbb{R}_+$ be such that $0 \leq R \leq E$ and $\sum c_i = KE + R$. Then a strategy profile is an equilibrium if and only if the following conditions are met:*

(i) Each component of the partition is claimed K times or $K + 1$ times.
(ii) If a component is claimed $K+1$ times, no agent claims it more than once.
(iii) If a component is claimed K times, no agent claims it more than twice.
(iv) If a component is claimed twice by some agent, the agent claims every component that is claimed K times. Also, $K \geq 4$.

The set of equilibrium payoff vectors is determined by a system of linear inequalities. For two claimants, it is still the case that there is a unique equilibrium payoff vector, the awards vector produced by applying concede-and-divide.

For problems in which some claim(s) may exceed the endowment, there may be no Nash equilibrium. When equilibria exist, they can be described,

[37] The analysis of this case is due to Atlamaz, Berden, Peters, and Vermeulen (2011), to whom the results described next are due.

but no simple formula is available. A critical parameter is the difference between the maximal and the minimal numbers of times a particular part of the endowment is claimed.

More can be said when two claims differ by at most the value of the endowment. For sequences of problems in which the endowment is fixed but claims tend to infinity, proportional division obtains at the limit. Finally, if agents are not restricted to claim each unit an integer number of times, but "claim height" can vary, then once again, proportional division is the limit of sequences of equilibrium outcomes, as claim height goes to zero.

14.2.2 Game of Rules

In our second type of strategic games, our starting point is a particular family of rules. Perhaps, the agents have not been able to reach agreement on a specific one, but at least they have agreed on a family; or it is a judge that has mandated guidelines for their negotiations. The family of rules may be specified by means of properties its members are required to satisfy, or it may be given explicitly. The idea here is that agents should be prevented from making unreasonable announcements, and the specification of a family of rules is intended to impose some discipline on what they may announce. In the theorem below, the family consists of all rules satisfying two basic properties. Now, each claimant is invited to choose one rule from the family. Our suggested compromise between their proposals is by means of the following recursive procedure: we apply the rules they all propose to the problem at hand and replace the claim of each agent by the maximal amount awarded to the agent by any one of them. This substitution, agent-by-agent, has the advantage of guaranteeing a well-defined claims problems at each step, but other formulas would make sense too. We reapply the rules agents have chosen to the revised problem, and make a further revision of their claims. We define the outcome function by taking the common limit point of the lists of awards vectors obtained at each step of the process if such a common limit point exists.[38] Clearly if no restriction are placed on the rules, no such common limit may exist. Indeed, if the sequential priority rules are allowed and each agent announces a sequential priority rule in which that agent is first, the process is stationary and the lists of proposed awards vectors do not have a common limit.

We refer to the game just defined as a **game of rules**. Given $(c, E) \in \mathcal{C}^N$, for each $t \geq 2$, we call c^t the claims vector obtained at the tth step of the process, $c^1 \equiv c$ being its initial value.

Figure 14.9 illustrates the process for two pairs of strategies. Let $N \equiv \{1, 2\}$. In panel (a), claimant 1 proposes the proportional rule and claimant 2

[38] This game was proposed by Chun (1989), to whom Theorem 14.6 is due. The game is inspired by a procedure developed for bargaining games by van Damme (1986). For another approach, see Mahanta (2018).

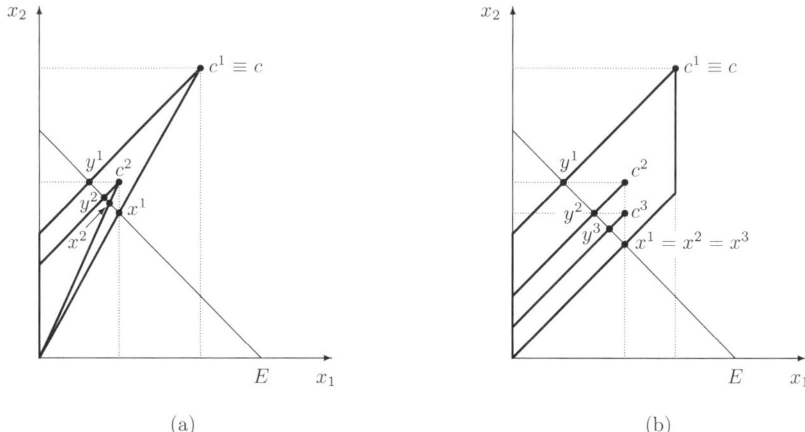

Figure 14.9: **A game of rules for two claimants.** Let $N \equiv \{1, 2\}$ and $(c, E) \in \mathcal{C}^N$. Showing how to revise the claims vector for two choices of strategies by the two claimants. The vectors x^1 and y^1 are obtained by applying to (c^1, E), where $c^1 \equiv c$, the rules S^1 and S^2 they announced. A revised claims vector c^2 is derived from these vectors. The vectors x^2 and y^2 are obtained by applying the rules S^1 and S^2 to the problem (c^2, E). The revised claims vector c^3 is derived from these vectors . . . (a) Claimant 1 chooses the proportional rule and claimant 2 the constrained equal losses rule. (b) Claimant 1 chooses the constrained equal awards rule and claimant 2 the constrained equal losses rule.

the constrained equal losses rule; both awards vectors are revised at each step. In panel (b), agent 1 proposes the constrained equal awards rule and claimant 2 the constrained equal losses rule: the awards vector obtained by applying by claimant 1's rule is stationary.

It turns out that the existence of a limit is guaranteed if the family satisfies some basic properties listed below, and that in the resulting game of rules, if the smallest claimant proposes the constrained equal awards rule, a rule that does satisfy these properties, then for each agent, the sequence of amounts this rule awards to the agent converges to the amount the constrained equal awards rule awards to the agent for (c, E). A consequence is a characterization of the equilibrium awards vector – it is unique – of the game.

Specifically, given a family Φ of rules, let $\Gamma^{rule,\Phi}(c, E)$ be the game of rules relative to Φ.

equilibria of game of rules

Theorem 14.6 *For each problem $(c, E) \in \mathcal{C}^N$, the game $\Gamma^{rule,\Phi}(c, E)$ associated with the family Φ of rules satisfying order preservation in awards and progressivity has a unique equilibrium outcome, which is the constrained equal awards vector of (c, E).*

Proof: Let $(c, E) \in \mathcal{C}^N$. To simplify notation, we choose $N \equiv \{1, \ldots, n\}$, and suppose that $0 < c_1 \leq \cdots \leq c_n$. Let $a \equiv CEA_n(c, E)$, $N' \equiv \{i \in N : CEA_i(c, E) = c_i\}$, and finally $N'' \equiv N \backslash N'$.

Let $(S^1, \ldots, S^n) \in \Phi^N$ be a profile of strategies. We claim that if $S^1 = CEA$, then for each $i \in N$ and each $S^i \in \Phi$, $\lim_{t\to\infty} S^i_i(c^t, E) = CEA_i(c, E)$.

First, since $S^1 = CEA$, then for each $t \geq 2$ and each $i \in N$, $\max_{j\in N}\{S^j_i(c^{t-1}, E)\} \geq CEA_i(c, E)$. Also, since each S_i satisfies *order preservation in awards*, then for each $t \in \mathbb{N}$, $c^t_1 \leq \cdots \leq c^t_n$, and thus, by *order preservation in awards* again, $S^i_n(c^t, E) \geq a$. Also, for each $t \in \mathbb{N}$ and each pair $\{i, j\} \subseteq N$, $S^i_j(c^t, E) \leq c_j$, and since $S^1 = CEA$, then for each $t \geq 2$ and each $j \in N'$, $c^t_j = c_j$.

We will show that for each $i \in N$, $S^i_n(c^t, E) \to CEA_n(c, E)$ as $t \to \infty$. By *order preservation in awards*, it will then follow that for each pair $\{i, j\} \subseteq N$, $S^i_j(c^t, E) \to CEA_j(c, E)$ as $t \to \infty$.

By *progressivity*,

$$(*) \quad \text{for each pair } \{i, j\} \subseteq N, c^2_j S^i_n(c^2, E) \leq c^2_n S^i_j(c^2, E).$$

Since for each $j \in N'$, $c^2_j = c_j$, $(*)$ applied to $j \in N'$ implies that for each $i \in N$ and each $j \in N'$, $c_j S^i_n(c^2, E) \leq c^2_n S^i_j(c^2, E)$. Summing these $|N'|$ inequalities, we obtain $\sum_{j\in N'} c_j S^i_n(c^2, E) \leq \sum_{j\in N'} c^2_n S^i_j(c^2, E) = c^2_n\{E - \sum_{j\in N\backslash N'} S^i_j(c^2, E)\}$, or equivalently

$$\{c^2_n + \sum_{j\in N'} c_j\} S^i_n(c^2, E) + c^2_n \sum_{j\in N''\backslash\{j\}} S^i_j(c^2, E) \leq E c^2_n.$$

Together with $(*)$ applied to each $j \in N''\backslash\{n\}$, we obtain

$$\{c^2_n + \sum_{j\in N'} c_j\} S^i_n(c^2, E) + S^i_n(c^2, E) \sum_{j\in N''\backslash\{n\}} c^2_j \leq E c^2_n.$$

Since $\sum_{j\in N''\backslash\{n\}} c^2_j \geq (|\, N'' \,| - 1)a$, we derive

$$\{c^2_n + (|\, N'' \,| - 1)a + \sum_{j\in N'} c_j\} S^i_n(c^2, E) \leq E c^2_n,$$

or equivalently

$$S^2_n(c^2, E) \leq \frac{E c^2_n}{c^2_n + (|\, N'' \,| - 1)a + \sum_{j\in N'} c_j}.$$

Since this inequality holds for each $i \in N$, we obtain

$$c^3_n \leq \frac{E c^2_n}{c^2_n + (|\, N'' \,| - 1)a + \sum_{j\in N'} c_j}.$$

Iterating, we calculate that for each $t \geq 2$,

$$(**) \quad c_n^{t+1} \leq \frac{Ec_n^t}{c_n^t + (|\, N'' \,| - 1)a + \sum_{j \in N'} c_j}.$$

The proof concludes by studying the function $f : \mathbb{R} \mapsto \mathbb{R}$ defined by

$$f(x) \equiv \frac{Ex}{x + (|\, N'' \,| - 1)a + \sum_{j \in N'} c_j}.$$

It is easy to see that f is increasing and concave, and that $x = a$ is the only positive solution to the equation $f(x) = x$. For each $t \in \mathbb{N}$, let $\bar{c}_n^t \equiv f(\bar{c}_n^t)$. Clearly, the sequence $\{\bar{c}_n^t\}$ converges to a. Finally, we claim that if $c_n^t \leq \bar{c}_n^t$, then $c_n^{t+1} \leq \bar{c}_n^{t+1}$. Indeed, using inequality $(**)$, the monotonicity of f, and the definition of $\bar{c}_n^t$, we obtain the string of inequalities $c_n^{t+1} \leq f(c_n^t) \leq f(\bar{c}_n^t) \leq \bar{c}_n^{t+1}$. Thus, for each $t \in \mathbb{N}$, $c_n^t \leq \bar{c}_n^t$, and since $a \leq \lim_{t \to \infty} c_n^t \leq \lim_{t \to \infty} \bar{c}_n^t = a$, we have $\lim_{t \to \infty} c_n^t = a$. Thus, for each $j \in N$, $\lim_{t \to \infty} S_n^j(c^t, E) = a$, and by *order preservation in awards*, for each $i \in N$, $\lim_{t \to \infty} S_i^j(c^t, E) = a$.

Altogether, we have shown that claimant 1 never receives more than $\min\{\frac{E}{n}, c_1\}$. By announcing the constrained equal awards rule, claimant 1 receives that amount. □

The same conclusion holds if we require rules to satisfy both parts of *order preservation* instead of *order preservation in awards* and *progressivity*.[39]

An alternative game can be defined in which at each stage, we award to each claimant the smallest amount that any of the rules chosen by the various claimants assigns to them (Figure 14.10), revise the claim down by that amount and revise the endowment down by the sum of the amounts awarded; we repeat the process. Figure 14.10 shows that each step is equivalent to moving the origin up by the vector of partial awards of that step, and translating the axes to the new origin. The geometry is similar to that developed in discussing *composition up*. The problem to be solved after one step is the "part" of the initial problem that lies above these axes. A result parallel to Theorem 14.6 holds, but this time, it is the constrained equal losses vector that emerges. This is because of the duality between the constrained equal awards and constrained equal losses rules, and the "duality" in the specification of the games. Let $\bar{\Gamma}^{rule,\Phi}$ denote this dual game:[40]

equilibria of game of rules

Theorem 14.7 *For each problem $(c, E) \in \mathcal{C}^N$, the game $\bar{\Gamma}^{rule,\Phi}(c, E)$ has a unique equilibrium outcome, which is the constrained equal losses vector of (c, E).*

[39] It also holds if agents are permitted to change their minds about which rule to promote along the process, provided the rules they use still satisfy the properties named in the specification of the game.

[40] This game is formulated and studied by Herrero (2003), to whom Theorem 14.7 is due.

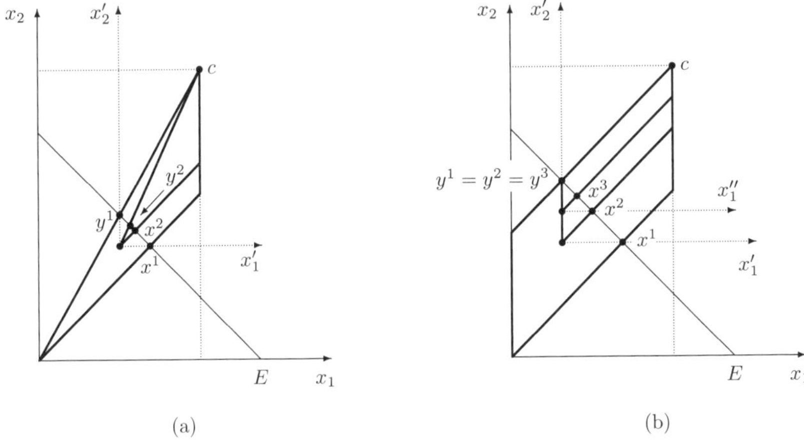

Figure 14.10: **A dual game of rules**. Let $N \equiv \{1, 2\}$ and $(c, E) \in \mathcal{C}^N$. Showing how to revise the claims vector for two choices of strategies by the two claimants. (a) Claimant 1 proposes the constrained equal awards rule and claimant 2 the proportional rule. (b) Claimant 1 proposes the constrained equal awards rule and claimant 2 the constrained equal losses rule.

An aside on a recursive process of assignments. In Subsection 3.4.2, we described the following process to obtain compromises for claims problems when no consensus has been reached on a single rule but there is agreement on a family of rules. Given a problem, we apply all the members of the family and calculate for each claimant the smallest amount awarded to that claimant by any rule in the family. We assign to each claimant this amount, revise claims and endowment accordingly; we repeat. If by proceeding in this way, the sequence of residual endowments converges to 0, and this is true for each problem, we have defined a rule.

When we introduced this process, we did not have all the necessary properties to be able to state any formal result. We now have them, and we can describe such a result. We state it here because of the conceptual connection to the material we just discussed.[41]

when limit of assignment process defines a rule

Theorem 14.8 *Consider a family of rules. Given a problem, assign to each claimant the smallest amount awarded to that claimant by any rule in the family. Revise claims and endowment accordingly and repeat: assign to each claimant the smallest amount awarded to that claimant by any rule in the family ...*

[41] Theorem 14.8 is due to Giménez-Gómez and Marco (2014). Giménez-Gómez and Peris (2014b) is along the same lines. Given a problem, they propose a way to recursively bound, below and above, its set of awards vectors. They show under very mild conditions convergence of the set of admissible awards vectors to a single point, thereby defining a rule.

(a) *Suppose the family consists of all rules satisfying order preservation. Then for each problem, the residual endowment converges to zero. The rule defined in the limit is the constrained equal losses rule.*
(b) *For $|N| = 2$. Suppose the family consists of all rules satisfying order preservation, endowment monotonicity, and the midpoint property. Then for each problem, the residual endowment converges to zero. The rule defined in the limit is the dual of the constrained egalitarian rule.*

For more than two claimants, and for the list of axioms of Theorem 14.8b, the rule defined in the limit may not be *endowment monotonic*. Thus, interestingly, but of course it is a disappointment, a rule obtained by the process for a particular list of properties does not necessarily satisfy all of these properties.

14.2.3 Sequential Game of Offers

Suppose that a two-claimant rule S has been selected. Let $(c, E) \in \mathcal{C}^N$. In the game defined next for an arbitrary claimant set N, the largest claimant, the "proposer" – let us index the proposer by p – proposes a division of the endowment, $x \in \mathbb{R}^N_+$. The proposer's award is tentatively set equal to x_p. Each claimant $i \in N \setminus \{p\}$ in turn is given the option of accepting or rejecting their component of it, x_i. If the claimant accepts it, they leave with it and the proposer's tentative award is left unchanged. If the claimant rejects it, they leave with what S would assign to the claimant in the problem that the proposer and the claimant would face if the amount available to them were the sum of what the proposer proposed for the two of them, $x_p + x_i$. The proposer's award is revised to what they are assigned in this two-claimant problem. The next claimant is then given the option of accepting or rejecting their component of x. The process continues until the last claimant. Let $\Gamma^{S,seq}(c, E)$ denote this game.[42]

equilibria of sequential game

Theorem 14.9 *Let S be a two-claimant rule satisfying endowment monotonicity, order preservation under endowment variations, and admits a consistent extension. (Results of Chapter 10 guarantee uniqueness of the extension.) Then for each problem $(c, E) \in \mathcal{C}^N$, the game $\Gamma^{S,seq}(c, E)$ has a unique Nash equilibrium outcome, at which each claimant receives what the consistent extension of S chooses for them. Moreover the outcome can be supported by a pure strategy subgame perfect equilibrium.*

[42] Theorem 14.9 is due to Dagan, Serrano, and Volij (1997). It generalizes an earlier result due to Serrano (1993). Serrano uses a form of *consistency* satisfied by the prenucleolus to construct a sequential game whose subgame perfect equilibrium outcome is the payoff vector the prenucleolus would choose.

If the proposer is not a largest claimant, uniqueness of the equilibrium may fail, but if S is *strictly endowment monotonic*, this property is recovered.[43]

(v) **An evaluation of the derivation of rules through the theory of noncooperative games.** We have seen that a number of the rules to which we had arrived on the basis of axiomatic considerations are given additional support when we take the noncooperative route. To the extent that the specification of a game is perceived as being fair by the participants, this approach may provide additional argument in favor of these rules. "Procedural fairness" is the expression that is often used to describe such a situation.

How these games are to be interpreted raises some delicate conceptual issues however. Are they meant to be formal representations of how agents would resolve on their own the conflict they face? Or are they chosen by some outside authority to help agents reach a compromise? If the latter, and given the wide range of rules that can be implemented by game forms, what would be the justification of choosing one game form over another? If the planner chooses a particular game form because of the rule it implements, given that the data of the game form may have to be public knowledge for the calculation of the outcome, isn't the planner de facto choosing the rule? On what basis should the planner do so? Is there a real benefit to letting agents choose the outcome through the strategies they select?

[43] Note that the outcome function of the game form requires the planner's knowledge of the claims. In a follow-up contribution, Dagan, Serrano, and Volij (1999) study the case when claims are unknown to the planner and can be misrepresented. They impose the natural restriction that only downward misrepresentation is possible and construct a general game form that can be specified so as to implement any *strictly claim monotonic* and *consistent* rule in subgame perfect Nash equilibrium.

In the game that Corchón and Herrero (2004) associate with a claims problem, agents propose payoff vectors that are bounded by claims. The proposals are combined by means of a "compromise function" to deliver a final outcome. They identify necessary and sufficient properties of a two-claimant rule for it to be implementable in dominant strategies in this way, and bring out the difficulties of extending the approach to problems with arbitrarily many claimants. García-Jurado, González-Díaz, and Villar (2006) associate with each rule in a broad class a normal form that implements it in Nash equilibrium as well as in strong Nash equilibrium.

An early contribution to the study of extensive-form games is Sonn (1992), who associates with each claims problem a game of demands similar to the game formulated by Rubinstein (1982) for bargaining games, and characterizes its subgame perfect equilibria. Chang and Hu (2008) and Li and Y. Ju (2016) associate with each rule in a large class an extensive-form game that implements it in subgame perfect equilibrium. Similar results are obtained by Li and Y. Ju (2016) for the constrained equal awards, constrained equal losses, and Talmud rules, by Moreno-Ternero, Tsay, Tsaur, and Yeh (2016) for the Talmud rule, by Hu (2010) for the constrained equal awards, constrained equal losses, and Talmud rules, and by Tsay and Yeh (2016) for the proportional, constrained equal awards, constrained equal losses, and Talmud rules.

CHAPTER 15

Variants and Generalizations of the Base Model

We introduce here variants and generalizations of our base model of adjudication of conflicting claims. A number of important classes of allocation problems have structures closely related to that of the class of problems studied in this book, and the theory we presented has been an important point of departure for handling them. Some have been obtained by restricting the domain of problems under consideration, others by widening it, and for others, it is the concept of a rule that has been reformulated. In each case, we note which differences with the base model are critical. We make no attempt at comprehensiveness in describing the literature here. For each variant of the base model, we simply give a few examples of rules and of characterizations in order to illustrate these developments. In many cases, much remains to be done.

15.1 CLAIMS PROBLEMS IN WHICH NO CLAIM EXCEEDS THE ENDOWMENT

A **simple claims problem** (briefly discussed in Section 1.2) is a claims problem $(c, E) \in \mathcal{C}^N$ in which each claim is at most as large as the endowment: for each $i \in N$, $c_i \leq E$ (Figure 15.1a). The contested garment problem of the Talmud and the estate division problem discussed by Ibn Ezra are examples.[1]

In practice, claims are often expressed as percentages of the endowment to which each claimant feels entitled or is actually entitled. Any such claim is at most as large as the endowment.

Much of the analysis we presented in this book applies to the domain of simple problems, but there are significant differences. In particular, the domain of simple problems is not closed under certain operations under which the base domain is closed. This means that certain properties cannot be applied, or cannot be applied directly. Consider, for example, *composition up* (Section 6.2). Recall that this says that if the endowment increases, the awards vector chosen

[1] O'Neill (1982) discusses this domain. Other studies are by Curiel, Maschler, and Tijs (1987), Moreno-Ternero (2006a, 2007), and Albizuri Leroux, and Zarzuelo (2010).

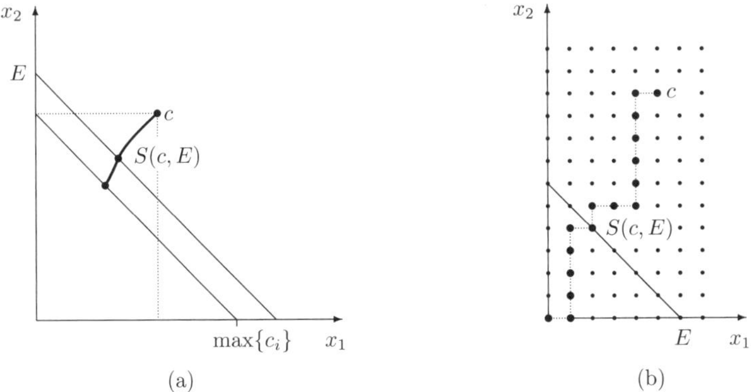

Figure 15.1: **Two models related to the base model of claims resolution**. Let $N \equiv \{1, 2\}$. (a) "Simple" claims problem: each claim is at most as large as the endowment, so the path of awards of a rule for a typical claims vector c goes from the line of equation $\sum t_i = \max\{c_i\}$ to c. (b) "Discrete claims problem": claims, endowment, and awards are natural numbers, so a path of awards is a discrete set. An example is the string of large dots from the origin to c.

for its larger value can be calculated in either one of two ways: directly, or in two steps, first dividing its smaller value and then, after revising claims down by the awards of that first step, dividing the increment. If the starting point is a simple claims problem, it could be that the problem of the second step violates the requirement that the endowment be at least as large as the largest claim. Thus, the property is not applicable as such. However a meaningful conditional version of it can be written according to which, *if* this inequality is satisfied, then the two ways of proceeding should indeed yield the same answer. For *composition down* (Section 6.1), no such proviso is necessary, however.

Consistency (Section 10.2) is another property for which an adjustment of the definition is necessary, as the domain of simple claims problems is not closed under the reduction operation: in some initial problem, each agent's claim may well be at most as large as the endowment, but this may not be the case in an associated reduced problem; indeed, claims are not revised down in a reduction, whereas the endowment is.

Importantly, notions of duality are not in general applicable here, the domain not being closed under duality, but this time, there is no interesting configuration of the parameters of the problems under which it is.

15.2 CLAIMS PROBLEMS IN WHICH THE DATA ARE NATURAL NUMBERS

In some situations, the data of a claims problem are natural numbers, and a rule is expected to select awards vectors whose coordinates are natural numbers too (Figure 15.1b): a **discrete claims problem with agent set N** is then a pair

$(c, E) \in \mathbb{N}^N \times \mathbb{N}$ such that $\sum c_i \geq E$, and rules take their values in $\mathbb{N}^N$. They are still required to satisfy *nonnegativity*, *claims boundedness*, and *balance*. In most cases, when there is a smallest unit of account in terms of which all of the variables of problems are expressed, this unit is sufficiently small in relation to the amounts involved that assuming instead that all variables are nonnegative reals is not a serious limitation. But in some contexts, the approximation is problematic. Think of the academic departments of a university requesting additional staff and faculty to handle increased student enrollments, or of the units of an expanding business in need of new personnel to accommodate a surge in orders, when the central administration or the head office do not have the resources to honor all of these requests.[2]

In a discrete version of the model, *single-valuedness* of allocation mappings is too much to demand in conjunction with our basic property of *equal treatment of equals*. To see this, consider a two-claimant problem with an odd number of units available for distribution. If the two agents have equal claims, their awards should be equal but that is not possible. Of course, this does not mean that nothing can be said about this situation – we could require that the difference between their assignments be at most one[3] – but it certainly complicates matters: a decision has to be made as to who gets more.

In a discrete model, it is also quite natural to turn to rules that select probability distributions over awards vectors, that is, **probabilistic rules**.[4] The implications of the same axiom system in the continuous and discrete versions of the model sometimes differ significantly. For example, a characterization of a unique rule, a probabilistic version of the proportional rule, has been obtained for the discrete model on the basis of axioms (*homogeneity*, *composition down*, and *composition up*) that, for the base model, are satisfied by a large family of rules (Theorem 6.7).

Enlarging the model so as to allow for variations in population and adding *consistency*, the rules that become available are defined as follows. An ordered partition of the set of potential claimants is specified; for each problem, the induced ordered partition on the set of claimants who are present is identified; then, proceeding from induced class to induced class, the claims of the members of each class are satisfied before anything is awarded to any member of a lower-priority class. If a class is induced from a reference priority class that

[2] Young (1994) discusses a special case. Moulin (2000) and Erlanson and Flores-Szwagrzak (2014) study versions of the model that accommodate both the continuous case and the discrete case. For additional results, see Herrero and Martínez (2004, 2008), Bergantiños and Vidal-Puga (2006), Fragnelli, Gagliardo, and Gastaldi (2014, 2016), Chen (2015), Fragnelli and Gastaldi (2016), and Giménez-Gómez and Vilella (2017).

[3] This is suggested by Balinski and Young (1982) in their study of apportionment, discussed next. Formulating strict versions of properties also requires care. For example, a strict version of *resource monotonicity* would say that if the endowment increases *by at least* $|N|$ *units*, then each claimant should get more than initially.

[4] Moulin (2002a) and Moulin and Stong (2002, 2003).

has more than two claimants, we have to apply the proportional rule however.[5] Again, this result should be compared to Theorem 11.8: in the continuous case, we had significantly more options.

The situation is similar for the list consisting of *claims truncation invariance*, *composition up*, and *consistency*. Theorem 11.9 had characterized the family of rules satisfying these axioms for the base model. The signature of such a rule consists of an ordered partition of the set of potential claimants together with a positive weight for each claimant. Then for each problem, the rule is defined by proceeding from induced class to induced class and within each class, applying the weighted constrained equal awards rule relative to the weights assigned to its members. For the discrete case, however, only the sequential priority rules satisfy the requirements.[6]

On the other hand, the recursive process studied in Subsection 3.4.2 can be adapted to handle problems with indivisibilities with no difficulties and the results are parallel.[7]

A class of problems that bear a close relation to the one studied in this subsection are **apportionment problems**: a certain number of seats in a House have to be allocated to States in proportion to their populations. Since exact proportionality is not in general possible, the issue that arises is how to approximate this ideal, to come up with a best way of "rounding." Here, the data of the problem as well as the recommendations allocation mappings make are lists of natural numbers. An important aspect of the situation however is that proportionality is usually seen as the only target worth considering, as the expression of the one man, one vote principle, and the theory of apportionment was developed under that presumption. However, rounding methods could conceivably be defined to approximate any *a priori* given method that cannot be implemented exactly because of integer constraints.[8]

15.3 CLAIMS PROBLEMS WITH A LARGE NUMBER OF CLAIMANTS

Some claims problems involve a large number of claimants whose claims are small in relation to the aggregate claim. An example is when the buyers of a defective product have to divide the amount they won in a class-action suit against the firm that sold them the product. We first model such situations by representing the set of claimants as an atomless continuum, skipping the technical details.[9]

[5] Moulin (2000).

[6] Flores-Szwagrzak (2015).

[7] Giménez-Gómez and Vilella (2017).

[8] For an extensive analysis of apportionment problems, and references to the relevant literature, see Balinski and Young (1982).

[9] This section is based on Chambers and Thomson (2002). We omit details having to do with integrability requirements for claims functions and award functions. Exchange economies in which

A claims problem with a measure set of claimants is informally defined as follows. The set of claimants is the unit interval [0, 1]. A claim profile is a function defined on that interval that specifies the claim of each agent. Aggregate claim is the integral of this function over the interval. The endowment is no greater than aggregate claim. A rule associates with each such problem a function defined on the interval whose integral equals the endowment.

Little has been done so far in the analysis of this model and we have only one result to report, a characterization of the proportional rule. It is essentially (that is, up to measure zero), the only one to satisfy the following version of *equal treatment of equal groups*: for each problem and each pair of subsets of [0, 1] such that the integral of the claim function over these subsets takes the same value, the integral of the award function over them also takes the same value.

This result should be compared to the characterization of this rule for the standard model on the basis of *claims continuity*, *equal treatment of equal groups*, and *replication invariance* (Theorem 12.5). Thus, when the set of claimants is modeled as a continuum, uniqueness is implied solely by *equal treatment of equal groups*. The main role of the replication property in the standard model is to make every claimant "small." This is automatically satisfied in a model with an atomless continuum of agents.

In practice, the case of a large number of claimants each of whom holds a claim that is small in relation to aggregate claim raises special issues. One is that claimants often do not bother identifying themselves or collecting their awards; the other is the administrative cost of implementing the chosen rule. This is the situation for some class action suits. Then some of the endowment ends up not being distributed. What should be done with the leftover? Commonly, courts award it to some nonprofit organization whose aim is to promote the interests of groups whose welfare is aligned with the claimants' welfare. For instance, if the suit has to do with the failure of a drug intended to combat some disease, the leftover may be assigned to an organization engaged in this activity. It has been argued that a full distribution that benefits the actual claimants *directly* would be preferable. For that purpose, the interesting proposal has been made that consists of drawing a random sample of claimants and distributing the endowment among them. The sample size would be chosen so that the selected claimants, or enough of them, would now have a sufficient incentive to pick up their awards; there would be no leftover, or at least the leftover would be seriously diminished, a first advantage. Another advantage is that the administrative costs of tracking down claimants and distributing the endowment would be considerably diminished. In practice, some of the

the set of traders is modeled as a continuum are studied by Aumann (1964). Another contribution to the literature on claims problems in which the claimant set is modeled as a continuum is Cetemen, Hasker, and Karagözoğlu (2015). Their main result is also a characterization of the proportional rule.

endowment is used to cover these costs, and the proposal would temper this waste.[10]

15.4 SURPLUS-SHARING PROBLEMS

Throughout this survey, we have only considered problems in which the endowment is insufficient to fully honor obligations that have been incurred. Of course, it may well be that there is more than enough – there is a surplus then – and the question arises of how to divide it.

A **surplus-sharing problem** with agent set N is a pair $(c, E) \in \mathbb{R}_+^N \times \mathbb{R}_+$ such that $\sum c_i \leq E$.[11] An illustration is when N is a group of investors and for each $i \in N$, c_i is the amount agent i invested in some joint venture. The venture turns out to be successful in that its worth, E, is greater than the aggregate investment, $\sum c_i$. How should the profit, $E - \sum c_i$, be distributed among the investors? Alternatively, the investors may have decided to sell the business and the issue they face is to distribute among themselves the proceeds from the sale.

There is an important mathematical difference between claims problems and surplus-sharing problems. For the former, awards are naturally bounded below, by 0, and above, by claims. For the latter, there is only one compelling bound: the claims vector should be a lower bound for the awards vector. Thus, certain properties that are meaningful for claims problems do not have counterparts for surplus-sharing. Examples are *composition down* and *self-duality*.

Central examples of rules here are the proportional rule (Figure 15.2a; the rule is well defined if $c \geq 0$) and the equal awards rule (Figure 15.2b).

One-parameter families of surplus-sharing rules that contain as particular cases the proportional rule and the equal sharing rule have been characterized.[12] The implications of monotonicity properties of rules are well understood for this model, and the model has also been analyzed from a noncooperative viewpoint.[13]

Situations in which there may be either a surplus or a deficit are also plausible of course.[14] Note however, that in the study of *consistency*, the subclass of claims problems is closed under the reduction operation for any rule such that, if the endowment is not sufficient to fully honor all claims, each agent is assigned at most his claim. The subclass of surplus-sharing problems is closed

[10] The idea is proposed and developed by Lavie (2011).

[11] This model is studied by Moulin (1985a,b), Chun (1989), Young (1987a), Kaminski (2000), Bergantiños and Vidal-Puga (2004, 2006), Yanovskaya (2003), and Laurent-Lucchetti and Leroux (2017).

[12] See Moulin (1985). One of the properties he imposes is *homogeneity*. Pfingsten (1991) describes how the family of admissible rules enlarges when this axiom is dropped.

[13] Chun (1987, 1989).

[14] Chae (1998), Herrero, Maschler, and Villar (1999), Shinotsuka (2000), Naumova (2002), and Sánchez-Pérez, Plata-Pérez, and Accinelli-Gamba (2015).

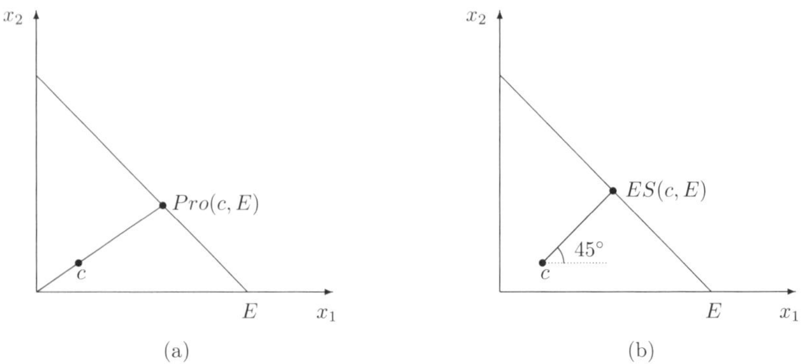

Figure 15.2: **Two rules for surplus-sharing problems**. Let $N \equiv \{1, 2\}$. (a) Proportional rule. (b) Equal-sharing rule.

under the reduction operation for any rule that satisfies the natural counterpart of this property, namely that in that case each agent be assigned at least their claim.

15.5 GENERALIZING THE NOTION OF A RULE

Next, we consider the domain of pairs $(c, E) \in \mathbb{R}^N_+ \times \mathbb{R}$ but without claims being commensurable with the quantity to divide. They could be interpreted instead as representing abstract notions of need or merit. In such a context, comparing $\sum c_i$ to E is not meaningful, and it may not make sense to impose any relationship between an agent's award and their claim of the type expressed in a requirement such as *claims boundedness*.

We have already argued that, in the context of taxation, *nonnegativity* may not be a desirable property either (think of negative income tax), and a theory that dispenses with that assumption is certainly worthwhile. For the generalization of the base model in these two ways, large families of rules have been identified that satisfy a number of important properties. These rules can be related to some of the rules that have come up repeatedly in our study.[15]

An example is a characterization of the family of rules satisfying *anonymity*, *continuity*, and *no advantageous transfer*. This family includes the proportional and equal award rules, and many others. Another is a characterization of the family of rules satisfying *anonymity*, *continuity*, and *endowment linearity*.

Characterizations have also been obtained concerning the case when awards vectors are allowed to have negative coordinates but are still required to satisfy *claims boundedness*.[16]

[15] Chun (1986), Ching and Kakkar (2001), Bergantiños and Méndez-Naya (2001), and Herrero, Maschler, and Villar (1999).

[16] This formulation is considered by Bergantiños and Méndez-Naya (1997) and Shinotsuka (2000). The former characterize a family of generalized solutions indexed by a vector of

15.6 COMPUTATIONAL ISSUES

Computer scientists have been taking an increasing interest in resource allocation but they have addressed questions that economists had traditionally ignored. Central to their concerns is whether allocation rules can be implemented on computers as the data of the problems to be solved become large. This question is relevant to the adjudication of conflicting claims when the number of claimants is large.

Although most of the central rules can be computed in polynomial time, the random arrival rule stands out as being in general at least as hard to compute as the hardest counting problems.[17]

These types of results should be balanced against what is known of the asymptotic behavior of rules. For the random arrival rule, for example, we have seen that if the number of agents becomes large, the rule makes recommendations that approach those made by the proportional rule (Theorem 12.8).

15.7 INCORPORATING ADDITIONAL INFORMATION INTO THE MODEL

In this section, we review a number of enrichments of our base model. Its simplicity obviously comes at a price: it is certainly a faithful description of some situations of interest, but it ignores various complications encountered in real life. However, the theory that has been developed for it can serve as a jumping point from which to handle these complications. We catalog next various types of problems whose study has been greatly helped by this theory. We eschew mathematical descriptions of models, and only give informal statements of a few results. Much remains to be done, and we hope that our readers will be inspired to join this ongoing research program.

- **Adding utility information.** What underlies the base model is the implicit assumption that the decision has been made to only pay attention to the monetary amounts claimants are owned and receive, or that they have linear utility over how much they receive, or to ignore possible nonlinearities in their utilities. In the nonlinear case, a transfer of the resource from one agent to another may not result in a one-for-one transfer of utility. As a result, the undominated boundary of the feasible set, instead of being a subset of a hyperplane normal to a vector of ones, has a more general shape. If the functions are concave however, its comprehensive hull (that is, the set of points that are dominated by some feasible point) is convex as in the classical theory of bargaining.

weights and defined by selecting for each problem, the awards vector whose associated vector of losses is proportional to the weight vector.

[17] Aziz (2013). For discrete claims problems, a polynomial computation time is achievable, however.

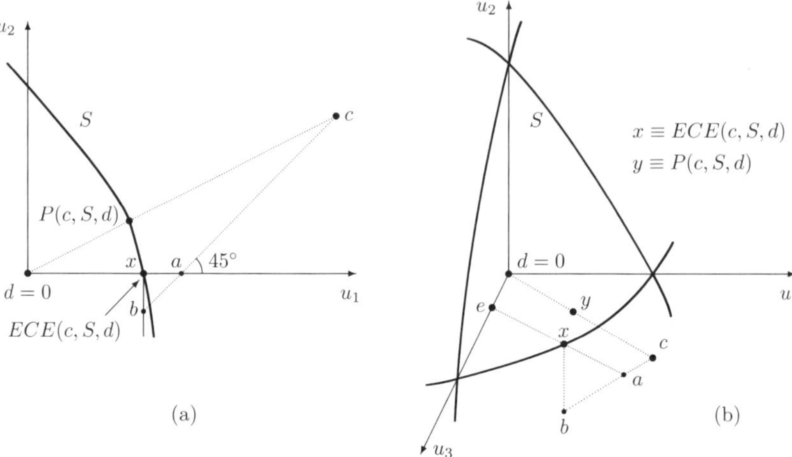

Figure 15.3: **Nontransferable utility claims problems.** The boundary of the feasible set is not a straight line of slope -1. Two solutions for such problems are illustrated here. (a) Let $N \equiv \{1, 2\}$. For the proportional solution, P, payoffs are proportional to claims. (b) Here, $N \equiv \{1, 2, 3\}$. For the extended claim-egalitarian solution, ECE, payoffs are obtained by imposing equal utility losses from the claims vector, subject to the constraint that no agent should end up with a negative payoff.

We then have what can be called a **bargaining problem with claims** (Figure 15.3).[18]

Allowing for a nonlinear boundary has a significant impact on the extent to which properties of interest can be satisfied. It also suggests additional properties pertaining to possible changes in the shape of this boundary.

A rule that has played a central role for this domain is the rule that selects the maximal feasible point on the ray from the origin to the claims vector, the straightforward extension of the proportional division rule (Figure 15.3a). This rule has been characterized in various ways.[19] The constrained equal losses rule has also played a role, but it had to be adapted in order to meet the nonnegativity constraints. This version, called the "claim-egalitarian" solution, has been characterized as well (Figure 15.3b).[20]

[18] Such a model is formulated and analyzed by Chun and Thomson (1992) and Herrero (1998, 2000). Recent studies of this model are by Dietzenbacher, Borm, and Estévez-Fernández (2017) and Dietzenbacher (2018). Carpente, Casas-Méndez, Gozálvez, Llorca, Pulido, and Sánchez-Soriano (2013) assume that utilities can be redistributed among agents. Herrero and Villar (2010) consider a version of the model in which the claims vector may be feasible. So does Naumova (2002). Grundel, Borm, and Hamers (2013) enrich it by adding production functions. For Gallice (2016), each claimant has so-called "rank-dependent preferences," specifically preferences that can be written as the sum of the claimant's award and some function of the loss the claimant incurs. Rong (2018) considers the case when utility functions are unknown.

[19] Chun and Thomson (1992). A variant of the rule is defined and characterized by Herrero (1998).

[20] Bossert (1992) and Marco (1995a).

A formulation of claims problems as nontransferable utility (NTU) coalitional games (as opposed to the transferable utility coalitional games of Subsection 14.1.2) has also been proposed.[21]

Under a certain smoothness property of feasible sets, the core and a version of the "prekernel" (Chapter 14) were shown to have a nonempty intersection. Characterizations of versions of the proportional, constrained equal awards, and constrained equal losses rules have also been obtained, patterned after results for the base model.

• **Adding unions.** Another enrichment of the base model is obtained by adding to it a partition of the set of claimants.

Extensions of the constrained equal awards, random arrival, and adjusted proportional rules have been proposed for this model, and axiomatized along the lines of characterizations for the base model.[22]

• **Adding group constraints.** Here, agents are organized in groups – the groups possibly overlapping – and in addition to an upper bound being specified on how much each agent can receive, there is an upper bound on how much each of these groups can receive. The upper bound faced by a group is at most as large as the sum of the upper bounds specified for its individual members. A special case is when the groups form a partition of the agent set. Then, the problem can be decomposed into a list of standard claims problems.[23]

Several rules defined for the base model have been extended to this kind of situations and characterized. They are the constrained equal awards, constrained equal losses, and proportional rules.

• **Adding a network structure.**

(i) In the base model, the endowment is a single entity. Instead it may be organized in distinct funds and, for each claimant, there may be a subset of the funds from which the claimant is allowed to receive compensation. These constraints can be formalized by adding a network structure to the base model.

Consistency has played a key role in the analysis of this enriched model, for which several families of rules have been characterized.[24]

(ii) When there are multiple funds to be used for compensating claimants, these funds may hold claims against one another. The possibility of mutual liabilities had actually been considered in a few papers that predate by quite a few years the literature reviewed in this book, and there has been a recent revival of interest in this issue.[25] It is one of great concern because the failure

[21] Orshan, Valenciano, and Zarzuelo (2003), Estévez-Fernández, Borm, and Fiestras-Janeiro (2014) and Dietzenbacher, Estévez-Fernández, Borm, and Hendrickx (2016).

[22] This model and the characterizations are due to Casas-Méndez, Garcia-Jurado, van den Nouweland, and Vásquez-Brage (2003) and Borm, Carpente, Casas-Méndez, and Hendrickx (2005).

[23] This model is proposed by Bergantiños and Sanchez (2002b) and further studied by Bergantiños and Lorenzo (2008) and Lorenzo (2010).

[24] The idea is formulated by Ilkılıç and Kayı (2014). See also Moulin and Sethuraman (2013).

[25] Benson (1935), Kocourek (1935) address this issue informally. Recent contributions are by Tyre (1980), Eisenberg and Noe (2001), Wood (2010), Karpov and Yurkov (2012),

of one financial institution may cause the failure of another; this in turn may cause the failure of some third one; these domino effects may cause a financial crisis.

A characterization of a version of the proportional rule has been established for this domain of problems.

For its analysis the concept of a "flow network" has been proposed and a number of rules that have been central in the literature on the base model have been considered in this context. Conceptual and technical challenges had to be addressed. A *consistency* axiom has been defined in terms of the flow network and the question asked whether certain two-claimant rules have *consistent* extensions to arbitrary populations. Similarly to what is the case for the base model, concede-and-divide and the constrained equal awards rules have been shown to have unique *consistent* extensions.[26]

• **Accommodating multiple claims vectors.** Imagine an estate division problem in which several documents have surfaced each of which specifying the amount to be awarded to some, possibly not all, heirs. Supposing that none of these documents has more validity than any other, how should they all be taken into account to come up with a recommendation?

A method has been proposed of completing incomplete documents when each of them specifies only one award. It involves filling in the blanks in a recursive manner. It delivers the random arrival rule.[27] The more general case when more than one heir may be named in one or several documents deserves further study.

• **Adding dimensions.** An agent's claim may have several components, each corresponding to one of several issues, but there might still be a single endowment to be used for compensations. Two definitions of a rule have been proposed for this type of situations: each agent may be assigned a single award; or each agent may be assigned one award for each of the issues.

Versions of the proportional, constrained equal awards, constrained equal losses, random arrival, and Talmud rules have been defined for this model and characterizations of most of them have been derived, as well as a version of the random arrival for a further extension of the model. A mixed rule based on the proportional and constrained equal awards rules has also come out of axiomatic work.[28]

O'Neill (2014), Groote Schaasberg, Reijnierse, and Borm (2018), Csóka and Herings (2017a, 2017b), and Stutzer (2015).

26 This formulation is due to Branzei, Ferrari, Fragnelli, and Tijs (2008) and Bjørndal and Jörnsten (2010).

27 This formulation is proposed by O'Neill (1982).

28 These problems are usually studied under the name of "multi-issue" claims problems. Papers on the subject are by González-Alcón, Borm, and Hendrickx (2003), Calleja, Borm, and Hendrickx (2005), Borm, Carpente, Casas-Méndez, and Hendrickx (2005), Lorenzo-Freire, Alsonso-Meijide, Casas-Mendez, and Hendrickx (2007), Moreno-Ternero (2009), Bergantiños,

• **Adding a reference point.** The base model can be enriched by adding a vector in awards space representing some reference that is judged relevant to the evaluation of proposed awards vectors. This point may or may not be feasible.

(i) A first formulation is when the reference point is exogenously specified.[29] To each rule for the base model can be associated a rule for the enriched model by replacing each claim by the corresponding coordinate of the reference vector truncated at the claim, applying the rule if the resulting vector is above the budget line; if not, using this vector as a vector of minimal rights, and then applying the rule. An alternative formulation involves applying the rule or its dual depending upon which case it is. Which properties of standard rules are inherited by their images under the operators just defined is well understood.

A formula has been proposed to convert such enriched problems into TU coalitional games, and a rule has been advocated to solve these problems, based on the τ-value (Subsection 14.1.2).

(ii) A second formulation is when the reference point is made to depend on the data of the problem: a baseline function associates with each problem a vector in awards space from which to evaluate proposed awards vectors.[30] Again, if the sum of its coordinates is smaller than the endowment, the vector is used to provide lower bounds on awards; if the opposite holds, to provide upper bounds. Thus, the lower bound functions and upper bound functions defined in Section 3.4 are examples of baseline functions.

Now, consider a baseline function that is continuous and, for each nonzero claims vector, specifies a vector with at least one positive coordinate and at least one coordinate that is smaller than the corresponding coordinate of the claims vector. Then, for each problem, recursively assigning the baseline amounts when it is feasible to do so and replacing claims by the baseline amounts when it is not, generates a sequence of problems in which the endowment converges to 0, thereby defining a rule. This convergence result can

Lorenzo, and Lorenzo-Freire (2010a, 2010b, 2011), Lorenzo-Freire, Casas-Mendez, and Hendrickx (2010), Hinojosa, Mármol, and Sánchez (2012a, 2012b), Sánchez (2012), Hougaard, Moreno-Ternero, and Østerdal (2013a,b), Flores-Szwagrzak (2015), and Borrero, Sánchez, Hinojosa, and Mármol (2017). Izquierdo and Timoner (2016) enrich the model by adding a constraint on how much can be spent on each issue. For Herrero (1998) and Ju and Moreno-Ternero (2017, 2018), each dimension corresponds to a commodity and they add information about the agents' preferences or about agents' utilities over commodity bundles.

[29] This formulation is proposed by Pulido, Sánchez-Soriano, and Llorca (2002), who require the sum of the coordinates of the reference vector not to exceed the endowment. Yager and Kreinovich (2000)'s proposal amounts to assuming that in addition, the reference vector is dominated by the claims vector. A follow-up is Woeginger (2006). Pulido, Borm, Hendrickx, Llorca, and Sánchez-Soriano (2008) do not make this assumption. Neither do Hougaard, Moreno-Ternero, and Østerdal (2013a,b). Related studies are by Giménez-Gómez and Osório (2015) and Giménez-Gómez, Osório, and Peris (2016).

[30] This proposal is due to Hougaard, Moreno-Ternero, and Østerdal (2012). Contributions by Timoner and Izquierdo (2016) and Izquierdo and Timoner (2016) are along the same lines.

be seen as a generalization of Theorem 3.2, which identified properties of lower bounds under which rules can be obtained by recursively assigning them.

The notion of duality applies to baseline functions. Also, with each baseline function can be associated an operator on the space of rules, as in Chapter 9.

The results pertaining to the composition of these operators with the duality operator that we presented in Chapter 9 extend to this formulation. Virtually all of the results concerning the claims truncation and attribution of minimal rights operators also extend to their reformulations in terms of baselines.

• **Adding uncertainty.** In practice, the data of a claims problem are often not known with certainty and the question arises of how to model this uncertainty.[31]

(i) One possibility is to add probabilistic information. A stochastic claims problem is a collection of standard claims problems indexed by states of nature together with a list of the claimants' utility functions.

A notion of core has been proposed for this type of situation. The constrained equal awards and the sequential priority rules select from it but none of the proportional, constrained equal losses, or Talmud rules do.[32]

Axioms of no-advantageous reallocations of claims across agents as well as across states have been formulated and characterizations of two versions of the proportional rule, an ex ante version and an ex post version, have been obtained, based principally on these axioms.[33]

When claims are uncertain, the endowment may turn out to exceed their sum. Waste is thereby generated and the issue has to be addressed of accommodating claims as well as possible, taking into consideration possible waste.

A family of rules that can be seen as generalizing Young's family, and a subfamily, have been characterized in this context on the basis of some of the axioms encountered for the base model, *strong composition down* and *consistency* being the central ones, as well as axioms pertaining specifically to the behavior of rules in this kind of situations.[34]

(ii) When there is uncertainty about claims that cannot be modeled probabilistically, one may specify each of these variables as an interval, the endowment being required to be no greater than the sum of the lower endpoints of the intervals so that for each realization of the claims profile, a well-defined claims problem results. A rule selects a nonnegative vector whose coordinates add up to the endowment and that is dominated by the vector of upper endpoints.

[31] The first study of this issue is due to Hougaard and Thorlund-Peterson (2001).

[32] This formulation and these results are due to Habis and Herings (2011, 2013).

[33] Ertemel and Kumar (2018).

[34] This formulation is due to Xue (2018). In a related contribution Long, Sethuraman, and Xue (2019) characterize another family of rules.

Such a problem can also be converted into a coalitional game and several ways have been proposed of applying solutions to coalitional games, in particular the Shapley value, to derive rules.[35] The possibility that the endowment be uncertain instead, or that both claims and endowment be uncertain, have been modeled in a similar way.[36]

• **Adding incentives issues.** In the context of bankruptcy, understanding the incentives that rules give agents to invest in a business that may go bankrupt and may have to be liquidated requires that the model be enriched. The literature is also developing in this direction. One can well imagine that there would not be a unique way of modeling this type of issues, a particularly important part of which is formalizing how uncertainty affects the endowment.

(i) A formulation has been proposed in which two firms compete for investors and each chooses a rule according to which its liquidation value would be divided among its investors should it fail. Investors maximize expected payoffs, taking into account this possibility.

It has been shown that, when the choice of rules is among the proportional, constrained equal awards, and constrained equal losses rules, each agent announcing the proportional rule is a subgame perfect equilibrium of the resulting game. Under certain conditions, it is the only such equilibrium.[37]

(ii) Another study offers comparative statics results on strategic equilibria of investment games concerning the total amount invested. It considers weighted averages of the proportional and equal awards rules as well as weighted averages of the proportional and equal losses rules.[38]

(iii) When there is uncertainty in the supply of a good in which several agents are interested, these agents need to protect themselves against possible shortages. They can do so by strategically choosing how much of a resource to invest. These choices depend on the rule that is used to allocate shortages.

An experimental study (See Section 15.8) of such situations has been conducted. It covers the proportional, constrained equal awards, and constrained equal losses rules.[39]

• **Adding heterogeneity to the dividend.** Consider a group of agents with conflicting claims over some piece of land. Land is not a homogeneous good, so the theory we have developed does not apply. However, it has been a point of departure for a noncooperative analysis. In particular, a game of stakes as in Subsection 14.2.1 has been studied in this context.[40]

[35] Branzei, Dimitrov, Pickl, and Tijs (2004).

[36] Branzei, Dimitrov, and Tijs (2003); Alparslan Gök, Branzei, and Tijs (2008); Branzei and Alparslan Gök (2008), Branzei and Dall'Aglio (2009), Branzei, Dall'Aglio, and Tijs (2013).

[37] This enrichment and this result are due to Karagözoğlu (2014).

[38] A. Kıbrıs and Ö. Kıbrıs (2013). A related study of surplus sharing is Kıbrıs (2016).

[39] Lefebvre (2013).

[40] Pálvödgyi, Peters, and Vermeulen (2013).

Existence of equilibrium has been established as a limit of approximate equilibria. In our base model, every division is Pareto efficient. Not surprisingly, this is not necessarily the case here. However, it turns out that no equilibrium outcome Pareto dominates any other.

• **Literature on claims problem as a source of inspiration.** The literature on the adjudication of conflicting claims has been a source of inspiration in handling several other classes of problems. We briefly review three applications.

(i) Deriving solutions to coalitional games from rules for claims problems. In Subsection 14.1.2 we discussed how the theory of coalitional games can help in solving claims problems. The reverse is possible too. Starting from a division rule for claims problems, and given a coalitional game, we convert the game into a claims problem, apply the rule to it, and choose the resulting awards vector as payoff vector for the game. An n-player coalitional game is an object of considerably larger dimension that an n-agent claims problems, and one would expect that restrictions should be imposed on games for a chosen conversion formula to be well defined and meaningful. That is indeed the case.

As an illustration of the kind of results that can be obtained by following this approach, on a domain of games for which a certain version of the core is nonempty, this process delivers a variant of the τ-value when the point of departure is the adjusted proportional rule, and it delivers the nucleolus when the point of departure is the Talmud rule.[41]

(ii) Museum pass problems. The museums in a city offer a pass: anyone purchasing it has access to all of them. How should the revenue generated by the sale of the pass be divided among the museums? Each museum has its own admission fee and for each museum, we have a record of how many of its visitors held a pass. A museum's "virtual revenue" is the amount the museum would collect if it charged all pass holders who visited it its regular fee. Assuming, as is natural, that an art lover buys a pass only if the price of the pass is no greater than the sum of the individual admission fees of the museums that the art lover would like to visit, simple algebraic manipulation shows that the total revenue from the sale of the pass is no greater than the sum of the museums' virtual revenues.[42] This opens up the possibility of using rules to solve claims problems in order to obtain recommendations for museum pass problems.

41 The first result is due to González-Díaz, Borm, Hendrickx, and Quant (2005). The second one to Quant, Borm, Reijnierse, and van Velzen (2005). Such results can be seen as counterparts of the "correspondence results" of Theorem 14.2(b)). Quant, Borm, Hendrickx, and Zwikker (2006) follow the same approach, using the random arrival rule to define a solution for coalitional games. Another contribution along these lines is by Estévez-Fernández, Fiestras-Janeiro, Mosquera, and Sánchez-Rodriguez (2012).

42 The museum pass problem is formulated by Ginsburg and Zang (2013). For a survey, see Casas-Méndez, Fragnelli, and García-Jurado (2014).

(iii) River sharing problems. A group of farmers are distributed along the slope of a mountain; sources of water for irrigation are located along the slope; the cost of moving water up is prohibitive; thus only downhill flow of water is possible. Finally, each farmer has a numerical claim over water. More generally, a group of agents are distributed along an ordered one-dimensional continuum. A resource is made available at various points but the resource can be transferred from one point to another only in a specific direction along this continuum. Also, each agent has a claim over the resource. A principal interpretation of the model is when the one-dimensional continuum is time and a resource can only flow from one generation to the subsequent generations. For this model, a version of the proportional rule has been characterized along the lines of a characterization of this rule for standard claims problems, the main axiom being a counterpart of "no transfer paradox." "Composition" properties have also been studied in this context.[43]

(iv) Coalition formation problems. A group of agents have to be partitioned into subgroups, called "coalitions." Each agent has preferences over the coalitions to which the agent belongs. A partition is stable if there is no group of agents each of whom prefers being part of the group to being part of the component of the partition that contains that agent. What properties of preference profiles guarantee the existence of stable partitions? This problem has been studied under the assumption that preferences over coalitions are derived as follows: there is one resource and each agent has a claim over the resource; each coalition, if it forms, has access to an amount of it that is insufficient to fully honor the claims of its members, a division rule for claims problems being applied to determine how much each of its members gets. An agent's preferences over coalitions are derived by a comparison of their induced payoffs. The existence of stable partitions then boils down to identifying properties of rules under which conditions on preference profiles that are known to guarantee stability for the abstract formulation of the problem are satisfied. These properties have been completely identified, *consistency* being a central one.[44]

15.8 EXPERIMENTAL TESTING

A considerable literature has recently emerged devoted to the experimental testing of economic theories but the theory developed here has just begun to be examined in the laboratory. The following questions can be asked.

[43] The river sharing model is formulated by Ambec and Sprumont (2002). For a study of composition properties in this context, see Ansink and Weikard (2012, 2015). A characterization of the family of rules obtained by taking convex combinations of the equal awards and proportional rules, based mainly on a form of immunity to reallocation of claims, is due to Oishi (2018). See also Madani, Zarezadeh, and Morid (2014) and Mianabadi, Mostert, Zarghami, and van de Giesen (2014). For a survey, see Béal, Ghintran, Rémila, and Solal (2013).

[44] This problem is formulated by Gallo and Iñarra (2018), to whom these results are due.

Do experimental subjects tend to express preferences for the recommendations made by particular rules? When they negotiate their own payoffs, can any regularity be observed in the eventual outcomes? Do these outcomes look like the payoffs that particular rules recommend? What if instead, subjects are asked their opinion as disinterested third parties? Also, in playing the cooperative and strategic games to which we confront them, do agents behave in the manner we postulate in our formal models? Perhaps more delicate is to elicit whether, and the extent to which, they care about the various properties that we consider in axiomatic theory, and to uncover the tradeoffs they see between properties or that are pointed out to them.

One should expect the answers to depend on the context. For instance, whether the issue is distributing a good in short supply among households or a profit among businesses is likely to matter. The values of the parameters of the problem may matter as well, how unequal claims are and how far the endowment is from covering them. The type of society in which the testing is performed may be relevant too, for example, whether it has a tradition of free enterprise or one of State intervention.[45]

This work is only starting but a legitimate hope is that in a few years, this approach will have been sufficiently developed to be a useful complement to the axiomatic work to which this book has mainly been devoted.

We do not see the results of experimental studies to be what ultimately should determine what rule to recommend however. Although they may tell us at a point in time and space how certain groups of experimental subjects view certain questions in particular controlled environments, the benefit of axiomatic work is to bring out important issues into the public debate, and eventually to help people form an opinion.

15.9 A CONCLUDING COMMENT

The general public is rarely offered choices illuminated by serious economic analysis, let alone axiomatic reasoning. Those of us engaged in the development of the design program hope that the principles that constitute its conceptual basis will come up in the conversation with increased frequency, and their evaluation inform the choices made in organizing societies.

Although the man on the street should eventually be the beneficiary of theoretical research, lawmakers and the entities in charge of implementing their decisions – bankruptcy courts, tax authorities, local governments – should already be able to take into account some of its lessons. With the development of economics education, responsible citizens today are in a much better

[45] Studies along these lines are due to Béhue (2003), Gächter and Riedl (2005, 2006), Bosmans and Schokkaert (2009), Herrero, Moreno-Ternero, and Ponti (2010), Cappelen, Luttens, Sorensen, and Tungodden (2013), Gaertner and Schwettmann (2017), and Büyüboyacı, Gürdal, A. Kıbrıs, and Ö. Kıbrıs (undated).

position to make judgments about economic decisions affecting their personal or public life than in the past. We hope that this book will contribute to widening the scope of this understanding so as to include a new set of issues having to do with the distribution of resources, and that it will help societies divide when there isn't enough.

CHAPTER 16

Summary Graphs and Tables

Although claims problems are among the simplest problems that one may encounter, we have discovered that the model of adjudication of conflicting claims is surprisingly rich. It is also remarkable how quickly the theory has reached maturity. In the space of a few years, many of the ideas that had been central in the development of the axiomatic program have been investigated in the context of this model, a number of properties that are specific to it have also been formulated, and very complete descriptions of the implications of these properties when imposed in various combinations obtained.

In order to facilitate assessing the relative merits of the most central rules, we illustrate here their paths of awards and present their properties in a single table. A second table summarizes what we have learned about the preservation of the central properties by the most important operators.

Each of the graphs of Figures 16.1 and 16.2 shows several paths of awards for one of twelve rules. We choose a typical claims vector and draw the construction lines that are needed to determine the path for that vector. We limit attention to claims vectors whose second coordinate is larger than the first. All of the rules represented are *anonymous*, so the paths of awards for claims vectors whose first coordinate is larger than the second are simply obtained by symmetry with respect to the 45° line. Also, all of the rules are *homogeneous*, so any path relative to a claims vector that is proportional to one already specified is simply obtained by a homothetic expansion or contraction of the path for that reference claims vector.

For two rules, the constrained egalitarian rule and the average of the constrained equal awards and constrained equal losses rules, two claims vectors are named, as the shape of the path depends on the relative values of the coordinates of the two claims. For the constrained egalitarian rule, the path for a claims vector c such that $c_1 \leq 2\frac{c_2}{3}$ consists of four segments, and the path for a claims vector c' such that $c'_1 \geq 2\frac{c'_2}{3}$ consists of five segments. For the average of the constrained equal awards and constrained equal losses rules, each path first follows the line of equation $x_2 = 3x_1$. The path for a claims vector c such that $c_1 \leq \frac{c_2}{3}$ does so until $(\frac{c_1}{2}, 3\frac{c_1}{2})$, then continues vertically until it meets the

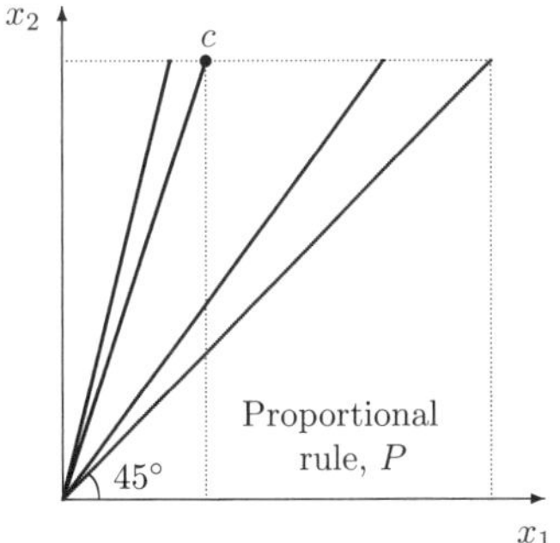

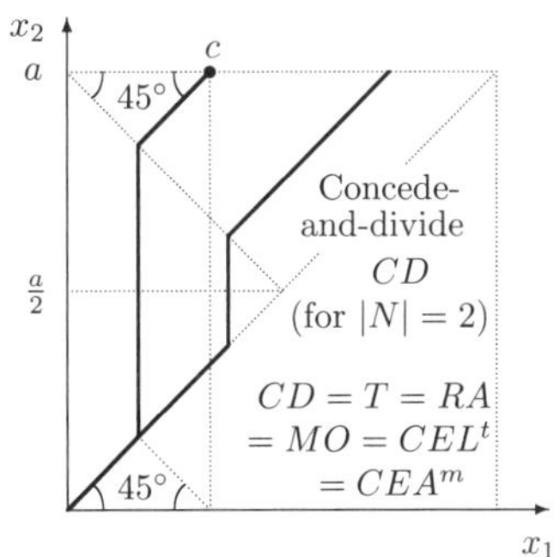

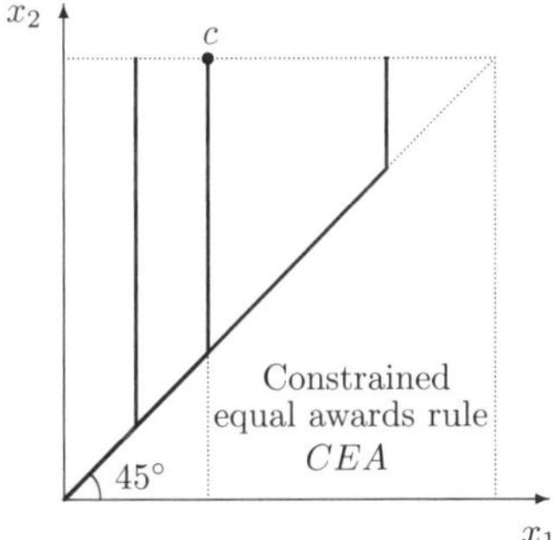

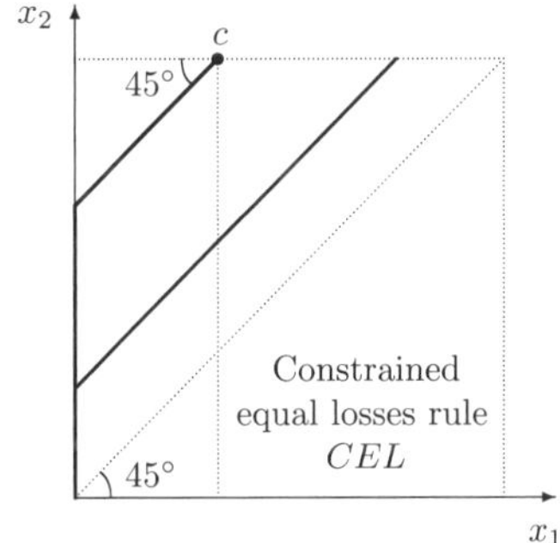

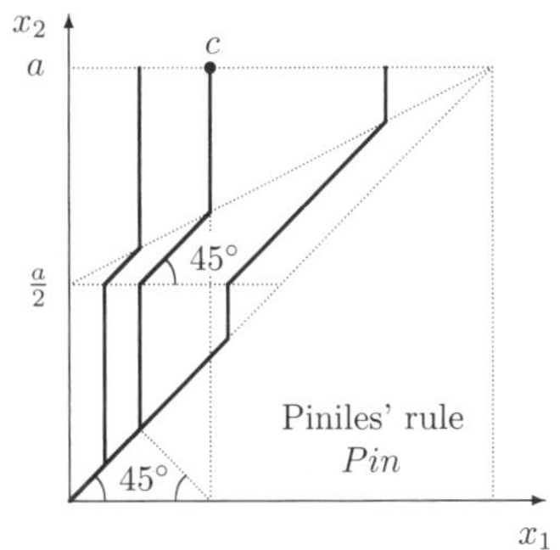

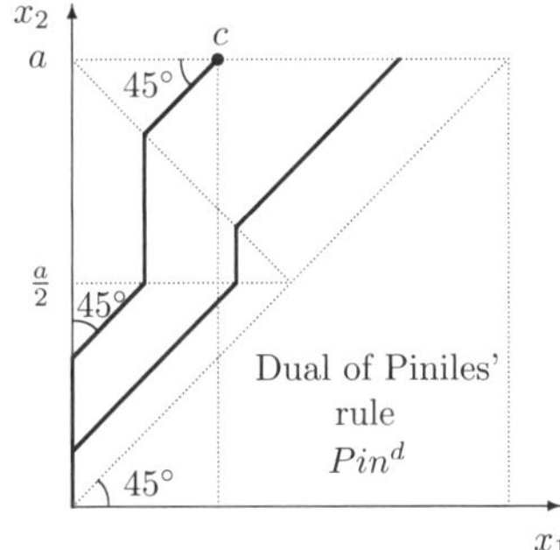

Figure 16.1: **Paths of awards for six rules in the two-claimant case.** In each case, we choose several claims vectors to illustrate the range of possible shapes for the paths.

line of equation $x_2 = c_2 - 3x_1$. For a claims vector c' such that $c'_1 \geq \frac{c'_2}{3}$, the first breakpoint is $(\frac{c'_2 - c'_1}{4}, 3\frac{c'_2 - c'_1}{4})$, then the path continues parallel to the 45° line until it meets the line passing through $(\frac{c'_2}{6}, \frac{c'_2}{2})$ and (c'_2, c'_2), and it terminates with a segment of slope 3.

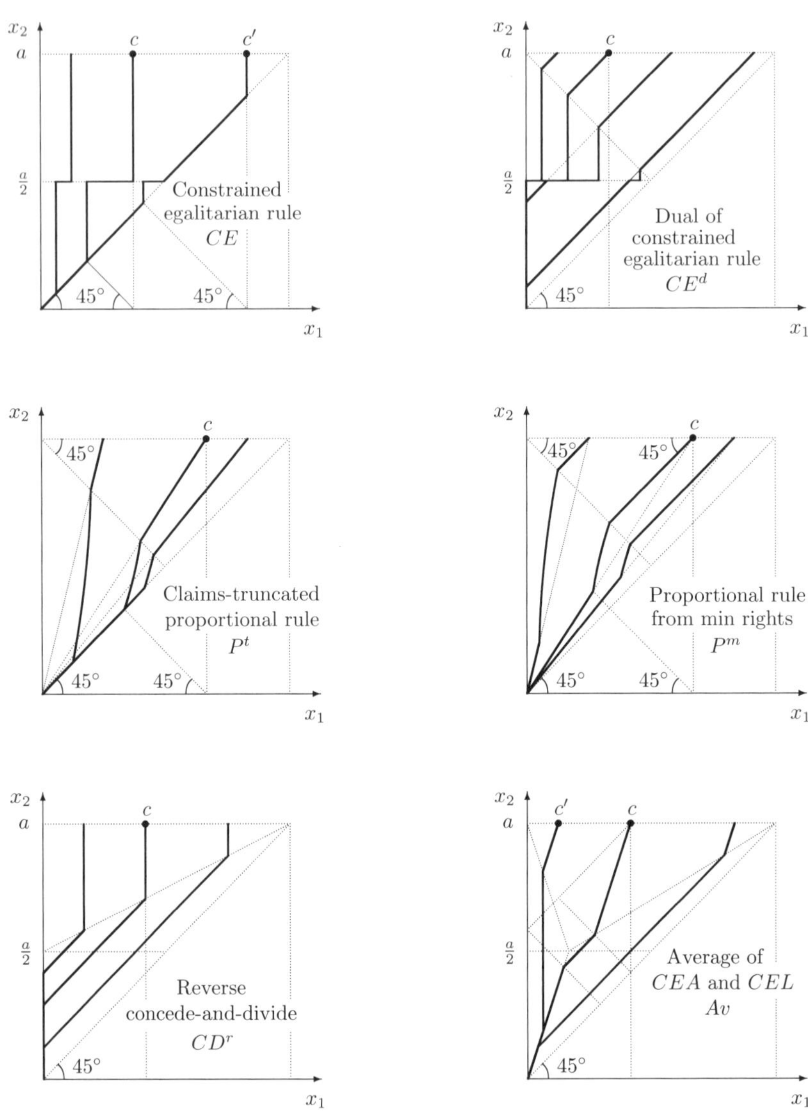

Figure 16.2: **Paths of awards for six more rules in the two-claimant case.** In each case, we choose several claims vectors to illustrate the range of possible shapes for the paths.

Table 16.1 collects the properties of the rules that have most often appeared in our study. A "+" in a cell at the intersection of a row and a column means that the property indexing the row is satisfied by the rule indexing the column, and a "–" means the opposite.

The assertions in the cells of Table 16.1 can be derived in a variety of ways, and in almost all cases, there are several ways of establishing them. (i) Some

Table 16.1: ***Showing which of the main properties the main rules satisfy***. *The notation "na" means that a certain property is not applicable. The notation $*$ in a cell of the column pertaining to the rules $D^{\prec}$ means that the property indexing the row is satisfied provided the orders $\prec$ corresponding to different populations are consistent. Dual properties are shown on consecutive lines.*

Prop \rules	P	CD	CEA	CEL	Av	CE	T	Pin	RA	MO	AP	$D^{\prec}$
$\frac{1}{\|N\|}$-trunc-claims lower bounds on awards	−	+	+	−	−	+	+	+	+	+	+	−
$\frac{1}{\|N\|}$-min-of-claims-and-deficit lower bounds on losses	−	+	−	+	−	−	+	−	+	−	+	−
Conditional full compensation	−	−	+	−	−	−	−	−	−	−	−	−
Conditional null compensation	−	−	−	+	−	−	−	−	−	−	−	−
Equal treat equals	+	+	+	+	+	+	+	+	+	+	+	−
Order preservation	+	+	+	+	+	+	+	+	+	+	+	−
Anonymity	+	+	+	+	+	+	+	+	+	+	+	−
Equal treat equal groups	+	na	−	−	−	−	−	−	−	−	−	−
Group order preservation	+	na	−	−	−	−	−	−	−	−	−	−
Regressivity	+	−	+	−	−	−	−	−	−	−	−	−
Progressivity	+	−	−	+	−	−	−	−	−	−	−	−
Continuity	+	+	+	+	+	+	+	+	+	+	+	+
Claim monotonicity	+	+	+	+	+	+	+	+	+	+	+	+
Linked claim-endowment monotonicity	+	+	+	+	+	+	+	+	+	+	+	+
No transfer paradox	+	+	+	+	+	+	+	+	+	+	+	+
Bounded impact of claims transfers	+	+	+	+	+	+	+	+	+	+	+	+
Endowment monotonicity	+	+	+	+	+	+	+	+	+	+	+	+
Concavity	+	−	−	+	−	−	−	−	−	−	−	−
Convexity	+	−	+	−	−	−	−	−	−	−	−	−
Homogeneity	+	+	+	+	+	+	+	+	+	+	+	+
Claims truncation invariance	−	+	+	−	−	−	+	−	+	+	+	+
Minimal rights first	−	+	−	+	−	−	+	−	+	+	+	+

Table 16.1 *(Cont.)*

Prop \rules	P	CD	CEA	CEL	Av	CE	T	Pin	RA	MO	AP	$D^{\prec}$
Composition down	+	–	+	+	–	–	–	–	–	–	–	+
Composition up	+	–	+	+	–	–	–	–	–	–	–	+
Self-duality	+	+	–	–	+	–	+	–	+	–	+	–
Midpoint property	+	+	–	–	+	+	+	+	+	–	+	–
No advantageous transfers	+	na	–	–	–	–	–	–	–	–	–	–
Summation independence	+	na	–	–	–	–	–	–	–	–	–	–
Claims separability	+	na	+	+	–	+	+	+	–	–	–	
Dual of claims separability	+	na	+	+	–	+	+	+	–	–	–	
Endowment convexity	+	–	–	–	–	–	–	–	–	–	–	–
Population monotonicity	+	na	+	+	+	+	+	+	+	+	–	+*
Linked endowment-population monotonicity	+	na	+	+	+	+	+	+	+	+	–	+*
No advantageous merging	+	na	+	–	–	–	–	–	–	–	–	–
No advantageous splitting	+	na	–	+	–	–	–	–	–	–	–	–
Division invariance	+	na	+	+	–	+	+	+	–	–	–	–
Replication invariance	+	na	+	+	–	+	+	+	–	–	–	–
Consistency	+	na	+	+	–	+	+	+	–	–	–	+*
Bilateral consistency	+	na	+	+	–	+	+	+	–	–	–	+*
Null claims consistency	+	na	+	+	+	+	+	+	+	+	+	+*
Null compensation consistency	+	na	+	+	+	+	+	+	+	+	–	+*
Full compensation consistency	+	na	+	+	+	+	+	+	+	+	–	+*
Converse consistency	+	na	+	+	+	+	+	+	–	–	–	+*
claim-endowment uniformity	+	na	+	+	–	+	+	+	–	–	–	
endowment-population uniformity	+	na	+	+	–	+	+	+	–	–	–	
claim-endowment separability	+	na	+	–	–	+	+	+	–	–	–	
Prop /rules	P	CD	CEA	CEL	Av	CE	T	Pin	RA	MO	AP	$D^{\prec}$

entries are obvious from the definition: for example, the fact that the constrained equal awards rule satisfies *equal treatment of equals* is immediate. (ii) Sometimes, we have given in the text an explicit proof that a particular rule satisfies a particular property, or we have constructed an example to show that the rule violates the property. (iii) Some entries can be obtained by exploiting logical relations among properties: for example, the fact that the proportional rule satisfies *order preservation* is a direct consequence of the fact that it satisfies the stronger property of *group order preservation*. (iv) Some entries can be deduced from characterizations: to illustrate, we can deduce that the minimal overlap rule violates *no advantageous transfer* from Theorem 8.1, stating that the proportional rule is the only rule satisfying the property (and the fact that the two rules are distinct).

Table 16.2 indicates which properties are preserved under the main operators.

Although one should not have expected a complete ranking to emerge from our investigation, axiomatic analysis has provided much support for the rule that is the most commonly used in practice, namely the proportional rule, but it has also brought out a number of arguments in favor of other rules such as the constrained equal awards, constrained equal losses, and Talmud rules. Particularly noteworthy is the large number of occasions in which the two-claimant rule we called concede-and-divide has come up. Since this rule is uniquely extended to general populations by requiring a natural consistency property, the case in favor of the rule that results, the Talmud rule, has been much strengthened by the recent literature.

More importantly, this study has illustrated the considerable help that the axiomatic method can provide in handling a class of allocation problems. Almost all of the principles that have played a role in this book are applicable in other contexts, where they have also allowed to thoroughly evaluate allocation rules and to identify certain rules as being worthy of particular attention.

Table 16.2: ***Showing which properties are preserved under the operators***. *In each cell for which a negative result holds, we indicate in parenthesis a rule allowing to prove the claim. For instance, the notation* (P) *at the intersection of the row labeled "Group order preservation" and column labeled "truncation" means that the proportional rule satisfies the property but that its version obtained by first truncating claims at the endowment does not. Dual properties are shown on consecutive lines.*

Prop \operators	convexity	duality	truncation	attrib of min rights	trunc ∘ attrib of min rights
$\frac{1}{\lvert N\rvert}$-trunc-claims lower bound (awards)	+	–	+	+	+
$\frac{1}{\lvert N\rvert}$-trunc-claims lower bound (losses)	+	–	+	+	+
Conditional full compensation	+	– (CEA)	–	– (CEA)	– (CEA)
Conditional null compensation	+	– (CEL)	– (CEL)	–	– (CEL)
Equal treat of equals	+	+	+	+	+
Order preservation	+	+	+	+	+
Anonymity	+	+	+	+	+
Equal treat of equal groups	+	+	– (P)	– (P)	– (P)
Group order preservation	+	+	– (P)	– (P)	– (P)
Regressivity	+	–(CEA)	+	– (P)	– (P)
Progressivity	+	– (CEL)	– (P)	+	– (P)
Continuity	+	+	+	+	+
Claim monotonicity	+	– (Prop 7.1)	+	– (Prop 9.5)	–
Linked claim-endowment monotonicity	+	– (Prop 7.1)	–	+	–
No transfer paradox	+	– (Prop 7.1)	–	–	–
Bounded impact of claims transfers	+	– (Prop 7.1)	–	–	–
Endowment monotonicity	+	+	– (CEL)	– (CEA)	– (CEA)
Concavity	+	– (CEA)	– (P)	– (P)	– (P)
Convexity	+	–(CEL)	– (P)	– (P)	– (P)
Homogeneity	+	+	+	+	+
Claims truncation invariance	+	– (CEA)	+	+	+
Minimal rights first	+	–(CEL)	+	+	+

Composition down	− (Av)	−	− (CEL)	− (CEA)	− (CEA)
Composition up	− (Av)	−	− (CEL)	− (CEA)	− (CEA)
Self-duality	+	+	− (P)	− (P)	+ (Cor 9.1)
Midpoint property	+	+	− (P)	− (P)	+ (Prop 9.6)
No advantageous transfer	+	+	− (P)	− (P)	− (P)
Summation independence	+	+	− (P)	− (P)	− (P)
Claims separability	+	−	− (P)	− (P)	
Dual of claims separability	+	−	− (P)	− (P)	
Endowment convexity	+	+	− (P)	− (P)	− (P)
Population monotonicity	+	− (Prop 12.1)	+	− (CEA)	− (CEA)
Linked endowment-population monotonicity	+	− (Prop 12.1)	− (CEL)	+	− (CEL)
No advantageous merging	+	−	−	− (P)	− (P)
No advantageous splitting	+	−	− (P)	−	− (P)
Division invariance	+	+	− (P)	− (P)	− (P)
Replication invariance	+	+	− (P)	− (P)	− (P)
Consistency	− (Av; Prop 10.3)	+ (Prop 10.4)	− (P; Prop 10.3)	− (CEA; Prop 10.3)	− (P; Prop 10.3)
Bilateral consistency	− (Av; Prop 10.3)	+ (Prop 10.4)	− (P; Prop 10.3)	− (CEA; Prop 10.3)	− (CEA; Prop 10.3)
Null claims consistency	+(Prop 10.3)	+ (Prop 10.4)	+(Prop 10.3)	+(Prop 10.3)	+
Null compensation consistency	+ (Prop 10.3)	− (Prop 10.4)	+(Prop 10.3)	+(Prop 10.3)	+
Full compensation consistency	+(Prop 10.3)	− (Prop 10.4)	+(Prop 10.3)	+(Prop 10.3)	+
Converse consistency	− (Av; Prop 10.3)	+ (Prop 10.4)	− (P; Prop 10.3)	− (CEA; Prop 10.3)	− (CEA; Prop 10.3)

CHAPTER 17

Appendices

This chapter collects a number of appendices. They are devoted to technical derivations that we felt were too lengthy to be included in the chapters to which they belong.

17.1 DERIVING A FORMULA FOR THE MINIMAL OVERLAP RULE

Proof of Proposition 2.1: (according to which the minimal overlap procedure produces a well-defined rule.)

We omit the straightforward proof for Case 1.

To handle Case 2, for simplicity let $N \equiv \{1, \cdots, n\}$ and assume $c_1 \leq \cdots \leq c_n$. Note that statement (b) in Case 2 is that the claims of all agents except those with the ℓ largest claims for some ℓ, are nested. For each $k \in \{0, 1, \ldots, n\}$, let E^k be the part of the endowment claimed exactly k times. Clearly, E^0 is empty, E^1 has positive size, and E^k has positive size for at least one other k. Let us arrange parts of the endowment in such a way that the part claimed the greatest number of times comes first, the part claimed the second greatest number of times comes second, and so on. Then E^1 is an interval of the form $[t^*, E]$ for some t^*. We should have $\sum_{i:\, c_i > t^*}(c_i - t^*) = E - t^*$.

We will show that if a configuration of claims achieves the objective stated in the definition of the rule, it satisfies (a) and (b) in Case 2.

To prove (a), suppose by contradiction that some agent $i \in N$ claims a positive part A of E^1, but that there is some positive part B of E^k, for $k \geq 2$, that agent i does not claim (Figure 17.1) and is claimed by some agent $j \in N$. Without loss of generality, assume that the size of B is twice that of A, and divide B into two subsets B' and B'' of equal sizes. Now, transfer agent i's claim on A to B', and agent j's claim on B'' to A. This transfer increases the size of E^{k-1} without decreasing the size of $E^{k'}$ for any $k' < k - 1$.

To prove (b), suppose by way of contradiction that some agent $i \in N$ who is not claiming any part of E^1 is also not claiming some positive part A of $[0, c_i]$. Let $k \in \mathbb{N}$ be the smallest integer such that agent i claims a positive part

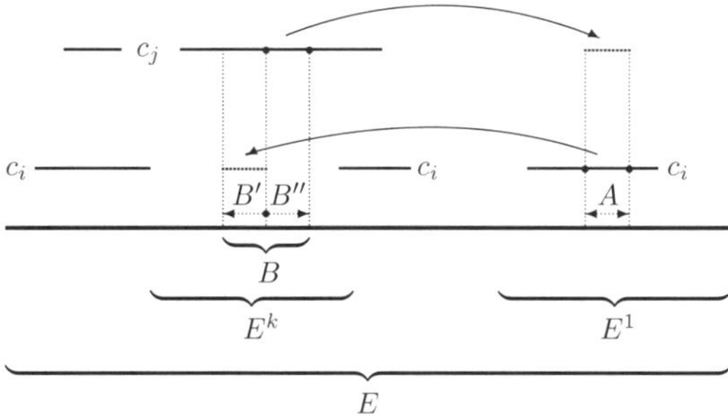

Figure 17.1: **Essential uniqueness of the configuration of claims yielding minimal overlap** (Proposition 2.1). Proof of part (a) of Case 2. Only the claims of agent i and j, between whom a transfer will take place, are indicated. Initially, agent i's claim covers three intervals and agent j's claim covers two intervals. The lower curvy arrow shows a transfer of part of agent i's claim from A to B', and the upper curvy arrow shows a transfer of part of agent j's claim from B'' to A.

of E^k. Then translating agent i's claim to the left so as to cover A necessarily increases the size of E^{k-1} without decreasing the size of $E^{k'}$ for any $k' < k-1$.

We have therefore established that if a configuration of claims solves our exercise, then a value t^* as described in Case 2 of the proposition exists. To calculate t^*, we solve the following simple equation. Say that a claimant as in (a) of Case 2 contributes to covering $[t^*, E]$. The value t^* should be such that the contributions of all such claimants cover the whole interval $[t^*, E]$. For each t, $L(t) \equiv E - t$ is the length of the interval $[t, E]$. If $t \in [0, c_1]$, then all agents contribute, for a total of $\sum(c_i - t)$. If $t \in [c_1, c_2]$, all agents except agent 1 contribute, for a total of $\sum_{N\setminus\{1\}}(c_i - t)$ ... More generally, if t falls in $[c_{k-1}, c_k]$, the total contribution, written as $C(t)$, is $\sum_{i\in[n-k+1,n]} c_i - (n-k+1)t$. Both L and C are continuous functions; also, $C(0) = \sum c_i > E = L(0)$ and $C(c_n) = 0 < L(c_n)$. Thus, there is t^* for which $C(t^*) = L(t^*)$. Moreover, at each t smaller than the second smallest claim, the slope of C, if well defined (it is well defined except at a number of points at most equal to the number of claimants), is smaller than -1, and at each t in the interval between the second largest and largest claims, it is equal to 1. Thus, such a t^* is unique except if E falls in that last interval, in which case the multiplicity of solutions is immaterial. □

17.2 MORE ABOUT THE CIC RULES

We describe in greater detail the CIC rules introduced in Subsection 2.2.3. These rules are parameterized by a pair of lists of functions of the claims vector $H \equiv (F^k, G^k)_{k=1}^{n-1}$, where $n \equiv |N|$, specifying when each agent comes into the distribution of each increment of the endowment and when they leave it. These functions have to be related by what we introduced there under the name of

CIC relations. Let us describe them. There are as many relations as claimants, but they are not independent: multiplying through the first one by n, the second one by $n-1$, ... and the last one by 1, and adding the results, we obtain an identity. When two agents have equal claims, the CIC relations imply that they come in together and that they drop out together. Thus, some of the parameters are equal then.

Let $H \equiv (F^k, G^k)_{k=1}^{n-1}$, where $n \equiv |N|$, be a list of pairs of real-valued functions of the claims vector such that for each $c \in \mathbb{R}_+^N$, the sequence $(F^k(c))_{k=1}^{n-1}$ is nowhere decreasing, the sequence $(G^k(c))_{k=1}^{n-1}$ is nowhere increasing, $G^1(c) \leq \sum c_i$, and

$$\begin{array}{ccccccc}
 & & \frac{-F^{n-1}(c)}{n} & + & \frac{G^{n-1}(c)}{n} & = & c_1 \\
c_1 & + & \frac{F^{n-1}(c)-F^{n-2}(c)}{n-1} & + & \frac{G^{n-2}(c)-G^{n-1}(c)}{n-1} & = & c_2 \\
\vdots & + & \vdots & + & \vdots & = & \vdots \\
c_{k-1} & + & \frac{F^{n-k+1}(c)-F^{n-k}(c)}{n-k+1} & + & \frac{G^{n-k}(c)-G^{n-k+1}(c)}{n-k+1} & = & c_k \\
\vdots & + & \vdots & + & \vdots & = & \vdots \\
c_{n-1} & + & \frac{F^1(c)}{1} & + & \frac{\sum c_i - G^1(c)}{1} & = & c_n
\end{array}$$

Let $\bar{\mathcal{H}}^N$ be the family of lists of pairs of functions $H \equiv (F^k, G^k)_{k=1}^{n-1}$ satisfying the CIC relations. We refer to the rules we have now defined as the "CIC rules" because each claimant's award, when plotted as a function of the endowment, is Constant over some initial interval, then Increases, then remains Constant until the endowment reaches the sum of the claims. Summarizing, we have the following definition:

CIC rule relative to $H \equiv (F^k, G^k)_{k=1}^{n-1} \in \bar{\mathcal{H}}^N$, CIC^H: For each $c \in \mathbb{R}_+^N$, the awards vector is given by the following algorithm as the endowment E increases from 0 to $\sum c_i$. Assuming for simplicity that $c_1 \leq \cdots \leq c_n$, as E increases from 0 to $F^1(c)$, claimant n receives everything. As E increases from $F^1(c)$ to $F^2(c)$, equal division of each increment prevails among claimants n and $n-1$. As E increases from $F^2(c)$ to $F^3(c)$, equal division of each increment prevails among claimants n, $n-1$, and $n-2$, and so on. This process continues until claimant 1 enters the scene. Equal division among all agents of each increment prevails until, when the endowment reaches $G^1(c)$, claimant 1 is fully compensated and is dropped off. Then equal division of each increment prevails among claimants 2 through n until, when the endowment reaches $G^2(c)$, claimant 2 is fully compensated and is dropped off, and so on. At the end of the process, claimant n is the only one left. Each increment goes entirely to claimant n until this final claimant is fully compensated.

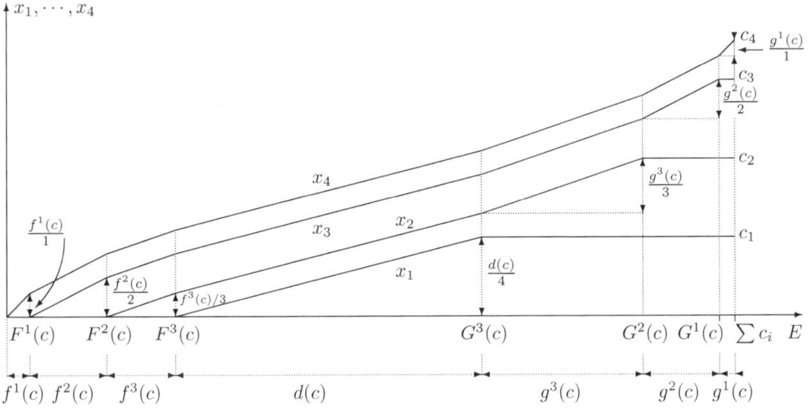

Figure 17.2: **Schedules of awards of a four-claimant CIC rule for a particular claims vector.** Here $N \equiv \{1, 2, 3, 4\}$ and $c \in \mathbb{R}^N_+$. The rule parameterized by $H \equiv (F^k, G^k)_{k=1}^3 \in \bar{\mathcal{H}}^N$ is denoted CIC^H. Let $f_1(c) \equiv F_1(c)$, and for $k = 2, 3$, let $f_k(c) \equiv F_k(c) - F_{k-1}(c)$. Let $g_1(c) \equiv \sum c_i - G_1(c)$, and for $k = 2, 3$, let $g_k(c) \equiv G_{k-1}(c) - G_k(c)$. Finally, let $d(c) \equiv G_3(c) - F_3(c)$.

As was the case for the ICI rules, there is an alternative way to describe a CIC rule. For each $k = 1, \ldots, n$ and each $c \in \mathbb{R}^N_+$ with $c_1 \leq \cdots \leq c_n$, let $\epsilon^k \equiv G^k(c) - F^k(c)$. We have:

$$\begin{array}{rcl} \epsilon^1(c) & = & c_1 + c_2 + \cdots + c_{n-3} + c_{n-2} + 2c_{n-1} \\ \epsilon^2(c) & = & c_1 + c_2 + \cdots + c_{n-3} + 3c_{n-2} \\ \cdots & = & \cdots + \cdots + \cdots + \cdots \\ \epsilon^{n-2}(c) & = & c_1 + (n-1)c_2 \\ \epsilon^{n-1}(c) & = & nc_1 \end{array}$$

Note that the sequence ϵ is the same for all CIC rules. Then, let us specify, for each $c \in \mathbb{R}^N_+$, a nowhere decreasing sequence $(F^k(c))_{k=1}^{n-1}$ of real numbers such that $F^1(c) \geq 0$. We then derive the sequence $(G^k(c))_{k=1}^{n-1}$ by adding to each $F^k(c)$ the parameter $\epsilon^k(c)$. The sequence $(F^k(c))_{k=1}^{n-1}$ should be nowhere increasing and such that $G^{n-1} \leq \sum c_i$.

Alternatively, we can specify a nowhere increasing sequence $(G^k(c))_{k=1}^{n-1}$ such that $G^{n-1}(c) \leq \sum c_i$, and derive the sequence $(F^k(c))_{k=1}^{n-1}$ by subtracting the sequence $(\epsilon^k(c))_{k=1}^{n-1}$. The sequence $(F^k(c))_{k=1}^{n-1}$ should be nowhere decreasing and such that $F^1(c) \geq 0$.

The next lemma identifies important CIC rules. The constrained equal awards and constrained equal losses rules, which are included, are the only ones to also be ICI rules.

Lemma 17.1 *The constrained equal awards, constrained equal losses, and reverse Talmud rules are CIC rules.*

Proof:

(a) Constrained equal awards rule: for each $c \in \mathbb{R}^N_+$, let $F(c) \equiv (0, \ldots, 0)$.
(b) Constrained equal losses rule: for each $c \in \mathbb{R}^N_+$, let $G(c) \equiv (\sum c_i, \ldots, \sum c_i)$.
(c) Reverse Talmud rule: for each $c \in \mathbb{R}^N_+$ such that $c_1 \leq \cdots \leq c_n$ say, let $F(c) \equiv (-\frac{c_{n-1}}{2} + \frac{c_n}{2}, -2\frac{c_{n-2}}{2} + \frac{c_{n-1}}{2} + \frac{c_n}{2}, \cdots, -k\frac{c_{n-k}}{2} + \frac{c_{n-k+1}}{2} + \cdots + \frac{c_n}{2}, \cdots, -(n-1)\frac{c_1}{2} + \frac{c_2}{2} + \cdots + \frac{c_n}{2})$. □

17.3 PATHS OF AWARDS OF THE DT RULE

We construct the paths of awards of the rule identified in Theorem 3.1 as resulting from the recursive application of the $\frac{1}{|N|}$-truncated-claims lower bounds on awards. In general, they consist of the concatenation of an infinite number of segments. A graphical representation is possible for $N \equiv \{1, 2\}$. The shape of the path for $c \in \mathbb{R}^N_+$ depends on the relative values of the claims. We distinguish two cases:

Case 1: $c_2 \leq 2c_1$. If $E \leq c_1$, $\mu(c, E) = (\frac{E}{2}, \frac{E}{2})$, so $DT(c, E) = (\frac{E}{2}, \frac{E}{2})$ (Figure 17.3a). If $c_1 < E \leq c_2$, $\mu(c, E) = (\frac{c_1}{2}, \frac{E}{2})$, and in the problem $(c - \mu(c, E), E - \sum \mu_i(c, E))$, the endowment is at most as large as the smaller claim, so equal division prevails. Thus, $DT(c, E) = (\frac{c_1}{4} + \frac{E}{4}, -\frac{c_1}{4} + 3\frac{E}{4})$. As E increases, $DT(c, E)$ moves up along a line of slope 3 (Figure 17.3a). The point reached when $E = c_2$ is $e^1 \equiv (\frac{c_1}{4} + \frac{c_2}{4}, -\frac{c_1}{4} + 3\frac{c_2}{4})$. If $c_2 < E$, $\mu(c, E) = \frac{c}{2}$. At first, equal division of any amount greater than c_2 prevails. We repeat the process described for $E \leq c_2$ for $E \leq \frac{c_2}{2}$ since this is the value of agent 2's revised claim (Figure 17.3b).

The path that results is as follows: divide box$[(0, 0), c]$ into four equal boxes by drawing the vertical line of abscissa $\frac{c_1}{2}$ and the horizontal line of ordinate $\frac{c_2}{2}$; divide the northeast box so defined into four equal boxes in a similar way; repeat. Let $d^1 \equiv (0, 0) + (\frac{c_1}{2}, \frac{c_1}{2})$, $d^2 \equiv (\frac{c_1}{2}, \frac{c_1}{2}) + (\frac{3c_1}{4}, \frac{3c_1}{4})$, $d^3 \equiv \frac{3}{4}(\frac{c_1}{2}, \frac{c_1}{2}) + (\frac{7c_1}{8}, \frac{7c_1}{8})$, and so on. Let $\sigma^1 \equiv$ seg$[(0, 0), d^1]$, $\sigma^2 \equiv$ seg$[\frac{c}{2}, d^2]$, $\sigma^3 \equiv$ seg$[\frac{3c}{4}, d^3]$, and so on. Let e^1 be the intersection of σ^2 with the line of slope 3 emanating from d^1, e^2 be the intersection of σ^3 with the line of slope 3 emanating from d^2, and so on. Now, the path for c is bro.seg$[(0, 0), d^1, e^1, d^2, e^2, \ldots]$ (Figure 17.3c).

The equality $c_2 = 2c_1$ identifies the boundary between Case 1 and Case 2 examined next. Then $e^1 = d^2$, $e^2 = d^3$, and so on. The segments of slope 1 are degenerate and we are left with a concatenation of segments of slope 3 from $(\frac{c_1}{2}, \frac{c_1}{2})$ to c. Altogether then, the path for c is bro.seg$[(0, 0), (\frac{c_1}{2}, \frac{c_1}{2}), c]$ (Figure 17.4a).

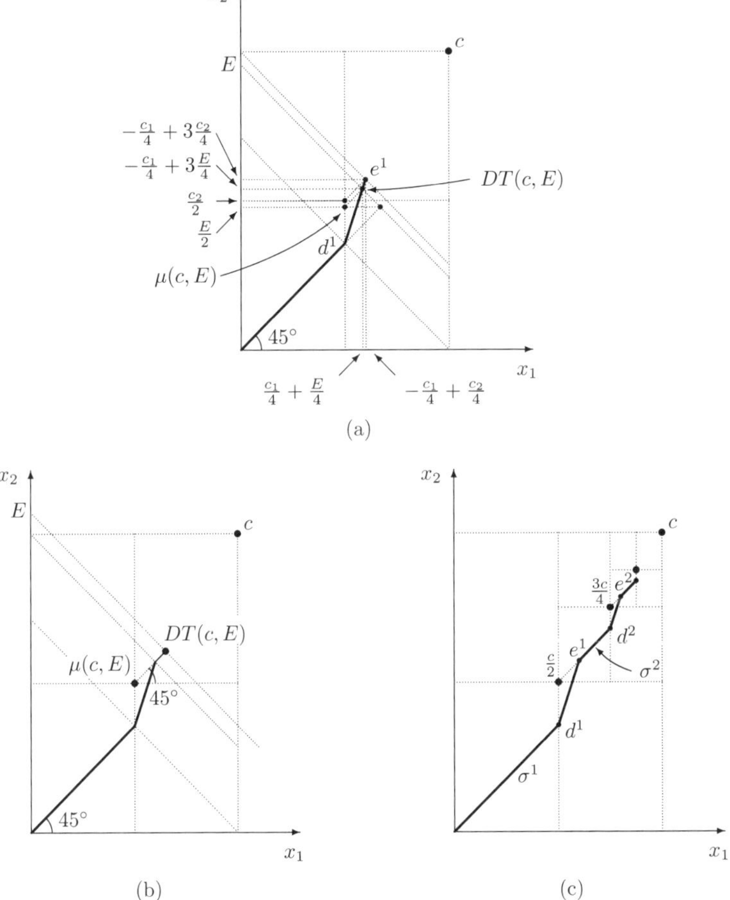

Figure 17.3: **Paths of awards of the DT rule.** Let $N \equiv \{1, 2\}$ and $c \in \mathbb{R}^N_+$ be such that $c_2 \leq 2c_1$. The path of DT for c is piece-wise linear. (a) We obtain the first and second segments by letting E vary in $[0, c_2]$. They are seg$[(0,0), d^1]$ and seg$[d^1, e^1]$. (b) Repeating the construction when E varies in $[c_2, \frac{c_1}{2} + c_2]$. (c) The third and fourth segments are seg$[e^1, d^2]$ and seg$[d^2, e^2]$.

Case 2: $c_2 > 2c_1$. The description of the path for this case is more complex because the direction of the inequality between agent 2's claim and the endowment may not change until several iterations. The path begins as in Case 1 with a segment of slope 1, and it continues with segments of slopes 3, 7,..., $2^k - 1$, and so on, until $\frac{E}{2} = \frac{c_2}{2}$, when we revise c_2 down to $\frac{c_2}{2}$ instead of to $\frac{E}{2}$. We refer to this sequence of steps as Stage 1. The greater c_2 is relative to c_1, the more steps in Stage 1. Stage 2 consists of a similarly defined sequence of steps, and the path continues with a sequence of segments of increasing slopes

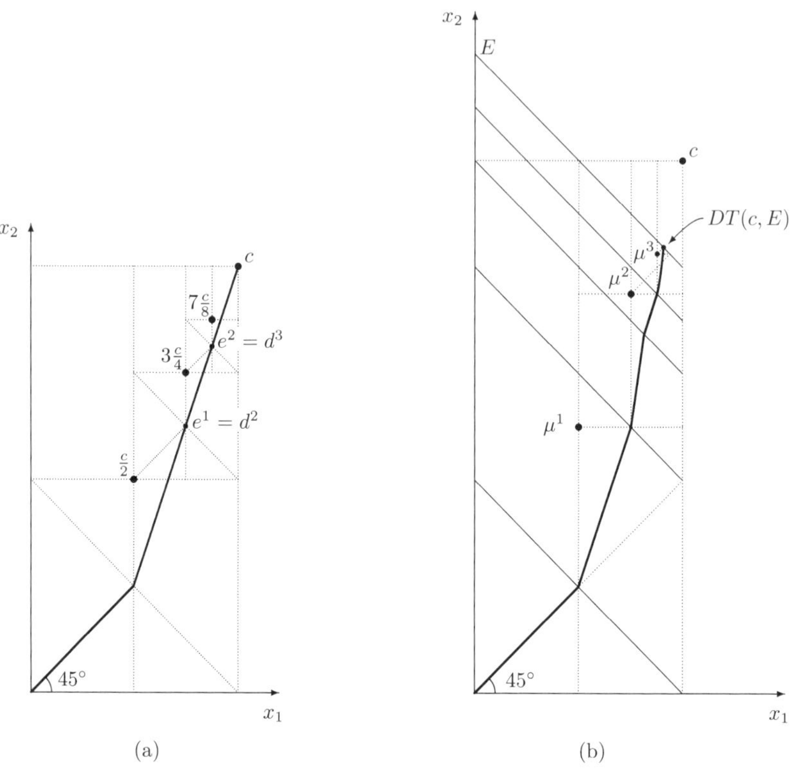

Figure 17.4: **Paths of awards of the DT rule (continued).** (a) The case $c_2 = 2c_1$. The path consists of only two segments. (b) The case $c_2 > 2c_1$. The path consists of parts, each of which consists of sequences of segments of increasing slopes, starting with a segment of slope 3. For short, we write μ^k for $\mu^k(c, E)$.

until once again, the direction of the inequality between agent 2's claim and the endowment changes. Figure 17.4b illustrates the construction when $c_2 = 2.5c_1$ and the endowment increases from 0 to $3c_1$.

17.4 NEITHER CLAIM MONOTONICITY NOR NO-TRANSFER PARADOX IS PRESERVED UNDER THE DUALITY OPERATOR

We identify here two properties that are not preserved under duality. First is *claim monotonicity*. We exhibit a rule that satisfies the property whereas its dual violates it. The rule is very well-behaved from a number of other viewpoints: it is *order-preserving*, *endowment monotonic*, and in particular *anonymous*, *homogeneous*, a fact that is used in the proof, and therefore its dual enjoys these properties too, since all of them are preserved under duality

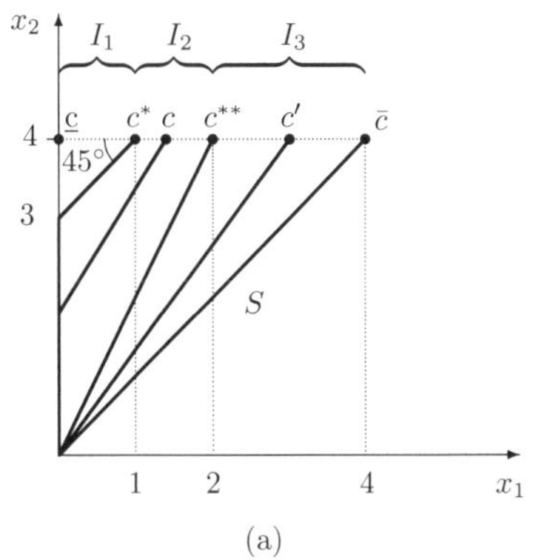

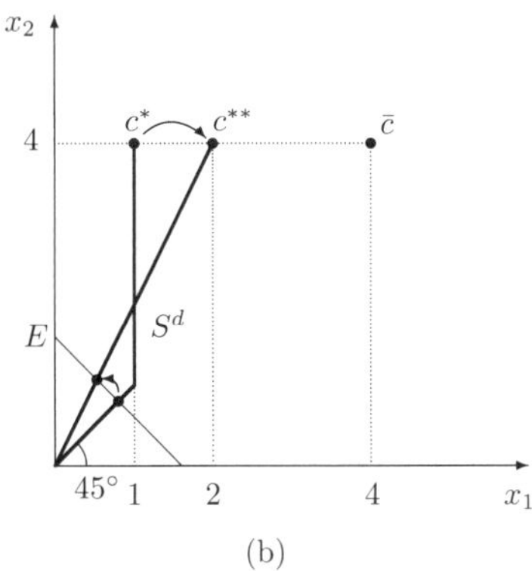

Figure 17.5: **Claim monotonicity is not preserved under duality** (Proposition 7.1). (a) Five paths of awards of Rule 17.1, denoted S in the proof. (b) Paths of the dual of S for c^* and c^{**}. If agent 2's claim is 4, the endowment is E, and agent 1's claim increases from c_1^* to c_1^{**}, but agent 1 receives less: S^d is not *claim monotonic*.

(Proposition 7.1). Thus, the additional properties do not help preserve *claim monotonicity*.

Proof of the assertion in Proposition 7.1 that claims monotonicity is not preserved under duality. The proof is by means of an example of a rule defined on $\mathcal{C}^N$, where $N \equiv \{1, 2\}$.

Step 1: Construction of Rule 17.1, denoted S.

Rule 17.1 (Figure 17.5a). Let $\underline{c} \equiv (0, 4)$, $c^* \equiv (1, 4)$, $c^{**} \equiv (2, 4)$, and $\bar{c} \equiv (4, 4)$. We first specify the path of awards of S for each $c \in \text{seg}[\underline{c}, \bar{c}]$. There are three cases. (i) For each $c \in I_1 \equiv \text{seg}[\underline{c}, c^*]$, the path is that of the constrained equal losses rule. (ii) For each $c \in I_2 \equiv \text{seg}[c^*, c^{**}]$, the path is piecewise linear in two pieces: given $0 \leq \lambda \leq 1$, the path for $\lambda c^* + (1 - \lambda)c^{**}$ is $\text{bro.seg}[(0, 0), \lambda(0, 3), \lambda c^* + (1 - \lambda)c^{**}]$. (Note that for $\lambda = 0$, the path is that of the proportional rule.) (iii) For each $c \in I_3 \equiv \text{seg}[c^{**}, \bar{c}]$, the path is that of the proportional rule.

For each $c \in \text{seg}[(4, 0), \bar{c}]$, the path of S is the symmetric image with respect to the 45° line of its path for (c_2, c_1). Finally, for each other $c \in \mathbb{R}_+^N$, the path is obtained by first calculating μ such that $\mu c \in \text{bro.seg}[(4, 0), \bar{c}, (0, 4)]$ and subjecting the path for μc to a homothetic transformation of ratio $\frac{1}{\mu}$.

Step 2: S is claim monotonic. Figure 17.6 shows that, no matter what the endowment is, when agent 2's claim is fixed at 4, and as agent 1's claim increases from 0 to ∞, agent 1's award does not decrease. *Claim monotonicity* of S is a consequence of this fact and of its being *anonymous* and *homogeneous*. The figure indicates the path of awards of S for each claims vector on the horizontal line of ordinate 4. Let us show that paths never cross.

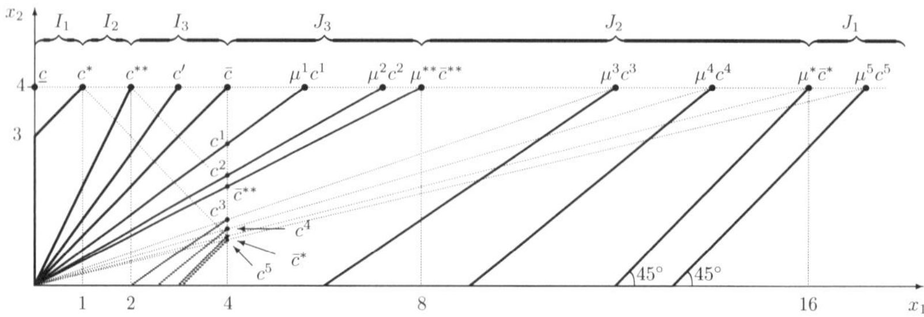

Figure 17.6: **Rule 17.1 is claims monotonic.** We represent the paths of awards for claims vectors of the form $(c_1, 4)$, giving to c_1 twelve different values chosen so as to illustrate all possible cases. The proof uses the fact that the path of S for each $c \in \text{seg}[(4,0), \bar{c}]$, where $\bar{c} \equiv (4,4)$, is the symmetric image of the path for the symmetric image of c with respect to the 45° line. We obtain the path for each $c \in J_3 \cup J_2 \cup J_1$ by a homothetic expansion of the path for the homothetic reduction of c that belongs to $\text{seg}[(4,0), \bar{c}]$. For each endowment, agent 1's award is a nowhere decreasing function of agent 1's claim: S is *claim monotonic*.

Given a pair $\{c_1, c'_1\} \subset [0, 4]$, the paths for $(c_1, 4)$ and $(c'_1, 4)$ were given explicitly and they clearly do not cross. Given any claims vector c of the form $c \equiv (c_1, 4)$ for $c_1 \in [4, \infty[$, there is a claims vector on $\text{seg}[(4,0), \bar{c}]$ that is proportional to it. We call $\mu \geq 1$ the expansion factor required to pass from the latter to the former, using the same superscript to keep track of this pairing, $\bar{c}^*$ and $\mu^*\bar{c}^*$ being another example of a pair so defined.

1. For each $c \in J_3 \equiv \text{seg}[\bar{c}, \mu^{**}\bar{c}^{**}]$, where $\bar{c}^{**}$ is the symmetric image of c^{**}, the path of awards of S is $\text{seg}[(0,0), c]$ (examples are the paths for μ^1c^1 and μ^2c^2).

2. For each $c \in J_2 \equiv \text{seg}[\mu^{**}\bar{c}^{**}, \mu^*\bar{c}^*]$, we obtain the path of awards of S by a homothetic expansion of its path for the reduced image of c that belongs to $\text{seg}[(4,0), \bar{c}]$. For example, consider two points in J_2, such as μ^3c^3 and μ^4c^4 in the figure, with μ^4c^4 to the right of μ^3c^3. Then the paths for these points are homothetic images of the paths for c^3 and c^4, with c^4 below c^3. The oblique segment in the path for c^4 is steeper than the oblique segment in the path for c^3. Thus, the same statement can be made about the oblique segments in the paths for μ^4c^4 and μ^3c^3. This implies that they do not cross.

3. Finally, for each $c \in J_1$, the horizontal half-line with $\mu^*\bar{c}^*$ as left endpoint, the path of awards of S consists of a horizontal segment with the origin as left endpoint, together with an oblique segment of slope 1.

Step 3: S^d is not claim monotonic. The paths of awards of S^d for c^* and c^{**} are the symmetric images of the paths of S for c^* and c^{**} with respect to the points $\frac{c^*}{2}$ and $\frac{c^{**}}{2}$ respectively. Figure 17.5b reveals that they cross, in violation of *claim monotonicity*. (In fact, for each endowment in the interval $]0, 3[$, agent 1 receives less if their claim increases from $c_1^* \equiv 1$ to $c_1^{**} \equiv 2$, agent 2's claim being kept fixed at 4.) □

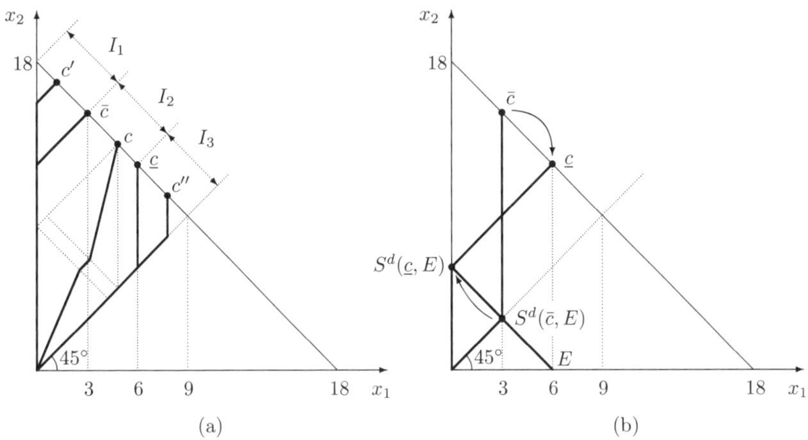

Figure 17.7: **No transfer paradox is not preserved under duality** (Proposition 7.1). (a) Sample paths of awards of Rule 17.2, denoted S in the proof. The rule satisfies *no transfer paradox*. (b) Paths of the dual of S for $\bar{c}$ and $\underline{c}$. As the claims vector changes from $\bar{c}$ to $\underline{c}$, for each endowment in the interval $]0, 12[$ (say, for $E = 6$, as shown in the figure), claimant 1 receives less and claimant 2 receives more: S^d violates *no transfer paradox*.

Strict claim monotonicity, the strengthening of *claim monotonicity* obtained by requiring that if an agent's claim increases, that agent should receive more (unless $E = 0$ of course), is not preserved under duality either. To see this, it suffices to modify the rule S used to prove Proposition 7.1. Without going into details, a simple way to obtain a rule that is *strictly claim monotonic* and whose dual is not is to adjust the paths of awards of S for each $c \in I_1 \cup I_2$ as follows: replace the vertical segment of the path for c by a very steep segment whose slope varies continuously and monotonically as $\frac{c_2}{c_1}$ varies between ∞ and $\frac{1}{2}$.

Proof of the assertion in Proposition 7.1 that no transfer paradox is not preserved under duality. The proof is by means of an example of a rule defined on $\mathcal{C}^N$, where $N \equiv \{1, 2\}$. The rule is constructed so as to be *anonymous* and *homogeneous*, a fact that is used in the proof.

Step 1: Construction of Rule 17.2, denoted S.

Rule 17.2 (Figure 17.7a) The rule is defined by first specifying its path of awards for each $c \in \text{seg}[(0, 18), (9, 9)]$. Let $\bar{c} \equiv (3, 15)$, $\underline{c} \equiv (6, 12)$, $I_1 \equiv \text{seg}[(0, 18), \bar{c}]$, $I_2 \equiv \text{seg}[\bar{c}, \underline{c}]$, and $I_3 \equiv \text{seg}[\underline{c}, (9, 9)]$. For each $c \in I_1$, the path of awards of S is that of the constrained equal losses rule. For each $c \in I_3$, it is that of the constrained equal awards rule. Finally, for each $c \in I_2$, it is that of the weighted average of the constrained equal losses and constrained equal awards rules with weights λ and $1 - \lambda$, where $\lambda \in [0, 1]$ is such that $c = \lambda\bar{c} + (1 - \lambda)\underline{c}$. This average is indicated for two critical budget lines, the one passing through the kink in the path of the constrained equal losses rule for c, and the one passing through the kink in the path of the constrained equal awards rule for c.

For each $c \in \text{seg}[(9,9),(18,0)]$, the path of S is the symmetric image with respect to the 45° line of its path for the symmetric image of c with respect to that line. For each other $c \in \mathbb{R}^N_+$, its path is obtained by a homothetic expansion or contraction, as the case may be, of its path for the claims vector on $\text{seg}[(0,18),(18,0)]$ that is proportional to c.

Step 2: S satisfies no transfer paradox. Indeed, no two paths relative to two claims vectors in $\text{seg}[(0,18),(9,9)]$ cross. It then suffices to observe that the rule is *anonymous* and *homogeneous*.

Step 3: S^d does not satisfy no transfer paradox. Inspection of Figure 17.7b shows that the paths of S^d for $\bar{c}$ and $\underline{c}$ cross. For $E \equiv 6$, agent 1 receives less after a claim transfer from agent 2 equal to $\bar{c}_2 - \underline{c}_2$. □

17.5 CLAIM MONOTONICITY IS NOT PRESERVED UNDER THE ATTRIBUTION OF MINIMAL RIGHTS OPERATOR

Proof of the assertion in Proposition 9.5 that claim monotonicity is not preserved under attribution of minimal rights. The proof is by means of an example of a rule defined on $\mathcal{C}^N$, where $N \equiv \{1,2\}$. The rule is constructed so as to be *anonymous*. It is also *order preserving*, *endowment monotonic*, and *continuous*.

Step 1: Construction of Rule 17.3, denoted S.

Rule 17.3 (Figure 17.8a). We first consider $c \in \mathbb{R}^N_+$ with $c_1 \leq c_2$. For each $c_2 \leq 2$, the path of awards of S is that of the proportional rule. For each $c_2 \geq 4$, its path is that of the constrained equal losses rule. For each $2 < c_2 < 4$ (the shaded region), its path is a linear combination (along lines of slope -1) of the paths of the proportional and constrained equal losses rules for c, using in the construction the function $g\colon [0,1] \mapsto [0,1]$ whose graph is $\text{bro.seg}[(0,0),(\frac{1}{2},\frac{1}{4}),(1,1)$. Now, let $k(c) \equiv g(\frac{c_2-2}{2})(c_2 - c_1)$, and let the path of S for c be $\text{bro.seg}[(0,0),(0,k(c)),c]$.

Finally, for each $c \in \mathbb{R}^N_+$ such that $c_1 > c_2$, the path of awards of S is the symmetric image with respect to the 45° line of its path for (c_2, c_1).

Step 2: S is claim monotonic. Since S is *anonymous*, it is enough to examine the rule for claims vectors in the region $\{c \in \mathbb{R}^N_+ : c_1 \leq c_2\}$. First, let $c_2 > 0$, and let $c_1, c_1' \in [0, c_2]$ be such that $c_1' < c_1$. There are three subcases. (i) If $c_2 \leq 2$, then the paths of S for c and c' are those of the proportional rule. Since this rule is *claim monotonic*, we are done. (ii) If $c_2 \geq 4$, the

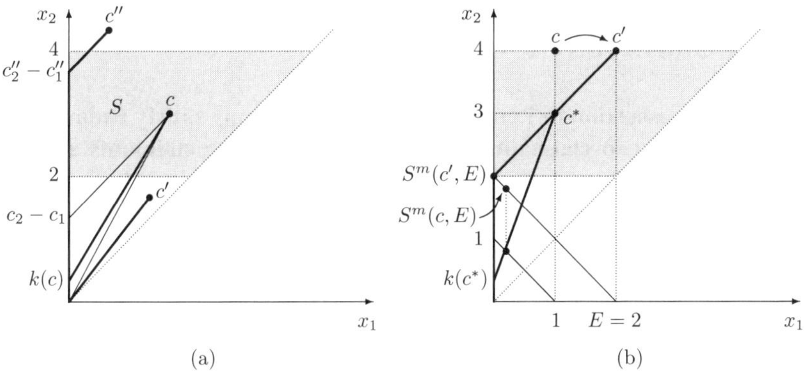

Figure 17.8: **Claims monotonicity is not preserved under attribution of minimal rights** (Proposition 9.5). (a) Sample paths of awards of Rule 17.3, denoted S in the proof. Its path for a claims vector c in the shaded region is a linear combination of the paths of the proportional and constrained equal losses rules for c. (b) Paths of S^m for c and c'. If the endowment is 2, as agent 1's claim increases from 1 to 2, agent 1 receives less.

paths of S for c and c' are those of the constrained equal losses rule. Since this rule is *claims monotonic*, we are done. (iii) If $2 < c_2 < 4$, the path of S for c is bro.seg$[(0, 0), (0, k(c)), c]$. The path of S for $c' \equiv (c'_1, c_2)$ is bro.seg$[(0, 0), (0, k(c')), c']$. The desired conclusion follows from the fact that $c_2 - c_1 < c'_2 - c'_1$, and since $c'_2 = c_2$, then $g(\frac{c_2-2}{2}) = g(\frac{c'_2-2}{2})$, so that altogether, $k(c) \equiv g(\frac{c_2-2}{2})(c_2 - c_1) < g(\frac{c'_2-2}{2})(c'_2 - c'_1) \equiv k(c')$.

Next, let $c_1 > 0$, and let $c_2, c'_2 \in [c_1, \infty[$ be such that $c_2 < c'_2$. The path of S for c is bro.seg$[(0, 0), (0, k(c)), c]$. The path of S for $c' = (c_1, c'_2)$ is bro.seg$[(0, 0), (0, k(c')), c']$. The desired conclusion follows from the fact that $c_2 - c_1 < c'_2 - c'_1$, and since g is increasing, $g(\frac{c_2-2}{2}) < g(\frac{c'_2-2}{2})$, so that altogether, $k(c) \equiv g(\frac{c_2-2}{2})(c_2 - c_1) < g(\frac{c'_2-2}{2})(c'_2 - c'_1) \equiv k(c')$.

Step 3: S^m is not claim monotonic (Figure 17.8b). To see this, let $c \equiv (1, 4)$, $c' \equiv (2, 4)$, and $E \equiv 2$. Note that $m(c, E) = (0, 1)$ and $m(c', E) = (0, 0)$. We have $S^m(c, E) = m(c, E) + S(c - m(c, E), E - \sum m_i(c, E))$. Let $c^* \equiv c - m(c, E)$. To calculate the second term in the expression for $S^m(c, E)$, we note that $c^* = (1, 3)$ and $E - \sum m_i(c, E)) = 1$. The path of S for c^* is, given that $k(c^*) = g(\frac{c^*_2-2}{2})(c^*_2 - c^*_1)$, bro.seg$[(0, 0), k(c^*), c^*]$. Since $g(\frac{c^*_2-2}{2}) = g(\frac{1}{2}) = \frac{1}{4}$, we have $k(c^*) = \frac{1}{4}(c^*_2 - c^*_1) = \frac{1}{2} < 1 = E - \sum m_i(c, E)$. So, $S^m_1(c^*, E) > 0$ and $S^m_1(c, E) > 0$. Also, $S^m_1(c', E) = S_1(c', E) = CEL_1(c', E) = 0$. Thus, as agent 1's claim increases from $c_1 = 1$ to $c'_1 = 2$, agent 1 receives less, in violation of *claim monotonicity*. □

17.6 LIFTING OF PROPERTIES BY BILATERAL CONSISTENCY

Proof of the assertion in Lemma 10.14 that a rule may satisfy endowment continuity for two claimants and self-duality for two claimants and be bilaterally consistent, but satisfy neither property in general. The proof is by means of an example of a rule defined on $\bigcup_{N \in \mathcal{N}} \mathcal{C}^N$.

Step 1: Construction of Rule 17.4, denoted S.

Rule 17.4 (Figure 17.9) Let $N \in \mathcal{N}$ and $(c, E) \in \mathcal{C}^N$.

Case 1: $1 \notin N$. Then $S(c, E) \equiv T^r(c, E)$ (recall that T^r refers to the reverse Talmud rule).

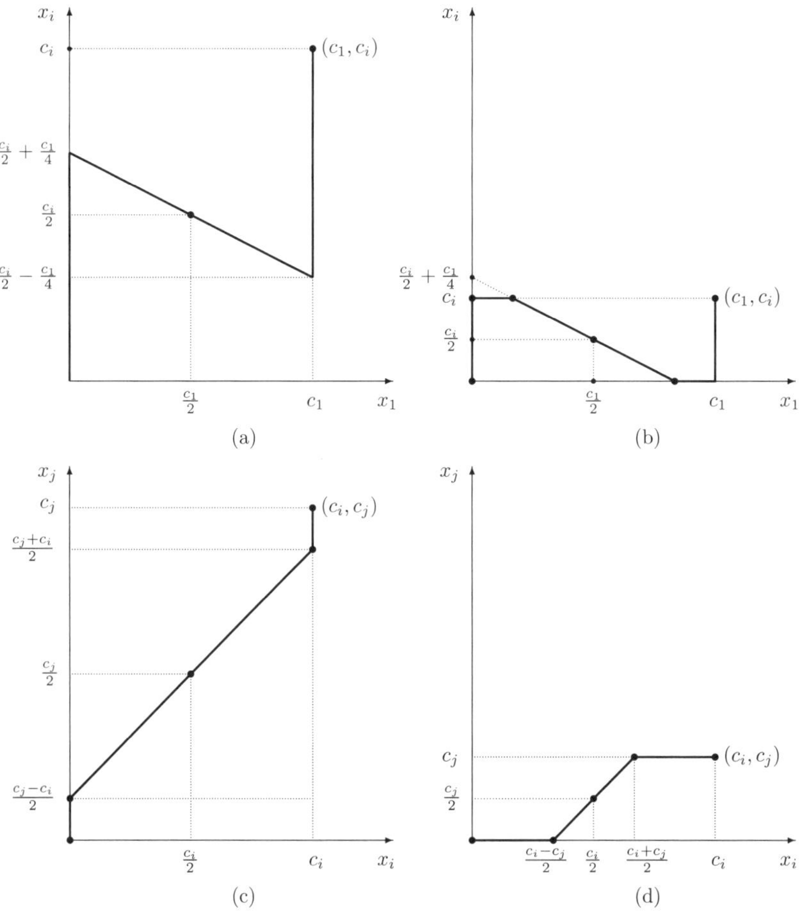

Figure 17.9: **Paths of awards of Rule 17.4** (Lemma 10.14a). (a) The path when $c_i \geq \frac{c_1}{2}$. (b) The path when $c_i < \frac{c_1}{2}$. (c) The path when $1 \notin \{i, j\}$ and $c_i < c_j$. (d) The path when $1 \notin \{i, j\}$ and $c_i > c_j$.

Case 2: $1 \in N$ and $|N| = 2$, say $N \equiv \{1, i\}$ for $i \in N \setminus \{1\}$. Then if $c_i \geq \frac{c_1}{2}$, the path of awards of S for c is bro.seg$[(0, 0), (0, \frac{c_i}{2} + \frac{c_1}{4}), (c_1, \frac{c_i}{2} - \frac{c_1}{4}), c]$ (Figure 17.9a); otherwise it is bro.seg$[(0, 0), (0, c_i), (\frac{c_1}{2} - c_i, c_i), (\frac{c_1}{2} + c_i, 0), (c_1, 0), c]$ (Figure 17.9b).

Case 3: $1 \in N$, $|N| \geq 3$, and $E < \sum_{i \in N \setminus \{1\}} \min \left\{c_i, \frac{c_i}{2} + \frac{c_1}{4}\right\}$. Then $S_1(c, E) \equiv 0$ and for each $i \in N \setminus \{1\}$, $S_i(c, E) \equiv T_i^r(c_{N \setminus \{1\}}, E)$.

Case 4: $1 \in N$, $|N| \geq 3$, $\sum_{i \in N \setminus \{1\}} \min \left\{c_i, \frac{c_i}{2} + \frac{c_1}{4}\right\} < c_1 + \sum_{i \in N \setminus \{1\}} \max \left\{0, \frac{c_i}{2} - \frac{c_1}{4}\right\}$, and E is equal to the left-hand side or lies strictly between these two quantities. Then $S_1(c, E) \equiv t$, and for each $i \in N \setminus \{1\}$, $S_i(c, E) \equiv T_i^r(c_{N \setminus \{1\}}, E - t)$, where $t > 0$ is the largest $t' \in [0, c_1[$ such that $t' + \sum_{i \in N \setminus \{1\}} \max \left\{\min \left\{c_i, \frac{c_i}{2} + \frac{c_1}{4} - \frac{t'}{2}\right\}, 0\right\} = E$.

Case 5: $1 \in N$, $|N| \geq 3$, $E \geq \max\{\sum_{i \in N \setminus \{1\}} \min \left\{c_i, \frac{c_i}{2} + \frac{c_1}{4}\right\}, c_1 + \sum_{i \in N \setminus \{1\}} \max \left\{0, \frac{c_i}{2} - \frac{c_1}{4}\right\}\}$. Then $S_1(c, E) \equiv c_1$ and for each $i \in N \setminus \{1\}$, $S_i(c, E) \equiv T_i^r(c_{N \setminus \{1\}}, E - c_1)$.

Note that the reverse Talmud rule is *continuous* and *self-dual*. From this fact and an inspection of Figure 17.9, we conclude that S is *continuous for two claimants* and *self-dual for two claimants*.

Step 2: S is bilaterally consistent. Let $N \in \mathcal{N}$ with $|N| \geq 3$, $(c, E) \in \mathcal{C}^N$, $x \equiv S(c, E)$, and $N' \subset N$ with $|N'| = 2$. We want to show that $x_{N'} = S(c_{N'}, \sum_{i \in N'} x_i)$. If $1 \notin N'$, then this equality holds since the reverse Talmud rule is *consistent* and for each $i \in N \setminus \{1\}$, $x_i = T_i^r(c_{N \setminus \{1\}}, E - x_1)$.

Suppose that there is $i \neq 1$ such that $N' = \{1, i\}$. Three of the cases listed in the definition of Rule 17.4 may apply to (c, E).

Case 3 applies: then $x_1 = 0$ and $x_i \leq \min \left\{c_i, \frac{c_i}{2} + \frac{c_1}{4}\right\}$.

Case 4 applies: then $x_i = \max \left\{\min \left\{c_i, \frac{c_i}{2} + \frac{c_1}{4} - \frac{x_1}{2}\right\}, 0\right\}$.

Case 5 applies: then $x_1 = c_1$ and $x_i \geq \max \left\{0, \frac{c_i}{2} - \frac{c_1}{4}\right\}$.

We can see on Figure 17.9 that in each case, (x_1, x_i) lies on the path of awards of S for (c_1, c_i).

Step 3: S is neither endowment continuous nor self-dual in general. Figure 17.10b shows that both properties fail for $E = \frac{\sum c_i}{2}$. *Self-duality* implies that when the endowment is equal to the half-sum of the claims, the half-claims vector is chosen, which we can see is not the case on the figures. It is also at that endowment that *continuity* is violated. □

17.7 CHARACTERIZING THE FAMILY OF EQUAL-SACRIFICE RULES

Proof of Theorem 10.11: (a characterization, on the domain of problems with positive claims, of the equal-sacrifice rules on the basis of *continuity*,

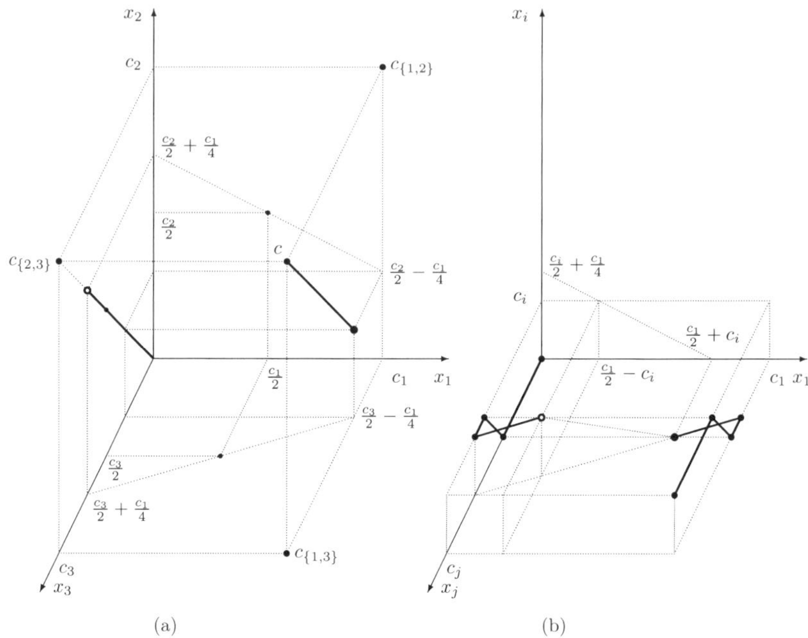

Figure 17.10: **Completing the proof of Lemma 10.14a.** Three-claimant problem revealing that Rule 17.4 violates *self-duality* and *endowment continuity*. (a) The path of the rule when $c_i > c_j > \frac{c_1}{2}$. (b) Its path when $c_j > \frac{c_1}{2} > c_i$.

strict endowment monotonicity, *strict order preservation in awards*, *composition down*, and *consistency*.) Clearly each equal-sacrifice rule satisfies the properties listed in the theorem. Conversely, let S be a rule satisfying these properties.

Step 1: Defining a function G to describe paths of awards and identifying three critical properties of G. Let $N \equiv \{i, j\}$. Let $G\colon]0, 1]^2 \mapsto \mathbb{R}_+$ be defined by the requirement that for each pair $\{x, y\} \subset]0, 1]$, the vector $(G(x, y), y)$ lies on the path for $(x, 1) \in \mathbb{R}^N_+$ (Figure 17.11a). (Draw the path for $(x, 1)$; $G(x, y)$ is the abscissa of the unique point on that path whose ordinate is y.) By *strict endowment monotonicity*, G is well defined. By *strict order preservation in awards*, S satisfies *equal treatment of equals*. In fact, since *equal treatment of equals* and *consistency* together imply *anonymity* (Lemma 10.9), S is *anonymous*. Thus, the function G is independent of i and j.

Substep 1-1: For each $\{x, y, z\} \subset]0, 1]$, $G(G(x, y), z) = G(x, G(y, z))$. Let $N' \equiv \{1, 2, 3\}$, and consider the point $(G(G(x, y), z), G(y, z), z)$ (Figure 17.11b). Note that in $\mathbb{R}^{\{2,3\}}$, $(G(y, z), z)$ lies on the path for $(y, 1)$. Also, in $\mathbb{R}^{\{1,3\}}$, $(G(x, y), z)$ lies on the path for $(G(x, y), 1)$. By *consistency*, this is possible only if in $\mathbb{R}^{\{1,2,3\}}$, $(G(G(x, y), z), G(x, y), z)$ lies on the

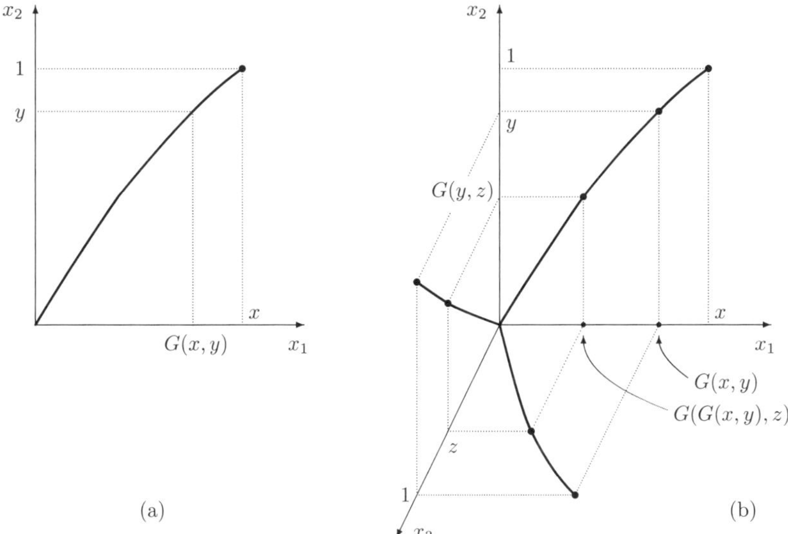

Figure 17.11: **Characterizing the family of equal-sacrifice rules** (Theorem 10.11). (a) Step 1: Defining the function G. (b) Substep 1-1: Uncovering a functional equation that G satisfies.

path for $(G(x, y), y, 1)$, and $(G(G(x, y), z), G(y, z))$ lies on the path for $(G(x, y), y)$.

By *composition down*, as in $\mathbb{R}^{\{1,2\}}$, $(G(x, y), y)$ lies on the path for $(x, 1)$ and $(G(G(x, y), z), G(y, z))$ lies on the path for $(G(x, y), y)$, then $(G(G(x, y), z), G(y, z))$ lies on the path for $(x, 1)$. Thus, $G(G(x, y), z) = G(x, G(y, z))$, as asserted.

Substep 1-2: for each $\{x, y, y'\} \subset]0, 1]$, if $G(x, y) = G(x, y')$, then $y = y'$; for each $\{x, x', y\} \subset]0, 1]$, if $G(x, y) = G(x', y)$, then $x = x'$. The first statement follows directly from *strict endowment monotonicity*. To prove the second statement, suppose that $x' > x$. Note that $(G(x, y), y)$ lies on the path for $(x, 1)$ and that $(G(x', y), y)$ lies on the path for $(x', 1)$. By *consistency* and *strict endowment monotonicity*, $(G(x, y), G(x', y), y)$ lies on the path for $(x, x', 1)$. By *strict order preservation in awards*, $G(x', y) > G(x, y)$, a contradiction.

Substep 1-3: G is continuous. This is because S is *continuous*. We omit the proof.

Step 2: Constructing u from G.

Substep 2-1: Constructing u on $]0, 1]$. By Substeps 1-1, 1-2, and 1-3, there is a continuous and strictly monotone function $u\colon]0, 1] \mapsto \mathbb{R}$ such that $G(x, y) = u^{-1}(u(x) + u(y))$ (Aczél, 1966, Section 6.2.2).

Substep 2-2: $u(1) = 0$ and for each $x < 1$, $u(x) < 0$. As $(1, 1)$ lies on the path for $(1, 1)$, $G(1, 1) = 1$. Thus, $1 = u^{-1}(u(1)+u(1))$, so that $u(1) = 2u(1)$, or $u(1) = 0$. Since u is strictly monotonic, for each $x < 1$, $u(x) < 0$.

Substep 2-3: $\lim_{x\to 0^+} u(x) = -\infty$. For each $x \in \mathbb{R}_+$, $u(G(x,x)) = 2u(x)$. Moreover, $0 < G(x,x) \leq x$. Hence, as $x \to 0$, $G(x,x) \to 0$. Thus, $\lim_{x\to 0^+} u(G(x,x)) = \lim_{x\to 0^+} u(x)$. But then, $\lim_{x\to 0^+} 2u(x) = \lim_{x\to 0^+} u(x)$, and as $u < 0$, $\lim_{x\to 0^+} u(x) = -\infty$.

Substep 2-4: Extending u to $[0,\infty)$. First, let $u(0) \equiv -\infty$. Next, for each $x > 1$, let $v \in \mathbb{R}_+$ be such that $(1, v)$ lies on the path for $(x, 1)$. Since S is *strictly endowment monotonic*, v is uniquely defined. Let $u(x) \equiv -u(v)$.

Step 3: S is the equal-sacrifice rule with respect to u.

Substep 3-1: Proving that $S = ES^u$ for $|N| = 2$. For each $x > 0$ and each pair $\{y, z\} \subset \mathbb{R}_+$, if (z, y) lies on the path for $(x, 1)$, then $u(z) = u(x) + u(y)$. This is clear if either y or $z = 0$ (because then they are both equal to zero, by *strict endowment monotonicity* and the fact that any path begins at $(0,0)$). So, assume that $y, z > 0$.

If $x \leq 1$, we already establish this fact, so assume that $x > 1$.

Case 1: $z \leq 1$. Let $v \in \mathbb{R}_+$ be such that $(1, v)$ lies on the path for $(x, 1)$. This number is uniquely defined. By *composition down*, (z, y) lies on the path for $(1, v)$. By *anonymity*, (y, z) lies on the path for $(v, 1)$. By definition of G then, $y = G(v, z)$ and by Substep 2-1, $u(y) = u(v) + u(z)$, so that $u(z) = u(y) - u(v) = u(y) + u(x)$.

Case 2: $z > 1$. Let $w, v \in \mathbb{R}_+$ be such that $(1, w, v)$ lies on the path for $(z, y, 1)$. Then in particular, $v \leq 1$, and as $y \leq 1$, $w \leq 1$. Invoking *consistency* and the definition of u repeatedly, we obtain:

- $(1, v)$ lies on the path for $(z, 1)$, so that $u(v) = -u(z)$.
- $(1, w)$ lies on the path for (z, y). As (z, y) lies on the path for $(x, 1)$, by *composition down*, $(1, w)$ lies on the path for $(x, 1)$. Thus, $u(w) = -u(x)$.
- (w, v) lies on the path for $(y, 1)$. As $y \leq 1$, $u(w) = u(v) + u(y)$.

Thus, $-u(x) = -u(z) + u(y)$, so that $u(x) - u(z) = u(1) - u(y)$.

Strict monotonicity of u over its whole domain is guaranteed.

Substep 3-2: Proving that $S = ES^u$ for $|N| \geq 3$. Let $(c, E) \in \mathcal{C}^N$. Then $S(c, E)$ lies on the path for c. Let $k \notin N$ and $N' \equiv N \cup \{k\}$. By *continuity* and *consistency*, there is $x \in \mathbb{R}_+$ such that $(S(c, E), x)$ lies on the path for $(c, 1)$. By *consistency*, for each $i \in N$, $(S_i(c, E), x)$ lies on the path for $(c_i, 1)$. But by definition then, $u(S_i(c, E)) = u(c_i) + u(x)$. Hence, for each pair $\{i, j\} \subset N$, $u(c_i) - u(S_i(c, E)) = -u(x) = u(c_j) - u(S_j(c, E))$. □

17.8 ON THE EXISTENCE AND UNIQUENESS OF AVERAGE CONSISTENT EXTENSIONS

Proof of Theorem 10.14: (which states the existence and uniqueness of an *average consistent* extension of any *endowment monotonic* rule S.) We will use the fact that *endowment monotonicity* implies *endowment continuity* (Section 4.1).

For each $x \in X(c, E)$ and each $i \in N$, let $f_i(x)$ be the average of the amounts awarded to claimant i in the reduced problems associated with x and the two-claimant subgroups of N to which claimant i belongs. Let $f(x) \equiv (f_i(x))_{i \in N}$. We will show that there is a unique $x \in X(c, E)$ such that $x = f(x)$. To simplify notation, we set $N \equiv \{1, \ldots, n\}$. Observe first that $X(c, E)$ is compact and that for each $x \in X(c, E)$, $f(x) \in X(c, E)$ (we omit the straightforward calculations). Second, f is continuous. The hypotheses of the Brouwer fixed-point theorem are met: there is x such that $f(x) = x$.

Next, we show that this fixed point x is unique by proving that f is a contraction for the norm $\| z \| \equiv \sum | z_i |$: this means that for each pair $\{x, y\} \subset X(c, E)$ with $x \neq y$, we have $\| f(x) - f(y) \| < \| x - y \|$. To see this, and dropping claims as an argument of S in order to simplify notation further, we first calculate that for each $i \in N$,

$$
\begin{aligned}
(n-1) \mid f_i(x) - f_i(y) \mid &= \Big| \sum_{j \in N \setminus \{i\}} S_i(x_i + x_j) - S_i(y_i + y_j) \Big| \\
&\leq \sum_{j \in N \setminus \{i\}} \mid S_i(x_i + x_j) - S_i(y_i + y_j) \mid .
\end{aligned}
$$

Summing over $i \in N$, we deduce that the expression $(n-1) \| f(x) - f(y) \|$ is smaller than or equal to:

$$
\begin{aligned}
&\sum_{i \in N} \sum_{j \in N \setminus \{i\}} \mid S_i(x_i + x_j) - S_i(y_i + y_j) \mid \\
\leq &\sum_{i \in N} \sum_{j \in N, j > i} (\mid S_i(x_i + x_j) - S_i(y_i + y_j) \mid \\
&+ \mid S_j(x_i + x_j) - S_j(y_i + y_j) \mid).
\end{aligned}
$$

By *endowment monotonicity* of S, the two expressions whose absolute values are taken are of the same sign. Thus we can write the double summation as:

$$
\begin{aligned}
&\sum_{i \in N} \sum_{j \in N, j > i} \mid S_i(x_i + x_j) - S_i(y_i + y_j) + S_j(x_i + x_j) - S_j(y_i + y_j) \mid \\
= &\sum_{i \in N} \sum_{j \in N, j > i} (\mid S_i(x_i + x_j) + S_j(x_i + x_j) - (S_i(y_i + y_j) + S_j(y_i + y_j)) \mid \\
= &\sum_{i \in N} \sum_{j \in N, j > i} \mid (x_i + x_j) - (y_i + y_j) \mid \\
= &\sum_{i \in N} \sum_{j \in N, j > i} \mid (x_i - y_i) + (x_j - y_j) \mid \\
< &\sum_{i \in N} \sum_{j \in N, j > i} (\mid x_i - y_i \mid + \mid x_j - y_j \mid),
\end{aligned}
$$

where the last inequality is because for each pair $\{i, j\} \subset N$, $|(x_i - y_i) + (x_j - y_j)| \leq |x_i - y_i| + |x_j - y_j|$, and that since $x \neq y$, there is $\{i, j\} \subset N$ such that $x_i > y_i$ and $x_j < y_j$, implying $|(x_i - y_i) + (x_j - y_j)| < |x_i - y_i| + |x_j - y_j|$.

Using the notation $a_{ij} \equiv |x_i - y_j|$, we can develop the last double summation as

$$\begin{array}{rlllllll} = & a_{11} + a_{22} & + & a_{11} + a_{33} & + & \dots & + & a_{11} + a_{nn} \\ & & + & a_{22} + a_{33} & + & \dots & + & a_{22} + a_{nn} \\ & & & & + & \dots & + & \dots \\ & & & & & & + & a_{n-1,n-1} + a_{nn} \\ = & (n-1)\sum_{i \in N} a_{ii} \\ = & (n-1)\sum_{i \in N} |x_i - y_i| \\ = & (n-1)\,\| x - y \| . \end{array}$$

Thus, $\| f(x) - f(y) \| < \| x - y \|$, as asserted.

Uniqueness of the fixed point of f follows directly. □

17.9 CONSTRUCTING CONSISTENT EXTENSIONS

Proof of Theorem 11.3: (according to which the two-claimant claims-truncated proportional rule has no *bilaterally consistent* extension.) Let us suppose that there is a *bilaterally consistent* rule S that coincides with P^t for two claimants. We will derive a contradiction to this supposition by considering the population of agents $N \equiv \{1, 2, 3\}$ when their claims are $c \equiv (2, 4, 6)$.

Step 1: Constructing the paths of awards of P^t for two claimants (Figure 17.12a). Let $\{i, j\} \subset N$, and $(c_i, c_j) \in \mathbb{R}_+^{\{i,j\}}$. Without loss of generality, suppose $c_i \leq c_j$. Then the path of awards of P^t for (c_i, c_j) is obtained as follows (the construction is briefly mentioned in Section 9.1):

Case 1: $E \leq c_i$. Both claims are truncated. After truncation, they are both equal to E, so that $P^t(c, E) = (\frac{E}{2}, \frac{E}{2})$. As E varies in $[0, c_i]$, $P^t(c, E)$ traces out seg$[(0, 0), (\frac{c_i}{2}, \frac{c_i}{2})]$.

Case 2: $c_i \leq E \leq c_j$. Only c_j is truncated, and $P^t(c, E)$ is the vector $x \in \mathbb{R}_+^{\{i,j\}}$ defined by (i) $x_i + x_j = E$, and (ii) for some $\lambda \in \mathbb{R}_+$, $x_i = \lambda c_i$ and $x_j = \lambda E$. As E varies in $[c_i, c_j]$, $P^t(c, E)$ traces out the part of the curve of equation $x_j = \frac{x_i^2}{c_i - x_i}$ (obtained by eliminating E and λ from (i) and (ii) above) that lies between the lines of equation $x_i + x_j = c_i$ and $x_i + x_j = c_j$. We denote by C this curve when $c_i = 2$, and for each $E \in \mathbb{R}_+$, we designate by $(f(E), g(E))$ the point of C that belongs to the line of equation $\sum x_i = E$. In Figure 17.12a, C is the very steep convex curve emanating from $(1, 1)$ and extending above the horizontal segment of ordinate 6. The critical observation to make here is that it is the same curve that generates the nonlinear parts of the paths for $(2, c_j)$ as c_j varies in $[c_2, \infty[$.

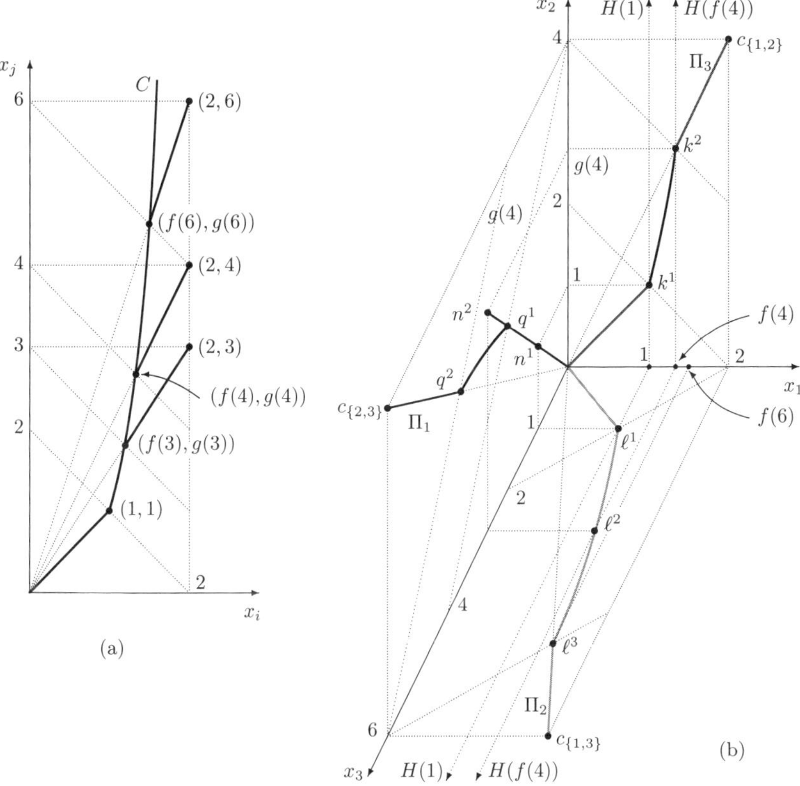

Figure 17.12: **Proof of Theorem 11.3.** (a) Step 1: Generating the paths of awards of P^t for (2, 3), (2, 4), and (2, 6). (b) Step 2-4: Deriving the contradiction. The path for $c_{\{2,3\}}$ in $\mathbb{R}_+^{\{2,3\}}$ consists of the union of seg$[(0, 0), q^1]$, a curvilinear segment from q^1 to q^2, and seg$[q^2, c_{\{2,3\}}]$. The projection onto $\mathbb{R}^{\{2,3\}}$ of the path for $c \equiv (2, 4, 6)$ of the *consistent* extension of P^t, if such an extension exists, contains seg$[n^1, n^2]$.

Case 3: $c_j \leq E$. No truncation takes place and $P^t(c, E) = P(c, E)$. As E varies in $[c_j, c_i + c_j]$, $P^t(c, E)$ traces out seg$[(f(c_j), g(c_j)), (c_i, c_j)]$.

Panel (a) of Figure 17.12 illustrates these conclusions for $c_i = 2$ and three values of c_j, namely 3, 4, and 6. Given $c_j \geq 2$, the path for $(2, c_j)$ has three parts: it consists of the union of seg$[(0, 0), (1, 1)]$, the part of C that lies between $(1, 1)$ and $(f(c_j), g(c_j))$, and seg$[(f(c_j), g(c_j)), (2, c_j)]$.

Step 2: Representing in $\mathbb{R}^N$ the paths of awards of P^t for $(c_1, c_2) = (2, 4)$, $(c_1, c_3) = (2, 6)$, and $(c_2, c_3) = (4, 6)$ (Figure 17.12b). We designate these paths by Π_3, Π_2, and Π_1 respectively.

• The path Π_3 of panel (b) is a copy of the path for (2, 4) of panel (a), with k^1 corresponding to (1, 1) and k^2 to $(f(4), g(4))$.

• The path Π_2 of panel (b) is a copy of the path for (2, 6) of panel (a), with ℓ^1 corresponding to (1, 1) and ℓ^3 to $(f(6), g(6))$.

• The path Π_1 of panel (b) is obtained by a homothetic expansion of factor 2 of the path for (2, 3) of panel (a). The points q^1 and q^2 correspond to the points obtained from (1, 1) and $(f(3), g(3))$ by subjecting them to this expansion.

Step 3: Constructing the projection onto $\mathbb{R}^{\{2,3\}}$ of Π, the path of awards of S for (2, 4, 6) (Figure 17.12b). Since Π_3 and Π_2 are strictly monotonic in the two-dimensional subspaces in which they lie, we can uniquely deduce Π from them. We can divide this path into four parts, separated by the planes parallel to the {2, 3}-coordinate subspace that contain either a kink of Π_3 or a kink of Π_2. For each $t \in [0, c_1]$, let $H(t)$ be the plane of equation $x_1 = t$. The important values of t, those for which $H(t)$ contains a kink or an endpoint of Π_3 and Π_2, are $t = 0, 1, f(4), f(6)$, and c_1. To avoid cluttering the figure, we do not represent Π itself. In fact, since this suffices for our purposes, we only identify in the next paragraph the part of it that lies between $H(1)$ and $H(f(4))$.

Let ℓ^2 be the point of Π_2 whose first coordinate is $f(4)$. The part of Π_3 that lies between k^1 and k^2 – let us call it C^3 – and the part of Π_3 that lies between ℓ^1 and ℓ^2 – let us call it C^2 – are both copies of the part of C that lies between (1, 1) and $(f(4), g(4))$, a strictly monotonic curvilinear segment. Thus, the part of Π whose projection onto $\mathbb{R}^{\{1,2\}}$ is C^3 and whose projection onto $\mathbb{R}^{\{1,3\}}$ is C^2 is a (strictly monotonic) curvilinear segment that lies in the plane of equation $x_2 = x_3$. Its endpoints are (1, 1, 1) and $(f(4), g(4), g(4))$. Its projection onto $\mathbb{R}^{\{2,3\}}$ is a segment that lies in the 45° line of that space, namely seg$[n^1, n^2]$, where $n^1 \equiv (1, 1)$ and $n^2 \equiv (g(4), g(4))$.

Step 4: Deriving the contradiction. We have just determined that the projection of Π onto $\mathbb{R}^{\{2,3\}}$ extends linearly beyond the line of equation $x_2+x_3 = c_2$. However, we had seen that this is not how Π_1 extends beyond that line.[1] □

17.10 ON THE CONSISTENT MEMBERS OF THE CIC FAMILY

In Subsection 11.2.3, we stated a theorem identifying the *consistent* members of the CIC family (Theorem 11.6), which we call CIC* rules. These rules belong to Young's family. Thus, they have Young representations, which we

[1] The four parts of Π are as follows. First is the segment in $\mathbb{R}^N$ whose projection onto $\mathbb{R}^{\{1,2\}}$ is seg$[(0,0), k^1]$ and whose projection onto $\mathbb{R}^{\{1,3\}}$ is seg$[(0,0), \ell^1]$. It is seg$[(0,0,0), (1,1,1)]$. Its projection onto $\mathbb{R}^{\{2,3\}}$ is seg$[(0,0), n^1]$. Second is the part described in the body of the proof. Third is the curvilinear segment whose projection onto $\mathbb{R}^{\{1,2\}}$ is seg$[k^2, (f(6), 2f(6))]$ and whose projection onto $\mathbb{R}^{\{1,3\}}$ is the part of Π_2 that lies between ℓ^2 and $\ell^3 \equiv (f(6), g(6))$. Its projection onto $\mathbb{R}^{\{2,3\}}$ is a curvilinear segment with endpoints n^2 and $(2f(6), g(6))$ (this segment is not represented). Fourth is the segment whose projection onto $\mathbb{R}^{\{1,2\}}$ is seg$[(f(6), g(6)), c_{\{1,2\}}]$ and whose projection onto $\mathbb{R}^{\{1,3\}}$ is seg$[(f(6), 2f(6)), c_{\{1,3\}}]$. Its projection onto $\mathbb{R}^{\{2,3\}}$ is seg$[(2f(6), g(6)), c_{\{2,3\}}]$, (a subset of seg$[q^2, c_{\{2,3\}}]$.

now describe. Given $\gamma \in \Gamma$, Figure 17.13a shows a representation of CIC^γ. Let $\underline{\lambda} = -\infty$ and $\bar{\lambda} = \infty$. Let $B^\gamma \equiv \{(c_0 - \gamma(c_0), c_0) \colon c_0 \in \mathbb{R}_+\}$. For each $c_0 \in \mathbb{R}_+$, let $f^\gamma(c_0, \cdot) \colon \mathbb{R} \mapsto \mathbb{R}_+$ be the function whose graph consists of the horizontal half-line $\{(t, 0) \colon t \in]-\infty, -\gamma(c_0)]\}$, the segment of slope 1 whose endpoints are $(-\gamma(c_0), 0)$ and $(c_0 - \gamma(c_0), c_0)$ (this second point is a point of B^γ), and the horizontal half-line $\{(t, c_0) \colon t \in [c_0 - \gamma(c_0), \infty[\}$. It is easy to see that the function $f^\gamma \colon \mathbb{R}_+ \times [\underline{\lambda}, \bar{\lambda}]$ satisfies the required properties to be a representation of a member of Young's family.

To see that indeed f^γ is a Young representation of CIC^γ, it is enough to consider the two-claimant case, as the logic is the same for the general case. Let $N \equiv \{1, 2\}$, $c_0, c_0' \in \mathbb{R}_+$ be such that $c_0 < c_0'$, and suppose that agent 1's claim is c_0 and agent 2's claim c_0'. The functions $f^\gamma(c_0, \cdot)$ and $f^\gamma(c_0', \cdot)$ are plotted in Figure 17.13a. As the endowment increases from 0 to $c_0 + c_0'$, the equilibrium λ (the value of the parameter for which *balance* is achieved) increases from $-\infty$ to $-\gamma(c_0')$, the graphs of both $f^\gamma(c_0, \cdot)$ and $f^\gamma(c_0', \cdot)$ follow the horizontal axis, and neither claimant gets anything. (We have what we called in Subsection 11.2.3 when discussing the ICI* rules a "dead interval.") As λ increases from $-\gamma(c_0')$ to $-\gamma(c_0)$, the graph of $f^\gamma(c_0, \cdot)$ remains horizontal but the graph of $f^\gamma(c_0', \cdot)$ starts rising. Thus, claimant 2 receives each increment of the endowment. As λ increases from $-\gamma(c_0)$ to $c_0 - \gamma(c_0)$, the graphs of both $f^\gamma(c_0, \cdot)$ and $f^\gamma(c_0', \cdot)$ are upwards sloping parallel lines, so equal division of each increment prevails. At $\lambda = c_0 - \gamma(c_0)$, claimant 1 is fully compensated. As λ increases from that point, the graph of $f^\gamma(c_0, \cdot)$ is horizontal, but that of $f^\gamma(c_0', \cdot)$ is still rising, so claimant 2 receives the totality of each increment. At $\lambda = c_0' - \gamma(c_0')$, claimant 2 is also fully compensated and claimant 2's graph also becomes horizontal. As λ increases beyond $c_0' - \gamma(c_0')$, we have another dead interval in which both awards remain stationary and

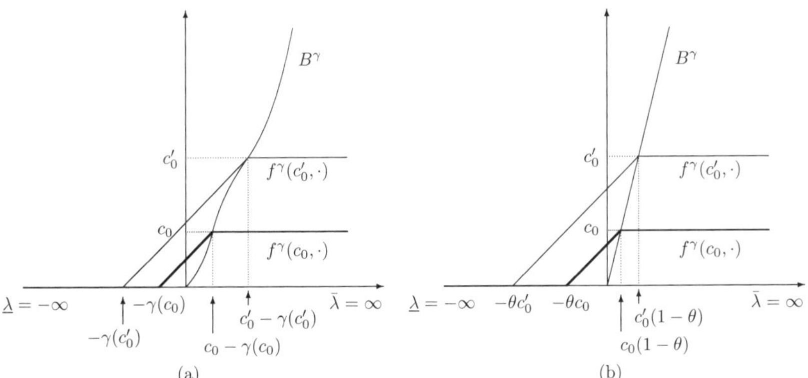

Figure 17.13: **Young representations of two CIC* rules.** (a) The curve B^γ is the locus of the point $(c_0 - \gamma(c_0), c_0)$ as c_0 varies in $\mathbb{R}_+$. Due to the properties of γ, it is a monotone path emanating from the origin. (b) If γ is a linear function, B^γ is a ray of slope greater than 1. The resulting rule is *homogeneous*.

equal to claims (as they should). Altogether, we have obtained the path of R^γ for (c_0, c'_0).

If $\gamma = 0$, B^γ is the 45° line; then $CIC^\gamma = CEA$. If $\gamma = e$, B^γ is the vertical axis, then $CIC^\gamma = CEL$. If $\gamma = \frac{e}{2}$, B^γ is the ray of slope 2; then $CIC^\gamma = T^r$. For each $\theta \in [0, 1[$, if $\gamma = \theta e$, B^γ is the ray of slope $\frac{1}{1-\theta}$ (for $\theta = 1$, B^γ is the vertical axis), and $CIC^\gamma = U^\theta$ (the reverse TAL rule of parameter θ).

Figure 17.13b shows a *homogeneous* CIC* rule: then there is $\theta \in [0, 1]$ such that for each $c_0 \in \mathbb{R}_+$, $\gamma(c_0) = \theta c_0$. Such a rule is a reverse TAL rule.

The CIC* family is not a convex family but it is closed under duality.

17.11 CHARACTERIZING A FAMILY OF SEQUENTIAL TALMUD RULES

In Subsection 11.3.1 we described two approaches to extend two-claimant asymmetric versions of the Talmud rule to general populations. In this appendix, we add details to the second approach.

Let $\preccurlyeq$ be a complete and transitive binary relation on the set of potential claimants $\mathbb{N}$. Let $w \in \mathbb{R}^{\mathbb{N}}_{++}$ be a list of positive weights. Let $\boldsymbol{\mathcal{P}^2}$ be the class of all such pairs $(\preccurlyeq, w)$.

Family $\mathcal{T}^2$ of sequential Talmud rules: For each $(\preccurlyeq, w) \in \mathcal{P}^2$, the member of the family associated with $(\preccurlyeq, \boldsymbol{w})$, $\overline{\boldsymbol{ST}}^{\preccurlyeq, \boldsymbol{w}}$, is defined as follows. Let $N \in \mathcal{N}$ and $(c, E) \in \mathcal{C}^N$. Let $(N^1, N^2, \ldots, N^K)$ be the ordered partition of N induced by $\preccurlyeq$. Let $E^1 \equiv \min\{E, \frac{1}{2}\sum_{i\in N^1} c_i\}$, $E^2 \equiv \min\{E - E^1, \frac{1}{2}\sum_{i\in N^2} c_i\}$, $E^3 \equiv \min\{E - E^2 - E^3, \frac{1}{2}\sum_{i\in N^3} c_i\}$, and so on.

For each $E \in \left]\frac{1}{2}\sum_N c_i, \sum_N c_i\right[$ and each $k \in \{1, 2, \ldots, K\}$, let F^k be defined as E^k was but replacing E by $E - \frac{1}{2}\sum_{N^k} c_i$, and each E^ℓ by F^ℓ.

Now, for each $N \in \mathcal{N}$ and each $i \in N$, let $\alpha_i \equiv \frac{w_i}{\sum_N w_j}$ and $\alpha \equiv (\alpha_i)_{i\in N}$. Then we define $\overline{ST}^{\preccurlyeq, w}(c, E)$ to be the awards vector x obtained by setting, for each $E \leq \frac{1}{2}\sum_N c_i$ and each $k \in \{1, 2, \ldots, K\}$,

$$x_{N^k} \equiv CEA^\alpha\left(\frac{1}{2}c_{N^k}, E^k\right),$$

and by setting, for each $E \in \left]\frac{1}{2}\sum_N c_i, \sum_N c_i\right]$ and each $k \in \{1, 2, \ldots, K\}$,

$$x_{N^k} \equiv \frac{1}{2}c_{N^k} + CEL^\alpha\left(\frac{1}{2}c_{N^k}, F^k\right).$$

Family $\mathcal{T}^2$ is closed under duality. We omit the proof of the following theorem, as much of it overlaps with that of Theorem 11.7.

Theorem 17.1 *Let S be a rule such that*

sequential Talmud rules characterized

(∗∗) *for each pair* $\{i, j\} \in \mathcal{N}$, *there is a vector of weights* $(\alpha_{ij}, \alpha_{ji}) \in \Delta^{\{i,j\}}$ *such that* $S|_{\mathcal{C}^{\{i,j\}}} = \overline{ST}^{(\alpha_{ij},\alpha_{ji})}$

and satisfies consistency. Then there is $(\preccurlyeq, w) \in \mathcal{P}^2$ *such that, for each pair* $\{i, j\} \in \mathcal{N}$, *the following relations hold:*

(i) $(\alpha_{ij}, \alpha_{ji}) = (1, 0)$ *if and only if* $i \prec j$;
(ii) $(\alpha_{ij}, \alpha_{ji}) \in int\{\Delta^{\{i,j\}}\}$ *if and only if* $i \sim j$ *and* $(\alpha_{ij}, \alpha_{ji})$ *is proportional to* (w_i, w_j).

In fact, S coincides with $\overline{ST}^{\preccurlyeq,w}$.

Conversely, for each $(\preccurlyeq, w) \in P^2$, $\overline{ST}^{\preccurlyeq,w}$ *satisfies condition* (∗∗) *and consistency. Here, for each pair* $\{i, j\} \in \mathcal{N}$, *the weights* $(\alpha_{ij}, \alpha_{ji})$ *are constructed from* $(\preccurlyeq, w)$ *by invoking conditions* (i) *and* (ii).

The requirement on the weight vectors chosen for the two-claimant populations is necessary for *consistency*. Another way to express it is as follows: if agent i belongs to a higher half-priority class than agent j, then $(\alpha_{ij}, \alpha_{ji}) = (1, 0)$, and if agents i, j, and k belong to the same half-priority class, then the weights $(\alpha_{ij}, \alpha_{ji})$ and $(\alpha_{jk}, \alpha_{kj})$ determine the weights $(\alpha_{ik}, \alpha_{ki})$. For example, if "agent 2 is twice as important as agent 1" and "agent 3 three times as important as agent 2," then "agent 3 is six times as important as agent 1."

Note that in our definition, the bias in favor of one claimant or the other is independent of the endowment. However, we could choose who is favored as a function of how much is available. This two-regime idea is part of the Talmud rule, which for each claims vector trades off particularly favorable treatment of the smaller claimants over half the range of the endowment for a particularly favorable treatment of the larger claimants over the complementary range. However, it does so in a way that respects *equal treatment of equals*. If this property is dropped, we have the option of choosing weights that depend on the regime. Still, for each regime, the weights should satisfy consistency conditions. These constraints are expressed in the theorem.

A special case is when a reversal of the weights occurs between the two regimes. Let $N \equiv \{i, j\}$. The suggestion here is to apply, for each claims vector, the weighted constrained equal awards rule with weights (α_i, α_j) for an endowment no greater than the half-sum of the claims (of course, still using the half-claims in the formula instead of the claims themselves), and the weighted constrained equal losses rule with weights (α_j, α_i) for an endowment greater than the half-sum of the claims (once again, using the half-claims).

If some weights are 0, *consistency* and this reversal have an interesting implication. Let $N \equiv \{1, 2, 3\}$ and $c \in \mathbb{R}^N_+$. Suppose that when the endowment is less than the half-sum of the claims, the associated weights are

$(\alpha_{12}, \alpha_{21}) = (1, 0)$, $(\alpha_{13}, \alpha_{31}) = (1, 0)$, and $(\alpha_{23}, \alpha_{23}) = (1, 0)$. Suppose also that the weights are reversed when the endowment is greater than the half-sum of the claims. Then a *consistent* rule that coincides with this two-claimant hybrid rule exhibiting reversal of the weights behaves as follows. As the endowment increases from 0, at first agent 1 gets everything, and continues to do so until reaching their half-claim; agent 2 receives the next increments until reaching their half-claim; then agent 3 receives the next increments until reaching their half-claim. At that point (all three claimants have now reached their half-claims), *consistency* forces us to reverse the half-priority relation: agent 3 receives the next increments until fully compensated; agent 2 comes next and is also fully compensated; and it is only then that agent 1 starts receiving more, and that continues until agent 1 is fully compensated.

17.12 COMPLETION OF THE PROOF OF THE CHARACTERIZATION OF FAMILY $\mathcal{M}$

The next two lemmas are steps in the proof of Theorem 11.8, a characterization of family $\mathcal{M}$ on the basis of *homogeneity*, *composition down*, *composition up*, and *consistency*.

Proof of Lemma 11.7: Without loss of generality, suppose $\bar{N} \equiv \{1, 2\}$.

Step 1: *K* is not an interior cone. We suppose otherwise, calling its boundary rays ρ and ρ', ρ being the steeper one in Figures 17.14–17.16.

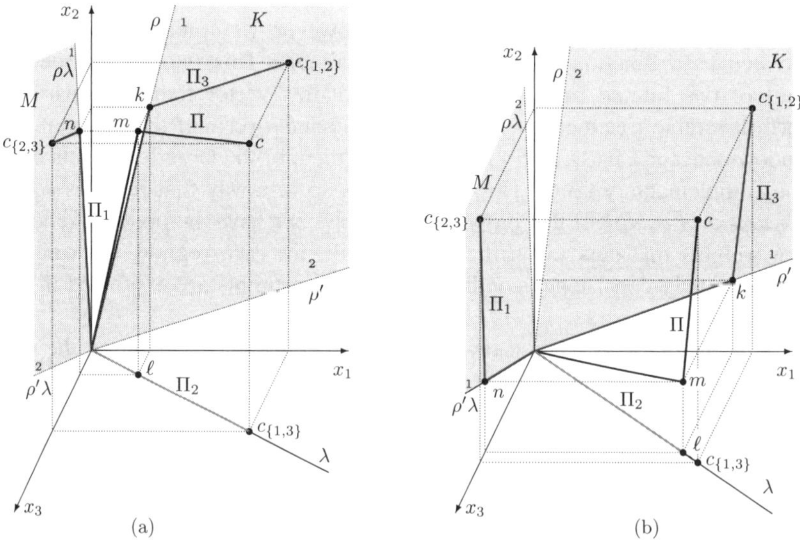

Figure 17.14: **Lemma 11.7, Substep 1-1.** The existence of an interior nondegenerate cone in the $\{1, 2\}$-partition, K, and a ray in the $\{1, 3\}$-partition, λ, reveal the existence of an interior nondegenerate cone in the $\{2, 3\}$-partition.

Substep 1-1: the {2, 3}-partition contains an interior nondegenerate cone. To prove this assertion, we use the fact that since $1 \sim 3$, the {1, 3}-partition contains at least one interior ray λ. Let $c \in \mathbb{R}^{\tilde{N}}$ be such that $c_{\{1,2\}} \in \text{int}\{K\}$ and $c_{\{1,3\}} \in \lambda$ (Figure 17.14a). Using the language introduced in connection to Theorem 11.8, we denote by M the cone in the partition of $\mathbb{R}^{\{2,3\}}$ revealed by the path for $c_{\{2,3\}}$. Its boundary rays are $d(\rho, \lambda)$ and $d(\rho', \lambda)$, this notation being simplified to $\rho\lambda$ and $\rho'\lambda$ in the figure (we use this compact notation in the remaining figures too). Both are interior rays. Also, $d(\rho, \lambda)$ is first in M if and only if ρ is first in K. In Figure 17.14a, ρ is first, and in Figure 17.14b, it is second.

Substep 1-2: in fact, the {1, 2}- and {2, 3}-partitions cannot both contain interior cones. For convenience, we illustrate the proof using the {1, 2}- and {1, 3}-partitions instead, calling L the cone in the {1, 3}-partition. (The reason why it is convenient to replace {2, 3} by {1, 3} is that in all of our other diagrams, we start from paths in $\mathbb{R}^{\{1,2\}}$ and $\mathbb{R}^{\{1,3\}}$. Thus, a little less mental gymnastics will be required of the reader.) Since the orientation of the two cones are related (last line of the previous paragraph), there are only two cases to consider. In Figure 17.15a, the first rays of K and L are both further from the axis shared by the spaces in which these cones lie – this axis is $\mathbb{R}^{\{1\}}$ – than their

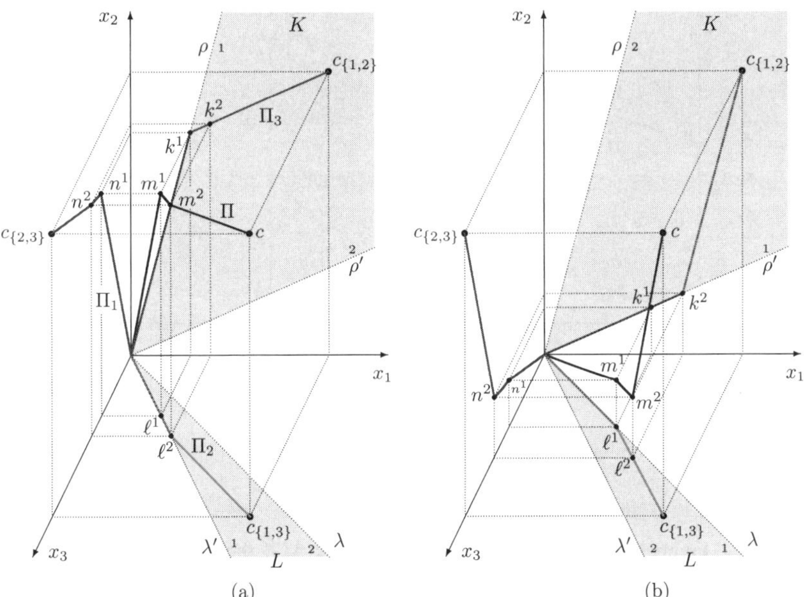

Figure 17.15: **Lemma 11.7, Substep 1-2:** the {1, 2}- and {1, 3}-partitions cannot both have nondegenerate interior cones K and L. (a) The boundary rays that are first for the two cones (ρ and λ') are the furthest from the axis shared by the spaces in which these cones lie, namely $\mathbb{R}^{\{1\}}$. (b) Here, the boundary rays that are first (ρ' and λ) are the closest to $\mathbb{R}^{\{1\}}$ for both cones.

second rays. In Figure 17.15b, they are both closer. In each case, we choose $c \in \mathbb{R}^{\tilde{N}}$ such that $c_{\{1,2\}} \in \text{int}\{K\}$, $c_{\{1,3\}} \in \text{int}\{L\}$, and the first coordinates of the kinks in the paths for $c_{\{1,2\}}$ and $c_{\{1,3\}}$ differ. (It is precisely because K and L are nondegenerate that this last restriction can be met.) In each case, we obtain a two-kink contradiction.[2]

This completes the proof of Step 1 of Lemma 11.7. It follows from this step that one boundary ray of K is an axis.

Step 2: Completing the proof of Lemma 11.7. We suppose, by way of contradiction, that the $\{1, 3\}$-partition contains at least two interior rays – let us call them λ and λ'. Let $c \in \mathbb{R}^{\tilde{N}}$ be such that $c_{\{1,2\}} \in \text{int}\{K\}$ and $c_{\{1,3\}} \in \lambda$ (Figure 17.16 only shows the construction for λ). The path for $c_{\{2,3\}}$ that we obtain reveals the existence in the $\{2, 3\}$-partition of a non-degenerate cone M having an axis as one boundary ray and $d(\rho, \lambda)$ as other boundary ray. Substituting λ' for λ, the existence in the $\{2, 3\}$-partition of a nondegenerate cone M' having that same axis as boundary ray and $d(\rho, \lambda')$ as other boundary ray is similarly revealed. Since $d(\rho, \lambda) \neq d(\rho, \lambda')$, M and M' overlap. There are four cases.

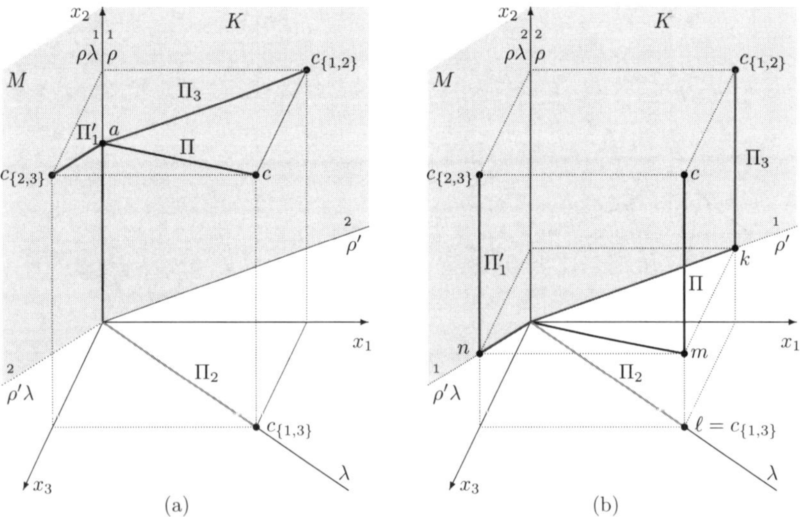

Figure 17.16: **Lemma 11.7, Step 2, Case 1:** if the partition of at least one two-dimensional awards space contains at least one nondegenerate cone, each other such space is partitioned into exactly two cones. Panel (a) pertains to (i) and panel (b) to (ii).

[2] In fact, one can show that more generally, the partitions of two adjacent two-dimensional spaces cannot both contain nondegenerate interior cones, independently of the orientations of these cones.

Case 1: the axis that is a boundary ray of K is $\mathbb{R}_+^{\{2\}}$.

(i) $\mathbb{R}_+^{\{2\}}$ is first in K (Figure 17.16a).

(ii) $\mathbb{R}_+^{\{2\}}$ is second in K (Figure 17.16b).

Case 2: the axis that is a boundary ray of K is $\mathbb{R}_+^{\{1\}}$.

(i) $\mathbb{R}_+^{\{1\}}$ is second in K (case not represented).

(ii) $\mathbb{R}_+^{\{1\}}$ is first in K (case not represented).

Thus, the $\{1, 3\}$-partition consists of exactly two nondegenerate cones and their boundary rays.

We now exchange the roles played by $\{1, 2\}$ and $\{1, 3\}$ in the above proof. Since the $\{1, 3\}$-partition contains at least one nondegenerate cone (an implication of the conclusion just reached), the $\{1, 2\}$-partition consists of exactly two nondegenerate cones and their boundary rays.

We can of course obtain the same conclusion for the $\{2, 3\}$-partition. □

Proof of Lemma 11.8:
Case 1: there is a two-claimant group $\bar{N} \subset \tilde{N}$ and a nondegenerate cone K in the $\bar{N}$-partition whose interior boundary ray is first.

Step 1: For each other two-claimant group $N' \subset \tilde{N}$, the central direction of the N'-partition is first. Without loss of generality, set $\bar{N} \equiv \{1, 2\}$. Also, suppose that $\mathbb{R}_+^{\{2\}}$ is a boundary ray of K.

First, we show that for both of the nondegenerate cones in the $\{1, 3\}$-partition, the central direction is first. Let L be one of these two cones, and suppose by contradiction, that its interior boundary ray is second. Let $c \in \mathbb{R}_+^N$ be such that $c_{\{1,2\}} \in \text{int}\{K\}$ and $c_{\{1,3\}} \in \text{int}\{L\}$.

(i) $\mathbb{R}_+^{\{2\}}$ is a boundary ray of L. Then Π has two kinks and so does Π'_1, resulting in a two-kink contradiction (Figure 17.17a).

(ii) $\mathbb{R}_+^{\{1\}}$ is a boundary ray of L. Here too, we obtain a two-kink contradiction (Figure 17.17b).

The lesson to be drawn from the argument just made is the following. Let K be a nondegenerate cone in the partition of the award space of some two-claimant group. Suppose that its interior boundary ray is first, and that some other two-claimant group does not contain the agent in the first group whose axis is a boundary ray of K. Then the interior rays of both nondegenerate cones in the partition for the second group are also first. Thus, since the central direction of the nondegenerate cone in the $\{1, 3\}$-partition that has $\mathbb{R}_+^{\{3\}}$ as boundary ray is first, the interior rays of both nondegenerate cones in the $\{1, 2\}$-partition are first (K is one of these cones, and the statement we reach for it is in fact our hypothesis). Also, since the central direction of the nondegenerate cone in the $\{1, 3\}$-partition that has $\mathbb{R}_+^{\{1\}}$ as boundary ray is

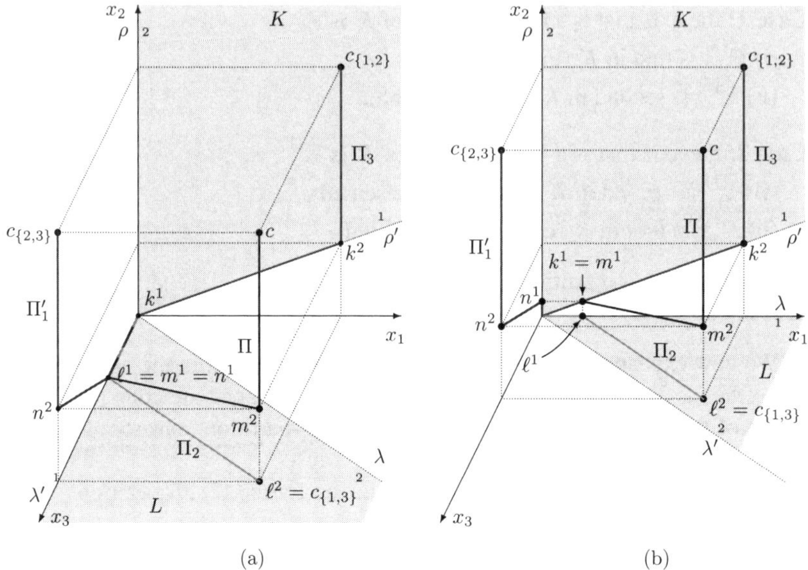

Figure 17.17: **Lemma 11.8**: the central directions all come first or they all come second. In both panels, $\mathbb{R}^{\{2\}}$ is a boundary ray of K. (a) Here, $\mathbb{R}^{\{1\}}$ is not a boundary ray of L. (b) Here, it is. In either case, the resulting three-dimensional path Π has two kinks, and its projection onto $\mathbb{R}^{\{2,3\}}$, Π'_1, also does.

first, then the interior rays of both nondegenerate cones in the $\{2, 3\}$-partition are first.

Step 2: The central directions are consistent. This follows from the fact that the central direction of the space associated with each two-claimant group $N \subset \tilde{N}$ is a cone in the N-partition. From the existence of interior rays ρ and λ in the $\{1, 2\}$- and $\{1, 3\}$-partitions, we deduce the existence of an interior ray in the $\{2, 3\}$-partition whose direction is $d(\rho, \lambda)$.

Case 2: the central direction of K is second. Then it follows from Case 1 that the central direction of each other cone in each partition is second. The proof of the consistency of the central directions also applies (Step 2). Altogether, we obtain that for each two-claimant group $N \subset \tilde{N}$, S coincides on $\mathcal{C}^N$ with a weighted constrained equal losses rule, and that the weights assigned to these two-claimant groups are consistent. □

17.13 POPULATION MONOTONICITY IS NOT PRESERVED UNDER DUALITY

Proof of Proposition 12.1: (according to which *population monotonicity* is not preserved under duality.) The proof is by means of an example of a rule S, defined on $\bigcup_{N' \subseteq N} \mathcal{C}^{N'}$, where $N \equiv \{1, 2, 3\}$.

Step 1: Construction of Rule 17.5, S.

Rule 17.5 (Figure 17.18). On the subdomain of two-claimant problems, S coincides with P. Now, let Q be the unit cube in $\mathbb{R}^N_+$, ∂Q the boundary of Q, and for each $t \in \{1, 2, 3\}$, F_t the face of Q consisting of all claims vectors $c \in \mathbb{R}^N_+$ such that $c_t = 1$. Given $c \equiv (c_1, 1, c_3) \neq (1, 1, 1)$, a typical claims vector in F_2, let L be the line passing through c and $e \equiv (1, 1, 1)$, x and y be the points of intersection of L with seg$[(\frac{2}{3}, 1, 1), (1, 1, \frac{2}{3})]$ and seg$[(0, 1, 1), (1, 1, 0)]$ respectively (we use parallel notation, L', x', y', for the corresponding objects associated with the claims vector c'). If $0 < c_1 + c_3 \leq 1$, the path of awards of S for c is that of the proportional rule (Figure 17.18a). If $1 < c_1 + c_3 \leq 1 + \frac{2}{3}$, the path of S for c is bro.seg$[(0, 0, 0), y, c]$ (consider c' in Figure 17.18a). If $1 + \frac{2}{3} < c_1 + c_3 \leq 2$, the path of S for c is piecewise linear in two pieces defined as follows: let $0 \leq \lambda \leq 1$ be such that $c \equiv \lambda x + (1 - \lambda)e$. Then the path is bro.seg$[(0, 0, 0), d, c]$, where $d \equiv \lambda y + (1 - \lambda)\frac{2}{3}e$. Finally, if $c = e$, the path is that of the proportional rule. We deduce the path of S for each $c \in F_1$ by symmetry with respect to the plane of equation $x_1 = x_2$ of the path of the symmetric image of c with respect to that plane; similarly, we deduce the path of S for each $c \in F_3$ by symmetry with respect to the plane of equation $x_2 = x_3$ of the path of the symmetric image of c with respect to that plane. If c is not in any of the faces F_1, F_2, and F_3, let μ be such that μc does belong to such a face. Such a μ exists uniquely. Then we obtain the path for c from the path for μc by the homothetic transformation of ratio $\frac{1}{\mu}$. This construction guarantees that S is *anonymous* and *homogeneous*.

Step 2: S is population monotonic. Let $E > 0$ and $c \equiv (c_1, 1, c_3)$ be an arbitrary point on F_2. We distinguish three cases.

Case 1: $0 < c_1 + c_3 \leq 1$. Then $S(c, E) \equiv P(c, E)$. Since $S(c_{N'}, E) \equiv P(c_{N'}, E)$ for each N' with $|N'| = 2$ and P is *population monotonic*, the *population-monotonicity* inequalities hold.

Case 2: $1 < c_1 + c_3 \leq 1 + \frac{2}{3}$. We imagine the departure of each agent in turn (Figure 17.18c).

Subcase 2.1: Claimant 1 leaves. We have to compare $z \equiv S(c, E)$ and $z' \equiv S(c_{\{2,3\}}, E)$. We assume that $E \leq 1 + c_3$ since otherwise there is nothing to check. Since y is the point of intersection of L with seg$[(0, 1, 1), (1, 1, 0)]$, then $y_1 + 1 + y_3 = 2$. Note that y belongs to the simplex in the plane of equation $\sum x_i = 2$. Thus, $z = \left(\frac{y_1 E}{2}, \frac{E}{2}, \frac{y_3 E}{2}\right)$. Also, $z' = \left(\frac{E}{1+c_3}, \frac{c_3 E}{1+c_3}\right)$. Then $z'_3 - z_3 = \frac{c_3 E}{1+c_3} - \frac{y_3 E}{2}$. Since $c_3 \geq y_3$ and $1 + c_3 \leq 2$, then $z'_3 - z_3 \geq 0$.

Also, $z'_2 - z_2 = \frac{E}{1+c_3} - \frac{E}{2}$. Since $1 + c_3 \leq 2$, then $z'_2 - z_2 \geq 0$.

Subcase 2.2: Claimant 2 leaves. We have to compare $z \equiv S(c, E)$ and $z' \equiv S(c_{\{1,3\}}, E)$. We assume that $E \leq c_1 + c_3$ since otherwise, there is nothing to check. Since y is the point of intersection of L with seg$[(0, 1, 1), (1, 1, 0)]$, as already calculated, $y_1 + 1 + y_3 = 2$. Thus, $z = \left(\frac{y_1 E}{2}, \frac{E}{2}, \frac{y_3 E}{2}\right)$. Also, $z' =$

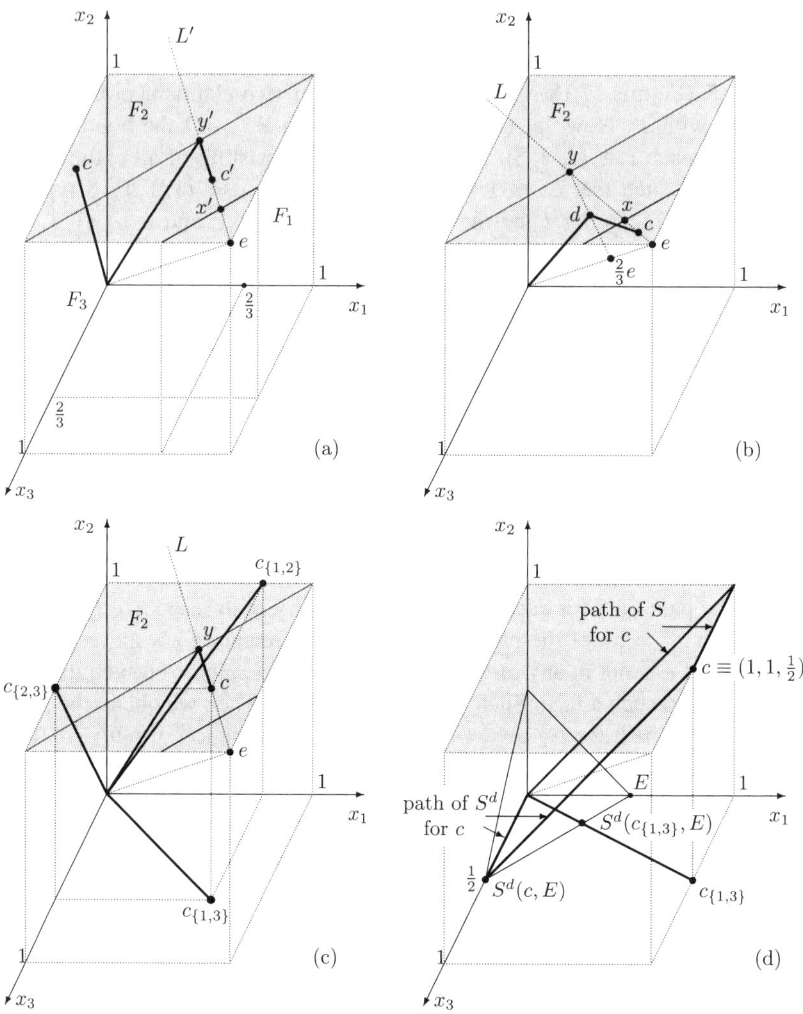

Figure 17.18: **Population monotonicity is not preserved under duality** (Proposition 12.1). The first two panels show the construction of Rule 17.5, denoted S (Step 1). (a) Paths of awards of S for $c \in \mathbb{R}^N_+$, where $N \equiv \{1, 2, 3\}$, such that $c_2 = 1$ and $c_1 + c_3 \leq 1$, and for $c' \in \mathbb{R}^N_+$ such that $c'_2 = 1$ and $1 < c'_1 + c'_3 \leq 1 + \frac{2}{3}$. (b) Path of S for $c \in \mathbb{R}^N_+$ such that $c_2 = 1$ and $1 + \frac{2}{3} < c_1 + c_3$. (c) The rule S is *population monotonic* (Step 2). Given a typical claims vector $c \in F_2$, the top face of the cube, we determine the path of S for c (it is a broken line segment), and its path for each of the projections of c onto the three two-dimensional coordinate subspaces (these paths are segments connecting the origin to these projections). Then, given $E \in \mathbb{R}_+$ such that $\sum_N c_i > E$, we calculate the awards vectors chosen by S for (c, E) and for each two-claimant subproblem of (c, E). (d) The rule S^d is not *population monotonic* (Step 3). Indeed, $S^d((1, 1, \frac{1}{2}), \frac{1}{2}) = (0, 0, \frac{1}{2})$ but for the two-claimant problem that results from the departure of claimant 2, we have $S^d((1, \frac{1}{2}), 1) = (\frac{1}{3}, \frac{1}{6})$: claimant 3 receives less.

$\left(\frac{c_1 E}{c_1+c_3}, \frac{c_3 E}{c_1+c_3}\right)$. Then $z'_1 - z_1 = \frac{c_1 E}{c_1+c_3} - \frac{y_1 E}{2}$. Since $c_1 \geq y_1$ and $c_1 + c_3 \leq 2$, then $z'_1 - z_1 \geq 0$.

Also, $z'_3 - z_3 = \frac{c_3 E}{c_1+c_3} - \frac{y_3 E}{2}$. Since $c_3 \geq y_3$ and $c_1+c_3 \leq 2$, then $z'_3 - z_3 \geq 0$.

Subcase 2.3: Claimant 3 leaves. We apply the same argument as in subcase 2.1.

Case 3: $1 + \frac{2}{3} < c_1 + c_3 \leq 2$. Let $\lambda \in [0, 1]$ be such that $c = \lambda x + (1 - \lambda)e$ and $d \equiv \lambda y + (1 - \lambda)\frac{2}{3}e$. Since $x \geq y$ and $e > \frac{2}{3}e$, then $c \geq d$.

Subcase 3.1: Claimant 1 leaves. We have to compare $z \equiv S(c, E)$ and $z' \equiv S\left(c_{\{2,3\}}, E\right)$. We assume that $E \leq 1 + c_3$ since otherwise there is nothing to check. Note that $d_1 + d_2 + d_3 = 2$ and $E \leq 1 + c_3 \leq d_1 + d_2 + d_3$, so $z = \left(\frac{d_1 E}{2}, \frac{d_2 E}{2}, \frac{d_3 E}{2}\right)$ and $z' = \left(\frac{E}{1+c_3}, \frac{c_3 E}{1+c_3}\right)$. Then $z'_3 - z_3 = \frac{c_3 E}{1+c_3} - \frac{d_3 E}{2}$. Since $c_3 \geq d_3$ and $1 + c_3 \leq 2$, $z'_3 - z_3 \geq 0$.

Also, $z'_2 - z_2 = \frac{E}{1+c_3} - \frac{d_2 E}{2}$. Since $1 \geq d_2$ and $1 + c_3 \leq 2$, then $z'_2 - z_2 \geq 0$.

Subcase 3.2: Claimant 2 leaves. We have to compare $z \equiv S(c, E)$ and $z' \equiv S\left(c_{\{1,3\}}, E\right)$. We assume that $E \leq c_1 + c_3$ since otherwise there is nothing to check. Note that $d_1 + d_2 + d_3 = 2$ and $E \leq c_1 + c_3 \leq d_1 + d_2 + d_3$, so $z = \left(\frac{d_1 E}{2}, \frac{d_2 E}{2}, \frac{d_3 E}{2}\right)$ and $z' = \left(\frac{c_1 E}{c_1+c_3}, \frac{c_3 E}{c_1+c_3}\right)$. Then $z'_1 - z_1 = \frac{c_1 E}{c_1+c_3} - \frac{d_1 E}{2}$. Since $c_1 \geq d_1$ and $c_1 + c_3 \leq 2$, then $z'_1 - z_1 \geq 0$.

Also, $z'_3 - z_3 = \frac{c_3 E}{c_1+c_3} - \frac{d_3 E}{2}$. Since $c_3 \geq d_3$ and $c_1+c_3 \leq 2$, then $z'_3 - z_3 \geq 0$.

Subcase 3.3: Claimant 3 leaves. We apply the same argument as in Subcase 3.1.

Step 3: S^d is not population monotonic (Figure 17.18d). Let $(c, E) \equiv ((1, 1, \frac{1}{2}), \frac{1}{2})$. The path of awards of S for c is bro.seg$[(0, 0, 0), (1, 1, 0), (1, 1, \frac{1}{2})]$. The path of S^d for c is obtained from the path of S for c by symmetry with respect to $\frac{c}{2}$. It is bro.seg$[(0, 0, 0), (0, 0, \frac{1}{2}), (1, 1, \frac{1}{2})]$. Then $S^d((1, 1, \frac{1}{2}), \frac{1}{2}) = (0, 0, \frac{1}{2})$.

Suppose claimant 2 leaves. Then $c_{\{1,3\}} \equiv \left(1, \frac{1}{2}\right)$. By definition of S, $S((1, \frac{1}{2}), \frac{1}{2}) = P((1, \frac{1}{2}), \frac{1}{2}) = (\frac{1}{3}, \frac{1}{6})$. Since the proportional rule is *self-dual*, $S^d\left((1, \frac{1}{2}), \frac{1}{2}\right) = \left(\frac{1}{3}, \frac{1}{6}\right)$. Since claimant 3 receives less in the two-claimant problem $((1, \frac{1}{2}), \frac{1}{2})$ than in the initial three-claimant problem, S^d violates *population monotonicity*. □

17.14 CHARACTERIZATION OF THE CONSTRAINED EQUAL AWARDS RULE AS OFFERING MAXIMAL GROUP GUARANTEES

Proof of Theorem 12.1: (according to which the constrained equal awards rule is the only rule to be *claims continuous*, *consistent*, and to *offer maximal average guarantees*.)

We already know that the constrained equal awards rule satisfies the first two properties and we omit the proof that it *offers maximal average guarantees*. To prove the converse, let S be a rule satisfying the properties listed in the theorem.

Step 1: S satisfies equal treatment of equals. Let $k, n \in \mathbb{N}$ with $2 \leq k < n$, $N \in \mathcal{N}$ with $|N| = n$, and $\delta \in \mathbb{R}_+$. Also let $i \in N$, $E \equiv k\delta$, $c^\delta \equiv (\delta)_{j\in N}$, and $x \equiv S(c^\delta, E)$. For each $S \subset N$ with $i \in S$ and $|S| = k$, $S(c^\delta_S, E) = (\delta)_{j\in S}$, so

$$\frac{k}{n} = ag^S(k, n-k) \leq \frac{1}{k}\sum_{j\in S}\frac{x_j}{\delta} = \frac{1}{E}\sum_{j\in S}x_j.$$

That is, $\sum_{j\in S} x_j \geq \frac{kE}{n}$. Now agent i is a member of C^{n-1}_{k-1} such subgroups and each other agent is a member of C^{n-2}_{k-1} such subgroups. Summing awards over these subsets,

$$\begin{aligned} C^{n-1}_{k-1}\frac{kE}{n} &= C^{n-1}_{k-1}\, x_i + C^{n-2}_{k-2}\sum\nolimits_{j\in N\setminus\{i\}} x_j \\ &= \left[C^{n-1}_{k-1} - C^{n-2}_{k-2}\right] x_i + C^{n-2}_{k-2}\sum\nolimits_{j\in N} x_j \\ &= \frac{n-k}{k-1}\, C^{n-2}_{k-2}\, x_i + C^{n-2}_{k-2}\, E. \end{aligned}$$

Rearranging,

$$\frac{n-k}{k-1}\, C^{n-2}_{k-2}\, x_i = \left[\frac{k}{n}\, C^{n-1}_{k-1} - C^{n-2}_{k-2}\right] E = \frac{n-k}{n(k-1)}\, C^{n-2}_{k-2}\, E.$$

Thus, $x_i = \frac{E}{n} = \frac{k\delta}{n}$. Let $c^\delta \equiv (\delta, \ldots, \delta)$. Since this is true for each $i \in N$, $S(c^\delta, E) = \left(\frac{k\delta}{n}, \ldots, \frac{k\delta}{n}\right) = CEA(c^\delta, E)$.

By *consistency*, for each pair $\{i, j\} \subset N$, $S\big((c^\delta_i, c^\delta_j), \frac{2k\delta}{n}\big) = \left(\frac{k\delta}{n}, \frac{k\delta}{n}\right)$. Moreover, the argument shows that this is true for each pair $\{k, n\} \subset \mathbb{N}$ with $2 \leq k < n$. For each $E \in [\delta, 2\delta]$ and each $\varepsilon \in \mathbb{R}_{++}$, there is a pair $\{k, n\} \subset \mathbb{N}$ with $2 \leq k < n$ such that $\left|\frac{2k\delta}{n} - E\right| < \varepsilon$. Then by *continuity*, $S(c^\delta, E) = CEA(c^\delta, E)$. Since $\delta \in \mathbb{R}_+$ was arbitrary, S satisfies *equal treatment of equals* on the domain of two-claimant problems. By *consistency*, S satisfies *equal treatment of equals* generally. Since S satisfies *equal treatment of equals*, *continuity*, and *consistency*, it also satisfies *endowment monotonicity*.[3]

Step 2: S=CEA on the domain of two-claimant problems. Let $N \in \mathbb{N}$ with $|N| = 2$, $(c, E) \in \mathcal{C}^N$ with $c_1 \leq c_2$, and $x \equiv S(c, E)$.

[3] Although Young (1987) invokes *continuity* with respect to both claims and endowment, the argument for this implication relies only on *endowment continuity*.

Case 1: $E \in [0, c_1]$. For each $i \in N$, $(c_i, E) \in \mathcal{C}^{\{i\}}$ and $S_i(c_i, E) = E$. Since $ag^S(1,1) = \frac{1}{2}$, $x_i \geq \frac{E}{2}$. This is true for both agents, so $x = \left(\frac{E}{2}, \frac{E}{2}\right) = CEA(c, E)$.

Case 2: $E \in [c_1, 2c_1]$. Suppose by way of contradiction that $x \neq \left(\frac{E}{2}, \frac{E}{2}\right)$ and label the agents so that $x_i < \frac{E}{2} < x_j$. Then there is $k \in \mathbb{N}$ such that $kx_i + E < (k+1)c_1$. Let $M \in \mathcal{N}$ with $N \cap M = \emptyset$ and $|M| = k$, $\hat{c} \equiv (c_i)_{h \in M}$. Then $((c_i, \hat{c}), kx_i + E) \in \mathcal{C}^{\{i\} \cup M}$. By *equal treatment of equals*, $S(c_{\{i\} \cup M}, kx_i + E) = \left(\frac{kx_i+E}{k+1}, \ldots, \frac{kx_i+E}{k+1}\right)$. Also, by *consistency*, for each $h \in \{i\} \cup M$, $S_h((c, \hat{c}), kx_i + E) = x_i$. Now comparing group guarantees,

$$\frac{k+1}{k+2} = ag^S(k+1, 1) \leq \frac{1}{k+1} \sum_{h \in \{i\} \cup M} \frac{S_h((c, \hat{c}), kx_i + E)}{S_h((c_i, \hat{c}), kx_i + E)}$$

$$= \frac{x_i}{(kx_i + E)/(k+1)}.$$

But then $E \leq 2x_i$, which contradicts $E = x_i + x_j > 2x_i$. Instead, $x_i = x_j = \frac{E}{2}$ and $x = CEA(c, E)$.

Case 3: $E \in [2c_1, c_1 + c_2]$ By Case 2, $S(c, 2c_1) = (c_1, c_1)$. By *endowment monotonicity*, for each $E \in [2c_1, c_1 + c_2]$, $S(c, E) = (c_1, E - c_1) = CEA(c, E)$. Thus, $S = CEA$ on the domain of two-claimant problems.

Step 3: S=CEA. By Step 2, $S = CEA$ for all two-claimant problems. As CEA is its own unique *consistent* extension from the two-claimant case, $S = CEA$ generally.[4] □

17.15 UNDER REPLICATION, THE RANDOM ARRIVAL RULE CONVERGES TO THE PROPORTIONAL RULE

Proof of Theorem 12.8: (according to which, under replication, the random arrival rule behaves more and more like the proportional rule.) Suppose, without loss of generality, that $N \equiv \{1, \ldots, n\}$, and let $(c, E) \in \mathcal{C}^N$. Let $k \in \mathbb{N}$. To calculate the random arrival awards vector of a k-replica of (c, E), we need to find out how much each agent is awarded at each permutation. At each permutation, an agent receives one of the following amounts: their claim, some positive amount smaller than their claim, or 0. In the k-replica of the problem, given $i \in N$, let $n_1(i, k)$ be the number of permutations at which the agent receives c_i, $n_2(i, k)$ the number of permutations at which the agent receives some positive amount smaller than c_i, and $n_3(i, k)$ the number of permutations at which the agent receives 0. For each $\ell = 1, 2, 3$, let $p_\ell(i, k)$ be the corresponding probability, that is, $p_\ell(i, k) = \frac{n_\ell(i,k)}{(kn)!}$.

[4] Since *CEA* is also *conversely consistent*, this step is an application of the Elevator Lemma.

At each permutation, claimant i receives c_i if the sum of the claims of the agents arriving before claimant i plus c_i is at most equal to kE. Let Π^{k*N} denote the class of bijections on $k*N$. Then for each $\pi \in \Pi^{k*N}$ and each $i \in k*N$, let $b^{\pi}(i)$ be the set of agents who arrive before i. For each $\{i, j\} \subset k*N$ and each $\pi \in \Pi^{k*N}$, let $\pi' \in \Pi^{k*N}$ be the permutation obtained from π by exchanging i and j.

For each pair $\{i, j\} \subset k*N$,

$$\begin{aligned}
p_1(i,k) &= Pr[\pi \in \Pi^{k*N} | \sum_{m \in b^{\pi}(i)} c_m + c_i \leq kE] \\
&= Pr[\pi \in \Pi^{k*N} | j \in b^{\pi}(i), \sum_{m \in b^{\pi}(i)} c_m + c_i \leq kE] + \\
&\quad Pr[\pi \in \Pi^{k*N} | j \notin b^{\pi}(i), \sum_{m \in b^{\pi}(i)} c_m + c_i \leq kE] \\
&= Pr[\pi \in \Pi^{k*N} | j \in b^{\pi}(i), \sum_{m \in b^{\pi}(i), m \neq j} c_m \leq kE - c_i - c_j] + \\
&\quad Pr[\pi \in \Pi^{k*N} | j \notin b^{\pi}(i), \sum_{m \in b^{\pi}(i)} c_m \leq kE - c_i] \\
&= Pr[\pi \in \Pi^{k*N} | j \in b^{\pi}(i), \frac{\sum_{m \in b^{\pi}(i), m \neq j} c_m}{k} \leq E - \frac{c_i}{k} - \frac{c_j}{k}] + \\
&\quad Pr[\pi \in \Pi^{k*N} | j \notin b^{\pi}(i), \frac{\sum_{m \in b^{\pi}(i)} c_m}{k} \leq E - \frac{c_i}{k}].
\end{aligned}$$

Similarly,

$$\begin{aligned}
p_1(j,k) &= Pr[\pi \in \Pi^{k*N} | i \in b^{\pi}(j), \frac{\sum_{m \in b^{\pi}(j), m \neq i} c_m}{k} \leq E - \frac{c_j}{k} - \frac{c_i}{k}] + \\
&\quad Pr[\pi \in \Pi^{k*N} | i \notin b^{\pi}(j), \frac{\sum_{m \in b^{\pi}(j)} c_m}{k} \leq E - \frac{c_j}{k}].
\end{aligned}$$

Let us compare $p_1(i,k)$ and $p_1(j,k)$.

$$\begin{aligned}
&Pr[\pi \in \Pi^{k*N} | j \in b^{\pi}(i), \frac{\sum_{m \in b^{\pi}(i), m \neq j} c_m}{k} \leq E - \frac{c_i}{k} - \frac{c_j}{k}] \\
&= Pr[\pi' \in \Pi^{k*N} | i \in b^{\pi'}(j), \frac{\sum_{m \in b^{\pi'}(j), m \neq i} c_m}{k} \leq E - \frac{c_j}{k} - \frac{c_i}{k}] \\
&= Pr[\pi \in \Pi^{k*N} | i \in b^{\pi}(j), \frac{\sum_{m \in b^{\pi}(j), m \neq i} c_m}{k} \leq E - \frac{c_j}{k} - \frac{c_i}{k}].
\end{aligned}$$

Moreover, if $c_i \leq c_j$, then

$$\begin{aligned}
&Pr[\pi \in \Pi^{k*N} | j \notin b^{\pi}(i), \frac{\sum_{m \in b^{\pi}(i)} c_m}{k} \leq E - \frac{c_i}{k}] \\
&\geq Pr[\pi \in \Pi^{k*N} | i \notin b^{\pi}(j), \frac{\sum_{m \in b^{\pi}(j)} c_m}{k} \leq E - \frac{c_j}{k}].
\end{aligned}$$

Thus, if $c_i \leq c_j$, then $p_1(i,k) \geq p_1(j,k)$.

Also, if $c_i \leq c_j$, then

$$\begin{aligned} p_3(i,k) &= Pr[\pi \in \Pi^{k*N} | \sum_{m \in b^{\pi}(i)} c_m \geq kE] \\ &\geq Pr[\pi \in \Pi^{k*N} | \sum_{m \in b^{\pi}(j)} c_m \geq kE] = p_3(j,k). \end{aligned}$$

At each permutation, at most one agent receives a positive amount smaller than their claim, so that $\sum_{j \in k*N} n_2(j,k) \leq (kn)!$. Moreover, since the random arrival rule satisfies *equal treatment of equals*, if i and i' are of the same type, then for each $\ell = 1,2,3$, $n_\ell(i,k) = n_\ell(i',k)$. Since there are at least k agents of the same type, $\sum_{j \in k*N} n_2(j,k) \leq (kn)!$ implies that for each $i \in k*N$, $n_2(i,k) \leq \frac{(kn)!}{k}$, or equivalently, $0 \leq \frac{n_2(i,k)}{(kn)!} \leq \frac{1}{k}$. As $k \to \infty$, $\frac{n_2(i,k)}{(kn)!} \to 0$. Consequently, as $k \to \infty$, for each $i \in k*N$, $p_2(i,k) \to 0$.

Let $\{i,j\} \subset k*N$ be such that $c_i \leq c_j$. Since $p_1(i,k)+p_2(i,k)+p_3(i,k) = p_1(j,k)+p_2(j,k)+p_3(j,k) = 1$, $\lim_{k\to\infty} p_2(i,k) = \lim_{k\to\infty} p_2(j,k)$ implies that $\lim_{k\to\infty}\{p_1(i,k)+p_3(i,k)\} = \lim_{k\to\infty}\{p_1(j,k)+p_3(j,k)\}$.

As discussed above, since the random arrival rule satisfies *equal treatment of equals*, $\sum_{i\in N} RA_i(k*(c,E)) = E$. Since $\sum_{i \in N} c_i p_1(i,k) \leq E \leq \sum_{i\in N} c_i p_1(i,k) + \sum_{i \in N} c_i p_2(i,k)$, as $k \to \infty$, $\lim_{k\to\infty} \sum_{i\in N} c_i p_1 (i,k) = E$. Thus, it follows that for each $\varepsilon > 0$, there is $K_1(\varepsilon) > 0$ such that for each $k > K_1(\varepsilon)$, we have $|E - \sum_{i \in N} c_i p_1(i,k)| < \varepsilon$.

Also, for each $\{i,j\} \subset k*N$, from $\{p_1(i,k) - p_1(j,k)\}\{p_3(i,k) - p_3(j,k)\} \geq 0$, we obtain

$$\begin{aligned} |p_1(i,k) - p_1(j,k)| &\leq |p_1(i,k) - p_1(j,k) + p_3(i,k) - p_3(j,k)| \\ &\leq |p_1(i,k) + p_3(i,k) - 1| + |p_1(j,k) + p_3(j,k) - 1|. \end{aligned}$$

Since $\lim_{k\to\infty}\{p_1(i,k)+p_3(i,k)\} = \lim_{k\to\infty}\{p_1(j,k)+p_3(j,k)\} = 1$, it follows that for each $\varepsilon > 0$, there is $K_2(\varepsilon,i,j) > 0$ such that for each $k > K_2(\varepsilon,i,j)$, we have $|p_1(i,k) - p_1(j,k)| < \varepsilon$. Let $K_2(\varepsilon) \equiv \max_{i,j\in N} K_2(\varepsilon,i,j)$. Then, for each $\varepsilon > 0$, each $\{i,j\} \subset k*N$, and each $k > K_2(\varepsilon)$, we have $|p_1(i,k) - p_1(j,k)| < \varepsilon$.

Now, we show that for each $i \in N$, $\lim_{k\to\infty} p_1(i,k) = \frac{E}{\sum_{j\in N} c_j}$. Indeed,

$$\begin{aligned} |\frac{E}{\sum_{j\in N} c_j} - p_1(i,k)| &\leq \frac{1}{\sum_{j\in N} c_j} |E - \sum_{j \in N} c_j p_1(i,k)| \\ &\leq \frac{1}{\sum_{j\in N} c_j} |E - \sum_{j\in N} c_j p_1(j,k)| \\ &\quad + \frac{1}{\sum_{j\in N} c_j} |\sum_{j\in N} c_j p_1(j,k) - \sum_{j\in N} c_j p_1(i,k)| \end{aligned}$$

$$\leq \frac{1}{\sum_{j\in N} c_j} |E - \sum_{j\in N} c_j p_1(j,k)|$$
$$+ \frac{1}{\sum_{j\in N} c_j} \sum_{j\in N} \{c_j |p_1(j,k) - p_1(i,k)|\}.$$

By setting $K(\varepsilon) = \max\{K_1(\frac{\sum_{j\in N} c_j \varepsilon}{2}), K_2(\frac{\varepsilon}{2})\}$, we deduce that for each $\varepsilon > 0$, and each $k > K(\varepsilon)$, $|\frac{E}{\sum_{j\in N} c_j} - p_1(i,k)| < \varepsilon$. Thus, as $k \to \infty$, for each $i \in k * N$, $RA_i(kc, kE) \to \frac{c_i}{\sum_{j\in N} c_j} E$, as announced. □

17.16 CONVEXITY OF THE TU COALITIONAL GAME ASSOCIATED WITH A CLAIMS PROBLEM

Proof of Proposition 14.1: (according to which the core of the TU coalitional game associated with any claims problem is convex.) Let $(c, E) \in \mathcal{C}^N$, $i \in N$, and $N', N'' \subseteq N$ such that $N' \subset N'' \subset N$, and $i \notin N''$ be given. For notational simplicity, we write v instead of $v(c, E)$. We need to show that

$$v(N' \cup \{i\}) - v(N') \leq v(N'' \cup \{i\}) - v(N''),$$

or, equivalently, that

$$\max\{E - \sum_{N\backslash N'\cup\{i\}} c_j, 0\} - \max\{E - \sum_{N\backslash N'} c_j, 0\}$$
$$\leq \max\{E - \sum_{N\backslash N''\cup\{i\}} c_j, 0\} - \max\{E - \sum_{N\backslash N''} c_j, 0\},$$

or, using the notation $\Delta \equiv \sum_N c_j - E$, that

$$\max\{-\Delta + \sum_{N'\cup\{i\}} c_j, 0\} - \max\{-\Delta + \sum_{N'} c_j, 0\}$$
$$\leq \max\{-\Delta + \sum_{N''\cup\{i\}} c_j, 0\} - \max\{-\Delta + \sum_{N''} c_j, 0\}.$$

For each $\bar{N} \subset N$, let $d(\bar{N}) \equiv \max\{-\Delta + \sum_{\bar{N}} c_j, 0\}$. Then the previous inequality becomes

$$\delta(N') \equiv d(N' \cup \{i\}) - d(N') \leq d(N'' \cup \{i\}) - d(N'') \equiv \delta(N'').$$

We distinguish two cases:

Case 1: $\sum_{N'} c_j \leq \sum_{N'\cup\{i\}} c_j \leq \sum_{N''} c_j \leq \sum_{N''\cup\{i\}} c_j$.

We compare Δ with each of the sums. We indicate how the desired conclusion is reached by calculating the differences $\delta(N')$ and $\delta(N'')$. There are five subcases:

Subcase 1.1:. $\sum_{N''\cup\{i\}} c_j \leq \Delta$. Then $d(N') = d(N'\cup\{i\}) = d(N'') = d(N''\cup\{i\})$=0, so that $\delta(N') = \delta(N'') = 0$.

Subcase 1.2: $\sum_{N''} c_j \leq \Delta \leq \sum_{N''\cup\{i\}} c_j$. We still have $\delta(N') = 0$, but $d(N''\cup\{i\}) > 0$ and $d(N'') = 0$, so that $\delta(N'') > 0$.

Subcase 1.3: $\sum_{N'\cup\{i\}} c_j \leq \Delta \leq \sum_{N''} c_j$. We still have $\delta(N') = 0$, but $d(N''\cup\{i\}) = -\Delta + \sum_{N''\cup\{i\}} c_j$, $d(N'') = -\Delta + \sum_{N''} c_j$, and $\delta(N'') = c_i$.

Subcase 1.4: $\sum_{N'} c_j \leq \Delta \leq \sum_{N'\cup i} c_j$. Then $d(N') = 0$, $d(N'\cup\{i\}) = -\Delta + \sum_{N'\cup\{i\}} c_j \leq c_i$, so that $\delta(N') < c_i$. As in Subcase 3, $\delta(N'') = c_i$.

Subcase 1.5: $\Delta \leq \sum_{N'} c_j$. Then $d(N') = -\Delta + \sum_{N'} c_j$, $d(N'\cup\{i\}) = -\Delta + \sum_{N'\cup\{i\}} c_j$, so that $\delta(N') = c_i$ and we still have $\delta(N'') = c_i$.

Case 2: $\sum_{N'} c_j \leq \sum_{N''} c_j \leq \sum_{N'\cup\{i\}} c_j \leq \sum_{N''\cup\{i\}} c_j$. Five parallel subcases have to be considered, and for each of them, the claim is proved in parallel fashion. □

17.17 PROOF OF THE CORRESPONDENCE BETWEEN THE TALMUD RULE AND THE NUCLEOLUS, AND OF THE CONSTRAINED EQUAL AWARDS RULE AND THE DUTTA–RAY SOLUTION

Proof of Proposition 14.2b: (according to which the Talmud rule corresponds to the nucleolus and that the constrained equal awards rule corresponds to the Dutta–Ray solution.) The proof is in five steps.[5]

Step 1: The Talmud rule is a *bilaterally consistent* and *conversely consistent* division rule (Sections 10.2 and 10.3).

Step 2: On the domain of all TU games, the prenucleolus is a *bilaterally max consistent* solution.[6]

To see this, let $N \in \mathcal{N}$, $v \in \mathcal{V}^N$, $i, j \in N$, $N' \equiv \{i, j\}$, and $x \equiv PreNuc(v)$. Let $\rho^x_{N'}(v) \in \mathcal{V}^{N'}$ denote the reduced game of v with respect to N' and x, and $y \equiv (y_i, y_j) = PreNuc(\rho^x_{N'}(v))$. We need to show that $x_{N'} = y$. Suppose not. Then without loss of generality, $x_i < y_i$. Now

$$\begin{aligned} \max_{M\subseteq N\setminus N'} [v(M\cup\{i\}) - \sum_M x_k] - x_i &> \rho^x_{N'}(v)(\{i\}) - y_i \\ &= \rho^x_{N'}(v)(\{j\}) - y_j \\ &> \max_{M\subseteq N\setminus N'}[v(M\cup\{j\}) \\ &\quad - \textstyle\sum_M x_k] - x_j \end{aligned}$$

[5] Alternate proofs are by R. Lee (1992), Benoît (1997), and Fleiner and Sziklai (2012). Neither one of the last two proofs invokes notions of consistency for coalitional form games. A related study is by Solymosi and Sziklai (2015).

[6] The prenucleolus is *max consistent* on the domain of all TU games but the proof for two players is considerably simpler than that for *n* players.

Let $\varepsilon > 0$ be such that

$$\max_{M \subseteq N \setminus N'} [v(M \cup \{i\}) - \sum_M x_k] - x_i - \varepsilon > \max_{M \subseteq N \setminus N'} [v(M \cup \{j\}) - \sum_M x_k] - x_j + \varepsilon.$$

Let $z \in \mathbb{R}^N$ be defined by

$$z_k \equiv \begin{cases} x_k & \text{if } k \notin N', \\ x_i + \varepsilon & \text{if } k = i, \\ x_j - \varepsilon & \text{if } k = j. \end{cases}$$

Note that $\sum z_k = v(N)$. Moreover, for each $M \subset N \setminus N'$,

$$\begin{array}{rcl} v(M) - \sum_M x_k & = & v(M) - \sum_M z_k \\ v(M \cup \{i\}) - \sum_M x_k - x_i & > & v(M \cup \{i\}) - \sum_M z_k - z_i \\ & > & \max_{M \subseteq N \setminus N'} [v(M \cup \{j\}) - \sum_M z_k] - z_j \\ & \geq & v(M \cup \{j\}) - \sum_M z_k - z_j \\ & > & v(M \cup \{j\}) - \sum_M x_k - x_j. \end{array}$$

Thus, $(v(M) - \sum_M z_k)_{M \subseteq N}$ is lexicographically greater than $(v(M) - \sum_M x_k)_{M \subset N}$, which contradicts $x = PreNuc(v)$.

Step 3: The operation consisting in converting a claims problem into a TU game commutes with the operation consisting in reducing a game with respect to a subset of the set of agents and a payoff vector (whether it is a claims problem or a TU game) (Figure 14.7).[7]

Step 4: For two claimants, the contested garment rule coincides with the rule that chooses, for each problem, the payoff vector obtained by converting the problem into a coalitional game and then solving this game by applying the nucleolus.

Step 5: Concluding by applying the Elevator Lemma (Section 10.4).

Proof of Proposition 14.2c: (according to which the constrained equal awards rule corresponds to the Dutta–Ray solution.) The proof is in five steps parallel to the five steps of the previous proof.

Step 1: The constrained equal awards rule is a *bilaterally consistent* and *conversely consistent* division rule (Sections 10.2 and 10.3).

Step 2: On the domain of convex games, the Dutta–Ray solution is a *bilaterally max consistent* solution. This follows directly from the definition of the Dutta–Ray outcome as selecting for each game the payoff vector that solves a certain minimization exercise.

Step 3: Same as Step 3 of Part (b).

Step 4: For two claimants, the constrained equal awards rule coincides with the rule that chooses, for each problem, the payoff vector obtained by converting

[7] This fact is proved by Aumann and Maschler (1985).

the problem into a coalitional game and solving this game by applying the Dutta–Ray solution.

To prove this, let $N \equiv \{i, j\}$ and suppose that $c_i \leq c_j$.

Then $\frac{v(N)}{2} = \frac{E}{2}$, and

$$\frac{E}{2} - v(\{i\}) = \begin{cases} \frac{E}{2} & \text{if } E \leq c_j, \\ c_j - \frac{E}{2} & \text{if } c_j < E, \end{cases}$$

$$\frac{E}{2} - v(\{j\}) = \begin{cases} \frac{E}{2} & \text{if } E \leq c_i, \\ c_i - \frac{E}{2} & \text{if } c_i < E. \end{cases}$$

If $\frac{E}{2} \leq c_i$, then $(\frac{E}{2}, \frac{E}{2}) \in C(v)$. Thus, $DR(v) = (\frac{E}{2}, \frac{E}{2}) =$*CEA* (c, E).

If $c_i < \frac{E}{2}$, then $(\frac{E}{2}, \frac{E}{2}) \notin C(v)$ and $\frac{E}{2} < v(\{j\}) = E - c_i$. Thus

$$DR(v) = E - v(\{j\}, v(\{j\}) = (c_i, E - c_i) = CEA\,(c, E).$$

Step 5: If $|N| \geq 3$, $DR(v)$ =*CEA* (c, E). Let $x \equiv DR(v)$. Then for each pair $\{i, j\} \subset N$, and since the Dutta–Ray solution is a *bilaterally max consistent* solution, $(x_i, x_j) = DR(\rho^x_{\{i,j\}}(v))$. By Step 3, this expression is equal to $DR(v((c_i, c_j), x_i + x_j))$ and since for two claimants, $DR =$ *CEA*, we obtain $(x_i, x_j) =$ *CEA* $((c_i, c_j), E)$. We conclude by applying the Elevator Lemma.) □

References

Aczél, J., *Lectures on Functional Equations and Their Applications*, New York, NY: Academic Press 1966.

Albizuri, M. J., J. Leroux, and M. Zarzuelo, "Updating claims in bankruptcy problems," *Mathematical Social Sciences* 60 (2010), 144–148.

Alcalde, J., M.-C. Marco, and J. A. Silva, "Bankruptcy problems and the Ibn Ezra's proposal," *Economic Theory* 26 (2005), 103–114.

"The minimal overlap rule revisited," *Social Choice and Welfare* 31 (2008), 109–128.

"The minimal overlap rule: restrictions on mergers for creditors' consensus," *TOP* 22 (2014), 363–383.

Ambec, S., and Y. Sprumont, "Sharing a river," *Journal of Economic Theory* 107 (2002), 453–462.

Anbarci, N., "Non-cooperative foundations of the area monotonic solution," *Quarterly Journal of Economics* 108 (1993), 245–258.

Ansink, E., "The arctic scramble: introducing claims in a contest model," *European Journal of Political Economy* 27 (2011), 693–707.

Ansink, E. and H.-P. Weikard, "Contested water rights," *European Journal of Political Economy* 25 (2009), 247–260.

"Sequential sharing rules for river sharing problems," *Social Choice and Welfare* 38 (2012), 187–210.

"Composition properties in the river claims problem," *Social Choice and Welfare* 44 (2015), 807–831.

Araujo, A. and M. R. Páscoa, "Bankruptcy in a model of unsecured claims," *Economic Theory* 20 (2002), 455–481.

Arin, J, and E. Iñarra, "A characterization of the nucleolus for convex games," *Games and Economic Behavior* 23 (1998), 12–24.

Arin, J., and J. Benito, "The lexmax rule for bankruptcy problems," *Contributions to Game Theory and Management* 6 (2013), 8–23.

Arin, J., J. Benito, and E. Iñarra, "The reverse Talmud family of rules for bankruptcy problems: a characterization," *Mathematical Social Sciences* 89 (2017), 43–49.

Arin, J, and I. Katsev, "The SD-prekernel for TU games," mimeo, 2016.

Aristotle, *Ethics*, J. A. K. Thompson, tr. Harmondsworth: Penguin, 1985.

Ashlagi, I., E. Karagözoğlu, and B. Klaus, "A non-cooperative support for equal division in estate division problems," *Mathematical Social Sciences* 63 (2012), 228–233.

Atlamaz, M., "Contests with fixed resources in a spatial model," mimeo, 2004.

Atlamaz, M., C. Berden, H. Peters, and D. Vermeulen, "Non-cooperative solutions for estate division problems," *Games and Economic Behavior* 73 (2011), 39–51.

Aumann, R., "Markets with a continuum of traders," *Econometrica* 32 (1964), 39–50.

"Some non-superadditive games, and their Shapley values, in the Talmud," *International Journal of Game Theory* 39 (2010), 3–10.

Aumann, R. and M. Maschler, "Game theoretic analysis of a bankruptcy problem from the Talmud," *Journal of Economic Theory* 36 (1985), 195–213.

Aumann, R. and B. Peleg, "A note on Gale's example," *Journal of Mathematical Economics* 1 (1974), 209–211.

Aziz, H., "Computation of the random arrival rule for bankruptcy problems," *Operations Research Letters* 41 (2013), 499–502.

Balinski, M. and P. Young, *Fair Representation*, New Haven, CT: Yale University Press, 1982.

Banker, R., "Equity considerations in traditional full cost allocation practices: an axiomatic perspective," in *Joint Cost Allocations* (S. Moriarity, ed), Norman, OK: University of Oklahoma Press, 1981, 110–130.

Béal, S., A. Ghintran, E. Rmila, and P. Solal, "The River Sharing Problem: A Survey," *International Game Theory Review* 15 (2013), 16 pages.

Béhue, V., "Opinions éthiques sur les règles de division concernant les problèmes de banqueroute et de taxation," mimeo, 2003.

Bénassy, J.-P., *The Economics of Market Disequilibrium*, Cambridge, MA: Academic Press, 1982.

Benoît, J.-P., "The nucleolus is contested-garment–consistent: a direct proof," *Journal of Economic Theory* 77 (1997), 192–196.

Benson, C., "Circuitry of lien—a problem in priorities," *Minnesota Law Review* 19 (1935), 139–162.

Bergantiños, G. and L. Lorenzo, "The equal award principle in problems with constraints and claims," *European Journal of Operations Research* 1 (2008), 224–239.

Bergantiños, G., L. Lorenzo, and S. Lorenzo-Freire, "A characterization of the proportional rule in multi-issue allocation situations," *Operations Research Letters* 38 (2010a), 17–19.

"Mixed rules in multi-issue allocation situations," mimeo, 2010b.

"New characterizations of the constrained equal awards rule in multi-issue allocation problems," *Mathematical Methods of Operations Research* 74 (2011), 311–325.

Bergantiños, G. and L. Méndez-Naya, "New properties in bankruptcy problems," University of Vigo discussion paper, 1997.

"Additivity in bankruptcy problems and in allocation problems," *Spanish Economic Review* 3 (2001) 223–229.

Bergantiños, G. and E. Sanchez, "Point solutions for PERT problems," *Operations Research Letters* 30 (2002a), 130–140.

"The proportional rule for problems with constraints and claims," *Mathematical Social Sciences* 43 (2002b), 225–249.

Bergantiños, G. and J. Vidal-Puga, "Additive rules in bankruptcy problems and in other related problems," *Mathematical Social Sciences* 47 (2004), 87–101.

"Additive rules in discrete allocation problems," *European Journal of Operational Research* 172 (2006), 971–978.

Bernheim, B., B. Peleg, and M. Whinston, "Coalition-proof Nash equilibria I: concepts," *Journal of Economic Theory* 42 (1985), 1–12.

Bjorndal, E. and K. Jörnsten, “Flow sharing and bankruptcy games,” *International Journal of Game Theory* 39 (2010), 11–28.

Borm, P., Carpente, L., Casas-Méndez, B. Hendrickx, “The constrained equal awards rule for bankruptcy problems,” *Annals of Operations Research* 137 (2005), 211–227.

Borrero, D. V., F. J. Sánchez, M. A. Hinojosa, and A. M. Mármol, “A random arrival rule for division problems with multiple references,” *International Transactions in Operational Research* (2017).

Bosmans, K. and L. Lauwers, “Lorenz comparisons of nine rules for the adjudication of conflicting claims,” *International Journal of Game Theory* 40 (2011), 791–807.

Bosmans, K. and E. Schokkaert, “Equality preference in the claims problem: a questionnaire study of cuts in earnings and pensions,” *Social Choice and Welfare* 33 (2009), 533–557.

Bossert, W., “Monotonic solutions for bargaining problems with claims,” *Economics Letters* 39 (1992), 395–399.

“An alternative solution to bargaining problems with claims,” *Mathematical Social Sciences* 25 (1993), 205–220.

Branzei, R. and S. Z. Alparslan Gök, “Bankruptcy problems with interval uncertainty,” *Economics Bulletin* 3 (2008), 1–10.

Branzei, R. and M. Dall’aglio, “Allocation rules incorporating interval uncertainty,” *Badania Operacyjne i Decysje* 2 (2009), 19–28.

Branzei, R., M. Dall’aglio, and S., Tijs, “On bankruptcy game theoretic interval rules,” mimeo, 2013.

Branzei, R., D. Dimitrov, S. Pickl, and S. Tijs, “How to cope with division problems under interval uncertainty of claims,” *International Journal of Uncertainty, Fuzziness and Knowledge-Based Systems* 12 (2004), 191–200.

Branzei, R., D. Dimitrov, and S. Tijs, “Shapley-like values for interval bankruptcy games,” *Economic Bulletin* 3 (2003), 1–8.

Branzei, R.,G. Ferrari, V. Fragnelli, and S. Tijs, “A flow approach to bankruptcy problems,” *AUCO Czech Economic Review* 2 (2008), 146–153.

van den Brink, R., Y. Funaki, and G. van der Laan, “Characterization of the reverse Talmud bankruptcy rules by exemption and exclusion properties,” *European Journal of Operational Research* 228 (2013), 413–417.

van den Brink, R. and J. Moreno-Ternero, “The reverse TAL-family of rules for bankruptcy problems,” *Annals of Operations Research* 254 (2017), 449–465.

Büyüboyacı, M., M. Gürdal, A. Kıbrıs, and Ö. Kıbrıs, “An experimental study of the investment implications of bankruptcy law,” mimeo, undated.

Calleja, P., P. Borm, and R. Hendrickx, “Multi-allocation situations,” *European Journal of Operations Research* 164 (2005), 730–747.

Callen, J., “A Medieval controversy about profit and loss allocations,” *Abacus* 23 (1987), 85–90.

Cappelen, A., R. I. Luttens, E. Sorensen, and B. Tungodden, “Fairness in bankruptcy situations: an experimental study,” *Management Science*, forthcoming, 2015.

Carpente, L., P. Borm, B. Casas-Mendéz, and R. Hendrickx, “The constrained equal award rule for bankruptcy problems with a priori unions,” *Annals of Operations Research* 137 (2005), 211–227.

Carpente, L., B. Casas-Méndez, J. Gozálvez, N. Llorca, M. Pulido, and J. Sánchez-Soriano, “How to divide a cake when people have different metabolism?,” *Mathematical Methods of Operations Research* 78 (2013), 361–371.

Casas-Méndez, B., V. Fragnelli, and I. Garcıa-Jurado, "Weighted bankruptcy rules and the museum pass problem," *European Journal of Operational Research* 215 (2011), 161–168.

"A survey of allocation rules for the museum pass problem," *Journal of Cultural Economics* 38 (2014), 191–205.

Casas-Méndez, B. I. Garcia-Jurado, A. van den Nouweland, and M. Vásquez-Brage, "An extension of the τ-value to games with coalition structures," *European Journal of Operational Research* 148 1 (2003), 494–513.

Cassel, G., "The theory of progressive taxation," *Economic Journal* 11 (1901), 481–491.

Cetemen, E. D., K. Hasker, and E. Karagözoğlu, "Rewards must be proportional in the core of large claim games," mimeo, 2015.

Chae, S., "Linked recapitalization agreement," Rice University, mimeo, 1998.

Chae, S. and J.-A. Yang, "The unique perfect equilibrium of an n-person bargaining game," *Economics Letters* 28 (1988), 221–223.

Chambers, C., "Asymmetric rules for claims problems without homogeneity," *Games and Economic Behavior* 54 (2006), 241–260.

Chambers, C. and J. Moreno-Ternero, "Taxation and poverty," *Social Choice and Welfare* 48 (2017), 153–175.

Chambers, C. and W. Thomson, "Group order preservation and the proportional rule for bankruptcy problems," *Mathematical Social Sciences* 44 (2002), 235–252.

Chang, C. and C.-C. Hu, "A non-cooperative interpretation of the f-just rules of bankruptcy problems," *Games and Economics Behavior* 63 (2008), 133–144.

Chen, S., "Systematic favorability in claims problems with indivisibilities," *Social Choice and Welfare* 44 (2015), 283–300.

Ching, S. and V. Kakkar, "A market approach to bankruptcy problem," City University of Hong-Kong discussion paper, February 2000.

"Diagnosing alternative characterizations of the proportional rule," City University of Hong-Kong discussion paper, September 2001.

Chun, Y., "The solidarity axiom for quasi-linear social choice problems," *Social Choice and Welfare* 3 (1986), 297–310.

"The proportional solution for rights problem," *Mathematical Social Sciences* 15 (1988a), 231–246.

"The equal-loss principle for bargaining problems," *Economics Letters* 26 (1988b), 103–106.

"A non-cooperative justification for egalitarian surplus sharing," *Mathematical Social Sciences* 17 (1989), 245–261.

"Equivalence of axioms for bankruptcy problems," *International Journal of Game Theory* 28 (1999), 511–520.

"Agreement, separability, and other axioms for quasi-linear social choice problems," *Social Choice and Welfare* 17 (2000), 507–521.

"A dual relation between the Talmud rule and the random arrival rule for 3-person bankruptcy problems," *Korean Economic Journal* 44 (2005), 509–515.

Chun, Y., I. Jang, and B.-G. Ju, "Priority, solidarity and egalitarianism," *Social Choice and Welfare* 43 (2014), 577–589.

Chun, Y. and J. Lee, "On the convergence of the random arrival rule in large claims problems," *International Journal of Game Theory* 36 (2007), 259–273.

Chun, Y. and H. Peters, "The lexicographic equal-loss solution," *Mathematical Social Sciences* 22 (1991), 151–161.

Chun, Y., J. Schummer, and W. Thomson, "Constrained egalitarianism: a new solution for claims problems," *Seoul Journal of Economics* 14 (2001), 269–297.

Chun, Y. and W. Thomson, "Bargaining solutions and relative guarantees," *Mathematical Social Sciences* 17 (1989), 295–295.

"Bargaining problems with claims," *Mathematical Social Sciences* 24 (1992), 19–33.

"Convergence under replication of rules to adjudicate conflicting claims," *Games and Economic Behavior* 50 (2005), 129–142.

Cohen Stuart, A. J, "On progressive taxation," in *Classics in the Theory of Public Finance* (R. A. Musgrave and A. T. Peacock, eds), New York, NY: McMillan, 1889.

Corchón, L. and C. Herrero, "A decent proposal," *Spanish Economic Review* 6 (2004), 107–125.

Csóka, P. and P. J. J. Herings, "Decentralized clearing in financial networks," *Management Science*, forthcoming, 2017a.

"An axiomatization of the proportional rule in financial networks," mimeo, 2017b.

"Liability games," mimeo, 2017c.

Curiel, I., M. Maschler, and S. H. Tijs, "Bankruptcy games," *Zeitschrift für Operations Research* 31 (1987), A143–A159.

Dagan, N., "On the least sacrifice principle in taxation," Hebrew University of Jerusalem mimeo, June 1994.

"New characterizations of old bankruptcy rules," *Social Choice and Welfare* 13 (1996), 51–59.

Dagan, N., R. Serrano, and O. Volij, "A non-cooperative view of consistent bankruptcy rules," *Games and Economic Behavior* 18 (1997), 55–72.

"Feasible implementation of taxation methods," *Review of Economic Design* 4 (1999), 57–72.

Dagan, N. and O. Volij, "The bankruptcy problem: a cooperative bargaining approach," *Mathematical Social Sciences* 26 (1993), 287–297.

"Bilateral comparisons and consistent fair division rules in the context of bankruptcy problems," *International Journal of Game Theory* 26 (1997), 11–25.

van Damme, E., "The Nash bargaining solution is optimal," *Journal of Economic Theory* 38 (1986), 78–100.

Davis, M. and M. Maschler, "The kernel of a cooperative game," *Naval Research Logistic Quarterly* 12 (1965), 223–259.

de Frutos, M. A. "Coalitional manipulation in a bankruptcy problem," *Review of Economic Design* 4 (1999), 255–272.

de Mesnard, L., "Three wives problem and Shapley value," *Revue de Philosophie Economique* 16 (2015), 145–169.

Dietzenbacher, B., "Bankruptcy games with nontransferable utility," *Mathematical Social Sciences 92* (2018), 16–21.

Dietzenbacher, B., P. Borm, and A. Estévez-Fernández, "NTU bankruptcy problems: consistency and the relative adjustment principle," mimeo, 2017.

Dietzenbacher, B., Estévez-Fernández, A., P. Borm, and R. Hendrickx, "Proportionality, equality, and duality in bankruptcy problems with non-transferable utility," mimeo, 2016.

Dominguez, D., "Lower bounds and recursive methods for the problem of adjudicating conflicting claims," *Social Choice and Welfare* 40 (2013), 663–678.

Dominguez, D and I. Morgenstern, "A characterization of the random arrival rule for claims problems," *Economics Letters* 174 (2019), 214–217.

Dominguez, D. and W. Thomson, "A new solution to the problem of adjudicating conflicting claims," *Economic Theory* 28 (2006), 283–307.

Driessen, T., "Tree enterprise and bankruptcy ventures: a game theoretic similarity due to a graph theoretic proof," *Discrete Applied Mathematics* 79 (1997), 105–117.

"The greedy bankruptcy game: an alternative game theoretic analysis of a bankruptcy problem," in *Game Theory and Applications IV* (L. A. Petrosjan and V. V. Mazalov, eds), New York, NY: Nova Science Publishers Inc., 1998, 45–61.

Dutta, B. and D. Ray, "A concept of egalitarianism under participation constraints," *Econometrica* 57 (1989), 615–635.

Eisenberg, L. and T. H. Noe, "Systemic risk in financial systems," *Management Science* 47 (2001), 236–249.

Erlanson, A. and K. Flores-Szwagrzak, "Allocating divisible and indivisible resources according to conflicting claims: collectively rational solutions," mimeo, 2014.

Ertemel, S. and R. Kumar, "Proportional rules for state contingent claims," *International Journal of Game Theory* 47 (2017), 229–246.

Estévez-Fernández, A., P. Borm and G. Fiestras-Janeiro, "NTU bankruptcy problems," mimeo, 2013.

Estévez-Fernández, A., G. Fiestras-Janeiro, M. A. Mosquera, and E. Sánchez-Rodriguez, "A bankruptcy approach to the core cover," *Mathematical Methods of Operations Research* 76 (2012), 343–359.

Fleiner, T., and B. Sziklai, "The nucleolus of the bankruptcy problem by hydraulic rationing," *International Game Theory Review* 14 (2012), 11 pages.

Flores-Szwagrzak, K., "Priority classes and weighted constrained equal awards rules for the claims problem," *Journal of Economic Theory* 160 (2015), 36–55.

Flores-Szwagrzak, K., Garcia-Segarra, J., and M. Ginés-Vilar, "Priority and proportionality in claims problems," mimeo, 2017a.

"Additive adjudication of conflicting claims," mimeo, 2017b.

Flores-Szwagrzak, K. and R. Treibich, "How much can you claim?," mimeo, 2016.

Fragnelli, V., S. Gagliardo, and F. Gastaldi, "Integer solutions to bankruptcy problems with non-integer claims," *TOP* 22 (2014), 892–933.

"Bankruptcy problems with non-integer claims: definition and characterizations of the ICEA solution," *TOP* 24 (2016), 88–130.

Fragnelli, V. and F. Gastaldi, "Remarks on the integer Talmud solution for bankruptcy problems," *TOP* 25 (2017), 127–163.

Gächter, S. and A. Riedl, "Moral property rights in bargaining with infeasible claims," *Management Science* 51 (2005), 249–263.

"Dividing justly in bargaining problems with claims: normative judgments and actual negotiations," *Social Choice and Welfare* 27 (2006), 571–594.

Gale, D., "Exchange equilibrium and coalitions: an example," *Journal of Mathematical Economics* 1 (1974), 63–66.

Gallice, A., "Bankruptcy problems with reference-dependent preferences," *International Journal of Game Theory* (2019), forthcoming.

Gaertner, W. and L. Schwettmann, "Burden sharing in deficit countries: a questionnaire-experimental investigation," *SERIEs* 8 (2017), 113–144.

García-Jurado, I, J. González-Díaz, and A. Villar, "A non-cooperative approach to bankruptcy problems," *Spanish Economic Review* 8 (2006), 189–197.

Giménez-Gómez, J. M., "A way to play claims problems," *Group Decision and Negotiation* 23 (2014), 617–627.

Giménez-Gómez, J. and M.-C. Marco, "A new approach for bounding awards in bankruptcy problems," *Social Choice and Welfare* 43 (2014), 447–469.

Giménez-Gómez, J. and A. Osório, "Why and how to differentiate in claims problems? An axiomatic approach," *European Journal of Operational Research* 241 (2015), 842–850.

Giménez-Gómez, J. M., A. Osório, and J. Peris, "From bargaining solutions to claims rules: a proportional approach," *Games* 6 (2015), 32–38.

"Bankruptcy problems with two references: an impartial compromise," *TOP* 24 (2016), 131–142.

Giménez-Gómez, J. and J. Peris, "A proportional approach to claims problems with a guaranteed minimum," *European Journal of Operational Research* 232 (2014a), 109–116.

"Mediations in claims problems," *SERIEs* 5 (2014b), 357–375.

"Participation and solidarity in redistribution mechanisms," *Czech Economic Review* 9 (2015), 36–48.

Giménez-Gómez, J., J. Teixedó-Figueras, and C. Vilella, "The global carbon budget: a conflicting claims problem," *Climatic Change* 136 (2016), 693–703.

Giménez-Gómez, J. M. and C. Vilella, "Recursive methods for discrete claims problems," *Economics Bulletin* 37 (2017), 1653–1665.

Ginsburg, V. and I. Zang, "The museum pass game and its value," *Games and Economic Behavior* 43 (2003), 322–325.

González-Alcón, C., P. Borm, and R. Hendrickx, "A composite run-to-the-bank rule for multi-issue allocation situations," *Mathematical Methods of Operations Research* 65 (2007), 339–352.

González Díaz, C., P. Borm, R. Hendrickx, and M. Quant, "A geometric characterisation of the compromise value," *Mathematical Methods of Operations Research* 61 (2005), 483–500.

Grahn, S. and M. Voorneveld, "Population-monotonic allocation schemes in bankruptcy games," *Annals of Operations Research* 109 (2002), 317–329.

Green, J., and J.-J. Laffont, *Incentives in Public Decision Making*, Amsterdam: North-Holland, 1979.

Groote Schaasberg, M., Reijnierse, and P. Borm, "On solving liability problems," *Mathematical Methods of Operational Research* 87 (2018), 383–409.

Grundel, S., P. Borm, and H. Hamers, "Resource allocation games: a compromise stable extension of bankruptcy games," *Mathematical Social Sciences* 78 (2013), 149–169.

Guiasu, S., "Three ancient problems solved by using the game theory logic based on the Shapley value," *Synthese* 181 (2011), 65–79.

Habis, H. and P. J. J. Herings, "Transferable utility games with uncertainty," *Journal of Economic Theory* 146 (2011), 2126–2139.

"Stochastic bankruptcy games," *International Journal of Game Theory* 42 (2013), 973–988.

Harless, P., "Endowment additivity and the weighted proportional rules for adjudicating conflicting claims," *Economic Theory* 63 (2017a), 755–781.

"Wary of the worst: maximizing award guarantees when new claimants arrive," *Games and Economic Behavior 105* (2017b), 316–328.

"Guarantee structures for claims problems; properties and comparisons among rules," mimeo, 2017c.

Harsanyi, J. and R. Selten, "A generalized Nash solution for two-person bargaining games with incomplete information," *Management Science* 18 (1972), 80–106.

Hart, S. and A. Mas-Colell, "Potential, value and consistency," *Econometrica* 57 (1989), 589–614.

Hendrickx, R., P. Borm, R. van Elk, and M. Quant, "Minimal overlap rules for bankruptcy," *International Mathematical Forum* 2 (2007), 3001–3012.

Herrero, C., "Bargaining with claims in economic environments," *Revista Espanola de Economia* 15 (1998), 3–13.

"Endogenous reference points and the adjusted proportional solution for bargaining problems with claims," *Social Choice and Welfare* 15 (1998), 113–119. Corrigendum, *Social Choice and Welfare* 17 (2000), 377–378.

"Equal awards versus equal losses: duality in bankruptcy," in *Advances in Economic Design* (M. Sertel and S. Koray, eds), Springer-Verlag, 2003, 413–426.

Herrero, C. and M.-C. Marco, "A note on the equal-loss principle for bargaining problems," University of Alicante working paper 92-02, 1992.

"Rational equal loss solutions for bargaining problems," *Mathematical Social Sciences* 26 (1993), 273–286.

Herrero, C. and R. Martínez, "Balanced allocation methods for claims problems with indivisibilities," *Social Choice and Welfare* 29 (2008), 603–617.

Herrero, C., M. Maschler, and A. Villar, "Individual rights and collective responsibility: the rights-egalitarian solution," *Mathematical Social Sciences* 37 (1999), 59–77.

Herrero, C., J. Moreno-Ternero, and G. Ponti, "On the adjudication of conflicting claims: An experimental study," *Social Choice and Welfare* 34 (2010), 145–179. Erratum in *Social Choice and Welfare* 33 (2009), 517–519.

Herrero, C. and A. Villar, "The three musketeers: four classical solutions to bankruptcy problems," *Mathematical Social Sciences* 39 (2001), 307–328.

"Sustainability in bankruptcy problems," *TOP* 10 (2002), 261–273.

"The rights egalitarian solution for NTU problems," *International Journal of Game Theory* 39 (2010), 137–150.

Hinojosa, M. A., A. M. Mármol, and F. Sánchez, "A consistent Talmud rule for division problems with multiple references," *TOP* 20 (2012a), 661–678.

"Leximin rules for bankruptcy problems under uncertainty," *International Journal of Systems Science* 45 (2012b), 20–28.

Hokari, T., "Axiomatic analysis of coalitional TU games: population monotonicity and consistency," University of Rochester Ph.D. Dissertation, 2000.

Untitled notes on claims problems, 2001.

"Consistency implies equal treatment in TU-games," *Games and Economic Behavior* 51 (2005), 63–82.

Hokari, T. and W. Thomson, "Claims problems and weighted generalizations of the Talmud rule," *Economic Theory* 21 (2003), 241–261.

"On properties of division rules lifted by bilateral consistency," *Journal of Mathematical Economics* 44 (2008), 211–231.

"Independence properties for claims problems," mimeo, 2010.

Hougaard, J. L., J. Moreno-Ternero, and L. P. Østerdal, "A unifying framework for the problem of adjudicating conflicting claims," *Journal of Mathematical Economics* 48 (2012), 107–114.

"Rationing in the presence of baselines," *Social Choice and Welfare* 40 (2013a), 1047–1066.

"Rationing with baselines: the composition extension operator," *Annals of Operations Research* 211 (2013b), 179–191.

Hougaard, J. L. and L. P. Østerdal, "Inequality preserving rationing," *Economics Letters* 87 (2005), 355–360.

Hougaard, J. L. and L. Thorlund-Peterson, "Bankruptcy rules, inequality, and uncertainty," mimeo, 2001.

Hu, C.-C., "Bidding for the award and the loss for bankruptcy problems," mimeo, 2010.

Huijink, S., P. Borm, J. J. Reijnierse, and J. Kleppe, "Bankruptcy and the per capita nucleolus: the claim-and-right rules family," *Mathematical Social Sciences* 77 (2015), 15–31.

Hwang, Y.-H., "Two characterizations of the random arrival rule," *Economic Theory Bulletin* 3 (2015), 43–52.

Hwang, Y.-A. and T.-F. Wang, "Population monotonicity, consistency, and the random arrival rule," *Economics Bulletin* 29 (2009), 2816–2821.

Ilkılıç R. and Ç. Kayı, "Allocation rules on networks," *Social Choice and Welfare* 43 (2014), 877–892.

Imai, H.,"Individual monotonicity and lexicographic maximin solution," *Econometrica* 51 (1983), 389–401.

Izquierdo, J. M. and P. Timoner, "Constrained multi-issue rationing problems," mimeo, 2016.

Ju, B.-G., "Manipulation via merging and splitting in claims problems," *Review of Economic Design* 8 (2003), 205–215.

"Coalitional manipulation on networks," *Journal of Economic Theory* 148 (2013), 627–662.

Ju, B.-G. and E. Miyagawa, "Proportionality and non-manipulability in claims problems," mimeo, 2002.

Ju, B.-G., E. Miyagawa, and T. Sakai, "Non-manipulable division rules in claims problems and generalizations," *Journal of Economic Theory* 132 (2007), 1–26.

Ju, B.-G. and J. Moreno-Ternero, "Progressivity, inequality reduction and merging-proofness in taxation," mimeo, 2006.

"On the equivalence between progressivity and inequality reduction in taxation," *Social Choice and Welfare* 30 (2008), 561–569.

"Progressive and merging-proof taxation," *International Journal of Game Theory* 40 (2011), 43–62.

"Fair allocation of disputed properties," *International Economic Review* 58 (2017), 1279–1301.

"Entitlement theory of justice and end-state fairness in the allocation of goods," *Economics and Philosophy*, forthcoming, 2018.

Juarez, R., "Convex rationing solutions," mimeo, 2013.

Kalai, E., "Proportional solutions to bargaining situations: interpersonal comparisons of utility," *Econometrica* 45 (1977), 1623–1630.

Kalai, E. and M. Smorodinsky, "Other solutions to Nash's bargaining problem," *Econometrica* 43 (1975), 513–518.

Kaminski, M., "Hydraulic rationing," *Mathematical Social Sciences* 40 (2000), 131–155.

"Parametric rationing methods," *Games and Economic Behavior* 54 (2006), 115–133.

Karagözoğlu, E., "A noncooperative approach to bankruptcy problems with an endogenous estate," *Annals of Operations Research* 217 (2014), 299–318.

Karpov, A. and S. Yurkov, "Generalized bankruptcy problem," mimeo, 2012.

Kasajima, Y. and W. Thomson, "Monotonicity properties of rules for the adjudication of conflicting claims," mimeo, 2011.

Kasajima, Y. and R. Velez, "Non-proportional inequality preservation in gains and losses," *Journal of Mathematical Economics* 46 (2010), 1079–1092.

"Reflecting inequality of claims in gains and losses," *Economic Theory* 46 (2011), 283–295.

Kıbrıs, Ö., "A revealed preference analysis of solutions to simple allocation problems," *Theory and Decision* 72 (2012), 509–523.

"On recursive solutions to simple allocation problems," *Theory and Decision* 75 (2013), 449–463.

Kıbrıs, A., and Ö. Kıbrıs, "On the investment implications of bankruptcy laws," *Games and Economic Behavior* 80 (2013), 85–99.

"On surplus sharing rules in partnerships," *Social Choice and Welfare* 47 (2016), 89–111.

Kocourek, A., "A first-rate legal puzzle—a problem of priorities," *Illinois Law Review* 29 (1935), 952–958.

Landsburg, S., "Incentive-compatibility and a problem from the Talmud," mimeo, 1993.

Laurent-Lucchetti, J., and J. Leroux, "Rights on what is left: an axiomatic discussion of grandfathering," mimeo, 2017.

Lavie, S., "Reverse sampling: holding lotteries to allocate the proceeds of small-claims class actions," *George Washington Law Review* 79 (2011), 1065–1102.

Lee, N.-C., "A simple generalization of the constrained equal award rule and its characterization," Keio University mimeo, 1994.

Lee, R., "Quick proof of a theorem concerning a Talmudic bankruptcy problem," Harvard University mimeo, 1992.

Lefebvre, M. "Can rationing rules for common resources impact self-insurance decisions?," *Strategic Behavior and the Environment* 3 (2013), 185–222.

Lefebvre, M., S. Thoyer, M. Tidball, and M. Willinger, "Sharing rules for common-pool resources when self-insurance is available," *Environment Modeling and Assessment* 19 (2014), 111–125.

Li, J. and Y. Ju, "Divide and choose: a strategic approach to bankruptcy problems," mimeo, 2016.

Littlechild, S. C. and G. Owen, "A simple expression for the Shapley value in a special case," *Management Science* 20 (1973), 370–372.

Long, Y., J. Sethuraman, and J. Xue, "Equal-quantile rules in resource allocation with uncertain demands," mimeo, 2019.

Lorenzo, L., "The constrained equal loss rule in problems with constraints and claims," *Optimization* 59 (2010), 643–660.

Lorenzo-Freire, S., J. Alsonso-Meijide, B. Casas-Mendez, and R. Hendrickx, "Balanced contributions for TU games with awards and applications," *European Journal of Operational Research* 182 (2007) 958–964.

Lorenzo-Freire, S., B. Casas-Mendez, and R. Hendrickx, "The two-stage constrained equal awards and losses for multi-issue allocation situations," *TOP* 18 (2010), 465–480.

Luttens, R., "Minimal rights based solidarity," *Social Choice and Welfare* 34 (2010), 47–64.

"Lower bound rules," mimeo, November 2010.

Ly, A. H., M. Zakharevich, O. Kosheleva, and V. Kreinovich, "An ancient bankruptcy solution makes economic sense," mimeo, 2017.

Madani, K., M. Zarezadeh, and S. Morid, "A new framework for resolving conflicts over transboundary rivers using bankruptcy methods," *Hydrology and Earth System Science* 18 (2014), 3055–3068.

Mahanta, A., "A non-cooperative solution to bankruptcy problems," mimeo, 2018.

Maimonides, Moses, [1135-1204], *Book of Judgements* (translated by Rabbi Elihahu Touger), New York, NY and Jerusalem: Moznaim Publishing Corporation, 2000.

Malkevitch, J., "Resolving bankruptcy claims," *American Mathematical Society*, www.ams.org/samplings/feature-column/fcarc-bankruptcy.

"Bankrupt," *Consortium* 95 (2008), 1–5.

"Taxes, bankruptcy and the Talmud," *Consortium* 97 (2009), 1–5.

Marchant, T., "Rationing: dynamic considerations, equivalent sacrifice and links between the two approaches," Ghent University, 2004.

"Scale invariance and similar invariance conditions for bankruptcy problems," *Social Choice and Welfare* 31 (2008), 693–707. Erratum in *Social Choice and Welfare* 31 (2008), 709–710.

Marco, M.-C., "An alternative characterization of the extended claim-egalitarian solution," *Economics Letters* 45 (1994), 41–46.

"Efficient solutions for bargaining problems with claims," *Mathematical Social Sciences* 30 (1995a), 57–69.

"The extended claim-egalitarian solution across cardinalities," University of Alicante mimeo, 1995b.

Martínez, R., "Strong composition down. Characterizations of new and classical bankruptcy rules," mimeo, 2008.

Maschler, M. and G. Owen, "The consistent Shapley value for hyperplane games," *International Journal of Game Theory* 18 (1989), 389–407.

Mianabadi, H., E. Mostert, M. Zarghami, and N. van de Giesen, "A new bankruptcy method for conflict resolution in water resources allocation," *Journal of Environmental Management* 144 (2014), 152–159.

Moreno-Ternero, J. "Composition, securement, and concede-and-divide," *Spanish Economic Review* 8 (2006a), 227–237.

"Proportionality and non-manipulability in bankruptcy problems," *International Game Theory Review* 8 (2006b), 127–139.

"Bankruptcy rules and coalitional manipulation," *International Game Theory Review* 9 (2007), 411–424.

"The proportional rule for multi-issue bankruptcy problems," *Economics Bulletin* 29 (2009), 474–481.

"A coalitional procedure leading to a family of bankruptcy rules," *Operations Research Letters* 39 (2011a), 1–3.

"Voting over piece-wise linear tax methods," *Journal of Mathematical Economics* 47 (2011b), 29–36.

"A Talmudic approach to bankruptcy problems," in *Game Theory and Management Accounting* (D. Mueller and R. Trost, eds), Berlin: Springer, 2017, 267–285.

Moreno-Ternero, J. and J. Roemer, "Impartiality, priority, and solidarity in the theory of justice," *Econometrica 74* (2006), 1419–1427.

"A common ground for resource and welfare egalitarianism," *Games and Economic Behavior* 75 (2012), 832–841.

Moreno-Ternero, J. and W. Thomson, "Between Aristotle and the Talmud," mimeo, 2017.

Moreno-Ternero, J., M.-H. Tsay, T.-W. Tsaur, and C.-H. Yeh, "A strategic justification of the Talmud rule for bankruptcy problems based on lower and upper bounds," mimeo, 2016.

Moreno-Ternero, J. and A. Villar, "The Talmud rule and the securement of agents' awards," *Mathematical Social Sciences* 47 (2004), 245–257.

"The TAL-family of rules for bankruptcy problems," *Social Choice and Welfare* 27 (2006a), 231–249.

"On the relative equitability of a family of taxation rules," *Journal of Public Economic Theory* 8 (2006b), 283–291.

"New characterizations of a classical bankruptcy rule," *Review of Economic Design* 10 (2006c), 73–84.

Moulin, H., "Egalitarianism and utilitarianism in quasi-linear bargaining," *Econometrica* 53 (1985a), 49–67.

"The separability axiom and equal-sharing methods," *Journal of Economic Theory* 36 (1985b), 120–148.

"The pure compensation problem: egalitarianism versus laissez-fairism," *Quarterly Journal of Economics* 101 (1987a), 769–783.

"Equal or proportional division of a surplus, and other methods," *International Journal of Game Theory* 16 (1987b), 161–186.

Axioms of Cooperative Decision Making, Cambridge: Cambridge University Press, 1988.

"Priority rules and other asymmetric rationing methods," *Econometrica* 68 (2000), 643–684.

"The proportional random allocation of indivisible units," *Social Choice and Welfare* 19 (2002a), 381–413.

"Axiomatic cost and surplus sharing," *Handbook of Social Choice* (K. Arrow and K. Suzumura, eds), Amsterdam: North-Holland, 2002b, 290–357.

Moulin, H. and J. Sethuraman, "The bipartite rationing problem," *Operations Research* 61 (2013), 1087–1100.

Moulin, H. and S. Shenker, "Distributive and additive cost-sharing of an homogeneous good," *Games and Economic Behavior* 27 (1999), 299–330.

Moulin, H. and R. Stong, "Fair queueing and other probabilistic allocation methods," *Mathematics of Operations Research* 27 (2002), 1–30.

"Filling a multicolor urn: an axiomatic analysis," *Games and Economic Behavior* 45 (2003), 242–269.

Myerson, R., "Conference structure and fair allocation rules," *International Journal of Game Theory* 9 (1980), 169–182.

Nash, J. F., "The bargaining problem," *Econometrica* 18 (1950), 155–162.

Naumova, N. I., "Non-symmetric equal sacrifice solutions for claim problem," *Mathematical Social Sciences* 43 (2002), 1–28.

von Neumann, J. and O. Morgenstern, *Theory of Games and Economic Behavior,* Princeton, NJ: Princeton University Press, 1944.

Oishi, T., "Legal and political agreements for sharing international rivers with water shortage," mimeo, 2018.

O'Neill, B., "A problem of rights arbitration from the Talmud," *Mathematical Social Sciences* 2 (1982), 345–371.

"Networks of rights in conflict: A Talmudic example," mimeo, 2014.

Orshan, G., "Non-symmetric prekernels," Hebrew University of Jerusalem, 1994.

Orshan, G., F. Valenciano, and J. M. Zarzuelo, "The bilateral consistent prekernel, the core, and NTU bankruptcy problems," *Mathematics of Operations Research*, 28 (2003), 268–282.

Ortells, T. and C. Santos, "The pseudo-average rule: bankruptcy, cost allocation and bargaining," *Mathematical Methods of Operations Research* 73 (2011), 55–73.

Otten, G.-J., H. Peters, and O. Volij, "Two characterizations of the uniform rule for division problems with single-peaked preferences," *Economic Theory* 7 (1996), 291–306.

Pálvödgyi, D., H. Peters, and D. Vermeulen, "A strategic approach to multiple estate division problems," June 2013.

Perles, M. A. and M. Maschler, "The super-additive solution for the Nash bargaining game," *International Journal of Game Theory* 10 (1981), 163–193.

Peters, H., M. Schröder, and D. Vermeulen, "A non-cooperative analysis of the estate division problem," mimeo, 2013.

Pfingsten, A., "Surplus-sharing methods," *Mathematical Social Sciences* 21 (1991), 287–301.

Piniles, H. M., *Darkah shel Torah*, Vienna: Forester, 1861.

Potters, J., R. Poos, S. Muto, S., and S. Tijs, "Clan games," *Games and Economic Behavior* 1 (1989), 275–293.

Pulido, M., P. Borm, R. Hendrickx, N. Llorca, and J. Sánchez Soriano, "Compromise solutions for bankruptcy situations with references," *Annals of Operations Research* 158 (2008), 133–142.

Pulido, M., J. Sánchez-Soriano, and N. Llorca, "Game theory techniques for university management: an extended bankruptcy model," *Annals of Operations Research* 109 (2002), 129–142.

Quant, M., "Interactive behavior in conflict situations," Ph.D. Thesis, Tilburg University, 2006.

Quant, M., and P. Borm, "Random conjugates of bankruptcy rules," *Social Choice and Welfare* 36 (2011), 249–266.

Quant, M., P. Borm, R. Hendrickx, and P. Zwikker, "Compromise solutions based on bankruptcy," *Mathematical Social Sciences* 51 (2006), 247–256.

Quant, M., P. Borm, and R. Maaten, "A concede-and-divide rule for bankruptcy problems," mimeo, 2005.

Quant, M., P. Borm, H. Reijnierse, and B. van Velzen, "The core cover in relation to the nucleolus and the Weber set," *International Journal of Game Theory* 33 (2005), 491–503.

Rabinovitch, N., *Probability and Statistical Inference in Medieval Jewish Literature*, Toronto: University of Toronto Press, 1973.

Rong, K., "Fair allocation when players' preferences are unknown," *Economic Inquiry*, (2018), forthcoming.

Rubinstein, A., "Perfect equilibrium in a bargaining model," *Econometrica* 50 (1982), 97–109.

Salonen, H., "On additivity of bankruptcy rules," University of Turku mimeo, October 2007.

Sánchez, F., "An algorithm to compute a rule for division problems with multiple references," *Revista Electronica de Communicaciones y Trabajo de ASEPUMA 13* (2012), 107–118.

Sánchez-Pérez, J., "On the linearity property for allocation problems and bankruptcy problems," *Journal of Dynamics and Games* 5 (2018), 9–20.

Sánchez-Pérez, J., L. Plata-Pérez, and E. Accinelli-Gamba, "Characterization of linear symmetric solutions for allocation problems," *Economic Letters* 130 (2015), 9–12.

Sanchez-Soriano, J., N. Llorca, and E. Algaba, "An approach from bankruptcy rules applied to the apportionment problem in proportional electoral systems," mimeo, 2016.

Schmeidler, D., "The nucleolus of a characteristic function form game," *SIAM Journal of Applied Mathematics* 17 (1969), 1163–1170.

Schummer, J. and W. Thomson, "Two derivations of the uniform rule," *Economics Letters* 55 (1997), 333–337.

Serrano, R., "Strategic bargaining, surplus-sharing problems and the nucleolus," *Journal of Mathematical Economics* 24 (1995), 319–329.

Shapley, L., "A value for n-person games," in *Contributions to the Theory of Games II* (Annals of Mathematics Studies 28), ed. by H. W. Kuhn and A. W. Tucker, Princeton, NJ: Princeton University Press, 1953, 307–317.

"Cores of convex games," *International Journal of Game Theory* 1 (1971), 11–26.

Shinotsuka, T., "Budget allocation problems," Otaru University mimeo, May 2000.

Solymosi, T. and B. Sziklai, "Characterization sets for the nucleolus in balanced games: the case of bankruptcy games," mimeo, 2015.

Sonn, S., "Sequential bargaining for bankruptcy problems," mimeo, 1992.

Sprumont, Y., "The division problem with single-peaked preferences: a characterization of the uniform allocation rule," *Econometrica* 49 (1991), 509–519.

Stovall, J., "Asymmetric parametric division rules," *Games and Economic Behavior* 84 (2014a), 87–110.

"Collective rationality and monotone path division rules," *Journal of Economic Theory* 154 (2014b), 1–24.

"Equal sacrifice taxation," mimeo, 2018.

Stutzer, M., "Decentralized clearing in financial markets," mimeo, 2016.

Tejada, O. and A. Álvarez-Mozos, "Vertical-syndication-proof competitive prices in multilateral assignment markets," *Review of Economic Design* 20 (2016), 289–327.

Thomson, W., "The fair division of a fixed supply among a growing population," *Mathematics of Operations Research* 8 (1983a), 319–326.

"Problems of fair division and the egalitarian solution," *Journal of Economic Theory* 31 (1983b), 211–226.

"Collective guarantee structures," *Economics Letters* 11 (1983c), 63–68.

"Monotonic allocation rules," mimeo, 1987.

"A study of choice correspondences in economies with a variable number of agents," *Journal of Economic Theory* 46 (1988), 237–254.

"Resource-monotonic solutions to the problem of fair division when preferences are single-peaked," *Social Choice and Welfare* 11 (1994a), 205–223.

"On the computational implications of converse consistency," mimeo, 1994b.

"Population-monotonic allocation rules," in *Social Choice, Welfare, and Ethics*, (W. A. Barnett, H. Moulin, M. Salles, and N. Schofield, eds), Cambridge: Cambridge University Press, 1995a, 79–124.

Bargaining Theory: The Axiomatic Approach, Cambridge, MA: Academic Press, forthcoming, 1996.

The Theory of Fair Allocation, book manuscript, 1998.
"Welfare-domination under preference replacement: a survey and open questions," *Social Choice and Welfare* 16 (1999a), 373–394.
"Options-monotonic allocation rules," mimeo, 1999b.
Condorcet Lecture, Fourth International Meeting of the Society for Social Choice and Welfare, Alicante, 2000.
"On the axiomatic method and its recent applications to game theory and resource allocation," *Social Choice and Welfare* 18 (2001), 327–387.
"Axiomatic and game-theoretic analysis of bankruptcy and taxation problems: a survey," *Mathematical Social Sciences* 45 (2003), 249–297.
"On the existence of consistent rules to adjudicate conflicting claims: a geometric approach," *Review of Economic Design* 11 (2007a), 225–251.
"Cost allocation and airport problems," mimeo, 2007b, revised 2016.
"The two-agent claims-truncated proportional rule has no consistent extension: a constructive proof," *Economics Letters* 98 (2008a), 59–65.
"Two families of rules for the adjudication of conflicting claims," *Social Choice and Welfare* 31 (2008b), 667–692.
"Consistency and its converse, an introduction," *Review of Economic Design* 15 (2011), 257–291.
"Lorenz orderings of rules for the adjudication of conflicting claims," *Economic Theory* 50 (2012a), 547–569.
"On the axiomatics of resource allocation: Interpreting the consistency principle," *Economics and Philosophy* 28 (2012b), 385–421.
"Game-theoretic analysis of bankruptcy and taxation problems: recent advances," *International Game Theory Review* (2013a), 14 pages.
"A characterization of a family of rules for the adjudication of conflicting claims," *Games and Economic Behavior* 82 (2013b), 157–168.
"Fully allocating a commodity when preferences are single-peaked," mimeo, 2014.
"Axiomatic and game-theoretic analysis of bankruptcy and taxation problems: an update," *Mathematical Social Sciences* 74 (2015a), 41–59.
"For claims problems, compromising between the proportional and constrained equal awards rules," *Economic Theory* 60 (2015b), 495–520.
"For claims problems, another compromise between the proportional and constrained equal awards rules," *Journal of Dynamics and Games* 2 (2015c), 363–382.
"For claims problems, a new proof of a characterization of the proportional rule," *Economics Letters* 145 (2016), 255–257.
Consistent Allocation Rules, Cambridge: Cambridge University Press, forthcoming, 2018a.
"Equal area rule to adjudicate conflicting claims," in *Social Design. Essays in Memory of Leonid Hurwicz*, (W. Trockel, ed), Springer Verlag, forthcoming, 2018b.
Let's Talk about Economic Design, mimeo, 2018c.
Thomson, W. and T. Lensberg, "Guarantee structures for problems of fair division," *Mathematical Social Sciences* 3 (1983), 205–218.
The Axiomatic Theory of Bargaining with a Variable Number of Agents, Cambridge: Cambridge University Press, 1989.
Thomson, W. and R. B. Myerson, "Monotonicity and independence axioms," *International Journal of Game Theory* 9 (1980), 37–49.

Thomson, W. and C.-H. Yeh, "Minimal rights, maximal claims, duality, and convexity for the adjudication of conflicting claims," mimeo, 2001.

"Operators for the adjudication of conflicting claims," *Journal of Economic Theory* 143 (2008), 177–198.

Tijs, S. H., "Bounds for the core and the τ-value," in *Game Theory and Mathematical Economics* (O. Moeschlin and D. Pallaschke, eds), Amsterdam: North-Holland, 1981, 123–132.

Timoner, P. and J. M. Izquierdo, "Rationing problems with ex-ante conditions," *Mathematical Social Sciences* 79 (2016), 46–52.

Tsay, M. H. and C.-H. Yeh, "Relations between the central rules in bankruptcy problems: a strategic implementation perspective," mimeo, 2016.

Tyre, A., "Circular priorities in secured transactions," *The American Mathematical Monthly* 87 (1980), 186–193.

Velez, R., "Generalized tree rules for claims problems," mimeo, 2007.

Woeginger, G. J., "A note on fair division under interval uncertainty," *International Journal of Uncertainty, Fuzziness and Knowledge-based systems* 14 (2006), 753–756.

Wood, R., "Circular priorities in secured transactions law," *Alberta Law Review* 823 (2010), 823–852.

Xue, J., "Fair division with uncertain needs," *Social Choice and Welfare* 51 (2018), 105–136.

Yager, R. and V. Kreinovich, "Fair division under interval uncertainty," *International Journal of Uncertainty, Fuzziness and Knowledge-based systems* 8 (2000), 611–618.

Yanovskaya, E., "Nonsymmetric consistent surplus sharing methods," mimeo, 2003.

Yeh, C.-H., "Two alternative formulations of equal treatment of equals in claims problems," mimeo, 2001.

"Sustainability, exemption, and the constrained equal award rule: a note," *Mathematical Social Sciences* 47 (2004), 103–110.

"Protective properties and the constrained equal awards rule for claims problems: a note," *Social Choice and Welfare* 27 (2006), 221–230.

"Secured lower bound, composition up, and minimal rights first for bankruptcy problems," *Journal of Mathematical Economics* 44, (2008), 925–932.

Young, P., "Methods and principles of cost allocation," Chapter 1 of *Cost allocation: Methods, Principles, Applications* (P.Young, ed), Elsevier Science Publishers, 1985, 3–29.

"On dividing an amount according to individual claims or liabilities," *Mathematics of Operations Research* 12 (1987a), 398–414.

"Progressive taxation and the equal sacrifice principle," *Journal of Public Economics* 32 (1987b), 203–214.

"When is a tax increase fairly distributed?," University of Maryland mimeo, 1987c.

"Distributive justice in taxation," *Journal of Economic Theory* 44 (1988), 321–335.

"Progressive taxation and equal sacrifice," *American Economic Review* 80 (1990), 253–266.

Index

Econometric Society Monograph Series *(continued from page ii)*

H. White, *Inference, Estimation and Specification Analysis*, 1994

J-J. Laffont (ed.), *Advances in Economic Theory, Sixth World Congress, Vols. I & II*, 1992

W. Härdle, *Applied Nonparametric Regression Analysis*, 1990

A. Roth & M. Sotomayor, *Two-Sided Matching*, 1990

T. Lancaster, *The Econometric Analysis of Transition Data*, 1990

L. G. Godfrey, *Misspecification Tests in Econometrics*, 1989

H. Moulin, *Axioms of Cooperative Decision-Making*, 1988

T. Bewley (ed.), *Advances in Economic Theory, Fifth World Congress, Vols. I, II, & III*, 1987

C. Hsiao, *Analysis of Panel Data*, 1986

J. Heckman & B. Singer, *Longitudinal Analysis of Labor Market Data*, 1985

A. Mas-Colell, *The Theory of General Economic Equilibrium: A Differentiable Approach*, 1985

R. J. Bowden & D. A. Turkington, *Instrumental Variables*, 1985

B. Peleg, *Game Theoretic Analysis of Voting in Committees*, 1984

F. M. Fisher, *Disequilibrium Foundations of Equilibrium Economics*, 1983

J.-M. Grandmont, *Money and Value*, 1983

G. Debreu, *Mathematical Economics*, 1983

G. S. Maddala, *Limited Dependent and Qualitative Variables in Econometrics*, 1983

W. Hildenbrand (ed.), *Advances in Economic Theory*, 1983

W. Hildenbrand (ed.), *Advances in Econometrics*, 1983